The SAGE Encyclopedia of
Psychology and Gender

Editorial Board

The SAGE Encyclopedia of Psychology and Gender

3

Edited by

Kevin L. Nadal
John Jay College of Criminal Justice and
The Graduate Center at City University of New York

SAGE reference

Los Angeles | London | New Delhi
Singapore | Washington DC | Melbourne

FOR INFORMATION:

SAGE Publications, Inc.
2455 Teller Road
Thousand Oaks, California 91320
E-mail: order@sagepub.com

SAGE Publications Ltd.
1 Oliver's Yard
55 City Road
London, EC1Y 1SP
United Kingdom

SAGE Publications India Pvt. Ltd.
B 1/I 1 Mohan Cooperative Industrial Area
Mathura Road, New Delhi 110 044
India

SAGE Publications Asia-Pacific Pte. Ltd.
3 Church Street
#10-04 Samsung Hub
Singapore 049483

Acquisitions Editor: Maureen Adams
Editorial Assistant: Jordan Enobakhare
Developmental Editor: Carole Maurer
Reference Systems Manager: Leticia Gutierrez
Production Editor: Tracy Buyan
Copy Editors: QuADS Prepress (P) Ltd.
Typesetter: Hurix Systems Pvt. Ltd.
Proofreaders: Lawrence Baker, Sarah Duffy, Annette Van Deusen
Indexer: Maria Sosnowski
Cover Designer: Candice Harman
Marketing Manager: Kate Brummitt
Cover images: Adam Hester/Getty Images
Thinkstock.com/Design Pics
©iStockphoto.com/SolStock
Roy Rochlin/Getty Images

Printed in the United States of America.

Library of Congress Cataloging-in-Publication Data

Names: Nadal, Kevin L., editor.

Title: The SAGE encyclopedia of psychology and gender / edited by Kevin L. Nadal, John Jay College of Criminal Justice.

Other titles: Encyclopedia of psychology and gender

Description: First Edition. | Thousand Oaks : SAGE Publications, [2017] | Includes bibliographical references and index.

Identifiers: LCCN 2017014081 | ISBN 9781483384283 (hardcover : alk. paper)

Subjects: LCSH: Gender identity. | Developmental psychobiology.

Classification: LCC BF692.2 .S234 2017 | DDC 155.3/3—dc23 LC record available at https://lccn.loc.gov/2017014081

This book is printed on acid-free paper.

17 18 19 20 21 10 9 8 7 6 5 4 3 2 1

Contents

Volume 3

List of Entries *vii*

Entries

J	*997*	O	*1247*
K	*1009*	P	*1253*
L	*1017*	Q	*1383*
M	*1091*	R	*1389*
N	*1221*		

List of Entries

Ability Status and Gender
Ability Status and Sexual Orientation
Abortion
Abstinence
Abstinence in Adolescence
Abstinence-Only Education
Acceptance and Commitment Therapy
Acquaintance Rape
Adlerian Theories of Gender Development
Adolescence and Gender: Overview
Affirmative Action
Ageism
Agender. *See* Genderqueer
Aging and Gender: Overview
Aging and Mental Health
Agoraphobia and Gender
Alcoholism and Gender
Alexithymia
Allies
Ambivalent Sexism
Androcentrism
Androgyny
Anorexia and Gender
Anti-Feminist Backlash
Antisocial Personality Disorder and Gender
Anti-Trans Bias in the *DSM*
Anxiety Disorders and Gender
Arab Americans and Gender
Arab Americans and Sexual Orientation
Arab Americans and Transgender Identity
Asexuality
Asian Americans and Gender
Asian Americans and Sexual Orientation
Asian Americans and Transgender Identity
Assisted Reproduction and Alternative Families
Assisted Suicide, Euthanasia, and Gender
Attraction
Avoidant Personality Disorder and Gender
Behavioral Approaches and Gender
Behavioral Disorders and Gender
Behavioral Theories of Gender Development
Bem Sex Role Inventory
Benevolent Sexism
Biculturalism and Gender
Biculturalism and Sexual Orientation
Biculturalism and Transgender Identity
Bi-Gender
Biological Sex and Cognitive Development
Biological Sex and Health Outcomes
Biological Sex and Language and Communication
Biological Sex and Mental Health Outcomes
Biological Sex and Social Development
Biological Sex and the Brain
Biological Sex Differences: Overview
Biological Theories of Gender Development
Biopsychology
Biphobia
Bipolar Disorder and Gender
Bisexual Identity Development
Bisexuality
Black Americans and Gender
Black Americans and Sexual Orientation
Black Americans and Transgender Identity
Body Dysmorphic Disorder and Gender
Body Image
Body Image and Adolescence
Body Image and Aging
Body Image Issues and Men
Body Image Issues and Women
Body Modification
Body Objectification
Borderline Personality Disorder and Gender
Brain Lateralization
Breastfeeding
Buddhism and Gender
Buddhism and Sexual Orientation
Bulimia and Gender

Bullying, Gender-Based
Bullying in Adolescence
Bullying in Childhood
Butch
Bystanders

Campus Rape
Career Choice and Gender
Career Choice and Sexual Orientation
Caretakers, Experiences of
Child Adoption and Gender
Child Neglect
Child Play
Childhood and Gender: Overview
Children With LGBTQ Parents
Children With Transgender Parents
Children's Cognitive Development
Children's Moral Development
Children's Social-Emotional Development
Christianity and Gender
Christianity and Sexual Orientation
Cisgender
Cissexism
Cognitive Approaches and Gender
Cognitive Disorders in Men
Cognitive Disorders in Women
Cognitive Theories of Gender Development
Colonialism and Gender
Coming Out Processes for LGBTQ Youth
Coming Out Processes for Transgender People
Community and Aging
Competition and Gender
Comprehensive Sexuality Education
Congenital Adrenal Hyperplasia
Consciousness-Raising Groups
Contraception
Conversion Therapy. *See* Sexual Orientation Change Efforts
Couples Therapy With Heterosexual Couples
Couples Therapy With Same-Sex Couples
Criminal Justice System and Gender
Criminal Justice System and Sexual Orientation
Criminal Justice System and Transgender People
Criminalization of Gender Nonconformity
Criminalization of Men of Color
Criminalization of Transgender People
Critical Race Feminism
Cross-Cultural Differences in Gender
Cross-Cultural Models or Approaches to Gender
Cultural Competence
Cultural Gender Role Norms
Cyberbullying
Cycles of Abuse

Date Rape
Delusional Disorder and Gender
Demasculation. *See* Masculinity Threats
Dependent Personality Disorder and Gender
Depression and Gender
Depression and Men
Depression and Women
Developmental and Biological Processes: Overview
Dialectical Behavior Therapy and Gender
Disability and Adolescence
Disability and Aging
Disability and Childhood
Discursive Approaches
Dissociative Disorders and Gender
Division of Domestic Labor
Doing Gender
Domestic Care Industry and Women
Dual Diagnosis and Gender
Dual Minority Status

Eating Disorders and Gender
Ecofeminism
Education and Gender: Overview
Egg Donation
Emasculation. *See* Masculinity Threats
Emotional Abuse
Emotions in Adolescence and Gender
End-of-Life and Existential Issues
Equal Employment Opportunity
Equal Pay for Equal Work
Equality Feminism
Estrogen
Ethics in Gender Research
Ethics in Psychotherapy and Gender
Ethics of Self-Care for Psychologists
Evolutionary Sex Differences
Exhibitionism and Gender
Existential Approaches and Gender
Existential Theories of Gender Development
Exoticization of LGBTQ People of Color
Exoticization of Women of Color

Family Relationships in Adolescence
Fat Shaming
Fatherhood

Female Sex Offenders
Femininity
Feminism: Overview
Feminism and Men
Feminist Identity Development Model
Feminist Psychology
Feminist Therapy
Femme
Fetal Programming of Gender
Fetal Sex Selection
Fetishism and Gender
First-Wave Feminism
Fraternities
Friendships in Adolescence
Frotteurism and Gender

Gambling and Gender
Gay Male Identity Development
Gay Men
Gay Men and Dating
Gay Men and Feminism
Gay Men and Gender Roles
Gay Men and Health
Gay Men and Romantic Relationships
Gender Affirming Medical Treatments
Gender and Society: Overview
Gender Balance in Education
Gender Bias in Education
Gender Bias in Hiring Practices
Gender Bias in Research
Gender Bias in the *DSM*
Gender Conformity
Gender Development, Theories of
Gender Discrimination
Gender Dynamics in Clinical Supervision
Gender Dynamics in Clinical Training
Gender Dynamics in Group Therapy
Gender Dynamics in Psychotherapy
Gender Dysphoria
Gender Equality
Gender Expression
Gender Fluidity
Gender Identity
Gender Identity and Adolescence
Gender Identity and Childhood
Gender Identity Disorder, History of
Gender Marginality in Adolescence
Gender Microinequities
Gender Nonconforming Behaviors
Gender Nonconforming People
Gender Nonconformity and Transgender Issues: Overview
Gender Norms and Adolescence
Gender Presentation and Childhood. *See* Gender Variant Role Expression in Childhood
Gender Pronouns
Gender Reaffirming Surgeries
Gender Role Behavior
Gender Role Conflict
Gender Role Socialization
Gender Role Strain Paradigm
Gender Role Stress
Gender Roles: Overview
Gender Segregation
Gender Self-Socialization
Gender Self-Socialization Model
Gender Socialization in Adolescence
Gender Socialization in Aging
Gender Socialization in Childhood
Gender Socialization in Men
Gender Socialization in Women
Gender Stereotypes
Gender Studies in Higher Education
Gender Studies in K–12 Education
Gender Tracking in Education
Gender Variant Role Expression in Childhood
Gender Versus Sex
Gender-Based Violence
Gender-Based Violence in Athletics
Gender-Based Violence in the Media
Gender-Biased Language in Research
Gendered Behavior
Gendered Behaviors in Adolescence
Gendered Organizations
Gendered Stereotyped Behaviors in Childhood
Gendered Stereotyped Behaviors in Men
Gendered Stereotyped Behaviors in Women
Genderqueer
Gilligan's Moral Development Theory
Glass Ceiling. *See* Women and Leadership; Women in Corporate Positions, Experiences of; Workplace Sexual Harassment
Government and Gender
Grieving and Gender

Hate Crimes Toward LGBTQ People
Health at Every Size
Health Issues and Gender: Overview
Hegemonic Masculinity

Help-Seeking Behaviors and Men
Help-Seeking Behaviors and Women
Heteronormative Bias in Research
Heteronormativity
Heterosexism
Heterosexist Bias in the *DSM*
Heterosexual Male Identity Development
Heterosexual Male Relationships
Heterosexual Men and Dating
Heterosexual Men and Feminism
Heterosexual Privilege
Heterosexual Romantic Relationships
Heterosexual Women and Dating
Heterosexuality
Histrionic Personality Disorder and Gender
HIV/AIDS
Homophobia
Homosexuality
Hormone Therapy for Cisgender Men and Women
Hormone Therapy for Transgender People
Hostile Sexism
Hostile Work Environment. *See* Women's Issues: Overview; Workplace Sexual Harassment
Human Rights
Humanistic Approaches and Gender
Humanistic Theories of Gender Development
Hypochondriasis and Gender
Hysterectomy

Identity Construction
Identity Development and Aging
Identity Formation in Adolescence
Identity Formation in Childhood
Immigration and Gender
Immigration and Sexualities
Immigration and Transgender Identity
Impostor Syndrome
In Vitro Fertilization
Inferiority Complex
Infertility
Institutional Sexism
Intermittent Explosive Disorder and Gender
Internalized Heterosexism
Internalized Sexism
Internalized Transphobia
International Perspectives on Women's Mental Health
Interpersonal Therapies and Gender
Intersectional Identities
Intersectional Theories
Intersex
Intimacy
Intimate Partner Violence
Intimate Partner Violence in Same-Sex Couples
Islam and Gender
Islam and Sexual Orientation
Isolation and Aging

Judaism and Gender
Judaism and Sexual Orientation
Juvenile Justice System and Gender

Kinsey Reports
Kinsey Scale, The
Kohlberg's Stages of Moral Development

Labor Movement and Women
Late Adulthood and Gender
Latina/o Americans and Gender
Latina/o Americans and Sexual Orientation
Latina/o Americans and Transgender Identity
Legal System and Gender
Lesbian, Gay, and Bisexual Children
Lesbian, Gay, and Bisexual Experiences of Aging
Lesbian Identity Development
Lesbians
Lesbians and Dating
Lesbians and Gender Roles
Lesbians and Health
Lesbians and Romantic Relationships
LGBQ Older Adults and Health
LGBTQ Athletes, Experiences of
LGBTQ Community, Experiences of Transgender People in
LGBTQ Community, Gender Dynamics in
LGBTQ People of Color and Discrimination
LGBTQQ-Affirmative Psychotherapy
Long-Term Care
Low Testosterone

Machismo
Male Privilege
Mania and Gender
Marianismo
Marriage
Marriage Equality
Masculinities
Masculinity Gender Norms

Masculinity Ideology and Norms
Masculinity in Adolescence
Masculinity Threats
Masturbation
Matriarchy
Measuring Gender
Measuring Gender Identity
Measuring Gender Roles
Measuring Sexual Orientation
Media and Gender
Men and Aging
Menopause
Men's Friendships
Men's Group Therapy
Men's Health
Men's Issues: Overview
Men's Studies
Menstruation
Mental Health and Gender: Overview
Mental Health Stigma and Gender
Microaggressions
Middle Adulthood and Gender
Military and Gender
Military Sexual Trauma
Minority Stress
Misogyny
Motherhood
Multiculturalism and Gender: Overview
Multiracial People and Gender
Multiracial People and Sexual Orientation
Multiracial People and Transgender Identity

Narcissistic Personality Disorder and Gender
Native Americans and Gender
Native Americans and Sexual Orientation. *See* Two-Spirited People
Native Americans and Transgender Identity
Nature Versus Nurture
Neofeminism
Neurofeminism
Neurosexism
Nonbinary Gender. *See* Gender Nonconforming People

Obsessive-Compulsive Disorder and Gender
Orgasm, Psychological Issues Relating to

Pacific Islanders and Gender
Pacific Islanders and Sexual Orientation
Panic Disorder and Gender
Pansexuality
Parental Expectations
Parental Messages About Gender
Parental Stressors
Parenting Styles, Gender Differences in
Passing
Pathologizing Gender Identity
Patriarchy
Pedophilia and Gender
Peer Pressure in Adolescence
Perimenopause
Perpetrators of Violence
Personality Disorders and Gender Bias
Physical Abuse
Physical Assault, Female Survivors of
Physical Assault, Male Survivors of
Physical Assault, Transgender Survivors of
Pornography and Gender
Postpartum Depression
Posttraumatic Stress Disorder and Gender
Posttraumatic Stress Disorder and Gender Differences in Children
Posttraumatic Stress Disorder and Gender Violence
Power-Control and Gender
Pregnancy
Pregnancy Discrimination
Pretend Play
Psychoanalytic Approaches and Gender
Psychoanalytic Feminism
Psychoanalytic Theories of Gender Development. *See* Psychodynamic Theories of Gender Development
Psychodynamic Approaches and Gender
Psychodynamic Feminism
Psychodynamic Theories of Gender Development
Psychological Abuse
Psychological Measurements, Gender Bias in
Psychological Measurements, Sexual Orientation Bias in
Psychopathy and Gender
Psychosexual Development
Psychosis and Gender. *See* Schizophrenia and Gender
Puberty
Puberty Suppression

Queer
Queerness

Quid Pro Quo. *See* Women's Issues: Overview; Workplace Sexual Harassment

Race and Gender
Racial Discrimination, Gender-Based
Racial Discrimination, Sexual Orientation–Based
Rape
Rape Culture
Reliability and Gender
Reparative Therapy. *See* Sexual Orientation Change Efforts
Reproductive Cancer and Mental Health in Men
Reproductive Cancer and Mental Health in Women
Reproductive Rights Movement
Research: Overview
Research Methodology and Gender
Revictimization
Role Models and Gender
Romantic Relationships in Adolescence
Romantic Relationships in Adulthood

Safe Sex
Safe Sex and Adolescence
Sampling Bias and Gender
Schizoid Personality Disorder and Gender
Schizophrenia and Gender
Second-Wave Feminism
Self-Fulfilling Prophecy and Gender
Self-Injury and Gender
Sex Culture
Sex Education
Sex Education in Schools
Sex Work
Sexism
Sexism, Psychological Consequences for Men
Sexism, Psychological Consequences for Women
Sexual Abuse
Sexual Assault
Sexual Assault, Adolescent Survivors of
Sexual Assault, Child Survivors of
Sexual Assault, Female Survivors of
Sexual Assault, Male Survivors of
Sexual Assault, Survivors of
Sexual Coercion
Sexual Desire
Sexual Disorders and Gender
Sexual Dysfunction
Sexual Harassment
Sexual Identity
Sexual Offenders
Sexual Orientation: Overview
Sexual Orientation as Research Variable
Sexual Orientation Change Efforts
Sexual Orientation Disturbance, History of
Sexual Orientation Dynamics in Clinical Supervision
Sexual Orientation Dynamics in Clinical Training
Sexual Orientation Dynamics in Group Therapy
Sexual Orientation Dynamics in Psychotherapy
Sexual Orientation Identity
Sexual Orientation Identity Development
Sexuality and Adolescence
Sexuality and Aging
Sexuality and Men
Sexuality and Social Media
Sexuality and Women
Sexually Transmitted Diseases
Sleep Disorders and Gender
Sleep Disorders and LGBTQ People
Slut Shaming
Social Anxiety Disorder and Gender
Social Class and Gender
Social Class and Sexual Orientation
Social Media and Gender
Social Role Theory
Sociodramatic Play/Role-Play
Socioeconomic Status and Gender
Sodomy Laws
Somatization Disorder and Gender
Sororities
Sperm Donor
Spirituality and Gender
Spirituality and Sexual Orientation
Sports and Gender
Spousal Rape
Stalking
STEM Fields and Gender
Stereotype Threat and Gender
Stereotype Threat in Education
Stigma of Aging
Stranger Rape
Street Harassment
Substance Use and Gender
Substance Use Disorders and Gender. *See* Substance Use and Gender
Subtle Sexism
Suicide and Gender
Suicide and Sexual Orientation
Superwoman Complex

Superwoman Squeeze
Surrogacy

Take Back the Night
Teacher Bias
Teaching Feminism
Teaching Human Sexuality
Teen Fathers
Teen Mothers
Testosterone
Theories and Therapeutic Approaches: Overview
Third Gender
Third-Wave Feminism
Title IX
Trans*
Transgender and Gender Nonconforming Adolescents
Transgender and Gender Nonconforming Identity Development
Transgender Children
Transgender Day of Action
Transgender Day of Remembrance
Transgender Experiences of Aging
Transgender People
Transgender People and Dating
Transgender People and Health Disparities
Transgender People and Resilience
Transgender People and Romantic Relationships
Transgender People and Violence
Transgender Research, Bias in
Transgender Studies
Transmisogyny
Transphobia
Transphobia Bias in the *DSM*. *See* Anti-Trans Bias in the *DSM*
Transsexual
Transvestic Fetishism
Turner Syndrome
Two-Spirited People

Validity and Gender
Vicarious Sexism
Vicarious Trauma
Victim Blaming
Violence Against Women Act
Violence and Gender: Overview
Voting and Gender
Voyeurism and Gender

White/European Americans and Gender
White/European Americans and Sexual Orientation
White/European Americans and Transgender Identity
Womanism
Women and Aging
Women and Leadership
Women and War
Women Athletes, Experiences of
Women in Academia, Experiences of
Women in Corporate Positions, Experiences of
Women in Government, Experiences of
Women in Public Safety, Experiences of
Women in Religious Leadership, Experiences of
Women in STEM Fields, Experiences of
Women in the Military, Experiences of
Women Leaders in Political Movements, Experiences of
Women of Color and Discrimination
Women's Friendships
Women's Group Therapy
Women's Groups
Women's Health
Women's Issues: Overview
Women's Studies
Womyn
Workplace and Gender: Overview
Workplace Sexual Harassment
Worldviews and Gender Research

Judaism and Gender

Much of the ideology that shapes Judaism is rooted in patriarchal traditions. Gender defines most of the roles in traditional Judaism, both inside the home and outside. The basis for Jewish law, or Halacha in Hebrew, is the Torah, which is the first five books of the Bible. Countless scholars have made interpretations of the Torah, leading to many different sects of Judaism and many different interpretations of the responsibilities of men and women. This entry provides a basic overview of the ways Judaism views gender differences with regard to roles and responsibilities, paying special attention to the roles and responsibilities of women. Domestic violence will be examined in this context to provide an example of the ways in which gender plays such an integral role in the intersection of psychology and Judaism.

Overview of Gender and Roles

Traditionally, Jewish men are the leaders of the family and are required to financially support their wives and children, while maintaining a religious presence in the congregation. In the strictest sects, women are considered to be subservient to men. This is an interpretation of the biblical story of Adam and Eve, whereby God made Eve from Adam's rib, suggesting that woman would not exist if not for man's existence. This is also interpreted in strict Jewish sects to mean that men are more focused on outer, public responsibilities and prayer while women are to be focused on the inner (as derived from the "inner" rib), taking responsibility for prayer and ritual inside the home. Men are expected to pray several times a day and to take part in a minyan, or a traditional prayer circle requiring 10 men, once or twice per day at their house of worship. In the most traditional or strict sects of Judaism, women are not allowed to pray in these circles or touch the Torah, the sacred Jewish scrolls and text. Also in the strict and orthodox sects, women and men are separated by a wall in the house of worship, or synagogue.

Women have traditionally held the responsibility for maintaining peace in the home, or *shalom bayit*. This generally includes cooking for the family and maintaining a kosher home, which involves strict laws about the types of food allowed in the home and the manner in which the food is handled. Following kashrut, or the kosher laws of Judaism, can be difficult while also trying to take care of the children and the other aspects of housekeeping. Women are also expected to follow Jewish laws pertaining to purity, which require women to bathe in a special bath, called the *mikvah*, each month, following their menstruation cycle. Gender role differences remain important in most traditional and strict orthodox sects and communities.

Another example of Jewish biblical laws that demonstrate the furthering of gender inequality in Jewish traditions and current interpretations is in the realm of sexuality. In the book of Deuteronomy, it states that a man who cheats on his wife and commits sexual adultery with another woman should be killed as he has stolen another man's property, while a man who rapes a virgin must marry the woman he raped as he has now taken ownership of this woman's body through sex. There are no considerations in these biblical laws about the woman's rights or her body in its own right. While these laws may not be interpreted in a literal sense in modern Judaism, the undertone may still be present, and it is more present in more traditional and orthodox sects.

In the Bible, which, as stated before, loosely remains the text on which modern Jewish law is based, women are described in terms of men. Women are described as wives, daughters, or mothers, as they relate to their husbands, fathers, or sons. Stories of biblical women such as Miriam, who can be viewed as a female leader in her own right, are rarely shared as such. Judaism believes that because Eve was derived from an inner part of Adam's body, women have more inner intuition than men and are more focused on relational issues whereas men are often focused on larger, bigger-picture issues. Many traditional, orthodox Jewish interpretations state that men and women were designed to exist together; however, more modern interpretations and sects of Judaism make different interpretations and are inclusive and welcoming of same-sex marriages and relationships.

Traditional Jewish interpretations suggest that women should not pursue higher education and training because there are concerns that these pursuits could take away from their primary roles of mother and wife. Thus, women in very orthodox, traditional communities rarely pursue college degrees or careers outside of the home. Within the home, women have several responsibilities, including lighting candles, which ushers in the Sabbath on Friday nights at sundown. Women are also responsible for maintaining separation from their husbands during their menstrual cycles and, as mentioned earlier, for visiting the *mikvah* to cleanse following the menstrual cycle.

Evolution of Gender Roles in Judaism

As Judaism has evolved over the past century and has been affected by the feminist movement, women's roles have evolved as well to some degree depending on the sect. In some orthodox communities, women have started their own prayer groups, while in other, more progressive orthodox communities, women are also allowed to touch the Torah scrolls and pray in the presence of men, undivided. More and more women in modern orthodox sects are becoming interested in and becoming scholars of Judaism and the Torah. In conservative and reformed Judaism congregations, women are allowed and encouraged to take on positions of leadership, including that of rabbi and congregation president. Women are also encouraged to pray with the entire congregation, in the company of men, and are believed to be equals.

Some Jewish women believe that the existing, traditional model of prayer and Jewish law is male dominated and patriarchal and that a different feminine model should be re-envisioned. Judith Plaskow, a scholar of Jewish feminism, argues that the Jewish texts and biblical readings should be evaluated from a female perspective and that women were far more involved in shaping Jewish tradition than the interpretations of male scholars put forth. Plaskow demonstrates that women held important roles in biblical times but that their stories are not given the same space or importance as the male stories. This is parallel to the ways women's roles have been understood in modern Judaism as well, such that women are considered important and given roles to maintain the family and a peaceful home but are often silenced in a male-dominated social culture. To re-envision women's roles in Judaism and to reexamine the historical context of women's roles, Plaskow believes that it is essential to analyze the Bible from a new, feminist lens. By doing so, women's roles and positions can be seen as more prominent, providing a new context for interpretation in today's society and Jewish culture.

Interpretations of the Torah and biblical text are most often done by men, leaving the stories that shape Jewish laws even today for the most religious sects up to male and patriarchal interpretation. The Torah forms the basis for many Jewish laws and interpretations of law in modern times. While men's interpretations of women's roles focus mostly on their family relationships and issues within the home, there are stories and instances where women had roles of leadership and power that have not been widely discussed. Jewish feminist scholars are now beginning to discuss these stories and interpret them, developing new traditions that modernize women's roles as well as bring attention to previously silenced stories. For example, Jewish women's organizations and sisterhood committees in synagogues are developing events such as a women's seder, during the holiday of Passover, where women congregate for a special seder meal and the story of Passover is told from a feminine lens. Others are creating new traditions, by adding an orange to the traditional seder plate items, to represent women's equality or liberation, in the name of Miriam, a Jewish leader in the Bible, who is rarely discussed. In addition, there are traditional prayers that have been revised in the reform and conservative prayer books to include the names of important female biblical figures, in addition to the male names.

Women of Reformed Judaism, an organization within the newest sect of Judaism, published a biblical commentary from the female perspective, providing an alternative interpretation to the traditional male interpretation. This interpretation of the Torah examines women's roles and gender differences from a historical perspective, understanding the ways in which society functioned in a much earlier time period. Women and men both made important contributions to the survival of the household, and the household would not have been able to survive without either of their contributions. Women produced food and other products from the land, as well as textiles, which contributed to the economy of that time. Men's interpretations of this work do not stress women's economic contributions to the household but mainly their domestic duties as wives and mothers. Archaeologists and historians have found tools and other concrete proof that Jewish women were involved in activities outside of domestic duties.

Most of the interpretations of Jewish biblical texts do not examine women's roles and do not use a lot of discussion space to deal with women's issues. Much of the reason why so many women's interpretations and voices have been heard so many years later is that women were not given access to the Torah or taught to read Hebrew until more modern times. There are certain places in the interpretive texts that do speak of women's roles and issues, but they do so in limited ways, often relegating them to the household and never speaking of the other important things that women did in the community and in society. Male rabbis and interpretive voices often denounced women for being immodest in public, without covering all parts of their bodies with clothing. Also, Jewish women were often denounced for trying to take on public roles and speaking out in public settings against injustices.

Gender-Related Issues in Traditional Jewish Homes

Silencing women by not telling all of their stories from the Bible has led to traditions that silence women in prayer and religious observance, leading them to believe that they have no place in many Jewish traditions and prayer rituals. Furthermore, discussion and interpretation of women's roles in the Bible often focus on issues of morality, leading one to believe that if a woman has been noticed in the Jewish tradition, then there must be some moral issue to contend with. All of this sometimes leads Jewish women to feel silenced in other ways as well. Women do not feel comfortable sharing the troubles that happen in the home, as they feel that their stories are not meaningful and will not be taken seriously. In traditional Jewish law, women are not entitled to be granted a divorce, even in cases of abuse, unless the husband releases them from marriage in a Jewish court of law. Women often rely on rabbis and other religious leaders to pressure men to release them from their marriage. This enables men to have an enormous power differential over their wives. Women who do become divorced are labeled negatively and shunned from the Jewish culture and society within which they have always existed. This can be psychologically damaging to women, making them afraid to leave abusive or dysfunctional relationships.

In 2003, Carol Goodman Kaufman, a Jewish scholar, wrote about the dichotomy in Jewish law, directing attention not only to the issues discussed in this entry but also to areas of Jewish writings that explicitly tell men not to harm their wives and to treat them with care. Goodman Kaufman talks at length about this dichotomy and the number of biblical stories informing Jewish law that direct men to be respectful of their wives as well as others that make it very difficult for women to do anything in situations of abuse or serious dysfunction.

Teaching Jewish women to break some of these silences can be difficult because of the gender separation and the design of religious traditions that are centered on this separation. Awareness regarding abuse in Jewish homes, however, is being raised in more modern sects, especially the reform and conservative movements. Public campaigns place information for women who are in abusive relationships in synagogue bathrooms and other locations that Jewish women frequent. Progressive Jewish women's movements campaign to have information placed in the *mikvah* facilities.

Raising awareness and campaigning to provide women with tools to find support in situations of abuse or dysfunctional marriages is a start. Various rabbinical groups and Jewish women's organizations are working hard to bring resources into communities. These efforts are often met with resistance by individual community groups and rabbis. The literature is sparse in this area of research, but the available work shows that many religious leaders in the Jewish community are still unaware that such abuse exists within their community. Rabbis are often approached for advice in handling issues related to marital conflict, and they work to restore peace between husband and wife.

Many believe that despite the tradition of separation and role differences in religious ritual, women should be treated equally and with respect at home. This does not always translate into specific advice or actions as such. For example, a leader in the community may believe theoretically that any abusive situation should not exist, but he does not acknowledge the rituals and traditions that separate the genders and lead to difficulties with handling such situations. Thus, the leader may work with the congregant or community member to find resources or referrals to help manage the household and restore *shalom bayit*. Knowledge of the dynamics of domestic violence increases the chances that the rabbi or community leader will understand the need to find help or referrals specifically dedicated to the issue of abuse. Many Jewish leaders, though, are not trained in these dynamics and do not feel confident about counseling women or couples in these situations.

Future Directions

Gender roles and differences are central to Jewish life, tradition, and culture. Traditional sects are more rigid with gender boundaries, keeping male and female roles separated, whereas more modern sects allow women to take part in traditionally labeled male rituals. Jewish biblical texts have traditionally been interpreted by men, leaving women's stories, texts, and voices silenced for hundreds of years. More recently, Reform Judaism groups as well as some Conservative Judaism groups are embracing feminist forms of Judaism and Jewish life, reexamining the texts from a woman's perspective and learning more about women's roles and lives during biblical times. These new examinations of text are influencing the ways in which Jewish laws are interpreted and the ways in which rituals are practiced, providing women with a more prominent role in Jewish life and culture, as well as ritual.

Domestic violence is an example of the ways in which the dichotomies of Jewish law and related gender issues can have a negative impact on women, silencing their voices. Future research and work in this area should focus on ways in which women's voices can be shared more openly. Furthermore, Jewish leaders and traditional communities should be educated and provided resources to handle issues such as domestic violence, so that women do not feel isolated and feel that there is some recourse to handle their situation safely, with support.

Amanda Sisselman-Borgia

See also Career Choice and Gender; Cultural Gender Role Norms; Feminism: Overview; Intimate Partner Violence

Further Readings

Eskenazi, T. C., & Weiss, A. L. (Eds.). (2008). *The Torah: A women's commentary*. New York, NY: URJ Press.

Jackson, S. (1997). God of our fathers: Feminism and Judaism—A contradiction in terms? *Women's Studies International Forum, 20*(1), 129–143.

Kaufman, C. G. (2003). *Sins of omission: The Jewish community's reaction to domestic violence*. New York, NY: Basic Books.

Plaskow, J. (1990). *Standing again at Sinai: Judaism from a feminist perspective.* San Francisco, CA: HarperCollins.

Judaism and Sexual Orientation

Jewish identity and nonheterosexual orientation (i.e., lesbian, gay, bisexual, and queer [LGBQ]) are typically seen as two separate identities, though both involve some form of identity negotiation. The presumption in some Jewish communities is that one is heterosexual, and the presumption in some LGBQ communities is that one is not religious. Thus, the intersection of Judaism and sexual orientation provides challenges and opportunities for growth, from attitudinal shifts and questioning of staid understandings of religion and sexual orientation to the recognition of multiple and intersecting identities. Lack of acceptance in each community of the other identity and in mainstream communities of both groups makes these negotiations rife with negative consequences, such as internalized identity gaps, relational stress, community rejection, and even violence. Research shows that individuals with stigmatized identities have developed strategies for negotiating these pressures. These strategies include separating or integrating their multiple identities. These strategies will evolve as norms and mores change, particularly those associated with same-sex marriage in the United States and other countries. This entry discusses the complex interplay between Judaism and sexual orientation.

Understanding Judaism and Sexual Orientation

Judaism and nonheterosexual orientation (i.e., LGBQ) are typically considered to be two separate identities or cultural groups. Individuals who identify with these minority groups have historically been stigmatized, and both identities have been hidden or closeted from the mainstream. Judaism is often seen as hereditary (i.e., inherited from one's mother); however, it is more accurately viewed as a volitional religious and cultural identity. In contrast, sexual orientation is viewed as having a biological basis in addition to cultural implications, though this basis is still not uniformly accepted. Thus, while Jewish identity often assumes heritability, the biological basis of nonheterosexual orientation is often denied. One can see reasons for overlap and divergence, then, in these identities.

Recent theorizing and research on culture and identity encourage examination of overlapping identities. The communication theory of identity, for example, explicitly assumes that people experience multiple interacting or interpenetrating identities at any one moment. One rarely perceives and behaves through a single identity frame or lens; rather, we are complex interactions of multiple identities. As a result, someone who identifies as Jewish is likely also to assume occupational, relational, and gender identities. Likewise, members of the LGBQ community are not only gay or lesbian but also friends, lawyers, and members of religions. It is this assumption of overlap that is considered in this discussion of these two identities, starting with the Jewish identity and its relationship to the religion, Judaism.

Judaism and Jewish Identity

Judaism is a religion with historical roots that trace back over 3,000 years to what some argue is the first monotheistic religion. Members of the religion have variously considered themselves (and been considered by others) to be a tribe, race, nationality, and cultural identity. Since the emergence of Christianity, Middle Eastern Islam, and Eastern European communism as dominant regional forces, Judaism has often been a stigmatized identity. At the same time, Jewish people have seen their associations evolve over time, often from a religious to a cultural identity.

For many, particularly in the United States, Jewish identity has transformed from an all-encompassing identity to one that exists alongside or in combination with other identities. The Jewish identity includes a complex interplay of religious, ethnic, racial, and cultural behaviors. Jewish education, membership in social groups, and philanthropic contributions constitute nonreligious behaviors, and the observance of Jewish laws and rituals constitute religious behaviors. While Jewish identity always included both religious and secular elements, for many Jews in the United States and elsewhere, the religious element has become subordinate to cultural or secular elements. For them, Jewish identity is not focused solely on images of God or religious practices as much as it represents a social style. Most American Jewish organizations, for example, consider Jewish identity to be a combination of both religious and ethnic characteristics. A synagogue not only has traditionally been a house of worship and study but also serves as a center for secular Jewish cultural and social activities. For example, a seemingly nonreligious Jewish philanthropic organization may close its offices during religious holidays and may coordinate a religious service for the Jewish homeless. At times, being Jewish has superseded other identities for group members in the face of oppression; during past historical epochs such as the Holocaust, one's Jewish identity often took on a monolithic or singular emphasis.

When others within and outside Jewish communities are determining who is Jewish, they may rely on the matrilineal principle where one's mother must be Jewish, the nonlineal principle of having one Jewish parent and being raised Jewish, or cultural indicators such as gastronomy, traditional family, and involvement in communal rituals, ceremonies, and identity. Others consider Jewish identity as contingent on community participation.

The embrace of modernism and individualism has shaped the identity of the Jewish community, as seen in the erosion of generational continuities by increased exposure to non-Jewish ideas and symbols. Jewish identity is formed from one's family life, religious beliefs, social network, and life experiences. Traditionally, Jewish life existed within a closed community whose members learned, worked, and prayed together using common languages reflecting a shared heritage and a unity of belief. Jewish identity was both central and salient, consisting of a pattern of prescribed and fixed actions and beliefs. The Jewish religion in the Unites States has changed to meet the needs of the individual, as evidenced by the variety of religious interpretations in Judaism, seen in the presence of four Jewish denominations: (1) Orthodox, (2) Conservative, (3) Reform, and (4) Reconstructionist. The transformation of religious life to meet the needs of the individual has created a shift from a religious to a nonreligious identity and from a community of shared belief to a community of shared identity. Thus, Jewish identity constitutes an ethnic and cultural identity as well as a religious one and includes individuals determining for themselves how they will define their Jewishness. One may identify as Jewish through affiliation with Jewish communities, religious affiliation, observed rituals, and/or personal conceptions of what being Jewish means.

LGBQ Jewish Identity

The relationship between LGBQ and Jewish identities may be quite complex. Some LGBQ Jews experience being Jewish as a bifurcated rather than integrated relationship; individuals may have to choose between being Jewish or LGBQ, depending on the kind of LGBQ and/or Jewish community present in their lives. Some, including many Conservative and Orthodox congregations, believe that Jewish law condemns homosexuality as contrary to the natural order and a rejection of the covenant between God and the Jews. Family embarrassment and concern pressure some individuals to hide being LGBQ from their Jewish communities and dissuade them from participating in communal prayers to remain a part of their Jewish communities.

Other Jewish communities, such as the Reconstruction and Reform communities, have moved beyond tolerance of LGBQ Jews and the injunctions against homosexuality in mainstream Judaism with their blessing of same-sex unions and the ordination of LGBQ rabbis. Beginning in the 1970s, organized movements of LGBQ Jews fought for integration, and in 1972, Beth Chayim Chadashim (an LGBQ synagogue) was built in Los Angeles, California, and was admitted to the Union of American Hebrew Congregations despite national controversy. In addition, the Union of American Hebrew Congregations passed the Human Rights of Homosexuals resolution 5 years later with 80% approval. In 1974, the Federation of Reconstructionist Congregations and Havurot supported gay and lesbian rabbinic ordination, and in 1993, they passed resolutions that explicitly welcomed LGBQ members into their congregations. In addition, congregations were asked to address heterosexist biases and affirm the right of Reconstructionist rabbis to perform same-sex commitment ceremonies.

Within a process called bifurcation, an individual may experience an "identity gap," which happens when one or more elements of a person's identities are discordant or even in conflict with other elements. As described earlier, Orthodox LGBQ Jews who have accepted religious condemnations of their gender orientation or LGBQ anti-Semitism are likely to experience gaps between and among these elements of their identities. Managing these gaps becomes a complex endeavor. LGBQ Jews may contend with minority stress, stigmatization, and feelings of bifurcation by separating their Jewish and LGBQ identities, integrating them, or segmenting their identities contingent on factors such as geography, community, and relationships. The LGBQ and Jewish communities surrounding LGBQ Jews influence the integration of their identities into their self-concepts, relationships, and perceptions of community. Some individuals choose to "out-marry," though some may desire a long-term relational partner who is Jewish because of a desire for shared cultural values, fear of anti-Semitism, and parental wishes for a Jewish pairing regardless of the partner's sex. The rejection of gay identity in the Jewish community and anti-Jewish sentiment in society can lead to LGBQ Jews internalizing negative attitudes toward LGBQ individuals and anti-Semitism and expressing this lack of self-acceptance, in part, through intergroup partnering.

Other LGBQ Jews use management of the conversation and relationship as well as self-statements to contend with anti-Semitism and homophobia. The continuum of responses from separation to integration demonstrate that, for some, the focus on parts of identity may help them manage anti-Semitism and homophobia. This management often includes choosing a specific relational partner (Jewish or not), neighborhood (predominately Jewish or LGBQ), social network (LGBQ or Jewish), or résumé list (Jewish or LGBQ organizations). It is also possible for LGBQ Jews to re-create communities and culture to make room for themselves, make a Jewish community, and create new forms of Jewish life. The kind of social support influences whether a person feels accepted, comfortable, and able to identify with Jewish and LGBQ communities. Another strategy for contending with the stigma of and negative reactions to being Jewish and LGBQ is to assimilate and pass as Christian and/or heterosexual. Some individuals experience being LGBQ as different from being Jewish; being LGBQ may influence daily life and decisions (e.g., talking about a relational partner at work) more than being Jewish, demonstrating that enactment of some identities may carry more consequences. Some use passing (closeting) as a strategy because of fears of rejection, violence, and misunderstanding, though others believe that being out is actually a religious obligation and not antithetical to Jewish practice in the Reform and Reconstructionist traditions. Those who integrate their LGBQ and Jewish identities, regardless of their experiences with anti-Semitism and negative attitudes toward LGBQ individuals, do not closet their identities and actively enact their identities through their work and choice of community. Being part of a Reconstructionist community is a way for LGBQ Jews to connect secular and religious life.

Even with these strategies, identity gaps may cause alienation and estrangement for all but the most secure. Persons experiencing identity gaps may experience embarrassment for themselves and/or for the group, or experience hostile reactions, resulting in an identity negotiation rife with risk. Negative attributions by others or self-expression puts persons at risk for an array of negative outcomes, from as minor as dissatisfying conversations in relationships to more significant outcomes such as depression, partner loss, job loss, internal anti-Semitism and negative attitudes toward LGBQ individuals, and alienation. Others, however, may try to honor both identities, and this may be challenging, particularly if there is insufficient means to form integrated relationships and communities. Relationally, gaps also can lead to disagreements over children's religious education, being outed, and/or finding an accepting community. More objectively, these problems are reflected in hate crime statistics, where both groups rank among the top victims.

Identity negotiations are not entirely negative. There are successes, too. For some, emphasizing one element of identity over the other (e.g., seeing themselves as primarily LGBQ or Jewish but not an LGBQ Jew) helps embed them in a single community that provides the support they need to thrive. For others, provisional and even compartmentalized moments of integrated identity may be a more reasonable goal.

Finally, an important part of negotiating identity is deciding if it is safe to disclose these identities. Members tend to appraise the situation and make judgments about the likelihood of rejection, misunderstanding, and even violence. But despite the odds, many LGBQ Jews find communities that provide love and acceptance, sometimes among others who share these two closetable identities, as reflected in research as well as popular anthologies of personal narratives about being LGBQ and Jewish. Thus, it is possible for LGBQ Jews to move beyond the "traditional dilemma of bifurcated selves" and the choice to either stay closeted within or leave entirely their Jewish communities.

Sandra L. Faulkner and Michael L. Hecht

See also Homophobia; Intersectional Identities; Judaism and Gender; Sexual Orientation Identity; Stereotype Threat and Gender

Further Readings

Alpert, R. T., Elwell, S. L., & Idelson, S. (Eds.). (2001). *Lesbian rabbis: The first generation.* New Brunswick, NJ: Rutgers University.

Balka, C., & Rose, A. (Eds.). (1989). *Twice blessed: On being lesbian, gay and Jewish.* Boston, MA: Beacon.

Brown, A. (2004). *Mentsh: On being Jewish and queer.* Los Angeles, CA: Alyson Books.

Coyle, A., & Rafalin, D. (2000). Jewish gay men's accounts of negotiating cultural, religious, and sexual identity: A qualitative study. *Journal of Psychology & Human Sexuality, 12*(4), 21–48. doi:10.1300/J056v12n04_02

Faulkner, S. L., & Hecht, M. L. (2011). The negotiation of closetable identities: A narrative analysis of LGBTQ Jewish identity. *Journal of Social and Personal Relationships, 28*(6), 829–847. doi:10.1177/0265407510391338

Schnoor, R. S. (2003). *Finding one's place: Ethnic identity construction among gay Jewish men* (Unpublished doctoral dissertation). McGill University, Montreal, Quebec, Canada.

Schnoor, R. S., & Weinfeld, M. (2005). Seeking a mate: Inter-group partnerships among gay Jewish men. *Canadian Ethnic Studies, 38*(1), 21–39.

Shneer, D., & Aviv, C. (Eds.). (2002). *Queer Jews.* New York, NY: Routledge.

Juvenile Justice System and Gender

The term *juvenile justice system* (JJS) refers to those parts of the legal system that deal with violations of the criminal law by young people. Juveniles are usually defined as those under the age of 18 years, but this is not true for all states in the United States. The JJS includes law enforcement, the courts, and the correctional system. Gender, like age, race, class, family composition, and other factors, often has an impact on a child or adolescent's experience in the JJS. Because youth who encounter the JJS do so when they are still growing and developing their gender identities, gender and the JJS intersect in a number of ways. These include the issues that bring these youth into the system as well as their treatment by the system. Young people's gender identity development includes their perceptions of their gender roles in the family, the neighborhood, and society at large—what it means to be a man, what it means to be a woman, and how gender identity shapes girls' and boys' actions. This entry provides a brief outline of the origins of the JJS and explores some of the ways in which gender shapes the JJS experience, including gender disparities in the system, risk factors and vulnerabilities, and interventions.

The JJS

The U.S. JJS originated in response to concerns about children and adolescents being imprisoned with adult offenders. Its founders believed that children had a greater potential to be rehabilitated, or made into law-abiding persons, than did adults and that this rehabilitation was more likely to occur in an environment where young people were protected from the presumed bad influence of adult offenders. The first juvenile court was established in Illinois in 1899, and the other states quickly followed suit. In most, but not all, states, a juvenile is defined as a person who has not yet attained his or her 18th birthday at the time of the charged offense. Some states set the age limit a year or two lower.

Even before separate juvenile courts existed, however, girls and boys tended to be brought before the courts for different reasons. Boys would often be arrested for offenses deemed to constitute a threat to the public, such as fighting or theft, whereas many girls were brought to court by their own families because they disobeyed parental rules or were suspected of sexual activity. Gender norms and prevailing ideas about which children were dangerous and which were in danger influenced the ways parents and courts responded to transgressions. The needs for protection, control, and regulation of the child were likely to be balanced differently depending on the child's gender. To a great extent, the modern JJS separates delinquency charges, which constitute the violation of a criminal law by a juvenile, from status offenses, which are the commission of an act by a juvenile that would be legal if committed by an adult. Examples of status offenses are failure to obey reasonable parental authority or running away.

Gender Disparities

Boys predominate in the JJS as a whole, and the proportion of boys to girls in the system tends to increase the deeper into the JJS continuum one progresses. Some official sources report that juvenile courts handle 2.5 times the number of cases involving boys as they do girls' cases. However, the number of boys sentenced to juvenile facilities can be more than 25 times the number of girls in such facilities. What is sometimes called the "funnel" of the JJS tends to filter out many more girls than boys along the way, through diversion, probation, dismissal, or other outcomes. There are many reasons for this, and two of the primary ones are the so-called chivalry effect and the differing risk factors and vulnerabilities faced by girls and boys.

The Chivalry Effect

People usually think of the JJS as what happens to juveniles in court and afterward in the correctional system. However, many events that take place earlier in the process, such as the initial police contact, arrest, charging, and detention decision, also have an impact on which cases are handled by the JJS. Gender bias in favor of girls is widely considered to be present in these early stages, resulting in girls often being diverted from the system instead of going to court. One example of such favorable treatment would be a police officer who warns a girl and returns her home to her parents for committing an offense but arrests and charges a boy who commits a similar offense. This practice of more lenient treatment for girls is sometimes referred to as the chivalry effect. It may pervade all phases of the JJS, from the original point of police contact through the disposition, or sentencing. Whether this more lenient treatment is ultimately beneficial or harmful to girls is subject to debate. At the same time, girls may be treated more strictly than boys are by the JJS when they are viewed as putting themselves in danger. This can be attributed to a more protective or paternalistic attitude toward girls, who are seen by many actors in the JJS as more vulnerable than boys in some ways and therefore needing more restrictions placed on their freedom of movement.

Some researchers argue, however, that in the 21st century girls are more likely to face charges, especially for offenses such as fighting in school, which might formerly have been handled administratively by school officials rather than legally by charging. Some attribute this shift in practice to zero-tolerance policies regarding school violence. Thus, changing perceptions of other threats, such as the risks inherent in school violence, as well as changing ideas about gender may affect the extent of gender disparities in the JJS.

Risk Factors and Vulnerabilities

Boys and girls each face unique gender-based risks and vulnerabilities that may bring them into contact with the JJS.

Boys

Gender often influences the path that brings a young person into the JJS. The strong associations in U.S. history and culture between men and guns or other weapons, and between men and violence, may lead some boys to believe that acquiring a gun or engaging in other forms of violence is part of becoming a man, particularly if the young man grows up in an environment where weapons and violence are common. In addition, the traditional role of men as providers often inclines boys, especially those living in homes with mothers who struggle financially, to take part in income-producing forms of delinquency, such as drug sales, robbery, burglary, or theft, while still in their early teens. Similarly, the traditional male role of protector may prompt boys to defend female family members or younger siblings by engaging in assaultive behavior against persons viewed as threatening their loved ones. Both provider and protector roles may be accentuated if the young man perceives himself to be functioning in the role of "man of the house." Regardless of a young man's environment, however, he may encounter sociocultural pressures that encourage male bonding through illegal activities such as vandalism, bullying, or harassment of out-groups.

Girls

While both boys and girls can be victims of sexual abuse, girls are more frequently victimized, and they, like boys, may be victims of physical abuse as well. Girls with a history of abuse may enter the JJS because of status offenses, such as running away, or sometimes because of other offenses precipitated by leaving home and fending for themselves, such as theft, prostitution, or drug offenses.

When girls are arrested for assaultive behavior, the behavior often occurs in their home against parents or siblings, or in school, often against other girls. Some fights may occur out in the streets of the neighborhood, occasionally involving weapons, especially box cutter knives and other types of blades. Relational issues, such as fights over boys, may give rise to such assaults. Girls' aggression and violence, whether against other girls, boys, or adults, may stem from a number of origins, including long-term anger from experiencing victimization.

While homicide, the taking of a human life, is most often associated with boys and men, one type of homicide is uniquely associated with girls and women because only they can bear children. Neonaticide is the killing of a newborn within 24 hours of its birth. Although a boy or a man may be charged with this offense, it is more likely that a girl or a woman will face this charge alone. In these situations, the juvenile girl may, out of fear, have concealed her unplanned pregnancy from those around her and may give birth at home in solitude. The newborn may die, whether from being smothered to conceal its crying from others, from being exposed to the elements if the baby is left outside, or from other causes. If the baby's mother is charged with homicide, the JJS must determine the appropriate disposition for the offense. Transfer of the case to adult court, incarceration in a facility for juvenile girls, and probation with psychological, psychiatric, or other counseling are all possibilities in such tragic cases.

Lesbian, Gay, Bisexual, Transgender, and Questioning Youth in the JJS

Lesbian, gay, bisexual, transgender, and questioning (LGBTQ) youth are believed to be overrepresented in the JJS, although obtaining an accurate estimate is difficult. While research into the experiences of LGBTQ youth in the JJS is in its early stages, several reasons have been proposed for this overrepresentation. These include the increased likelihood of LGBTQ youth being runaways, homeless, or victims, and being arrested for status offenses and other nonviolent offenses. Once detained, they may be less likely to be released during the pretrial stage of court proceedings, due to problems at home, than heterosexual youth in custody for similar offenses. If an LGBTQ youth is sentenced to a secure juvenile facility, he or she may face an increased risk of victimization by other residents. This can result in the youth being placed in protective isolation, which presents additional risks to the young person's physical or mental health and interferes with the juvenile's opportunity to participate in reentry programming. Staff and volunteers at juvenile facilities receive training to help them understand and be attentive to the rights and vulnerabilities of LGBTQ residents.

Interventions

Although boys outnumber girls in the JJS, the term *gender specific* has traditionally been used to refer to programming specifically designed for girls. Only since the late 20th century has attention been given to addressing issues specific to masculinity. This is partially due to the evolution of the men's movement, which has focused attention on the ways in which masculine gender can affect psychosocial processes and influence behavior. JJS interventions, such as fatherhood programs as part of reentry curricula, have begun to address risk factors and identity processes specific to boys. Programming for girls in residential, secure, or probationary dispositions often includes health awareness, with a focus on how the body functions as well as the importance of physical exercise and healthy self-esteem. In addition, girls receive education about child development, as many of the young women are mothers or are taking care of children. Programming is also likely to include workshops discussing particular types of victimization to which a girl, especially a girl who enters the JJS, may have been especially vulnerable, whether as a victim or a witness. These services might focus on domestic violence, child or adolescent sexual abuse, or other types of physical abuse.

Residential programs and secure facilities for adjudicated juveniles, which are segregated by gender, often feature occupational training that follows traditional gender career paths, such as auto mechanics for boys and cosmetology for girls. Both boys' and girls' facilities may also offer training in more gender neutral vocations, such as graphic arts, as well as opportunities to finish high school and take college courses.

Diane Marano

See also Criminal Justice System and Gender; Criminal Justice System and Sexual Orientation; Criminal Justice System and Transgender People; Masculinity in Adolescence; Sexual Assault, Adolescent Survivors of

Further Readings

Barrett, C. L. (2013). *Courting kids: Inside an experimental youth court.* New York: New York University Press.

Chesney-Lind, M., & Shelden, R. G. (1998). *Girls, delinquency, and juvenile justice* (2nd ed.). Belmont, CA: West/Wadsworth.

Development Services Group. (2014). *LGBTQ youths in the juvenile justice system* [Literature review]. Washington, DC: Office of Juvenile Justice and Delinquency Prevention. Retrieved from http://www.ojjdp.gov/mpg/litreviews/LGBTQYouthsintheJuvenileJusticeSystem.pdf

Fader, J. J. (2013). *Falling back: Incarceration and transitions to adulthood among urban youth.* New Brunswick, NJ: Rutgers University Press.

Messerschmidt, J. W. (1993). *Masculinities and crime: Critique and reconceptualization of theory.* Lanham, MD: Rowman & Littlefield.

Schaffner, L. (2006). *Girls in trouble with the law.* New Brunswick, NJ: Rutgers University Press.

Schneider, E. C. (1992). *In the web of class: Delinquents and reformers in Boston, 1810s–1930s.* New York: New York University Press.

Silver, L. J. (2015). *System kids: Adolescent mothers and the politics of regulation.* Chapel Hill: University of North Carolina Press.

Kinsey Reports

The Kinsey Reports are the collective name for two volumes authored by Alfred C. Kinsey and colleagues: *Sexual Behavior in the Human Male* (1948) and *Sexual Behavior in the Human Female* (1953). They describe, exhibit, and interpret interview data from more than 18,000 participants that Kinsey and his coresearchers collected from the late 1930s through 1950. The analysis in the Kinsey Reports also incorporates extensive historical research and the team's own original (sometimes participatory) research using still photography and film. The Kinsey Reports remain noteworthy in studies of sexual behavior for their size, thoroughness, and impact through the present.

Historical Development

Kinsey began the research that would become the Kinsey Reports in the mid-1930s as a zoology professor at Indiana University, Bloomington, where he had been working since 1920. His interest in sex research developed out of his biology pedagogy teaching, the professional decline in his preferred field methods for entomological studies, his extensive reading in sexology, and students approaching him during the leadership of a noncredit marriage course starting in the summer of 1938. At the same time, he also began traveling to Chicago and northern Indiana to interview men who identified as gay. In the fall of 1940, the university president granted him permission to devote his research to human sexual behavior. Two co-investigators, Wardell B. Pomeroy and Clyde E. Martin, soon joined him.

Kinsey developed a questionnaire and a form of interviewing that he taught to Pomeroy and Martin. The questionnaire contained approximately 300 questions for most individuals, but additional questions (up to 521) were possible for those with homosexual, sadomasochistic, or prostitution experience. The questions covered an individual's sex history comprehensively and used orgasm as a measure of whether a sexual experience occurred. The team memorized the questions and recorded answers in a secret code on a preformed single interview sheet. The team gathered interview subjects using a 100% group sampling method: They became acquainted with the leaders of specific groups and used their influence to convince all members of the group to participate in private individual interviews. Standard interviews took roughly 90 minutes to complete; more complex histories took up to 3 hours. The interview data were transferred onto punched cards and processed in punched-card machines for statistical analysis. Kinsey chose W. B. Saunders, a conservative medical press in Philadelphia, as the publisher for the first volume in a planned multivolume series on human sexual behavior. That first volume was *Sexual Behavior in the Human Male*, released in January 1948.

Sexual Behavior in the Human Male

The *Male* volume presented data from 5,300 White American male interviewees, some of whom were or had previously been incarcerated. It was organized in three sections. The first section described the history of sexology and explained the reasons for the current study, the interview methods, the statistical methods, and the justifications for the validity of the data. The second section outlined child and adolescent sexual behavior and factors that influenced adult sexual behavior, including age, age at adolescence, social class, stability of social class, rural/urban background, and religious background. The third section examined sexual behavior by the circumstance in which the subjects experienced orgasm: masturbation, heterosexual petting (foreplay), nocturnal emissions, premarital intercourse, marital intercourse, extramarital intercourse, prostitution, homosexual contact, and animal contact. The volume concluded with a set of clinical tables for physicians, social workers, legal professionals, and others who would find the average amounts of behavior shown for different types of men useful in their professional practice.

The volume included hundreds of pages of statistics displayed in graphs, charts, and tables, but some of the most striking statistics were in the chapters on extramarital intercourse and homosexual behavior. Fifty percent of the interviewees admitted to extramarital intercourse, and 37% of all interviewees admitted to at least one homosexual experience to orgasm. Ten percent of the interviewees stated that they had exclusively homosexual experiences for a 3-year period. The volume was also notable for the presentation and description of a 0 to 6 scale later known as the Kinsey Scale, which plotted an individual's behaviors, fantasies, and desires on a scale from 0 (*completely opposite sex*) to 6 (*completely same sex*).

Sexual Behavior in the Human Female

The second Kinsey Report was published in August 1953 and centered on women's sexual behaviors and comparisons between men and women. (The team now included Paul H. Gebhard.) The *Female* volume was based on 5,940 interviews with White American women who had never been incarcerated. It included two sections similar to two in the *Male* volume: one on methodology and the second on sources of sexual outlet. However, the *Female* volume did not include a section on factors affecting sexual outlet, in part because social class did not appear to affect women's sexual behavior as it did men's and in part because Kinsey and his growing research team instead devoted five chapters to similarities and differences in men's and women's sexual bodies and minds. They presented findings on the anatomical, physiological, psychological, hormonal, and neurological aspects of sexual behavior. They concluded that men's and women's bodies were largely the same anatomically and physiologically, though men were more impressionable psychologically. The research team found inconclusive data on the role of hormones and brain function in determining sexual response and orgasm, concluding that if gender difference in human sexuality existed, that difference may manifest in the brain.

Due to Kinsey's untimely death in August 1956, no further volumes were published as part of the Kinsey Reports, though the Kinsey Institute published additional books based on the original interview data. The two Kinsey Reports stand as landmarks in American history and the history of sexology.

Donna J. Drucker

See also Bisexuality; Heterosexuality; Homosexuality; Identity Construction; Kinsey Scale, The; Measuring Sexual Orientation; Pansexuality; Sexual Identity

Further Readings

Drucker, D. J. (2014). *The classification of sex: Alfred Kinsey and the organization of knowledge.* Pittsburgh, PA: University of Pittsburgh Press.

Kinsey, A. C., Pomeroy, W. B., & Martin, C. E. (1948). *Sexual behavior in the human male.* Philadelphia, PA: W. B. Saunders.

Kinsey, A. C., Pomeroy, W. B., Martin, C. E., & Gebhard, P. H. (1953). *Sexual behavior in the human female.* Philadelphia, PA: W. B. Saunders.

Kinsey Scale, The

Biologist and sex researcher Alfred C. Kinsey created the Kinsey Scale, also known as the 0–6 scale or heterosexuality-homosexuality scale, in 1940. The Kinsey Scale was first published in Kinsey's coauthored book *Sexual Behavior in the Human Male* (1948) and reprinted in the subsequent volume, *Sexual Behavior in the Human Female* (1953). The Kinsey Scale was a visual representation of human sexual behavior, desire, and fantasy on a 7-point spectrum from 0 (*completely heterosexual*) to 6 (*completely homosexual*). Since its initial publication, the Kinsey Scale remains a popular tool for individuals to consider their sexual identity without using the words *heterosexual*, *bisexual*, and *homosexual*.

Historical Development

Quantitative research using large data sets rose in popularity in the 1920s and 1930s among U.S. social and human scientists, including sex researchers Robert Latou Dickinson and Katharine Bement Davis. Kinsey, who had collected more than 6 million individual gall wasps during his entomological research in the 1920s and 1930s, turned his interest in large sample sizes and quantitative data methods to studying human sexual behavior. Beginning in the summer of 1938, he began leading a marriage course at Indiana University, Bloomington, and collecting data in private interview sessions from the students, faculty, and faculty spouses who attended the course. After the marriage course concluded in August 1940 and Kinsey turned to sex research full-time, he developed an interview method and used punched-card machine technology to organize the data. That September, he wrote a letter to Glenn V. Ramsey, an Indiana University graduate student whose own research with adolescent boys in Peoria, Illinois, found that approximately one third of them engaged in homosexual behavior. Kinsey compared Ramsey's research with his own findings, and in the letter, he described the development of a numerical method and image to represent a range of sexual behavior that decoupled behavior from the standard categories of "homosexual" and "heterosexual." After the creation of the scale, Kinsey showed it to interviewees and asked them to place themselves on the scale. The interviewer would also include his own perception of the interviewee's scale number on the interview sheet.

The Kinsey Scale in *Sexual Behavior in the Human Male*

The Kinsey Scale was printed in the *Male* volume's chapter on homosexual behavior, which compiled data from 5,300 White male interviewees. Kinsey and his coauthors described the scale as a continuum, arguing that interviewees' sexual behavior, desire, and fantasy rarely fell into the easy black-and-white categories that law, medicine, religion, and broader U.S. society had established and enforced. According to the authors, human sexual experiences should not be dichotomized into "normal" or "abnormal," "acceptable" or "unacceptable," or "heterosexual" or "homosexual." Instead, it was more accurate to represent the diversity of sexual experience based on the relative amounts of heterosexual and homosexual experiences in an individual's history. In the *Male* volume, the percentage of Kinsey zeros ranged between 61.2 and 86.5 (depending on age, educational level, marital status, rural/urban background, and religious background), with the rest of the values between "X" (asexual) and 1 through 6. In the *Female* volume, the percentage of Kinsey zeros similarly ranged between 61 and 90 (depending on age, educational level, and marital status), with the rest of the values between "X" and 1 through 6. As Kinsey and his coauthors noted, however, the single-digit values were only placeholders—there were infinite ways in which a person could identify using the scale's numbers.

Furthermore, the authors argued that the word *homosexual* should be used to describe same-sex encounters and fantasies regardless of physical position or the number of times an encounter or fantasy occurred; rather, the proportion of heterosexual and homosexual behaviors was most important. They found that 46% of men had experienced some sexual arousal from other men and that 37% of men (and 13% of women) had homosexual contact that led to orgasm. Since same-sex physical encounters were illegal across the United States until the late 20th century, Kinsey and his team argued that given their evidence, all homosexual behavior should be destigmatized and legalized.

One of the statistics derived from the Kinsey Scale became a critical figure in both antihomosexual campaigns and the gay and lesbian rights movement. Kinsey and his colleagues found that

10% of men had lived exclusively homosexual lives for at least 3 years between the ages of 16 and 55. The figure of 10% became fixed as the overall percentage of gays and lesbians in U.S. society. Antihomosexual campaigns of the 1950s claimed that 10% of federal government employees were homosexual and must be discovered and removed from employment. Gay and lesbian political movements, first beginning in the 1950s and growing much larger by the 1970s, proudly proclaimed that they made up 10% of the U.S. population and deserved full legal rights.

Long-Term Legacy

The Kinsey Scale has been reused by sex researchers and adapted into other forms, including Fritz Klein's Klein Sexual Orientation Grid, which added the dimension of time, and Michael D. Storms's Storms Scale, which differentiated sex role and erotic orientation. It is being reprinted widely online in the early 21st century and used by individuals as a self-discovery instrument. Kinsey's goal of changing "heterosexual" and "homosexual" to descriptors for behaviors alone and not identities or persons was not successful. However, using Kinsey numbers as personal descriptors remains current in early-21st-century GLBT (gay, lesbian, bisexual, and transgender) culture, as reflected by entities such as the "dragapella" group Kinsey Sicks, a band called "The Kinsey Scale," and a Wisconsin support organization for bisexual and pansexual individuals called 521 (five-to-one).

Donna J. Drucker

See also Bisexuality; Heterosexuality; Homosexuality; Identity Construction; Kinsey Reports; Measuring Sexual Orientation; Pansexuality; Sexual Identity

Further Readings

Drucker, D. J. (2012). Marking sexuality from 0–6: The Kinsey Scale in online culture. *Sexuality and Culture, 16*, 241–262. doi:10.1007/s12119-011-9122-1

Kinsey, A. C., Pomeroy, W. B., & Martin, C. E. (1948). *Sexual behavior in the human male*. Philadelphia, PA: W. B. Saunders.

McWhirter, D. P., Sanders, S. A., & Reinisch, J. M. (Eds.). (1990). *Homosexuality/heterosexuality: Concepts of sexual orientation*. New York, NY: Oxford University Press.

Kohlberg's Stages of Moral Development

Lawrence Kohlberg's theory of moral development originated out of his studies on the development of children's and adolescents' moral thinking. Building on the theories of John Dewey and Jean Piaget, Kohlberg identified six developmental stages of moral reasoning. Successive stages represent increasing complexity and psychological adequacy in solving moral problems. According to this theory, moral development is a process of organized mental transformations regarding social interactions and concepts. This entry further describes Kohlberg's stages and how they are identified, discusses their relation to gender and culture, and examines the challenges and revisions to Kohlberg's theory.

Justice and Perspective Taking

In this developmental process, the individual internalizes, actively organizes, and becomes capable of carrying out more advanced and complex modes of moral thinking. Throughout development, there is an increase in *moral perspective taking*, which is the basic developmental phenomenon underlying moral stages. According to Kohlberg, moral perspective taking is about justice, as it is based on rights, duties, and obligations. Throughout development, the individual's conception of what constitutes justice undergoes transformation.

Each successive stage represents a more inclusive and more complex moral perspective taking. In this sense, Kohlberg's theory is a theory of increasing moral awareness. As the *level of sociomoral perspective* improves, moral awareness develops. Each stage includes the concerns of the earlier stages but also transforms their meaning on behalf of its own, more complex framework of priorities. At each successive stage, there is a different structure of thinking, which transcends, reorganizes, and replaces the earlier structure.

Characteristics of Stages

As part of the cognitive-developmental tradition, Kohlberg's theory is based on the following characteristics of stages: (a) qualitative distinctions, (b) structured wholeness, (c) invariant sequence, and (d) hierarchical integration. First, different stages represent qualitatively different thinking patterns that correspond to different ages. Second, the type of thinking that characterizes a particular stage is expected to manifest consistently across various contexts. Third, development over time follows an invariant sequence of stages. That is, all individuals are expected to move forward from earlier to later stages in step-by-step fashion, without the possibility of skipping stages or moving backward. Fourth, higher stages incorporate the cognitive capacities of the earlier stages. Because of their inclusivity and comprehensiveness, higher stages have adaptive advantage. Therefore, the natural course of development is toward higher stages. As *logical necessities*, higher stages emerge out of and incorporate the earlier stages.

Descriptions of Stages

Kohlberg proposed three levels, each representing a distinct socio-moral perspective. Each level has two stages. The second stage of each level is the fuller articulation and more adequate fulfillment of the level's socio-moral perspective.

The preconventional level represents the *concrete individual perspective*, according to which the self experiences duties, obligations, and rules externally, without internalization. Stage 1 is the *punishment-and-obedience orientation*, based on an appeal to power and authority as ultimate realities. Stage 2 is the *instrumentalist-relativist orientation*, through which the individual is primarily motivated to fulfill personal needs. At this stage, justice is based on crude reciprocity. Recognition of other people's needs is a means toward the primary goal of satisfying one's own needs.

The conventional level represents the *member-of-society perspective*, representing the internalization of and identification with social rules and expectations. Stage 3 is *the interpersonal concordance or "good boy/nice girl" orientation*, based on being nice to others and winning their approval. At this stage, the individual feels identified with a system of interpersonal relationships that extends beyond the individual's personal needs. Stage 4 is *the law-and-order orientation* toward social order. Moral thinking is in terms of the existing social system of rules and laws.

The postconventional level represents the *prior-to-society perspective*, based on autonomously chosen principles that transcend external rules and expectations. This level identifies morality with objective obligations as parts of natural moral law. Stage 5 is *the social-contract, legalistic orientation* toward the greatest good for the greatest number of people in society. This *utilitarian* orientation represents pluralism that observes the rights and welfare of all members of society. Right action or judgment is based on the acknowledgment and utilization of the relative value of diverse perspectives, and the need to achieve social consensus beyond the dictates of social rules and regulations. According to this stage, the construction and application of laws and duties must be based on a rationally achieved understanding of overall social welfare. With the exception of certain universal principles such as life and liberty, rules and laws are relative based on the ideal of utmost social utility. Stage 6 is *the universal-ethical-principle orientation*, through which the individual's conscience is identified with moral principles that are universally valid. At this stage, moral reasoning, judgment, and action reflect the conscience of humanity based on individually chosen universal principles such as respect for human dignity.

The Moral Judgment Interview and the Standard Issue Scoring System

Using a series of hypothetical dilemmas, the Moral Judgment Interview elicits responses that reflect the participant's developmental stage. According to Anne Colby and colleagues, a major aim is to understand and explicate the conceptual significance of the participant's responses to moral dilemmas beyond and underlying the utterances. For each dilemma, the interviewer asks the participant a series of standard questions, in addition to various spontaneously emerging questions to clarify the subjective meaning of the responses.

The Standard Issue Scoring System is designed to use and move beyond the content of responses in order to identify the underlying moral structure clearly. This scoring system is the result of a substantial revision that improved the ability of the theory to account for data in terms of its basic premises of structured wholeness and invariant sequence of stages. This system deemed as mere content a large variety of responses that were previously considered as indicative of higher stages. With the strict interpretation of and criteria for what constitutes higher structures, Stage 6 was removed from the scoring system. It became possible to identify individuals more reliably to be at one of the first five stages or in transition between two adjacent stages. As a result, the moral ideal of the theory (Stage 6) remained as a hypothetical state.

Moral Orientation and Gender

Carol Gilligan criticized Kohlberg's theory for overemphasizing and overgeneralizing an orientation toward justice and independence and for neglecting or underestimating the relational moral orientations of females. As a result of comprehensive analyses, Lawrence Walker demonstrated that males and females are very similar in moral reasoning and Kohlberg's theory is not biased against females. In contrast, Diana Baumrind pointed out evidence that Stages 5 and 6 are disproportionately represented between males and females and between Western and Eastern cultures. Baumrind further criticized Kohlberg for equating certain natural cultural differences with moral deficits.

There may be stylistic differences between males and females in the content of moral reasoning and meaning making. For example, based on a content analysis of real-life moral dilemmas of adolescents and young adults, Gilligan and Jane Attanucci found support for the existence of two distinct moral orientations: (1) justice and (2) care. The justice orientation is more sensitive to oppression and prioritizes fairness and equal rights, whereas the care orientation is more sensitive to relational isolation and prioritizes attachment and attending to people's needs. In this study, the majority of participants used both orientations, but females were more likely to emphasize care, and males were more likely to emphasize justice considerations. This evidence is interpreted by Gilligan and Attanucci as supporting the assertion that Kohlberg's theory favors the justice orientation and downplays the care orientation of females. Moreover, it is possible that these orientations represent content-based rather than structural differences. Furthermore, in their meta-analysis, Sara Jaffee and Janet Shibley Hyde found only small differences for females to use the care orientation and males to use the justice orientation. Moral orientation appears to be one of the many psychological variables in which the genders are more similar than different.

According to Gilligan and Attanucci, increased capacity to use both orientations is an indication of moral maturity. This postulation is not incompatible with Kohlberg's theory if, as Kohlberg asserted, moral development represents both improvements in the adequacy of justice conceptions and increased capacity for empathy. Consistently, as Walker and colleagues found, individuals who scored at higher stages of moral development according to Kohlberg's theory were likely to use both orientations (justice and care).

According to the developmental tradition of Dewey, Piaget, and Kohlberg, moral development is a process of increased moral autonomy. This view is likely to seem problematic as gender and culture biased when autonomy is construed as individualism and independence. When autonomy is more accurately understood as self-regulation, the story of increased moral autonomy is more likely to represent moral development universally.

Kohlberg's Theory and Culture

According to Richard Shweder, there are *divergent rationalities* in morality, of which Kohlberg's theory provides one example based on individualism, secularism, and free choice. Shweder and colleagues proposed that there are alternative forms of postconventional morality not accounted for by Kohlberg's theory. That is, Kohlberg's form of postconventional morality is a Western version that takes the individual as the ultimate and independent moral agent. By contrast, Hindu culture emphasizes social customs and duties as objective responsibilities and moral principles. According to Shweder and colleagues, natural moral order as an ultimate vision for moral development can alternatively be constructed on the basis of status or role obligations. From the perspective of these researchers, conventional morality does not precede postconventional morality for Hindu children or adults. Rather, in an affect-laden learning process of daily interactions, Hindu children are directly socialized to adopt a specific kind of postconventional morality: a sense of natural moral law based on Hindu beliefs and customs that bind individuals strongly to society around central concepts such as purity, cleanliness, and status.

A related challenge to Kohlberg's theory was proposed by Elliot Turiel that young children can recognize objective moral principles to be categorically valid independently of their conventional status. However, Shweder and colleagues asserted that the distinction between social conventions and morality is itself a culturally specific experience, while many people around the world (like the Hindu Brahmans) experience most conventions in moral terms. According to Shweder and colleagues, such an experience represents a different kind of postconventional morality as natural moral law but may be identified with and underestimated as conventional morality according to Kohlberg's theory. Shweder and colleagues asserted that conventional morality is peculiar to Western individualism and not a necessary development for the emergence of an objective moral obligation that is characteristic of postconventional morality. A plausible implication of Shweder's research is that there may be a strong postconventional sentiment in many participants who are considered to be conventional thinkers according to Kohlberg's theory and methodology.

Revisionist Models

According to Kohlberg, people's reasoning about moral issues represents the essence of their sociomoral perspective and reflects its developmental quality. For most individuals (with the exception of those transitioning between two adjacent stages), the cognitive structure of a single stage characterizes and unites the entire moral domain. However, there has been a growing consensus that a single structure of reasoning is insufficient to account for the complexity of an individual's moral judgment and action.

Dennis Krebs and colleagues offered an interactional model that connects structural regularity with contextual variability in moral judgment. According to this model, a combination of Stages 2 to 4 is operative in the moral judgments of most adults, but different contexts exert different influences toward the operation of particular structures. Other revisionist models of Kohlberg's theory were offered by James Rest and colleagues (the Defining Issues Test and the schema theory) and by John Gibbs and colleagues (Sociomoral Reflection Objective Measure). Unlike the production task of the Moral Judgment Interview, both of these neo-Kohlbergian approaches offered a recognition task: Statements that represent various stages are evaluated by participants in the context of standard moral dilemmas.

Krebs and colleagues found evidence that moral judgments on a wide range of moral issues are structured in terms of Kohlberg's stages. This assertion is consistent with recent evidence by Ulas Kaplan and Terrence Tivnan from a dynamic motivational reformulation of Kohlberg's stages as soft assembled (contextually emerging and dynamically variable) structures that are used within person in multiplicity. Based on this reformulation, adolescents and young adults were found to use a wide range of developmental structures, with particularly strong operations of postconventional motivations. Furthermore, college students' responses to both hypothetical and public policy dilemmas revealed meaningful distinctions among judgment choices based on the degrees of specific stage operations.

Ulas Kaplan

See also Children's Moral Development; Children's Social-Emotional Development; Gilligan's Moral Development Theory; Psychosexual Development

Further Readings

Colby, A., Kohlberg, L., Gibbs, J. C., & Lieberman, M. (1983). A longitudinal study of moral judgment. *Monographs of the Society for Research in Child Development, 48*(1/2, No. 200), 1–124. doi:10.2307/1165935

Gilligan, C. (1977). In a different voice: Women's conceptions of self and of morality. *Harvard Educational Review, 47*(4), 481–517. doi:10.17763/haer.47.4.g6167429416hg5l0

Gilligan, C., & Attanucci, J. (1988). Two moral orientations: Gender differences and similarities. *Merrill-Palmer Quarterly, 34*(3), 223–237.

Jaffee, S., & Hyde, J. S. (2000). Gender differences in moral orientation: A meta-analysis. *Psychological Bulletin, 126*(5), 703–726. doi:10.1037/0033-2909.126.5.703

Kaplan, U., & Tivnan, T. (2014). Moral motivation based on multiple developmental structures: An exploration of cognitive and emotional dynamics. *Journal of Genetic Psychology: Research and Theory on Human Development, 175*(3), 181–201. doi:10.1080/00221325.2013.838936

Kaplan, U., & Tivnan, T. (2014). Moral motivational pluralism: Moral judgment as a function of the dynamic assembly of multiple developmental structures. *Journal of Adult Development, 21*(4), 193–206. doi:10.1007/s10804-014-9191-0

Kohlberg, L. (1969). Stage and sequence: The cognitive developmental approach to socialization. In D. A. Goslin (Ed.), *Handbook of socialization theory and research* (pp. 347–480). Chicago, IL: Rand McNally.

Kohlberg, L. (1984). Moral stages and moralization: The cognitive developmental approach. In L. Kohlberg (Ed.), *The psychology of moral development: The nature and validity of moral stages* (pp. 170–205). San Francisco, CA: Harper & Row.

Kohlberg, L., & Hersh, R. H. (1977). Moral development: A review of the theory. *Theory Into Practice, 16*(2), 53–59. doi:10.1080/00405847709542675

Lapsley, D. K. (2006). Moral stage theory. In M. Killen & J. Smetana (Eds.), *Handbook of moral development* (pp. 37–66). Mahwah, NJ: Lawrence Erlbaum.

Shweder, R. A., Mahapatra, M., & Miller, J. G. (1987). Culture and moral development. In J. Kagan & S. Lamb (Eds.), *The emergence of morality in young children* (pp. 1–83). Chicago, IL: University of Chicago Press.

Turiel, E. (1983). *The development of social knowledge: Morality and convention.* Cambridge, England: Cambridge University Press.

Walker, L. J. (1984). Sex differences in the development of moral reasoning: A critical review. *Child Development, 55*(3), 677–691. doi:10.2307/1130121

Walker, L. J., de Vries, B., & Trevethan, S. D. (1987). Moral stages and moral orientations in real-life and hypothetical dilemmas. *Child Development, 58*(3), 842–858.

Labor Movement and Women

The labor movement is a primary source of social change in the United States. In striving to improve workers' rights, unions have fostered social change for women by promoting gender equality in the workplace. Often, the most significant advances in the workforce have been the inadvertent results of overall social and industrial change in the United States. Although the goals of the labor movement and the women's movement have seemingly diverged over time, there are still many areas of common ground between the two.

Industrial Revolution

Women played an essential role in labor movements, starting from the Industrial Revolution. From the late 1700s into the early 1800s, textile mills became a central point of industrial advancement. Mills during this era employed a primarily female workforce (about 75% of all employees), ranging in age from 15 to 30 years. For women, the mills offered opportunity for social growth. As compared with traditional occupations, the mill life allowed women to earn a substantial income and to leave farms for the advantages of a city. Mill laborers lived in boarding houses where they had access to musical instruments, libraries, and lectures by prominent individuals. Magazines published by the mill workers also encouraged free speech and intellectual growth. Even women of prominent families would choose to work in the mills for a period of time (often until the point of marriage), to gain access to the social and educational opportunities they were otherwise denied.

Despite the benefits of mill labor, there were also disadvantages. Women were expected to work from dawn to dusk, with only a half-hour lunch break. Air quality was poor, creating numerous health problems. While working in the mills paid more than other occupations, women still earned much less than their male counterparts, with wages taken out for room and board. They were also subjected to a paternalistic system of being monitored by male supervisors and patrolled by matrons at the boarding houses, all to "protect their moral standing."

While labor unions were illegal in the United States at the time, this did not stop women from protesting their working conditions and organizing. Among the earliest agitators was Susan Bagley, a worker at the Lowell mill, who had written editorials espousing the virtues of mill life earlier in her career. As time went on, Bagley and other laborers began to note the problems with their working conditions, which were ignored by their supervisors. The women at the Lowell mill staged their first walkout in 1834, in response to a threatened 15% wage reduction. Although this first strike was short-lived due to the factory owners firing and blacklisting the leaders, a second, more organized strike occurred in 1836. This time, a third of the workforce of several mills walked out, resulting in an overall reversal of proposed increases in room and board fees.

While the striking women during this time were often ridiculed for their unfeminine behavior, their methods proved effective. By 1842, the right to organize and form a peaceful strike was upheld in *Commonwealth vs. Hunt*. In 1844, Bagley helped organize the Lowell Female Labor Reform Association as a branch of the overall New England Workingmen's Association. Bagley was also among the first women to speak before the Massachusetts legislature about the poor conditions for mill workers.

Early Women's Movement

Many of the original efforts of Bagley and her fellow agitators were unfruitful. The women never gained the 10-hour work day, one of their most heavily fought for demands, and no formal inquiries were ever made into mill conditions. However, their early efforts set in motion a string of events that formed the beginnings of the women's rights movement. The 1848 Seneca Falls Convention resulted in the creation of the "Declaration of Sentiments and Resolutions," drafted by Elizabeth Cady Stanton, an early manifesto primarily outlining women's stance on abolition, though the convention also heavily focused on women workers' rights and saw the beginnings of discussions on suffrage. Later, in 1860, Caroline H. Dall published "Women's' Right to Labor," a seminal work outlining the imperative need for equality in the workplace. As the influence of textile workers diminished following the Civil War, the consciousness of the early women's movement continued. Especially as male slaves were granted the right to vote, the issue of women's suffrage began to gather more momentum.

Internal Division

One of the early problems identified during those years was the need for striking groups to be able to join forces across the lines of economic class, race, and gender. Many men viewed women in the workforce as a threat to their finances as women took much less pay. Men's labor groups were hesitant to even include women in organizational meetings. These attitudes began to change in 1860, when female shoe workers in Pennsylvania were finally able to convince their male counterparts that lobbying for increased women's wages could help both groups. Women also began to refuse to operate as scabs against male strikers, instead joining their efforts in walkouts and on the picket line. These difficulties in getting disparate groups to work together have continued to be a primary issue in the success of labor unions.

New Deal Era Reforms and Agitators

As the women's movement began to form in its own right, a number of women continued their efforts of agitation in the name of labor, including Emma Goldman, Mother Jones, Elizabeth Gurley Flynn, and Frances Perkins. Women-specific unions continued to grow during this time, with wider unionization across different industries. Women of the upper and middle class often joined working-class women in their striking efforts, helping bring significantly more attention to their causes. Even during men's strikes, it became a regular practice to include women on the picket lines as a sympathetic face for the union and also as a shield against violence, as confrontations between unions and police forces became more extreme.

Triangle Fire

One particular incident that brought attention to the struggles of female laborers was the fire at the Triangle Shirtwaist factory in 1911. Having resisted the striking efforts of the Women's Trade Union League and the International Ladies Garment Workers Union between 1903 and 1910, Triangle remained one of the few nonunion garment factories in New York City. As a result, when a fire broke out on the eighth floor of the building on a Saturday afternoon in March, the fire escape doors for all of the floors were locked. All 146 women on the ninth floor of the building either died in the blaze or jumped to their deaths in a scene that was widely witnessed by public onlookers, the police, and firefighters, who could do nothing to help the women. This incident gained much public support for unions, particularly as many aspects of the incident could have been prevented had Triangle adhered to the union requests of the time (primarily, cleaner working conditions, adequate fire escapes, and fewer work hours).

Workplace Reform

Following the Triangle Fire, Frances Perkins, among others, became an outspoken advocate for the improvement of working conditions and the regulation of industrial hazards. Perkins and Alice Hamilton (the first female faculty member at Harvard Medical School) were highly influential in pushing forward reforms that would eventually lead to the formation of the Occupational Safety and Health Administration. In 1933, Perkins was appointed by President Franklin Roosevelt as secretary of the Department of Labor, making her the first woman to serve as a cabinet member.

Sexual Revolution

Many female leaders in the labor movement embraced the ethos of women's liberation in their personal lives and actions. Goldman first became prominent in the movement following her involvement with Alexander Berkman and their failed assassination attempt in 1889 on the chairman of the Carnegie Steel Company. Despite Goldman's tumultuous entry into the movement, she continued throughout the 1900s to be a prominent figure, known for her moving writing and lecturing styles. In addition to her support of labor, Goldman also stood out as a prominent figure in terms of women's rights. Arrested for distributing information about birth control, Goldman encompassed what would be later known as the anarcha-feminist movement, as demonstrated by her opposition to traditional marriage and advocacy for women's sexual freedom.

Women and Children

While living untraditional lives themselves, Elizabeth Flynn and Mother Jones appealed to the public sympathies through their use of wives, mothers, and children in their propaganda. Jones, a widow who had lost her husband and four children to yellow fever, was primarily known for her advocacy for child laborers, using tactics that often provoked a visceral response, such as locking children in circus cages or organizing marches of young workers to the front doors of politicians. Flynn, who was first arrested at the age of 16 years for demonstrating in Times Square with her father, was a vibrant (and attractive) face of the Industrial Workers of the World, colloquially known as the Wobblies. While Flynn's agitational efforts did not solely focus on women's rights, she was an active organizer in the export of more than 100 children of mill workers from Lawrence, Massachusetts, to New York City in 1910, an effort to lighten the financial burden of strikers while creating a large-scale public demonstration. Similarly, Jones worked to bring the wives of strikers to the picket lines to help in the protests, resulting in 200 miners' wives being arrested along with Jones for a public march in Trinidad, Colorado, in 1914.

World Wars I and II

The onset of worldwide war created conditions in the United States that allowed and encouraged women to enter the workforce in greater numbers and expanded the occupations available to them. However, socially these changes were unsustainable, leading women to return to traditional roles during peacetime. Starting with World War I in 1914, the significant number of men abroad due to military service allowed women to make up 24% of the workforce in aviation plants across the United States. The demands of World War II saw this number jump to 57% of the overall workforce. While women's roles in the war industry are well documented, as demonstrated by the popular image of Rosie the Riveter, women took up positions across the workforce, from farm labor to jobs in the federal government. While riveting was strongly emphasized due to its similarities with sewing (a natural transition for the average housewife), women took on essential roles in engineering and industrial settings, seeing projects through from conceptualization to construction, and women were noted to have higher productivity rates than their male counterparts.

Prior to World War II, there were 19 million women active in the U.S. workforce. This number increased by 3 million during the war, but many of this later group subsequently returned to their homes, and the women who continued to work generally returned to more traditional occupations, due to heavy pressure to allow men to take back their prewar positions. While women would not reenter the labor force in such large numbers until the 1970s, the efforts of women laborers during this time had a significant impact on perceptions about labor and gender roles in U.S. society.

Current State of Women and the Labor Movement

The women's movement and the labor movement have shared numerous successes. The public accessibility of birth control and abortion has increased women's ability to participate in the workforce. In addition, the winning of suffrage and the outlawing of gender-based discrimination (among numerous other legal successes) have given women a more equal position in society. The beginning of the 21st century saw the development of a culture that allows women to set their own standards and choose their own paths, traditional or not. The battle for women to be perceived as equal to men in intelligence, strength, and ability has widely been won, most notably codified in the lifting of the ban on women soldiers serving in combat zones in 2013. By the early 2000s, women had a majority presence at colleges and universities across the United States, and in 2009, women outnumbered men in the workforce, largely as a result of the Great Recession.

While many battles have been won for the women's movement and the labor movement, there are many still left to fight. Abortion and reproductive rights continue to be issues of debate. Despite social gains, on average, women continue to earn 5% to 7% less pay than men, and they continue to have unequal representation in many of the STEM (science, technology, engineering, and mathematics) fields. In the workforce, paid maternity (and paternity) leave is also a growing issue, with many other prominent nations offering significantly more benefits to new parents than the United States. The modern labor movement continues to focus more specifically on the rights of the lower classes, including the rights of illegal and legal Latina women working in sweatshops and the hotel and restaurant industry, as well as lobbying for an increased national minimum wage. The continued overlap between these two movements will likely continue to result in many significant partnerships for social change in the future.

Maya Elace Pignatore

See also Feminism: Overview; First-Wave Feminism; Gender Bias in Hiring Practices; Gender Discrimination; Neofeminism; Reproductive Rights Movement; Second-Wave Feminism; Third-Wave Feminism

Further Readings

Commonwealth v. Hunt, 45 Mass. 111 (1842).

Dray, P. (2010). *There is power in a union: The epic story of labor in America.* New York, NY: Doubleday.

Drinnon, R. (1961). *Rebel in paradise: A biography of Emma Goldman.* Chicago, IL: University of Chicago Press.

Foner, P. S. (1979). *Women and the American Labor Movement: From colonial times to the eve of world war.* New York, NY: Free Press.

Goldman, E. (1906). *The tragedy of woman's emancipation.* New York, NY: Mother Earth.

Gorn, J. (2002). *Mother Jones: The most dangerous woman in America.* New York, NY: Hill & Wang.

Rayback, J. G. (1966). *A history of American labor.* New York, NY: Free Press.

Late Adulthood and Gender

Researchers estimate that by 2030, one in five Americans (i.e., about 72 million people) will be 65 years of age or older. As the total population of older adults continues to grow, and as the average life expectancy keeps increasing, it becomes particularly important to ensure that quality of life is maintained throughout later adulthood. It is necessary not only to address the physical concerns and changes that are so characteristic of old age but to focus on the mental and social aspects of healthy aging as well. One way to examine these primary domains of functioning (i.e., physical, mental, and social) is to consider how the construct of gender interacts with the major changes that occur throughout later adulthood. This entry discusses later adulthood issues among cisgender women, cisgender men, and transgender elders.

Cisgender Women and Later Adulthood

For many aging cisgender women, menopause is a particular topic of interest. Menopause, which signals the end of a woman's fertile phase, typically begins before the late-adulthood stage; however, many of the associated side effects remain present for years after. Primarily, most of these issues are driven by an abrupt drop in sex hormones. This major shift in hormones may lead to a wide range of physiological and psychological difficulties that can last throughout later adulthood for many women. Physiologically, some common concerns include reduced bone density, sexual dysfunction, and increased risk for cardiovascular disease. There also appear to be higher rates of psychiatric issues such as anxiety and mood disorders for a number of older women—these are also exacerbated by many of the major life stressors that typically occur near this time (e.g., children leaving home, retirement). Furthermore, research suggests that there is a subset of women who display a "second peak" of diagnosis for schizophrenia around menopause; this is particularly salient given the lack of any corresponding pattern in men. Despite these concerns, there is also research to suggest that later adulthood is a period of solid coping strategies and good psychological functioning for the majority of individuals.

In terms of neuropsychological functioning, it appears that much of the established differences between genders across specific domains remain relatively stable throughout old age (e.g., women still outperform men on tasks of verbal fluency, and men outperform women on tests of visuospatial skills). Despite this consistency, some research suggests that women's overall cognitive functioning may be spared in comparison with men's during later adulthood and that women may demonstrate less age-related cognitive decline overall. Proposed theories for this discrepancy point to more innate differences that may be present in the female brain versus the male brain (e.g., greater complexity in frontoparietal regions, more gray matter despite smaller whole-brain volumes, and increased bilateralization for specific functions). These differences are thought to be protective and may allow women to compensate more effectively in response to the broad, age-related changes that typically occur (e.g., increased bilateralization of specific functions, mild reductions in gray matter volume). In terms of risk for dementia, there is some evidence suggesting that women may experience greater benefits from engaging in intellectual activities and/or regular exercise than men; nevertheless, additional research is necessary before any conclusions can be made.

There are a large number of social and cultural issues that are highlighted for many women during later adulthood. A major theme for this phase of life is the concept of "loss of roles." Shifting from regular work to retirement is a major role transition for a large number of women during this time. Another major adjustment period that many must come to terms with during later adulthood is the death of their partner. Widowhood, which is significantly more likely to occur to women than to men, is a very difficult time of adjustment, particularly for women who have always been financially dependent on their husbands. However, research suggests that having strong social support is especially valuable for those grieving during this period.

It is also useful to consider how the intersection of gender and aging influences various social perceptions and stereotypes of women during later adulthood. At a very basic level, women are labeled as "elderly" at a younger age than men, suggesting that problems such as ageism may affect women much earlier. In addition, given that a woman's perceived value in society has often been associated with her level of physical attractiveness, many women have "more to lose" as they age than their male counterparts, who often are more defined by their wealth or status. Furthermore, some research suggests that the major physical features of aging (e.g., gray hair, wrinkles) are seen as less acceptable for women than for men.

Despite these concerns, recent research has indicated that elderly women are perceived more positively than elderly men overall, though further research is needed to explore this pattern more fully.

Cisgender Men and Later Adulthood

Although men and women experience many of the same concerns and stressors as they age (e.g., declining health, role transitions), there are several issues particularly relevant to the male older adult population. One topic that has become increasingly popular in recent years has been the concept of "andropause," typically billed as the parallel to female menopause. According to some researchers, men will also experience a notable decline in sex hormones, but it occurs much more gradually.

Erectile dysfunction is an issue that affects millions of older men and is often linked to changes in hormone levels that occur with aging. Male sexual dysfunction has been shown to negatively affect the overall quality of life for many men, both physically and psychologically. However, medicine has become increasingly successful at diagnosing and treating erectile dysfunction for many men, and there is much more awareness and recognition than ever before.

Another major topic of concern within the intersection of aging and gender is suicide. Estimates suggest that although older adults only make up about 12% of the population, they account for 18% of all suicide deaths. Older men in particular have very high rates of completed suicide, which is partly attributed to the methods used (e.g., firearms, hanging, drowning). Furthermore, it is believed that elder suicide may be significantly underreported (i.e., by up to 40%), as many deaths may be "silent suicides" (e.g., overdose, self-starvation, dehydration, "accidents") and never reported as such.

Although awareness of this issue is increasing, there are still many obstacles associated with identifying and treating individuals at the highest risk. Researchers have suggested that some factors that contribute to the highest risk of attempting suicide are being divorced, increasing age, Caucasian race, having a current psychiatric disorder (e.g., depression), alcohol misuse, and presence of a chronic medical condition or disability. Other possible risk factors include recent loss and grief, family discord, and financial difficulty. It is not uncommon for many older men to report feeling like they are a "burden," either financially or care-wise. In addition, there is also significant difficulty related to identifying these individuals and providing appropriate services; the majority of older adults (and especially older men) will not seek treatment for mental health problems. Although elder suicide remains a major public health concern, awareness is continuing to increase, and there are many organizations attempting to educate the community and provide appropriate resources.

Transgender Elders

The term *transgender* encompasses the diverse group of individuals whose biological (or assigned) sex is different from their gender identity. A 2012 report by the National Center for Transgender Equality estimated that transgender individuals make up between 0.25% and 1% of the population—significantly higher than the previously reported rates per the American Psychiatric Association, which suggested that only 1:30,000 men and 1:100,000 women were transgender. Nevertheless, there is still only very little known about how experiences of being transgender affect outcomes across the life span and into old age. At a time when the older adult population is growing rapidly, the intersection of being transgender and growing old is becoming an area of increasing interest. Although many aging-related challenges that transgender adults face are similar to those of the cisgender population, there are additional concerns unique to this group.

Much of the recent research on transgender aging has focused on the long-term consequences of transphobia and discrimination over the life span. The widespread discrimination practices that many transgender individuals experience over their lifetime often influence various aspects of functioning in later adulthood. For many, discriminatory educational policies and practices during childhood (e.g., rigidly gendered dress codes and hostile classroom environments) were just the start of a pattern that would follow them for the remainder of their lives. Workplace discrimination is another area of significant concern. In a 2011 survey of transgender adults over 65 years of age, 90% reported experiencing transphobic discrimination at work and 70% reported delaying transitioning to avoid employment discrimination. Furthermore, current unemployment rates for transgender elders are double the national average.

These issues have contributed to the disproportionally high rates of economic instability for many transgender older adults, who are then more likely to experience a wide range of negative outcomes including homelessness, risky sexual behavior, substance abuse, and mental illness. Moreover, this lack of stable employment often leads to insufficient contributions to Social Security, so that when many transgender adults reach retirement age, they are at further economic disadvantage due to inadequate resources to meet even the most basic of needs.

Housing discrimination is another area in which many transgender adults often experience inequality. Not only do a significant number report being denied a house or apartment at some point in their lifetime, but also many transgender adults without a home altogether are frequently denied access to homeless shelters. Although this is in part due to the gendered nature of many of these spaces, it can leave many of these adults without any options.

Legal issues are often complex for transgender elders. Despite the high rates of discrimination and transphobia, antidiscrimination laws rarely include transgender people, leaving these individuals without legal protections as they age. Obstacles related to documentation and identification records are also prevalent, and governmental requirements for legally changing one's gender are often burdensome and expensive. Spousal benefits related to tax breaks and employment benefits are generally not guaranteed to partners or families of transgender individuals, regardless of their sexual orientation. End-of-life issues also become a concern for many transgender elders, as existing laws on power of attorney, property rights, and inheritance can create barriers for transgender adults or even exclude them altogether. Overall, it is clear that the legal rights of transgender people are lacking, often leading to major negative consequences across the life span.

Access to health care and insurance coverage are other realms in which transgender elders experience significant disparities. Many older transgender adults are highly distrustful of health care providers, in part due to a history of (real or perceived) negative interactions over their lifetime. It is not uncommon for transgender elders to report past experiences of care refusal, harassment by health care staff, and an overall lack of appropriate clinical and cultural competence on transgender issues. Often, this fear and apprehension lead to a number of transgender older adults forgoing a primary care physician and regular doctor's visits, delaying seeking treatment for an illness or ailment, and, for some, feeling too uncomfortable to disclose their status as transgender to their health care providers altogether. Ultimately, this contributes to greater negative health outcomes as these individuals grow older and contend with the health consequences of aging.

Another key health issue in transgender aging is the increased potential for polypharmacy and dangerous drug combinations. There is very little research on how long-term hormone replacement use may interact with various medications commonly taken by aging adults, and as some older adults feel uncomfortable disclosing their transgender status to their health care providers, the potential for dangerous drug interaction issues may increase substantially.

Another particularly pressing issue associated with the aging transgender community is HIV/AIDS. Older adults—including those who are transgender—constitute one of the fastest-growing groups with new HIV/AIDS infections in North America. Some of this has been attributed to the lack of attention to transgender sexuality in existing sex education programs aimed at older adults. There is also a suggestion that some adults who transition later in life are unaware of the risks for transmission of HIV/AIDS.

Many transgender elders experience notable mental health issues during their lifetime. Transgender older adults are at increased risk for depression and anxiety and are almost twice as likely as their cisgender lesbian, gay, and bisexual counterparts to have considered suicide. In the absence of adequate mental health treatment or social support, many transgender older adults turn to risky behaviors such as drug use, self-harm, risky sex, and suicide.

Many of these mental health issues are exacerbated by a shortage of social support; studies have shown that transgendered elders typically have less social support than nontransgender older adults and often feel socially isolated as a result. Although positive social interaction and community engagement have proven to be protective against many of these negative psychological and mental health outcomes, many transgender older adults report feeling unwelcome or estranged from their local communities and thus are left with few opportunities for social support or engagement. Although research in this area is scarce, it appears that this lack of support becomes particularly problematic for those who require assistance or caregiving. Many transgender adults do not have the family or economic resources necessary for the provision of adequate care as they grow older. This can lead to significant concerns about how to handle end-of-life situations for those who are no longer able to live independently or who require assistance.

Transgender older adults tend to experience disproportionately high rates of interpersonal and domestic violence. Unfortunately, much of this is perpetrated by those who are meant to protect and care for them. Reports of police brutality and negligence are not uncommon among transgender adults, and many remain distrustful enough to avoid law enforcement workers altogether. Health care facilities are another setting in which transgender adults are at increased risk for victimization, and those older adults living in assisted living facilities are at particular risk. Transgender elders in these settings experience disproportionally high rates of abuse and neglect, but much of it is never reported.

Brittany E. Hawkshead and L. Stephen Miller

See also Ageism; Aging and Gender: Overview; Health Issues and Gender: Overview; Middle Adulthood and Gender; Transgender Experiences of Aging

Further Readings

Barrett, A., & von Rohr, C. (2008). Gendered perceptions of aging: An examination of college students. *International Journal of Aging and Human Development, 67,* 359–386.

Finkenauer, S., Sherratt, J., Marlow, J., & Brodey, A. (2012). When injustice gets old: A systematic review of trans aging. *Journal of Gay & Lesbian Social Services, 24,* 311–330.

Kryspin-Exner, I., Lamplmayr, E., & Felnhofer, A. (2011). Geropsychology: The gender gap in human aging—a mini-review. *Gerontology, 57,* 539–548. doi:10.1159/000323154

Persson, D. (2009). Unique challenges of transgender aging: Implications from the literature. *Journal of Gerontological Social Work, 52*(6), 633–646. doi:10.1080/01634370802609056

Service and Advocacy for GLBT Elders, & National Center for Transgender Equality. (2012). *Improving the lives of transgender older adults: Recommendations for policy and practice.* Retrieved from http://www.transequality.org/sites/default/files/docs/resources/TransAgingPolicyReportFull.pdf

Latina/o Americans and Gender

The purpose of this entry is to highlight the influence of gender socialization in the lives of Latina/o Americans. First, this entry presents information on who may identify as Latina/o American. The entry then acknowledges the many ways in which Latina/o and U.S. cultures interact to influence gendered behaviors and gender roles within the Latina/o American community. Specifically, Latina/o gender expression is dependent on the strength of individuals' ties to their cultures of origin and the U.S. culture, along with their nationality, race, ethnicity, reasons for immigration, and phenotype. This entry also attends to the influence of the overarching Latina/o cultural value of interdependence and related values (e.g., *familismo*, *simpatía*, *personalismo*, *respeto*, and *fatalismo*). These values serve to tie Latina/o communities together, often leading to similarity across gender roles for Latina/o Americans. In addition, specific Latina/o gender roles, namely *marianismo* and servant leadership for Latinas and *machismo* and *caballerismo* for Latinos, are explored. Finally, the lived experiences of transgender and gender nonconforming Latina/o Americans are highlighted. Latina/os who identify as transgender and nonconforming face anti-transgender bias within and outside the Latina/o community, particularly in education, employment, housing, and health care settings. The split in the Latina/o community where only half the Latina/o transgender and gender non-conforming individuals receive family support, and the other half do not, is highlighted, with emphasis on family support as a protective factor against harassment and discrimination for Latina/os who identify as transgender and gender nonconforming.

Who Are Latina/o Americans?

Latina/o Americans, or Latina/os, are individuals residing in the United States who often share similar cultural characteristics, values, beliefs, practices, and traditions that have been influenced by their respective indigenous cultures, Spanish colonization, and the dominant U.S. culture. Representing various races, ethnicities, and nationalities, Latina/os have cultural roots in Mexico, Central America, South America, and the Caribbean. When asked, most Latina/os identify by their families' country of origin (e.g., Costa Rican). The majority of Latina/os identify as Mexican or Mexican American. However, recent changes in immigration patterns have increased the number of Latina/os identifying as hailing from countries in Central America (e.g., Bolivia), South America (e.g., Peru), and the Caribbean (e.g., Dominican Republic). Whereas many Latina/os emigrated to the United States from their countries of origin (e.g., Guatemala, El Salvador, Colombia), other Latina/os have resided in the United States for many generations due to changes in the U.S.-Mexico geographic border. Specifically, the U.S. states of California, Nevada, Utah, Arizona, New Mexico, and Texas, along with parts of Colorado, Wyoming, Oklahoma, and Kansas, were once a part of Mexico.

Furthermore, Puerto Rican Americans have a unique and complicated relationship with the United States in that their home country is a U.S. commonwealth. For example, although Puerto Ricans were granted U.S. citizenship in 1917, allowing them to move freely between Puerto Rico and the United States, they have not been granted full political participation as U.S. citizens if they remain on the island. For those who crossed borders to live in the United States, it is important to acknowledge the various reasons they had for doing so, including, but not limited to, escaping poverty, political instability, and violence, along with gaining educational and occupational opportunities. Finally, the historical intersections of European, African, Asian, and Indigenous cultures in the Americas and the Caribbean contribute to the diversity of races and phenotypes among Latina/os. Latina/os often identify as and/or phenotypically appear White, although others may identify as and/or appear Indigenous, Black, or Asian. Some Latina/os also may identify as some other race or appear racially ambiguous. Overall, Latina/os' national origins, racial self-identification, ethnic backgrounds, reasons for immigration, and phenotypes affect their lived experiences.

Gender Role Socialization in the United States

Along with race, ethnicity, nationality, and phenotype, gender is a dominant organizing influence on Latina/os' lived experiences. Gender within the Latina/o culture is often tied to a person's biological sex, resulting in gender being seen as solely binary (male vs. female). This is most likely due to its roots in a patriarchal system that privileges maleness over femaleness. The gender binary and patriarchy within the Latina/o community lead to differential gender role expectations based on biological sex and to the devaluing of those who may not identify with their biological sex and/or the gender binary. It is important to consider that Latina/o migrants or immigrants in the United States who have spent the majority of their lives in their home country may exhibit cultural values and gender roles that are more congruent with those in their place of origin. Latina/os who have been in the United States for many years or even over several generations may have been influenced by the process of acculturation and have found ways to negotiate values from the United States and their country of origin. Thus, gender roles of Latina/os are unique based on the interplay between the values of their cultures of origin and the values associated with the majority U.S. culture. At the same time, Latina/os share cultural values and are often socialized into specific Latina/o gender roles, resulting in similarities in gendered behaviors and expressions. These Latina/o cultural values and specific gender roles are explored in the following subsections.

Gendered Expression of Latina/o Cultural Values

In general, the Latina/o community share a number of values that demonstrate their interdependence. Namely, these values are familismo, simpatía, personalismo, and respeto. Latina/o culture is collectivistic, resulting in Latina/os working hard to develop and maintain strong family ties. This sense of closeness is not limited to family members but extends also to close friends with whom they have developed bonds. Familismo serves as a protective factor in which the family is a strong foundation of support, a source of advice and comfort, and an influence on the individual's identity. Latinos often express the value as being the primary "breadwinner" and disciplinarian of the family. Latinas, similarly, take on the responsibility of maintaining family cohesiveness. Latinas are considered the "glue" of the family, carry on family traditions, and are the family confidants. For both Latinos and Latinas, family is central to their presumed purpose in life.

Simpatía and personalismo are integral parts of an interpersonal style that tends to be represented in the Latina/o culture. The values of simpatía and personalismo strive to uphold relationship over discord. They promote kindness and pleasantries in the face of conflict or discomfort. It may appear as if the individual is avoiding a situation or is in denial of the circumstances; however, the individual may just be making an effort to sustain harmony in the interaction. These values are most often witnessed in the Latina. It is considered rude and disrespectful for a Latina to defend her position, be assertive, and/or disagree with another's voice that may be perceived as more important than hers (i.e., her parents or husband). Conversely, it is found to be more acceptable for Latinos to disagree, prove their point in arguments, and/or make executive decisions regardless of the opinions of anyone else. In some families, however, it is not uncommon to see Latino adult males defer to their mother or grandmother.

Respeto is simply defined as respect and is a value that is upheld in all relationships, especially with elders in the family and other persons of authority. Respeto also helps maintain the elder hierarchy naturally found in the Latina/o family model of grandparents, parents, and children. The Latina/o family model is collectivistic in nature, and thus aunts, uncles, cousins, and even close friends are also considered *familia*. The value of respeto is most actively expressed as deference. It is not uncommon to see it being demonstrated by a Latina hesitating to ask questions or express dissent against anyone in authority (e.g., parent, employer), or obeying family norms without question. Latinos often command this sense of respeto from others as well, thus maintaining the gendered division of who gives respect and who gets it.

Last, it is important to consider a Latina/o community's worldview and sense of control over their world. Cultures have different perceptions of fate and the power of changing one's own course in life. Latina/os tend to believe that no matter their actions, they cannot alter fate. This value of fatalismo is commonly tied to religious affiliation and the belief that God is omniscient and controls one's course in life. Fatalismo within the Latina/o culture may promote despair, hopelessness, and a sense of helplessness that situations are irreversible and cannot be helped unless God wants it differently. This external locus of control strongly influences an individual's behavior and how they navigate the world. For example, Latina/os may believe that they must adhere to gender roles ascribed to them within their families and communities.

Although all of the values of Latina/os are considered the foundation of the community, the values are expressed differently for men and women. The expressions of these values are also colored by country of origin (e.g., Mexican vs. Argentinian cultures), religion (e.g., Santeria vs. Roman Catholicism), and level of acculturation to the United States, among other variables.

Specific Latina/o Gender Roles

Apart from the universal values represented in the Latina/o community, there are specific gender roles subscribed to Latinas and Latinos. These gender roles are often considered to be complementary, but in actuality they are expressed in a number of different ways. According to the scholarly literature, *marianismo* and machismo serve as the traditional views of the Latina female and Latino male gender roles, respectively.

Marianismo was first conceptualized in the 1970s by Evelyn Stevens, a political scientist who was studying rural communities in Mexico. She described Mexican women as passive and subservient to males, pure and chaste; she associated these traits with the women's devotion to the Virgin Mary. Stevens's conceptualization, however, failed to recognize the theology of the Virgin Mary, according to Roman Catholic scholars. Although the Virgin Mary was chaste and pure, she was not subservient. On the contrary, she was, and remains, a powerful figure in the Roman Catholic religion and to the Latina/o community in particular. She exhibited assertiveness and selflessness both at the same time. Roman Catholic Latina/os are strongly devoted to their patron Virgin Mary, or *Virgencita*, as she represents strength in times of adversity and compassion toward all. Latina/os who are not Roman Catholic are also drawn to the Virgin Mary and offer devotion to her.

Over time, the *marianista* gender role has been applied to Latinas' lives in a rather rigid way. Latinas are often perceived to be uneducated, submissive to men, and unable to fulfill a role like head of the household. Moreover, Latinas are objectified in the media and considered "exotic," and their strengths are seldom given the same rate of attention. Cynthia E. Guzmán argued that *marianismo* is much more flexible than how today's society perceives it to be. She also argued that it is expressed in a much more contextualized and diverse way than Stevens first posited. *Marianismo* today can be seen in the Latina activist and Latina businesswoman, among other roles. A Latina marianista may not just be a passive, stay-at-home mom who defers her own personal goals for the sake of the family; Latinas are also quite influential. For this reason, Guzmán argued for a more robust understanding of *marianismo* that also included the acknowledgment of Latinas as servant leaders.

"Servant leadership" is a concept borrowed from the business literature but one that has become increasingly applicable to interpersonal relations across multiple settings. Servant leadership is built on the premise that everyone has value. Servant leaders empower others to be the best individuals they can be and are literally leaders who "serve" others, rather than the traditional hierarchy of others serving the leader. Think of Mahatma Gandhi, Nelson Mandela, or Martin Luther King Jr. Guzmán explained that *marianismo* today is inclusive of qualities that have been associated with the term *servant leadership*. Latinas embody the value of generosity to others before self-interest, also sacrificing themselves for the benefit of the family or community.

Machismo is known in popular culture as the archetype of how a Latino behaves and what he believes. In fact, societal discourse often labels the Latino male as *machista*. The use of this term refers to the traditional gender role of machismo. It is largely associated with hypermasculinity and a rejection of any characteristics associated with femininity. Under this gender role, the Latino is expected to be the primary provider and protector of the family. The label "machista" has been widely used in pop culture to discriminate against men, specifically Latinos. It is not uncommon to hear a Latino male being assumed to be a machista (i.e., violent toward women, gang affiliation). G. Miguel Arciniega was among the first to consider a more contemporary view of this otherwise rigid construct. In his view, caballerismo may more appropriately describe the Latino male today. A man who is a *caballero* is one who genuinely cares for the well-being of his family and is not necessarily interested in just being the most powerful one in command or in charge of his family's every move.

Together, *marianismo* and machismo are seen as complementary, and the literature has previously alluded to one not being present without the other. However, it is important to consider that the community is diverse, with numerous within-group differences. Women who behave in ways congruent with the *marianismo* and servant leadership models are not always married or even partnered with a man. For example, a Latina woman who identifies as lesbian, bisexual, or transgender may or may not behave in marianista ways. Or take, for instance, the Latino man who is a stay-at-home dad.

Considerations for Latina/os Who Identify as Transgender or Gender Nonconforming

In recent years, there has been an increase in literature that describes the experiences of transgender or gender nonconforming people within the Latina/o community; in fact, there has been a movement for the Latina/o community to embrace the usage of Latina/o/x or Latinx in order to be inclusive of those who may not identify strictly as a woman or a man. Latina/o/x transgender and gender nonconforming individuals face anti-transgender bias along with the structural racism associated with being Latinx, together leading to discrimination across multiple life domains (e.g., education, employment, housing, health care, and family life). The National Transgender Discrimination Survey provides a glimpse at what the lives of these Latinx individuals may be like. The results from that survey are detailed in the following paragraphs.

The majority of Latinx respondents who identified as transgender and gender nonconforming reported being harassed by both teachers and peers during their kindergarten through 12th-grade education. Many reported experiences of physical and sexual assault and harassment that led to them leaving school voluntarily or being expelled from school. These patterns of harassment and abuse seemed to follow these respondents from the educational system into the world of work. That is, the majority reported being harassed at work, with reports of physical and sexual assaults. In addition, Latinx people who identified as transgender and gender nonconforming tended to have higher rates of unemployment than others in the survey and in the general U.S. population. They also reported losing or being denied jobs due to anti-transgender bias. Two thirds of the Latinx survey respondents reported that they had to participate in sex work or drug sales to financially survive. Finally, the Latina/o transgender and gender nonconforming respondents reported experiencing housing discrimination (e.g., being refused a home or apartment, being evicted unjustly), being less likely to own a home, and experiencing homelessness at some point in their lives. In fact, their rates of homelessness were four times greater than the national average.

The harassment and abuse faced by Latinx transgender and gender nonconforming individuals in education, employment, and housing have been associated with health disparities. Specifically, one fourth of the Latinx respondents reported being denied medical care due to anti-transgender bias, with even more reporting delaying seeking care due to concerns about such bias. They also reported high rates of substance use and abuse (e.g., nicotine, alcohol, and drugs). Nearly half the Latinx respondents reported attempting suicide. Finally, significantly more Latinx transgender and gender nonconforming respondents reported being HIV positive when compared with others in the survey and the general U.S. population.

It is important to note that nearly half the Latinx transgender and gender nonconforming respondents reported that their families were accepting of their gender identities, with slow improvements over time. Family acceptance is significant, particularly in the Latinx community, and often helps partially protect Latinx transgender and gender nonconforming individuals from the negative effects of anti-transgender and racial harassment and discrimination. More attention to increasing family acceptance of transgender and gender nonconforming respondents within the Latinx community is needed.

Cynthia E. Guzmán and Rachel L. Navarro

See also Latina/o Americans and Transgender Identity; Machismo; *Marianismo*; Parental Messages About Gender; Spirituality and Gender

Further Readings

Anzaldúa, G. (1987). *Borderlands/la frontera: The new Mestiza* (1st ed.). San Francisco, CA: Spinsters/Aunt Lute Book.

Arciniega, G. M., Anderson, T. C., Tovar-Blank, Z. G., & Tracey, T. J. G. (2008). Towards a fuller conception of machismo: Development of a traditional machismo and *caballerismo* scale. *Journal of Counseling Psychology, 55,* 19–33.

Blanchard, K. H. (2010). *Leading at a higher level: Blanchard on leadership and creating high performing organizations.* Upper Saddle River, NJ: FT Press.

Guzmán, C. E. (2011). *Toward a new conceptualization of marianismo: Validation of the Guzmán Marianismo Inventory* (Unpublished doctoral dissertation). New Mexico State University, Las Cruces.

National Center for Transgender Equality. (2012, September 11). *Injustice at every turn: A look at Latino/a respondents in the National Transgender Discrimination Survey.* Retrieved June 15, 2015, from http://transequality.org/sites /default/files/docs/resources/ntds _latino_english_2.pdf

Pew Hispanic Center. (2012). *When labels don't fit: Hispanics and their views of identity.* Washington, DC: Author.

Raffaelli, M., & Ontai, L. L. (2004). Gender socialization in Latino/a families: Results from two retrospective studies. *Sex Roles, 50,* 287–299.

Santiago-Rivera, A. L., Arredondo, P., & Gallardo-Cooper, M. (2002). *Counseling Latinos and la familia: A practical guide.* Thousand Oaks, CA: Sage.

Stevens, E. P. (1973). *Marianismo*: The other face of machismo in Latin America. In A. Decastello (Ed.), *Female and male in Latin America* (pp. 88–109). Pittsburgh, PA: University of Pittsburgh Press.

Latina/o Americans and Sexual Orientation

Within psychology and other social science disciplines, scholars have increasingly recognized the ways dimensions of identity—such as race, ethnicity, and sexual orientation—shape the experiences, behavior, and well-being of diverse groups. Although this scholarship has undeniably enhanced the understanding of groups such as people of color and lesbian, gay, and bisexual (LGB) people, it is common for research to focus on one dimension of identity in isolation. Thus, research is less likely to focus on populations with multiple minority identities, such as LGB people of color.

Indeed, a recent review of psychological scholarship produced between 1998 and 2007 found that only 4% of sexual orientation–focused articles and 1% of race/ethnicity–focused articles dealt specifically or substantially with LGB people of color.

Such findings suggest that increased attention to the intersections of race, ethnicity, and sexual orientation is an important direction for future psychological research. This entry focuses specifically on sexual orientation among Latina/o Americans. The entry begins with a brief sketch of the demographic characteristics of Latina/o Americans. Subsequently, it discusses cultural factors that may affect Latina/o Americans' understanding and experience of sexual orientation. Next, it briefly reviews research on contextual factors, such as racism, heterosexism, and acculturation, that may affect the mental health of Latina/o Americans. The entry concludes with suggestions for future scholarship in this area.

Demographics: Latina/o Americans Overall

As of 2012, the number of people residing in the United States who identified as Latina/o or Hispanic was approximately 53 million, which constitutes 17% of the total U.S. population. Although the terms *Latina/o* and *Hispanic* have distinct origins and connotations, they are often used interchangeably to refer to people with cultural origins in Cuba, the Dominican Republic, El Salvador, Puerto Rico, Mexico, or other Spanish- or Portuguese-speaking countries in Central and South America. The majority of Latina/o Americans were born in the United States, but a substantial minority (36%) were born outside the United States. Latina/o Americans as a group are diverse with regard to race, religion, and socioeconomic status, but shared linguistic and historical factors (e.g., the legacy of Spanish or Portuguese colonialism) unify them as a large, influential ethnic group in the United States.

LGB Latina/o Americans

It is relatively more difficult to produce estimates of the number of people, regardless of race or ethnicity, who identify as LGB or some other sexual minority (e.g., asexual, queer). These reasons include the invisible, concealable nature of sexual orientation; heterosexist stigma that may motivate LGB people to conceal their identities from researchers; and ambiguous definitions of what constitutes an LGB identity (e.g., same-sex attraction, same-sex behavior, explicit identification as LGB). Despite these methodological limitations, large, national, population-based surveys estimate that 2.2% to 4% of the U.S. population identify as LGB or transgender.

Estimates of the Latina/o American population who identify as LGB or transgender are quite similar to those for the general population. The proportion of Latina/o Americans who identify as LGB or transgender is 4.3% (approximately 1.4 million people), which is quite similar to estimates for the general population. Based on data from couples in the United States, it appears that Latina/o Americans in same-sex couples are more likely than those in mixed-sex couples to be born in the United States, to be employed, and to have completed a college degree.

Cultural Factors and Heterosexism

A prominent assumption of psychological scholarship focused on racial or ethnic minority LGB people is that racial or ethnic minority communities espouse more negative attitudes toward homosexuality, bisexuality, and LGB people than the general population. In turn, the greater prevalence of heterosexist (i.e., anti-LGB) prejudice in racial or ethnic minority communities is thought to affect LGB people of color (e.g., Latina/o American LGB people) by exposing them to greater heterosexist discrimination, promoting their internalization of heterosexist prejudice (i.e., internalized heterosexism or homophobia), and reducing the likelihood of their disclosing their LGB identities to others. These assumptions characterize what has been called the "greater risk" perspective by scholars. There are several cultural factors that are thought to contribute to greater heterosexism within Latina/o American communities, with two of the most commonly discussed being traditional gender roles and religiosity. Following an overview of these cultural factors, evidence for the greater risk perspective will be reviewed and critiqued.

Latina/o Gender Roles: Machismo and Marianismo

One popular explanation for the greater heterosexism in Latina/o communities points to traditional Latina/o gender role norms, such as *machismo* and *marianismo*. Machismo has traditionally referred to a hypermasculine Latino gender role that emphasizes traits such as assertiveness, dominance over others (particularly girls and women), and aggression. However, scholars have recently critiqued such conceptualizations of machismo as focusing too narrowly on the negative aspects of Latino masculinity to the exclusion of potential positive aspects. Thus, more contemporary definitions of machismo distinguish between the aforementioned traditional machismo and *caballerismo* (from *caballero*, the Spanish word for "gentleman"), which entails nurturance and a focus on familial relationships. *Marianismo* is a Latina gender role that emphasizes qualities traditionally associated with the Virgin Mary, such as self-sacrifice, caretaking, passivity, and sexual conservativeness.

Together, machismo and *marianismo* are thought to define, reflect, and perpetuate what is considered appropriate, "gendered" behavior for Latina/o American men and women in society. Thus, for example, a Latina American woman enacts her proper role in society by being partnered with a man, having children, and placing the needs of her husband and children over her own. In turn, her husband fulfills his role in society by exerting power over his wife and children. Same-sex attractions, behaviors, and identities violate key assumptions of these gender roles—for example, that men and women need to be in romantic and sexual relationships with each other to be truly whole. Thus, the greater endorsement of machismo and *marianismo* among Latina/o Americans and Latina/o American communities is thought to promote more negative attitudes toward homosexuality and bisexuality.

There has been some empirical support for the association between traditional gender roles and heterosexist prejudice. Indeed, research in the United States with predominantly European American samples has consistently shown that more traditional gender role attitudes are associated with greater heterosexist prejudice among heterosexuals and greater internalized heterosexism among LGB people. Moreover, LGB individuals with more gender nonconforming appearance and behavior—which is presumably related to less adherence to traditional gender roles—report experiencing more heterosexist harassment and discrimination. This pattern of findings is replicated among Latina/o American samples. Thus, adherence to traditional gender roles is associated with greater heterosexist prejudice in samples of heterosexual Mexican American people, traditional machismo (but not caballerismo) is associated with higher internalized heterosexism among Mexican American men, and gender nonconformity is associated with greater exposure to heterosexist discrimination among Latino gay and bisexual men. Notably, less research has focused specifically on the relation of *marianismo* and gender nonconformity with internalized heterosexism and heterosexist discrimination among Latina lesbian and bisexual women.

Religiosity

A second factor thought to promote greater heterosexism among Latina/o communities is religiosity. Research with predominantly European American samples has consistently demonstrated that religiosity is associated with heterosexist prejudice among heterosexuals. This relation has been demonstrated using several indicators of religiosity, including self-reported religiosity and attendance at religious services, but the relation is particularly robust for people who are members of ideologically conservative religious denominations that endorse heterosexist teachings about same-sex attractions, behaviors, and identities. Membership in conservative religious denominations has also been associated with higher internalized heterosexism in samples of predominantly European American LGB people.

Given the relation between religiosity and heterosexism in the general population, scholars have argued that religiosity is also associated with heterosexism among Latina/o Americans. The majority (55%) of Latina/o Americans identify as Catholic, 22% identify as Protestant, and 18% identify as unaffiliated. As in research with the general population, studies of heterosexual Latina/o Americans find that greater religious attendance and membership in conservative religious denominations (e.g., Evangelical Protestantism) is associated with higher heterosexist prejudice and lower support for pro-LGB legislation, such as same-sex marriage. With regard to LGB people, there is some evidence that greater exposure to nonaffirming religious communities accounts for higher levels of internalized heterosexism among Latina/o American LGB people relative to European American LGB people.

Greater Risk Perspective

The greater risk perspective assumes that communities of color, such as Latina/o American communities, are more likely to espouse heterosexist prejudice for a variety of reasons, including greater adherence to traditional gender roles and conservative religious traditions. As previously described, there is some evidence that Latina/o gender roles such as machismo and *marianismo* and membership in nonaffirming religious communities are associated with heterosexist prejudice among heterosexual Latina/o Americans and greater internalized heterosexism and exposure to heterosexist discrimination among LGB Latina/o Americans. However, these relations are also evinced in predominantly European American samples of heterosexual and LGB people, which makes it difficult to state that Latina/o communities are relatively more heterosexist than the dominant, European American culture. A more direct test of the assumptions of the greater risk perspective for Latina/o communities would compare levels of heterosexism, such as heterosexuals' heterosexist prejudice or LGB people's internalized heterosexism or exposure to heterosexist discrimination, across racial/ethnic groups.

A small body of research has conducted such comparisons, and the results are largely inconsistent with the greater risk perspective. With regard to heterosexuals' attitudes toward homosexuality and bisexuality, studies have not consistently shown that Latina/o Americans possess more heterosexist prejudice than European Americans. Indeed, data from large, nationally representative data sets suggest that Latina/o Americans' attitudes toward homosexuality and LGB people and support for pro-LGB legislation are remarkably similar to estimates for the general population.

Studies have also compared manifestations of heterosexism between Latina/o American and European American LGB people. Again, research has not consistently demonstrated that Latina/o American LGB people are exposed to greater heterosexist discrimination or that they possess higher levels of internalized heterosexism relative to European American LGB people. The only consistent group difference to emerge from such comparisons is that Latina/o American LGB people appear to disclose their identities to family members less often than European American LGB people. This group difference also emerges for other racial/ethnic minority groups, such as African Americans and Asian Americans. Although it is possible to interpret Latina/o American LGB people's lower levels of disclosure to their families as evidence that Latina/o families (and, by extension, communities) are more heterosexist, alternative interpretations that do not pathologize Latina/o communities are also possible. For example, Bonnie Moradi and colleagues proposed that the lower levels of identity disclosure among racial/ethnic minority LGB individuals could be interpreted as a protective strategy in the context of experiencing both racism and heterosexism. That is, because racial/ethnic minority people often depend on family to cope with the racism that they encounter, they may be more cautious about disclosing stigmatized LGB identities and potentially jeopardizing an important source of support.

Given the mixed empirical support for the propositions of the greater risk perspective, scholarship focused on Latina/o American LGB people would benefit from shifting attention to other topics, such as the factors that contribute to the well-being of this population. In the next section, research that has investigated contextual issues that affect the mental health of Latina/o American LGB people will be reviewed.

Contextual Influences and Latina/o American Mental Health

Data from large, national, population-based studies suggest that, relative to heterosexual people, LGB people are at higher risk for psychiatric disorders and mental health concerns. Moreover, risk estimates do not appear to vary substantially between Latina/o American and European American LGB people. Nonetheless, the factors that contribute to mental health concerns among diverse LGB people may vary according to social context. That is, because of their racial/ethnic and sexual minority statuses, Latina/o Americans must contend with social stressors stemming from societal racism as well as heterosexism.

Social stressors arising from societal heterosexism, such as heterosexist discrimination (both interpersonal and institutional), internalized heterosexism, and expectations of rejection based on one's sexual orientation, have been identified as factors causing mental health concerns among LGB people. Indeed, a substantial body of research with predominantly European American LGB samples shows that higher levels of discrimination, internalized heterosexism, and expectations of rejection are associated with higher levels of overall psychological distress, depression, anxiety, and posttraumatic stress symptoms and lower self-esteem and life satisfaction.

A parallel body of research has investigated how stressors associated with racial or ethnic minority identities may negatively affect mental health among Latina/o Americans. One stressor that may be particularly salient for Latina/o Americans is acculturative stress, which is the difficulty experienced by recent immigrants during the process of acclimating to the dominant, Eurocentric culture of the United States. Such difficulty may include linguistic barriers or discrepancies in cultural beliefs and values. Another, related concept is racial or ethnic discrimination, which for Latina/o Americans may manifest as exposure to hurtful stereotypes (e.g., the assumption by others that one does not speak English), differential treatment from authority figures or institutions (e.g., being stopped by police officers and asked for one's "papers"), being called racist epithets, or racially motivated hate crime victimization. Research with predominantly heterosexual Latina/o Americans has consistently demonstrated that acculturative stress and racist or ethnic discrimination are associated with poorer mental health outcomes.

Some studies have focused specifically on the ways multiple forms of oppression combine to affect Latina/o American LGB people. For example, one study of this population by Brandon L. Velez and colleagues found that heterosexist discrimination, internalized heterosexism, racist discrimination, and internalized racism contributed additively and interactively to mental health outcomes. Another study of gay and bisexual Latino men by Rafael M. Díaz and colleagues found that heterosexist discrimination and poverty contributed independently to psychological distress. Finally, some studies have taken a more intersectional approach by investigating forms of oppression that are specific to LGB people of color. For example, with a sample of racial and ethnic minority LGB people that included Latina/o Americans, Kimberly F. Balsam and colleagues found that heterosexism experienced in the context of communities of color and racism experienced in the context of LGBT relationships were both associated with depression and stress. These studies point to the importance of tailoring psychological research and intervention efforts to the particular characteristics of the populations under investigation.

Future Research Directions

Scholarship on Latina/o Americans and sexual orientation has provided valuable insights into the ways in which race, ethnicity, and sexual orientation combine to shape the experiences of diverse populations. Overall, research has shown that Latina/o American LGB people have many of the same experiences as LGB people from other racial or ethnic groups, but they may also contend with social stressors that are specific to the Latina/o American experience.

One of the most important considerations for future research with this population is greater inclusion of girls and women. As noted by Yu-Ping Huang and colleagues, the vast majority of research on LGB people of color uses samples of Latino American and African American gay or bisexual men. In large part, the absence of Latina American (as well as African American, Asian American, and Native American) lesbian or bisexual girls and women reflects the tendency for research on racial or ethnic minority LGB people to focus on the risk factors for and consequences of HIV/AIDS. Because public health data show that Latino and African American gay and bisexual boys and men are disproportionately affected by HIV/AIDS, it is vitally important for research to identify ways to reduce the impact of HIV/AIDS on this population. However, it is also important for research to attend to topics that are salient to lesbian and bisexual girls and women of color broadly and Latina American girls and women specifically. For example, in addition to contending with heterosexism and racism, Latina American women must also contend with the negative impact of sexism on their mental, physical, social, and economic well-being. Furthermore, the racism or heterosexism Latina American women encounter may be "gendered" or shaped by their experiences as women. Thus, diversifying the composition of samples has the added benefit of expanding the range of topics that could be fruitfully examined in research.

Brandon L. Velez

See also Arab Americans and Sexual Orientation; Asian Americans and Sexual Orientation; Black Americans and Sexual Orientation; Two-Spirited People; White/ European Americans and Sexual Orientation

Further Readings

Balsam, K. F., Molina, Y., Beadnell, B., Simoni, J., & Walters, K. (2011). Measuring multiple minority stress: The LGBT People of Color Microaggressions Scale. *Cultural Diversity and Ethnic Minority Psychology, 17,* 163–174. doi:10.1037/a0023244

Cochran, S. D., Mays, V. M., Alegría, M., Ortega, A. N., & Takeuchi, D. (2007). Mental health and substance use disorders among Latino and Asian American lesbian, gay, and bisexual adults. *Journal of Consulting and Clinical Psychology, 75,* 785–794. doi:10.1037/0022-006X.75.5.785

Díaz, R. M., Ayala, G., Bein, E., Henne, J., & Marin, B. V. (2001). The impact of homophobia, poverty, and racism on the mental health of gay and bisexual Latino men: Findings from 3 U.S. cities. *American Journal of Public Health, 91,* 927–932.

Herek, G. M., & Gonzalez-Rivera, M. (2006). Attitudes toward homosexuality among U.S. residents of Mexican descent. *Journal of Sex Research, 43,* 122–135.

Huang, Y., Brewster, M. E., Moradi, B., Goodman, M. B., Wiseman, M. C., & Martin, A. (2010). Content analysis of literature about LGB people of color: 1998–2007. *The Counseling Psychologist, 38,* 363–396. doi:10.1177/0011000009335255

Moradi, B., Wiseman, M. C., DeBlaere, C., Goodman, M. B., Sarkees, A., Brewster, M. E., & Huang, Y. (2010). LGB of color and white individuals' perceptions of heterosexist stigma, internalized homophobia, and outness: Comparisons of levels and links. *The Counseling Psychologist, 38,* 397–424. doi:10.1177/0011000009335263

Velez, B. L., Moradi, B., & DeBlaere, C. (2015). Multiple oppressions and the mental health of sexual minority Latina/o individuals. *The Counseling Psychologist, 43,* 7–38. doi:10.1177/0011000014542836

Williams Institute. (2013). *LGBT Latino/a individuals and Latino/a same-sex couples.* Los Angeles, CA: Author. Retrieved from http://williamsinstitute.law.ucla.edu/wp-content/uploads/Census-2010-Latino-Final.pdf

Latina/o Americans and Transgender Identity

Latina/o (Latinx) Americans are a very diverse group of people, and country-of-origin and cultural differences between multiple ethnic groups create significant intragroup diversity. Each country has differences in language, colonization, history, economy, immigration challenges, and sociopolitical environment, among others, thus making generalizations difficult at best. Latinxs are considered the fastest-growing ethnicity in the United States, according to the 2010 U.S. Census data. On immigration to the United States, Latinx Americans also differ in the level of enculturation and how identified they remain with their families' countries of origin. While most Latinxs share the colonial legacy of imperialistic Catholic countries and linguistic roots in their Latin-derived languages, their histories of resistance to colonization and their indigenous roots make for regional differences in gender roles and, sometimes, gender categories. Although, historically, indigenous and African influences often defied binary gender assumptions, at present, many countries have cultures that define strict gender roles and struggle with the legacy of machismo, gender inequality, sexism, and heterosexism. Research on trans Latinxs remains scarce and, when present, focuses almost exclusively on female identified transgender populations. Part of the challenge of doing research with trans Latinxs is that those who transgress the gender binary with their identity, expression, and/or behavior do not always assume the term *transgender* as their identity. Trans Latinx Americans face high levels of discrimination, harassment, and violence, which create barriers to education, health care, gender affirming treatments, socioeconomic stability, and access to safe housing. Due to the intersectionality of their marginalized identities, trans Latinxs are often criminalized and face unwarranted stops and arrests by law enforcement agencies. This entry focuses on the various factors that affect gender in Latin America and Latinx Americans, including gendered language, colonization, and stigmatization.

Latinxs and Latin America

Latina/o American is used to describe the ethnic identity of people born in one of the more than 26 countries and dependent territories in Central, South America, and the Caribbean that were colonized by Spain, Portugal, and France. People who live in this geographical area call themselves *latinoamericanos* or Latin Americans. In the United States, the term *Latina/o American* is used to describe people whose families emigrated from a Latin American country. The term *Latinx* is used throughout this entry instead of *Latina/o* to also include people who do not conform to the gender binary.

Latinxs are grouped together under the word *Latin* as they share a history of colonization by countries whose language is a Romance language. The diversity of cultures in Latin America is exponentially augmented when considering that there are at least 522 indigenous groups that inhabit the land that encompasses the region. This diversity makes it hard to generalize about Latinxs on any topic regarding identity, gender, and psychology.

Latinxs are the fastest-growing ethnic group in the United States according 2010 Census data, which also project that they will be the majority ethnic group in various states by 2050. By this year, the United States will become the country with the most Spanish speakers in the world, followed by Mexico. According to calculations by the Pew Research Center in 2010, almost half (45%) the Latinxs in the United States live in metropolitan areas, including six areas in California (e.g., Los Angeles), New York–New Jersey, three areas in Texas (e.g., San Antonio), Chicago in Illinois, Miami in Florida, and Phoenix in Arizona.

Latinx Nonbinary Gender History and Resistance

The precolonial indigenous societies of the Americas had different gender roles and hierarchies from those of the colonizers. In many indigenous groups, the relationship between men and women was more egalitarian than that of their colonizers. Several indigenous groups categorized gender differently, and some continued to do so despite colonization. The *omegiids* within the Kuna in Panama are assigned males who exhibit female characteristics (i.e., feminine mannerisms). As they enter adolescence, they assume the identity of omegiids and are allowed to engage in traditionally female activities such as the sewing of the *molas* (Kuna women's shirts). Among the Zapotec indigenous groups in Mexico, the Oaxacan *muxhes* and Teotitlán *biza'ah* are also considered separate genders, equally legitimate as male and female.

Some (but not all) Latinxs who challenge, question, or transgress gender norms identify as trans. Some gender variant Latinxs prefer the term *queer* or *genderqueer*, as this term has often been used by nonheterosexual people of color who have experienced marginalization by the LGB movement due to the intersectionality of their identities (including their ethnic/racial, socioeconomic, and/or gender identity/expression). In many countries, there are local words that gender variant Latinxs identify with: For example, in Brazil, *travesti* is used by some female identified trans Latinxs; *jota* is a reappropriated pejorative term sometimes used by female identified trans Mexicans; in Puerto Rico, the term *bucha* (similar to *butch*) is often preferred by male identified trans people (although many buchas consider themselves female and lesbian), and *draga/drago* is used by drag queens/kings. Some gender variant Latinxs may prefer the label *genderfluid*, as it represents their experience of gender transcending closed categories and shifting according to context or mood. Latinx Americans who strongly identify with their indigenous roots sometimes identify as *Two Spirit*, a term used by queer and LGBT people of indigenous descent in the United States. Finally, other gender variant Latinxs may not use any labels for their gender identity at all.

Latinxs and Gendered Language

Although the countries that colonized Latin America brought with them three different languages (Spanish, French, and Portuguese), their origin in Latin makes one thing similar: All are gendered languages. *Gendered language* refers to a language in which most nouns are assigned a gender that is evident in the spelling of the word and in the article that precedes it. For example, in Spanish "the dog" is translated as *el perro* or *la perra*, depending on the gender of the dog. Thus, it is possible to immediately tell the gender of a word by how it is written. Other nouns like "the sky" are translated as *el cielo*, which means the sky's gender is male. Although each language may assign different genders for the same noun (e.g., "the map" is *el mapa* in Spanish, which is masculine, whereas it is *la carte* in French, which is feminine), the experience of understanding the world as gendered from the time that we name it is similar across the three languages. Most of the nouns in Spanish, Portuguese, and French have one of two possible genders: masculine or feminine. There are few gender neutral nouns. Thus, for the most part, the world is named and perceived in two discrete gender categories: male and female.

This has important implications for gender development and the internalization of hegemonic masculinity and gender roles in Latin Americans. Because of the constant gendered experience of the world, gender indoctrination occurs via language acquisition and conversation on a constant basis. This recurrent affirmation of a gender binary deems invisible the possibility of other, nonbinary genders. Moreover, the appearance of other gender possibilities or the transgression of the binary can appear as aberrant, enabling the stigmatization of variance. Finally, with gendered languages, it is virtually impossible to speak in a gender neutral way: Even when the gender of a person or object is unknown, the default is to use masculine descriptors and articles.

Colonization

In addition to language, the legacies of colonization affect gender in multiple ways in Latin America. Religion was a significant part of the colonization agenda of all three countries, as they were intent on converting all indigenous and African people to Catholicism. The gender roles prescribed by the Church of the time were tied to their doctrines. The culture of the colonizer was also imposed by explicit (i.e., language, laws) and implicit (i.e., schools) means. As the colonizers engaged in consensual and forced (rape) coupling with indigenous and African women, new generations of multiracial and multicultural progeny began to emerge.

The reality of people who have been colonized is marked by multiple paradoxes, as the work of Frantz Fannon, Albert Memmi, Linda Tuhiwai Smith, and other scholars points out. Identity is particularly sensitive to this, as it bears witness to the intertwining of multiple cultures in the intersectionality of many aspects of the self. People from colonized countries, in multiple ways, have to cope with having parts of their selves contain aspects of both the colonizer and the colonized. Even through resistance of colonization, people from colonized countries are often faced with the recognition that their innermost fibers of *being* contain multiple apparent contradictions.

Transgender

Transgender (*trans*) is an umbrella term that refers to the gender identity of people who challenge gender norms in various ways. It includes people who feel that the gender they are assigned at birth (assigned gender) does not correspond to their gender identity, as well as people who feel that their gender identity does not follow the traditional binary of masculine and feminine. People whose assigned gender corresponds to their gender identity are called *cisgender*. Under the umbrella of "transgender," there are other terms that people use to define their gender identity, such as *androgynous, transsexual, boi, masculine of center, aggressive, stud, gender variant, genderqueer, pangender, genderfluid*, and *gender nonconforming*, among others. Other identities that also transgress gender norms include, among others, *drag queen/king, cross-dresser*, and *genderbender*; people who hold these identities may or may not identify as trans.

People who identify as trans may or may not choose to hormonally, surgically, and/or socially modify their bodies and gender expression to align with their gender identity. When people choose to align their gender expression with their gender identity, this process is known as transitioning.

Stigmatization and Violence

For many Latinxs, there is a lot of pressure to conform to traditional, binary gender roles, which also demand heterosexuality. The binary is, in many countries, so polarized that correct performance of gender implies hypermasculinity or hyperfemininity. Hegemonic masculinity is enforced, exhibited, and professed in many countries as *machismo*. Countries where machismo is prevalent often experience high levels of gender violence. Gender violence encompasses what has been usually denominated domestic violence, *crímenes pasionales* ("passion crimes"), and other misogynistic, homophobic, and transphobic violence.

The correct performance of masculinity is more violently policed than the performance of femininity, which puts boys and men who are seen as effeminate at risk of being targeted for bullying, harassment, and physical, verbal, emotional, and sexual violence. This is particularly true for trans identified and/or gender variant people. A 2013 report from the Latin American Organization RED LACTRANS and the International HIV/AIDS Alliance presented figures from the 2011 Trans Murder Monitoring Project (2008–2011) and found that 80% of transgender murders in the world took place in Latin America. With 826 total murders of trans people from 2008 to 2011, this sum represents an estimate of one trans identified individual being killed every other day in Latin America.

The pressures to conform to femininity standards for assigned women are remarkably strong as well. While families may not always embrace nonheterosexual identities, they can often be better tolerated if the person's gender expression does not transgress gender norms. Many gender nonconforming, assigned-female Latinxs describe experiences where their families of origin had stronger reactions to their masculine gender expression than when they started dating women. In some Latin American countries, masculine-of-center, assigned-female Latinxs often identify as buchas; transgender identity can be seen as a foreign phenomenon, another level of colonization. This often renders trans-masculine communities invisible and increases the challenges for research and outreach.

Nevertheless, prevalence studies seem to suggest that Latinx trans women are more at risk and less tolerated than Latinx trans men. In Latin American societies that are *machistas*, Latinx trans men who reflect some of the masculine attributes that are valued in society can find some acceptance in certain contexts. Within these same societies, sexism, gender violence, and misogyny combined with transphobia can create a lethal combination that results in sanctioned violence toward trans women.

Violence toward trans Latinxs occurs at multiple levels, and its perpetrators often enjoy impunity. Street verbal and physical harassment and physical, emotional, and sexual assaults are frequent in the lives of trans Latinxs in Latin America. However, despite the high numbers of crimes of violence committed against trans Latinxs, these are rarely prosecuted. RED LACTRANS has documented a history of inaction on the part of governmental authorities (i.e., judges, prosecutors, the police), whereby they do not bring the perpetrators of violence against trans Latinxs to justice. Moreover, some of the perpetrators of crimes against trans Latinxs are police officials themselves: 80% of trans activists interviewed by REDLACTRANS had experienced violence or threats to their safety from the police and/or within government facilities. This renders this population particularly vulnerable to violence and harm.

Immigration

There are many economic and sociopolitical reasons why people emigrate to the United States. For many trans Latinxs, the violence and discrimination they face in their countries of origin is severe enough for them to qualify for asylum. In addition, the possibility of feeling freer and safer to express their gender identity in the United States, and thus have a better quality of life, motivates many trans Latinxs to immigrate. However, apart from seeking asylum, there are structural barriers that make it harder for trans identified Latinxs to immigrate to the United States legally. Discrimination at the workplace and family rejection make work visas and family petitions more challenging for trans identified Latinxs. Furthermore, identity documents can be hard to obtain or may be in their assigned gender and difficult to change. The intersection of gender, ethnic/racial background, and immigration status puts trans identified Latinxs at a disadvantage in work settings and at increased risk for interpersonal violence and discrimination.

In the United States, trans Latinxs also experience high levels of discrimination and are subject to violence at higher rates. A 2011 report by the National Gay and Lesbian Task Force, the National Center for Transgender Equality, and the League of United Latin American Citizens stated that trans Latinxs experience among the highest levels of discrimination in the United States. Trans Latinxs had the highest unemployment rate (20%); 28% had a household income of less than $10,000 per year; 47% reported having attempted suicide; 27% had experienced homelessness; 23% had been refused medical care due to their identity; and 77% had experienced harassment in school. In addition, 29% were refused housing, and 15% were evicted due to bias. Eight percent were HIV positive. All these numbers were higher for trans Latinxs than for cisgender Latinxs, non-Latinx transgender people, and the general population.

Nevertheless, not all the numbers are disheartening: 47% of Latinx trans and gender nonconforming people reported being accepted by their families, with 65% reporting that their relationships with their family slowly improved after coming out as trans. Trans Latinx who were accepted by their family were less likely to face discrimination, experience homelessness, or attempt suicide.

Multiple Marginalizations

Another aspect of the stigmatization that trans Latinxs face is the criminalization of trans identity at the intersection of racial/ethnic background. Trans Latinxs and other trans people of color are often profiled by law enforcement. The victimization and discrimination that many trans Latinxs and other trans people of color experience can lead to homelessness and to survival practices, which may include survival sex (i.e., trading sex for shelter, food, or money). Discrimination and harassment at homeless shelters often push trans Latinxs out of resources and further marginalize them. Profiling trans Latinxs as sex workers or criminals leads to overpolicing of this population: Often, trans Latinxs describe being stopped just for "walking while trans," as police stop them due to their gender identity and ethnic background under the assumption that they are about to engage in criminal activities.

Although trans Latinas often face higher rates of overpolicing, masculine trans Latinxs also face additional scrutiny due to their gender identity. Masculine trans Latinxs face increased safety challenges as their gender expression becomes increasingly masculine and/or after transitioning. While trans Latinos at times may seem to enjoy some of the privileges of masculinity in a sexist and heterosexist society, they can also face increased oppression due to the intersection of their ethnic/racial identity and their gender identity and the demonization of Black and Brown masculinity.

The impact of the intersectionality of multiple marginalized identities also can be seen in the scarcity of research about trans Latinx populations. Most of the studies of trans Latinxs focus on trans women, sex work, and HIV status. The impact of discrimination and victimization on trans Latinxs as well as their resiliency need to be further documented. Studies on masculine identified trans Latinxs are needed. Finally, interdisciplinary approaches to the study of trans Latinxs are warranted: Trans Latinxs have long documented their experiences in the arts and literature as well as through their activism. Although the lack of visibility of some trans Latinxs and the lack of uniformity in nomenclature (i.e., how people choose to name their gender) can be a challenge to identify and conduct research with this population, a decolonizing, community-based, and multiculturally sensitive approach to research can help overcome these hurdles.

Trans Latinxs and Visibility

Latinxs have been transgressing traditional gender roles throughout history. During the early 1900s, Frida Kahlo, one of Mexico's most influential artists, pushed gender boundaries publicly: She would occasionally dress as male and engage in traditionally masculine behaviors (e.g., smoking, swearing, seducing women). Around the same time, Luisa Capetillo, a Puerto Rican writer, labor leader, and women's rights activist, was pushing gender norms with her political work and wearing pants in public (a "crime" for which she was arrested). While neither assumed a trans identity, they are both examples of Latinxs who transgressed gender norms.

Trans Latinxs have also been at the forefront of LGBTQ rights activism in the United States, contributing to the movement since its beginnings. Sylvia Rivera was a trans Latina who was part of the Stonewall riots in 1969. She was also a founder/founding member of various advocacy organizations, such as the Street Transvestite Action Revolutionaries, the Gay Liberation Front, and the Gay Activists Alliance, among others. José Sarria, a drag queen and LGBT activist in San Francisco since the 1950s, was the first openly gay person to run for public office in the United States. He founded the League for Civil Education, the Society for Individual Rights, and the Imperial Court of San Francisco.

Contemporary Latinx performers who push gender boundaries include Carmelita Tropicana, Marga Gómez, Janis Astor del Valle, and Antonio Pantojas. Current public figures who identify as trans include Endry Cardeño, Florencia de la V., Alejandra Bogue, Ignacio G. Rivera, Paxx Moll, Diego Sánchez, and Raffi Freedman-Gurspan. Some trans identified Latinx scholars include Andrés Ignacio Rivera Duarte, Brigitte Luis Guillermo Baptiste, and Luis Felipe (Luisa Fernanda) Díaz. Trans Latinxs have been featured in documentaries such as *Mala mala* (2015), which depicts the transgender community in Puerto Rico. Increased visibility is considered a positive step toward equality for trans Latinxs.

María R. Scharrón-del Río

See also Colonialism and Gender; Criminalization of Gender Nonconformity; Criminalization of Men of Color; Hegemonic Masculinity; Intersectional Identities; Latina/o Americans and Gender; Machismo; Transgender People and Resilience; Transgender People and Violence

Further Readings

Cerezo, A., Morales, A., Quintero, D., & Rothman, S. (2014). Trans migrations: Exploring life at the intersection of transgender identity and immigration. *Psychology of Sexual Orientation and Gender Diversity, 1*(2), 170–180. doi:10.1037/sgd0000031

Harrison-Quintana, J., Perez, D., & Grant, J. (2012). *Injustice at every turn: A look at Latino/a respondents in the national transgender discrimination survey.* Washington, DC: National Center for Transgender Equality and National Gay and Lesbian Task Force.

Lambert, N. (2010). *Understanding transgender identity and activism in Latin America.* Paper presented at the annual meeting of the American Sociological Association, Atlanta, GA. Retrieved from http://citation.allacademic.com/meta/p_mla_apa_research_citation/4/1/0/2/2/p410226_index.html

Morales, E. (2013). Latino lesbian, gay, bisexual, and transgender immigrants in the United States. *Journal of LGBT Issues in Counseling, 7*(2), 172–184. doi:10.1080/15538605.2013.785467

REDLACTRANS. (2012). *"The night is another country": Impunity and violence against transgender women human rights defenders in Latin America.* Buenos Aires, Argentina: International HIV/AIDS Alliance.

Santini, A., & Sickles, D. (Producers/Directors). (2014). *Mala mala* [Motion picture]. Culver City, CA: Strand Releasing.

Legal System and Gender

The U.S. legal system is very complex in terms of the types of cases heard, jurisdictions, types of courts, and specific processes within each court. The common denominator for all courts is that they are either criminal or civil courts and that they follow the stages of the judicial process; these steps will be elaborated on later in this entry. The primary difference between a criminal and a civil court depends on the type of case that is heard—essentially who brings the case to the court's attention. In civil cases, a party approaches the legal system to seek resolution to some issue or dispute; this usually entails the examination of some relief as the plaintiff believes that they have been harmed in some way by the defendant. This relief can come in the form of financial compensation for some damage, an order or protection, or a court order implementing the cessation of some activity. Involvement in a criminal court involves an allegation that an individual has broken a law and is tried to determine whether or not a punishment can be levied. In this court, the prosecutor, who represents the people, brings the case against the person who allegedly committed the crime.

The role of gender in the legal system is important; its impact cannot be understated. For the purposes of this entry, the terms *gender* and *sex* are used interchangeably, even though *gender* refers to behaviors and roles in society and *sex* refers to the biological and physiological characteristics of a person. This entry compares and contrasts the fields of criminal justice, criminology, and law; introduces the Federal Bureau of Investigation's Uniform Crime Report; outlines the judicial process; examines the role of gender and crime; examines the components of gender and the legal system, including role congruity theory; and concludes with a discussion on future directions.

Criminal Justice, Criminology, and Law

In terms of legal system involvement, there are three major fields of study that must be understood individually, and how they overlap, to understand the others: (1) criminal justice, (2) criminology, and (3) law. Criminal justice refers to the primary focus on the societal systems or laws implemented to address some criminal act or behavior. The implementation of systems addressing crime, detention of alleged offenders, and prosecution are key components of criminal justice. Common criminal justice personnel include law enforcement officers, correctional officers, probation officers, and special agents. Criminology, on the other hand, is the analysis of crime. More specifically, criminologists seek to identify the causes, associated costs, and consequences of crime. There are many specialties in criminology; however, a majority of careers are centered on data collection to identify causality. The field of law focuses on the laws surrounding crime as opposed to policy or psychosocial aspects of the legal system. Although the three fields have characteristics that make them distinct, there is some overlap.

Uniform Crime Report

The Uniform Crime Report (UCR) was developed by the Federal Bureau of Investigation (FBI) to tally arrests, citations, and summons based on a variety of offenses. The UCR reflects the number of arrests as opposed to the number of people who are arrested, given that a person may be arrested multiple times in the span of 1 year. The FBI also provides information on age, race, and gender. Because gender is an important variable in research, the UCR is an excellent resource when comparing type of crime and demographic variables such as gender.

The Judicial Process

In criminal and in civil cases, the individual is involved in the judicial process. This process has steps through which the individual proceeds: (a) pretrial, (b) trial, (c) disposition, and (d) appellate stages. In the pretrial stage, the information discovered is made available to the other side, there is an initial appearance or arraignment, and in most cases, there is negotiation between both sides. In the trial stage, evidence, witnesses, consultants, and experts are presented to provide the jury (trial jury) or the judge (bench trial) information about their case. The next stage is the disposition stage. This is when a judge or jury renders a verdict of guilty or not guilty, and if guilty, a sentence is imposed. Last, in the appellate stage, the unsuccessful party has a variety of options to appeal the judgment.

Race and Legal Involvement

The relationship between criminal involvement and race has long been a controversial topic. The U.S. Census Bureau has identified that African Americans constitute between 10% and 15% of the U.S. population, and the FBI has identified that between 25% and 30% of individuals arrested were African Americans. Social psychologists have identified two theories to explain this phenomenon: normative and conflict. In the former, the enforcement of laws is unbiased; therefore, consideration of the offender's race, ethnicity, and gender is nonexistent in terms of criminal culpability. In the latter, the elevated levels of arrests of African Americans can be viewed as discriminatory policing, and criminal law is protecting the powerful and wealthy citizens.

Regardless of the theory, this is a significant issue that begs the academic community for an answer. In the normative theory, it would be unrealistic to believe that people are unbiased since many opinions are based on personal experiences, including those of law enforcement and legal professionals. In the conflict theory, it may be far-fetched to state that the law is protecting the powerful. To address this issue, intervention at the law enforcement, judicial, and policy levels is necessary.

Gender Nonconformity and Legal Involvement

Gender nonconformity refers to the level of incongruence between the sex of persons at birth and their gender role; the higher the level, the greater the incongruity between the person's appearance, interests, or behaviors and societal expectations of masculinity and femininity. Individuals who do not conform to gender roles experience more rejection, discrimination, and stigmatization than those who conform to gender roles or who have lower levels of gender nonconformity. Historically, there are two marginalized groups who face stigma for not conforming to gender role expectations. First, there are lesbian, gay, bisexual, and queer people, who defy gender norms through their sexual orientation identities, sexual behaviors, and romantic relationships. Some, but not all, may also participate in other gender nonconforming behaviors including in dress, speech, and presentation. Second, transgender and gender nonconforming people defy gender norms by identifying as something other than their assigned birth sex. Many, but not all, transgender people may seek gender affirming medical treatments, whereas most, but not all, gender nonconforming people (or genderqueer people) do not.

Regarding the legal system, there is some research on the experiences of lesbian, gay, bisexual, and queer and transgender and gender nonconforming people with the police, the courts, and other aspects of the criminal justice system. In their work reviewing victim experiences of hate crimes, Gregory Herek, J. Roy Gillis, and Jeanine Cogan found that individuals who do not conform to traditional gender roles experience more extreme forms of discrimination. Furthermore, they may become a victim of a crime, and this victimization further increases the likelihood that gender nonconforming individuals will be involved in the legal system. Individuals with higher levels of gender nonconformity who are arrested due to their involvement in criminal activity are more likely to experience discrimination at all stages of the judicial process.

Gender and Crime

It has been well established that men commit crime at significantly higher rates than women. On review of the 2014 UCR by the FBI, men accounted for approximately 73% of all arrests within a given year. It has also been well supported in the literature that men are involved in more violent offending and have higher rates of recidivism. The 2014 UCR also supports this finding as it has been identified that approximately 80% of violent crime was perpetrated by males. Historically and currently, the data have supported the idea that men are responsible for more criminal offenses, but the continued open-ended question is what it is about men that they commit more crime. To date, there is no answer to this question; however, there is the intriguing theoretical research on masculinity and crime by Raewyn Connell, James Messerschmidt, and Tony Jefferson.

Gender and the Legal System

At its onset, positions in the legal system were occupied primarily by males. Through awareness, education, and training, the number of females in legal positions is increasing; however, the majority are still male. In essence, a majority of crime is committed by males, and thus a significant majority of the individuals in the legal system are males. The marriage of law and gender has been very slow moving; therefore, research focusing on the crossing of law and gender is necessary. By combining the various theories of gender with the types of research in the legal system, a better understanding of law that has a gender component may enrich overall understanding and inform future law. For future research on gender and law, Carrie Menkel-Meadow and Shari Seidman Diamond recommended that future researchers complete studies on narrowing the gender gap in law; investigate women's issues such as intimate partner violence, child law, and divorce; develop theories that are gender based; and include both women and men in making, participating in, and interpreting law.

Gender Stereotyping

Alice Eagly found that gender stereotypes identify females as more empathic, nurturing, and understanding, whereas males are considered to be more independent, ambitious, and better leaders. These stereotypes propel males into more leadership positions and demote females to more supportive roles. In his work examining different forms of discrimination, salary, hiring practices, and occupational prestige, Peter Glick identified that males and females are informally "matched" to positions based on these gender stereotypes. In the criminal justice and legal systems, leadership and independence are valued traits; therefore, the gender stereotypes for males are more attractive than for females. Although this does not fully explain the gender gap in position representation in the legal system, it is one component.

Role Congruity Theory

The role congruity theory of prejudice, as examined by Eagly and Steven Karau, stated that when there is incongruity between a group stereotype, such as gender, and the expectation or requirement of a social role, prejudice will become more prevalent. Furthermore, with regard to leadership roles, they identify two specific forms of prejudice: prejudice toward (1) a potential role occupant and (2) current role occupants. The amount of prejudice depends on group stereotypes and role requirements; there appears to be a positive correlation. For example, if there is a significant discrepancy between the identified group stereotype for gender and the requirement for the role, it is likely that there will be greater prejudice.

Prejudice Toward Females

In their work on role congruity theory, Eagly and Karau also found that females receive less favorable evaluations of their potential for a role in leadership or another male-dominated position as it is thought that females will not be able to fulfill the responsibilities of those roles. In terms of gender prejudice, when females fulfill their duties in their incongruent role, gender prejudice remains a constant. For example, if the female is successful in the leadership position, meaning that she possesses the male-dominated characteristics for the position, she may fail to exhibit feminine behaviors (which males may expect) and may exhibit more masculine behaviors. The violations of these gender-based norms can lower the evaluation of a female in a current role.

Prejudice Toward Males

Generally, there are far fewer males who seek to work in female-dominated professions. The prejudice toward men is significantly less than that experienced by females. However, Eagly and Anne Koenig, in their examination of gender prejudice and occupying incongruent roles, identified that when this prejudice does occur, the same happens to males as does to females; prejudice increases when males try to occupy or currently occupy female-dominated positions.

Future Directions

It has been well supported in the academic literature that males encompass a significant majority of arrests. It has also been well supported that males hold significantly more leadership positions in the legal system than females. This gender gap is a significant area to address, and only some components could be included in this brief entry. Further research that aims to explain what exactly these differences are that account for such a large gap between genders in terms of arrest, violence, and occupational leadership roles is warranted.

Greg Bohall

See also Criminal Justice System and Gender; Criminal Justice System and Sexual Orientation; Criminalization of Gender Nonconformity; Gendered Stereotyped Behaviors in Men; Gendered Stereotyped Behaviors in Women; Masculinity Gender Norms; Violence and Gender: Overview

Further Readings

Bartlett, K. T., & Rhode, D. L. (2013). *Gender and law: Theory, doctrine, commentary.* Frederick, MD: Wolters Kluwer Law & Business.

Bartlett, K. T., Rhode, D. L., Grossman, J. L., & Buchalter, S. L. (2014). *Gender law and policy.* Frederick, MD: Wolters Kluwer Law & Business.

Eagly, A. H., & Karau, S. J. (2002). Role congruity theory of prejudice toward female leaders. *Psychological Review, 109*(3), 573–598. doi:10.1037//0033-295X.109.3.573

Eskridge, W. N., Jr., & Hunter, N. D. (2011). *Sexuality, gender, and the law* (3rd ed.). St. Paul, MN: Foundation Press.

Gill, M. J. (2004). When information does not deter stereotyping: Prescriptive stereotyping can foster bias under conditions that deter descriptive stereotyping. *Journal of Experimental Social Psychology, 40*(5), 619–632. doi:10.1016/j.jesp.2003.12.001

Heilman, M. E., Wallen, A. S., Fuchs, D., & Tamkins, M. M. (2004). Penalties for success: Reactions to women who succeed at male gender-typed tasks. *Journal of Applied Psychology, 89*(3), 416–427. doi:10.1037/0021-9010.89.3.416

Prentice, D. A., & Carranza, E. (2002). What women and men should be, shouldn't be, are allowed to be, and don't have to be: The contents of prescriptive gender stereotypes. *Psychology of Women Quarterly, 26*(4), 269–281. doi:10.1111/1471-6402.t01-1-00066

Vescio, T. K., Gervais, S. J., Snyder, M., & Hoover, A. (2005). Power and the creation of patronizing environments: The stereotype-based behaviors of the powerful and their effects on female performance in masculine domains. *Journal of Personality and Social Psychology, 88*(4), 658–672. doi:10.1037/0022-3514.88.4.658

Lesbian, Gay, and Bisexual Children

This entry discusses the current state of research on lesbian, gay, and bisexual (LGB) children from a psychosocial perspective. The discussion encompasses issues of prevalence, the unique challenges LGB children face, and the consequences of these challenges on their health and well-being. In this discussion, the term *lesbian, gay, and bisexual* (LGB) is used to refer to individuals whose sexual orientation is nonheterosexual. A nonheterosexual orientation can be manifested in a few ways, including self-identification as LGB, sexual attraction toward people of the same sex/gender (gay or lesbian) or both sexes/genders (bisexual), or sexual behavior with people of the same sex/gender (gay or lesbian) or both sexes/genders (bisexual). The term *children* is used to refer to individuals whose age ranges from 12 to 24 years, and it is therefore inclusive of youth and young adults. Although LGB children encompass all races, ethnicities, ages, social classes, religions, nationalities, and cultures, this discussion is focused on LGB children in the United States.

Because questions about LGB identity are not included in national, population-based surveys conducted in the United States, it is still not known what percentage of the U.S. children population are LGB. However, current estimates suggest that approximately 3% to 4% of U.S. adults self-identify as LGB. When assessing sexual orientation by asking about sexual behavior, approximately 25% of U.S. adults report engaging in homosexual or bisexual behavior. This is mainly because some individuals may engage in homosexual or bisexual behavior but self-identify as heterosexual.

Although LGB and heterosexual children go through many similar experiences during their lives, LGB children face unique challenges based on their sexual orientation. One such challenge is the formation of an LGB identity and its sharing with others, a process also known as *coming out*.

Coming Out

Scholars have described the process of forming one's LGB identity and coming out using stage models. These stage models involve individuals passing through different phases before they come to completely forming their sexual identity. Although these stage models offer different trajectories, they all include similar milestones, namely (a) the realization and self-awareness of being attracted to the same sex/gender or both sexes/genders; (b) sexual experimentation accompanied by internal struggles, along with shame and guilt (a process also known as internalized homophobia); (c) interacting with other members of the LGB community; (d) acceptance of one's LGB identity; and (e) finally, the integration of one's LGB identity into a holistic, multidimensional self.

Some scholars have criticized the aforementioned stage models because the models assume that the development of one's sexual orientation is linear and cannot deviate from a set path. This critique is based on studies that have found that disclosing one's sexual orientation and engaging in sexual behavior with people of the same sex/gender can happen at different times. Some people experiment first, whereas others disclose first. In response to this critique, other scholars have suggested an alternative conceptualization of the process of LGB identity formation by using developmental milestones. According to this approach, LGB children go through critical milestones in their sexual identity development in a nonlinear and subjective way. Put differently, most LGB children face similar challenges in their coming out process, but the time of occurrence differs from one individual to another.

The age of coming out among LGB individuals in the United States is averaged at 18 to 21 years. According to previous studies, the average age gay men thought they knew their sexual orientation was 10 years, they reported knowing for sure at age 15 years, and they first told someone about their sexual orientation at age 18 years. Lesbian women reported first thinking about their sexual orientation at age 13 years, they knew for sure at age 18 years, and they first told someone about it at age 21 years. Similarly, bisexual people thought they knew at age 13 years, knew for sure at age 17 years, and first told someone when they were 20 years old. It should be noted that most researchers believe that sexual identity development, and specifically the process of coming out, should be viewed as an ongoing process rather than a single event at a certain time point. This is mainly due to the ongoing stigma and discrimination LGB children face throughout their lives, as well as the internalization of LGB stigma.

Stigma and Discrimination

Despite the apparent positive changes in the general public attitude toward LGB individuals and issues, LGB children still encounter stigma and discrimination based on their sexual orientation in many aspects of their lives. Homophobia and heterosexism, defined as explicit and implicit negative attitudes toward LGB individuals, respectively, are a significant barrier to the self-realization and well-being of LGB children. From a young age, LGB children are exposed to homophobic beliefs, values, and attitudes through their interactions with family members, at school, and in the media, among others. These stigma-related experiences, also known as discrimination, are combined with the general stressors of adolescence and coming out. The added psychological burden of managing the various societal demands and experiences puts LGB children at a greater risk of developing negative mental and physical health outcomes compared with their heterosexual counterparts.

LGB Children at School

Compared with their heterosexual counterparts, LGB children's negative experiences can be categorized by violence, bullying, general safety, and school policies. Between 12% and 28% of LGB students reported being threatened with a weapon on school property, 36% were physically harassed in the past year because of their sexual orientation, and 17% were physically assaulted (e.g., punched, kicked, injured with a weapon). LGB students also fall victim to anti-LGB remarks. More than 70% of LGB students heard the word "gay" used in negative ways frequently, and more than 90% said that they felt distressed because of this language. As a result, 56% of LGB students reported that they felt unsafe at school because of their sexual orientation, and 30% had missed at least one day of school in the past month because they felt unsafe or uncomfortable at their schools. Other anti-LGB remarks heard at school include name-calling (e.g., "dyke" or "faggot"; 65%) and negative remarks about gender expression (56%).

LGB children also experience homophobia directed at them by their schoolteachers and staff. Indeed, 51% of students frequently hear homophobic remarks from their teacher or other school staff. A small minority—10% of students—reported that their school's antibullying policy included penalties for bullying based on sexual orientation and gender expression. More than half of the LGB students who were harassed or assaulted in school did not report the incident, because they believed that nothing would happen or an ineffective intervention would take place and possibly make the situation worse. Of those students who did report the harassment to staff, 62% said that the school staff did nothing in response. In addition, some schools prohibit students from creating a Gay-Straight Alliance, or a similar safe space, and discussing or writing about LGB topics in school assignments. Others prevent LGB students from attending a dance or function with someone of the same sex/gender. LGB children were also up to three times more likely than their heterosexual peers to receive punishment from schools, the police, or courts, even though there is no difference in the likelihood of troublesome behavior between LGB and heterosexual children. This gap can be explained by discriminatory practices by authority representatives.

The constant victimization LGB children face at their schools can have many adverse effects on their academic achievement and self-image. Those who experienced high levels of victimization due to their sexual orientation were more than three times as likely to have missed school in the past month, had lower grade point averages, were twice as likely to report that they did not plan to pursue any postsecondary education, and had a lower self-esteem when compared with students who were less often harassed. LGB children also face a plethora of negative mental and physical health outcomes because of stigma and discrimination.

Health and Well-Being of LGB Children

LGB children face many health disparities (i.e., differences between LGB and heterosexual children in disease distribution). LGB individuals have higher rates of negative mental and physical health outcomes due to the stigma, discrimination, and prejudice attached to their identities. This means that although fewer people self-identify as LGB compared with heterosexuals, the proportion of LGB children who experience certain negative mental and physical health outcomes is overwhelming. One of the most widely used theories for explaining the development of health disparities among LGB children is the minority stress model.

Minority Stress Among LGB Children

According to minority stress theory, children who self-identify as LGB are members of at least one stigmatized group (i.e., the LGB community). Experiencing stigma and discrimination because of one's LGB identity leads to additional stress burden along with general life stressors. This additional stress burden, in turn, increases the likelihood of LGB children developing negative mental and physical health outcomes. Put differently, children encounter various stressful life events, such as academic failures, ending a relationship, and graduation. These stressful life events jeopardize their health and make them more likely to develop negative health outcomes. The minority stress model suggests that LGB children experience *additional* stress because of their stigmatized LGB identity. As mentioned earlier, many LGB children experience harassment, teasing, and bullying in their schools because of their LGB identity. These stressful incidents of bullying are considered additional stress that is experienced along with the general stressful life events that every individual faces regardless of sexual orientation.

Mental Health of LGB Children

The majority of LGB children do not report mental health problems, but they are still at a higher risk due to the stigma and discrimination they often face. LGB children are two to three times more likely to experience generalized anxiety disorder, major depression, and conduct disorder than their heterosexual counterparts. LGB children are also at an increased risk for suicide ideation and attempts as well as depressive symptoms compared with heterosexual peers. This increased rate of suicidality compared with heterosexual children is consistent across age-groups, gender, race/ethnicity, and differing definitions of sexual orientation.

Physical Health Among LGB Children

Due to stigma and discrimination, LGB children are more likely to use substances than their heterosexual counterparts. For example, lesbian and bisexual girls were 10 times more likely than heterosexual girls to have smoked in the past week, but bisexual females were the most likely to have used marijuana or other illicit drugs. LGB children also engage in riskier sexual behaviors, such as unprotected sexual intercourse (anal or vaginal), which in turn puts them at higher risk of being affected by a sexually transmitted disease and/or HIV.

Protective Factors

When considering the health and well-being of LGB children, it is crucial to consider protective (resilience) factors that alleviate the negative consequences of stigma and discrimination on their lives. Connectedness to the broader LGBT community, social support, familial support, and self-accepting one's LGB identity are some of the well-documented factors that protect the health of LGB children.

That is, LGB children who are respected and supported by their friends and family are better able to cope with or manage the external stressful events they face due to stigma and discrimination. An emerging field in the study of LGB health is the strengths of LGB children. It is proposed that LGB children may develop positive psychological attributes (i.e., strengths) despite, and perhaps even because of, their exposure to stigma and discrimination. For example, because of their experiences with stigma and discrimination, LGBT children may develop a heightened sense of empathy and compassion toward the suffering of other people. These strengths may in turn counteract the negative consequences of stigma and discrimination as they may facilitate an increased connection to others and therefore easier access to social support.

Nadav Antebi-Gruszka

See also Homophobia; Homosexuality; Identity Formation in Childhood; Psychosexual Development; Sexual Orientation: Overview; Sexual Orientation Identity Development

Further Readings

Institute of Medicine. (2011). *The health of lesbian, gay, bisexual, and transgender people: Building a foundation for better understanding.* Washington, DC: National Academies Press.

Meyer, I. H., & Northridge, M. E. (2007). *The health of sexual minorities: Public health perspectives on lesbian, gay, bisexual, and transgender populations.* New York, NY: Springer.

Mustanski, B. (2015). Future directions in research on sexual minority adolescent mental, behavioral, and sexual health. *Journal of Clinical Child & Adolescent Psychology, 44*(1), 204–219.

Savin-Williams, R. C. (2009). *The new gay teenager.* Cambridge, MA: Harvard University Press.

Lesbian, Gay, and Bisexual Experiences of Aging

In the United States, it is estimated that there are between 1.75 and 4 million lesbian, gay, bisexual (LGB), and transgendered individuals over the age of 60 years. Around the globe, the older adult population, inclusive of all sexual orientations and gender identities, is growing and is marked by incredible diversity. There are many factors that encompass one's personal identity, and these elements intersect and include age, sexual orientation, gender identity, race, ethnicity, national origin, culture, religion, language, ability, socioeconomic status, as well as unique life experiences. Hence, there is no homogeneous LGB older adult population or community. Rather, LGB older adults reflect the broad tapestry of diversity observed in all aged populations. This entry focuses on the experiences of aging for LGB older adults.

Challenge of Definitions and Research

Limited research exists concerning older LGB adults and their experience of aging. Three significant problems exist in relation to LGB gerontological research. First, the heterosexual versus homosexual, or straight versus lesbian, gay, or bisexual, individual definitional systems are limiting. Sexual orientation, much like gender identity, is not only biologically based but also personally, socially, and culturally determined and, as such, is marked by an incredible diversity of experience. Moreover, sexual orientation, particularly for women, exists on a continuum and is often fluid across the life span, inclusive of old age. In addition, individuals who identify as transgender, intersex, third gender, or nongender are largely invisible within the traditional classification systems used by researchers studying LGB aging. The ambiguity and interplay between all of these factors and the addition of other arenas of diversity such as ethnicity, race, and religion make simple, nonfluid sexual orientation definitions incredibly challenging.

Second, cohort effects significantly affect research concerning LGB individuals' experience of aging. Older adults in the United States and other countries lived through, experienced, and grew up in very different social and historical contexts. By necessity, most LGB elders kept their sexual orientation hidden during their youth through middle-adulthood years due to the threat of stigma, discrimination, or violence, and legal concerns. Indeed, in response to social and cultural pressures, they never may have identified as LGB but rather defined themselves according to their unique relationship (e.g., roommates, best friends) or maintained normative heterosexual marriages with special, alternative relationships on the side. Many older LGB adults reported experiencing significant instances of discrimination or violence directly related to their sexual orientation at some point in their lives. These traumas change individuals and hence can affect their experience of aging. As such, information from research gathered concerning current LGB older adults' experiences of aging includes a number of cohort effects and may not reflect research outcomes in the future.

Third, around the globe, many LGB individuals are hidden from view due to cultural, religious, or legal strictures. In most countries, individuals who identify as LGB may risk discrimination, banishment, prison time, or death. Even within the United States, older LGB adults may continue to remain hidden due to stigma and stereotype. Older individuals, after a lifetime of remaining private about their sexual orientation, may be reticent to self-identify as LGB due to fears concerning family, confidentiality, or internalized heterosexism and homophobia. As such, researchers largely have limited their study of LGB older adults to a very select group of the population—typically, White, formally educated, urban, upper middle class, and predominantly individuals who could be classified as middle-aged to early old age. As such, research findings may be skewed due to nonrepresentative samples. In response to this problem, researchers are currently exploring new methodologies such as the use of the Internet for research purposes and the use of alternative and qualitative methodologies.

Stereotype and Stigma

Stereotypes exist concerning both younger and older LGB individuals. The most prominent stereotype of older LGB individuals portrays them as depressed, isolated, and desperate people who are either sexless or lusting after individuals they can no longer attain due to the ravages of age—a stereotype that is not supported by the research literature. Older LGB adults' lives are comparable with the lives of older heterosexual adults. Nonetheless, older LGB adults experience challenges from, at a minimum, a dual stigma in American and some other societies—sexual orientation and old age. Throughout their lives, older LGB individuals have had to deal with stereotypes, prejudice, and discrimination prior to their experience of ageism. Individuals who have positively dealt with LGB bias often have developed resiliency concerning new forms of stigma, which makes adjusting to the bias against old age less difficult. Older LGB individuals have been found to have developed greater self-acceptance and self-confidence, affording them the skills to successfully deal with the stigma of aging.

Similarities and Differences

LGB individuals' experiences of aging are both similar to and different from the experiences of individuals who primarily identify as heterosexual. When looking at differences, it is important to remember that the heterosexual experience should not be viewed as normative or ideal when compared with LGB experiences. Rather, the similarities and differences are only reflective of research findings related to differing older adult populations. Common areas of research related to LGB aging include physical and mental health, family, retirement, and a host of social concerns (e.g., housing, employment, legal concerns), noting that these are not mutually exclusive categories.

LGB older adults' experiences of physical aging are largely identical to those of older heterosexual adults. Certainly, the physiology of aging is comparable, and LGB adults express similar fears related to heart disease, cancer, dementia, and other physical concerns. However, due to a lifetime of possible employment discrimination and lower-wage jobs, older LGB individuals are at greater risk for a variety of health concerns correlated with poverty. Rates of obesity and heart disease, for example, are higher in older LGB adults than in heterosexual elders. These health risks are also documented in other marginalized populations. HIV status remains a concern among the gay male population, but of course, all individuals who are sexually active or who come in contact with infected blood (e.g., shared needles) are at risk for HIV/AIDS.

Problems associated with access to health care and bias within the health care community remain barriers for many LGB older adults. Most physicians are not trained to address LGB health care concerns, and some are even blind to the existence of LGB elders. Health care services and educational materials are typically aimed at a heterosexual population. In addition, older LGB patients today, and certainly earlier in their lives, may have been afraid to discuss health concerns, particularly sexual health issues, with their physicians for fear of bias and discrimination. Historically, some older LGB individuals may have faced psychiatric hospitalization, if they were open with their physicians about their sexual orientation during their youth. The inability to communicate honestly with a health care professional can negatively affect treatment. Discrimination in certain hospitals and health care facilities may further negatively affect health care for LGB older adults. Despite marriage equality, older LGB spouses/partners may have difficulty visiting their loved ones in the hospital and may be denied participation in the health care decisions of their life partner.

LGB older adults' experiences of psychological processes and health are largely similar to those of older heterosexual adults. For example, the cognitive changes associated with age and processes such as life review are similar for LGB elders and heterosexual older adults. However, some research studies have found that rates of depression, anxiety, and substance abuse are higher for older LGB adults, perhaps reflective of a lifetime of discrimination, victimization, and lower socioeconomic status, as well as minority stress. LGB older adults who bear the scars of chronic discrimination and have internalized negative stereotypes associated with LGB identification are at greater risk for mental health problems. Certainly, older individuals who believe the negative stereotypes and religious/cultural proscriptions about LGB individuals have a more difficult time adjusting to their own sexual orientation.

Although some research focuses on the impact of poverty, discrimination, minority stress, violence, and trauma on mental health factors such as depression, anxiety, and substance abuse during the lifetime of an LGB elder, more recent research focuses on psychological strengths. A growing literature exists related to resiliency and the development of positive coping skills in response to negative life events—valuable skills that increase the psychological well-being of older LGB individuals. For example, LGB individuals who experience trauma related to their sexual orientation (e.g., a physical attack, being shunned by family, loss of a job) often develop a skill called crisis competence. Having learned how to successfully handle a trauma, integrate the traumatic experience into their life in a positive manner, and move from survival of trauma to thriving, the LGB individual feels empowered and can apply those same skills to new life challenges and continue to flourish as a person. Similar patterns of psychological hardiness, resiliency, and positive coping can be found in other marginalized populations.

LGB elders are more likely to have a broad network of close friends than heterosexual older adults. Typically, older heterosexual individuals are most closely connected to biological family as opposed to outside friendships. LGB elders often have developed a community of friends that constitute a self-created family—a safe haven in what has been a largely hostile world. This community of friends has often been essential to the LGB elder as their family of origin may not have been aware of or supportive of their life and relationships. The community affords LGB older adults the opportunity to meet new people, socialize, and form new friendships, with both young and old, as well as providing support during times of crisis and need. The conscious establishment of friendship networks or communities and personally selected role models appears to make the aging process easier for LGB elders.

Retirement, for many LGB elders, has an additional positive benefit. While in the workforce, the threat of job loss on the basis of sexual orientation is a constant source of concern for many LGB workers. The LGB individual may subsequently view retirement as freedom from this source of financial concern. On retirement, many LGB older adults, if in good health, begin to engage more in social and political causes than before, when disclosure of sexual orientation might have threatened their employment status. In addition, retirement also translates into a loss of workplace friendships for many individuals. However, as LGB older adults are less likely to disclose and become close friends with work peers, but rather rely on a separate community, the LGB elder's network of friends may remain relatively unchanged with retirement.

LGB elders experience a host of additional concerns that may affect their daily lives. In terms of employment and housing, LGB older adults are at risk for the same forms of discrimination as their younger counterparts. For example, an older LGB individual may be forced out of their rental apartment due to their sexual orientation, with little to no recourse. Older LGB couples may not be allowed to live together in retirement facilities, and sexual relations between same-sex individuals may be prohibited in a nursing home, while heterosexual relationships are condoned. When LGB elders' primary relations are discounted, ignored, or institutionally prohibited, it creates pain, trauma, and loss. As such, LGB elders often express a desire to live in communities that are either predominately LGB or, at least, sensitive to the needs of older LGB individuals. However, these options are limited.

Older LGB individuals face myriad housing, employment, and legal concerns due to institutionalized discrimination. Although marriage equality has remedied a number of legal concerns, many problems remain. LGB elders need to explore alternative legal protections when evaluating issues such as long-term care, end-of-life problems, health care directives, and other concerns affecting those without the protections of legal marriage.

Resources

In recognizing the needs of older LGB individuals, the U.S. Administration on Aging provides funding so that programs can create resources aimed at education, training, and services related to the needs of LGB elders. SAGE (originally Senior Action in a Gay Environment but now Services and Advocacy for GLBT Elders) was a recipient of such funding and developed the National Resource Center on LGBT Aging website. This website provides information by state on lesbian, gay, bisexual, and transgendered (LGBT) resources, as well as information on relevant topical issues, training, and local events. Originally formed in New York City, SAGE meets the needs of active LGBT elders and includes a range of programs from opportunities for socialization to a home visitation program for shut-in LGBT older adults. Groups such as SAGE and alternative programs, which are listed in the National Resource Center guide, also provide services to individuals exploring their LGB identity for the first time as an older adult.

Linda M. Woolf

See also Ageism; Aging and Mental Health; Bisexuality; Community and Aging; Gay Men; Internalized Heterosexism; Lesbians; Minority Stress; Research: Overview; Sexual Orientation Identity; Stigma of Aging; Transgender Experiences of Aging

Further Readings

Kimmel, D. (2014). Lesbian, gay, bisexual, and transgender aging concerns. *Clinical Gerontologist: The Journal of Aging and Mental Health, 37,* 49–63.

Kimmel, D., & Martin, D. L. (Eds.). (2001). *Midlife and aging in gay America: Proceedings of the SAGE Conference.* New York, NY: Routledge.

Kimmel, D., Rose, T., & David, S. (2006). *Lesbian, gay, bisexual, and transgender aging: Research and clinical perspectives.* New York, NY: Columbia University Press.

LGBT Movement Advancement Project, & SAGE. (2010). *Improving the lives of LGBT older adults.* Retrieved from https://www.americanprogress.org/wp-content/uploads/issues/2010/04/pdf/lgbt_elders.pdf

Metlife Mature Market Institute, & American Society on Aging. (2010). *Still out, still aging: TheMetLife Study of Lesbian, Gay, Bisexual, and Transgender Baby Boomers.* Retrieved from https://www.metlife.com/assets/cao/mmi/publications/studies/2010/mmi-still-out-still-aging.pdf

Orel, N. A., & Fruhauf, C. A. (Eds.). (2015). *The lives of LGBT older adults: Understanding challenges and resilience.* Washington, DC: American Psychological Association.

Witten, T. M., & Eyler, A. E. (Eds.). (2012). *Gay, lesbian, bisexual, and transgender aging: Challenges in research, practice, and policy.* Baltimore, MD: Johns Hopkins University Press.

Websites

National Resource Center on LGBT Aging: http://lgbtagingcenter.org/

Lesbian Identity Development

Identity development is a central psychological task for all people. Each person's identity is made up of the intersection of many dimensions of social location, as well as a unique individual personality, skills, and interests. In today's society, gender and sexual orientation are two of the key components of identity. This entry defines the term *lesbian* and provides a brief history of the term. The changing psychosocial context is described, including long periods of widespread antigay attitudes that have had a powerful influence on lesbian identity development. The divergent ways of thinking about lesbian identity—essentialism and postmodern social construction—are explained. Next, the models of lesbian identity development available in the past 100 years are described: lesbianism as pathology, gay-affirmative stage theories, and theories of life span identity processes. Finally, 21st-century changes in understanding lesbian identity development are discussed; these include lesbian-specific theorizing, intersectionality, fluidity, queer theory, the impact of reduced stigmatizing, and the contribution of technology.

A lesbian is a woman whose primary erotic, psychological, emotional, and social interest is in other women. To have a lesbian identity is more than to have feelings or thoughts about women; it is more than having romantic/sexual relationships with women. To have a lesbian identity is to feel that a lesbian is who one is, how one thinks of oneself. A lesbian identity is similar in some ways to one's ethnic or racial identity or one's gender identity—it is an aspect of who one is, and it puts one in a "category" of people who are similar in some way.

The concept of "lesbian" is a relatively new idea, less than 150 years old. While romantic couple relationships between women have been documented across thousands of years in many countries and cultures, they were not labeled "lesbian," nor were they considered part of an identity. In the late 1800s, sex began to be studied scientifically; these scientists were called sexologists. They created the labels of heterosexual, homosexual, bisexual, and asexual, and these became identity terms. *Lesbian* became the term for a female homosexual.

In these past 150 years, homosexual people—gay men and lesbian women—have been subjected to a great deal of stigma, prejudice, and discrimination. As a result, when a woman considered accepting an identity as a lesbian, she had to grapple with accepting a stigmatized identity. This made the identity development process much more arduous, often painful and filled with doubt, than it is today (at least for some people). Alternatives were to deny or hide one's identity (remain "in the closet") or to accept an identity as an outcast and create a subculture of one's own (this was particularly prevalent in the first half of the 20th century but still continues today in some areas). Today, in many parts of North America, Europe, and some other countries, the stigma against gay and lesbian people has markedly diminished. As a result, the process of developing a lesbian identity, too, has changed.

Essentialism and Postmodern Social Construction

In the past 50 years, theorists have become increasingly aware of two divergent ways of thinking (epistemologies): (1) the lens of essentialism and (2) the lens of postmodern social construction. The essentialist view is that people are born with a sexual orientation, that it is an essential and enduring aspect of who they are, and that it is not a choice and is not changeable. This has been the prevailing view held by scientists for the past 50 years. By contrast, the postmodern social construction view sees sexual orientation as constructed by the society and the times. Presented with the options and the associations of the social context, each woman makes choices, which may be stable or may change, in part depending on her current social context. Lesbian identity development, from this perspective, is profoundly shaped by what it means in today's society to be a lesbian; it is not inborn, it is learned, and it can change.

Theories of Lesbian Identity Development

Lesbianism as Pathology

In the first two thirds of the 20th century, ideas about lesbian identity were framed within the premise that there was something wrong or sick about being a lesbian; therefore, the literature tried to suggest what was wrong and how (or whether) it could be fixed. The late 1970s brought in a new era—discussions of lesbian identity presumed that it is one of several normal variations of sexual orientation. This was consistent with larger changes in society; the American Psychiatric Association had labeled homosexuality (including lesbian sexuality) as a mental disorder in its diagnostic manual of 1952, but it was just about to eliminate that view in its new edition of the manual, published in 1981.

In this new era, theories of lesbian identity focused on the resolution of internal conflicts about adopting an identity that was seen in such a negative light by much of society. These theories saw the completion of the lesbian identity development process as a psychologically healthy outcome.

Early theories and models, written mainly in the 1970s and 1980s, were about developing a nonheterosexual identity; they grouped lesbian identity development together with gay men's identity development and the bisexual identity development of both men and women. These theories described LGBQ (lesbian, gay, bisexual, queer) identity development against a backdrop of cultural homophobia and heterocentrism, and frequent legal and social discrimination that made lesbian lives difficult and worrisome.

Stage Theories

In 1979, Vivienne Cass, an Australian psychologist, created one of the first theories of homosexual identity development, and it is the theory that has been most thoroughly researched. It emphasizes both the personal and the interpersonal (social) aspect of a person's identity. As a woman moves toward a fully realized lesbian identity, there is an agreement between who she thinks she is, who she claims to be, and how others view her. Cass points out that this is a multidimensional process and may vary from person to person, situation to situation, and period to period (in history); however, most of the people she spoke with were White and middle class. In recent years, there has been continued research on her theory, and she has taken a social-constructionist position, whereby current ideas about sexual orientation and identity are specific to Western cultures at this particular period of history.

Cass created a stage theory, describing a series of steps toward a lesbian identity:

Prestage: Cass believes that, because such a large majority of women identify as heterosexual, a woman who begins to develop a lesbian identity will also start out by thinking that she is heterosexual.

Stage 1, identity confusion: In this stage, the woman realizes that she has thoughts or feelings or actions that could be labeled lesbian. This recognition opens up the question "Who am I?" Key questions at this time are about how the woman views her own thoughts and feelings—whether these feelings are correct and acceptable, correct but undesirable, or incorrect and undesirable. Depending on how the woman answers these questions, she may consider the possibility of a lesbian identity or reject that possibility entirely. A woman can foreclose her identity and stop the developmental process at any point in any of the stages.

Stage 2, identity comparison: During this stage, the woman compares herself with heterosexual women and becomes more aware of how she is different from them, but her sense of identity is very tentative. Women at this stage are not yet ready to claim a minority sexual orientation identity.

Stage 3, identity tolerance: The woman begins to think that she probably is a lesbian. She makes contact with lesbian/gay people, either in person or through a wide array of Internet sites. Positive contacts cause her to feel better about who lesbians "are" and to increase contact with the LGB community. If her experiences are negative, however, she may withdraw. In this stage, a woman is willing to tell some other gay people that she, too, is queer.

Stage 4, identity acceptance: In this stage, the woman internalizes her lesbian identity and increases contact with the lesbian community. She moves beyond tolerating her lesbian identity to accepting it and begins to tell a few friends and family members about this aspect of herself. She is more frequently identified by others as lesbian, and this furthers her understanding of herself as queer. This stage is slowed if she recognizes truely antagonistic friends and family or feels strongly that gay people are a negatively valued group.

Stage 5, identity pride: Now the woman is proud of being a lesbian. She now sees other lesbians as important and credible and is angry about society's stigmatizing of lesbian women. She is interested in telling friends and family about her sexual orientation identity. Referred to as "coming out," this kind of self-disclosure is a developmental effort unique to the lives of gay men and lesbian women. When others respond well, coming out can be an affirming experience of deep connection, as one confides this important and private information to people one cares about. If others respond with distress or rejection, there may be confrontations, conflicts, sorrow, guilt, or grief. Research has suggested that long-standing personality styles may affect the timing and prevalence of coming out; having an avoidant attachment style may be associated with a reluctance to do so.

Stage 6, identity synthesis: In this final stage, sexual orientation becomes less central and is integrated as one part of a many-sided identity. Anger and pride become less intense, and previous feelings of dissimilarity fade as the lesbian woman recognizes that she is similar in many ways to heterosexual women and also dissimilar from some lesbians. She lives her life in such a way that her lesbian identity is not hidden and disclosure is no longer an issue. Views of self, claims about the self, and others' view of self then become synthesized into an integrated identity that unites both private and public aspects, giving rise to feelings of peace and stability.

Several other stage theories have been offered, attempting to refine the description of the lesbian identity development process. Their themes are similar to the themes of Cass's stages, but some have fewer stages or label them somewhat differently.

Life Span Theories

There has been criticism of the basic idea that identity development could best be described as a series of stages. One problem with the stage model is that it seems to offer a sequence where one stage follows the other; actual experience may not be so linear for many people. However, the stages are intended to be like a road map—and when a person is driving down the road, they may decide to stop for a while, or turn and change direction, or even go back to where they were before. The same idea describes the "map" of stage theories, which are different from the actual "journey" of real women.

In addition, the stage model implies that development is completed at a certain point; researchers have pointed out that the coming out process is lifelong and that some people (perhaps many) may have multiple sexual identities in the course of their lifetime, so an accurate model must leave room for a much longer time frame and an array of possible options at any time.

Anthony R. D'Augelli has offered a life span model that attempts to address these and other limitations of the stage models. He identifies six "identity processes." Each of these can operate independently of the others—so there is no sequence—and can be operating (or not) at any time in the life span. The processes are as follows: (1) exiting heterosexuality, (2) developing a personal lesbian identity, (3) developing a social lesbian identity, (4) becoming a lesbian offspring of parents, (5) developing a lesbian intimacy status, and (6) entering a lesbian community.

Individuals may differ in the extent to which they have developed through each of these processes. For example, a woman may have a strong sense of herself as a lesbian but may have little contact with a lesbian community; another may have an intimate partner and have developed a social identity but may not have come out to her parents. Each woman may also change where she is in relation to each process; for example, if a woman moves to a new job and a new city, she may have to begin again in order to create a social identity as a lesbian. These variations may be influenced by other dimensions of that woman's identity and also by the particular psychosocial context she is in at different times during her life.

Twenty-First-Century Changes in Understanding Lesbian Identity Development

Awareness of Gender Differences and Intersectionality

More recently, several authors have suggested that while the general themes of identity development (awareness, exploration, increasing acceptance and commitment, disclosing to others, internalization/synthesis) are the same for men and women, there are important differences. Women tend to experience awareness and exploration of their attraction to women at later ages, and their experience is often less sexually driven than that of men and more ambiguous and fluid. Because they are women, their experience is also affected by sexism, the dynamics of institutionalized power inequities, and the imposition of expectations that they live out traditional gender roles, which often include subservience to men and involvement in gendered work and family roles. These differences cause the process of identity development to be lesbian specific in many ways.

Just as sex differences make for differences in identity development, researchers have also become increasingly aware of the intersection of all the dimensions of identity—and how each person's embodiment of intersecting social locations creates a different identity development process for that person. Key dimensions of identity that must be considered are how sexual orientation and gender intersect with race, ethnicity, social class, religion, education, age, and ability/disability. So, for example, a 25-year-old, college graduate, middle-class, Catholic, able-bodied African American woman will have an experience of lesbian identity development that differs in important ways from the experience of a 45-year-old, high school graduate, working-class, nonreligious White woman who has a hearing impairment. Personality differences, too, can affect the identity development process.

Fluidity and Queer Theory

Emerging in the 1990s, queer theory uses deconstruction, an aspect of the social construction approach, to take apart (deconstruct), make visible, and then question (or problematize) ideas about sexual orientation and gender at different times in recent history. For example, it disputes the popular view that one's (anatomical) sex should be linked to one's gender and that they both should be linked to sexual orientation. The essentialist view is that everyone has a sex at birth, that it is an essential part of who each person is (their gender identity), and that it does not change. Gender is seen as a binary—male or female—two mutually exclusive categories. In contrast, queer theories suggest that everyone "performs" their gender, that it is a performance that is learned rather than something people inherently are. Queer theory disputes the idea of a gender binary and sees the binary as a class system that privileges the masculine "class." Queer theorists note that the binary overlooks many people (intersex, transgender, and genderqueer people—who are born with ambiguous genitalia and so cannot be classified into a binary system, who feel that the sex they were assigned at birth does not fit them so they want to change, or who prefer to combine both masculine and feminine traits, interests, or appearance, respectively). They also dispute ideas about what society views as "normal" and what it views as "variant," starting with the idea that heterosexuality is normal and other orientations are not. From the perspective of queer theory, both gender and sexual orientation can be not only changeable but also fluid; queer theory is hesitant to apply gender or sexual labels. This point of view asks everyone to question their understanding of their own gender and sexual identity, and it may lead people away from establishing or claiming an identity, because they have come to see it as a dimension of social location rather than as an aspect of an essential and stable self.

A More Accepting Society

The reduction of stigma has also profoundly changed the process of lesbian identity development. The legalization of same-sex marriage and the widespread recognition of lesbian two-mom families raising children have created a vision of the relational life of lesbians that is markedly different from that of the 20th-century stereotypes; this vision has a powerful impact on a woman who is considering a lesbian identity.

The Information Superhighway

In earlier times, it was common for a lesbian to begin her process of identity formation without ever knowing another lesbian woman. This left her at the mercy of stereotypes and misinformation, and feeling very much alone. Today, the availability of the Internet allows a woman to gather information and even to engage in chatroom or forum conversations, to meet and get to know other lesbians while at the same time maintaining anonymity (if she feels safer doing so). In addition, the visibility of lesbians in the media, popular culture, and public life has brought forward real people, so that the image of the lesbian is no longer dehumanized (as it once was).

Valory Mitchell

See also Feminist Identity Development Model; Lesbian, Gay, and Bisexual Children; Lesbians and Gender Roles; Sexual Orientation Identity; Sexual Orientation Identity Development

Further Readings

Brown, L. (1995). Lesbian identities: Concepts and issues. In A. D'Augelli & C. Patterson (Eds.), *Lesbian, gay and bisexual identities over the lifespan: Psychological perspectives* (pp. 3–23). New York, NY: Oxford University Press.

D'Augelli, A. (1994). Identity development and sexual orientation: Toward a model of lesbian, gay and bisexual development. In E. Trickett, R. Watts, & D. Birman (Eds.), *Human diversity: Perspectives on people in context* (pp. 312–333). San Francisco, CA: Jossey-Bass.

Greene, B. (1994). Mental health concerns of lesbians of color. In L. Comas-Diaz & B. Greene (Eds.), *Women of color and mental health* (pp. 389–427). New York, NY: Guilford Press.

Kitzinger, C. (1987).*The social construction of lesbianism.* London, England: Sage.

McCarn, S., & Fassinger, R. (1996). Revisioning sexual minority identity formation: A new model of lesbian identity and its implications for counseling and research. *The Counseling Psychologist, 24,* 508–534.

Mitchell, V. (2012). Coming out to family: Adrift in a sea of potential meanings. In J. Bigner & J. Wetcher (Eds.), *Handbook of LGBT-affirmative couple and family therapy* (pp. 131–148). London, England: Routledge.

Mohr, J., & Fassinger, R. (2003). Self-acceptance and self-disclosure of sexual orientation in lesbian, gay and bisexual adults: An attachment perspective. *Journal of Counseling Psychology, 50*(4), 582–495.

Reynolds, A., & Hanjorgiris, W. (2007). Coming out: Lesbian, gay and bisexual identity development. In R. Perez, K. Debord, & K. Bieschke (Eds.), *Handbook of counseling and psychotherapy with lesbian, gay and bisexual clients* (pp. 35–56). Washington, DC: American Psychological Association.

Rust, P. (2003). Finding a sexual identity and community: Therapeutic implications and cultural assumptions in scientific models of coming out. In L. Garnets & D. Kimmel (Eds.), *Psychological perspectives on lesbian, gay and bisexual experiences* (pp. 227–269). New York, NY: Columbia University Press.

Sophie, J. (1986). A critical examination of stage theories of lesbian identity development. *Journal of Homosexuality, 12*(2), 39–51.

Lesbians

The term *lesbian* was developed in the 20th century to differentiate women who experience same-sex attraction from gay men. Individuals who identify as lesbians are women whose primary affectional, emotional, physical, and other attractions are to individuals of the same gender. The term highlights the diversity of experiences among sexual minority individuals that cuts across gender lines. Sexual orientation is a construct that is deeply tied to gender, as the two, despite constituting independent identities, are often conflated in research, the literature, and daily life. This entry describes gender identity among lesbian communities, the consequences of conflating gender and sexual orientation, and gender identity politics that are important to lesbian communities, concluding with a discussion of the intersections of sexual identity in lesbians with other identities, particularly racial and ethnic identities.

Gender Identity in Lesbian Communities

Gender identity refers to a deeply felt, psychological sense of oneself as a gendered being, usually in identification with being male, female, or another gender. This construct is distinct from one's attraction to the same or another gender, and one's gender identity may or may not be associated with one's sex assigned at birth. Because lesbians typically identify as women, and this gender has traditionally been associated with femininity, the construct of femininity is relevant to the study of lesbians. Masculinity is also relevant, especially as prevailing stereotypes conflate gender and sexual orientation and often link masculinity to lesbian identity.

Defining femininity is often difficult as it is constructed in a binary contrast with masculinity. As a result, the construct of femininity has been developed within the context of the subordination of women to men. In lesbian communities, sexuality and gender are viewed differently by various cultures and social groups, so gender identity among lesbians is culturally bound. As defined by mainstream Western society, however, the most common lesbian gender expression has been that of *butch/femme.* In accordance with typical dominant culture definitions of gender as binary, butch/femme expressions exist as binary as well.

Since the early 20th century, and until recently, lesbian sexuality has been largely defined within butch/femme frameworks, which served to regulate clothing, gender roles, and gender behavior. To be femme meant that one was emotionally supportive, in accordance with traditionally feminine roles, and to be butch meant carrying oneself with traditionally masculine behavior and appearance. While some see butch-femme relationships as constructing a lesbian sexuality that is grounded in love, courage, and autonomy, a debate exists within feminist and lesbian communities as to whether the butch and femme identities reinforce heterosexual hegemony or challenge it by reworking it in a lesbian-normed context. Regardless, it is critical to note that a far more fluid understanding of gender identity exists within lesbian cultures today.

Lesbian stereotypes persist, however, and most are tied to gender expression, such as images of "lipstick lesbians" (feminine lesbians who desire other feminine women), "bull dykes" (masculine or butch lesbians, who are seen as aggressive, stoic, and tough), and "lesbian soccer moms" (White, upper-middle-class lesbians who epitomize motherhood and domesticity). These oversimplified, stereotypical images promulgated by the media and dominant Western culture risk construing lesbianism from heterosexual male perspectives, while simultaneously catering to heterosexual fears and fantasies. Moreover, such stereotypes, as reinforced by dominant heteronormative cultures, position lesbians within a gender binary and may discredit the free flow of gender expression among lesbians. More recently, with the increasing social acceptance of lesbian lifestyles in the larger society, a broader, more fluid understanding of gender is expressed within lesbian communities.

Few models of gender identity take into account the experiences of lesbian women. Of note, Susan R. McCarn and Ruth E. Fassinger proposed a model of sexual identity development (SID) that incorporated insights from racial/ethnic identity and gender identity models. Unique to SID is the idea that political activism and consciousness are important but not essential to identity development. SID also proposes a dual process that takes into account the reality of factors such as racial and/or ethnic group membership, work environment, and geographic location, embracing multiple realities by proposing separate sexual identity and group membership identity processes. The SID model applies to both men and women, although there are likely differences in the coming out process and the lifelong development of sexual identity in lesbians as compared with gay men, due in part to differences in gender socialization. For instance, it is generally more accepted for women to be emotionally and physically close with other women, so lesbians might engage in these behaviors at a younger age than gay men. Also, even though butch/femme roles may be enacted by a lesbian couple, this role-play may not necessarily signify the dominance of one partner over another, as might be presumed among heterosexual couples. Lesbian couples may have to be aware of others, such as mental health professionals and researchers, who may impose male/female gender role expectations on their relationship. While some researchers have begun to ask how the development of self-concept and gender socialization might be unique for lesbians, particularly how gender socialization might affect self-concept in lesbians, much is left unknown and remains a major area for future research.

Conflation of Gender and Sexual Orientation

Throughout Western society, gender is thought to exist in a man/woman binary, in which each is defined in opposition to, or as a complement of, the other. Moreover, while gender is currently understood as socially constructed, it has historically been thought to have biological bases and to be conflated with sex. The dominant discourse on gender and sex in Western societies has primarily focused on Whites, males, men, and heterosexuals. A major consequence of this is that gender and sexual orientation are often conflated, because men, simply due to their gender identity and expression, are assumed to be attracted to women, and vice versa.

In terms of gender expression and presentation (e.g., style of dress, outward appearance, and body language), under such a narrowly conceptualized gender binary, individuals' ascription to traditionally feminine or masculine presentations is mistakenly used as a proxy for sexual orientation. Individuals who do not conform to the gender binary within mainstream society, including sexual minority individuals, are often considered to be less psychologically adjusted. It also may be presumed by those in the larger society that to conform to gender role stereotypes indicates a heterosexual identity and the failure to conform to gender role stereotypes indicates a gay or lesbian identity. Therefore, a woman who wishes to "pass" as heterosexual may employ gender role stereotypes to do so—by dressing as a traditionally feminine women, she may avoid the assumption of others that she is lesbian.

Antilesbian prejudices may come from individuals' discomfort with lesbians' perceived lack of ascription to the female gender role (or perceived gender role deviance). The conflation of gender and sexual orientation can be damaging both to individuals' conception of self and to sexual minority communities as a whole. Among lesbians, for example, such expectations can work to reinforce rigid expectations and stereotypes, which may become internalized and further reinforced.

Lesbian Gender Identity and Politics

Lesbian communities have had a strong presence in the women's movement and the fight for gender equality. Bearing the sexual minority marginalized status, lesbians have often fought for equality within feminist movements as well. Since the 1960s, *lesbian feminism* has been central to the social and political struggle to change women's feelings about same-sex sexuality such that shame is replaced with pride. Lesbian feminism is an identity, a theory, and a political movement that emerged out of the sexual revolution, gay liberation, and women's liberation in the 1960s. Lesbian feminism contests the assumption of heterosexuality and maleness as "normal" and has been instrumental in furthering understandings of the nature of power and gender. Early lesbian feminists included members of the Daughters of Bilitis, which was formed in 1955 and was the first national organization for lesbian women. The goals of Daughters of Bilitis included greater social acceptance, educating lesbians about legal rights, and addressing the social isolation many lesbians felt at the time. During the second-wave feminism of the 1960s, the concerns of the lesbian community became more prominent in the fight for gender equality, but this did not occur without pushback, and lesbians were deemed the "lavender menace" by mainstream feminists in the late 1960s. As a stigmatized group, lesbians were feared by other feminists as detracting from the feminist movement's overarching goals. Lesbian feminism emerged from this political climate as a means to empower female sexual minorities during the 1960s and 1970s.

According to lesbian feminist thought, heterosexuality works to perpetuate women's secondary status while also offering women certain privileges, such as economic benefits and social status in their partnerships with men. Lesbian feminists also emphasized their connection to larger feminist goals and emphasized the need to build community among all women. Although some lesbian feminists were criticized as endorsing conformity by viewing lesbians as the best representation of women's liberation, the feminist movement did much in bringing greater acceptance for those who identify as lesbian. Since its beginnings, lesbian feminism has adapted to developing ideas about sexual identity and feminist strategies, particularly by de-emphasizing separatism and fostering more solidarity with men and heterosexual women. Lesbian feminists have done much to point out the social constructions of gender roles and sexuality. Today, queer activists and third-wave feminists share with lesbian feminists a common commitment to resisting traditional gender and sexual identities.

Lesbians of Color

In most discussions of gender and sexual orientation, individuals of color are overlooked, missing, or overgeneralized to the experiences of White individuals. This often happens when intersectionality (or the interplay of one's various social identities—e.g., race, gender, and sexual orientation) is not considered. Intersectionality refers to the notion that people do not experience life through a single identity; when considering lesbians of color, at least three oppressed identities are present, based on race/ethnicity, gender, and sexual orientation. Intersectional approaches suggest that one's identities rely on one another for meaning, and unique contextual meanings are created by the convergence of gender, race/ethnicity, and sexual identity for lesbians of color. At various times and in different situations, any one of these identities might be more or less salient to an individual, but there is also a cumulative and overlapping effect on people's lives.

In terms of gender identity construction, lesbians of color are tasked with managing their gender and sexual orientation identities in light of their own racial/ethnic community standards, along with those of the larger LGBT community as well as the dominant Western society in which they live. For example, a Latina lesbian may experience homophobia or heterosexism within her Latino/a community, while she experiences sexism and racism from the larger society. A sense of fragmentation of identity and negative self-evaluation may result, because forming an integrated sense of self becomes a complex task of negotiating multiple forms of oppression at once. For some women of color, it is important to maintain ties to their racial/ethnic community's expectations and definitions of gender and sexual orientation in order to preserve connection with their racial/ethnic groups. In this way, lesbians of color may experience and integrate their sexual orientation identity differently than how traditional sexual identity models delineate. Feelings of hostility, betrayal, devaluation, alienation, and disconnection may also result from intragroup differences between lesbians of color and White lesbians.

For lesbians of color, the idea of having to "choose" one community over another can be difficult. Often, one's racial/ethnic reference groups, LGBT community, and feminist community exist separate from, and even in contrast to, one another. In this way, negotiating allegiances to different communities (women/feminists, sexual minorities, people of color) may create unique psychological stressors. Lesbian individuals of color often must simultaneously develop strategies to construct and maintain a sense of cultural meaning among their racial/ethnic groups, self-defined scripts relative to gender and sexual identity, and self-conceptualizations of what it means to be a non-White and nonheterosexual individual. It is important that future research addresses how racism, dual and multiple marginalized identities, and reference group salience affect lesbians of color. There has been some research on sexual minority status among different racial/ethnic groups, such as African Americans, Latina/o and Hispanic Americans, Asian Americans, and Native Americans.

For African American communities, kinship and community values are often described as important. Such an emphasis on community means that African American lesbians might not be comfortable disclosing their sexual identity for fear of alienation and loss of group support. As same-sex attraction is considered a sin in some religious doctrines, strong adherence to religious beliefs and traditions might contribute to the prejudice that African American lesbians face from their peers. When there is a supportive family environment, many African American lesbians come out exclusively to family members, due to the fear of disapproval from the broader racial/ethnic community. African American lesbians also may find themselves at the crossroads of gender-based expectations from their ethnic community, from their lesbian community, and from the larger society, which can feel confusing, conflicting, and compromising of how they self-identify as a gendered being. In addition, not fitting within the preconstructed, gender-based mold of any of these communities could leave them susceptible to negative intrapsychic and interpersonal consequences.

Latina/o communities, like African American communities, are family and community oriented and closely knit. *Machismo*, or masculinity and male dominance, can be a prominent force in many Latina/o families, and lesbians are often seen as existing in defiance of it. In addition, Latina lesbians may be at odds with the heteronormative expectations of how a Latina woman should be (i.e., be happy with her *husband*, not seek to be more than a housewife, and not forsake tradition), much of which is heavily entwined with religious values. The strong tradition of Catholicism, with its disapproval of homosexuality, may increase the prejudice Latina lesbians face within their ethnic communities. Latina lesbians are more likely than African Americans but less likely than White Euro-Americans to disclose their lesbian identities, and Latinas/os are more likely to disclose this sexual identity to their immediate family than to others.

Many Native American cultures historically have viewed homosexuality as "two spirited" and are more accepting than the dominant Western society of sexual minority identities. In contemporary Native American tribes, acceptance of gender and sexual diversity is not universal, but as compared with other racial/ethnic groups, Native American sexual minorities are more likely to be openly involved in the LGBT community. Although in mainstream U.S. culture, those who do not fit the gender binary are considered to be nonconforming or androgynous, many Native Americans do not believe that such an identification exists, as this contradicts a basic indigenous belief that all persons are an embodiment of part femaleness and part maleness. That is, compartmentalizing one's gender identity into either the U.S. binary or nonconformity conflicts with Native American beliefs of the interconnectedness of gender.

Asian American communities, like Latina/o and African American communities, tend to be community based, and group needs take precedence over individual needs. For an Asian American lesbian, being a sexual minority is likely to be seen as putting her individual needs ahead of the group's values. Coming out may be seen as a statement on her family's status and may distance her from her cultural community. As a result, lesbians of Asian descent are less likely than other lesbians to partake in LGBT communities, and they are less likely to come out to either family members or others. In addition, Asian American lesbians, as with other lesbians of color, face a multitude of cultural expectations and gender-based stereotypes that align with the intersection of being both a person of color and a woman. Asian American lesbians find themselves having to negotiate the gender-based expectations of their Asian American communities (i.e., being passive and subservient to men) and the stereotypes ascribed to them by the larger society based on their racial/ethnic identity (i.e., being the model minority). Compromising on either set of expectations has accompanying repercussions, with psychological and social consequences.

Across racial/ethnic groups, lesbians of color face discrimination not only from their families and racial/ethnic communities but from the dominant LGBT community as well. Many people of color have consequently created their own LGBT communities to foster safe environments where both sexual diversity and racial/ethnic diversity are celebrated.

Naomi Rayfield, Mariel Buque, and Marie L. Miville

See also Sexual Orientation: Overview; Sexual Orientation Identity

Further Readings

Broido, E. M. (2006). Constructing identity: The nature and meaning of lesbian, gay, and bisexual identities. In K. J. Bieschke, R. M. Perez, & K. A. DeBord (Eds.), *Handbook of counseling and psychotherapy with lesbian, gay, bisexual, and transgender clients* (2nd ed., pp. 13–33). Washington, DC: American Psychological Association.

Ferguson, A. D., Carr, G., & Snitman, A. (2014). Intersections of race-ethnicity, gender, and sexual minority communities. In M. L. Miville & A. D. Ferguson (Eds.), *Handbook of race-ethnicity and gender in psychology* (pp. 45–63). New York, NY: Springer.

Greene, B. (1997). *Ethnic and cultural diversity among lesbians and gay men* (Vol. 3). Thousand Oaks, CA: Sage.

Greene, B., & Herek, G. M. (1994). *Lesbian and gay psychology: Theory, research, and clinical applications* (Vol. 1). Thousand Oaks, CA: Sage.

McCarn, S. R., & Fassinger, R. E. (1996). Revisioning sexual minority identity formation: A new model of lesbian identity and its implications for counseling and research. *The Counseling Psychologist, 24,* 508–534.

Reynolds, A. L., & Hanjorgiris, W. F. (2006). Coming out: Lesbian, gay, and bisexual identity development. In K. J. Bieschke, R. M. Perez, & K. A. DeBord (Eds.), *Handbook of counseling and psychotherapy with lesbian, gay, bisexual, and transgender clients* (2nd ed., pp. 35–55). Washington, DC: American Psychological Association.

Lesbians and Dating

Dating is typically defined as a social engagement or an informal interaction for assessing another's romantic potential. Given the recent advances in same-sex marriage equality, it is important to understand how two women meet, date, and develop and maintain an intimate relationship. The focus of this chapter is on what is known about this topic, exploring both unique aspects of lesbian dating and those that are similar to heterosexual dating.

History

Lesbian dating must be understood in the context of societal heterosexism, including laws and cultural prohibitions against homosexuality, which kept lesbian dating largely underground throughout history. During the early 20th century, magazines welcomed stories about "intense, romantic friendships" between two women—until the 1920s, when homosexuality became associated with mental and medical illness. Political and social changes in the late 1960s to 1970s, including the removal of homosexuality from the *Diagnostic Statistical Manual of Mental Disorders* and the rise of the gay rights movement, led more lesbians to openly come out and initiate romantic relationships in the public eye. In the 1980s and 1990s, friendship networks and gay bars became common turf for lesbian dating and still represent enticing dating atmospheres today, given their visible representation of lesbian, gay, bisexual, transgender, and queer (LGBTQ) life, and an opportune space to meet other women seeking women in person.

The rise in the accessibility of the Internet and availability of mobile dating apps has made the ability to connect with and date other women even easier. Dating websites and apps such as OkCupid and Tinder provide women with opportunities to screen prospective dates easily and quickly. By specifying geographical location, individuals are able to filter their dating search to a specific radius. Because these sites are relatively safe and private, lesbians may experience a sense of safety while reducing exposure to social scrutiny. Dating sites can help lesbians "know" whether women are also seeking other women by their self-generated profile. Meeting online provides a preemptive medium to assess and decide, before committing to meet in person, whether one's demographic information, photographs, career path, recreational interests, and more are a compatible fit.

Dating Scripts

A script is a schema of stereotypical actions understood through cultural norms that organizes people's feelings and behaviors in particular situations. Heterosexual dating is affected and shaped by gender role expectations and the historical roots of sexism. Historically, the subjugation of women and sexual minorities was significantly influenced by hegemonic masculinity, which continues to infiltrate the expectations of gender role scripts and heteronormative culture. Lesbian scripts are inherently different because they do not map onto traditional roles associated with gender and power.

Lesbian scripts involve three patterns: (1) romance, (2) friendship, and (3) sex. The romance and friendship scripts are the most commonly used by lesbians, with the focus on emotional and physical intimacy. Many lesbians have reported that the friendship script provides a secure basis for long-term commitment. When two women build an intimate friendship, a deep emotional commitment is established that may or may not include sex. The sexually explicit script involves sharing sexually pleasurable experiences together without the requirement of commitment. Many lesbians develop a blended combination of scripts that has been described as playful, intimate, and exciting. Gay men's dating scripts focus on physical attractiveness and sex over emotional commitment, which suggests that it is not uncommon for gay men to have sex on a first date. In contrast, lesbians tend to be more concerned about personality and emotional intimacy over physical appearance.

Gender Roles

Traditional gender roles require men to initiate a relationship (active role) and women to wait for the offered initiation (reactive role). Since women have been historically socialized to wait for someone to approach them, lesbians have notoriously been described as "procrasti-daters." While heterosexual men have been conditioned to directly initiate verbally and choose their woman of interest, lesbians' pursuit involves a nonverbal process that is uniquely different. Lesbians are more likely to partake in a nonverbal proceptive behavioral approach (i.e., a darting glance, smiling, a light touch) than a directive approach. Other lesbians who do not adhere to gender stereotyped roles use a direct approach in addition to the initial, skilled nonverbal cues. The chosen date environment and activity are similar across lesbians, gay men, and heterosexual individuals. However, expectations during the date may differ as a function of gender roles. While heterosexual dating scripts tend to adhere to traditional gender roles, many lesbians share the responsibility in arranging, maintaining, and paying for dates. Friendship and the lack of traditional gender roles in lesbian dating have been found to result in egalitarian relationship development.

Gender identities shape interpersonal interactions that may or may not mirror heterosexual dating. While some lesbians are coupled in butch-femme relationships, others prefer butch-butch or femme-femme relationships, and some women are androgynous and do not identify as either butch or femme. Although butch-femme interactions may mirror heterosexual scripts, lesbians tend to value a more equal or fluid power dynamic in dating than do their heterosexual counterparts. Many lesbians engage in an egalitarian approach when developing and maintaining a relationship, and they may shift and mix aspects of both traditional and nontraditional gender roles. The division of responsibilities is often negotiated by the personal preference of each partner, regardless of butch, femme, or androgynous identities. Studies comparing heterosexual and same-sex couples have found very few differences in relationship quality.

It is important to recognize that lesbian dating, including methods of meeting potential partners, dating scripts, and gender roles, has varied and will continue to vary as a function of sociocultural context. Recent advances in marriage equality as well as the shifting public acceptance of LGB people have made lesbian dating more visible and will inevitably continue to shape the experience of lesbians who seek to initiate intimate relationships. In addition, it is important to note that the context and form of lesbian dating can vary according to other cultural identity factors such as race, ethnicity, age, disability status, and socioeconomic status. Future research should expand the knowledge base by examining lesbian dating within these diverse groups to understand the full range of the lesbian experience.

Kimberly F. Balsam and Jessica Simonetti

See also Lesbians; Lesbians and Gender Roles; Lesbians and Romantic Relationships; Marriage; Marriage Equality

Further Readings

Faderman, L. (1991). *Odd girls and twilight lovers.* New York, NY: Columbia University Press.

Klinkenberg, D., & Rose, S. (1994). Dating scripts of gay men and lesbians. *Journal of Homosexuality, 26*(4), 23–35. doi:10.1300/j082v26n04_02

Moore, M. (2006). Lipstick or timberlands? Meanings of gender presentation in black lesbian communities. *Signs: Journal of Women in Culture and Society, 32*(1), 113–139. doi:10.1086/505269

Tea, M. (2000). *Valencia.* New York, NY: Seal Press.

Lesbians and Gender Roles

Lesbian is a term that refers to a woman identified person who is sexually, romantically, and/or emotionally attracted to another woman identified person. The term is applicable for individuals with *any* sex identity—meaning, whether a person is biologically male, female, other, and beyond. For example, a biologically male person who identifies as a woman (e.g., a transgender woman) may identify as a lesbian if she is primarily attracted to other lesbian, bisexual, or queer women.

Gender role describes a set of socially and culturally constructed beliefs, behaviors, expectations, and attributions (e.g., the way a person thinks, speaks, dresses, and interacts with others in a public or private domain) that are generally based on an individual's actual or perceived gender. Gender roles are learned and developed during the formative years, which can be influenced by several factors not limited to ethnicity, race, social class, education, age, and religion. Although sex is a biological characteristic and gender is a social construct, gender roles are commonly perceived as binary, biological sex roles. In other words, women in the United States are expected to take on the role of child rearing, interact in a submissive or accommodating manner toward men, and demonstrate ease in emotion expression and physical affection. Gender roles for women also include ways of dressing and maintaining their physical appearance (e.g., wearing skirts/dresses, wearing form-fitting clothing, utilizing cosmetic makeup, and/or maintaining long hair). On the contrary, men are expected to exemplify qualities of leadership, independence, and authority and to serve as the breadwinner for the family. Physical embodiment of masculinity is typically construed as being physically strong and brawny, and maintaining a short hair length. This entry focuses on the various gender roles in the lesbian community.

Replications of Heterosexual Gender Roles

Dichotomous gender roles among heterosexuals are sometimes observed in the lesbian community, which is frequently characterized as the butch/femme dynamic. *Butch* is a term that describes a masculine identified lesbian who embodies physical, mental, and emotional traits typically ascribed to heterosexual men (e.g., competitive, strong, emotionally stoic). *Femme* is a word that describes a lesbian who epitomizes physical traits and personality characteristics commonly associated with heterosexual women (e.g., soft, supportive, submissive). Some butch-femme lesbian relationships mimic the rigid gender roles of heterosexual relationships. In other words, butch identified lesbians may behave in a dominant manner whereby they hold specific assumptions, including the initiation of sexual acts in the bedroom and/or assumption of financial responsibility on a date. Femme identified lesbians may hold contrasting beliefs, including the expectation to be asked out on a date and/or not being the first to initiate sex in a romantic relationship. Replication of heterosexual gender roles in this manner arguably perpetuates the power dynamic germane in most heterosexual relationships; however, the aforementioned butch/femme binary gender roles do not epitomize all lesbian relationships.

Continuum of Gender Roles Among Lesbians

Widespread iterations of various gender roles are prevalent in the lesbian community and reach beyond the butch/femme binary. Butch identified lesbians are not always limited to gender roles typically associated with men in heterosexual relationships (e.g., emotional reticence, sexual aggression/initiation, leadership role in household decisions). Similarly, gender roles of femme identified lesbians are not circumscribed to exhibiting a delicate, sensitive, or gentle way of being.

While the butch-femme dyad is arguably an organizing principle for the larger society, many lesbian relationships do not replicate the heterosexual dynamic commonly observed in U.S. culture. Lesbian relationships comprise wide-ranging gender presentations, gendered behaviors, and gender roles that span across the continuum and typically do not fall into discrete categories of masculine (e.g., boi, dyke, or butch) and feminine (e.g., femme AG or lipstick lesbian). Gender roles in lesbian relationships are more complex and ambiguous as they are not guided by the traditional gender roles of men and women in heterosexual relationships. Furthermore, gender roles among lesbians are not neatly defined by one's gender presentation (e.g., butch, femme, androgynous). As such, lesbian couples have opportunities to negotiate different ways of being and are not restricted to a specific set of behaviors or beliefs typically ascribed to one's gender. Lesbian relationships challenge societal gender-based assumptions as lesbians can exhibit a blend of gender roles (e.g., caretaker and income provider) irrespective of their gender presentation. For example, when a lesbian woman exhibits a feminine appearance, it does not necessarily indicate that she adopts the stereotypical gender roles of heterosexual women, such as being the caretaker in the family. Butch identified lesbians may take gender roles akin to heterosexual women, including acting as the more sexually passive partner, wearing makeup, or valuing emotional expression.

Challenging Heteronormativity and Heterosexism

Gender roles among lesbians challenge the deeply entrenched American beliefs of heteronormativity (i.e., the tendency for individuals to be categorized as discrete genders of either man or woman) and heterosexism (i.e., the belief that opposite-sex romantic relationships are the norm). Given that lesbians are women identified, the concept of gender hierarchies inherent in heterosexual relationships (i.e., men hold more power and authority over women) is arguably deconstructed, although power dynamics may play out in different ways (e.g., butch identified women may take on a more assertive role). Unlike the traditional gender roles in the heterosexual American culture, gender roles in lesbian relationships are dynamic, evolve over time, and require increased communication and negotiation. Initiating sex, expressing feelings, providing the primary income, grocery shopping, and engaging in manual labor (e.g., mowing the lawn, maintaining the car) are responsibilities and roles that vary within a lesbian relationship. Perhaps lesbian relationships can be construed as more egalitarian compared with their heterosexual counterparts.

Preservation of Culture Through Gender Roles

One of the primary ways in which individuals retain and/or express their cultural values, identity, and beliefs is through gender roles. However, discussion of gender roles in the United States is oftentimes conceptualized through a White American, middle-class, and heterosexual lens. Gender roles for women of color can be vastly different from White American gender roles, highlighting the within-group differences. For example, women outside the White American culture may play a matriarchal role, such as managing the household finances and taking major decisions related to the family. Other cultures outside the United States may hold more extreme examples of gender inequity compared with the American culture. In some cultures in the Middle East and in East Asia, women are generally discouraged from obtaining a higher education, employment, or a driver's license. Therefore, lesbians of color in the United States are faced with learning and redefining gender roles across the life span. Deviation from traditional gender roles may be perceived as abandonment of one's cultural heritage, rejection of familial values and beliefs, or rejection of family membership.

Melissa J. Corpus

See also Androgyny; Butch; Femme; Gender Role Socialization; Gender Role Stress; Lesbians and Dating; Lesbians and Romantic Relationships

Further Readings

Miville, M. L., Darlington, P., Whitlock, B., & Mulligan, T. (2005). Integrating identities: The relationships of racial, gender, and ego identities among White college students. *Journal of College Student Development, 46*(2), 157–175.

Miville, M. L., & Ferguson, A. D. (2006). Intersections of sexism and heterosexism with racism: Therapeutic implications. In M. G. Constantine & D. W. Sue (Eds.), *Addressing racism: Facilitating cultural competence in mental health and educational settings* (pp. 87–103). Hoboken, NJ: Wiley.

Lesbians and Health

Research has compared lesbian and heterosexual women across a variety of health outcomes and concluded that health disparities exist across many samples and methodologies. Lesbians are at increased risk for a variety of health problems compared with their heterosexual counterparts. Recent reports published by the Institute of Medicine and the U.S. Department of Health and Human Services have classified lesbians and other sexual and gender minorities as an at-risk and underserved population. This entry examines some of these health disparities as well as the reasons for them. In addition, the entry provides recommendations for culturally affirmative practices and future research.

Health Disparities

Research shows that lesbians are more likely to have diabetes, heart disease, and multiple risk factors for cardiovascular disease than their heterosexual counterparts. Lesbians report higher rates of asthma, putting them at more risk for malignant neoplasm, coronary artery disease, hypertension, peripheral vascular disease, and chronic pulmonary conditions.

Population-based data indicate that lesbians have twice the odds of being overweight and obese as heterosexual women. Higher prevalence of obesity is observed among lesbian women of color, especially African American lesbians. Although lesbians are at higher risk for obesity than heterosexual women, they are less likely to consider themselves overweight. In addition, there is some preliminary evidence that, when compared with heterosexual women, lesbians are at greater risk for health problems that are associated with obesity. Lesbians also report engaging in more maladaptive eating and dieting behaviors than heterosexual women. In studies of siblings, lesbian women are more likely to have a higher body mass index score, waist circumference, and waist-to-hip ratio than their heterosexual sisters. It has been hypothesized that lesbians, in comparison with heterosexual women, possess somewhat different attitudes about beauty and are more apt to reject the cultural norms of excessive thinness in women.

Sexual Health and Cancer

Lesbians have a higher 5-year and lifetime risk of developing breast cancer compared with heterosexual women. Many studies have found that they are less likely to get screened for other forms of cancer. Since many lesbians do not use birth control pills or other contraceptives, they are less likely to receive routine breast cancer screenings and gynecological examinations. This lack of gynecological care might cause higher morbidity and mortality rates for lesbians from undiagnosed and untreated gynecological cancers, especially ovarian cancer. Lesbians have traditionally been less likely to bear children, and hormones released during pregnancy and breast-feeding are believed to protect women against breast, endometrial, and ovarian cancers.

A common misconception is that lesbians have little to no risk of contracting sexually transmitted diseases (STDs), when in fact sexual activity between women can still transmit many different kinds of sexually transmitted infections, including human papillomavirus (the virus that causes cervical cancer) and trichomonas. Bacterial vaginosis, a common vaginal infection, occurs in lesbians, and if one woman in a couple has it, it is likely her partner has it too. Lower infection rates may exist among lesbians for some STDs such as gonorrhea and syphilis; however, similar rates as seen in heterosexual women may be present for other types of STDs (e.g., human papillomavirus) and genital herpes. Studies show that many women who have sex with women have had past sexual relations with men, and some continue to have sex with men, putting sexual minority women at risk of contracting virus-based STDs.

There are few documented cases of woman-to-woman transmission of HIV. This may be because, in part, cases are attributed to traditionally accepted risk factors such as illicit drug use or high-risk heterosexual actions. But many HIV-positive women report having sex with other women and are often unaware of the possible risk for HIV. The fairly common belief that lesbian women are immune may lead these women to reject safer sex practices.

Substance Use

Estimates of substance use among lesbians vary depending on how sexual orientation and substance use were measured. The recent trend toward assessing multiple dimensions of sexual orientation, including sexual attraction, sexual behavior, and sexual identity, is considered a methodological improvement over previous research. Data from population-based health studies indicate that lesbians have higher rates of alcohol use and alcohol dependence relative to heterosexual women. Lesbians are less likely to abstain from alcohol use, more likely to consume greater amounts of alcohol at a time, and more likely to report having sought treatment for their alcohol use. Alcohol dependence is highest in incidence among lesbians who are not in committed relationships. Sexual minority women with lifetime alcohol use disorders are at heightened risk for co-occurring psychiatric disorders compared with heterosexual women with lifetime alcohol use disorders. Researchers and practitioners attribute the higher rates of alcohol use in this population to the impact of minority stress and the fact that gay bars have been such a significant and safe place for socializing.

Many studies have found that lesbians are roughly twice as likely as heterosexual women to smoke cigarettes, and their smoking has been linked to many negative health consequences, such as elevated rates of asthma. Sexual minority women are also at greater risk for drug use disorders than heterosexual women. Recent research suggests that drug use patterns in younger lesbians are affected by socioeconomic status and by racial, ethnic, and gender identity and expression. For example, in White working-class lesbians, the most commonly abused substance is alcohol; in African American women in urban settings, it is crack and marijuana; in prep schools and colleges, it is methamphetamine, ecstasy, and marijuana; and more recently, there has been increased heroin use on college campuses affecting college-age lesbians. Finally, methamphetamine and oxycodone continuous-release use is found in pockets around the country in small towns and rural areas, where those drugs are commonly abused. In one study, young butch lesbians (displaying traditionally masculine traits) reported smoking more cigarettes and using marijuana more frequently than young femme lesbians (displaying traditionally feminine traits).

Mental Health Issues

Mental health is a state of being where persons engage in productive activities and meaningful relationships, adjust to change, and cope with adversity. Mental disorders are health concerns that are distinguished by changes in thinking, attitudes, behavior, or a combination of these factors. With the inclusion of questions on sexual identity in an increasing number of national, population-based health surveys, a growing body of research is documenting that lesbians are at higher risk for poor mental health, psychological distress, suicidal ideation, self-harm, and mental health disorders (e.g., depression and anxiety) than heterosexual women and men. For example, data from the National Comorbidity Survey indicated that women reporting a same-sex partner were at a twofold greater risk for any mood and anxiety disorder compared with heterosexual women. Lesbians are more likely than heterosexual women to experience childhood and adulthood adversity and trauma (e.g., sexual/physical/emotional abuse and/or assault, school victimization, intimate partner violence).

Why Health Disparities?

Minority stress theory suggests that lesbians are at greater risk for health problems than heterosexual women because they experience greater stress by virtue of the social stigma associated with their sexual orientation. Lesbians may experience everyday discrimination, including microaggressions and slights, hate crimes, expectations of rejection, concealment, and internalized homophobia. Lesbians report hostile health care environments and, as a result, are reluctant to disclose their orientation to providers and generally avoid medical care. For example, in a recent Behavioral Risk Factor Surveillance System survey with population-based samples of U.S. adults in 10 states, lesbians had more than 30% decreased odds of having an annual routine physical exam.

Health care professionals have also reported feeling uncomfortable dealing with lesbians and avoid discussions about their sexuality. Training about LGBT health issues is sparse in medical schools; a recent report demonstrated that a median of only 5 hours during clinical training was devoted to LGBT issues at U.S. and Canadian medical schools.

Possible barriers to accessing health services for lesbians include lack of health insurance. Research indicates that many lesbians may pay higher rates for insurance than the general population. Lesbians and their partners often face additional challenges such as lack of availability of health care providers offering fertility services to women who identify as lesbian.

Future Recommendations for Culturally Affirmative Practices

Appropriate health interventions for lesbians and other sexual and gender minorities are needed. Without clear and visible signals from health care facilities and verbal interactions with health care professionals that demonstrate acceptance, LGBT persons may not feel safe and welcome. The need to improve the cultural competency of health care providers who work with lesbian elders is especially imperative. Recent findings suggest that mainstream aging services and nursing and long-term care facilities may not be adequately addressing the needs of LGBT elders, and consequently, many midlife lesbians experience significant apprehension about their future health care needs. Clinicians and researchers have just begun to develop specialized treatment protocols and prevention programs for sexual and gender minority mental health and substance abuse clients. However, research on the efficacy and effectiveness of these treatment programs is limited. Clinical treatment for lesbians with substance use and other co-occurring psychiatric disorders is especially complex, and empirically based and culturally sensitive interventions are needed.

To ensure inclusive and appropriate health care for lesbians, health care personnel need to understand the relationships between discrimination, health status, and health risk behaviors. Interventions based on minority stress theory might aim to change how situations are appraised and to develop strategies to cope with stressful conditions such as discrimination. Clinicians, for example, might assist their lesbian clients in reducing their negative self-perceptions and attitudes (i.e., internalized shame and negative self-acceptance) and in reevaluating their coping skills for dealing with discrimination.

Future Research

Historically, health researchers have mainly utilized deficit-focused models to understand health disparities and poor health outcomes in LGBT populations. However, there has been a recent emergence of interest in the study of resilience and strengths in LGBT persons. There is also a growing recognition among researchers that the LGBT community is not a homogeneous group. There remain significant gaps in the understanding of lesbians, particularly in exploring similarities and differences across age, racial, ethnic, and socioeconomic lines. For example, much of what was known about racial and ethnic differences in LGBT communities was based solely on research with men who have sex with men with regard to HIV/AIDS infection and, therefore, did not necessarily resonate with the experiences of lesbians. In seeking to understand health disparities, researchers have begun to focus on important intersections of social categories to gain a nuanced understanding of multiple identities.

A small amount of research suggests that assessments of stigma from co-occurring identities may yield more comprehensive results about health outcomes than assessment of stigma from any one identity. The recent introduction of the Health Equity Promotion model builds on minority stress theory by focusing on the ways in which both sexual and gender minorities build supportive networks and develop coping skills in the face of marginalization. The Health Equity Promotion model integrates a life course development perspective within a health equity framework to highlight how socioeconomic status, age, race/ethnicity, and individual and environmental contexts intersect with health-promoting and adverse pathways to influence possible health outcomes in sexual minorities.

Lynne Carroll

See also Health Issues and Gender: Overview; Mental Health and Gender: Overview; Minority Stress; Sexual Orientation: Overview

Further Readings

Balsam, K. F., Blayney, J. A., Yamile, M., Dillworth, T., Zimmerman, L., & Kaysen, D. (2015). Racial/ethnic differences in identity and mental health outcomes among young sexual minority women. *Cultural Diversity and Ethnic Minority Psychology, 21*(3), 380–390.

Fredriksen-Goldsen, K. I., Simoni, J. M., Hyun-Jun, K., Walters, K. L., Yang, J., Hoy-Ellis, C. P., . . . Muraco, A. (2014). The health equity promotion model: Reconceptualization of lesbian, gay, bisexual, and transgender (LGBT) health disparities. *American Journal of Orthopsychiatry, 84*(6), 653–663.

Lehavot, K. (2012). Coping strategies and health in a national sample of sexual minority women. *American Journal of Orthopsychiatry, 82*(4), 494–504.

Taliaferro, J. D., Lutz, B., Moore, A. K., & Scipien, K. (2014). Increasing cultural awareness and sensitivity: Effective substance treatment in the adult lesbian population. *Journal of Human Behavior in the Social Environment, 24,* 582–588.

Lesbians and Romantic Relationships

Although there is a decline in the stigma associated with same-sex-attracted people, gay and lesbian people still experience difficulty in finding acceptance. The number of lesbians in society is difficult to ascertain, and reported numbers vary depending on how the question about sexual orientation in the surveys was phrased. Regardless of the number of same-sex-attracted women in society, many of these women are in a romantic relationship. Beginning in the early 1980s, researchers became more interested in studying lesbian relationships. A substantial body of this research indicates that lesbian relationships generally operate on the same principles as heterosexual relationships. However, a few differences have been found. This entry provides an overview of current research on gender roles, sexuality, and relationship satisfaction in lesbian couples.

Gender Roles

In heteronormative societies, people often assume that same-sex couples adopt husband-wife roles in their relationships. In fact, when studying lesbian relationships, researchers have distinguished between butch and femme lesbian roles for many years. Butch lesbians were expected to appear and behave in a stereotypically masculine manner, whereas femme lesbians were expected to perform in a feminine fashion. However, these two lesbian gender roles are different from heterosexual roles in terms of sexual behavior and economic dominance. The role of butch or femme is not related to who most often initiates sexual activity in the relationship. With a more equal power distribution in lesbian couples, egalitarianism is often practiced, whether it is a conscious decision or not. Often, both lesbian partners are employed, and neither of them is the exclusive breadwinner. Although equal sharing is hard to achieve, lesbian couples tend to be more equitable with regard to household work than heterosexual couples.

Sexuality

Generally, sexual relationship satisfaction has been found to be comparable among same-sex and heterosexual couples. For all kinds of couples, greater sexual satisfaction is associated with greater overall relationship satisfaction, and sexual frequency tends to decline the longer a couple has been together. Lesbian couples, compared with gay males and heterosexuals, engage in less frequent sexual activity. A large research study conducted by Philip Blumstein and Pepper Schwartz on U.S. couples found that only 20% of lesbian couples reported having sexual relations at least three times a week, compared with 55% of heterosexual couples. However, comparisons of sexual activity between gay, lesbian, and heterosexual couples have been criticized in recent years. Many researchers have argued that gay, lesbian, and heterosexual adults may have different definitions of, and desires for, sex. Questions regarding sexual relationships may be answered differently by these various types of couples. For lesbian couples particularly, the description of sexual activities has been limited by the heteronormative nature of language, and many behaviors relevant to lesbian sex were not included in the surveys. More recently, researchers have used updated assessments and consistently found that frequency of sexual activity in lesbian couples was comparable with that in heterosexual couples.

Relationship Commitment and Satisfaction

Partners in gay and lesbian relationships experience less social support than heterosexual partners from outside sources, such as family, which leads same-sex partners to rely more on each other for support. Statistically, lesbian relationships tend to be more monogamous than those of gay men. Recent data have shown that gay men reported having had more sexual partners than lesbians did, even when in committed relationships. Although marriage for same-sex couples is relatively new in the United States (beginning with a few states in the early to mid-2000s, before a 2015 Supreme Court ruling made it legal nationwide), two thirds of reported same-sex marriages are lesbian marriages and one third involve gay men. Furthermore, fewer lesbian marriages have ended in divorce than gay or heterosexual marriages.

Researchers have compared same-sex and heterosexual couples on their relationship satisfaction. The findings consistently show no significant differences in relationship satisfaction between diverse samples of gay, lesbian, and heterosexual couples. If anything, research indicates that lesbian couples report slightly higher satisfaction than gay or heterosexual couples.

Lesbian couples demonstrate a high capacity for mutual empathy, empowerment, and authenticity in their relationships. Also, lesbian partners are especially effective at interacting with each other and working together harmoniously compared with other couple types. Because same-sex partners have variations of the same gender role development as heterosexuals, partners in lesbian relationships can have an increased understanding of each other, which may contribute to their slightly higher levels of intimacy and satisfaction compared with heterosexual couples. Moreover, similarities in gender role socialization between partners may result in lesbians showing more emotional expressiveness, exhibiting greater egalitarianism, and sharing more responsibility than opposite-sex partners. Lesbian couples also report more cohesion, trust, and equality than gay and heterosexual couples.

Regarding conflict resolution, lesbians are more likely than heterosexual couples to discuss problems positively, use more communication skills, show more joy/excitement, and resolve conflict effectively. Also, members of lesbian couples show more empathic attunement to their partner's nonverbal signals and consciously avoid expressions of contempt. These latter findings may be due to the presence of shared power between partners. However, the equivalence of lesbian partners also increases conflicts. Without gender expectations, virtually all decisions (e.g., division of labor, finances, whose career takes priority) can be stressful, even when couples possess the necessary skills to resolve matters smoothly.

In conclusion, regardless of sexual orientation, successful relationships share the same features, and the factors predictive of relationship satisfaction are the same for all kinds of couples. For example, relationship satisfaction is higher when partners trust each other, care for each other, and have positive communication styles. Current knowledge about lesbian romantic relationships indicates that many lesbian couples can and do build healthy, satisfying, and committed relationships. However, the limitation of demographic homogeneity of participants in past research should be mentioned. The majority of lesbian couples in previous studies were White, well-educated, middle-class Americans. The topic merits further attention, specifically regarding the experiences of working-class or ethnic-minority lesbian couples.

Shu Yuan, Jennifer L. Lindsey, and Sylvia Niehuis

See also Gender Role Socialization; Lesbians and Dating; Lesbians and Gender Roles

Further Readings

Kurdek, L. A. (2005). What do we know about gay and lesbian couples? *Current Directions in Psychological Science, 14,* 251–254.

Markey, P. M., & Markey, C. N. (2013). The complementarity of behavioral styles among female same-sex romantic couples. *Personal Relationships, 20,* 170–183.

Peplau, L. A., & Fingerhut, A. W. (2007). The close relationships of lesbians and gay men. *Annual Review of Psychology, 58,* 405–424.

LGBQ Older Adults and Health

Lesbian, gay, bisexual, and queer (LGBQ) people, particularly those who are older in age, continue to face a plethora of health disparity issues. The 2015 Supreme Court landmark decision in *Obergefell v. Hodges* legalized same-sex marriages in the United States, yet it is not clear how this watershed moment will affect those who have lived for years in nontraditional marriage arrangements, particularly those who are older. A paucity of research addressing the health and aging needs of LGBQ older adults currently prevents full exploration of this underserved population. The Institute of Medicine's 2011 Report on LGBTQ Health identifies the need for more research among this population, which faces a multitude of risk environments.

This entry examines the health of sexual minority populations who are 50 years of age and older. The entry is organized around several thematic areas: (a) physical health, (b) mental health, (c) key indicators of health and health care access, and (d) structural explanations contributing to health disparities among this underserved population. Integrated within each section is a focus on those who are at the nexus of being racial/ethnic minorities who are also LGBQ older adults, as well as on gendered differences and partnership statuses. Last, the entry discusses recent research on community-related factors, which provides evidence of potential resiliency factors.

Physical Health

Older adults who are members of socially disadvantaged groups are at higher risk for poor physical and mental health than their counterparts who are members of more advantaged groups. It has been identified that roughly 26% of LGBQ older adults are at risk of being obese. In addition, data drawn from the Washington State Behavioral Risk Factor Surveillance System indicated that 44.27% of sexual minority women and 38.27% of sexual minority men reported being at risk for disability. Conversely, 36.87% of heterosexual women and 33.96% of heterosexual men reported being at risk for disability. Similarly, 15.92% of sexual minority women and 13.09% of sexual minority men reported frequent poor mental health days, whereas only 9.36% of heterosexual women and 6.88% of heterosexual men reported frequent poor mental health days. Also, 20.57% of sexual minority women and 15.52% of sexual minority men reported having asthma. However, only 15.89% of heterosexual women and 11.56% of heterosexual men reported having asthma. Moreover, older LGBQ adults are more likely to report physical disability and chronic disease. It is important to consider gendered differences and sexual orientation differences in the patterning of physical health concerns among LGBQ older adults.

Research has shown that lesbian and bisexual older women are less likely to have an annual routine checkup and more likely to be obese than gay and bisexual older men. Interestingly, gay and bisexual older men (compared with lesbian and bisexual older women) are more likely to report higher rates of smoking and excessive drinking, higher rates of lifetime victimization, and more internalized stigma (i.e., the absorbing, either cognitively or emotionally, of assumptions and stereotypes that are often viewed unfavorably in society, particularly in relation to mental health). Similarly, gay and bisexual older men are more likely to report having less social support and smaller social networks. Compared with older lesbians and bisexual men, bisexual older women report a higher degree of internalized stigma and a higher likelihood of sexual identity concealment. In addition, bisexual older women also report lower rates of physical activity and less social support than older lesbians, whereas older lesbians are more likely to indicate a higher degree of lifetime victimization than bisexual older women. Research has persistently demonstrated the importance of social networks in facilitating higher levels of physical activity and, subsequently, decreased physical illness. However, as a result of older sexual minority women and men having smaller social networks, this might amplify health inequities in this population.

Research has also demonstrated that partnered LGBQ older adults are significantly younger than those without partners. Interestingly, it has been identified that partnered older LGBQ adults are more likely to be female and White and often have relatively a higher education and income than unpartnered LGBQ older adults. Older LGBQ adults in same-gender relationships, particularly women in same-gender relationships, have been shown to be more likely than their heterosexual partnered counterparts to need assistance with activities of daily living, which have been traditionally conceptualized, and subsequently quantitatively measured, as consisting of needing assistance with dressing, bathing, and doing errands.

Mental Health

Mental health among LGBQ populations has been shown to be deleterious compared with their heterosexual counterparts. For example, research has demonstrated that depression is particularly heightened among older LGBQ adults. Depression in older LGBQ adults is shaped by dynamic social influences. In addition, financial barriers to health care and smoking worsen depressive symptomatology in older LGBQ adults, as do victimization and internalized stigma. On the other hand, research has shown that higher social support and increased social networking decreased the odds of depressive symptomatology among older LGBQ adults—working in a protective manner. Related to mental health is the higher use of substances among older LGBQ adults. For example, research has shown that older LGBQ adults are at higher risk for alcohol use compared with their heterosexual counterparts.

It is important to note that health outcomes and behaviors among older LGBQ adults have been shaped by experiences of social discrimination more intensely than among younger cohorts. For example, homosexuality was listed in the *Diagnostic and Statistical Manual of Mental Disorders* as a mental health disorder until 1973. Thus, it is quite plausible that the current cohort of older LGBQ adults were coming into their sexuality when—and living in contexts where—disclosure of one's sexuality was negatively accepted within society. Mental health quality of life has been demonstrated to have an inverse relationship with lifetime victimization, discrimination, and lack of identity disclosure for older LGBQ adults. On the other hand, research has identified that mental health quality of life for older LGBQ adults improves when they exhibit a higher sense of sexual identity, larger social network size and social support, and greater levels of physical activity.

There are many gendered dynamics concerning mental health outcomes among older LGBQ adults. Research has shown that lesbian populations experience higher depression (roughly 14% to 18%) rates than their heterosexual counterparts (11%). Similarly, older gay men also experience greater feelings of depression than their heterosexual counterparts. Suicide has been a major problem within sexual minority communities and among sexual minority populations. Lesbians have increased suicidal thoughts when compared with their heterosexual counterparts, and this is even more pronounced among gay men in comparison with their heterosexual counterparts. In addition, older LGBQ women are at increased risk for suicide mortality compared with their heterosexual counterparts.

Social Conditions Shaping Health

Social conditions and dynamics can also shape health disparities. This section focuses on three major areas undergirding social determinants of health: (1) relationship status, (2) income dynamics, and (3) housing dynamics. Relationship statuses have long been important factors contributing to health variations and thus warrant attention. Also, income has been a major driver of health disparities, with low income contributing deleteriously to health. Last, focusing on housing permits exploration into broader social conditions among older LGBQ adults as a prism to understand health.

Research has shown that both lesbian and gay older individuals tend to have larger social networks comprising other LGBQ adults. This is important to note because successful aging can be largely affected by social networks. Studies among LGBQ older adults have demonstrated that successful aging also depends heavily on maintenance of high life satisfaction, being physically active, and not feeling marginalized as a result of the interaction between ageism and homophobia. A major influence on these dynamics is whether older LGBQ adults are partnered in some form or fashion.

Roughly 30% of older LGBQ adults live in poverty, measured as at or below 200% of the federal poverty level. Bisexual older women (≈48%) and bisexual men (≈47%) are more likely to live in poverty than lesbians and gay men, respectively. Moreover, research has shown that economic resources decline among older LGBQ adults, particularly among those who have experienced chronic stress as a result of experiencing discrimination based on sexual orientation and/or identity. Studies indicating this finding highlight a bidirectional relationship between income and health, wherein each influences the other. Supporting this is research that has indicated that resiliency among older LGBQ populations is statistically significant and positively correlated with having a higher income.

Housing is another important social determinant, which is also closely related to income and relationship status. Older lesbian and gay adults are more likely to live alone than their heterosexual peers, even though they are more likely to have more peers in their social networks (particularly other older LGBQ adults). Interestingly, while older LGBQ adults may live alone, they may also have partners with whom they do not physically reside. Older LGBQ adults have shown greater delay in entering residential care, which can be largely shaped by economic resources and/or residential care lacking culturally appropriate delivery of services geared toward LGBQ older adults.

The implications of housing arrangements are important for another reason related to health outcomes, specifically mental health. LGBQ older adults who live alone, compared with their peers living with a partner or spouse, are more likely to report higher degrees of loneliness. Researchers have been able to explore what social factors contribute to this relationship and have identified that other forms of social support, social network size, and internalized stigma partially account for the relationship between living arrangement and loneliness. Loneliness can be utilized as a proxy measure for mental health; thus, greater loneliness among older LGBQ adults has been shown to be correlated with poorer mental health.

Kasim Ortiz and Devon Tyrone Wade

See also Aging and Gender: Overview; Lesbian, Gay, and Bisexual Experiences of Aging; Transgender Experiences of Aging

Further Readings

Battle, J., Daniels, J., & Pastrana, A., Jr. (2015). Civic engagement, religion, and health: Older Black lesbians in the Social Justice Sexuality (SJS) Survey. *Women, Gender, and Families of Color, 3*(1), 19–35. doi:10.5406/womgenfamcol.3.1.0019

Fredriksen-Goldsen, K. I., Emlet, C. A., Kim, H.-J., Muraco, A., Erosheva, E. A., Goldsen, J., & Hoy-Ellis, C. P. (2013). The physical and mental health of lesbian, gay male, and bisexual (LGBQ) older adults: The role of key health indicators and risk and protective factors. *The Gerontologist, 53*(4), 664–675. doi:10.1093/geront/gns123

Fredriksen-Goldsen, K. I., & Kim, H.-J. (2015). Count me in response to sexual orientation measures among older adults. *Research on Aging, 37*(5), 464–480. doi:10.1177/0164027514542109

Fredriksen-Goldsen, K. I., Kim, H.-J., Muraco, A., & Mincer, S. (2009). Chronically ill midlife and older lesbians, gay men, and bisexuals and their informal caregivers: The impact of the social context. *Sexuality Research and Social Policy Journal of NSRC, 6*(4), 52–64. doi:10.1525/srsp.2009.6.4.52

Henning-Smith, C., Gonzales, G., & Shippee, T. P. (2015). Differences by sexual orientation in expectations about future long-term care needs among adults 40 to 65 years old. *American Journal of Public Health, 105*(11), 2359–2365. doi:10.2105/AJPH.2015.302781

Stanley, I. H., & Duong, J. (2015). Mental health service use among lesbian, gay, and bisexual older adults. *Psychiatric Services (Washington, D.C.), 66*(7), 743–749. doi:10.1176/appi.ps.201400488

Williams, M. E., & Fredriksen-Goldsen, K. I. (2014). Same-sex partnerships and the health of older adults. *Journal of Community Psychology, 42*(5), 558–570. doi:10.1002/jcop.21637

LGBTQ Athletes, Experiences of

An athlete is a person who recreationally or competitively participates in an individual or team sport. Gender and sexual norms are central to the organization and ethos of athletic competition. Along with restrooms, sports may be one of the most explicitly gendered environments in Western society. Because sports is considered a masculine domain, involvement carries different societal meaning for men and women. Whereas sports participation can reinforce perceptions of masculinity and heterosexuality among men, for women participation may raise questions about their femininity and sexual orientation. This relationship between societal gender and sexual norms structures the experiences of all athletes, in particular those who identify as lesbian, gay, bisexual, transgender, and queer (LGBTQ). Due to the stereotype that gay men are effeminate and lesbians are masculine, gay men are thought to be nonexistent in sports, whereas lesbian women are caricatured as ubiquitous. Although participation in sports can have many positive psychological outcomes (including but not limited to increased self-esteem and self-efficacy, a sense of belonging, and lower levels of anxiety and depression), due to the heteronormative culture of sports, such benefits may be less readily available to LGBTQ athletes.

Gender Norms and Heteronormativity

Expectations for how individuals should appear and behave based on the gender they were assigned at birth is deeply embedded within Western cultures. Characteristics such as aggression, strength, and dominance are expected features of masculinity among men, whereas traits such as passivity, subordination, and dependence are expected features of femininity among women. These gendered characteristics are presumed to be opposite and complementary—that is, males should always be masculine, and females should always be feminine. The term *heteronormativity* defines this interdependent relationship and characterizes how within institutions and social relations, heterosexuality is seen as the "natural" expression of gender and sexuality. In having same-gender desire and/or identifying with a gender other than the one they were assigned at birth, LGBTQ athletes challenge societal expectations of heteronormativity. Violation of these deeply entrenched norms greatly shapes their experiences: Within sports, LGBTQ athletes confront both heterosexism (discrimination based on sexual orientation) as well as transphobia (discrimination based on gender identity).

Gay, Bisexual, and Queer Male Athletes

Throughout its history, sports have been considered a mainstay for the acquisition and appearance of heterosexual masculinity among boys and men. Through direct competition, athletics provide a training ground for masculine ideals: Aggression, strength, and dominance are rewarded, while passivity, weakness, and submission are punished. Aggressive team sports such as football, hockey, and basketball have a reputation for being more masculine, whereas individual and aesthetic sports such as gymnastics, figure skating, swimming, and running are considered less masculine. Because masculinity is defined by what it is not—homosexuality and femininity—male gay, bisexual, and queer (GBQ) athletes are thought to be nonexistent in sports.

Throughout all levels and types of sports, antigay prejudice and discrimination are commonplace. It is quite normal for coaches—as well as players—to use antigay or sexist slurs as a means to shame players in their performance or to motivate them to play better. Calling players a "fag" or a "sissy" or criticizing their performance as "like a girl" implies that expressing emotion, vulnerability, or weakness (stereotypically feminine characteristics) is unacceptable. Antigay and sexist pejoratives rebuke the existence of homoerotic desire in sports. By maintaining a heterosexist environment within athletics, intimate forms of physically relating (e.g., hugging, slapping of the buttocks, nakedness) are protected from homoerotic accusations. The open acknowledgment of GBQ male athletes, in contrast, draws attention to the physical and emotional intimacy among athletes and the possibility of homosexual desire within all-male spaces.

The heterosexist climate in sports pressures GBQ athletes to hide their sexual orientation and limits the number of GBQ men who decide to play sports, as well as the type of sport they choose to play. GBQ male athletes may decide, for example, to play an individual sport instead of a team sport, as team sports environments and locker rooms are fiercer sites of heteronormative disciplining. Others may quit altogether to avoid harassment. Overwhelmingly, GBQ male athletes choose to keep their sexual identities hidden. Players' nondisclosure is motivated by a desire not only to buttress ridicule but also to preserve team cohesion. Because a considerable amount of antigay discrimination and sexual harassment comes from coaches and fellow players, GBQ athletes may experience feelings of isolation and exclusion from their teammates and reinforce feelings of internalized homonegativity—that is, shame or hatred of one's nonheterosexual sexual orientation.

For those who do disclose their sexuality, adherence to traditional expressions of masculinity can help them avoid ridicule of their sexual orientation. The more skilled an athlete is, for example, the higher his value to the team and greater the esteem he receives from his teammates, coaches, and administration. Similarly, a player who is "out" about his sexuality and is more traditionally masculine will be less scrutinized than a player of comparable skill who is effeminate. Regardless, a culture of "Don't ask, don't tell" endures in men's sports. Many athletes—including GBQ athletes—believe that conversations about same-gender attractions do not have a place within locker rooms. Because sexual orientation does not affect athletic ability, the argument goes, discussion about same-gender attractions is unwarranted. Although this same logic could apply to discussion of heterosexual attractions, conversations about women and heterosexual exploits are commonplace within men's sports.

Lesbian, Bisexual, and Queer Female Athletes

Whereas masculinity and athletic participation are viewed as naturally well matched, femininity and sports participation are considered to be at odds. Female athletes continuously confront accusations of being "mannish" or lesbians, particularly in traditionally male-dominated team sports (e.g., football, hockey, basketball, baseball). In and outside of competition, women are pressured to accentuate their femininity and heterosexuality. Within all levels of mainstream sports, the use of the "lesbian" label functions pejoratively and negatively affects heterosexual and nonheterosexual athletes alike. Homophobic sports environments deter lesbian, bisexual, and queer (LBQ) athletes from coming out, while simultaneously silencing the heterosexual teammates who support them. Many LBQ athletes choose not to disclose their sexual identities and/or attempt to "pass" as heterosexual. For example, some may laugh at "gay jokes," use gender neutral pronouns when discussing their partners, and avoid situations where their sexuality could be exposed. Somewhat paradoxically, LBQ female athletes may choose to remain "in the closet" precisely because of the stereotype that all women athletes are lesbians. Although participation in sports can foster social relationships, many LBQ female athletes may not feel genuinely accepted due to the stigma that surrounds their sexual orientation.

Despite the sexual shaming and stigmatizing of LBQ women in sports, a number of LBQ athletes compete in mainstream athletics. Within women's sports, a number of professional female athletes have come out, helping normalize the existence of LBQ female athletes. Importantly, the Women's National Basketball Association, which had denied its largely lesbian identified fan base since the league's inception, became the first American professional sports league in 2014 to openly cater to and recruit LGBTQ fans. More generally, women's sports has been a space in which LBQ women have found and developed community. In the face of the pressure to feminize appearances, sports continues to be one of the few socially acceptable venues within which women can express nonconventional gender attitudes and behaviors and be aggressive, competitive, and dominant. Although it is not a universal experience, some LBQ female athletes who are out to their athletic teams receive support from their teammates and coaches. With such support, LBQ athletes self-censor less and are able to concentrate more on athletic success.

Transgender Athletes

Sexual orientation and gender identity are separate concepts, and identifying as gay, lesbian, bisexual, or queer neither precludes nor assumes identification as transgender. *Transgender* (*trans*) is an umbrella term used to describe individuals whose psychological gender identity is different from the gender they were assigned at birth. Because the structure of sports is rooted in the belief that gender is a binary—that is, male/female—athletes must identify as either "man" or "woman" to compete. Identifying as both, neither, or another gender identity is not an option. The existence of trans athletes in sports raises fundamental questions about the biological and psychological characteristics that "make" individuals "male" or "female." A number of trans individuals decide not to participate in athletics because of the unwelcoming environment created by rigid gender and sexual norms.

The separate categories of sports competition for men and women reflect the traditional assumption that men are naturally better athletes than women due to innate biological differences. Not all athletic organizations have explicit policies for the inclusion of transgender athletes. For those that do, policies vary by level of play. Trans advocates recommend that children in grades K–12 be allowed to participate in their affirmed gender, but few school districts have policies for transgender inclusion. At college and professional levels of competition, many policies focus on the potential advantage that androgenic hormones—in particular testosterone—may provide due to the effects these hormones have on the musculoskeletal system (e.g., bone growth and increases in strength and muscle mass). Within the National Collegiate Athletic Association, trans athletes must compete in the gender role consistent with their hormonal makeup. In women's sports, trans men are allowed to compete provided they have not undergone testosterone hormone therapy, while trans women can participate after having undergone 1 year of estrogen therapy. It is believed that the athletic advantages trans women may have from natural levels of testosterone dissipate after 1 year of estrogen therapy. At one of the highest levels of competition—the Olympic Games—requirements for trans athletes are more extensive. To compete on the team that matches their gender identity, trans athletes must have undergone sex reassignment surgery, have legal recognition of their affirmed gender, and have taken at least 2 years of either testosterone suppression or testosterone supplementation.

The developmental time period in which trans individuals come out and/or decide to transition affects their decision to participate or continue to participate in athletics. Those who come out as trans during adolescence or in college may feel that they have to choose between living authentically—that is, as the gender that aligns with their sense of self—and their identity as an athlete. Because of the various policies surrounding transgender inclusion in sports, trans athletes may delay receiving identity affirming medical interventions, while others may leave sports altogether. For those who have college scholarships or forms of financial endorsement, the decision to transition and to what extent (e.g., clothing, pronouns, hormonal supplementation, genital surgery) can add additional stress on top of what is already a significant life change.

Gay Identified Sport

In response to the heteronormative environments that exist within mainstream sports for LGBTQ athletes, since the 1990s, gay identified sports leagues and international events have been developed regionally, nationally, and internationally. Gay identified sports refers to sports leagues, sporting events, or teams that publicly self-identify as "gay." These alternative sports spaces strive to establish a venue for athletic participation that is free from discrimination based on sexual orientation, gender, race, class, national origin, and ability.

They also seek to promote an ethos of participation, inclusion, and personal best. Hallmark events such as the Gay Games and the Outgames host thousands of athletes every 4 years, and numerous gay identified recreational sports leagues exist throughout the United States. For many individuals who participate, the importance of gay sports lies not in the actual competition but, rather, in the atmosphere that characterizes these spaces. Compared with mainstream sports settings, athletes describe experiencing a greater sense of belonging as well as a greater ability to express their individuality in gay identified sports. Although these athletic spaces are intended to be fully inclusionary, trans athletes may experience unfair treatment due to concerns about "fair" competition and essentialist beliefs about gender.

Stephanie M. Anderson

See also Femininity; Gender Stereotypes; Heteronormativity; Masculinity Ideology and Norms; Queer; Women Athletes, Experiences of

Further Readings

Anderson, E. (2005). *In the game: Gay athletes and the cult of masculinity.* Albany: State University of New York Press.

Caudwell, J. (Ed.). (2006). *Sport, sexualities and queer/theory.* New York, NY: Routledge.

Griffin, P. (1998). *Strong women, deep closets: Lesbians and homophobia in sport.* Champaign, IL: Human Kinetics.

Messner, M. A. (2002). *Taking the field: Women, men and sports.* Minneapolis: University of Minnesota Press.

Moiser, C. (n.d.). *TRANS*ATHLETE.* Retrieved June 10, 2015, from http://www.transathlete.com

Symons, C. (2010). *The gay games: A history.* New York, NY: Routledge.

Wilchins, R. A. (2014). *Queer theory, gender theory: An instant primer.* Bronx, NY: Magnus Books.

LGBTQ Community, Experiences of Transgender People in

This entry describes the experiences of transgender people within the lesbian, gay, bisexual, transgender, and queer (LGBTQ) community. This entry first describes the definition of community and the history of how transgender people were included within and excluded from the LGBQ community. The entry then discusses the importance of community, emphasizing the different types of communities transgender people seek and the types of communities available to transgender people. Next, this entry discusses both the negative and the positive aspects of the transgender community, focusing on the juxtaposition of experiences of transphobia against experiences of group cohesion.

History of the LGBTQ Community

The phrase *LGBTQ community* has been used historically as an umbrella term to bring together a variety of identities that refer to sexual orientation (lesbian, gay, bisexual, queer) and gender identity (transgender). There are other acronyms for the LGBTQ community that include and name other identities, most commonly *queer*, *questioning*, *intersex*, and *asexual*. There are many other sexual orientations and gender identities that fall under the larger umbrella of LGBTQ community.

Shared values and common movements also define the LGBTQ community. Some of the shared values that LGBTQ people celebrate are sexuality, gender expression, individuality, and equality. Many of the movements in LGBTQ communities have been rooted in these values and promote equity and equality for LGBTQ people. There have been movements in the United States around visibility for LGBTQ people, equal access to marriage, access to employment and housing without discrimination, bullying and violence that target LGBTQ people, and many more. Often LGBTQ movements fight discrimination and cultural practices such as homophobia, biphobia, transphobia, heterosexism, and misogyny. LGBTQ community movements have been rallying points to bring community members together, and they have also been divisive by issue and identity. There has been a great deal of discourse around the idea that many movements that build equality for LGBTQ people have not been inclusive of transgender and gender nonconforming people.

History of the *T* Being Included in "LGBQ"

As mentioned, in the LGBTQ community, there are two distinct identity groups: (1) identities based on sexual orientation (lesbian, gay, bisexual, queer)

and (2) identities based on gender identity (transgender). These are two different identity constructs that have been conflated and often confused when describing the LGBTQ community. Sexual orientation refers to a person's sexual, romantic, and emotional attraction to other people. Gender identity refers to a person's internal sense of their own gender, which can be feeling like a man, feeling like a woman, not identifying as a man or a woman, identifying as both a man and a woman, identifying as somewhere in between a man and a woman, completely rejecting the idea of man and woman, and many others. Often, these two constructs are confused with gender expression, which is how a person displays their gender and gender identity to the world. There are many nontransgender identified people in the LGBQ community whose gender expression is different from the presumed gender expression of their sex assigned at birth, which creates an array of gender expressions across the LGBTQ community. An example of this is a lesbian woman who presents by wearing masculine clothing and hair or a gay man who embodies a feminine presentation. This is important in understanding the history of why transgender people have been included in LGB communities. It is because there is a common history of discrimination based on perceived gender identity and perceived gender expression. LGB people and transgender people have been harassed and bullied because of the many different gender expressions in the communities.

Along with gender identity being conflated with sexual orientation, coming out constitutes another reason why the "T" has been included within the broader LGBTQ community. Transgender identity, as well as sexual orientation, requires a person to come out and let others know about their internal feelings about their gender and/or attractions to others. Because this identity information may not be readily apparent to others, these identities are considered "invisible identities." While the coming out processes may look very different for transgender people and LGBQ individuals, the internalized shame and invisibility of the identities can draw the communities together. In addition to coming out, the majority of transgender individuals identify as a sexual minority, thus indicating considerable overlap among LGBTQ identities.

There was a turning point in LGBTQ history that many describe as the birth of the modern LGBTQ movement: the Stonewall Riots. The Stonewall Riots were a series of violent riots near the Stonewall Inn in New York City that were catalyzed by police raids and violence in local inns and bars that had LGBTQ clientele in the area. The outcome of the Stonewall Riots was an increased visibility and awareness of LGBTQ identities and communities and the discrimination that LGBTQ people faced at the time, as well as the formation of the Gay Liberation Front to start combating discrimination. Many of the leaders and people engaged in the riots were transgender women, particularly transgender women of color. At the moment when the modern gay rights movement was coalescing, transgender people were at the forefront, particularly transgender community icons Sylvia Rivera and Marsha P. Johnson. It is often difficult for people in transgender communities to hear this history because of the erasure of transgender people from this history, as well as the erasure of transgender people in gay liberation after the Stonewall Riots.

Importance of Community

Transgender people find community in the LGBTQ community and within their own communities as well. The importance of community to transgender people cannot be understated with regard to finding support and friendship. Transgender people have created their own communities and networks in different communities, who come together to provide resources to one another, provide support around different struggles and life events, and share similar experiences. Oftentimes, transgender communities come together to build movements around struggles that are unique to transgender communities. An example of this is The Shot Clinic in Minneapolis, a transgender-led organization that provides hormone shots to transgender and gender nonconforming people who do not want to do their hormone shots alone. This community space also has clothing resources for people transitioning, such as chest binders, wigs, and clothes, as well as regular discussion and social groups. It is important for transgender people to have their own community space and also to be welcomed into LGBTQ community spaces. Research ubiquitously indicates that community and social support are two primary protective factors in assisting transgender people with their physical and mental well-being.

Negative Experiences of Transgender People Within the LGBQ Community

Transgender people have a variety of different labels and gender expressions, which can make it difficult to generalize what types of experiences everyone has in relation with the LGBQ community. However, transgender and gender nonconforming people have experienced many different types of transphobia from within the LGBTQ community. Transphobia is defined as prejudice, dislike, and unfair treatment toward transgender people and their loved ones.

First, as mentioned in relationship to the Stonewall Riots, there are many transgender people who feel as though their identities and experiences have been erased from the LGBTQ community narrative and history. Another example of this was during the early HIV/AIDS crisis in the 1980s and 1990s, when gay male culture was pushed into the mainstream media but transgender people affected by HIV/AIDS were very rarely discussed or seen, leading to transgender women being one of the most disproportionately affected groups later in the epidemic.

Second, there have been many instances of transgender people being excluded and ejected from lesbian and gay community spaces because of their transgender identities. An example of this is the Michigan Women's Musical Festival, where transgender women have not been permitted because they were not "womyn born womyn." This type of discourse has created a great rift between lesbian and gay people and transgender people because this is a form of invalidating a transgender person's identity. At the Michigan Women's Music Festival, transgender women who identify as women were told that they were not woman enough to be in a woman-only space. This created a huge controversy and an entire movement of artists and activists protesting the music festival.

There are larger instances of erasure and rejection from within the LGBTQ community, however; transgender people have also faced harassment and microagressions from within the community, which has created a divide between transgender people and lesbian and gay communities (bisexual communities have also faced biphobia from within the LGBTQ community, which has led to similar circumstances, which is why bisexual communities are not mentioned in this commentary).

In addition to transgender people experiencing erasure within the gay and lesbian communities, transgender people of color experience even more exclusion and discrimination within their own communities. The LGBTQ community has often been considered a "White space," whereby political agendas tend to influence policy and practice centered on LGBTQ individuals who come from White, high-socioeconomic communities. Many of the health disparities and the most severe discrimination (e.g., murders that end in hate crimes) are highlighted within transgender communities of color; however, transgender people of color often feel as though they do not fit in.

Positive Experiences of Trans People Within the LGBQ Community

The cohesion of the LGBTQ movement since the Stonewall Riots has created a space for transgender and gender nonconforming people to build community and movements that otherwise may have been more difficult. Across the United States, LGBTQ community centers have emerged in many urban areas, and these centers have often created space for transgender specific support groups and social opportunities. Community centers have also been working with transgender people to conduct community education about transgender identity in order to create a more affirming place for transgender people to live.

Transgender individuals indicate two primary factors that have assisted them through their identity process: (1) having a sense of community and (2) feeling as though they belong. Many transgender individuals will reach out to other LGBTQ people on the Internet when they are first realizing a sense of their identity. Some younger transgender individuals will have access to LGBTQ groups within their school or community (e.g., GSAFE) that will help them meet other transgender individuals. These LGBTQ groups will often provide a sense of normalization of transgender identity and also a space where individuals can be their authentic selves.

In addition, LGBQ cisgender people have been great advocates and allies of transgender individuals. Much of the legislation that has attempted to exclude transgender people from LGB rights has been critiqued and shut down by LGBQ allies who resist the unfairness of a disconnected movement. Transgender people have been at the forefront of much of the policy movements for transgender rights, with LGBQ individuals fighting alongside to improve health and well-being for transgender individuals.

Stephanie Budge and shor salkas

See also Gender Identity; LGBTQ Community, Gender Dynamics in; LGBTQ People of Color and Discrimination; Transgender People and Resilience; Transphobia

Further Readings

Barr, S. M., Budge, S. L., & Adelson, J. L. (2016). Transgender community belongingness as a mediator between transgender self-categorization and wellbeing. *Journal of Counseling Psychology, 63,* 87–97.

Budge, S. L., Katz-Wise, S. L., Tebbe, E. N., Howard, K. A., Schneider, C. L., & Rodriguez, A. (2013). Transgender emotional and coping processes facilitative and avoidant coping throughout gender transitioning. *The Counseling Psychologist, 41*(4), 601–647. doi:10.1177/0011000011432753

Burdge, B. J. (2007). Bending gender, ending gender: Theoretical foundations for social work practice with the transgender community. *Social Work, 52*(3), 243–250.

Factor, R. J., & Rothblum, E. (2008). Exploring gender identity and community among three groups of transgender individuals in the United States: MTFs, FTMs, and genderqueers. *Health Sociology Review, 17*(3), 235–253.

Ghaziani, A. (2011). Post-gay collective identity construction. *Social Problems, 58*(1), 99–125. doi:10.1525/sp.2011.58.1.99

Monro, S. (2005). Activism: Tensions and alliances. In S. Monro (Ed.), *Gender politics* (pp. 91–118). Ann Arbor, MI: Pluto Press.

Stone, A. L. (2010). Diversity, dissent, and decision making: The challenge to LGBTQ politics. *GLQ: A Journal of Lesbian and Gay Studies, 16*(3), 465–472.

LGBTQ Community, Gender Dynamics in

For the lesbian, gay, bisexual, transgender, and queer (LGBTQ) community in the United States, gender has been a central organizing feature. Gay men and lesbians, for instance, experience gender nonconformity more often and in higher degrees in early childhood than their heterosexual counterparts. This can lead to more concern and anxiety about gender performance and affect interactions in places like schools, athletic teams, and other social events. In addition, LGBTQ individuals have historically been considered gender dysfunctional by religious, law enforcement, medical, and psychological institutions in the United States, resulting in persecution, alienation, and even, in some cases, incarceration. The American Psychological Association removed homosexuality from the *Diagnostic and Statistical Manual of Mental Disorders* in 1973 and removed any definition of homosexuality as a disorder in 1986. This entry describes how gender continues to play an integral role in the LGBTQ community.

The LGBTQ Community

The LGBTQ community, as it is known today, became visible in the United States in the early 1970s. Before that, LGBTQ individuals remained largely under the radar because homosexuality was illegal in most states. The Gay Liberation Movement is often cited as originating in the protests at the Stonewall Inn in 1969, when the local community aggressively resisted police intervention. Visibility increased exponentially as LGBTQ communities rose in mostly urban areas and open LGBTQ individuals became prominent national figures in activism (especially, but not limited to, HIV), sports, the creative arts, politics, and business.

Gender among the transgender community has been pathologized to a larger extent than perhaps any other segment of the LGBTQ community. Even within the LGBTQ community, there is a dearth of understanding and acceptance of transgender individuals. Often, this is epitomized by tokenization, such as using transgender individuals as performers or public figures without concomitant advocacy, education, and acceptance.

The use of *LGBTQ* as an acronym reflects a shift in gender awareness within the community. The utilization of *gay* as a term to describe the entire spectrum of sexual minority experience is restrictive, excluding lesbians, bisexual individuals, and transgender individuals. Therefore, the term *LGBTQ* articulates the diversity and differences among those considered sexual minorities in the United States.

External Perceptions of LGBTQ Gender

For generations, stereotypes of LGBTQ gender—for example, gay men as effeminate, outrageous, and physically meek and lesbians as masculine, ugly, and aggressive—have existed. These stereotypes are supported by representations of gay men and lesbians within popular media. Such stereotypes of gender feed homophobia and heterosexism and are often used to justify discriminatory public policies, including acting against same-sex relationships and LGBTQ adoption rights. Homophobia and heterosexism about gender performance can lead to more serious interpersonal conflicts.

Bullying has come to the spotlight in recent years, most notably bullying due to gender nonconformance. LGBTQ youth are more likely than non-LGBTQ peers to avoid school and other social arenas due to fear of harassment and bullying. In some states, LGBTQ middle school students reported missing at least 1 day of school in the past month due to fear.

While bullying may be more apparent, microaggressions about gender performance occur constantly. Microaggressions are subtle actions and words that denigrate, intentionally or not, persons due to a particular facet of their identity, such as LGBTQ sexuality or gender nonconformance. In these interactions, language such as "That's so gay" (connoting "bad" or "stupid") or even "Don't walk like a girl" (meaning effeminate and somehow wrong) serves to undermine the targeted individual's well-being. Nonverbal communication such as making a face or backing away from an LGBTQ or gender nonconforming individual is also a microaggression.

Such perceptions about gender nonconformity can lead to violence. Homophobic violence remains a concern globally, in particular the high rates of violence against transgender and gender nonconforming persons. In the United States, incidents of violence against transgender and gender nonconforming individuals include public stripping, beatings, immolation, and even murder. Because law enforcement across the country does not track gender data in a consistent manner, it is difficult to capture the full picture.

Such external perceptions and beliefs about gender in the LGBTQ community can be traumatic for LGBTQ individuals, resulting in debilitating wounds. However, there is a dearth of resources to address these. Clinical psychology can play an integral role in coping with sexuality and gender nonconformance.

Gender Within the LGBTQ Community

While external perceptions affect LGBTQ persons, there is a wide range of beliefs about gender within the LGBTQ community. When considering same-sex relationships, gender becomes instrumental in creating difference. Feminists have advocated for understanding the difference between gender and sex. Often, this is simplified as gender is how one acts and sex is biology. In practice, this separation is more complex, as sexual variation is not as binary as once thought.

For decades, the notions of "butch/femme" or "active/passive" were pervasive within the LGBTQ community. This pairing indicated that one partner was more masculine and the other more feminine (regardless of biological sex). These kinds of gendered performances are coded by culture and socioeconomic class; that is, members of similar groups understand specific ways of being masculine or feminine. Non–group members may also observe and react to the gendered performance but may not respond appropriately. In-group members will recognize the gender performance.

Masculinity is complicated within the LGBTQ community. Some gay and bisexual men are heteronormative in their beliefs about gender. In this case, they expect other gay and bisexual men to "act like real men" and will disparage more effeminate gay and bisexual men. Masculinity is always coded by culture and socioeconomic class. Some gay and bisexual men utilize this knowledge to portray masculinity as meant to communicate a different cultural background or socioeconomic class. Definitions of masculinity also change, as evidenced in the shift from a muscular, shaved body to a scruffy, less muscular look as a sign of masculinity in the gay community.

Other gay and bisexual men believe that masculinity is something to play with, and they purposefully deploy different kinds of masculinity depending on their intent. This includes gay and bisexual men who are flamboyant or effeminate. Some, such as the Radical Faeries, organize a network of communities that actively choose to resist gender norms and have created sanctuaries on the west and east coast of the United States, as well as in Australia and Italy.

Among lesbian and bisexual women too, masculinity is complex. More masculine women were once referred to as "butch" or "tomboy" and often were associated with partnering with a feminine woman, also known as a "femme." As with other gender performances, masculinity is coded through culture and socioeconomic class; therefore, individuals may choose to act out their masculinity as a person from another culture or socioeconomic class.

Femininity among lesbian and bisexual women has had multiple views. Within the LGBTQ community, feminine women are often seen as privileged through heteronormativity, and feminine lesbian and bisexual women struggle to differentiate their sexuality from that of their heterosexual counterparts. On the other hand, feminine lesbian and bisexual women can also be subversive in the utilization of heteronormative trappings, often by partnering with masculine women.

Transgender individuals learn gender codes at early ages and are forced to strategize about how, when, and where to comply or resist societal gender codes. As such, transgender persons have a wide gender vocabulary and a range of options along the spectrum of genders. Transgender persons have challenged and advanced the general knowledge about gender in the LGBTQ community. Transgender individuals differ widely in their gendering, including whether or how far to pursue surgical gender shifting. Transgender partner choice is also not prescribed; that is, people who identify as transgender women do not necessarily partner with heterosexual men. Instead, transgender individuals have a wide range of sexuality.

Within the LGBTQ community, gender consists of a complex assemblage of acts, cultural codes, nuanced reading, and performances made visible through interaction. LGBTQ people utilize a wide range of tactics and have vastly different beliefs about gender. The LGBTQ community's movement regarding gender seems less about categories and more about possibilities.

Beyond Categories: Queer, Trans*, and Gender Nonconforming

In the 1990s, queer politics and identity emerged as an organizing tool in the HIV epidemic. While at first a derogative term, *queer* came to exemplify a resistance to societal norms and values about a wide range of subjects including sexuality. Activists, academics, and community members chose to identify as queer to signify their disavowal of ideas such as what is good, what is proper, and what is acceptable. Queer politics were central in the expansion and undoing of gender norms.

Within the LGBTQ community, the movement for transgender rights has expanded policy, education, and knowledge on gender. Like other identity movements, transgender rights activists have recognized the importance of names. To accommodate the range of possibilities for transgender individuals, the transgender rights movement uses *trans** or just *trans* as a means of self-definition.

Focus on the transgender community has also enriched knowledge on gender nonconforming individuals as a whole. Gender nonconforming individuals can be of any sexuality, but they resist the socially valued standard for gender performance (i.e., masculine for men, feminine for women). This has resulted in an examination of how all gender nonconforming individuals experience discrimination, as well as processes of adjustment.

Research Directions

Psychological research on gender in the LGBTQ community looks at both perceptions external to the community and the dynamics within the community. These have included the examination of discrimination, violence, social roles, conformity, development, adjustment, health, and the intersections of race, culture, and nationality with gender in the LGBTQ community. Psychologists have extensively looked at the impact of HIV/AIDS, especially among gay and bisexual men. Research on transgender populations has increased since 2010, with more promising research on the horizon. In addition, there remains a dearth of research that utilizes intersectional identity as the center; instead, much of the research focuses on race or gender, socioeconomic class, sexuality, or some subset of these identities. Accordingly, it is crucial for future research to examine intersectionalities in all aspects of the LGBTQ community in order to address all the dynamics that occur.

Andrew Spieldenner

See also HIV/AIDS; Internalized Heterosexism; LGBTQ Community, Experiences of Transgender People in

Further Readings

Butler, J. (2006). *Gender trouble: Feminism and the subversion of identity.* New York, NY: Routledge.

Clarke, V., Ellis, S. J., Peel. E., & Riggs, D. W. (Eds.). (2010). *Lesbian, gay, bisexual, trans and queer psychology: An introduction.* Cambridge, MA: Cambridge University Press.

Diaz, R. M. (1997). *Latino gay men and HIV: Culture, sexuality, and risk behavior.* New York, NY: Routledge.

Golden, C. (1996). What's in a name? Sexual self-identification among women. In R. C. Savin-Williams & K. M. Cohen (Eds.), *The lives of lesbians, gays, and bisexuals: Children to adults* (pp. 229–249). Fort Worth, TX: Harcourt Brace.

Herek, G. M. (1996). "Some of my best friends": Intergroup contact, concealable stigma, and heterosexuals' attitudes toward gay men and lesbians. *Personality and Social Psychology Bulletin, 22,* 412–424.

Hill, S. E., & Flom, R. (2007). 18- and 24-month-olds' discrimination of gender-consistent and inconsistent activities. *Infant Behavior and Development, 30,* 168–173.

Nadal, K. L. (2013). *That's so gay! Microaggressions and the lesbian, gay, bisexual and transgender community.* Washington, DC: American Psychological Association Books.

Parent, M. C., DeBlaere, C., & Moradi, B. (2013). Approaches to research on intersectionality: Perspectives on gender, LGBT, and racial/ethnic identities. *Sex Roles, 68,* 639–645.

Stryker, S. (2008). *Transgender history.* Berkeley, CA: Seal Press.

Toomey, R. B., Ryan, C., Diaz, R. M., Card, N. A., & Russell, S. T. (2010). Gender non-conforming lesbian, gay, bisexual, and transgender youth: School victimization and young adult social adjustment. *Developmental Psychology, 46*(6), 1580–1589.

Yep, G. A., Lovaas, K., & Elia, J. P. (Eds.). (2003). *Queer theory and communication: From disciplining queers to queering the discipline(s).* Binghamton, NY: Harrington Park Press.

LGBTQ People of Color and Discrimination

Lesbian, gay, bisexual, transgender, and queer (LGBTQ) people of color experience multiple sources of societal discrimination in the world. While LGBTQ people face heterosexism, homophobia, biphobia, and transphobia in society, LGBTQ people of color may experience racism and other oppressions in addition to LGBTQ discrimination. For instance, Beverly Greene termed the oppression that African American lesbians face as a *triple jeopardy* of heterosexism, racism, and sexism. In this entry, the microaggressions and overt discrimination that LGBTQ people of color experience are described, as well as the resilience that LGBTQ people of color may develop as they navigate multiple oppressions. In addition, the discrimination experiences that LGBTQ people of color have and liberation movements that LGBTQ people of color participate in around the world are described.

Microaggressions and Overt Discrimination Against LGBTQ People of Color

In 1970, psychiatrist Chester Pierce described *microaggressions* as the brief, insidious, everyday experiences of verbal and nonverbal discrimination that African Americans face in society. Microaggressions have an influence on the mental health of historically marginalized groups as the oppression can be not only a regular occurrence but also subtle and difficult to identify as discrimination in the moment. Psychologist Derald Wing Sue further developed Pierce's work in the counseling and psychological field and used *microaggressions* to describe the everyday, small experiences of discrimination that could also influence the counselor-client relationship. In 2013, Kevin Nadal, in his text *That's So Gay! Microaggressions and the Lesbian, Gay, Bisexual, and Transgender Community*, and Kimber Shelton, in a research study, further applied the microaggressions historically marginalized groups experience in counseling and psychology to describe the experiences of brief, multiple, and everyday encounters with discrimination that LGBTQ people of color have. Each of these scholars asserted the insidiousness of microaggressions in terms of the impact on mental health, as well as the institutional systems that support and reify environments where microaggressions can occur. For example, a transgender Latina woman may hear microaggressive comments at work such as "You look good for a woman" or "Are you in the right bathroom?" In 2011, Kimberly Balsam and colleagues published the LGBT People of Color Microaggressions Scale to encourage further research on the experiences that LGBTQ people of color have of racism within LGBTQ communities, heterosexism within communities of people of color, and racism in interpersonal relationships (e.g., dating, friendship). Initial research suggested that African Americans and Latina/os scored lower than Asian Americans on this scale and men had higher rates of microaggression than women, whereas gay men and lesbians experienced higher rates of microaggression than bisexual men and women.

LGBTQ people of color experience microaggressions that emerge from overt discrimination in society. This includes legal, policy, and other systemic discriminations that influence the lives of LGBTQ people of color. The same transgender Latina woman may be at risk of being fired due to her gender identity and gender expression if she happens to live in a city or state that does not have employment nondiscrimination policies that protect the employment rights of LGBTQ people. A large-scale national research study examining the experiences transgender people had of societal discrimination found that transgender people of color had more negative health outcomes than White transgender people across many domains: education, housing, employment, health care access, and income. The intersection of microaggressions and overt discrimination set the stage for negative mental and physical health outcomes. For instance, when transgender people of color are unable to access employment opportunities at a living wage, then they also are likely unable to access general and transgender specific health care. Without employment and health care access, many transgender people of color may turn to survival sex work (i.e., trading sex for food, shelter, or other needs) to generate the financial resources to obtain needed health care and housing. Research has also suggested that transgender people of color are at risk for HIV infection and homelessness. Discrimination in the lives of LGBTQ people of color is not limited to one particular stage of life, yet it is also often shaped by a person's particular life stage. LGBTQ youth of color and aging individuals experience racist and heterosexist discrimination, and these specific acts may manifest very differently (e.g., First Nations lesbian youth experiencing heterosexism from a teacher vs. an elder African American bisexual man experiencing racism in an assisted living facility).

LGBTQ People of Color and Individual and Community Resilience

Research has suggested that resilience is an important construct to consider when seeking to understand the lives of LGBTQ people of color. LGBTQ people of color may develop individual sources of resilience, such as having pride in one's racial/ethnic and LGBTQ identity, connecting with LGBTQ-affirming people, cultivating hope for the future, and—for some—practicing religion/spirituality. There may also be community sources of resilience that LGBTQ people of color find supportive. In 2012, Sel Hwahng and colleagues noted that communities of LGBTQ people of color may develop "thick trust" (e.g., friendships, social networks) with one another through multiple interactions, connecting one another with social support and other resources for LGBTQ people of color, and providing strategies on how to navigate challenging systems (e.g., health care, housing).

Other research has noted the importance of community resilience to individual sexual orientation identity development. For instance, in many White, Western models of sexual orientation development, there is a focus on the individual "coming out," whereby sexual orientation identity disclosure to family, friends, and/or work colleagues is prized as a critical point of identity development. This coming out process has also been extensively studied for majority, White LGBTQ people, connecting sexual orientation identity disclosure with increased well-being. For LGBTQ people of color, however, identity disclosure may not be a developmental point on the way to increased wellness. LGBTQ people of color may experience more resilience and wellness in their racial/ethnic straight communities and may not feel the need to disclose their LGBTQ identity. An example might be a Latino, queer, cisgender man who is out in his LGBTQ community but when he visits his family in Argentina may choose not to disclose his identity. It may be more important for his mental health to maintain connections with his family, which may increase his resilience, rather than risk rupturing those relationships. In other words, he may not view his queer identity disclosure in opposition to his racial/ethnic ties to his family and/or community and may be comfortable holding both spaces with different identity disclosure strategies. For other LGBTQ people of color, it may be a threat to their resilience that they do not feel safe disclosing their LGBTQ identity to their families and/or racial/ethnic communities. Shannon J. Miller studied lesbian identity disclosure of African American lesbians to their mothers and found that participants were often greeted with a "Don't ask, don't tell" response from their mothers, indicating that their mothers were accepting of them but asked their daughters not to share with extended families. Scholars have hypothesized that this may be due to families and communities of color being concerned about their LGBTQ children experiencing not only racial oppression but also LGBTQ oppression.

There has also been scholarship examining the influence of religious and spiritual beliefs as a source of resilience for LGBTQ people of color. Religion and spirituality for LGBTQ people of color may be a complex area that has been a source of both discrimination or harm and resilience. Research on the resilience that transgender people of color experience while navigating transgender oppression has suggested that being connected with spiritual beliefs is a source of coping that increases well-being and the ability to navigate anti-transgender prejudice. Studies have examined the religious and spiritual coping of African American gay men living with HIV/AIDS, finding that the use of religious and spiritual coping with regard to their racial/ethnic and sexual orientation, along with their HIV/AIDS status, involved some dissonance in integrating these identities and experiences but ultimately increased well-being.

Scholars in anthropology and gender studies have also researched the elevated status that queer and transgender people often had in the precolonization religious and spiritual traditions of communities of people of color. Although communities of transgender people of color have been largely decimated in terms of their societal value around the world after colonization, some of them have persisted. For instance, the *hijra* are the transgender people of South Asia, who often live in large communities where there is an emphasis on taking care of one another as chosen family and bringing blessings when births or marriages occur. Colonization histories have similarly destroyed queer histories of fluid sexuality orientations around the world. For example, in Hinduism, there are numerous stories of sexual and gender fluidity.

Liberation Movements of LGBTQ People of Color

LGBTQ people of color have been building a variety of movements around the world in response to multiple experiences of discrimination. LGBTQ people of color have created language movements, and often reinvent language to describe their sexual orientation and gender identities, such as *same-gender loving* to describe an LGBQ identity, *stud* to describe a lesbian identity, and *masculine of center* to describe a transgender identity. Also, in 2014, the Black Lives Matter movement in the United States had strong constituents of queer- and transgender-led organizations that demanded an intersectional analysis. Organizations such as Solutions Not Punishment in Atlanta, Georgia, have challenged institutional and structural racism in addition to heterosexism and transphobia. The Brown Boi Project in Oakland, California, developed online resources and a text advocating for the needs of transgender men of color.

In addition to U.S.-based movements of LGBTQ people of color, there are also international movements that have existed over time, often in the face of significant danger. For example, anti-LGBTQ laws have increased in countries on the African continent, such as Nigeria and Uganda, and are often fueled by Western-based Christian missionaries. Some of these anti-LGBTQ laws have penalties ranging from imprisonment to death for "homosexual acts." The International Gay & Lesbian Human Rights Commission and International Lesbian, Gay, Bisexual, Trans and Intersex Association chapters around the world work actively on issues of LGBTQ people of color, challenging anti-LGBTQ policies and laws.

Anneliese A. Singh

See also Dual Minority Status; Heterosexism; Intersectional Identities; Microaggressions; Racial Discrimination, Sexual Orientation–Based

Further Readings

Chin, S. (2010). *The other side of paradise: Memoir about growing up poor, half-black and half-Chinese, and lesbian in Jamaica*. New York, NY: Scribner.

Cole, B., & Han, L. (2011). *Freeing ourselves: A guide to health and self love for brown bois*. Oakland, CA: Brown Boi Project.

Greene, B. (1997). Lesbian women of color: Triple jeopardy. *Journal of Lesbian Studies: Classics in Lesbian Studies, 1*(1 [Special issue]), 49–60.

Pierce, C. (1970). Offensive mechanisms. In F. Barbour (Ed.), *The Black seventies* (pp. 265–282). Boston, MA: Porter Sargent.

LGBTQQ-Affirmative Psychotherapy

Lesbian, gay, bisexual, transgender, queer, and questioning (LGBTQQ)–affirmative psychotherapy emerged in response to the rise of the gay rights movement in the late 1960s. For many decades, the mental health profession considered any sexual orientation apart from heterosexuality to be a form of psychopathology. This was true until the mid-1970s, when the diagnostic labels for homosexuality were removed by major mental health organizations. Recognition of normative variability in gender identity has been slower to emerge, but affirmative therapies for people whose gender identity is different from their sex assigned at birth have also been developed. LGBTQQ-affirmative psychotherapy is based on one basic premise: There are varieties of sexual orientations and gender identities that are normal variants of human development. This entry describes the core ideas and development of LGBTQQ-affirmative therapies, provides an overview of affirmative psychotherapy, and uses a case example to illustrate the experience of a person in LGBTQQ-affirmative therapy.

LGBTQQ-Affirmative Therapies

Evelyn Hooker was the first American researcher to affirm that gay men showed no more evidence of a mental health disorder than their heterosexual peers. Her work is consistent with the work of Alfred Kinsey, whose research on sexuality in the United States showed that human sexuality was on a continuum from exclusively heterosexual to exclusively homosexual and that many individuals' sexual orientation resided on a continuum between those two poles. Given the increasing evidence that there is nothing inherently pathological about homosexuality or bisexuality, treatments for these "disorders" became increasingly suspect.

Affirmative treatments that have developed from the basic idea that there is normal variation of sexual orientations and gender identities have drawn from several therapeutic orientations. Feminist, client-centered/existential, and, more recently, cognitive behavioral psychologies have been the primary perspectives to study and promote affirmative therapies. Affirmative approaches in psychodynamic or psychoanalytic therapy have also been proposed. LGBTQQ affirmative therapy is not associated with any single theoretical psychotherapeutic orientation.

Another core idea in LGBTQQ-affirmative therapies is that there are important acute and chronic stressors for LGBTQQ people (hereafter referred to as "sexual and gender minorities") that place them at greater risk for certain mental and behavioral health problems, mostly mediated by environmental factors and accounted for in minority stress models. Therefore, from an affirmative stance, it is clear that there is nothing inherently pathological about being a member of a sexual or gender minority but this population is more vulnerable to certain psychological problems, including higher rates of depression and anxiety, as a result of unique environmental stressors such as social stigma, discrimination, and internalized oppression. There have been similar findings on the vulnerability of people from ethnic and racial minorities, and these differences in vulnerability to certain behavioral health problems are generally considered to result from the increased stress of being a member of a minority group.

Development of Affirmative Therapies

Prior to declassifying homosexuality as psychopathology, psychotherapeutic interventions had already been developed under the presumption that sexual and gender minorities were essentially mentally disordered. Behaviorists had used aversive conditioning procedures, for example, showing gay men erotic photos of men and providing an electric shock until the participants turned to an image of a woman, at which point of time the shock was removed. Such treatments rarely produced changes in sexual behavior and never actually changed the sexual orientation. Not only did these treatments fail to deliver the promised outcomes, but also many men and women who underwent such treatments went on to experience depression, increased anxieties, and sexual dysfunction as a result of the treatments.

Overview of Affirmative Psychotherapy

Since psychotherapists practice from a variety of theoretical orientations including psychodynamic, behavioral, and humanistic, therapy that is affirmative of sexual and gender minorities is not rooted in any one of those particular modes of treatment. Rather, affirmative treatment is defined largely by the ethical and professional guidelines put forth by a variety of professional organizations such as the American Psychological Association and the National Association of Social Workers. These guidelines articulate ethically and professionally competent use of language, the exercise of nondiscrimination in professional practice, the right of sexual and gender minority clients to exercise self-determination, and recognition of the deleterious effects of social stigma and discrimination on the mental health of sexual and gender minorities.

LGBTQQ-affirmative psychotherapy relies on culturally competent use of language that reflects the use of nonstigmatizing, LGBTQQ-normative words, while also responding empathically and respectfully to the ways in which clients identify themselves. Professional associations have identified contemporarily preferred terms that reflect competent and ethical practice with sexual and gender minorities (e.g., using *lesbians* and *gay men* rather than *homosexuals*). However, LGBTQQ-affirmative psychotherapy must respect the self-determination and self-identification of clients, taking into account the variability of acceptable language choices across generational cohorts and between subpopulations. For example, during much of the 20th century, *queer* was a term of derision, and as a result, many sexual and gender minority older adults continue to consider the word pejorative and insulting. However, more recently, the word *queer* has been embraced by many who have come to reclaim it as a means of confronting heteronormative assumptions and claiming self-empowerment. Similarly, there are clear professional guidelines regarding language about gender identity (e.g., preferring the term *transgender* to *transgendered*). However, an increasing number of individuals deploy alternative terminology for their gender identity, such as *genderqueer*, potentially rejecting the presumption of a gender binary. LGBTQQ-affirmative psychotherapy is predicated on an understanding of the prevailing professional norms regarding the language used about sexual and gender minority individuals, communities, and concerns, but truly affirmative psychotherapy requires therapists to competently assess the words clients use to identify themselves. This includes asking clients what pronouns they prefer, rather than assuming gender pronouns that correspond to social assumptions based on gender presentation or the perception of the therapist. Affirmative therapy requires a familiarity with the history and social context of stigmatizing and affirming language choices, as well as intentional respect for the self-determination of clients to identify in ways most meaningful to them.

LGBTQQ-affirmative therapy targets interventions toward mitigating the harmful effects of a hostile social environment for sexual and gender minorities. As stated earlier, the basic premise of affirmative psychotherapy is that variations in sexual orientation and gender identity are normal variants of the human condition and not indicative of a mental or behavioral disorder. Therefore, therapists practicing from this standpoint affirm sexual and gender minority clients as productive members of society without having a need to change their sexual orientation or gender identity.

Experiencing the stress of societal prejudice, discrimination, or, in some cases, physical threat increases the vulnerability of some sexual and gender minority individuals to developing mental health problems. Such problems are related to sexual and gender minority status only in that the individual may not have developed such problems had they not been discriminated against or mistreated in some way due to their sexual orientation or gender identity. Individuals from sexual and gender minorities do not need to have been direct victims of discrimination or violence to have increased stress and distress. The pervasive attitudes of the dominant culture, including attempts to legislate discriminatory practices, an assumed right to talk about sexual and gender minorities as if they are "other" and not full members of society, or, in a milder form, the absence of role models in popular media, can affect those whose sexual orientation or gender identity differs from the dominant culture.

Unlike other minorities, sexual minority individuals also face potential bias and rejection from their own families of origin. Certainly, many people have familial problems, but rarely are people disenfranchised from their families due to ethnicity, race, or socioeconomic status. For example, given that sexual minority individuals are often the only members of their families with their particular sexual orientation, they can face rejection by parents, siblings, or extended family for being different. This is particularly true for those from highly conservative religious backgrounds, who may be seen as sinful or defying the laws of a particular deity or religious doctrine. Therefore, the affirmative psychotherapist works with clients to cope with distress that is related to minority status and that may contribute to other emotional or behavioral problems. Affirmative psychotherapy employs interventions to minimize the negative effects of a stigmatizing and hostile social environment.

Affirmative therapists have the challenge of finding the proper balance between recognizing when sexual or gender minority status is relevant to a client's problems and when it has little to do with the problem presented. As normal variations of human sexuality and gender identity, LGBTQQ statuses reflect only in part the complexity and richness of any particular person. Mistakes in therapy can occur when insensitive or biased therapists assume that being a member of a sexual or gender minority is, in itself, a problem and become inappropriately focused on this when the client is troubled by unrelated concerns.

However, LGBTQQ-positive therapists can also overemphasize the centrality of stigma and discrimination in responding to a client's report of distress. Sexual and gender minority clients often present symptoms or concerns that may be primarily not related to their LGBTQQ identity, and focusing too exclusively on the deleterious outcomes of social stigma may overlook more direct causes and solutions in many circumstances. Equally hazardous is the possibility of underemphasizing the pervasive impact of stigma and discrimination. While client complaints of work-related stress or chronic depression may not, at first glance, include content directly attributable to stigma and discrimination, even supportive therapists may miss issues of internalized homonegativity or transphobia if they simply assume that sexual or gender minority status is only central when explicitly identified as the problem. It is most appropriate to consider the experience of each client and to assess where problems exist and where they do not. LGBTQQ-affirmative therapy requires the skilled assessment and identification of how salient sexual and gender minority statuses are to a particular client and a specific case presentation.

A majority of psychotherapists come from the predominant culture or, in other words, are likely to identify as heterosexual and cisgender (i.e., not transgender). This is simply a matter of numbers, since more people identify as heterosexual and cisgender. Psychotherapists from the dominant culture pursuing the practice of LGBTQQ-affirmative therapy need first to be aware of their own privilege as a member of the majority culture, the group that tends to make the rules for everyone else. There are hierarchies of privilege. White heterosexual men earn more money than women on their jobs, are not routinely victims of police violence, and can freely assert their sexuality without fear of ostracism or violence. Thus, White heterosexual men are typically free to go wherever they want, whenever they want, without needing to fear for their safety or integrity. White heterosexual women are more vulnerable by virtue of being women; that is, they may be more likely to be the victims of sexual violence or face an uphill battle to achieve professional stature and income security similar to what their male counterparts get. Men and women of color have increased vulnerability to societal prejudice and systemic racism. Therefore, psychotherapists who identify as heterosexual will have varying degrees of privilege based on their gender, ethnicity, and so forth.

Stating that one holds certain privileges does not imply that one does not have challenges to overcome in life but simply that one can take for granted certain advantages that others cannot. Affirmative psychotherapists need to be aware of their own privilege. For example, heterosexual persons do not need to make a decision about disclosing their heterosexuality to family or friends; it is assumed and typically expected. This is a privilege that those who are members of sexual and gender minorities do not have. Privilege does not imply that any individual has had a particularly easy life, and this is often a misperception when those from a privileged group are facing unemployment, financial stress, or other life problems. Nevertheless, during the same hard times experienced throughout society (e.g., during national economic troubles), as a group, those from the dominant culture will likely have greater potential to advance than those from a minority group who face discrimination.

Everyone has privilege, and everyone has challenges. Being a member of a sexual or gender minority does not remove certain privileges provided by society and culture. For example, a White gay man has access to more privilege than, for example, most African American lesbian women. Being a member of a sexual or gender minority also does not qualify one as an expert on those communities. Behavioral health practitioners who are members of sexual or gender minorities still need professional preparation to work with this population and need to be aware of their own values and biases. For example, a lesbian psychotherapist may have experienced a great deal of freedom and joy by disclosing her sexual orientation and becoming involved with community activism groups, but her experience will not necessarily generalize to the experience of all the clients she sees. She may work with clients who wish to remain hidden and not disclose their sexual minority status. The affirmative psychotherapist would certainly need to understand how much internalized homonegativity or fear influences a client's decision, but it would be inappropriate to push an agenda that "coming out" is always a positive experience.

Case Example

Because LGBTQQ-affirmative therapy crosses therapeutic orientations, it makes sense to describe some basic experiences that a client being seen by an affirmative therapist would experience. To bring this to life, a fictional client, Jeri, will serve as an example. Jeri, a 23-year-old client, saw Dr. L.Z. for therapy. At the intake appointment, Jeri was required to complete paperwork. Jeri was pleased to see that the paperwork allowed an option for "other" or "do not define" in listing gender rather than simply saying "male" or "female." In addition to gender, Jeri also had the option to identify as transgender. Likewise, the intake form listed relationship status as an open-ended question rather than a forced choice of "single," "married," "divorced," or "widowed." A brief personal history sheet also allowed for options to talk about "parents or parental figures," and the question "Who is your current family?" accompanied questions of biological family history. The forms were also free of any potentially offensive words such as the phrase *homosexual experiences*.

Just like Dr. L.Z.'s intake forms, Dr. L.Z. was very open and matter of fact during discussions of sexuality. Dr. L.Z. asked if Jeri was currently in a relationship and did not use any gender pronouns to predetermine the kind of relationship. The same strategy was used in asking about past relationships. Dr. L.Z. then asked, "Do you typically date men, women, or both?" Jeri, who identified as genderqueer, did not like to put former relationships in a gender binary box, and Dr. L.Z. was very accepting when Jeri said, "I prefer to date people." Dr. L.Z. recognized that Jeri's concerns were about dealing with anxiety and mild depression and not about sexual orientation.

Throughout treatment, Jeri was able to talk about feelings of isolation and sadness that were a result of living in a new city and beginning a new job. Dr. L.Z. focused on what Jeri presented as the connections between emotions and context, without suggesting that sexual orientation was a factor. However, when Jeri was particularly sad over the Thanksgiving holiday, Dr. L.Z. recognized not only that Jeri was far away from biological family but also that the biological family had been critical and rejecting and that there were other functions of the holiday (e.g., having a nice meal with people one cares about) that were missing because Jeri had not gotten to know anyone close enough to receive a dinner invitation.

Dr. L.Z. was alert as a therapist and would question Jeri when certain self-critical statements sounded as though they were coming from internalization of a negative stereotype. In one session, for example, Jeri made frequent references to being "very selfish." Dr. L.Z., who never experienced Jeri as particularly selfish or self-centered, asked how Jeri had formed that conclusion. It became clear that it was Jeri's biological parents who repeatedly said that LGBTQQ people were "self-centered" and "narcissistically in love with themselves." While Jeri rejected this notion as applying to LGBTQQ people in general, Jeri had internalized the idea and made harsh self-judgments and frequently interpreted making reasonable requests of others as being self-centered.

Jeri's problems were relatively uncomplicated, and Jeri was seen for only a brief course of therapy, lasting only 4 months. With the help of Dr. L.Z., Jeri confronted the anxiety and approached social situations that held hope for making new friendships in a new city. Dr. L.Z. also helped Jeri differentiate when difficulties on the new job were the logical consequence of being new at something rather than a personal failure. Over the course of therapy, Jeri's anxiety was greatly reduced, and Jeri did not report feeling depressed.

Christopher R. Martell and Mark E. Williams

See also Coming Out Processes for LGBTQ Youth; Coming Out Processes for Transgender People; Couples Therapy With Same-Sex Couples; Feminist Therapy; Gay Men; Lesbian, Gay, and Bisexual Experiences of Aging; Lesbians; Queer

Further Readings

American Psychological Association. (2012). Guidelines for psychological practice with lesbian, gay, and bisexual clients. *American Psychologist, 67(1)*, 10–42.

Bieschke, K. J., Perez, R. M., & DeBord K. A. (Eds.). (2006). *Handbook of counseling and psychotherapy with lesbian, gay, bisexual, and transgender clients.* Washington, DC: American Psychological Association.

Bigner, J. J., & Wetchler, J. L. (2012). *Handbook of LGBT-affirmative couple and family therapy.* New York, NY: Routledge.

Coleman, E., Bockting, W., Botzer, M., Cohen-Kettenis, P., DeCuypere, G., Feldman, J., Fraser, L., . . . Zuker, K. (2011). Standards of care for the health of transsexual, transgender, and gender nonconforming people, Version 7. *International Journal of Transgenderism, 13,* 165–232.

Hunter, S., & Hickerson, J. C. (2003). *Affirmative practice: Understanding and working with lesbian, gay, bisexual, and transgender persons.* Washington, DC: National Association of Social Workers Press.

Lev, A. I. (2004). *Transgender emergence: Therapeutic guidelines for working with gender-variant people and their families.* New York, NY: Haworth Press.

Long-Term Care

Long-term care involves medical and nonmedical personal care provided to individuals who have difficulty caring for themselves independently. People of all ages require long-term care for a multitude of different reasons, including chronic and terminal illness, traumatic injury, developmental disabilities, congenital abnormalities, serious mental health conditions, and general declines in physical abilities as a result of normal aging processes. Long-term care can take place in a variety of settings, including one's own home, group homes, or other types of long-term care communities. The term itself is misleading as *long-term care* can refer to care provided for either a short or a long period of time. In the United States, health insurance and government-sponsored financial need-based programs sometimes cover part of the expense of long-term care. However, many older Americans who live above the federal poverty line often pay for such care out of pocket at an immense cost. A small percentage of Americans also purchase long-term care insurance; however, such programs vary widely in their coverage and can be quite expensive. Overall, unpaid family members provide most long-term care within individuals' private homes. This entry explores various types of long-term care, with a special emphasis on sexual and gender identity expression.

Sexuality, Sexual Orientation, and Gender Identity in Long-Term Care

Most long-term care facilities do not have policies with regard to sexual expression and/or gender identity. In addition, most long-term care staff do not receive training regarding sexuality as part of their initial or ongoing professional development. As a result, long-term care residents are often restricted in their right to express themselves sexually both with themselves (i.e., masturbation) and/or with intimate partners. Lesbian, gay, bisexual, and transgender adults face particular difficulty regarding sexual and gender expression. For fear of discrimination and potential physical abuse, some lesbian, gay, and bisexual residents opt to conceal their sexual orientation. Some gender nonconforming and/or trans identified older adults are so fearful of how they will be treated or mistreated in long-term care facilities that they attempt to conceal their trans identity and/or begin the process of de-transitioning. Even if they do not conceal their true gender identity, some trans and gender nonconforming adults are denied gender affirming care and may even be forced to room with someone of a different gender.

Community-Based Long-Term Care

Community-based long-term care programs differ from county to county and state to state. Such programs are often supplemented by state and local government funds and provided by both for-profit and not-for-profit social service agencies, such as local corporations on aging. Services provided by such programs include home meal deliveries, adult day care, in-home health aid services, case management, adult and child protective services, transportation services, senior community centers and social activities, and respite care. Respite care is short-term care provided to an individual to allow caregivers to have a rest and/or attend to their own needs while not having to provide care for their loved one. These services, including respite care, are often provided based on medical and/or financial need, but they can also be acquired via private funds.

Long-Term Care Facilities

Long-term care encompasses a large, profit-driven, highly regulated industry within the United States, including adult foster care, boarding homes, independent and assisted living facilities, nursing homes, continuing care retirement communities, and long-term care hospice facilities. These facilities provide various services depending on the emotional and physical needs of their residents. Not all long-term care facilities can provide comprehensive nursing and medical care; therefore, individuals may have to transition through various communities as they age and become increasingly dependent.

Boarding Homes

Boarding homes, also known as residential facilities, care homes, or group homes, are smaller private homes, usually with 20 or fewer residents. Individuals residing in group homes may occupy a private or shared dormitory. Residents receive round-the-clock personal care and meals; however, medical and nursing care is most often not provided. As medical needs increase, residents will often receive services from visiting home care agencies or transition to nursing homes where medical care can be provided 24 hours per day.

Independent and Assisted Living Facilities

Independent and assisted living facilities are typically occupied by older Americans who require some assistance with activities of daily living but are not yet at a point where they require 24-hour care. Within these facilities or communities, ranging vastly in size, residents typically occupy private rooms with shared bathrooms or apartments with private amenities. Some services, such as three meals per day, are included in the daily room and board fee, whereas others, such as medication management, are an additional cost. Usually, services within these facilities can be increased as the residents require additional assistance with age. The cost of independent and assisted living facilities is not covered by health insurance but is paid via private funds and/or long-term care insurance.

Nursing Homes

Nursing homes, referred to as long-term care facilities, provide 24-hour personal and medical care for residents. Nursing homes often provide two types of care: (1) short-term acute rehabilitation (fewer than 3 hours of rehabilitation per day) and (2) long-term custodial care. Typically, short-term rehabilitation is covered either in part or whole by medical insurance, whereas long-term custodial care is paid for either privately or via a state government–sponsored program for those with low incomes. Nursing homes also differ in size and can be either privately owned or owned by a local municipality. Some nursing homes and assisted living facilities offer locked units specifically designated for individuals with Alzheimer's disease or other types of dementia.

Continuing Care Retirement Communities

These communities often combine independent and assisted living facilities with nursing homes, providing typically three different levels of care to their residents. Such communities allow for residents to buy into the community at one level and then transfer to the other levels of care as needed.

Long-Term Care Hospice Facilities

Although rare, long-term care hospice facilities exist. These facilities are typically privately paid or based on financial need. According to Medicare guidelines, one qualifies for hospice care with a prognosis of 6 or fewer months. Most inpatient hospice units provide for short-term symptom management, with the goal of transferring the patients back to their home or to a more appropriate long-term care facility once the symptoms are better managed. Long-term care hospice facilities, however, allow residents to stay for typically 3 to 6 months or until their death. For example, Sacred Heart Free Home in the city of Philadelphia, Pennsylvania, is a free hospice home funded by the Catholic Church for individuals with a cancer diagnosis and financial need. Also, some veterans' hospitals operate inpatient hospice units that allow residents to remain long term. Last, some inpatient hospice units provide residents with upscale, private rooms for which they are able to pay for room and board privately, even if they do not have active symptoms to be managed.

Stephanie C. Chando and Eli R. Green

See also Aging and Gender: Overview; Aging and Mental Health; Community and Aging; Disability and Aging; End-of-Life and Existential Issues; Gender Socialization in Aging; Identity Development and Aging; Isolation and Aging; Lesbian, Gay, and Bisexual Experiences of Aging; Men and Aging; Sexuality and Aging; Stigma of Aging; Transgender Experiences of Aging; Women and Aging

Further Readings

Auldridge, A., Tamar-Mattis, A., Kennedy, S., Ames, E., & Tobin, H. J. (2012, May). *Improving the lives of transgender older adults: Recommendations for policy and practice.* Washington, DC: Services and Advocacy for GLBT Elders & National Center for Transgender Equality. Retrieved from http://www.lgbtagingcenter.org/resources/pdfs/TransAgingPolicyReportFull.pdf

Chernof, B. (2011). The three spheres of aging in America: The Affordable Care Act takes on long-term-care reform for the 21st century. *Generations, 35*(1), 45–49.

Doll, G. A. (2012). *Sexuality and long-term care: Understanding and supporting the needs of older adults.* Baltimore, MD: Health Professions Press.

National Institutes of Health. (2015). *Long-term care.* Bethesda, MD: Author. Retrieved from http://nihseniorhealth.gov/longtermcare/whatislongtermcare/01.html

Low Testosterone

Psychological studies investigating the hormone testosterone and its associated social behaviors, cognitive effects, and personality traits commonly define testosterone levels in a relative sense.

As such, low testosterone is defined here as *low* relative to other members of a given sample and excludes individuals with atypically low levels due to medical conditions. Generally, testosterone is associated with a variety of human social behaviors, including dominance, concern for status, and cooperation. Specifically, low testosterone is implicated in attenuated dominance, diminished proclivity to seek and maintain high status, and increased cooperative behavior.

Variability of Testosterone Levels

Baseline testosterone levels vary naturally between individuals but also within an individual, with testosterone rising at the onset of puberty and decreasing in old age—particularly among males. Testosterone levels can also vary within an individual on a smaller time frame based on social context (e.g., winning or losing a competition can result in temporary changes in testosterone levels). The largest difference in testosterone levels is between the sexes, with males having seven to eight times the amount of circulating testosterone found in females. For example, low levels of testosterone in a given male individual may still be equal to or exceed the average levels of testosterone in a sample of females.

Relationship to Social Behavior

Much like in nonhuman animals, testosterone has been linked to aggression in humans, with lower testosterone levels being associated with lower levels of aggression. However, among humans, such findings are inconsistent and, when present, show smaller effects in comparison with nonhuman animal models. Often, aggression is interpreted as a manifestation of dominance. Dominance is a general proclivity to acquire and maintain higher rank within a social hierarchy. Behavioral displays of dominance are varied but may include assertiveness, intimidation, coercion, extended stare duration, body posturing that conveys superiority, and, in some contexts, physical violence. From this perspective, the role of testosterone becomes clearer, as the relationship between it and dominance, rather than aggression per se, is more robust. (Two predominant theories that attempt to explain this relationship are the challenge hypothesis and the biosocial theory of status.)

Typically, individuals with low baseline testosterone exhibit less dominance than their higher-testosterone contemporaries. This is measured in a variety of ways. For example, individuals with low baseline testosterone exhibit less dominant behaviors in competitive social interactions than individuals with high baseline testosterone. Individuals with low testosterone also show diminished selective attention to angry faces, which are often indicators of social threat. The hormone cortisol is frequently used as a measure of stress, with increases in cortisol usually indicating a stressful event. When their status is threatened, individuals with low testosterone show reduced cortisol reactivity (i.e., reduced stress) in comparison with individuals with high testosterone. Beyond seemingly not seeking higher status, individuals with low testosterone appear not to prefer high status even when it is freely given. That is, when placed in a position of higher status, individuals with low testosterone have shown declined cognitive performance, increased physiological arousal, and increased negative emotions (all indicators of stress).

Individuals with low testosterone appear to be more inclined toward cooperative behavior. Prior to a team competition, individuals with low testosterone have shown increased team bonds. Although outperformed by their higher-testosterone contemporaries in individualistic competitions, those with low testosterone performed better than those with high testosterone in intergroup, cooperation-based competitions. In economic decision games, people with low baseline testosterone are more likely to accept offers perceived as unfair, suggesting a diminished concern for perceived threats to status as well as increased proclivity to cooperate.

Caveats

Although baseline testosterone has been linked to various social behaviors, evidence suggests that the stronger predictor of competitive and aggressive behaviors (i.e., dominant behaviors) is changes in testosterone in response to an event, rather than baseline testosterone per se. For example, individuals with decreases in testosterone after a competitive event were less likely to engage in further competitive tasks than those whose testosterone remained steady or increased. No such association was found when investigating differences in baseline testosterone. Furthermore, the relationship between context-related testosterone dynamics and dominance is less consistently found in women, though frequently found in men. This latter inconsistency may be due to actual differences in psychobiological processes between the sexes. However, it may instead be due to methodological issues in measurement sensitivity, given that women have far less circulating testosterone than men and, thus, changes in testosterone are difficult to measure accurately in women.

Jason Isbell and Pranjal Mehta

See also Estrogen; Gendered Behavior; Hormone Therapy for Cisgender Men and Women; Hormone Therapy for Transgender People; Testosterone

Further Readings

Archer, J. (2006). Testosterone and human aggression: An evaluation of the challenge hypothesis. *Neuroscience & Biobehavioral Reviews, 30*(3), 319–345.

Mazur, A., & Booth, A. (1998). Testosterone and dominance in men. *Behavioral and Brain Science, 21,* 353–397.

Machismo

Machismo is a socially constructed term that encompasses a variety of stereotyped male roles typically associated with traditional, hyper- or hegemonic masculinity, whereby men occupy a socially dominant position and women a subordinate one. At an individual level, machismo's stereotypical, exaggerated characteristics may include overreliance on the self, toughness, impulsivity, and recklessness. At an interpersonal level, machismo can include implicit and explicit dynamics that assert male superiority, dominance in the form of patriarchy, and further oppressive practices toward not only females but other males too. Machismo may be learned and reinforced in the interplay of social dynamics within families, educational institutions, organized sports, sex-segregated restrooms and locker rooms, communities, work environments, leisure and civic activities, and social structures.

While previously yet inaccurately associated only with Latino males, contemporary perspectives on machismo acknowledge its presence in all patriarchal societies and advance a more distinct understanding of the construct, placing it at an extreme of the range of masculinities within communities and societies while offering possibly contrasting constructs, including, for example, *caballerismo* among Latinos. This entry details the male characteristics associated with machismo, discusses its assessment, and offers clinical recommendations to practitioners.

Machismo as a Social Construct

Although the terms *male*, *man*, and *masculinity* are at times used interchangeably, it is important to distinguish how these terms can be used differentially. The stereotypical characteristics of a male (*macho* in Spanish) include being strong, virile, even irresponsible, and a womanizer. In contrast, a man is stereotypically characterized as being respectful, a protector of the family, and self-sacrificing. Masculinity encompasses the roles, behaviors, characteristics, and beliefs ascribed to men and manifests differently within and across cultures, races, classes, and generations; therefore, it is more appropriate to refer to masculinities, emphasizing their plurality.

Within the spectrum of masculinities, machismo can be placed at an extreme, stereotyped end. In its most traditional, caricatured, albeit pernicious form, it is represented by males who exhibit a particular set of personal and interpersonal characteristics. Besides exaggerated self-reliance, toughness, impulsivity, bravado, and recklessness, males who exhibit machismo at a personal level may also display arrogance, invulnerability, and restricted emotionality beyond anger. Similarly, they are perceived as highly competitive, intimidating, rude, and overbearing and are likely to strive for overachievement while demanding respect from others. They are more likely to act daringly and defiantly to the point of unanticipated self-harm. They may pride themselves for their alcohol tolerance and heavy drinking to the point of intoxication and even alcohol poisoning. There is a sense of being the law or "above the law" in their actions. They may brag about their physical and sexual prowess, virility, and insatiable sexual appetite and are likely to be described as womanizers. They tend to demonstrate objectifying attitudes toward sexuality and homophobia (i.e., fear, aversion, and discrimination toward lesbians, gay men, and bisexual persons) while overcompensating for aspects of themselves that may not exactly meet the strict standards of maleness that they set out for themselves. While machismo has been constructed as a form of heteronormative masculinity, this norm has been found in the gay community as well. Like heterosexual men, some gay men exhibit behaviors, characteristics, and values that align with machismo. Moreover, the endorsement of machismo has been found to be positively associated with experiencing internalized homophobia.

Interpersonally, machismo manifests itself in strictly hierarchical relationships that consistently and systematically assert male superiority not only toward females but also, at times, toward other males. The social construction of machismo involves the denigration of stereotypical female activities for the express purpose of asserting male superiority, while interfering with, if not impeding, female self-determination and perpetuating a patriarchal social structure. The oppressive and oppressing actions of males in the context of machismo are expressed in the form of interpersonal violence; prototypically, though not exclusively, as intimate partner violence or domestic abuse; force-based child discipline practices; and other violent crimes. Males exhibiting high levels of machismo are more likely to be described as misogynist, sexist, and chauvinistic while promulgating the objectification of women. They are more likely to engage in harassing women through socially inappropriate actions (e.g., whistling, leering, following) as well as through socially sanctioned behavior (e.g., groping). They are also more likely to engage in discrimination against gays, lesbians, and transsexual and transgender people. In addition, the endorsement of gender inequality is often a risk factor for becoming a victim or a perpetrator of violence. The World Health Organization indicates that 38% of female murders were committed by an intimate partner, while 35% of women experience intimate partner violence or sexual violence.

Machismo must be understood in the context from which it acquires its meaning and purpose: the particular, unequal interplay between gender roles in a patriarchal society. That is, machismo exists in the context of nonegalitarian, patriarchal societies, where the social order and status quo are maintained by the existing power structure, which is typically populated or dominated by males. Machismo serves and perpetuates patriarchy through the gender role subjugation and oppression of women while elevating male roles. In other words, machismo as a social construct in a patriarchal society serves the purpose of socially construing women as inferior, framing their societally limited activities as less prestigious, preventing their upward mobility advertently or inadvertently, and ultimately causing women to be rewarded less for equal work. Moreover, machismo limits the range not only of masculinities but also of femininities while promulgating homophobia.

Socialization theories posit that from an early age boys are anticipated to emulate gender stereotyped expectations, which they, in turn, learn and internalize through observation and modeling from various sources (e.g., family, schools, peers and peer pressure, recreational activities). This learning is reinforced in children through the affirmation of gender congruent and the disaffirmation of gender incongruent comportment, inclusive of thoughts, feelings, behaviors, and meaning making.

Machismo and Latinos

Machismo has been stereotypically albeit erroneously ascribed exclusively to Latin American males, communities, and societies, in part because of essentialist, grand narratives (i.e., overencompassing yet simplifying objectifying theories based on narrow stories) in the second half of the 1900s, in part due to the Spanish origin of the term. *Macho* means "male," and the suffix *-ismo* (for *-ism*) denotes "a reduction of the male gender role." Yet the association of machismo with Latino males in the United States obscures the role played by factors such as social class, marginalization, discrimination, ethnocentrism, racism, and the concomitant historical disempowerment of those belonging to this group. Although misguided and inexcusable, these individuals may be seeking to overcome or compensate for their socially stressed self-agency by oppressing their partners in their domestic environment. It should be noted that the characteristics typically associated with machismo in the United States are referred to as *machista* (i.e., "male chauvinist," "sexist") in the Latin American culture in the United States and throughout Latin America.

Contemporary masculinities within Latin American cultures embrace multiple identities that challenge machismo to the point of contradicting its stereotyped definition and reclaim empowering, strength-based narratives grounded in affirmative relational ethics. In fact, in an effort to diversify the discourse concerning Latino men and to reflect contemporary rather than traditional societies, there has been a resurgence of contrasting if not opposing terms for machismo in the U.S. Latin American literature. For example, *hombre noble* ("noble man"), *hombre de verdad* ("a true man"), and *caballero* ("gentleman") emphasize culturally congruent values (e.g., *familismo*, *personalismo*, *respeto*) and have received theoretical and empirical attention. Perhaps the most studied one is *caballerismo* ("the practice of being chivalrous or gentlemanly"), which has been used to highlight other masculine ideologies, those that characterize men's (i.e., caballeros) expected gender roles within a positive framework. Caballeros are expected to be responsible, perseverant, protective, loyal, hardworking, courageous, and appropriately assertive yet polite. Similarly, they are expected to honor family, be nurturing and respectful of women's individuality, as well as be emotionally connected and engaged in domestic responsibilities including child rearing and parenting. Nonetheless, there has been some criticism of caballerismo, where it is perceived as benevolently sexist, all the while obscuring patriarchy, and furthering classism.

Finally, it is of utmost importance to acknowledge the ongoing evolution of gender roles taking place among Latinos/as in the United States and throughout Latin America as well. Immigrants to the United States from Mexico and other Latin American countries are likely to encounter significant shifts in gender dynamics, relatively better protection for women's rights, and potentially greater opportunities for upward mobility of women, all dimensions that may challenge the status quo of family dynamics. Similarly, as they visit their countries of origin, they are likely to notice these changes there as well.

Assessment of Machismo

A number of measures have been developed to evaluate attitudes and behaviors related to machismo. However, several considerations must be taken into account when assessing the construct of machismo. General considerations such as test reliability, validity, sample validity, and currency should be taken into account when choosing any assessment tool. Specific considerations such as the conceptual and operational definition of machismo, as well as the context and the time period in which it is assessed, are important to entertain. Regarding definitions of machismo, some measures reflect traditional, gender stereotyped behaviors, attitudes, and beliefs about a single masculinity, which differ from other measures that place and therefore assess machismo within a wider spectrum of masculinities. Regarding context and as previously discussed, *machismo* is a socially constructed term that acquires its meaning within a person's culture, community, ethnic identity, acculturation level, education, age, and socioeconomic status, among other factors. Expressions of machismo may vary based on the community the client lives in, with salient differences between rural versus urban settings (i.e., rural patriarchies contrasted with urban ones). Furthermore, adherence to traditional gender roles such as those associated with machismo may change with age, with more stereotyped attitudes being held by younger generations. Therefore, all these dimensions must be taken into account when seeking to assess machismo.

As indicated, some scales operationalize machismo through traditional gender roles and a single, restricted masculinity, whereas other scales complement those traditional views of machismo with others, reflecting a spectrum of masculinities. Similarly, some items within machismo scales reflect traditional, stereotypical behaviors, attitudes, and beliefs that are congruent with patriarchal social arrangements, whereas others emphasize egalitarian, contemporary roles. In short, as gender roles have evolved in societies, so has the assessment of machismo.

An example of traditional, stereotypical machismo representation is captured by the 17-item machismo subscale of the Multiphasic Assessment of Cultural Constructs, developed by B. Arnold and J. Cuéllar. Examples of items in this scale include "A man should not marry a woman who is taller than him," "Boys should not be allowed to play with dolls and other girls' toys," "There are some jobs that women simply should not have," "Men are more intelligent than women," and "It is important for a man to be strong."

An example of a more sophisticated assessment of machismo within broader masculinities is a scale developed by James Alan Neff with 13 items that include positive representations associated with contemporary male gender roles and negative representations associated with traditional machismo (i.e., male dominance, macho risk taking, male independence). The scale emphasizes the multidimensionality of gender roles and resorts to three dimensions to organize the items: (1) emotion regulation (e.g., "A man should not show emotions"), (2) honor (e.g., "It is important for a man to be respected by others"), and (3) egalitarianism in gender roles (e.g., "Men should share housework with their wives"). The scale has been used with different ethnic groupings, such as U.S. Anglos, African Americans, and Mexican Americans, resulting in similarities across groups while undermining the exclusive association of machismo with Latino men.

Finally, a scale developed by G. Miguel Arciniega and collaborators, a 20-item, bidimensional, two-factor structure measure, assesses cognitive and behavioral expressions of both stereotyped machismo and more contemporary, albeit old-fashioned, patriarchal aspects of male gender roles (i.e., caballerismo). Examples of items within the traditional machismo factor include the following: "In a family, a father's wish is law," "Real men never let down their guard," "Men are superior to women," and "A man should be in control of his wife." Examples of items within the caballerismo factor include "Men must display good manners in public," "A woman is expected to be loyal to her husband," and "Men should respect their elders."

It is important to note that the majority of the assessments developed thus far rely heavily on self-reported information. More inclusive and complete assessment tools are needed to measure machismo within the spectrum of masculinities in order to provide a more comprehensive view of the construct not only in definition but also in the way it is presented across different groups and contexts.

Clinical and Research Recommendations

Practitioners and researchers should examine their own views on males, men, and masculinities, including stereotyped ones such as machismo, paying close attention to the evolution of their own views on the matter, the influence of their socioeconomic status, and their education on such views, in addition to their personal histories. Such ongoing examination and humble appreciation of themselves as cultural, gendered beings facilitate the consideration of expressed masculinities when working with clients and research participants.

Clinicians and researchers alike may want to concern themselves with the extent to which stereotyped, rigid masculinities such as machismo may help explain differential patterns in help seeking, access and utilization of health and mental health care, and sexual practices. In fact, men who score high on machismo scales are likely to present in therapy with rigid expectations regarding treatment preferences and are more likely to struggle with treatment adherence to health and mental health care regimes. Similarly, they are more likely to have sex with multiple partners and contract and transmit sexual infections. They are less likely to engage in safe sex or take responsibility for birth control (e.g., use of a condom) and more likely to exhibit homophobic attitudes.

Clinicians and researchers may want to consider their clients' and participants' view of themselves as males and men, including their identification with stereotyped masculinities such as machismo and the *machista* attitudes associated with it, particularly in the context of paternal involvement in child rearing and in their children's schooling. Men who exhibit machismo are less likely to be involved and engaged as fathers and believe those tasks to be ones done by women exclusively. To the extent that machismo has been associated with a range of problematic behaviors such as maladaptive coping patterns (e.g., passive-aggressive behavior and wishful thinking) and interpersonal difficulties (e.g., aggressiveness and antisocial behavior), clinicians and researchers alike are encouraged to assess the extent to which clients or research participants may construct their masculinities in such a stereotyped, rigid manner. Furthermore, men who exhibit conduct congruent with machismo tend to present with higher levels of alexithymia (i.e., difficulties accessing one's own feelings) and of depression and stress, particularly in the context of gender role conflicts. In short, machismo is potentially harmful not only to others but also to those who identify with it. Although machismo may indicate a higher need for services, it may make it more difficult to access and utilize the available services.

Culturally competent clinicians and researchers refrain from assuming that Latino clients embrace rigid, stereotyped masculinities such as machismo. They take into consideration the role that immigration status, educational level, and socioeconomic status may play in the endorsement of stereotyped gender roles. Similarly, they are attentive to the role that social desirability may play in the concealment or the exhibition of machismo, and they remain mindful of the power differential in health care or research encounter, which could bring about interpersonal defiance or even stoicism in the initial and subsequent visits or create marked difficulties in treatment adherence.

Clinicians and researchers alike are encouraged to consider the extent to which masculinities, even a stereotyped, rigid one such as machismo, may have served their clients and research participants well in their own contexts. An understanding of such matters can help build a bridge of empathy, which can, in turn, make treatment and research possible.

Andres J. Consoli, Ana Romero Morales, and Gina Vanegas Martinez

See also Hegemonic Masculinity; Help-Seeking Behaviors and Men; Latina/o Americans and Gender; Male Privilege; *Marianismo*; Masculinity Gender Norms; Masculinity Ideology and Norms; Matriarchy; Patriarchy

Further Readings

Arciniega, G. M., Anderson, T. C., Tovar-Blank, Z., & Tracey, T. J. G. (2008). Toward a fuller conception of machismo: Development of a traditional machismo and caballerismo scale. *Journal of Counseling Psychology, 55,* 19–33.

Arnold, B., & Cuéllar, J. (1985). *Development of a bilingual multiphasic inventory for measurement of clinically relevant constructs in the Mexican American culture.* Unpublished manuscript. University of Texas—Pan American.

Casas, J. M., Wagenheim, B. R., Banchero, R., & Mendoza-Romero, J. (1994). Hispanic masculinity: Myth or psychological schema meriting clinical consideration. *Hispanic Journal of Behavioral Sciences, 16,* 315–331.

Estrada, F., Rigali-Oiler, M., Arciniega, G. M., & Tracey, T. J. G. (2011). Machismo and Mexican American men: An empirical understanding using a gay sample. *Journal of Counseling Psychology, 58,* 358–367.

Falicov, C. J. (2010). Changing constructions of machismo for Latino men in therapy: "The devil never sleeps." *Family Process, 49,* 309–329.

Félix-Ortiz, M., Abreu, J. M., Briano, M., & Bowen, D. (2001). A critique of machismo measures in psychological research. In F. Columbus (Ed.), *Advances in psychology research* (Vol. 3, pp. 63–90). Hauppauge, NY: Nova Science.

Guttman, M. C. (Ed.). (2003). *Changing men and masculinities in Latin America.* Durham, NC: Duke University Press.

Guttman, M. C. (2006). *The meanings of macho: Being a man in Mexico City* (10th Anniversary ed.). Berkeley: University of California Press.

Mirandé, A. (1997). *Hombres y machos: Masculinity and Latino culture.* Boulder, CO: Westview Press.

Neff, J. A. (2001). A confirmatory factor analysis of a measure of "machismo" among Anglo, African American, and Mexican American male drinkers. *Hispanic Journal of Behavioral Sciences, 23,* 171–188.

Tello, J. (1998). El hombre noble buscando balance: The noble man searching for balance. In R. Carrillo & J. Tello (Eds.), *Family violence and men of color: Healing the wounded male spirit* (pp. 31–52). New York, NY: Springer.

Welland, C., & Ribner, N. (2008). *Healing from violence: Latino men's journey to a new masculinity.* New York, NY: Springer.

Male Privilege

Male privilege refers to the structural differentiations within a patriarchal society wherein males are conferred societal entitlements and advantages that are denied to those who identify as female, transgender, or gender nonconforming. Conceptually, male privilege is cut from the same theoretical cloth as other forms of epistemic privilege that accompany membership within dominant or ruling social groups such as White privilege, class privilege, heterosexual privilege, and cisgender privilege. Like all of these forms of societal privilege, male privilege is not earned, not acquired by merit, and not conferred on men because of anything they have done or have failed to do. Men acquire this privilege simply by being born biologically male while simultaneously taking up a traditional male gender identity and performing male gender roles.

The Theoretical Inception of Male Privilege

In 1955, Simone de Beauvoir wrote *Privileges*, a collection of reflective essays on the privileges associated with class, education, sex and nationality, and the question of how those with privilege should negotiate their unmerited social advantages. For Beauvoir, social privilege is about not only unmerited social advantages but also the systemic denial of such advantages. Beauvoir held that our social systems are designed to obfuscate, rationalize, and deny the dominant groups' privileged status. For men, the relative comfort of remaining unaware of their own privilege (i.e., the luxury of obliviousness) has been downloaded into our society's patriarchal operating system and is an integral aspect of male privilege itself.

Influenced by Beauvoir, Peggy McIntosh, in 1989, applied the construct of privilege to racial identity. In her essay "White Privilege: Unpacking the Invisible Knapsack," McIntosh defined privilege as an invisible package of unearned assets that White people can count on cashing in each day but about which they are "meant" to remain oblivious. It was this essay that catapulted the political theory of epistemic privilege to greater social and academic awareness. McIntosh suggests that privilege comes in two types: (1) unearned entitlements and (2) conferred dominance.

Unearned Entitlements

Unearned entitlements are valuable forms of social capital that everyone should have. For example, everyone should have the freedom to walk through a parking garage without the fear of sexual assault, the right to career advancement without fear of hitting a gender-related glass ceiling, or the opportunity to attend a party without having to vigilantly protect one's drink from being drugged. Males have these unearned entitlements. Women and transgender identified persons do not. When an unearned entitlement is restricted to certain dominant groups such as males, it becomes a form of privilege that is called an unearned advantage.

Conferred Dominance

Conferred dominance is the form of privilege that gives one group social power over another. Social dominance naturally follows from unearned advantages. In a patriarchal society, this results in males having an unequal share of social power and control. Conferred dominance is readily identified by paying attention to which group is highly visible if not always present and which group is silenced and/or absent in social spaces. For example, it is acceptable, if not expected, for men to control conversations, to take the driver's seat, and to manage the family finances. Women are underrepresented in films, managerial positions, and elected offices. When women do break the corporate glass ceiling and attain the title of CEO, they are often paid millions less than their male counterparts. Conferred dominance is also evident when nondominant groups are exoticized or objectified by society. The portrayal of female bodies as objects for male sexual consumption is ubiquitous within our patriarchal society. Finally, conferred dominance is demonstrated through gender appropriation, such as when men construct what is deemed as acceptable standards for women and then only view women who meet those standards as worthy of attention and praise.

Male Privilege in Everyday Life

Numerous scholars and theorists have adapted McIntosh's groundbreaking knapsack of White privilege to convey the privileges that come with male identity. Just a few of the many male privileges that have been identified now follow:

- If a man fails in his job or career, the failure will not be perceived as an example of his entire gender's capabilities.

- In most professions, men are held against a lower standard than women. It is easier for a "good but not great" male lawyer to make a partner than it is for a comparable woman.
- If a man chooses not to have children, his masculinity will not be called into question.
- If a man has children and a career, no one will think that he is selfish for not staying at home.
- Men can assume that when they go out in public they will not be sexually harassed or assaulted just because they are male, and if they are victimized, they will not be asked to explain what they were wearing or what they were doing there.
- Men are more likely to have their ideas and contributions taken seriously, even those that were previously suggested by a woman and dismissed or ignored.
- When men ask to "see the person in charge," they are likely to face a person of their own gender. The higher-up in the organization the person is, the more likely this is the case.
- Men do not have to deal with the endless and exhausting stream of attention drawn to their physical appearance.
- If a man does not meet the cultural standards of male beauty, the disadvantages are relatively small and will have little impact on his professional status.
- If men have sex with multiple partners, they will not be stigmatized and are likely to be praised and achieve higher social status.
- The ordinary language of day-to-day existence consistently reinforces the notion that to be a "man" is the standard (e.g., "All men are created equal," whether mailman, chairman, or businessman).

Lance C. Smith

See also Heterosexual Privilege; Patriarchy; Sexism

Further Readings

Beauvoir, S. de. (1955). *Privileges*. Paris, France: Gallimard.

Coston, B. M., & Kimmel, M. (2012). Seeing privilege where it isn't: Marginalized masculinities and the intersectionality of privilege. *Journal of Social Issues, 68,* 97–111. doi:10.1111/j.1540-4560.2011.01738.x

Johnson, A. G. (2006). *Privilege, power and difference.* New York, NY: McGraw-Hill.

Kruks, S. (2005). Simone de Beauvoir and the politics of privilege. *Hypatia, 20,* 178–205.

McIntosh, P. (2000). White privilege: Unpacking the invisible knapsack. In J. Noel (Ed.), *Notable selections in multicultural education* (pp. 115–120). Guilford, CT: Dushkin/McGraw-Hill.

Mania and Gender

Gender affects the course of presentation and treatment of mania. The *Diagnostic and Statistical Manual of Mental Disorders, Fifth Edition* (*DSM-5*), defines mania as a mental state of elevated, expansive, or irritable mood and persistently increased level of energy. Manic episodes may be specified as mild, medium, moderate to severe, or severe and are found in varying degrees in people with bipolar disorders and, parenthetically, in some instances, substance-related disorders that may or may not be comorbid. In bipolar I disorder, the manic episode is persistently elevated, expansive, and sufficiently severe so as to cause marked impairment in work or social activities. In bipolar II disorder, diagnosis occurs after at least one depressive episode and an episode of hypomania, which is defined as an abnormality of mood resembling mania but of less intensity. Both *mania* and *hypomania* are terms used to describe symptoms of cyclothymic disorder, which is a chronic disorder involving many periods of hypomanic and depressive symptoms, though less severe than those of the bipolar disorders.

Manic episodes can present not only as euphoric, where the mood is one of elation, but also as dysphoric, with the mood characterized by agitation, anger, and depression. Because effective treatment protocols depend on it, Steven Dilsaver and colleagues stressed the importance of distinguishing the phenomenology of the mood states. For the very same reason, it is at least equally important to recognize how mania presents differently in men and in women.

Studies of Mania and Gender

What was classically called manic depressive disease occurs equally in women and men. Because of this, it had been assumed that its course and treatment would be the same for both women and men. Before the latter part of the 20th century, scant effort was made to study the symptoms of mania and the treatment of mania differential to gender. Mood disorders, particularly mania and mixed mania, are prevalent and dangerous in both men and women, with suicide not an infrequent outcome. Thus, subsequent to the woman's movement, in the latter part of the 20th century, a new scientific interest in women's health was born, and from the end of the 20th century to the present day, there have been numerous studies addressing how men and women in manic states react to both symptoms and treatment differently. Some studies have been designed to determine the efficacy of psychopharmacological interventions and psychotherapy. Not only the efficacy but also the safety of various medications have been researched.

Findings demonstrate that there is no one treatment for everyone and there is no medication that is harmless during all periods of the life cycle. Some medications helpful to men are harmful to women, especially during pregnancy and during the postpartum period—times that may be challenging for women in general but more so for women who experience bouts of mania. Hormones are related to gender and are typically related to the experience of mania. In 2006, Jayashri Kulkarni and colleagues conducted a pilot study related to hormones as a treatment for mania and found that women who completed treatment with hormonal agents showed significant improvement. A. C. Viguera and colleagues have reported findings consistent with earlier studies related to pregnancy and postpartum issues. In part due to hormonal changes, there are substantial risks for the occurrence of mixed manic episodes during pregnancy and especially during the postpartum period. The women most at risk are those diagnosed with bipolar I disorder, the most serious of the mood disorders, in which elevated, expansive, exuberant, euphoric mania can cause activity that may be a danger to the individual and to society.

In 1996, Ellen Leibenluft reviewed the then existent literature related to depression and rapid cycling (which occurs when a person experiences shifts between mania and depression). She also looked at the effect of women's reproductive life cycle. Leibenluft's study pointed to the need for more research on the topics of the menstrual cycle, pregnancy, postpartum issues, menopause, and the use of oral contraceptives as related to their influence on manic behavior. Many of these studies are yet to be done.

In 2000, Victoria Hendrick and associates conducted a 3-year study of 131 patients (63 women and 68 men) admitted to the University of California mood disorders program and found no significant difference in gender for hospital admittance due to depression. However, at the time of hospital admission, there were some gender differences: Women registered four times the rate of alcohol consumption that men registered, while men had a higher rate than women for a comorbid substance abuse disorder. Related to mania, one major gender difference was that women were found to experience more rapid cycling than men.

Summary of Study Findings

The studies mentioned herein are just a few of the many studies that have been conducted on the subject of mania and gender. The criteria for bipolar disorder are basically the same for men and women; however, depression and mania are experienced differently in those who experience it. The following list summarizes research findings of the most researched gender differences:

Men tend to be more prone to manic episodes, whereas women tend to be more prone to depressive episodes.

Men tend to develop bipolar illness at an earlier age than women.

Men tend to seek help less than women, perhaps leading to substance abuse, which aggravates bipolar symptoms.

During manic episodes, men tend to act out more than women and resort to fighting, drinking, and substance abuse.

Women tend to experience more depressive episodes and fewer manic episodes than men.

Women face the difficulty of managing bipolar illness during pregnancy and the postpartum period.

Women are denied the benefits of some newer helpful medications such as valproic acid and carbamazepine during pregnancy and the lactating period due to possible harm to the fetus and the baby. The medicines that are less harmful to women during these times are older and less effective medications such as lithium, haloperidol, and chlorpromazine.

Women have eating disorders more frequently than men, comorbid with mania and mixed mania.

Men have a greater genetic history with the disorder, though a genetic history is common to both genders.

Men tend to be more overt and more aggressive than women during manic episodes.

Gender-Related Diagnostic Issues and Commentary

The *DSM-5* contains several paragraphs about gender-related diagnostic issues in the discussion of bipolar I and bipolar II disorders. Based on empirical studies, the *DSM-5* describes gender issues in bipolar I disorder, including that women are more likely to experience rapid cycling and mixed states and to have patterns of comorbidity that differ from those of men, including higher rates of eating disorders. The *DSM-5* also states that women with bipolar I and II disorders are more likely to experience depressive symptoms than males, that women also have a higher lifetime risk for alcohol use disorder than males, and that women with bipolar I disorder are more likely to use alcohol than women in the general population.

In the gender-related diagnostic issues for bipolar II disorder, there is a caveat that indicates that while the gender ratio for bipolar I is equal, findings for bipolar II disorder vary depending on the sample. Bipolar II disorder seems to be more common in females than males, but this may be due to data relative to who seeks treatment. Many people with bipolar II disorder see mania as a natural state rather than as a diseased state. Females are more likely than males to report hypomania with mixed depressive features and a rapid cycling course. Elevated highs and subsequent depression are common in about half of the women who report having highs during the postpartum period. The *DSM-5* advocates for future research to understand how postpartum affects women with symptoms of mania, as well as to prevent suicide and infanticide. This is very important because the lifetime risk for suicide in individuals with bipolar disorder is known to be 15 times that of the general population.

Children and Adolescents

The topic of mania in children and adolescents is very complex. Children with mood disorders can move from a happy and joyful state to an extremely sad state in a very short span of time. They can have racing thoughts, can be hypersexual, may be in need of little sleep, and experience all the symptoms of mania. However, one's ability to distinguish true mania from the mood swings and associated behaviors that are normal in children may be quite limited. Bipolar disorder can exist in the preteen years and should be diagnosed by a specialist, such as a pediatric psychiatrist who specializes in bipolar disorders. Little if anything is known about gender differences in children's manic behavior.

Future Directions

There is evidence that people with bipolar disorder have a different brain function and structure compared with people who do not have the disorder. The irrational and risky behavior that characterizes mania is correlated with these differences. Advances in neuroscience may facilitate further investigation of differences in manic behavior between men and women. In addition, psychopharmacological advances may offer new treatments, and genetic research could possibly offer a cure in the distant future. Future research should focus on how the life cycles of men and of women influence manic behavior, as well as its medical and psychosocial treatment.

Lee Joyce Richmond

See also Bipolar Disorder and Gender; Depression and Gender; Dialectical Behavior Therapy and Gender; Schizophrenia and Gender

Further Readings

Dilsaver, S. C., Chen, Y. R., Shoaib, A. M., & Swann, A. C. (1999). Phenomenology of mania: Evidence for distinct depressed, dysphoric, and euphoric presentations. *American Journal of Psychiatry, 156*(3), 426–430.

Frye, M. A., Altshuler, L. L., McElroy, S. L., Suppes, T., Keck, P. E., Denicoff, K., & Post, R. M. (2003). Gender differences in prevalence, risk, and clinical correlates of alcoholism comorbidity in bipolar disorder. *American Journal of Psychiatry, 160*(5), 883–889.

Hendrick, V., Altshuler, L. L., Gitlin, M. G., Delraim, S., & Hammen, G. (2000). Gender and bipolar illness. *Journal of Clinical Psychiatry, 61*(5), 393–396.

Kulkarni, J., Garland, K. A., Scaffidi, A., Headey, B., Anderson, R., de Castella, A., . . . Davis, S. R. (2006). A pilot study of hormone modulation as a new treatment for mania in women with bipolar affective disorder. *Psychoneuroendocrinology, 31*(4), 543–547.

Leibenluft, E. (1996). Women with bi-polar illness: Clinical and research issues. *American Journal of Psychiatry, 153*(2), 163–173.

Viguera, A. C., Tondo, L., Koukopoulos, A. E., Reginaldi, D., Lepri B., & Baldessarini R. J. (2011). Episodes of mood disorders in 2,252 pregnancies and postpartum periods. *American Journal of Psychiatry, 168*(11), 1179–1185.

Websites

National Institute on Mental Health, Bipolar Disorder: http://www.nimh.nih.gov/health/topics/bipolar-disorder/

MARIANISMO

Marianismo refers to the traditional female gender role based on the values of Catholicism and traditional Latin American cultural norms, with its roots stemming from the Spanish conquest. In the simplest terms, *marianismo* is the ideal female role that includes qualities such as sexual purity, self-sacrifice, and suffering. Other major concepts include the emphasis on the role of mother, moral strength, caretaking, submission and passivity, and duty and honor. *Marianismo* is significant because it defines the female roles in Latin American culture, dictating behaviors that are acceptable and unacceptable as well as beliefs and values related to women. This entry briefly defines the different aspects of *marianismo* and discusses how it plays a significant role in the psychosocial adjustment of Latin American women in the United States. The entry concludes with an overview of criticisms in the research literature.

Aspects of *Marianismo*

First coined by Evelyn P. Stevens in her 1973 political essay "Marianismo: The Other Face of Machismo in Latin America," *marianismo* is a social process that stereotypes the female gender role in Latin American societies and is historically sensitive, with its definition shifting across generations. The traditional male gender role counterpart is known as *machismo*, defining a man's role as the protector and provider of the family, who ideally demonstrates characteristics such as chivalry, honor, responsibility, and courage, as well as dominance over women and virility.

Marianismo has its origins in the belief that Mary, Mother of God, was a virgin when she gave birth to Jesus, leading to her veneration and admiration by followers of Christianity. This led to the idea that women should ideally be pure and self-sacrificing, with the role as mother being the most important. Therefore, traditional *marianismo* is understood as an ideal emulation of the Virgin Mary—"Maria" (hence *maria*-nismo)—who is characterized by virtuous purity, chastity, self-sacrifice, and being eternally self-giving. The Virgin Mary is seen as the epitome of true femininity, a virgin who nurtured and cared for not only her son Jesus but also the world. A symbol of humility and patience, the Virgin Mary is the ultimate role model for Latin American women, whose virtues are seen as the ideal and reinforced by members of their society. Her image is a powerful one, representing an entity that understands the pain and suffering of childbirth, child rearing, and losing one's child. She exudes virtue, strength, and patience.

Stemming from these beliefs of the Virgin Mary, sexual innocence and purity are highly valued in *marianismo*. Women are to wait until marriage to have sexual relations, and once married, each woman is expected to remain faithful to her husband. The woman is seen as almost asexual, whereas the man is seen as sexually hungry, morally inferior to her, and unable to control his sexual desires. Women are viewed as morally strong and spiritually superior to men and are expected to tolerate men's imperfections. Thus, if a woman has sexual relations before marriage or out of wedlock, she is generally seen as immoral and weak, dishonoring herself and her family. Women who consent to sex before marriage are generally seen as in opposition to the *marianista* (a term used to refer to a worldwide family of men and women consecrated to Mary and her evangelizing mission), as the *puta* ("whore"), giving rise to dichotomous thinking of the female role in Latin American cultures. These women are seen as loose and promiscuous, a *mujer mala* ("bad woman") lacking in virtue, whose behavior is seen as inappropriate, resulting in being ostracized by both men and women.

Self-sacrifice is greatly exemplified by the Virgin Mary and is reflected in *marianismo* by the expectation that a woman should attend to her children's and husband's needs before her own. Women are seen as the ones who give birth, nurture the children, and control the domestic home. The woman lives in the shadows of her husband and children, continuously supporting them as well as putting the needs of extended family, friends, and community members above her own. Thus, a woman's self-worth is largely measured by what she can do for others. The *marianista* is able to withstand extreme suffering and sacrifices for the sake of the family. This self-sacrifice, likened to the sacrifice of the Virgin Mary, enables traditional Latin American women to gain the respect and admiration of others in their society. In turn, Latin American women obtain their identity through adherence to this gender role, gaining their power and self-worth.

Significance in Mental Health

Marianismo can be utilized as a foundational framework for understanding some of the experiences of Latin American women in U.S. mainstream society. For example, *marianista* values and beliefs can come into conflict with U.S. culture, resulting in psychological distress. Mental health practitioners commonly encounter Latin American clients who present with struggles of differing gender role expectations or interpersonal conflicts. When presented with these cases, the cultural phenomenon of *marianismo* can help guide understanding and inform clinical interventions.

Marianismo is a sacred duty or code of behavior for how a *mujer buena* ("good woman") is supposed to act and is an intergenerational phenomenon. It is essential in understanding the basic, traditional gender role beliefs of some Latin American cultures and thus the basic underpinnings of traditional Latino romantic and familial relationships. Children and adolescents learn the gender role scripts that orient them to act according to (conforming) or to deviate from (not conform) their culture norms. Gender role socialization occurs not only via the parent-child relationship but also from siblings, extended family, friends, and other ethnic group members. *Marianismo* may be embedded in the child's or adolescent's cultural norm expectations based on tradition, the Latin American cultural background, and the level of acculturation.

Intergenerational tension may arise if adolescent girls being raised in the United States do not subscribe to *marianismo*'s guiding principles. Grandmothers, mothers, aunts, female cousins, and even the males in the family expect the adolescent female to behave within the parameters set forth by *marianismo*. The emphasis on high sexual morality can lead to conflict between U.S. dating norms and the family's restrictiveness. Moreover, the *marianista* values of sexual purity, submissiveness to men, and enduring suffering may place adolescent females at risk of not questioning their partner's fidelity and/or sexual behaviors, utilizing sexual protection, and/or becoming involved in a violent relationship due to misinterpretation of the *marianista* (and *machista* [a term used to refer to a strong or exaggerated sense of traditional masculinity, placing great value on physical courage, virility, domination of women, and aggressiveness]) values.

At times, the complementary traditional gender roles of *marianismo* and machismo can play a large part in relationship conflicts. Due to the values of being pure and morally superior to men, Latin American women face great pressure to live up to these values in every aspect of their daily lives. Financial dependence on their husband is a natural consequence of staying at home to take care of domestic duties and the needs of the children and husband. A combination of these factors and a perversion of the values of *marianista* submission and the *machista* belief that men's sexual urges are uncontrollable can lead to domestic abuse—psychological, physical, and/or sexual. Moreover, a request by the woman to utilize a condom or other sexual protection may be interpreted as an accusation that the man is unfaithful or an admittance that she herself is unfaithful. When these cultural beliefs and values are utilized to legitimize or rationalize actions that are harmful in nature to women (and men), they must be challenged and role expectations reshaped.

Marianismo may also create conflicts for Latin American women who identify as lesbian, bisexual, transgender, and/or queer. For example, the importance of marriage, motherhood, and being sexually "pure" may lead a lesbian woman to enter into a heterosexual marriage because of the pressure to conform to these values. *Marianista* ideals privilege heterosexual women, with little room for homosexuality or bisexuality, which are seen as transgressions against the *marianismo* gender ideal. Hence, Latin American women who identify as lesbian, bisexual, transgender, and/or queer may feel invisible with respect to their gender identities if attempting to fulfill the traditional female gender role. However, if and when these *marianista* values do not prohibit Latin American women from choosing their partners, these roles can also be adopted in same-gender relationships. The values of procreation, motherhood, and marriage can be demonstrated in marriage, long-term committed relationships, and having children among lesbian couples.

There is great variability in *marianismo* values within each Latin American woman. Thus, when a gender role conflict emerges, learning to negotiate conflicting values and identify areas of change is essential for psychosocial health. Latin American women who are able to examine their *marianista* values; decide what they want to keep, dismiss, or modify; and choose in which environments to do some, none, or all of these values tend to be more psychosocially adjusted than their counterparts who are not able to negotiate their values to fit their life situations. In many ways, this process is akin to the concepts of acculturation (i.e., the process of cultural change) and bicultural identity (i.e., being a part of two cultures).

Although *marianismo* has often been misinterpreted, misapplied, and manipulated, the phenomenon may have some empirical value in understanding the gender role values of some Latin Americans that only further research can uncover.

Criticisms

Latin American countries have fostered and honored women who followed the script of *marianismo*. Thus, the *marianista* has been protected from loneliness and want by gaining respect, religious superiority over men, and a place in society as a wife and mother. Her level of power is reflected in the fact that she is able to give life (just like the Virgin Mary), and because of this, *marianistas* who have children have a higher status in the community. These values and beliefs have been taught and learned through generations of Latin American women, who have continued to maintain *marianismo* within Latin American cultures.

However, that empowerment and honor can at times not be as adaptive, especially for Latin American women acculturating to the U.S. mainstream culture. Alternatively, even in traditional gender role partnerships, *marianismo* can become problematic if the woman's self-sacrifice and tolerance of suffering is taken advantage of. In other words, if adherence to *marianismo* causes the woman to be tolerant of abuse or other behaviors that hurt her physically, sexually, or emotionally, then it can be said that the role may not be best suited for that woman's situation. In fact, it is this last description of *marianismo* that has been the talking point of many critics who say that there is a lot of negativity regarding the definition of *marianismo*.

Critics have taken multiple perspectives when defining and studying *marianismo*. For example, some feminist critics dismiss the notion of *marianismo* as an excuse for the social conditions of women in Latin American countries, whereas other critics believe that the phenomenon exists but the extreme idealizing is not representative of the reality of how it is expressed or understood by Latin American women. The latter group argue that *marianismo* seemingly represents a negative stereotype for Latin American women and caution that cross-ethnic group differences and individual context should be taken into account. Furthermore, some critics point out that not all Latin American women have adopted all (or any) of these values or beliefs and that *marianismo* should not be utilized as a blanket label for Latin American women. Hence, some critics have adopted the term *maternalismo* to avoid utilizing what they believe has become a negative stereotype as well as to take away the religious connotation of the origin of the term *marianismo*.

At the very least, *marianismo* provides a basic understanding of the idealized beliefs and values of the gender role that has influenced the normative beliefs of Latin American women and how they should behave. Stevens's essay has provoked much debate on the phenomenon among critics and researchers. Whether all Latin Americans subscribe to these values and beliefs and to what extent remain to be proven, and those applying this concept to individuals should do so with caution.

Rebecca Rangel Campon

See also Biculturalism and Gender; Gender Conformity; Gender Expression; Gender Role Conflict; Gender Socialization in Adolescence; Machismo

Further Readings

Comas-Diaz, L. (1988). Mainland Puerto Rican women: A sociocultural approach. *Journal of Community Psychology, 16,* 21–31.

D'Alonzo, K. T. (2012). The influence of marianismo beliefs on physical activity of immigrant Latinas. *Journal of Transcultural Nursing, 23*(2), 124–133.

Gil, R. M., & Vasquez, C. I. (1996). *The Maria paradox.* New York, NY: G. P. Putman's.

Hussain, K. M., Leija, S. G., Lewis, F., & Sanchez, B. (2015). Unveiling sexual identity in the face of marianismo. *Journal of Feminist Family Therapy, 27*(2), 72–92.

Stevens, E. (1973). Machismo and marianismo. *Transaction Society, 10,* 57–63.

Marriage

Marriage is the joining of two people through legal, social, or religious ceremonies. The marital relationship has a long-standing tradition in society and has been found in human cultures since the beginning of time. During the 2000s, legal conceptualizations of marriage expanded to include same-sex couples. Same-sex marriage is legal in many countries, and in those where it is not legal, legislation is often in place to provide the same rights and benefits to same-sex partners that opposite-sex partners have. Apart from the legal benefits conferred by marriage, marriage often has financial benefits due to shared resources as well as psychological and physical health benefits. Gender differences exist in many of these benefits, however.

Health Benefits of Marriage

Compared with those who are divorced or widowed, individuals who are married tend to enjoy better physical and psychological health and engage in healthier behaviors. This may be due, in part, to the social resources that marriage provides. Specifically, the marital relationship is a primary source of social support and social control (influence), and it provides individuals with an increased sense of purpose and meaning. The health benefits of marriage, however, are not uniform. Compared with unmarried men, married men experience better health. However, the health benefits of marriage for women are less pronounced. Among those who are married, those with higher marital quality enjoy greater health benefits. Little research has focused on the health benefits of marriage in same-sex couples. However, because many individuals from LGBT communities may experience sexual minority stress and are at risk for negative health outcomes, the recent shift toward legalizing same-sex marriage may have positive health benefits for this at-risk community.

Gender Roles in Marriage

In addition to the different factors promoting health within the marital relationship, gender roles may play a role in both marital quality and the physical and psychological health of marital partners. Gender roles are pervasive in the marital relationship, and most married couples develop a gendered division of labor and responsibilities within the relationship. Traditional gender roles prescribe that women are the caregivers and homemakers, whereas men have authority and hold the financial responsibility of the marriage. Since the 1950s, cultural norms regarding gender roles in marriage have shifted, mostly due to the increasing number of women in the workforce. Now, most view marriage in a more egalitarian perspective, and both partners share in financial responsibilities, child rearing, housework, and making major decisions. However, the division of these responsibilities may still be heavily gender based. For example, men may be in charge of major household repairs, whereas women are responsible for the cooking and cleaning. Gender roles play an important role in shaping the expectations of the marital relationship. Unrealistic expectations about the roles of each partner in the relationship can lead to marital conflict or discord.

Marital Conflict

All marriages experience some degree of marital conflict. Marital conflicts that occur frequently, become severe, and do not get resolved tend to have a negative effect on the entire family unit. Patterns of marital conflict appear to be stable over time. For example, in couples with lower marital satisfaction, it is common to see more negative and fewer positive statements during a conflict. A demand-withdraw pattern, where husbands withdraw and wives respond with hostile or negative behaviors, is also commonly observed in distressed couples. Nondistressed couples engage in reparative or restorative behaviors and are able to withdraw more easily from negative exchanges during a conflict.

Marital conflict is associated with poorer psychological well-being and health behaviors, including depression, eating disorders, and problem drinking. Negative and hostile behaviors during marital conflict are also associated with impaired immune and endocrine function as well as elevated blood pressure. These negative effects may be stronger for women than for men, in part because women are more likely to construe their sense of self in terms of their relationship and be more emotionally attuned to how well their marriage is functioning. Over time, these physiological changes can also lead to chronic illnesses such as heart disease, cancer, and chronic pain.

Marital Therapy

When conflict or relational concerns (e.g., communication difficulties, role expectations, sexual dissatisfaction, infidelity) arise within a marriage, some couples choose to seek marital therapy through conjoint counseling. Although several modalities of couples therapy exist, the two orientations that have been evaluated in most clinical trials are (1) behavioral couple therapy and (2) emotion-focused couple therapy, both of which appear to be highly effective. Other therapeutic orientations include insight-oriented couples therapy, integrated systemic couples therapy, and integrative behavioral couples therapy.

With regard to gender differences in marital therapy, women, overall, tend to be more involved in the marital therapy–seeking process, such that they are more likely to recognize a problem within a marriage, consider treatment options, and initiate treatment seeking. When the couple adheres to traditional gender roles, men are even less likely to be involved in the therapy-seeking process. Exceptions arise when the perceived problem pertains to sexual dissatisfaction, in which case men are more apt to note marital discord. Explanations for why men are less likely to seek and initiate the marital therapy are twofold. First, it is possible that men do not possess the same level of emotional self-awareness that women exhibit, which causes them to be less attuned to relational dynamics. Second, it may be that men do recognize and acknowledge the existence of marital discord, yet they prefer to keep such problems to themselves, possibly the result of early gender role socialization. Once couples have entered therapy and initiated treatment, gender differences in problem perception dissipate, and their reports on relational matters (e.g., level of happiness, communication difficulties) tend to be consistent.

Erin M. Fekete and Kasey E. Windnagel

See also Couples Therapy With Heterosexual Couples; Gay Men and Romantic Relationships; Gender Roles: Overview; Lesbians and Romantic Relationships; Marriage Equality; Men's Health; Women's Health

Further Readings

Doss, B. D., Atkins, D. C., & Christensen, A. (2003). Who's dragging their feet? Husbands and wives seeking marital therapy. *Journal of Marital and Family Therapy, 29*(2), 165–177.

Loscocco, K., & Walzer, S. (2013). Gender and the culture of heterosexual marriage in the United States. *Journal* of *Family Theory & Review, 5*(1), 1–14. doi:10.1111/jftr.12003

Robles, T. F. (2014). Marital quality and health: Implications for marriage in the 21st century. *Current Directions in Psychological Science, 23*(6), 427–432. doi:10.1177/0963721414549043

Wanic, R., & Kulik, J. (2011). Toward an understanding of gender differences in the impact of marital conflict on health. *Sex Roles, 65*(5–6), 297–312.

Marriage Equality

In June 2015, Justice Anthony Kennedy of the U.S. Supreme Court changed the course of history by writing for the majority opinion in *Obergefell v. Hodges*, which established the constitutional right of same-sex couples to marry throughout the United States. The effect was immediate jubilation among the gay community, particularly in those 13 states where marriage equality did not exist. Predictably, the backlash among conservative religious groups that had opposed marriage equality was equally immediate. This entry reviews the history of this issue and its relatively rapid progression through the cultural, political, and judiciary processes. The effects of marriage equality on lesbian and gay individuals and families are also reviewed, in addition to the impact on the larger sociocultural environment.

Historical Perspective

Marriage equality has been a primary focus of the gay civil rights movement in the United States, particularly since the turn of the 21st century. This issue had its genesis rather accidentally in 1990, when three same-sex couples sought marriage licenses from the state of Hawaii. A judge subsequently held that preventing the couples from obtaining marriage licenses was a constitutional breach of their civil rights; thus, the modern marriage equality movement was born. The foremost legal activist behind subsequent judicial and electoral victories in this area was Evan Wolfson, an attorney with the Lambda Legal organization. The next 25 years bore witness to a seesaw battle that was fought in legislatures, courtrooms, and the arena of public opinion. Space does not permit a detailed examination of the marriage equality timeline, but the following stand out as signal events, on both sides of the issue:

1996: Partly in response to the possibility of same-sex marriage, Congress enacted the Defense of Marriage Act (DOMA), a federal statute defining marriage as between one man and one woman.

2000: Vermont became the first state to provide a mechanism for legal recognition of same-sex relationships, called "civil unions."

2004: The Massachusetts Supreme Court ruled prohibitions against same-sex marriage unconstitutional, establishing it as the first state in the nation to legalize gay marriage.

2006: In response to a growing effort to legalize same-sex relationships, either through civil unions or marriage, 26 states adopted a Republican Party–led drive to establish constitutional bans on same-sex marriage.

2008: After a campaign funded by religious groups predicated on the notion that same-sex marriage threatens the traditional heterosexual family, Proposition 8 was passed in California (where civil unions had been authorized in 2000), defining marriage as between one man and one woman.

2012: President Barack Obama came out in support of same-sex marriage; the same year, it was legalized by popular vote in Washington State, Maryland, and Maine. Proposition 8 was declared unconstitutional in California. Public opinion turned quickly from majority opposition to support for same-sex marriage.

2013: The U.S. Supreme Court overturned DOMA and refused to hear plaintiffs' case to reestablish Proposition 8. Thereafter, states' bans on same-sex marriage were almost universally declared unconstitutional by the courts. By 2014, same-sex marriage was legal in 36 states and the District of Columbia.

2015: The U.S. Supreme Court declared same-sex marriage a constitutional right and thus to be legal nationwide.

Shifts in Public Opinion

The foregoing history is important because it provides a sociopolitical context from which to understand marriage equality. One might wonder how the United States progressed from a 1986 Supreme Court decision upholding a state sodomy statute to full marriage equality in slightly fewer than 30 years. First, there was a shift in public opinion about gay people and the rights they should have, and these changes were reflected in laws and ultimately in judicial decisions. According to the American Enterprise Institute, more than 73% of respondents in 1973 indicated that homosexual relations were "always wrong"; in 2010, this number was less than 40%. Similarly, an overwhelming majority of Americans believe that lesbians and gay men should be protected from discrimination in housing and employment and should be allowed to serve openly in the military, and—for the first time—a substantial majority (58%) believe that same-sex couples should have the right to marry. Many scholars attest that this rapid shift in public opinion would eventually have had an effect on the reasoning of state and federal judges, particularly in viewing the constitution in a socio-evolutionary context.

Scholars attribute this shift in public opinion to three related factors: (1) exposure to lesbian, gay, bisexual, transgender, and queer (LGBTQ) people; (2) evolution of legal understanding; and (3) experience with same-sex marriage laws already in place. Social psychology suggests that there is no more potent antidote to bias and prejudice than personal exposure. In 1973, 22% of respondents to a Pew Research Center survey indicated that they knew a person who was openly gay; by 2015, that number had risen to 73%. This survey further showed that one third of the respondents had changed their mind about same-sex marriage because they knew someone who is gay or lesbian. In addition, for those without a known LGBTQ individual in their social circle, there has been increased visibility of LGBTQ people (with a recent increase in transgender person visibility) in television, films, and other media sources—creating a secondary level of social exposure. The lives of LGBTQ persons, and their relationships, are seen as not so different from the often mundane hum of life among heterosexuals—save, of course, for the added burdens of prejudice, discrimination, and social marginalization.

Changes in the judiciary reflected changes in social views of gay and lesbian persons. The 1996 U.S. Supreme Court case *Evans v. Romer* was pivotal in that it put a stop to states (in this case, Colorado) enacting laws prohibiting antigay discrimination ordinances. Enacting such legislation was, as Justice Kennedy put it, to "deem a class of persons a stranger to its laws," which "Colorado cannot do." Quite a shift already was in progress, considering that just 5 years earlier the Court had upheld a sodomy statute based on society's "moral discomfort" with homosexuality. Clearly, as our society became less "uncomfortable," judicial validation of constitutional protections for gay men and lesbians increased considerably. The prelude to the Supreme Court's 2015 ruling on marriage equality was the double ruling of the previous year, in which the DOMA was ruled unconstitutional and the proponents of California's Proposition 8 were denied standing for an appeal. This set the stage for federal appeals courts in all circuits, save one (Circuit 4, including Michigan, Ohio, Kentucky, and Tennessee, where same-sex marriages were put on hold), to lead to the explosion of marriage equality in 36 states plus the District of Columbia.

Last, experience itself and the passage of time have proven to be important in shifting public opinion in favor of same-sex marriage. All of the dire predictions about the unraveling of the social fabric and the ultimate destruction of the nuclear heterosexual family simply have not come true in the 10+ years that same-sex marriage has been legal in at least one state. The truth is that despite same-sex marriage, heterosexual people continue to marry—and divorce—at approximately the same rate as before and are twice as likely to divorce as same-sex couples. Some conservative religious groups claim that same-sex marriage infringes on their religious freedom, whereas others claim victimization simply because their prejudice is no longer condoned.

Benefits of Marriage Equality

Justice Kennedy, in his opinion, established marriage as a constitutional right that in part protects lesbians and gay men from being condemned to loneliness. The legal validation of same-sex relationships elevates all lesbians and gay men, whether or not they choose to marry, to an equal status with heterosexuals—culturally, socially, and politically.

No longer are people in same-sex relationships relegated to a second-class status by virtue of civil unions or domestic partnerships—designations that, in most jurisdictions, did not provide the full range of benefits available to married couples. Furthermore, the tangible benefits now available to same-sex couples in every state enhance physical and mental well-being and legally protect their families.

It has long been established that marriage confers physical benefits in terms of physical health and longevity and that LGBTQ individuals in general tend to experience greater physical health challenges. In addition, research indicates that the mental health of lesbians and gay men living in jurisdictions that do not prohibit same-sex marriage is significantly better than that of individuals living in places without such rights. Sharon Rostosky and her colleagues found that lesbians and gay men who lived in states with constitutional bans on same-sex marriage, prior to such laws having been invalidated by the U.S. Supreme Court, experienced higher rates of depression and anxiety than their counterparts living in states without such bans. However, the aggregate stress of living in states where voters may be given the opportunity to invalidate one's relationship is now a thing of the past. With nationwide protections, further research should explore the mental health status of lesbians and gay men in America.

The benefits of marriage equality extend beyond the psychological realm. Legally, same-sex married couples are now entitled to the rights that heterosexual married couples have always enjoyed. From health care benefits to hospital visitation rights, Social Security and Veterans' benefits, and inheritance, the rights now available to all same-sex married couples number more than 1,000. For elder lesbian and gay Americans, same-sex marriage affords protection in terms of health care, institutional protection, and rights of survivorship.

One pivotal argument in support of same-sex marriage involved the children who are in families with same-sex parents. It is estimated that more than 2 million American children are living in same-sex households, and their lives changed as well with the marriage equality ruling. Opponents of marriage equality attempted to advance the notion that same-sex marriage is contrary to the "purpose" of marriage, which is procreation. This argument was rejected by the court, however, based on several fronts: Many heterosexual couples do not procreate, and many same-sex couples do—through surrogacy, sperm donation, or adoption. In 2015, Columbia Law School conducted a meta-analysis of 77 studies in the literature that discredits the notion that children raised by same-sex parents suffer any deficits.

Backlash

All social change—especially as rapid and as culturally sensitive as same-sex marriage—brings with it the prospect of a cultural backlash. Marriage equality, in the context of time, moved relatively quickly through society and, as a result, the courts. Predictably, some in the conservative religious end of the sociopolitical spectrum fear that their own rights are jeopardized by the recognition of same-sex marriage. Marriage is often viewed as a cornerstone of social organization, and these religious groups are faced with relinquishing ownership of the very "definition" of marriage. For some, marriage equality is difficult to accept because they are no longer able—legally at least—to devalue same-sex relationships as somehow less worthy than their own. They may see the removal of their social license to discriminate as an oppression of religious freedom. In fact, there are many religious organizations that do not discriminate against same-sex couples, and no religious institution is compelled to marry same-sex couples.

This issue becomes more complicated, however, when it comes to public accommodation. For example, a lesbian couple in Oregon successfully sued a homophobic baker for refusing to make a cake for their wedding. The baker claimed that this was an infringement on her religious freedom. The courts, however, saw it as a matter of discrimination. Just as it is illegal to refuse service to the public based on race, ethnicity, or any number of other factors, refusal to serve same-sex couples for whatever reason constitutes discrimination. This issue has been playing out in the courts in a variety of ways for some time, as in the case of a university counseling student who was dismissed based on her refusal to adhere to the program's diversity requirements, claiming religious objections.

Future Directions

Opponents of marriage equality often based their objections on the premise that same-sex marriage imposed an unwelcome and dangerous redefinition of the institution of marriage. This view, however, is derived from a culture-bound perspective for those with short memories. The truth is that marriage, like most social institutions, has been in a constant state of evolution since the beginning of recorded time. In antiquity, marriage was a proprietary relationship in which men exerted ownership over women. Even as recently as the 19th century, marital relationships were the province of gender-based ownership. The rise of women's rights, and ultimately feminist theory, was the prelude to today's marriage equality. In this evolution, marriage has become an institution that is based on personal freedoms central to the pursuit of happiness—and guaranteed by the constitution.

Although the future of marriage equality in the United States is still unknown, one may consider examining the Scandinavian countries, The Netherlands, Belgium, and even Spain, where marriage equality has been a social reality for many years. In those countries, which are admittedly more socially progressive than the United States, same-sex marriage has simply been absorbed into the country's cultural fabric, with no negative social effects or diminishment of heterosexual relationships. For the foreseeable future, one can expect to hear protests from those whose religious orientations will not permit them to accept same-sex people, let alone same-sex relationships. The mainstream, however, will ultimately continue its integration of same-sex marriage into the tidal shift of public opinion in favor of marriage equality—ultimately, removing the prefix *same-sex* and the suffix *equality* and simply referring to it as *marriage*.

Douglas C. Haldeman

See also Gay Men and Romantic Relationships; Heterosexism; Human Rights; Lesbians and Romantic Relationships; Marriage

Further Readings

Badgett, M., & Mallory, C. (2014). *New data from marriage licenses for same-sex couples*. Los Angeles, CA: Williams Institute. Retrieved from http://williamsinstitute.law.ucla.edu/research/census-lgbt-demographics-studies/relationship-data-2014/

Evans v. Romer, 517 U.S. 620 (1996).

Human Rights Campaign. (2014). *Overview of federal benefits granted to married couples*. Washington, DC: Author.

Obergefell v. Hodges, 576 U.S. ___ (2015).

Robles, T., Slatcher, R., Trombello, J., & McGinn, M. (2014). Marital quality and health: A meta-analytic review. *Psychological Bulletin, 140,* 140–187.

Rostosky, S. S., Riggle, E. D. B., Horne, S. G., Denton, F. N., & Huellemeier, J. D. (2010). Lesbian, gay, and bisexual individuals' psychological reactions to amendments denying access to civil marriage. *American Journal of Orthopsychiatry, 80,* 302–310.

Masculinities

Masculinities refer to the characteristics that define what it means to be a man or to be masculine. The scholarly discussion surrounding what makes someone a man or a woman has received much attention in recent years. In the past, many would argue that one's masculine or feminine characteristics were determined by genitalia. In the present time, when modern medicine makes it feasible to alter these biological attributes, the question of how *masculine* and *feminine* are defined begs to be asked.

For decades, researchers and scholars have been examining gender formation and maintenance across a number of fields. Scholars have posited a number of theories related to gender development that often consider the nature versus nurture debate. Gender development has even been a point of discussion in political deliberations, as evidenced by political pundits discussing whether rights should or should not be afforded to the LGBTQ community. There are those who assert that if gender were completely a result of nature or evolutionary factors, then that would have implications for social equality. Others have argued that it would give rise to further discrimination and derision.

This entry begins by defining some basic terms and concepts related to gender. Then, the entry focuses on the research on masculinity and the negative consequences that the socially accepted ideologies of masculinity can have for men. The entry concludes by discussing the argument for reimagining masculinity in society.

Sex Versus Gender

To begin this discussion on masculinities, it is important to clarify some basic terms. *Sex* refers to biological differences that are typically associated with females and males. Differentiations that are typically associated with sex include characteristics pertaining to height, physical strength, and voice tone. *Gender* refers to characteristics used to differentiate between masculine and feminine, typically based on social structures that delineate male and female roles. In society, terms such as *gender* and *sex* are used interchangeably, which is often incorrect. Furthermore, the differences across gender, which are typically discussed as points of controversy, often include intelligence and displays of emotion.

Gender Identity

Researchers have looked at individuals' inner self-concepts and the piece of their identity that gives them an understanding of their role as members of a particular gender. Gender identity often refers to one's self-concept and understanding of how one is expected to exist, relate, and interact with the world based on masculine and feminine ideologies. These ideologies are often socially constructed and have varying characteristics based on culture and region. Gender, and how one creates one's own understanding of this concept, has been the fodder for much scholarly discussion and disagreement. Researchers have looked to theories of gender identity and the role that these characteristics play in one's life. Gender identity, like many concepts, should be viewed through a cultural lens and cannot be used to explain or label "all" members of any group. It is important to note that since gender roles are socially and culturally constructed, they are not universal, even within a given subgroup.

Again, as with many pieces of one's identity, the attributes that one ascribes to one's gender begin to develop at an early age. When children are young, they begin by modeling the behaviors of their parents and others in their immediate social network. Often, children learn, through subtle and overt cues displayed by their caretakers, that there are gender specific behaviors that are socially acceptable. When children develop and grow older, they learn these same cues from other children in their social networks, on the playground, at school, and in other various social contexts. Researchers and scholars often see gender roles as representative of socially constructed attitudes, rules, and expectations. These expectations often influence behavior and play a vital role in how one interacts with the surrounding world. Attitudes and behaviors that are influenced by these socially constructed expectations may become so ingrained in one's personality that they are not easily extracted. Masculine and feminine characteristics develop through a series of social interactions that become the foundation of individuals' identities. Traditionally, gender roles were viewed as predetermined and based on one's sex. More recently, some researchers have acknowledged the nuances that exist in the understanding of gender and gender identity.

Masculinity

Researchers have found that some of the most commonly socialized ideas and behaviors among young boys are avoiding weakness, limiting the range of emotions, instilling the importance of power and competition, and maintaining control at all cost. While these thoughts and behaviors may not be endorsed by all men in society, they are similarly held beliefs pertaining to men across many cultures. With that said, men typically develop in a community where they learn that deviating from the traditionally held beliefs and behaviors will have consequences. Men are taught at an early age that displays of weakness, such as backing down from confrontation or crying, are taboo and will not be tolerated by most people in society. For example, a boy who cries in the schoolyard after injuring himself will most likely be ridiculed by other children in his peer group, which may at times include female peers. Thus, lessons that are ingrained in the mind of young boys at home by their immediate social group will be reinforced by their peer network outside the home. If a young man wishes to deviate from the norm, he is shown from a young age that he will be ridiculed, humiliated, and possibly injured by others in his peer group. Although these learned behaviors reveal themselves differently based on the individual and cultural upbringing, there are commonalities that exist among most studied cultures.

Boys are also taught from early on that they have to be strong in the face of all things. They are shown that there are certain emotions that they can and cannot display. As stated earlier, boys are socialized to believe that a show of weakness is unacceptable. This is also true for any emotion that might be interpreted as weak. For example, sadness, pain, and fear are emotions that are typically taboo for boys who are transitioning into manhood. Moreover, boys are conditioned to believe that emotions such as anger and frustration are socially acceptable and can be displayed without fear of reprisal. Boys are also socialized to believe that anger and violence are acceptable reactions to conflict. In addition, boys are often conditioned to believe that they are superior to their female counterparts as well as any males who do not conform to this masculine ideology. Researchers have noted that these behaviors and beliefs are even more resilient when they are reinforced by early female influences, such as mothers and female teachers. Researchers have also discovered that boys are socialized to seek out competition and are rewarded for assertiveness and dominance.

This holds true in the realm of personal and romantic relationships as well. Men are socialized to believe that they must be self-assured, and this behavior, in turn, is reinforced by women who find this display attractive as well as by men who are envious. Men are also conditioned to believe that it is acceptable, if not desirable, to be sexually uninhibited and take many partners as a testament to one's standing as a virile man. Men may discuss the number of their sexual "conquests" as a way to bolster their identities among their peers. This characteristic leads to questions regarding sexual orientation, as traditionally, same-sex relationships were viewed as counter to accepted norms and grounds for exclusion and denigration in society.

A Manly Toll

Researchers have discovered that the accepted masculine ideologies do take a toll on the psyches of men who adhere to them. As stated earlier, due to the consequences of failing to adhere to traditional norms, boys and men are burdened with the anxiety of abiding by rules that can be demoralizing and overwhelming. These destructive tolls can lead to feelings of insecurity and despair when one fails to uphold unrealistic expectations. A boy who fears his own inability to live up to these imposed standards, even if only anticipated, may experience a level of impairment that affects his ability to function. Research has documented that these disappointments may lead to acting out violently, depressed mood, isolation, and self-harm. It has also been documented that these feelings may translate into a negative self-image and cause one to develop an unhealthy self-concept. Ultimately, boys who fail to attain the pinnacle of this socially acceptable masculine ideology may experience substance abuse, depression, and other mental health issues, including suicidality. Also young boys who feel rejected by their peers may lash out violently. Even men who have attained this masculine identity may experience unwanted stress related to maintaining this status. This can be especially true for married men who are the sole or primary providers for their families. Given the uncertainty in today's turbulent economy, the fear of losing one's economic standing may produce copious amounts of unwanted anxiety. This, in turn, can affect the individual's ability to perform successfully at work and may also lead to on-the-job accidents. Researchers have found that stress also produces unwanted physical and psychological anguish.

Future Directions

Many have argued for a reimagination or reclassification of how masculinity is defined in current society. Researchers and scholars have looked at the consequences of adhering to a stringent and traditional view of how one should behave as a member of one's gender. They have also pointed out the inequities that fundamentally exist in a society where one is expected to adhere to strict rules that affect several areas of one's life. It seems logical that a first step in this reimagining would be to look at the messages that we as a society are sending to young boys about how they should behave in society. For example, as parents, when our young son falls and scrapes his knee, do we comfort him and give him the space to express his emotions? Or do we tell him that he must bury those feelings and present a strong front? When our teenage son tells us that he is trading in his football helmet for ballet shoes, do we accept and nurture his interest, or do we ridicule him for this choice? When we see a male nurse in our local doctor's office, do we assume that he was not smart enough or determined enough to become a doctor? Do we label him a failure and hold him up as an example of what we do not want our sons to imitate? If we as a society are to reimagine the ideas and beliefs that define masculinity, it is important to first reexamine our own biases and stereotypes pertaining to gender roles, including what is acceptable masculine behavior, in order to obtain a true representation of what needs to be studied and altered.

Sidney Smith

See also Gender Role Conflict; Hegemonic Masculinity; Heteronormativity; Masculinity Gender Norms; Masculinity Threats; Patriarchy

Further Readings

Addis, M. E., & Mahalik, J. R. (2003). Men, masculinity, and the contexts of help seeking. *American Psychologist, 58*(1), 5–14.

Bem, S. (1993). *Lenses of gender: Transforming the debate on sexual inequality.* New Haven, CT: Yale University Press.

Halpern, D. F. (2013). *Sex differences in cognitive abilities.* New York, NY: Psychology Press.

Hirsh, J. B., & Kang, S. K. (2016). Mechanisms of identity conflict uncertainty, anxiety, and the behavioral inhibition system. *Personality and Social Psychology Review, 20*(3), 223–244. doi:10.1177/1088868315589475

Levant, R. F. (1995). Toward the reconstruction of masculinity. In R. Levant & W. Pollack (Eds.), *A new psychology of men* (pp. 229–251). New York, NY: Basic Books.

Levant, R. F. (1996). The new psychology of men. *Professional Psychology: Research and Practice, 27*(3), 259–265.

Levant, R. F. (2011). Research in the psychology of men and masculinity using the gender role strain paradigm as a framework. *American Psychologist, 66*(8), 765–776. doi:10.1037/a0025034

Levant, R. F., Hirsch, L. S., Celentano, E., & Cozza, T. M. (1992). The male role: An investigation of contemporary norms. *Journal of Mental Health Counseling, 14*(3), 325–337.

Levant, R. F., & Rankin, T. J. (2014). The gender role socialization of boys to men. In R. Burke & D. Major (Eds.), *Gender in organizations: Are men allies or adversaries to women's career advancement?* (pp. 55–72). Northampton, MA: Edward Elgar. doi:10.4337/9781781955703.00011

Mahalik, J. R., & Burns, S. M. (2011). Predicting health behaviors in young men that put them at risk for heart disease. *Psychology of Men & Masculinity, 12,* 1–12. doi:10.1037/a0021416

O'Neil, J. M. (2008). Summarizing 25 years of research on men's gender role conflict using the gender role conflict scale: New research paradigms and clinical implications. *The Counseling Psychologist, 36*(3), 358–445. doi:10.1177/0011000008317057

Reilly, E. D., Rochlen, A. B., & Awad, G. H. (2014). Men's self-compassion and self-esteem: The moderating roles of shame and masculine norm adherence. *Psychology of Men & Masculinity, 15*(1), 22–28.

Thompson, E. H., & Pleck, J. H. (1986). The structure of male role norms. *American Behavioral Scientist, 29*(5), 531–543. doi:10.1177/000276486029005003

Masculinity Gender Norms

The ways in which individuals construct and understand gender, especially masculinity, tend to be fairly limited by time, culture, and geography. At any given time, there are multiple forms of masculinity being cultivated and endorsed, but many people are not aware of these various forms of masculinity. The ever-adolescent man who never seems to grow up, the metrosexual male who favors fashion, or the lumberjack man (i.e., lumbersexual) who idolizes "outdoorness" are examples of different forms of masculinity, each with an ideology, norm, and script for men who endorse these ideals. Masculine ideals and expectations vary across time as well. There was a time when the aristocratic man, affluent and avoidant of work, was the highest ideal of masculinity. The aristocratic man was the ideal contrast to men who were manual laborers (e.g., farmers) and regarded to be more beast than human. These perceptions and stereotypes of who was the ideal man influenced how men of color (men who are African, Asian, Latino, or Native American) were treated. Men of color also were contrasted as the "not-real men" to the ideal White male norm. White masculinity had to be the opposite of what men of color were: rapists, beasts, uneducated, dirty, and uncivilized.

Describing these various forms of masculinity allows one to see that masculinity is much better understood as multiple masculinity or masculinities. In addition, masculinity, like the concept of gender, is malleable (changeable) as well as adaptable to the prevailing cultural demands of a particular time and context or situation. If there are all these forms of masculinity, then what is masculinity, and how do men learn to be men? This entry explores these questions.

Masculinity, first and foremost, is a social construction; masculinity is not genetic or based in temperament. As a social construction, masculinity is the expression of a collection of cultural expectations, historical needs, and communal standards. It is far beyond this brief entry to note, but readers should be aware that masculinities are quite varied in expression across context and time.

There are notions of what is construed as traditional masculinity, but even those conceptualizations have changed with respect to what is considered "traditional." Some scholars have attempted to denote traditional aspects of masculinity to mean expectations such as to "be a big wheel," "be assertive," "be in control," or "be a sturdy oak." Yet even the degree to which one is expected to subdue one's feelings and emotions (e.g., be a sturdy oak) is different across cultures. In some cultural groups, emotional expression is very much nurtured and endorsed, but the expression of feelings and emotions is different if a man is interacting with in-group versus out-group members. Similarly, even among "traditional men," emotions are appropriate to express but only in certain contexts, such as if one has experienced an extreme trauma (e.g., in combat), witnessed the birth of a child, or just scored a winning touchdown. The codes and expectations for men can be complex if one did not grow up in that culture. In those instances, boys and men learn quickly from other men how to act.

These masculine expectations are considered to be aspects of a masculine ideology or script within a particular culture. These scripts are essentially ways in which men are expected to think and behave. Scripts and ideologies may seem innocuous, yet when men endorse these scripts and attempt to fulfill the expectations, the consequence for men is largely negative. Rather than being helpful and fulfilling for many men, these ideologies and scripts tend to be mostly restricting and confining. Research, for instance, shows that boys want to show emotions and are full of feelings, but the scripts and ideologies for boys and men are just the opposite: be emotionless, stoic, and restrained. Boys learn quickly via bullying, teasing, or physical abuse that the expression of emotions is considered within their culture to be "feminine" and therefore to be avoided.

Within any culture, the degree to which these gender and masculine expectations are seamlessly integrated into and synthesized with other expectations for an individual marks the extent to which these masculine expectations are regarded as normative. Masculine role norms in many cultures and societies are difficult to discern because the expectations for men are not in isolation from other cultural expectations and institutions. For instance, in considering what traditional masculinity is for many men in the United States, one has to see that the expectations for men are also tied to what is expected for women. Men are to be tough and strong, whereas the stereotype for an ideal woman in the United States is to be soft and nurturing. Men who venture away from the "strong" expectation are likely to be labeled as "gay," "weak," or "feminine."

Institutions also help support traditional masculinity. Schools teach that frontiersmen founded the United States and that military men fought wars of liberation and freedom. Some religious institutions subscribe to dogmas that reify the man as the head of the household, whose purpose is to lead the family and be the breadwinner. For many, what is considered to be normative masculinity is constantly reinforced via popular culture and the media. Thus, normal masculinity will be regarded as timeless, traditional, normal, and most healthy.

The problem many boys and men experience within their culture is that because masculinity is a social construction, many boys and men (a) have difficulty finding contexts and communities that nurture minority forms of masculinity and (b) have difficulty performing masculinity outside the expectation. Social construction of masculinity is not a passive-receptive experience; instead, social construction means that individual boys and men are active participants in how masculinity is shaped. Being active in the social construction of masculinity entails accepting how family, friends, and peers construct masculinity and then demonstrating one's acceptance of these expectations by "living" that masculinity. This interactive process of masculinity means that potentially shifting away from these expectations also implies that the man may lose those important relationships. It is not an easy prospect for many men to consider alternative forms of masculinity since the loss of important relationships that were tied to how they learned to be a man are likely in jeopardy. For scholars and psychologists, men have to be regarded as actors within a larger play and not as autonomous figures who can decide not to follow a masculine script.

Scholars have identified aspects of what they consider to be traditional masculine norms. Some of these male role norms revolve around strength, honor, action, being a provider, and being a protector. Men have to endorse hypermasculine styles such as stoicism, violence, and taking personal risks. James Mahalik's work on the Conformity to Masculinity Norms Inventory suggests that there might be as many as 11 norms that men are asked to endorse. His colleagues speculated that these factors are (1) winning, (2) emotional control, (3) risk taking, (4) violence, (5) power over women, (6) dominance, (7) being a playboy, (8) self-reliance, (9) the primacy of work, (10) disdain for homosexuals, and (11) the pursuit of status. Ron Levant also found similar constructs in his work on the Male Role Norms Inventory. In his scale, he found that men are expected to endorse the restriction of emotions, avoid being feminine, focus on being tough, be self-reliant, make achievement a priority, not focus on relationships, objectify sex, and be homophobic. All of these masculine role norms are within an original conceptualization by Deborah Sarah David and Robert Brannon, who suggested that men have to adhere to the following standards: (a) no sissy stuff, (b) be a big wheel, (c) be a sturdy oak, and (d) be aggressive (or give 'em hell).

William Ming Liu

See also Alexithymia; Gender Role Conflict; Hegemonic Masculinity; Heteronormativity; Masculinities; Masculinity Threats; Patriarchy

Further Readings

Addis, M. E., & Mahalik, J. R. (2003). Men, masculinity, and the contexts of help-seeking. *American Psychologist, 58,* 5–14.

David, D., & Brannon, R. (Eds.). (1976). *The forty-nine percent majority: The male sex role.* Reading, MA: Addison-Wesley.

Kindlon, D., & Thompson, M. (2000). *Raising Cain: Protecting the emotional life of boys.* New York, NY: Ballantine Books.

Levant, R. F., Hirsch, L., Celentano, E., Cozza, T., Hill, S., MacEachern, M., . . . Schnedeker, J. (1992). The male role: An investigation of contemporary norms. *Journal of Mental Health Counseling, 14,* 325–337.

Levant, R. F., & Richmond, K. (2007). A review of research on masculinity ideologies using the Male Role Norms Inventory. *Journal of Men's Studies, 15,* 130–146.

Mahalik, J. R., Good, G. E., & Carlson, M. (2003). Masculinity scripts, presenting concerns and help-seeking: Implications for practice and training. *Professional Psychology: Research and Practice, 34,* 123–131.

Mahalik, J. R., Locke, B., Ludlow, L., Diemer, M., Scott, R. P. J., Gottfried, M., & Freitas, G. (2003). Development of the Conformity to Masculine Norms Inventory. *Psychology of Men & Masculinity, 4,* 3–25.

Masculinity Ideology and Norms

Masculinity ideology and masculine norms are closely related concepts. Whereas masculinity ideology refers to a set of beliefs about how boys and men should or should not act, think, or feel, masculine norms, like other social norms, are the specific prescriptions and proscriptions for how boys and men should or should not act, think, or feel, as expressed in the commonly heard exhortation "Boys don't cry." Both traditional masculinity ideology and traditional masculine norms play a central role in the gender role strain paradigm, the dominant theory in the psychology of men and masculinities. This entry reviews the social-scientific foundations of masculinity ideology and masculine norms, describes the relevance of differing ideologies and norms, and reviews current empirical literature related to the endorsement and measurement of masculinity ideologies and masculine norms.

Social-Scientific Foundations of Masculinity Ideology

The term *masculinity ideology* refers specifically to beliefs about how a man should or should not think, feel, and behave. Masculinity ideology plays a central role in the gender role strain paradigm, a feminist and social learning perspective. The focus on socialized masculinity and on beliefs regarding men's roles was a departure from the literature on the psychology of gender from 1930 to 1980, in which the gender role identity paradigm reigned supreme. The gender role identity paradigm focused on the personality traits stereotypically associated with one's biological sex. This was an important distinction in that masculinity ideology corresponds to an individual's endorsement of how men should think, feel, and act, while masculine personality traits focused on a man's self-description of his personality in terms of sex-typed traits, which implies a biological cause, given that temperament is biologically based. Viewing masculinity from a perspective of ideology, rather than based on personality traits, moves the discourse away from essentialism.

This perspective in psychology has counterparts in other social science disciplines. Anthropologists have observed that the requirements for masculinity often transcend cultures, noting that most (though not all) cultures require men to be providers, protectors, and procreators. Sociologists have developed the construct of hegemonic masculinity, a social structure that serves to subordinate women to men, marginalize men of color in the United States, and subjugate sexual minority men. Psychologists refer to traditional masculinity ideology to refer to a similar phenomenon, namely the masculinity ideology that prevailed in the United States prior to the challenges of second-wave feminism in the 1960s and which is to some extent the dominant form in the Western world today. This construct—which could more accurately be termed *traditional White Western masculinity ideology*—like the anthropologists' construct of the requirements for masculinity and the sociologists' construct of hegemonic masculinity, is postulated to serve the function of maintaining the patriarchal social system that exists in most societies.

Differing Masculinity Ideologies

As masculinity ideology is based on social norms, it is important to note that there is no universal standard for masculinity, nor is there a single masculinity ideology. Elements of an individual's national and local culture as well as the cultures surrounding one's identities (i.e., race, ethnicity, gender, sexual orientation, age/cohort, socioeconomic status) play various roles in the development of an individual's masculinity ideology. Because of these local influences, we refer to masculinity ideologies to highlight the fact that the different social identities construct differing ideals for manhood. Prior research on different masculinity ideologies defined by race/ethnicity or nationality was done by looking for differences in the endorsement of the specific norms of traditional masculinity rather than developing different masculine norms for different cultural or identity groups. More recent research has attempted to develop a different set of masculine norms for different cultural or identity groups, often using qualitative and mixed-methods research.

The central role of traditional White Western masculine norms may play a part in the disparate masculinity experiences of individuals of different racial and ethnic groups. Non-White males have been found to experience pressure to change and adapt to traditional White Western masculine norms. This undermines the cultural differences among individuals of differing social identities, where many non-White men may receive the message that they are not men because they are acting in ways that are not seen as masculine by those on whom traditional White Western masculine norms are based (i.e., White men in the Western world). For example, a lower-socioeconomic-status Black man may not be able to fulfill the role of good provider for his family due to racism and the lack of economic opportunity and thus might be subjected to disparagement that he is not "man enough." The plural term *masculinity ideologies* also reflects the idea that complex masculinity ideologies might exist due to the intersection of several social identities, such as those based on gender (i.e., man), race (e.g., Black), sexual orientation (e.g., gay), age (e.g., older man), and/or ability/disability status (e.g., a man in a wheelchair).

Demographic Differences in the Endorsement of Traditional White Masculinity Ideology

Differences in the level of endorsement of the traditional White Western masculinity ideology have been found among individuals of differing identities. Some of the differences that have been most studied exist within the identities related to race, ethnicity, nationality, and gender. Research into differing masculinity ideologies has focused on comparing groups of differing identities on the basis of their responses to measures examining the endorsement of male role norms. A group of Russian men and women and a group of American men and women were found to have significant differences in the endorsement of traditional White Western masculine norms. The Russian men and women were more likely than the American men and women to endorse traditional White Western masculine norms, and the men participants were more likely than the women participants to endorse these norms. African American and White men and women in the United States responded significantly differently on similar measures, with women being less likely to endorse traditional White Western masculine norms than men and African American men being more likely to endorse traditional White Western masculinity ideology than White men. An investigation of the differences in the endorsement of traditional White Western masculinity ideology among African American, Hispanic, and White men and women found that the men participants endorsed traditional White Western masculine norms to a greater extent than the women participants and both Hispanic and African American individuals endorsed a more traditional White Western masculinity ideology than the White participants in the study, with the African American individuals endorsing a more traditional White Western ideology than the Hispanic individuals.

Measurement of Masculinity Ideology

It is arguable that measures of masculinity should utilize absolute norms, which focus on masculine behavior by itself, rather than relative norms, which compare masculine behavior with feminine behavior. A foundational review of extant masculinity measures identified that the Male Role Norms Inventory (MRNI) was the only measure that utilized absolute norms, while displaying consistent reliability and construct validity. Unlike the other three measures described, the MRNI has since been revised, and a short form of the revised version was also recently developed. These revisions have similarly exhibited adequate internal consistency reliability while maintaining a valid, seven-factor structure that maintains the multidimensional structure and allows for the assessment of specific masculine norms. All three versions of the MRNI focus on men's and women's endorsement of male role norms rather than on men's conformity to masculine norms.

A recent review detailed a significant shift in the measurement of masculinity ideology and masculine norms over 20 years. In addition to the development of new measures of masculinity, an increase has been evident in the focus on the normative (i.e., socially and culturally developed) approach to masculinity measurement. A corresponding decrease in focus on an ingrained trait perspective of masculinity measurement has also been observed. In addition, a distinction has been made between masculinity ideologies, which reflect the aforementioned social and cultural norms, and masculinity beliefs, which represent one's own internalization of these norms.

Recent literature has stated that while masculinity ideologies and femininity ideologies may overlap, they are not related when examined empirically. Studies measuring both femininity ideologies and masculinity ideologies have typically found that they had less than half of their variance accounted for in common.

Several new measures of masculine norms have emerged. Of these, the Conformity to Masculine Norms Inventory has not only been widely used but has also been revised for the development of a short form. The measure focuses on self-reported conformity to mainstream (i.e., traditional White Western) masculine norms, examining cognitive, affective, and behavioral conformity to these culturally dominant influences. Also of note is the Traditional Attitudes About Men scale. This scale focuses on personal norms, rather than making a comparison with global or culturally dominant norms, and does so with a succinct format.

New measures such as the Machismo Measure, the Macho Scale, and the Russian Male Norms Inventory have focused on specific ethnic identities' endorsements of masculinity ideology. As part of this trend, a more encompassing Multicultural Masculinity Ideology Scale has also been developed. This measure, whose questions ask about "a man," "guys," or "male friends" when querying about masculinity ideologies, has identified both etic (common) aspects and emic (disparate) aspects of masculinity ideology among several non-U.S. samples.

These newer measures, viewed as a second wave of masculinity ideology and masculine norm measurement, provide for the investigation both of the more socially located masculinity ideologies and the more internally focused masculinity beliefs. While both socially and culturally influenced, the incorporation of both elements into the methodology allows for a greater breadth in the research and a more nuanced understanding of masculinity and masculine norms

Ronald F. Levant and Eric R. McCurdy

See also Gender Role Strain Paradigm; Masculinities; Masculinity Gender Norms; Men's Issues: Overview

Further Readings

Chan, J. (2001). *Chinese American masculinities: From Fu Manchu to Bruce Lee.* New York, NY: Routledge.

Gilmore, D. (1990). *Manhood in the making: Cultural concepts of masculinity.* New Haven, CT: Yale University Press.

Levant, R. F. (2011). Research in the psychology of men and masculinity using the gender role strain paradigm as a framework. *American Psychologist, 66,* 762–776.

Levant, R. F., Cuthbert, A. C., Richmond, K., Sellers, A., Matveev, A., Matina, O., & Soklovsky, M. (2003). Masculinity ideology among Russian and U.S. young men and women and its relationship to unhealthy lifestyle habits among young Russian men. *Psychology of Men & Masculinity, 4,* 26–36.

Levant, R. F., Majors, R. G., & Kelley, M. L. (1998). Masculinity ideology among young African American and European American women and men in different regions of the United States. *Cultural Diversity & Mental Health, 4,* 227–236.

Pleck, J. H. (1995). The gender role strain paradigm: An update. In R. F. Levant & W. S. Pollack (Eds.), *A new psychology of men* (pp. 11–32). New York, NY: Basic Books.

Smiler, A. P. (2004). Thirty years after the discovery of gender: Psychological concepts and measures of masculinity. *Sex Roles, 50,* 15–26.

Thompson, E. H., & Bennett, K. M. (2015). Measurement of masculinity ideologies: A (critical) review. *Psychology of Men & Masculinity, 16,* 115–133. doi:10.1037/a0038609

Thompson, E. H., & Pleck, J. H. (1995). Masculinity ideology: A review of research instrumentation on men and masculinities. In R. F. Levant & W. S. Pollack (Eds.), *A new psychology of men* (pp. 129–163). New York, NY: Basic Books.

Masculinity in Adolescence

Adolescence is a period in life that begins at the onset of puberty and continues until adulthood. More specifically, it marks a transition from childhood to adulthood. There is debate about when someone officially moves into adulthood, and this is contextually dependent. Since the 2000s, in the United States, there is a phenomenon known as extended adolescence or emerging adulthood. This time frame extends into the mid-20s as a period when children are independent and have certain privileges (e.g., voting) but are still financially dependent on their families. According to Erik Erikson, the central developmental task during adolescence is identity development, including development of one's gender identity and expression.

Masculinity is a type of gender expression referencing qualities traditionally associated with men. These qualities may include independence, stoicism, and athleticism. While masculinity is often associated with the "natural" expression of a male identity, expressions of genders are socially constructed. Women can be perceived as masculine based on their adherence to certain characteristics.

This "natural" expression of manhood is referred to as hegemonic masculinity. Hegemonic masculinity is the idea that there is a culturally sanctioned way to be masculine. In the United States, this tends to be a White, middle-class, able-bodied, heterosexual type of masculinity. It is also an idealized masculinity rooted in a historical romanticism and, due to its fluid definition, is unattainable. Despite this type of masculinity being unattainable in adolescence, there is a pressure to perform as close to this idealized man as possible. In addition to hegemonic masculinity making an unrealistic standard for heterosexual men to achieve, it serves to oppress women and gay men, because they are both judged for deviating from this standard and held to this standard. This double bind is a part of the oppression of gay men and women.

This entry provides a rationale for the fluidity in masculinity, followed by examining masculinities across societies. After exploring those areas, the entry focuses on adolescent socialization around masculinity and concludes with two case examples from different cultural contexts.

Fluidity in Masculinity

Presenting as masculine in adolescence is a fluid, dynamic process. As Judith Butler discusses, masculinity is one type of gender performance that shifts based on the context. For example, masculine behavior in a basketball game might constitute engagement and athletic prowess; however, in a high school cooking class, masculinity may be experienced by perceived incompetence and a degree of disengagement. How masculinity is acted out and perceived also changes based on what other individuals encourage and promote.

This contextualization informs what type of masculinity is present in the historical moment. Some theorists believe that the type of masculinity that is encouraged in a given society is related to the historical moments that dictate masculinity. A masculinity that is affected by war and violence will socialize boys to be aggressive and emotionally dissociated. These are coping strategies for a boy to prepare for the traumatic and difficult situations he will face.

A historical shift in masculinity is evident in U.S. history. As the nation was being founded, a new type of masculinity arose. This type of masculinity focused on independence and individuality. The focus centered on a man changing his life based on his needs. With this shift in ideal masculinity, the British form of masculinity was vilified, primarily by the increased belief that British men were effeminate. These changes arose at the time the United States was forming a national identity. In other words, the United States needed a different type of masculinity to match their developing national identity.

Masculinities Across Societies

Masculinity is communicated to young boys and adolescents through social construction and social learning. These theories indicate that gender expression is learned and not innate. Social construction states that culture informs what types of expressions are perceived as masculine. It goes on to state that these perceptions are often fluid and change based on the context. There is no objective masculinity. Instead, masculinity is different in different settings. Social learning theory purports that individuals can observe behavior and be influenced without replicating it themselves. This theory relates to masculinity in adolescence as adolescents form impressions about what masculinity looks like based on what they see in their families, among friends, and in the media. Acknowledging the fluidity of masculinity, it is impossible to talk about a single type of masculinity. Therefore, it is more accurate to discuss masculinities.

Even within one society or context, there are different manners of socializing masculinity in adolescence based on racism and other marginalized identities. It is necessary to examine masculinity through an intersectional lens, looking at all the social identities. Someone who has more power in society will experience a different type of masculinity from someone at the margins of society. In addition, stereotypes about minority groups tend to proliferate, and there is a desire for individuals to not fulfill these stereotypes. An example is a young Black teenager in the United States who may be experienced as angry or dangerous. His parents may encourage politeness or avoidance of police officers as a way to cope with these personal and systemic biases.

Adolescent Socialization

Masculinity is socialized. This socialization takes place through families, peer, and the media. This experience of socialization can also make men feel conflicted or confused when they do not embody these ideals, wondering what type of a man they are. Part of socialization around masculinity involves socializing about affective expression. Traditionally in Western cultures, men are taught to inhibit emotional expression, with the exception of anger.

As previously mentioned, there are a variety of masculinities that differ based on culture and society. Therefore, making generalizations is difficult, but there are also some elements of masculinity in adolescence that are common. John Hill and Mary Lynch proposed gender intensification theory to indicate that adolescence is a period of heightened socialization and adherence to traditional gender roles.

Research examining gender intensification theory is mixed. There is also some evidence that individuals exhibit an experience of resistance to masculine cues. This resistance is because boys and men are actively engaged in socialization processes. At the beginning of adolescence, boys are open about their needs for interdependence and are looking for intimate emotional connections. Over time, boys' resistance may decrease due to acts by their peers, referred to as policing of masculinity. This policing of masculinity is frequently done through espousing homophobic and misogynistic comments. These biases are often communicated through bullying, but they can be communicated through what appear as casual comments from friends. Misogynistic and homophobic comments serve to communicate when someone acts in an effeminate way. There has been some literature that may indicate a link between masculinity performance, bullying, and school violence. Research indicates that being called homophobic names leads to calling others homophobic names. While at times this expression is playful, it also has a deleterious effect, particularly in creating hostile environments for LGBT students.

One shift in adolescence is that peer relationships begin to become more important than familial relationships. Peers also tend to dictate what is perceived as masculine. Early adolescence is a period of time when relationships with members of the opposite sex become more frequent. There is evidence that in adolescence male same-sex friendships entrench masculine behaviors, while friendships with women tend to lead men to identify more with feminine traits. In addition, based on the cues for the situation, men and women will identify as more masculine if they are presented with a task that is perceived to be more masculine. An example of a perceived masculine task is one that encourages competition, and a perceived feminine task is one that encourages cooperation.

Within male relationships, research indicates the frequency of competition between males. Michael Kimmel discusses how all male peer groups discuss sexual behavior as a way to show their masculinity. This discussion is often embellished, and in interviews, men acknowledge the role of bragging about their sexual relationships in their initiating of sexual behavior. There is evidence that during adolescence the pressure to perform in a sexually charged way is high, particularly for adolescents who identify as heterosexual.

The media also portray a certain kind of masculinity. These images are frequently mediated by race. Adolescent boys tend to look up to certain types of men in popular culture: musicians, athletes, and movie stars. These images teach young men what type of masculinity they should embody. An example is messages that exist in gangster rap of the 1990s, a type of music performed by mostly Black men but enjoyed by mostly White adolescent teenagers. This music connoted a type of masculinity, often steeped in misogyny, and that focused on violence and an explicit rebellion from authority. This is one of a multitude of media messages that young men consume, all of which shape their views of what it means to be a "real man."

Cultural Contexts

Shifts in masculinity are complex and can vary within different contexts. For instance, Jason Hart presents an ethnographic study about masculinity in adolescence with Palestinian youth living in a refugee camp. He describes masculinity in the Palestinian refugee camp as focusing on being extroverted and being strong and willing to fight for friends but never initiating fights with peers. He also describes masculinity as being aggressively protective of women (deemed as weak and requiring male protection) while also being knowledgeable about Islam. Finally, he finds that masculinity involves expressing overt sexual desire and that sexual desire between boys is not considered homosexual. In fact, penetrative anal sex appears common and is discussed gleefully and is a subject of jokes among friends. The adolescent boy proudly claims to be the inserter in anal sex—usually with younger boys. Neither the younger boys nor the older boys are concerned that penetrative anal sex indicates that they are homosexual or less masculine. However, if peers engage in anal intercourse, there is a bias that the inserted partner is perceived as less of a man. Hart discusses how these particular experiences are contextually embedded, including the fact that women are unavailable for sexual practices and are fiercely guarded by siblings. The general experience of encouraging adolescent aggression coexists within a context defined and shaped by a war and a forced expulsion.

Meanwhile, consider Black male adolescents in the United States, who are the victims of systemic oppression and violence. These young men cope with their experiences by coming across in a "cool pose." Richard Majors and Janet Mancini Billson describe this cool pose as a type of disengagement or presenting mild disinterest but in reality a protection against institutional systems of oppression. Some drawbacks of the cool pose are that it correlates with academic disengagement and underachievement. When African American boys are with friends, it may be frowned on to show any vulnerability or to explore any emotions that would be labeled as weak or feminine. Boys are taught overtly and covertly that they should be tough, be open to fighting to show their strength, and not cry or display "feminine" behaviors. However, they are also taught positive messages, including that they should be responsible, make good decisions, and be loyal to their family. Their parents often have "the talk" about how they should behave in public spaces, particularly with law enforcement, to protect their children from police brutality, violence, or even death.

Given these two examples, it is crucial to understand the many contextual factors that may influence how masculinity is taught in different cultural groups. In some ways, teaching masculinity can be a way to cope with, or fight against, systemic oppression. In other ways, teaching masculinity can prohibit the expression of emotions or the ability for young men to be vulnerable.

Matthew LeRoy

See also Adolescence and Gender: Overview; Hegemonic Masculinity; Homophobia; Male Privilege; Masculinities; Masculinity Gender Norms; Masculinity Ideology and Norms; Misogyny

Further Readings

Hart, J. (2008). Dislocated masculinity: Adolescence and the Palestinian nation-in-exile. *Journal of Refugee Studies, 21*(1), 64–81. doi:10.1093/jrs/fem050

Howard, L. (2012). Performing masculinity: Adolescent African American boys' response to gender scripting. *Journal of Boyhood Studies, 6*(1), 97–115. doi:10.3149/thy.0601.97

Kimmel, M. (2006). *Manhood in America: A cultural history* (2nd ed.). New York, NY: Oxford University.

Kimmel, M. (2008). *Guyland: The perilous world where boys become men: Understanding the critical years between 16 and 26.* New York, NY: HarperCollins.

Leszcynski, J. P., & Strough, J. (2008). The contextual specificity of masculinity and femininity in early adolescence. *Social Development, 17*(3), 719–736. doi:10.1111/j.1467-9507.2007.00443.x

Pascoe, C. J. (2005). "Dude, you're a fag": Adolescent masculinity and the fag discourse. *Sexualities, 8*(3), 329–346. doi:10.1177/1363460705053337

Reigeluth, C. S., & Addis, M. E. (2015). Adolescent boys' experiences with policing of masculinity: Forms, functions, and consequences. *Psychology of Men & Masculinity, 17*(1), 74–83. doi:10.1037/a0039342

Way, N., Cressen, J., Bodian, S., Preston, J., Nelson, J., & Hughes, D. (2014). "It might be nice to be a girl. . . . Then you wouldn't have to be emotionless": Boys' resistance to norms of masculinity during adolescence. *Psychology of Men & Masculinities, 15*(3), 241–252. doi:10.1037/a0037262

Masculinity Threats

With the start of the 21st century, traditional gender norms in many parts of the world became more flexible and frequently challenged. Yet in spite of this evolution, boys and men continue to experience masculinity threats throughout their social, emotional, and psychological development.

Masculinity threats can be defined as instances in which a boy or man experiences a threat from his external environment, with the potential to expose him as insufficiently masculine and failing to fulfill gender expectations. To further explore this topic, this entry provides an overview of different masculinity threats, the sources from which they originate, developmental and cultural differences, and social and psychological consequences.

The Origin of Masculinity Threats

Masculinity threats originate from societies and gender norms all over the world. Throughout history, the majority of societies have constructed and utilized gender norms and roles as an organizing structure and a means to establish criteria for masculine and feminine behaviors. The terms *gender* and *sex* can be mistakenly used interchangeably, but *gender* means socially constructed differences between males and females, whereas *sex* refers to biological differences (e.g., anatomy and physiology). Through prescribed gender roles and customs, societies establish clearly defined behavioral expectations and rules that differentiate boys and men from girls and women. For example, with the start of the 21st century, societies continued to establish gender norms through a host of conventions, such as clothing codes, hairstyles, toy and color preferences, occupational divisions, and wage disparities. Out of gender differences and institutional practices to preserve patriarchal privileges, the social practice of masculinity threats has grown.

Dominant Masculine Norms and Related Theories

When societal institutions and people issue masculinity threats, they often attempt to modify boys' and men's behaviors according to dominant masculine norms while punishing their target for failure to adequately conform. Commonly recognized and globally relevant masculine norms include aggression and dominance, toughness, control, emotional restriction, sexual prowess, financial caretaking, and the avoidance of anything perceived as "feminine" or "gay." Dominant masculine norms come together to form hegemonic masculinity, a theory attributed to R. W. Connell and others. A major premise underlying hegemonic masculinity is that it sets an unattainable and illusory gender standard that boys and men can never satisfy. Even the most celebrated and powerful boys and men in a society, such as White, wealthy, heterosexual males, can never fully embody or attain hegemonic masculinity. In considering hegemonic masculinity's unwavering requirements, such as emotional restriction, dominance, and sexual prowess, it likely becomes clearer why these standards would be difficult for a socially, emotionally, and biologically complicated human being to meet. Yet the dominant masculine norms represented within hegemonic masculinity are the criteria that institutions and individuals strive to uphold when issuing masculinity threats.

Researchers have also established that, in contrast to feminine norms (e.g., to be compassionate, nurturing, and emotionally sensitive), masculine norms need to be proven and achieved on an ongoing basis. Thus, many boys and men issue masculinity threats through which to engage in a cycle of precarious manhood. As Joseph Vandello explains, boys and men can experience society's manhood requirements as a precarious undertaking as they receive constant pressure to demonstrate their masculine status but can never fully satisfy those demands.

Masculinity Threats: Forms and Appearances

Masculinity threats take on many forms and appearances, from a high school adolescent male being called "gay" or "a pussy" to an older male feeling insecure after watching a commercial for erectile dysfunction medication. One of the most commonly experienced and pervasive forms of masculinity threats is policing of masculinity (POM). POM is any action intended to prevent or punish behaviors perceived as insufficiently masculine. The most commonly researched examples include homophobic and misogynistic (antifemale) epithets, such as "gay," "fag," "poofter," "bitch," and "pussy." Thus, in addition to directing a boy or man to change his behavior in line with dominant masculine norms, POM also serves to denigrate women and gay men with the suggestion that those groups possess inferior and undesirable characteristics. Recently, researchers have identified other verbal behavioral forms of POM, including manhood insults (e.g., "Man up"), performance insults (e.g., "Suck it up"), and physical body insults (e.g., "shorty" or "skinny boy"). In addition, boys and men can utilize physical behaviors to police and threaten masculinity, such as challenges and dares (e.g., roughhousing or drinking games) and physical aggression (e.g., fighting or physical abuse). In reporting on the functions of these behaviors, boys and men identify masculine norm enforcement, status elevation and preservation, and friendship enhancement as primary reasons for engaging in POM.

As the definition states, POM can be used to prevent and/or punish behaviors perceived as insufficiently masculine. Punishment happens when a boy or man is exposed and reprimanded in response to a perceived gender deviation, whereas prevention occurs when the recipient, along with other boys and men in the vicinity, is reminded of the importance of personifying masculine norms. Boys and men on the receiving end of masculinity threats likely experience an increase in threat level and ongoing punishment if they fail to appease the instigators. While researchers initially established POM as a victimization process used by high-status boys to bully lower-status boys, recent studies have also identified POM as a normative gender regulation process that threatens all boys and men to varying degrees.

Not only do boys and men experience masculinity threats through POM, but they can also feel threatened by institutional messages, popular media, and other communication mediums. Common media outlets that issue frequent threats include magazines, video games, and/or movies directed at a male audience. For example, a beer advertising campaign from 2010 featured men being accused of behaving in an insufficiently masculine manner, including for failure to consume the beer the advertisement was marketing. Ultimately, these men are shamed and told to "man up." Another common example of masculinity threats includes movies that feature hypermasculine, emotionless, and sometimes sex-obsessed male protagonists, such as Sylvester Stallone in *Rambo*, Arnold Schwarzenegger in *The Terminator*, and films such as *American Pie* and *Think Like a Man*. These films share the commonality of featuring characters who embody hegemonic masculinity. In response, male viewers can consciously or unconsciously draw comparisons between themselves and these unrealistic but idealized masculinity personifications. With regard to magazines, boys and men can experience a range of threats, such as physical body and sexual performance insecurities. For example, *Men's Health* magazine frequently features bare-chested young men standing next to slogans such as "The Body You Want" and "Six-Pack Abs." Boys and men viewing these covers likely experience varying levels of threat through feeling physically inadequate for not meeting this societal ideal.

Other common examples of masculinity threats that apply more to boys in indigenous societies include rites of passage ceremonies. These ritualized events typically involve challenges that an adolescent boy must endure and accomplish to be indoctrinated into "manhood" by his community. Some examples include a fire ant ceremony in the Amazon and a blood initiation rite in Papua New Guinea. Rites of passage ceremonies share the commonality of requiring boys to stoically pass tests of endurance, strength, and pain tolerance to "successfully" transition to manhood. Boys who fail these trials experience ongoing social punishment and masculinity threats through shaming and rebuke. Boys who satisfy these requirements also continue to experience masculinity threats through pressure to demonstrate power, procreation capabilities, and financial caretaking as they enter manhood. While they differ from traditional rites of passage, some common rituals in the United States and other Western countries that utilize masculinity threats include fraternity hazing and initiation ceremonies.

Masculinity Threats Through the Life Span

As researchers have established, masculinity threats affect boys starting at a young age. Between the ages of 3 and 5 years, boys have formed a gender identity and start to distance themselves from behaviors and things perceived as feminine. Masculinity threats play an integral role in teaching boys, through reinforcement, punishment, and fear-based learning, the behaviors required for social acceptance and status elevation. One of the earliest examples of masculinity threats is the statement "Big boys don't cry." Researchers have found that parents, teachers, and other authority figures can use this and other masculinity threats to restrict boys' emotional expressiveness, while providing girls with greater expressive freedom and support. Thus, from a young age to when masculinity threats peak in high school, boys receive a barrage of messages, insults, and other communications that threaten their masculine status and pressure them to conform to dominant masculine norms. The question of masculinity threats peaking in adolescence can be answered, in part, through the gender intensification hypothesis. The gender intensification hypothesis states that as boys and girls go through puberty and start to appear more physically different from each other, they experience greater levels of social pressure to conform to dominant notions of masculinity and femininity. However, the adolescent escalation of masculinity threats does not continue unabated, and with transitions to adulthood and the diminishing influence of the peer group, adult men generally experience masculinity threats to lesser degrees.

Consequences of Masculinity Threats

Researchers have identified a range of consequences associated with masculinity threats, with some boys and men reporting minimal psychological consequences and others endorsing acute psychological distress. At the most fundamental level, masculinity threats are intended to pressure boys and men to conform to dominant masculine norms while exposing and punishing behaviors perceived as insufficiently masculine. Thus, a pervasive consequence of masculinity threats for all boys and men is the experience of pressure to appear "appropriately" masculine and prove one's manhood in different contexts. This pressure to conform to masculine norms can result in behavioral constrictions and impositions that manifest differently for different boys and men.

Specific psychological consequences associated with masculinity threats and conformity to masculine norms include emotional silence and invisibility, externalizing disorders, aggression and violence, substance abuse, heightened risk for suicide, diminished help seeking, homophobic and misogynistic attitudes, and gender role strain and conflict. Emotional silence and invisibility refer to some boys' and men's experience of being less emotionally connected to themselves and others due to social pressures to conceal vulnerability; the suicide rate spikes for boys in adolescence, and from that period through old age, boys and men are four to six times more at risk for suicide than girls and women; resistance to help seeking signifies ambivalence and/or unwillingness to present to medical providers, psychologists, and other helpers for fear of appearing weak and vulnerable; and gender role strain refers to stress and negative outcomes associated with "straining" to conform to dominant masculine norms.

With regard to these and other outcomes, masculinity threats affect boys and men differentially and to varying degrees. Some boys and men report that masculinity threats are "no big deal" and "boys are just being boys," and others experience overt victimization and emotional distress. The most hostile form of masculinity threats occurs when boys and men who identify as homosexual, queer, or transgender, or are simply perceived as feminine or gay, are threatened and accosted with physical violence (e.g., hate crimes). While the psychological and emotional consequences can differ greatly for individual boys and men, masculinity threats share the universal commonality of inciting varying levels of fear and shame in response to the prospect of appearing insufficiently masculine.

Christopher S. Reigeluth and Michael E. Addis

See also Bullying, Gender-Based; Competition and Gender; Cyberbullying; Gender Role Conflict; Gender Role Strain Paradigm; Gender Role Stress; Hegemonic Masculinity; Heterosexism; Homophobia; Masculinity Ideology and Norms; Peer Pressure in Adolescence; Power-Control and Gender

Further Readings

Addis, M. E. (2011). *Invisible men: Men's inner lives and the consequences of silence*. New York, NY: Times Books.

Connell, R. W. (2000). *The men and the boys*. Berkeley: University of California Press.

Kimmel, M. S. (1994). Masculinity as homophobia: Fear, shame, and silence in the construction of gender identity. In H. Brod (Ed.), *Theorizing masculinities* (pp. 119–141). Thousand Oaks, CA: Sage.

Newsom, J. S., Congdon, J., & Anthony. J. (Producers). (2015). *The mask you live in* [DVD]. Retrieved from http://therepresentationproject.org/films/the-mask-you-live-in/

Pascoe, C. J. (2007). *Dude you're a fag: Masculinity and sexuality in high school.* Berkeley: University of California Press.

Pleck, J. H. (1995). The gender role strain paradigm: An update. In R. F. Levant & W. S. Pollack (Eds.), *A new psychology of men* (pp. 11–32). New York, NY: Basic Books.

Reigeluth, C. S., & Addis, M. E. (2016). Adolescent boys' experiences with policing of masculinity: Forms, functions, and consequences. *Psychology of Men & Masculinity, 17*(1), 74–83.

Vandello, J. A., Bosson, J. K., Cohen, D., Burnaford, R. M., & Weaver, J. R. (2008). Precarious manhood. *Journal of Personality and Social Psychology, 95*(6), 1325–1339.

Masturbation

Masturbation is the act of touching or otherwise stimulating one's own body, particularly one's genitals, for the purpose of sexual pleasure and/or orgasm. The term is most commonly used to describe solitary masturbation, in which people provide themselves with sexual stimulation while they are physically alone. Mutual masturbation is when two or more people manually stimulate their own body or each other's bodies. Masturbation usually involves stimulation of the clitoris for women and the penis for men, but many other body parts may also play a role, including the nipples, vagina, anus, labia, testicles, thighs, breasts, buttocks, and any other conceivable erogenous zone. Since most sexuality researchers agree that the entire body can act as an erogenous zone, there are countless methods of stimulating pleasure through masturbation.

Masturbation is a common and healthy sexual behavior. Nationally representative data indicate that the vast majority of Americans (about 73% of women and 88% of men) have masturbated. People of all ages masturbate, including young children, and masturbation is a developmentally appropriate behavior for adolescents and children as young as infancy. Gynecologists have even recorded a female fetus masturbating to orgasm in the womb, indicating that masturbation is a perfectly normal and natural behavior, regardless of age or gender.

Cultural Stigma

Although no evidence suggests that masturbation is in any way harmful, the behavior has historically been shrouded in stigma and sometimes considered a sin. Physicians in the 18th and 19th centuries believed that masturbation (particularly male masturbation) could cause any number of ailments, including weakness, blindness, and death. Although modern medicine has dispelled these myths, the stigma persists, and several religious groups continue to view masturbation as sinful. Public discussions of masturbation are rare and sometimes volatile. In 1994, U.S. Surgeon General Joycelyn Elders was fired for suggesting that masturbation could potentially be mentioned in school sexual education courses. Since the turn of the 21st century, masturbation has become increasingly acceptable but is still rarely discussed openly. This social stigma may explain why people sometimes feel guilty or ashamed about their masturbation.

Benefits of Masturbation

Masturbation has been linked to positive psychological health, including increased sexual self-esteem and sexual satisfaction. Masturbation can also provide relaxation, sexual release, and a greater understanding of one's body and the types of sexual stimulation one prefers. Because masturbation can be used as a tool for increasing comfort with one's body and sexual preferences, sex therapists have recommended masturbation to individuals and couples for decades with considerable success. There is no evidence to support the myth that people masturbate only when they are lonely or when they do not have a sexual partner. In fact, some people may masturbate more frequently when they are having frequent partnered sexual encounters.

Masturbation also has medical benefits. One study has linked male masturbation to a decreased likelihood of developing prostate cancer; researchers believe that regular ejaculation may prevent the buildup of cancerous substances in the prostate. Similarly, for women, masturbation to orgasm may help prevent cervical infection. Masturbation and orgasm are also helpful in reducing the pain associated with menstrual cramps and childbirth. Contrary to cultural myth, masturbation does not decrease clitoral or penile sensitivity. Masturbation (including mutual masturbation) is often considered the safest sexual behavior for both men and women because there is little to no risk for unintended pregnancy or transmission of sexually transmitted infections.

Masturbation Techniques

The most common form of masturbation for both men and women is the use of one's hands on the genitals. Masturbation may also include the use of various arousal aids, and both women and men may use synthetic lubrication to prevent chafing. Fantasy and imagination are common during masturbation, and sexual fantasies do not necessarily indicate behaviors a person would like to experience in reality. Both men and women also enjoy pornography and erotic literature.

A woman generally rubs her clitoris or vulva and may insert fingers into her vagina or anus. Women may also masturbate using vibrators, dildos (for vaginal or anal insertion), and/or running water. Some women obtain arousal from rubbing their genitals against pillows or other objects or squeezing their thighs together. Women may stimulate their genitals while simultaneously stimulating their breasts, nipples, or other erogenous zones. Many women report that to reach orgasm, they must remove all distractions and use their mental energy to focus. Many women also enjoy stimulation of the anterior (front) wall of the vagina, which is known as the *G-spot*. Women may use curved dildos or vibrators to stimulate the G-spot.

A man generally grips his penis with his hand and moves up and down along the shaft and/or glans (tip) of his penis. If a man is uncircumcised, he may move the foreskin back and forth. Men sometimes masturbate by rubbing their penis against an object or by using masturbation sleeves, and they may also use anal dildos, vibrators, or enemas to stimulate the prostate gland. Some men enjoy inserting tubes or objects into the urethral opening. Particularly flexible men may also be able to engage in auto-fellatio, which involves stimulating the penis with one's own mouth.

Gender Socialization

Most men learn to masturbate as children or adolescents, but fewer women do. While boys can easily explore their genitalia because they are external to their bodies, girls' genitalia are hidden from view. Girls and boys are not always taught the proper names of female genital anatomy (e.g., vulva, clitoris, labia) or shown accurate representations thereof. These conditions may socialize girls and women to feel ashamed of or detached from their genitals and may explain their lower rates of masturbation throughout life. Whereas boys' first experiences of arousal and sexual pleasure are often through self-exploration, girls' first experiences are more likely to occur in a dating situation. In other words, boys tend to learn about their arousal through self-exploration, whereas girls tend to learn about their own arousal from boys. Psychologists argue that this imbalance in heterosexual relationships underscores the importance of masturbation for young people—girls and boys alike—as a critical step in healthy sexual development.

Christin P. Bowman

See also Gender Role Socialization; Pornography and Gender; Safe Sex; Safe Sex and Adolescence; Sex Education; Sexual Desire

Further Readings

Bockting, W. O., & Coleman, E. (2003). *Masturbation as a means of achieving sexual health*. Binghamton, NY: Haworth Press.

Dodson, B. (1996). *Sex for one: The joy of self-loving*. New York, NY: Random House.

Stengers, J., & Van Neck, A. (2001). *Masturbation: The history of a great terror* (K. Hoffman, Trans.). New York, NY: Palgrave.

MATRIARCHY

Matriarchy describes a social system in which women have power and authority; this means that female contributions are not only valued but also that women make decisions that affect their individual lives, their families, the community, and the larger society. Single females or groups of women occupy leadership positions across the public and private spheres. A feminine perspective undergirds all social institutions, including the economy, education, politics, and religion. This entry begins by addressing some types of social systems described by the term *matriarchy*; it then discusses matriarchal and patriarchal societies, using the Cherokee and U.S. societies as examples, and offers two theories to explain the existence and understanding of matriarchy in these societies.

Social Systems

There have been many known matriarchal societies throughout the world and throughout history—mostly consisting of indigenous, noncolonized societies in Asia and North America. In Asia, precolonized Philippines was said to be a matriarchal society, led by the Babaylan (or chief priestesses), who people believed had special spiritual powers. Historians have also believed that some of these priestesses were transgender women (they had male sexual organs but lived as women or gender nonconforming persons). Despite this, when the Spanish colonized the Philippines, they introduced Catholicism and patriarchy—which obliterated matriarchy across the various islands. In addition, in Asia, there is also the Mosuo culture (an ethnic group in China near Tibet) and the Minangkabau tribe (one of the largest ethnic groups in Indonesia)—both groups that are also said to be matriarchal. Women are the heads of households and the business decision makers. Inheritance is also passed down through the female line. In North America, Native American tribes are said to be matriarchal, in that gender roles (e.g., chores, child care, providing for the family) are equally distributed between men and women. For example, Hopi women have historically been the political decision makers; traditionally, the tribe has also been matrilineal (i.e., lineage is passed through female lines) and matrilocal (i.e., the husband moves to live with the woman's family after marriage).

While originally *matriarchy* was used to describe whole societies, countries, or tribes that were run by women, some have used *matriarchy* to describe instances in which women are in the most powerful positions in given countries or societies. According to the World Economic Forum, 63 of 142 world nations have had a female head of government or state between 1964 and 2014; and in 2015, there were 17 countries with female world leaders. Despite this, it is important to note that most of these countries have had only one female leader within this 50-year span and that most female leaders served for a short period of time. In fact, half of these countries had women who served for fewer than 4 years, and 17% had women who served for less than 1 year. Given this, it is important to recognize that having a woman leader (e.g., president, prime minister) does not necessarily make a society matriarchal, in that there may still be historic sexism that prevents women from having equitable rights or opportunities as men.

Contemporary matriarchy has also been used to describe families that are led by women (e.g., single mothers, grandmothers, same-sex lesbian or queer women couples). Some research has found that children of single-mother homes achieve academically just as well as those from two-parent homes—debunking myths that having a mother and a father is necessary to attain success. Preliminary research has found that children of same-sex couples achieve academically as well as children of opposite-sex couples, with some studies finding that children of same-sex lesbian or queer women couples perform even better. Such research debunks myths that children need a male "father figure" in their life or that children of same-sex couples would have academic or psychological deficiencies.

Black matriarchy is a term that has been controversial since it was first introduced in the late 1800s to describe African American households led primarily by women. Because U.S. Census data have found that there were a higher number of single-parent families led by Black women, White scholars at the time perpetuated the belief that Black men abandoned their families and Black women had the same types of family responsibilities as White men. Today, Black scholars (and others) view such notions as racially problematic, in that they fail to consider the systemic reasons for these statistics. For instance, Black men are arrested, convicted, and incarcerated more than any other racial and gender group—often for crimes they did not commit or for lesser felonies with longer sentences. Black men are also killed by police officers and by hate violence, they experience overt and covert racism on systemic and interpersonal levels, and they may die at earlier ages due to preventable diseases such as cardiovascular disease or diabetes. Social class also determines whether Black families will be led primarily by women, in that middle-class to upper-middle-class Black families tend to have two parents in charge, whereas lower- or working-class Black American families tend to have women as the head of the household.

Despite these false premises in the initial use of the term, some scholars have argued in favor of some positive aspects of Black matriarchy. They recognize the role of Black women (particularly grandmothers and older female adults) in the family—especially as a source of power and wisdom. Black women tend to encourage their family members to uphold tradition, particularly religious and spiritual traditions, which may be a source of healing and collectivism for the family members. Finally, Black women are taught to be strong and self-sufficient, which may encourage the family members to be independent and goal driven. In this way, Black matriarchy may be reframed as a positive concept.

Matriarchy has also been used to describe female power, as opposed to patriarchy, which is used to describe male power. When men use (or abuse) their power, they are said to be patriarchal; such patriarchal behavior can be seen in family dynamics (e.g., fathers or brothers who force mothers or sisters to do chores), workplace environments (e.g., male supervisors who only promote other men and belittle the accomplishments of female employees), and school environments (e.g., male teachers who encourage male students to succeed, without encouraging female students in the same way). On the other hand, matriarchal power does not describe the opposite—in that women only support other women and belittle men. Instead, matriarchy involves the empowerment of other women to have equal opportunities as men and to succeed just as much as men. In this way, matriarchy also involves teaching men to view women as equals, as well as teaching men to advocate for the equality of genders.

Example of a Matriarchal Society

One example of a matriarchy is the traditional Cherokee society. Women held positions of power and leadership in the family and in the community. In terms of politics, two chiefs who alternated their positions led the Cherokees. A peace chief directed the tribe primarily; however, if there was a conflict with another tribe, a war chief would be in charge. Although a male chief may have served in this role, women constituted his advisement council, and any major decision was informed and guided by this female group.

Women are also represented in spiritual stories, particularly with women and the processes associated with pregnancy and birth as the basis for numerous traditional stories related to tribal origins. As women aged, they gained wisdom that was respected in spiritual and political circles. The importance of older females is evidenced in the tribal naming of a spiritual meeting place as "grandmother."

Work was divided based on gender—women were involved in agriculture, gathering, and preparing animal skins, while men were predominantly hunters. However, the tribal ideologies, based on balance and connectedness, did not elevate the status of male labor above female work. Both types of labor were valued as necessary for the health of the tribe, and females controlled the products of their labor.

Women owned the family home, and a wife indicated divorce by placing her husband's items outside the door of the home. On birth, a child belonged to the mother's clan. A clan can be considered as similar to the concept of the extended family in western European traditions. However, clan membership was an essential form of identity and guided many behaviors and customs. Marriage within a clan was prohibited. Once a person had married someone from another clan, the children born from that marriage took the mother's clan name, while the father remained affiliated with his mother's clan. Regarding child rearing, the brother of a child's mother (the child's uncle) was the male who disciplined the child—not the biological father. This uncle would instead be expected to be the disciplinarian for his sister's children (his nieces and nephews).

Representation in tribal government was organized by clan membership. The traditional tribal council meeting structure would contain seven areas that were designated by the clan. On entering the structure, the mother and the children would walk to her clan section and sit, while the father would sit with his mother's family. Finally, violence against women was prohibited, signifying that women were to be respected and honored.

Example of a Patriarchal Society

The United States is an example of a patriarchal social system. Men are dominant across all realms of society, ranging from private life (e.g., family situations, social circles) to political life (e.g., heads of government, heads of institutions). Children are socialized into a world where the male experience is the norm that defines what is valued and rewarded. Throughout U.S. history, policies across various sectors have overtly defined women as deficient in their thinking and behavior based on genetics.

In modern times, an overwhelming majority of government representatives are males, and they control the policy decisions that affect the nation. Because of this, male leaders advocate for, and vote on, laws that negatively affect women (e.g., women's reproductive health, women's civil rights). U.S. patriarchy has also resulted in devaluing females to the point of violent oppression, with women enduring higher rates of physical and sexual violence at the hands of males. Despite this, the criminal justice system has historically failed women with regard to violence, in that many perpetrators of physical or sexual assault do not serve time for their crime.

Leaders within the religious sphere are predominantly male—across most major religions but particularly in Christianity (the dominant religious group across the United States). Religious teachings are used to define the female role as being subservient to men. Many religious groups disallow women from having leadership positions (e.g., priest, rabbi), and most major religious groups celebrate the lives of male figures more than female figures.

Men dominate in the workforce in terms of leadership roles and income. Even within predominantly female professions such as nursing and teaching, males occupy management positions that do not correspond to their ratio of workers. A wage gap exists across all ethnic groups, with men commanding more for their labor than women who possess the same education and experience. This inequity in pay is evidenced in the higher percentages of women in poverty. A majority of heterosexual women who marry will take their husbands' last name. Although some women may hyphenate their last names, it is rarely that men will do the same. It is also expected that children will take their father's last name.

Within families, gender roles are uneven, in that women are expected to take on traditionally feminine roles (e.g., household chores, raising children) while men are expected to work and provide financially for the family. In traditional White American families, sons are allowed more freedom than girls—they are allowed to date at earlier ages, stay out later with friends, and have more independence and alone time. Furthermore, sons can have more power over their adult mother at a young age, particularly if the father is absent.

Matriarchy Meets Patriarchy Through Colonization

At a 1757 trade meeting in South Carolina, a male Cherokee leader asked the governor where the White women were. The tribal leader did not understand why there were no women present to advise the governor. After several days, the governor responded that he did trust women but only after he had made sure that their hearts were good. Colonization exposed the Cherokee tribe to values of male and female that were vastly different from those to which the Cherokee people were accustomed. As it gained more power, the United States began to assert a preference for dealing only with men in meetings that affected the tribe economically, politically, and spiritually. This dynamic affected the leadership roles of women. Patriarchal repercussions eventually appeared within the family, hastened by intermarriage with Europeans. Later generations saw a shift toward patriarchy—as evidenced by male ownership of land and property, male-dominated tribal politics, and domestic violence. The first written record of domestic violence in the Cherokee Nation was in 1805, in a journal kept by missionaries residing on a Cherokee plantation.

While Cherokee culture was affected by this colonization, matriarchy is still practiced and respected in present Cherokee tribes. Contemporary Cherokee people value women in the family as decision makers and cultural teachers, and women are making inroads into leadership positions in tribal government.

Theories Explaining Matriarchy

Social Construction Theory

Social construction theory explains the existence of matriarchy and patriarchy by examining the interactions among people and the shared realities that develop. Rather than accepting the assertion that men are biologically superior to women and that tribal cultures are inferior and uncivilized, this theory looks to common understandings related to what it means to be female and male in a particular society. Furthermore, the theory focuses on the sociopolitical environment and history to understand human behavior and cultural variance in the practices associated with matriarchal and patriarchal societies. When considering the history of matriarchy in Cherokee and U.S. societies, social construction theory would focus on the social and political interactions between the two societies to understand the changes that resulted from colonization until today.

Postcolonial Indigenous Feminist Theory

Postcolonial indigenous theory is congruent with the reality of Cherokee and other tribal women. Postcolonial indigenous feminist theory rejects a universal female experience and does not impose definitions of oppression and empowerment on tribal women. For example, a majority of tribal nations in North America have practices and rituals related to menstruation whereby girls and women are separated from the community while menstruating. Western feminist theorists might interpret these behaviors as evidence of female oppression because women are isolated during menstruation as they are viewed as dirty. Postcolonial indigenous feminist theory would not impose that view but would consider the indigenous women as the authorities. In this cultural explanation, females are isolated during menstruation not because of uncleanliness but because menstruating females are seen as too powerful. Once this cultural reference is known, then tribal women are in a position to determine if the practice is oppressive and needs to be changed. This allows tribal women to be authentic to their entire experience as a communal culture that is focused on balance, cooperation, and harmony. If these elements are lost, then the tribal female experience is distorted. This theory is open to the utilization of multiple theories originating from Western and multiple non-Western sources.

Lisa G. Byers and Kevin L. Nadal

See also Asian Americans and Gender; Black Americans and Gender; Native Americans and Gender; Pacific Islanders and Gender; Patriarchy

Further Readings

Bagele, C. (2012). *Indigenous research methodologies.* Thousand Oaks, CA: Sage.

Cheung, M. (1997). Social construction theory and the satir model: Towards a synthesis. *American Journal of Family Therapy, 25*(4), 331–343.

Johnson, A. G. (2010). Patriarchy, the system: An it, not a he, a them, or an us. In M. Adams, W. Blumenfeld, R. Castañeda, H. Hackman, M. Peters, & X. Zúñiga (Eds.), *Readings for diversity and social justice* (2nd ed., pp. 332–337). New York, NY: Routledge.

Johnston, C. (2003). *Cherokee women in crisis.* Tuscaloosa: University of Alabama Press.

Mills, T. (2010). *The house on diamond hill: A Cherokee plantation story.* Chapel Hill: University of North Carolina Press.

Measuring Gender

Many Americans see little difference between the terms *sex* and *gender* and consider them synonyms. Yet some individuals see the two terms as representing related but different ideas, or constructs. Recognizing and understanding the differences between these constructs is very important to psychologists as producers and consumers of research and in both research and applied settings. The connections between sex and gender are sufficiently important that the *Publication Manual of the American Psychological Association* (hereafter, *APA Publication Manual*), which provides the common standard for professional writing among social scientists, devotes several pages to the topic.

The related but overlapping nature of these constructs makes it a challenge to measure them effectively. However, measuring ideas and variables effectively is the researcher's task and, in many ways, is central to the idea of conducting scientific research. This entry discusses some of the factors that make asking questions about sex and gender more complicated than might seem at first glance, while also offering guidance about how young researchers might achieve this goal.

What Is Gender?

The *APA Publication Manual* has explicitly stated that *gender* is cultural and is the term to use when referring to women and men as social groups. *Sex* is biological; it is used when the biological distinction is predominant. This pair of definitions specifies that sex relates specifically to an individual's biological chromosomal allotment, typically XX for females and XY for males.

By contrast, gender refers to an individual's display of social or cultural characteristics that are assumed or expected for the individual's sex. In other words, females are expected to adopt the female or feminine gender role, whereas males are expected to adopt the male or masculine gender role. The APA recommends using *women* and *men* (or *girls* and *boys*) when discussing gender and using *female* and *male* when discussing sex.

Not all people are adequately described by these two pairs of terms. On the biological side, as many as 1 in 100 people may be intersexual. These persons are individuals who have been diagnosed with a disorder of sexual development (DSD). Some DSDs refer to atypical chromosomal patterns, such as Turner syndrome (XO), Klinefelter syndrome (XXY), or another pattern. Other DSDs describe hormonal problems such as congenital adrenal hyperplasia, in which a female (XX) embryo is exposed to high levels of androgens in utero and as a result becomes masculinized, and androgen insensitivity syndrome, in which a male (XY) body is unable to process androgens and the male genitalia develop either partly or not at all.

Transgender (or trans) individuals have become very visible in U.S. society in the past several years. Three well-known transgender Americans are (1) actress Laverne Cox, (2) athlete turned reality television star Caitlyn Jenner, and (3) Chaz Bono, the child of entertainers Cher and Sonny Bono. Cox, Jenner, and other transgender women may identify as women or trans women, or as male-to-female transgender women. Bono and other trangender men may identify as men or trans men, or as female-to-male men. Many transgender people do not feel comfortable with the sex or gender that is assigned to them at birth and instead identify more strongly with another gender. Some transgender people may seek gender affirming medical treatments or surgeries to align their gender identity and sex.

Other individuals may experience discomfort and disconnection between their biological sex and their culturally assigned gender but do not seek gender affirming medical treatments. These individuals might describe themselves as trans, queer, genderqueer, gender fluid, or some other label. Some may identify as gender neutral or gender nonconforming, or may identify as part of both genders.

Trans people (broadly defined) have begun the practice of using the prefixes *trans-* and *cis-* prior to the terms *female* and *male*. The sex (female or male) is determined by how persons identify themselves in public; the *cis-* prefix indicates a match between biological characteristics and identity, whereas the *trans-* prefix indicates a disjunction between the two. Thus, Caitlyn Jenner is a trans woman, and Katy Perry is a cis-woman (or cis-female). The term *transsexual*, although still used in some contexts (and considered appropriate by some), is not a commonly used term.

The broad array of labels and terms has caused some authors to differentiate between *gender* and *gender identity. Gender identity* refers to the way in which individuals identify their own gender and thus is distinct from the culturally imposed gender roles assigned by society. Thus, while the culture might assume that an individual with a male body, male-typical clothing, and a male hairstyle is a man and can be referred to using the pronoun *him*, that person might identify as genderqueer, for example, and choose a pronoun such as *ze* (pronounced "zhee") or *they*.

It is important to note that *sex*, *gender*, and *gender identity* are distinct from *sexual orientation*, *sexual identity*, and *sexual orientation identity*. These latter terms refer to an individual's romantic and sexual attractions and behaviors. Commonly used terms are *heterosexual*, *homosexual*, *bisexual*, and *pansexual*, although there are many other options.

The Background Binary

One of the challenges to measuring both gender and sex comes from the American cultural assumption that there are only two categories (*sex:* female and male; *gender:* feminine and masculine). The notion that there are only two categories comes with the corollary that these categories are opposites, which is why many people refer to the "opposite sex." Together, these assumptions are sometimes known as the gender binary because they specify a two-category, either/or set of options.

As described earlier, other categories exist, even though they account for a small percentage of the population. Nor is the notion of opposites correct. Male and female bodies are highly similar, with a small number of differences; for example, all humans have breasts and hips, but their size and shape are different for the two sexes. Gender roles rely on a similar distinction in which "differences" are often described as "opposites."

The binary helps obscure individuals who have DSDs, are trans people, or are a variety of "third" genders found around the world. In the either/or binary, individuals must fit themselves into one box or the other. The APA directs authors to use *other sex* instead of *opposite sex* because *opposite sex* implies that there are only two sexes, that there are significant differences between the two sexes, or both.

Measurement: Practical Suggestions

In any research project, it is important to consider why sex or gender will be measured. In psychological research, best practice requires researchers to report the sex of their participants when describing the research sample. If that is the extent of a researcher's interest, then the following question is probably sufficient:

> What is your sex? (select one)
> Female:
> Male:
> Trans:
> Other:

The responses here include the option "Trans," instead of asking about DSDs. The presence or absence of a medical condition is typically considered sensitive information that should be requested only when specifically relevant to a study's goals.

For researchers who are more explicitly interested in gender and gender-related phenomena, some form of the following question can be used:

> What is your gender? (select one)
> Female:
> Genderqueer:
> Male:
> Trans:
> Other:

The option "Genderqueer" can be replaced by "Queer," and the options "Genderqueer" and "Trans" could be listed together as "Queer/Trans." The response options could be expanded, assuming that there is a relevant reason to do so and that the researcher is explicitly drawing from these gender minority populations. At this level of detail, gender may be considered sensitive information. When in doubt, and especially when gender minority communities are explicitly recruited as research participants, it is best to solicit input from leaders of those communities to determine the most relevant and appropriate terms to use.

An alternate form of this question is the open-ended version:

> What is your gender? _________. (or "What is your sex?" or "What is your gender identity?")

From the perspective of demonstrating respect for research participants, this option allows participants to select their own label instead of selecting one from a list created by the researcher. It creates an additional step during the data entry process and requires the researcher (or data analyst) to make decisions about how to create categories. For example, should a response of "trans woman" be categorized as trans or woman or both, or should it be categorized as trans woman? Would there be a sufficient number of trans women in the study to allow analysis, or would the category only be capable of analysis when a researcher is able to combine data from multiple data sets across multiple studies?

Another possibility is to ask,

What gender pronoun(s) do you use? (e.g., *he, she, them*) __________.

This option provides a slightly less direct approach. However, when combined with a question such as "What is your sex?" or "What is your gender?" responses from the two questions can be combined to create a more specific set of categories.

The level of detail required—and thus the number of questions necessary to ask—depends on the specific goals of the research study and may be influenced by who the research participants are. Participants who are only familiar with the binary, due to age, developmental level, or belief system, may find a series of questions in which they provide the same answer (*sex:* female; *gender:* female; *gender identity:* female) to be off-putting, which may influence their behavior during the remainder of the study. In this case, limiting the number of these questions or moving them to the end of the research protocol may be beneficial.

Avoiding Bias

Regardless of the question or questions employed, it is important that researchers do their best to avoid bias. Bias can appear both in the way questions are asked and in the way data are presented. Stated differently, word choice is important.

When asking questions, whether in a written or verbal format, one way to avoid bias is to always provide at least three specific options, with *other* appearing as the fourth (or later) option. Providing three or more options communicates that the researcher team is aware of and trying to move beyond the binary by using some of the most popular and relevant terms. When providing a list of response options, listing them alphabetically also helps avoid bias (but *other* is always provided last and nonalphabetically).

Using the most relevant terms also helps reduce bias. Preferred terms can change over time and often vary across cultures, so the sample questions listed in this entry may not be the best options in all situations. Researchers may need to seek input from local leaders in order to ensure that the terms chosen are most appropriate for the research population.

Writing and speaking in the most accurate terms is also a component of avoiding bias. Data analysts and researchers need to use the most relevant terms, both when collecting and when analyzing data. As noted earlier and detailed in the *APA Publication Manual*, *female* and *male* are preferred when discussing sex, whereas *men* and *women* (and *boys* and *girls*) are preferred when describing gender. For plurals, researchers can alternate between *men and women* and *women and men*, or use terms such as *participants* and *people*; researchers are advised not to use either *men* or *women* to refer to mixed-sex or mixed-gender groups.

Use of the most accurate and precise terms also applies to the names of categories (or research questions), not just to the response options. *Sex*, *gender*, and *gender identity* each refer to a distinct construct and should be used specifically for that construct, not interchangeably. Similarly, *gender identity* should not be shortened to *gender*. One result of this focus on the most accurate terms is that written and verbal reports may have a repetitious quality because the same words are used repeatedly—unlike creative writing, where such repetition is discouraged.

Andrew P. Smiler

See also Cisgender; Gender Bias in Research; Gender Nonconformity and Transgender Issues: Overview; Genderqueer; Intersex; Masculinity Gender Norms; Measuring Gender Identity; Measuring Gender Roles

Further Readings

American Psychological Association. (2010). *Publication manual of the American Psychological Association* (6th ed.). Washington, DC: Author.

American Psychological Association. (2015). Guidelines for psychological practice with transgender and gender nonconforming people. *American Psychologist, 70*(9), 832–864. Retrieved from http://www.apa.org/practice/guidelines/transgender.pdf

Diamond, M. (2002). Sex and gender are different: Sexual identity and gender identity are different. *Clinical Child Psychology and Psychiatry, 7*, 320–334.

Herdt, G. (1994). *Third sex, third gender: Beyond sexual dimorphism in culture and history*. New York, NY: Zone books.

Vilain, E., Achermann, J. C., Eugster, E. A., Harley, V. R., Morel, Y., Wilson, J. D., & Hiort, O. (2007). We used to call them hermaphrodites. *Genetics in Medicine, 9*, 65–66.

Measuring Gender Identity

Psychologists have measured gender identity for the purpose of understanding an individual's identification with the cognitive, behavioral, emotional, and interpersonal differences that are thought to be inherent to either the male or the female sex. Gender identity has also been measured in clinical settings for the assessment and treatment of individuals who have experienced gender identity–related physical and mental health symptoms. Through the investigation and development of gender identity measures, researchers have learned the cultural valuations of gendered traits that exist within the constructs of both gender and identity. This entry describes the way in which psychologists define, understand, and measure gender identity in empirical research. What follows is an examination of both the social understandings and the empirical measurements of gender identity. For contextual purposes, brief definitions of gender identity and gender role norms are also provided.

Foundations for the Gender Identity Construct

Gender is typically defined as a sociological construct that involves classifying traits, behaviors, and attitudes that are traditionally associated with the male and female sexes. As such, the measurement of gender in psychology involves examining the commonalities in the sexes and the differences between them. Measurement of gender also involves identifying and defining gender role norms.

Gender role norms are socially imposed expectations for traits and behaviors ascribed to the male or the female sex that are thought to govern an individual's personality, including physical appearance, interpersonal behaviors, emotional expression, and self-concept. Gender role norms shape the way in which psychologists measure gender identity by providing a framework or schema of gendered behaviors. Some gender role norms rely on binary and exclusionary interpretations, such as "Males do 'X,' and females do not do 'X.'" Other gender role norms rely on gradations of a trait, such as "Females do 'X' more frequently than males do 'X.'"

Gender identity, though independent of an individual's sex, is nonetheless framed by traditional gender role norms. This framing provides the boundaries for the conforming and nonconforming classifications of gender identity and expression. Psychological frames of gender identity are filtered through a collective interpretation and comparative assessments of an individual's emotions, behaviors, cognitions, and physical appearance. Gender identity also provides the structure wherein an individual's inferred cultural value as a male or a female can be cultivated and transformed over time.

Measuring Gender Identity in the 20th and 21st Centuries

In the 20th century, researchers in psychology measured gender identity to note the social and behavioral differences between cisgender men and women. By examining the stereotypes and common traits within a gender identity, researchers were able to make observations about the influence of gender identity on personal characteristics such as decision making, styles of interpersonal communication, social development within children and adults, academic achievements, and propensity for violence, depression, emotionality, and compassion.

Gender identity researchers have developed and used two distinct types of measures: (1) trait measures and (2) ideology measures. Trait measures require participants to rate and/or report their identification with items on a list of gendered traits (e.g., independent, cheerful, moody, or forceful). In contrast, ideology measures of gender identity examine the extent to which an individual endorses traditional gender role norms (e.g., "Taking care of children is extremely fulfilling."). This endorsement can relate to the way subjects perceive themselves, or to the way they perceive others, as adhering to or violating cisgender, heterosexual gender role norms.

Trait Measures

The most widely known measure of gender identity from the 20th century, the Bem Sex Role Inventory (BSRI), is a trait measure. The BSRI was developed and validated on samples of Stanford University undergraduate students in the 1970s. To decide the list of 60 traits to be used in the first iteration of the BSRI, students narrowed down a list of 400 traits that they found most desirable in women and men. The short form of the scale was published in 1981 and contained 15 Likert-type scale items each for femininity and masculinity. An individual's score on the BSRI was thought to illustrate the person's level of psychological androgyny, which Bem theorized to be advantageous over an exclusive identification as either feminine or masculine.

The method of scoring resulted in labels of feminine, masculine, androgynous, and undifferentiated personalities. These labels indicate the number of times an individual endorsed the traits from separate scale components. For example, a feminine label resulted from an individual's high score in femininity and a low score on the traits identified as masculine. The masculine label identified those participants who had scored high on the masculine items (e.g., athletic) and low on the feminine items (e.g., sympathetic). The individuals who were labeled as androgynous had scored high on both masculine and feminine items. The undifferentiated personality label was associated with low scores on both masculine and feminine items on the BSRI.

Methodological criticisms specific to the BSRI include reliability in scoring the inventory and construct validity. In addition to those criticisms, researchers have questioned its utility for measuring gender identity in the 21st century. One source of concern over the BSRI is that the traits and gender role norms for the scale were identified in the 1970s, derived from a narrow demographic of Stanford University undergraduate students, and may therefore be less applicable to a 21st-century understanding of gender identity.

Another popular trait measure of gender identity is the Personal Attributes Questionnaire (PAQ). The PAQ was developed during the mid-to-late 1970s and was validated using male and female samples of children, undergraduates, scientists, and individuals of varying sexual orientations. A group of undergraduate students narrowed down the initial pool of 155 traits. The students were asked to select the traits that they saw as most desirable in men and women and the extent to which they themselves identified with the trait. The resulting list of 24 traits consists of 8 feminine traits (e.g., helpful to others), 8 masculine traits (e.g., stands up well under pressure), and 8 traits that represent the opposition between masculine and feminine characteristics (e.g., the need for approval of others and the need for security). The creators of the PAQ described the scale as measuring "instrumental" interpersonal styles, which they associated with masculinity, and "expressive" interpersonal styles, which they associated with femininity.

Ideology Measures

In contrast to listing adjectives and characteristics in a descriptive manner, as researchers have done with trait measures, ideology measures of gender identity examine the prescriptive norms associated with the male and female sexes. The items for the ideology measures are often phrased in sentences about the cognition, self-reflection, and cultural ideals of males and females. As such, many of the ideology measures examine the norms of one gender exclusively. For masculine gender identity measurement, the Male Role Norms Scale (1986), the Male Roles Attitudes Scale (1993), and the Adolescent Masculinity in Relationships Scale (2005) each use factor structures that identify, through an all-male sample, what it "means to be a man" in their culture. This includes measured endorsements of norms regarding how men should act with their families and friends, toward other men, and toward women, as well as achievement ideals, agency, and assertiveness. Similarly, the Male Role Norms Inventory (1992) and the Conformity to Male Norms Inventory (2003) used the same proscriptive ideologies of male gender norms as the Male Role Norms Scale, the Male Roles Attitudes Scale, and the Adolescent Masculinity in Relationships Scale, yet were validated on mixed, female and male, samples.

Other ideology measures of gender identity explore traditional gender norms for women. The Adolescent Femininity Ideology Scale (2000), the Femininity Ideology Scale (2007), and the Conformity to Feminine Norms Inventory (2005) measure gender identity through ideals about physical appearance and attractiveness, intelligence, emotionality, relationships with men, caretaking, and deference. The Adolescent Femininity Ideology Scale was validated on a female-only sample, but the Femininity Ideology Scale and the Conformity to Feminine Norms Inventory were validated on mixed, female and male, samples.

Measuring Gender Identity in Children and Adolescents

The goal for gender identity measurement in children is to observe the inception of a child's gender identity and how that identity develops through adolescence. Measuring a child's gender identity often involves observing or testing how the child detects or discerns their own absolute membership in a gender category, how they develop a taxonomy of gender- or sex-typed attributes, how they understand the constancy of gender, and how they understand their own self-perceived gender representativeness or typicality. Research with transgender children indicates that trans boys' scores were consistent with those of cisgender boys and that trans girls' scores were consistent with those of cisgender girls. These responses also illustrate that, at least with children and adolescents, the gender identity construct is not constrained by an individual's male or female sex classification.

Criticisms of Gender Identity Measures

To measure the construct of gender identity, researchers must first be able to define the construct of gender identity. These definitions are largely dependent on the prevalent gender role norms within a culture and its subcultures. These norms change between cultures so that what is considered feminine in one subculture could be characterized as masculine or androgynous in another subculture. In addition, how norms are characterized in someone's culture affects the context imposed on that person and may determine if the person's gender presentation is classified as conforming or nonconforming.

Issues of Reliability and Construct Validity

The biggest obstacle to creating a reliable measure of gender identity lies in the construct validity issues that are inherent to the measurement of gender identity. First, there are many ways to conceptualize gender identity, including through personality characteristics, hobbies and interests, sexual orientation, interpersonal style, and partner preference. This process makes creating a global conceptualization of gender or of gender identity elusive. Second, gender identity cannot be measured within a vacuum. The individuals who complete these measures are aware of gender stereotypes and of their own gender. It is extremely difficult to measure gender identity and exclude any comparative thoughts or ideals from an individual. Individuals are aware of their gender, and they have an awareness of societal thoughts and ideals about the ways in which people of their gender should laugh, cry, dress, speak, work, exercise, and provide care to others, and of other behaviors that have been sex typed.

Gender identity measurement is often measured using the degree to which one identifies with and embodies one's own gender and the degree to which one does not identify with or disembody the characteristics of a different gender. Measuring the presence, absence, and level of knowledge, agreement, and identity of one set of gender stereotypes and comparing it or combining it with the presence, absence, and level of knowledge, agreement, and identity of another set of gender stereotypes is the most comprehensive and most complicated way to measure gender identity. The complications inherent in reliably measuring self-reports of gendered behavior subsequently dilute the construct validity of gender identity measures.

Because there are so many manifestations of gender presentation and identity, it is difficult to understand what any given measure is quantifying or qualifying. A review of the gender identity literature demonstrates that, in addition to societal changes of the gender construct, self-perception in a single domain of gender identity can also change over time. Thus, self-perceived gender identity can be dynamic, even within a single person on a single dimension (e.g., physical appearance in public).

To combat this problem of construct validity, many of the aforementioned gender identity scales utilize a multifactor structure; there are minor scales within the major scale. By acknowledging and integrating these multiple facets of gender, these measures help capture a comprehensive conceptualization of gender identity. For this reason, researchers who measure gender identity must take caution in describing the implications of their findings. Gender identity is a difficult construct to measure, but when gender identity is measured for a specific purpose with a specific population, it helps develop the greater landscape of the gender identity construct.

Much of the published research on measuring gender identity has been conducted with cisgender and, often, heterosexual participants. It is unclear if the trait or ideology measures would have the same psychometric properties when administered to a noncisgender or nonheterosexual individual. As suggested by their higher rates of gender nonconformity, LGBTQ individuals may not identify with commonly held stereotypes about what defines their gender identity. Specifically, some gender identity measures assume heterosexual attraction and use it to contextualize other gendered traits. These measures contain items for behaviors in which a lesbian or gay participant does not engage. Subsequently, the masculine or the feminine label that researchers attached to the item is inadequate to measure behaviors common among male or female identified individuals of all sexual orientations and gender presentations.

The Effects of Cultural Shifts in Gender Roles

As cultures change over time, so too do the roles of men and women within those cultures. Sex-typed behaviors that, in the early 20th century, indicated a feminine gender identity (e.g., as homemaker or primary caregiver) faded as more women entered the workforce and more men adopted caregiving roles. Behaviors that were previously binary typed according to sex were subsequently viewed as androgynous or spectrum-typed characteristics. These shifts can be attributed to the diversification of the workforce, LGBTQ rights movements, women's rights movements, legislation promoting equality, and the presence and diversity of male and female role models. This diversity influences the populations on which researchers focus and publish, which in turn influences the scholarly discourse on gender identity.

Measurement of gender identity within populations that did not garner attention in previous research can help calibrate new measures of gender identity, with broader or more specialized constructs of gender. In the 21st century, more researchers and institutions became interested in measuring the gender identity of noncisgender and nonheterosexual populations. This shift in interest requires some shifts in measurement as populations that were traditionally considered to be gender nonconforming helped shape the new ideals of gender identity and expression.

Alexis Forbes

See also Ethics in Gender Research; Gender Bias in Research; Gender-Biased Language in Research; Heteronormative Bias in Research; Measuring Gender; Transphobia

Further Readings

Bem, S. L. (1981). Gender schema theory: A cognitive account of sex typing. *Psychological Review, 88,* 354–364.

Chu, J. Y., Porche, M. V., & Tolman, D. L. (2005). The Adolescent Masculinity Ideology in Relationships Scale: Development and validation of a new measure for boys. *Men and Masculinities, 8,* 93–115. doi:10.1177/1097184X03257453

Levant, R., Richmond, K., Cook, S., House, A. T., & Aupont, M. (2007). The Femininity Ideology Scale: Factor structure, reliability, convergent and discriminant validity, and social contextual variation. *Sex Roles, 57,* 373–383. doi:10.1007/s11199-007-9258-5

Pleck, J. H., Sonenstein, F. L., & Ku, L. C. (1993). Masculine ideology: Its impact on adolescent males' heterosexual relationships. *Journal of Social Issues, 49,* 11–29.

Smiler, A. P., & Epstein, M. (2010). Measuring gender: Options and issues. In J. C. Chrisler & D. R. McCreary (Eds.), *Handbook of gender research in psychology* (pp. 133–157). New York, NY: Springer Science + Business Media.

Spence, R. L., Spence, J. T., & Wilhelm, J. A. (1981). A psychometric analysis of the Personal Attributes Questionnaire. *Sex Roles, 7,* 1097–1108. doi:10.1007/BF00287587

Thompson, E. H., Jr., & Pleck, J. H. (1986). The structure of male role norms. *American Behavioral Scientist, 29,* 531–543. doi:10.1177/000276486029005003

Tolman, D. L., & Porche, M. V. (2000). The Adolescent Femininity Ideology Scale: Development and validation of a new measure for girls. *Psychology of Women Quarterly, 24,* 365–376. doi:10.1111/j.1471-6402.2000.tb00219x

Measuring Gender Roles

Some researchers are primarily interested in determining if one sex is at a greater risk for—or is more "protected" from—a specific, undesirable outcome than another sex. Other researchers focus on the differences within a single sex to determine who is at a greater risk for or more protected from those outcomes. For example, a researcher might want to know if "macho" men have more sexual hookups than their nonmacho counterparts, or whether "girly girls" are more susceptible to body image and eating disorders than their less feminine peers.

These questions require researchers to move beyond large group differences based on biological sex. Instead, they need to examine gender and gender roles and the cultural assumptions and expectations based on sex. This entry discusses current approaches to assessing these types of differences.

Underlying Assumptions

Before discussing specific types of measures, it is important to acknowledge that these measures are designed by researchers and reflect the researchers' understandings and assumptions about gender (or any topic). As such, measures are not inherently neutral or objective; instead, they reflect a particular conceptualization of the thing being measured. Four key assumptions are highlighted here.

Relative Positions

One key assumption addresses the relative positions of masculinity and femininity. The first efforts to measure gender, published in the 1930s, positioned masculinity and femininity as the opposite ends of a spectrum. After completing the scale, participants received a score indicating whether they were feminine, a negative number, or masculine, a positive number. In theory, it is possible for a participant to have a score of zero and thus be gender neutral. The notion of femininity and masculinity as opposites was embedded in all measures published until the mid-1970s.

Alternately, femininity and masculinity may be positioned as separate entities, each with its own (sub)scale scores. This approach allows individuals to possess aspects of both femininity and masculinity, although in different "quantities." The pair of scores would then indicate if the individual was more feminine, more masculine, or equally feminine and masculine (androgynous). Participants can also be classified as sex typed (masculine men and feminine women), cross-sex typed (masculine women and feminine men), or androgynous.

Number of Components

Another key assumption refers to the number of components measured. Scale developers must determine if femininity and masculinity consist of only one component or multiple components and whether they want their scale to provide subscale scores for each component. For example, the Boy Code identifies four relatively distinct aspects of masculinity (No Sissy Stuff, [Be a] Sturdy Oak, [Be a] Big Wheel, and Damn the Torpedoes, Full Speed Ahead [risk taking]). There is no universal agreement regarding the best approach—paralleling the debate on intelligence: Is intelligence a singular phenomenon best represented by a single IQ score, or are there multiple intelligences, each with their own score?

Predictor or Outcome?

In any given research study, gender role adherence may serve as the predictor or the outcome. As a predictor, the research question might take the form of "Do higher levels of masculinity predict higher levels of promiscuity?" or "Do people with high levels of femininity report more body image concerns than people with low levels of femininity?" Alternately, gender roles may serve as the outcome of a research study, with researchers examining questions in the form of "Do these two groups enact masculinity (or femininity) in different ways?" Note that this is an issue for researchers, not for scale developers.

Psychometrics

The term *psychometrics* refers to a set of statistical procedures and measures used to determine if a scale is sufficiently robust in terms of reliability and validity to be used for scientific research. Psychometrics is a subfield of psychology, and the full list of factors that make a good scale is too extensive for this entry, but any scale published in a peer-reviewed journal will have met at least the minimum standard.

Regardless of the underlying assumptions, most gender measures ask participants to indicate how strongly they disagree or agree with or believe a survey item or to indicate how strongly that survey item describes them. Responses are typically provided on a scale from 1 to 4, 1 to 5, or 1 to 6. Higher scores indicate greater endorsement or enactment of the gender role; relatively few scales use a multiple-choice format.

Behavior, Trait, and Ideology Measures

Many gender researchers rely on measures that position masculinity and femininity as separate entities, often with multiple components. Published in 1974, Sandra Bem's Sex Role Inventory (BSRI) was the first scale to adopt this approach. The BSRI was followed shortly by the Personal Attributes Questionnaire (PAQ). Both the BSRI and the PAQ focus on traits, such as "forceful" or "sympathetic," and provide separate scores regarding masculinity and femininity. Both scales have been criticized for focusing on positive traits, although there is an Extended PAQ that includes negative traits and provides negative femininity and negative masculinity scores in addition to the original positive femininity and masculinity scores.

However, the BSRI and the PAQ are both more than 40 years old, and average scores on both measures have tended to increase over the following decades. The BSRI also has psychometric problems. Accordingly, commentators currently recommend against using the BSRI and using the PAQ cautiously.

A related set of measures examined the beliefs or "ideology" regarding gender roles. They drew inspiration from Deborah David and Robert Brannon's 1976 discussion of the four principles of masculinity, which have subsequently been renamed as the Boy Code and the Man Box. The first set of measures focused specifically on masculinity, and subsequent measures have focused specifically on masculinity or femininity. Measures of this sort rarely address both femininity and masculinity.

The masculinity ideology measures typically include some version of anti-femininity that reflects cultural injunctions to "not be like a girl," and so these measures position masculinity and femininity as partial opposites. Femininity ideology measures do not include an anti-masculinity component and thus maintain femininity and masculinity as wholly distinct entities.

Ideology measures vary, with some assessing beliefs as a singular construct and others assessing as many as 9 feminine or 11 masculine (sub)components; each (sub)component typically generates its own score and contributes to the total score. Popular measures here include the Conformity to Masculine Norms Inventory and the Conformity to Feminine Norms Inventory.

The trait and ideology measures typically serve as predictor (or independent) variables, with researchers examining the extent to which femininity, masculinity, or some specific component predicts some outcome (or dependent variable).

Another set of measures tends to focus on behaviors, highlighting toy choice (e.g., dolls or trucks) and activities (e.g., sports, tea parties), as well as comfort with one's biological sex. These measures are used almost exclusively by researchers who study or work with children whose gender-typed behavior differs dramatically from our cultural expectations. These may be children with disorders of sexual development (also known as "intersexual") as well as children being assessed for a gender identity disorder. The gender dysphoria/identification is a good example of this class of measures.

Based on these measures, femininity and masculinity are typically positioned as opposites. The measures tend to employ a multiple-choice format for activities and often use the 1–*x* format when assessing comfort.

The behavioral measures often serve as outcomes, with researchers attempting to document if a clinical group differs from a gender-typical group or clinicians assessing the extent of a child's gender typicality.

Sexism

Sexism refers to the relative position and power of men versus women at the cultural or societal level. Although focused on the societal level and a comparison between the two sexes, these measures also provide a reasonable index of gender roles. Sexism measures were first published in the 1970s.

The Attitudes Toward Women (AWS) and the Attitudes Towards Women Scales for Adolescents have been very popular. These were published in 1972 and 1985, respectively. Because of their age, as well as evidence to prove that average scores with American samples have changed over time to reflect a less sexist and more egalitarian approach, the AWS should no longer be used. The Attitudes Towards Women Scales for Adolescents should be used cautiously until an updated scale for adolescents has been developed.

More recent measures include the Old-Fashioned Sexism (OFS) and the Modern Sexism scales. The authors of the OFS and the Modern Sexism scales sought to differentiate between the older and more obvious forms of sexism (e.g., "Women are generally not as smart as men") and the newer and subtler forms of sexism (e.g., "On average, people in our society treat husbands and wives equally" [which research demonstrates is not the case]). The OFS scale is quite similar to the AWS.

Another current measure is the Ambivalent Sexism Inventory, which contains separate subscales for hostile and benevolent sexism. These authors sought to identify beliefs and behaviors that are more blatantly sexist and offensive (e.g., "Women are too easily offended"), similar to the AWS. They also wanted to assess subtler aspects of benevolent sexism that are meant to help or protect women but simultaneously serve to limit them. For example, the idea that "women should be cherished and protected by men" assumes that women are incapable of protecting themselves and thus require men's assistance.

Choice among the newer sexism measures reflects the researchers' specific questions.

Femininities and Masculinities

A more holistic approach to gender focuses on the existence of masculinities and femininities. These plural terms emphasize that there is more than one way to be masculine or feminine and that each variation includes a relatively distinctive combination of behaviors, beliefs, and traits. These different versions might also be conceptualized as (social) identities or stereotypes, such as jocks, nerds, and players, as well as housewife, feminist, and career woman. Masculinities and femininities can also be based on demographic categories, such as ethnicity (e.g., strong Black woman), social class (e.g., working-class masculinity), or sexual orientation (e.g., [butch] lesbian).

There are no published scales for the assessment of femininities and masculinities. Consistent with the identity and stereotype literatures, participants might be asked to indicate the extent to which each term (e.g., *jock*, *career woman*) represents them using a 1–x scale, or they might be asked to select the single best term in a multiple-choice format. In these approaches, gender is typically the predictor.

Alternately, the goal might be to describe or define a demographically specified version of femininities or masculinities by examining how all the relevant participants answer other questions. For example, in an assessment of working-class masculinity, participants' perceptions of the importance of being the primary breadwinner might be the focus of the investigation.

Andrew P. Smiler

See also Bem Sex Role Inventory; Gender Nonconformity and Transgender Issues: Overview; Hostile Sexism; Masculinity Gender Norms; Measuring Gender; Measuring Gender Identity; Measuring Sexual Orientation; Sexism

Further Readings

Connell, R. W., & Messerschmidt, J. W. (2005). Hegemonic masculinity: Rethinking the concept. *Gender & Society, 19,* 825–859.

Glick, P., & Fiske, S. T. (1996). The Ambivalent Sexism Inventory: Differentiating hostile and benevolent sexism. *Journal of Personality and Social Psychology, 70,* 491–512.

Mahalik, J. R., Locke, B. D., Ludlow, L. H., Diemer, M. A., Scott, R. P. J., Gottfried, M., & Freitas, G. (2003). Development of the Conformity to Masculine Norms Inventory. *Journal of Men and Masculinity, 4,* 3–25.

Mahalik, J. R., Morray, E. B., Coonerty-Femiano, A., Ludlow, L. H., Slattery, S. M., & Smiler, A. P. (2005). Development of the Conformity to Feminine Norms Inventory. *Sex Roles, 52,* 417–435.

Morawski, J. G. (1985). The measurement of masculinity and femininity: Engendering categorical realities. *Journal of Personality, 53,* 196–223.

Smiler, A. P. (2004). Thirty years after gender: Concepts and measures of masculinity. *Sex Roles, 50,* 15–26. doi:10.1023/B:SERS.0000011069.02279.4c

Smiler, A. P., & Epstein, M. (2010). Measuring gender: Options and issues. In J. C. Chrisler & D. R. McCreary (Eds.), *Handbook of gender research in psychology: Vol. 1. Gender research in general and experimental psychology* (pp. 133–157). New York, NY: Springer Science + Business Media.

Thompson, E. H., & Pleck, J. H. (1995). Masculinity ideologies: A review of research instrumentation on men and masculinities. In R. F. Levant & W. S. Pollack (Eds.), *A new psychology of men* (pp. 129–163). New York, NY: Basic Books.

Measuring Sexual Orientation

Sexual orientation is a multifaceted construct, commonly defined in terms of the sex of individuals to whom one is affectionately and sexually attracted, one's behaviors, and one's sense and labeling of one's own identity. Rather than reflecting an essential quality of humans (e.g., something that is biological, immutable, and the same across time and across all humans), sexual orientation is socially constructed. This means that definitions and categories used to label people as a particular sexual orientation are different across cultures and time. What are understood as common categories of sexual orientation (e.g., lesbian, gay, bisexual, heterosexual, asexual, queer) in the current context of the United States have not always existed in their current forms and do not exist across all cultures and geographic locations. For example, the term *homosexual* was not used until the late 1800s, when cultural views on sexuality shifted from a focus on individual behaviors or acts to a focus on biology and individual identity. This term became the label for a diagnosable mental disorder listed in the American Psychiatric Association's *Diagnostic and Statistical Manual of Mental Disorders* in the 1950s, but it was removed in 1973 as methodologically rigorous research debunked the heterosexist notion that possessing a nonheterosexual sexual orientation is pathological. In the 1990s, the American Psychological Association officially recommended against the use of the term *homosexuality* in its recommendations for avoiding bias in language in its *Publication Manual of the American Psychological Association.*

In spite of the shifting language use and conceptualizations of sexual orientation, its measurement has implications for research on the experiences of sexual minorities, particularly in the domains of physical health and psychosocial well-being and for informing public policy. As such, it is important for psychologists to understand the measurement methods, challenges, and ethical issues associated with operationalizing sexual orientation and the cultural considerations.

Measurement Methods

Although same-sex attractions, behaviors, and relationships are not new, the measurement of individuals' sexual orientation is relatively recent; prior to the late 1800s, same-sex sexual behaviors did not define one's identity. Since that time, there has been consistent interest on the part of researchers, health care providers, and policymakers in measuring the sexual orientations of individuals, and a variety of methods have been developed that purport to measure aspects of sexual orientation, including continuous and categorical self-reports, physical measures, and implicit and indirect measures.

Continuous and Categorical Self-Reports

In their famous studies on male and female sexuality, Alfred Kinsey and his colleagues addressed the measurement of sexual orientation directly. They were surprised to find that more than one third of all men reported some form of same-sex sexual encounter and noted that this included married men in heterosexual relationships. This finding highlighted for them the complications with categorizing individuals as exclusively heterosexual or exclusively homosexual. Instead, they suggested that sexual orientation be measured using a scale ranging from 0 for *exclusively heterosexual* to 6 for *exclusively homosexual.* A scale such as this, they pointed out, allowed for gradations, rather than forcing individuals into two (or three, including bisexual) sexual orientation categories. The use of scales that allow for sexual orientation to be considered a continuous variable has continued to be a common practice.

More recent conceptualizations of sexual orientation have further complicated the construct of sexual orientation as a multidimensional construct. For example, Ruth Fassinger and Julie Arseneau's model of identity enactment of gender transgressive sexual minorities describes the necessity to understand a broader picture of sexual orientation that also includes one's gender orientation, other sociodemographic variables, and time. This model suggests that sexual orientation exists not as a binary from homosexual to heterosexual but rather as a multidimensional landscape. The Klein Sexual Orientation Grid takes a similar approach, incorporating sexual attractions, sexual behaviors, sexual fantasies, emotions, social preferences, self-identification, and lifestyle (referring to with whom one lives or spends most of one's time).

In addition to using continuous variables for assessing different dimensions of sexual orientation, another common practice in the measurement of sexual orientation is the inclusion of items that assess one's self-identity in a sexual orientation category. The strength of this method is that it is relatively easy and addresses the important dimension of self-identity, which may have strong connections to psychological constructs. A challenge, however, is that those constructing these types of measures must make a decision about which categories they will include as options for respondents, from a complex and constantly evolving list of possibilities (e.g., lesbian, gay, bisexual, heterosexual, asexual, queer, bi-curious, pansexual, heteroflexible).

Physical Measures

The socially constructed nature of sexual orientation suggests that it cannot be understood outside a cultural and temporal context. Still, as with most other socially constructed identities, researchers have used a wide variety of physical measures that seek to identify essential, immutable biological markers of one's sexual orientation. For example, the social psychologists Nicholas Rule and Nalini Ambady and their colleagues have found that individuals are more accurate in their judgments of someone's sexual orientation based on characteristics like face, eyes, and body movements than would be predicted by chance.

Phallometric testing is another physical measure that has been used since the 1950s to make claims about the "true" sexual orientations of men based on their levels of arousal to various sexual stimuli. Tom Waidzunas and Steven Epstein suggest, however, that technologies that claim to reveal the "truth" about people through measures of physical and biological functioning (including fMRI [functional magnetic resonance imaging]) must be understood in the context of the social worlds in which they are developed and used. Furthermore, they suggest that these technologies, themselves, help create the very categories they seek to measure—in the case of phallometry, arousal becomes sexual orientation.

Implicit and Other Indirect Measures

Similar to the aforementioned physical measures, others have used implicit and indirect measures to assess sexual orientation. For example, Caoilte Ciardha and Michael Gormley describe the use of the Implicit Association Test and a pictorial modified Stroop task for determining sexual interest. These measures collect data based on reaction times to various stimuli, with the underlying assumption being that slowing in reaction time reflects cognitive processes and attentional biases that can be interpreted as indicating sexual interests. These measures have been found to provide some window into sexual schema and interests, but they are not always able to accurately classify people according to their self-identified sexual orientation categories, highlighting again the multidimensional nature of sexual orientation. There may be myriad other reasons for differential reaction times and attentional focus, besides one's sexual orientation, which must also be considered in the interpretation of implicit and other indirect measures.

Challenges in Operationalizing Sexual Orientation

One of the most basic challenges to measuring sexual orientation is in the defining and operationalizing of the construct for any given study. Sexual orientation is a complicated construct that includes attractions, affections, behaviors, cognitions, and self-identity. Thus, researchers need to determine which of the components they choose to measure. For example, measures that assess only behavior (e.g., sexual activity) may not reflect the ways in which one self-identifies. This has implications for understanding individuals' experiences with many psychological constructs, such as perceived discrimination, or institutional policies that favor heterosexuality, which may have a different impact on a person who has same-sex sexual encounters but does not identify as lesbian, gay, or bisexual. If researchers choose instead to focus on individuals' self-identities, they must then make decisions about what options respondents have to choose from. For example, a researcher might choose to include response options of lesbian, gay, bisexual, and heterosexual, based on the perception that these are common labels for sexual orientation categories. This, however, leaves out or may force an inaccurate label on individuals who may identify as queer, questioning, asexual, or other labels. One option researchers might consider is including an "other" option, with a way for individuals to include a specific label that they prefer. Even this option, however, leaves researchers with the challenge of needing to decide how they will treat the data of individuals who self-identify as belonging to a sexual orientation other than those for which they have been provided choices. Labels for sexual orientations are different across cultures and across times and will continue to evolve; those measuring sexual orientation must continue to attend to the cultural and temporal contexts in which they are conducting their measurements.

Cultural Considerations

As with any construct measured in psychology, there are important cultural considerations that need to be made in the measurement of sexual orientation. For example, in a recent review of the literature on the measurement of sexual orientation, Dominic Beaulieu-Prévost and M. Fortin highlighted the connection between the ways in which sexual orientation is defined and the ways in which it is measured. As a socially constructed identity, sexual orientation categories and other measurement tools can only be understood in their sociohistorical contexts. This means that not all measurement tools will be equally valid across time, geographic location, or cultural group. Recent research has suggested that cultural differences exist in responses to measurement techniques (e.g., the relevance of the Kinsey scale across cultures) and responding patterns. When measuring sexual orientation, one must also consider the social and political implications of the question and the responses. Given that heterosexism remains prominent across many cultural and religious groups, individuals may feel uncomfortable or be unable to provide accurate responses for fear of real or perceived consequences. For example, in some countries where same-sex sexual relationships are outlawed, an individual may not be able to disclose a nonheterosexual relationship without the threat of punishment. Similarly, individuals of certain religious backgrounds may not wish to disclose a nonheterosexual identity for fear of social sanctions from their families, social groups, and/or religious communities. Therefore, it is important that those measuring sexual orientation take the social and political consequences of their measurements into account.

The measurement of sexual orientation remains a complicated and imperfect science given the socially constructed and multidimensional nature of sexual orientation. Measurement can have important policy and practice implications, such as understanding and addressing the mental and physical health disparities that exist between LGB people and their heterosexual counterparts. Researchers should choose measures based on the specific purpose of their research and their goals for future interventions.

Joseph R. Miles and Kevin M. Fry

See also Ethics in Gender Research; Gender Bias in Research; Gender-Biased Language in Research; Heteronormative Bias in Research; Measuring Gender; Transphobia

Further Readings

Beaulieu-Prévost, D., & Fortin, M. (2015). The measurement of sexual orientation: Historical background and current practices. *Sexologies, 24,* e15–e19. doi:10.1016/j.sexol.2014.05.006

Burleson, W. E. (2008). The Kinsey Scale and the Pashtun: The role of culture in measuring sexual orientation. *Journal of Bisexuality, 8,* 259–264. doi:10.1080/15299710802501850

Ciardha, C. Ó., & Gormley, M. (2012). Measuring sexual interest using a pictorial modified Stroop task, a pictorial implicit association test and a choice reaction time task. *Journal of Sexual Aggression, 19,* 158–170. doi:10.1080/13552600.2012.677486

Gonsiorek, J. C., Sell, R. L., & Weinrich, J. D. (1995). Definition and measurement of sexual orientation. *Suicide and Life-Threatening Behavior, 25,* 40–51.

Kim, H.-J., & Fredriksen-Goldsen, K. I. (2013). Nonresponse to a question on self-identified sexual orientation in a public health survey and its relationship to race and ethnicity. *American Journal of Public Health, 103,* 67–69. doi:10.2105/AJPH.2012.300835

Kinsey, A. C., Pomeroy, W. B., & Martin, C. E. (1948). *Sexual behavior in the human male.* Philadelphia, PA: W. B. Saunders.

Klein, F., Sepekoff, B., & Wolf, T. J. (1985). Sexual orientation: A multi-variable dynamic process. *Journal of Homosexuality, 11,* 35–49. doi:10.1300/J082v11n01_04

Matthews, D. D., Blosnich, J. R., Farmer, G. W., & Adams, B. J. (2014). Operational definitions of sexual orientation and estimates of adolescent health risk behaviors. *LGBT Health, 1,* 42–49. doi:10.1089/lgbt.2013.0002

Ridolfo, H., Mille, K., & Maitland, A. (2012). Measuring sexual identity using survey questionnaires: How valid are our measures? *Sexuality Research and Social Policy, 9,* 113–124. doi:1007/s13178-011-0074-x

Rule, N. O., Ambady, N., & Hallett, K. C. (2009). Female sexual orientation is perceived accurately, rapidly, and automatically from the face and its features. *Journal of Experimental Social Psychology, 45,* 1245–1251. doi:10.1016/j.jesp.2009.07.010

Waidzunas, T., & Epstein, S. (2015). "For men arousal is orientation": Bodily truthing, technosexual scripts, and the materialization of sexualities through the phallometric test. *Social Studies of Science, 45,* 187–213. doi:10.1177/0306312714562103

Media and Gender

The media have had an enormous impact on how gender and gender roles are perceived culturally. "Media" is generally understood to be a form of communication that is less direct than face-to-face communication, including a number of different media forms that influence and have been influenced by gender roles. These include, but are not limited to, television, advertising, animated media forms, video games, and books.

Television

Some examples illustrate the way the portrayal of genders has evolved over the decades since the advent of this media format in the late 1940s. Women in television traditionally were portrayed as domestic and supported by men. Women were supposed to be thin and youthful in order to be considered attractive.

The development of the crime drama, to give one example, proceeded with a "one step forward, two steps back" sequence with respect to women. *Cagney and Lacey*, in the 1981 made-for-TV movie, was a crime show in which the protagonists were both women who solved crimes without the help of men. However, when this show was made into a weekly series, a woman who had a "softer" and more feminine look replaced one of the actresses. Network producers, who at that time were mostly male, persisted in trying to keep the characters in line with a more traditional and less threatening image, at least to men it seems. Other popular crime dramas of the late 20th century like *Matlock*, *Moonlighting*, and *Murder She Wrote* mixed characters of both genders with an occasional crime-solving woman (like Jessica Fletcher in *Murder She Wrote*).

By the first decade of the 21st century, crime dramas had made some progress in the depiction of both female and male characters and how they were portrayed with respect to gender roles. *The Mentalist*, a top-rated show, had a woman as the lead detective and the "boss" over most of the other characters. The lead male character was a man who had given up his original profession to pursue the killer of his wife and daughter; he was shown to be vulnerable, manipulative, winsome, charming, and persuasive—all qualities more usually ascribed to female characters.

The popular crime drama *NCIS*, and its spin-offs (*NCIS LA* and *NCIS New Orleans*), showed a number of women in nonstereotypical roles, including a forensic scientist, an Israeli Mossad assassin, a coroner, a bureau chief, and various other scientific and leading roles. Leroy Jethro Gibbs (*NCIS*), one of the more popular characters on television for this era, while having a stoic and unemotional demeanor, also had a soft side showing a nurturing and paternal relationship with his female subordinates rather than the cliché of the older man having affairs with younger women. Indeed all of Gibbs's romantic partners were age appropriate for his character and more average in looks, rather than the under-40, model-type good looks more expected of such characters in the late 20th century. In another leading show, *Bones*, the main character, a female forensic anthropologist, was the unemotional, logical, and distant character, while her counterpart was a more emotionally driven and flawed man. Although certain stereotypes persist on television in these and other shows, women are being shown in more diverse roles with more diverse ages and body types than was true in earlier decades on television. *Body of Proof*, *Rizzoli and Isles*, and *Person of Interest* are other examples of women in crime-fighting shows who have had more instrumental roles that were less dependent on men for success.

Science fiction is another popular television form. In many ways, it has been progressive since its inception, although not without difficulty. The original *Star Trek* show (1966–1969), created by Gene Roddenberry, had a woman first officer in the pilot's seat, but when the network objected to that as being unbelievable, the actor was moved over to portray a nurse. The other progressive element was Lieutenant Uhura (played by Nichelle Nichols), a Black female bridge officer who, while she usually just answered the "space telephone," was cited by Martin Luther King Jr. as being significant by her very presence on the show. Nichols shared an anecdote of Dr. King talking her out of leaving the show at the end of the first season because of what she represented by being there.

When *Star Trek* was reconceptualized in the late 1980s, both the female officers portrayed traditional nurturing roles—as a doctor and a counselor. However, as that show progressed, women admirals, captains, and other women of power emerged on the show, in spite of the fact that in the earlier original *Star Trek* show women were not allowed to serve as captains. *Star Trek Deep Space Nine* debuted in 1993 with a woman first officer; however, the producers, afraid that they were losing their male 18- to 45-year-old demographic, "prettied up" the character at the beginning of Season 4 while adding a macho Klingon (a warrior race) character and a war ship. *Star Trek Voyager* debuted in 1995 with a woman captain and a woman chief engineer. The first woman producer in *Star Trek* history (Jeri Taylor) played a large role in *Voyager*, although she had done some work in key episodes on *Star Trek: The Next Generation*, in particular writing an episode about an androgynous society (*The Outcast*). While women were shown in progressively more traditional masculine roles, men persisted in being stereotypically masculine on all the *Star Trek* shows right up through *Enterprise*, which aired from 2001 to 2005.

Similar examples about gender could be offered about situation comedies, or sitcoms, which started with very traditional roles for women in the 1950s. While some progress has been made, gender stereotypes still abound. For example, *Modern Family* (2009–), a show that is considered progressive, still shows both genders in very stereotypical ways (e.g., an episode where the three women in one family were all shown as simultaneously having terrible moods during their menstrual periods—a depiction not supported by research).

One of the areas where considerable progress has been made is in the depiction of nontraditional relationships, most notably the depiction of same-sex relationships. A large shift in programming began with *Will and Grace* in 1998, a show with two regular characters who were gay, although certainly earlier programs paved the way for the popularity of that show. For example, *Ellen* (1994–1998) and *Soap* (1977–1981) were programs in which lesbian and gay male characters were portrayed as the main characters. The parasocial contact hypothesis has suggested that people's attitudes toward same-sex couples will become more favorable as they are exposed to these characters and relationships in primetime programming. *Modern Family* debuted in 2009 and depicted a gay male couple raising a family as part of a larger extended family structure, showing the struggles that one of the fathers has in adjusting to his expanding view of family and marriage. While such programming is becoming normative in the media, attitudes are changing toward non-traditional families. Further research is needed to look at the cause-and-effect possibilities involved.

While depictions of transgender persons are still rather limited in network television, there have been some cases where these individuals have had their stories told. *Glee* (2009–2015) is a television show that has expanded the boundaries of storytelling with two transgender characters. Unique Adams is a transgender student, while football coach Shannon Beiste transitions to male (Sheldon Beiste) during the sixth season of this show. In addition, *Glee* has other diverse characters, such as a student in a wheelchair who sings and performs choreography from his wheelchair, a student with Down syndrome, and openly gay boys and girls. *CSI*, *Bones*, *Law and Order*, *NCIS*, *Orange Is the New Black*, and *Pretty Little Liars* are all popular shows that have included stories featuring transgender characters. In July 2015, a reality show/docudrama titled *I Am Cait* debuted, featuring the story of the transition of Caitlyn Jenner.

Various racial/ethnic groups have struggled to be represented on television, and their depictions started out being stereotypical, with many African American characters being most often portrayed as domestics (for women) and as sports figures (for men). However, progress has been made as well with the emergence of female characters like Clair Huxtable on *The Cosby Show* (1984–1992), who portrayed an attorney; Olivia Pope, a crisis manager for a consulting firm on *Scandal*, which premiered in 2012; Dr. Camille Saroyan, head pathologist for *Bones*, which debuted in 2005; and Miranda Bailey, a surgeon on *Grey's Anatomy*, which also debuted in 2005. Male characters who broke away from early stereotypes include Cliff Huxtable, an obstetrician on *The Cosby Show*; Detective Ron Harris on *Barney Miller* (1974–1982); Benjamin Sisko, captain of *Star Trek Deep Space Nine* (1993–1999); and Geordi La Forge, engineer on *Star Trek: The Next Generation* (1987–1994), who in addition to being African American also depicted a character with a visual disability.

Those of Asian, Latino, Native American, Arab, and other diverse ethnic groups have also been underrepresented on television. Dr. Julian Bashir of *Star Trek Deep Space Nine* was a rare depiction of a positive character of Arab descent. Lieutenant Sulu on *Star Trek* was a prominent character of Asian descent, as was Harry Kim (*Voyager*), whereas Chakotay of *Star Trek Voyager* represented a character of Native American descent. Clearly, *Star Trek*, mentioned many times in this section, was a pioneering force in the depiction of diverse backgrounds on television beginning in the 1960s. Women on *Star Trek* were equally diverse, with the already mentioned Lieutenant Uhura, Hoshi Sato of *Star Trek Enterprise*, and B'Elanna Torres of *Voyager*, whose human father is Hispanic. *Star Trek* also pioneered a number of characters who showed obvious disabilities—for example, the already mentioned Geordi La Forge; Melora of *Deep Space Nine*, who was in a wheelchair; and Nog, who persisted with his Starfleet career after losing a leg in battle in *Deep Space Nine*.

With the 2014–2015 television season premieres, there were 10 new shows featuring non-White characters. In 2015, *Fresh off the Boat* was the first Asian American sitcom in 20 years, since *All-American Girl*, which ran for just one season in 1994. *Black-ish* and *Empire* are examples of other newer programming featuring diverse casts of both men and women.

Advertising

Killing Us Softly is a video series produced by Jean Kilbourne and used extensively in various academic settings. The main thesis of this production is the idea that women are portrayed in advertising in ways that exploit women by sexualizing and objectifying them. Many of these assertions have been supported by independent research.

Gender stereotypes in advertising are not limited to women being sexualized and objectified. Overall, advertising directed toward women involves beauty products, cleaning products, and other items that emphasize women in a domestic role. In spite of a trend to use more women as spokespersons for products, there is still a tendency to fall back on sexist language and stereotypes—for example, the "Progressive Girl" as the spokesperson for Progressive Insurance, in spite of the fact that she is clearly an adult and not a child. Using this kind of language infantilizes women. Men are portrayed in stereotypical ways in advertising as well, shown in sporty cars, as construction workers, in beer commercials, and in other ways that tie masculinity to consumerism.

Advertisers are not as prone to using diverse characters in commercials, nor are television programs. However, one exception was an ad aired just before Caitlyn Jenner received the Arthur Ashe Courage Award on the ESPY awards in July 2015, depicting the transition of Jacob, a transgender female-to-male man, and City Gym, a transgender affirmative gym in Kansas City, Missouri. Commercials featuring gay males and lesbians are equally rare. An early pioneer was Absolut Vodka, which began publishing ads in magazines like *The Advocate* as early as 1989. In 1995, Guinness made a commercial that depicted gay characters; however, it was never aired because it was deemed too controversial. Recent advertisements featuring mostly gay male couples and families have run for Toyota, Ray Ban, Chevrolet, Amtrak, and JC Penney, but these types of commercials are still not prevalent in contemporary times.

Animated Media Forms

Comic books started out being marketed to girls, focusing on a variety of subjects ranging from female-masked superheroes (*Wonder Woman*, *Supergirl*) to portrayals of teenage girls as being boy crazy and superficial (*Betty and Veronica*). *Brenda Starr, Reporter* was an early comic strip that showed a woman as a newspaper reporter, albeit an attractive younger woman. As the media form evolved, the format shifted to an emphasis on marketing to boys with stories and characters focusing more on male superheroes. Women in comic books tend to have exaggerated body types, with an emphasis on large breasts and unrealistically small waists, in contrast to male forms, who have exaggerated muscles and large body size. Jessica Rabbit (*Who Framed Roger Rabbit*) is an example of a female animated character with such exaggerated features.

Newspaper comic strips and animated television programs (e.g., *The Simpsons*, *Inspector Gadget*, *The Flintstones*, *Dagwood and Blondie*, *The Jetsons*) portrayed a number of gender stereotypes. A common theme is the young girl savant who is the real problem solver in the company of adults (e.g., *Inspector Gadget*, *The Simpsons*). Another common stereotype is the father figure as a bumbling and incompetent fool (e.g., *Family Guy*, *Dagwood and Blondie*, *Drabble*, *The Simpsons*, *The Jetsons*, *The Flintstones*, *Inspector Gadget*). Another common stereotype is the young boy as a troublemaker and intelligent underachiever (*Dennis the Menace*, *The Simpsons*). The mother in various comic forms is often portrayed as capable and intelligent but still in a traditional role as mother and nurturer (*Flintstones*, *Jetsons*, *Dagwood and Blondie*, *Baby Blues*). There are several popular comic forms that do not portray adults at all—the main characters are all or mostly children (*Peanuts*, *South Park*), and these characters represent various gender stereotypes—for example, Lucy in *Peanuts* as the young girl savant and Charlie Brown as the lead male character who is incompetent if well meaning. The evil older woman is another animation stereotype (Maleficent in *Sleeping Beauty* and Cruella De Vil in *101 Dalmatians*). Overall, animation is a microcosm of other media forms and the way in which the genders are portrayed, in general, in the media.

Video Games

Video games have become increasingly popular, with online gaming continuing to expand as Internet access becomes better and faster. Studies of video games have shown that women are consistently underrepresented in games and that when they are portrayed in games they tend to be sexualized, with exaggerated physical features (e.g., large breasts). While female video game characters are hypersexualized, male characters have exaggerated aggression and an emphasis on brawn over brains (e.g., *World of Warcraft*). The *Grand Theft Auto* series of games is an example of women being sexualized and violence against women being treated as normative.

While women gamers are a growing segment of gamers, they are mostly ignored by the industry. In 2014, a major controversy in social media surrounding women game developers became known as "Gamergate" and involved significant backlash and harassment toward prominent women in game development. Gamergate was seen as a kind of cultural war against diversifying the traditionally male-dominated gaming industry.

Books

Research on books, particularly children's books, has shown consistently that gender stereotypes and sexism persist in these books. Textbooks written for children still picture mostly men as scientists; meanwhile, in storybooks, women are shown in domestic and other stereotypical roles, while men are rarely shown as caregivers. In fact, fathers are nearly absent from the depiction of most domestic scenes. Adult textbooks follow the same pattern; for example, textbooks on the history of psychology tend to only feature a history of almost exclusively male psychologists.

A recent trend has been to publish books that challenge these stereotypes, and so books like *Marty McGuire* (about a girl who likes to do "boy" things, written by Kate Messner) and *Ballerino Nate* (about a boy who loves ballet, by Kimberly Bradley) are part of a new wave of children's books. *Guess How Much I Love You* (Sam McBratney) and *Shopping With Dad* (Matt Harvey) are newer children's books written about relationships between fathers and their children. Research has shown that books have a large effect on the development of children's attitudes about gender roles.

Books depicting same-sex families have become quite easy to find—for example, *My Two Moms*, by Zach Wahls; *Invisible Families: Gay Identities, Relationships, and Motherhood Among Black Women*, by Mignon Moore; and *This Is My Family: A First Look at Same-Sex Parents*, by Pat Thomas. Books supporting the transgender people experience include *Some Assembly Required*, by Arin Andrews, and *The Flowers of Transition: Bach Flowers for the Transgender and Transsexual Path*, by Claudia Valsecchi. The availability of books on this subject has increased in recent years with the prominence of individuals like Laverne Cox, Chaz Bono, and Caitlyn Jenner.

Gayle Stever

See also Gender and Society: Overview; Gender Stereotypes; Gender-Based Violence; Intersectional Identities; Sexism

Further Readings

Anderson, D. A., & Hamilton, M. (2005). Gender role stereotyping of parents in children's picture books: The invisible father. *Sex Roles, 52*(3–4), 145–151.

Carter, C., Steiner, L., & McLaughlin, L. (2014). *The Routledge companion to media and gender*. New York, NY: Routledge.

Conley T. D., & Ramsey, L. R. (2011). Killing us softly? Investigating portrayals of women and men in contemporary magazine advertisements. *Psychology of Women Quarterly, 35*(3), 469–478.

Petersona, S. B., & Lach, M. A. (1990). Gender stereotypes in children's books: Their prevalence and influence on cognitive and affective development. *Gender and Education, 2*(2), 185–197.

Rawson, C. H., & McCool, M. A. (2014). Just like all the other humans? Analyzing images of scientists in children's trade books. *School Science & Mathematics, 114*(1), 10–18.

Schiappa, E., Gregg, P. B., & Hewes, D. D. (2005). The parasocial contact hypothesis. *Communication Monographs, 72*(1), 92–115.

Williams, D., Martins, N., Consalvo, M., & Ivory, J. D. (2009). The virtual census: Representations of gender, race and age in video games. *New Media & Society, 11*(5), 815–834.

Men and Aging

Understanding the unique gender differences in the aging process has become a matter of increased importance due to the aging of the baby boomer generation. The specific needs of older men have been of particular interest due to the unique medical and mental health needs of the male population and the difficulties that arise in engaging men in the health care system. This issue is even more complex when it comes to addressing the needs of male ethnic/racial and sexual minorities.

Health Differences

Overall, the health of the aging U.S. population has continually improved over the course of the

20th and 21st centuries. Even the "oldest old" (80+ years of age) are displaying higher levels of independent functioning than ever before. Despite the natural, physical, and cognitive changes that develop with age, most older adults report positive well-being and life satisfaction.

Differences in life expectancy rates between the sexes are seen across groups regardless of ethnicity, race, or nationality, suggesting that these are reflective of core aspects of the human condition. With humans, as with most animal species, females tend to outlive their male counterparts. Among humans, a large part of this difference is due to the disproportionate number of male deaths that occur between birth and young adulthood, while mortality rates tend to stabilize after middle age. Personality and lifestyle factors are also associated with earlier mortality, along with high levels of hostility and more risk-taking behaviors (both more common among men).

Starting in the 20th century, life expectancies in the United States have increased significantly. This is due to considerable advances in access to health care and living conditions. According to the Centers for Disease Control and Prevention (CDC), the average life expectancy for men in the United States in 1980 was 70 years, whereas in 2012, it jumped to 76.4 years. Along with these improvements, the difference in life expectancy between men and women has also dropped from 7.4 years to 4.8 years. If rates continue along the current trend, this will likely result in a larger male representation among older adult cohorts, which will change the overall care needs of this population.

As lives lengthen, issues related to disease and health management become more significant. The leading causes of death for men over the first decade of the 21st century have been cancer and heart disease. Chronic disease management is a significant medical issue for older men, which is exacerbated by the fact that men have lower health care utilization rates than women. In addition to differences in disease rates, men continue to have higher rates of tobacco use and heavy drinking than women, and they are also less likely to exercise, see a primary care doctor, or have insurance. Positive health behaviors are fewer for men who are single, widowed, or divorced. On a more positive note, men do have lower rates of disability than their female counterparts, with lower rates of chronic pain problems and vision problems, lesser impairment in activities of daily living, and lower likelihood of reporting serious psychological distress, according to the CDC. Men are also more likely to be cohabitating with a female partner at the end of their lives, whereas women are more likely to be widowed, again reflecting differences in mortality.

Sexual Functioning With Aging

While changes in sex hormones are an expected part of aging in women, men's changes in testosterone and sexual functioning are less acknowledged. Typically, testosterone levels begin to steadily decline in men starting at the age of 50 years, though most older individuals maintain an interest in sex throughout their lives. Testosterone deficiency can mimic the symptoms of dysthymic disorder as well as reduce sexual desire. A variety of other endocrine disorders and psychosocial and mental health issues can also negatively affect sexual desire and functioning. Erectile dysfunction is a common sexual problem for older men, occurring in up to 40% of men by the age of 40 years and continuing to increase with age, according to the Massachusetts Male Aging Study. Medical problems and medications can further affect this area of older men's functioning, including obesity, diabetes, and vascular disorders. Men who experience changes in their sexual functioning with age are at risk for depression, negative self-esteem, and increased conflict with sexual partners.

Mental Health and Aging in Men

In general, depression is more likely to go unrecognized and untreated in older adults than in younger groups. For older men in particular, depression poses a serious health risk due to the high rates of suicide in this population. Depression rates appear to peak for men between the ages of 40 and 59 years (7% prevalence), reducing to 5% for men who are 60 years of age and older. However, men who are 85 years of age and older have the highest suicide rate of any group in the United States, suggesting that mental health issues in this oldest cohort are going unrecognized and untreated.

Across all age-groups, men are at higher risk of dying by suicide or homicide than women. In the

United States, Caucasian men have the highest suicide rate than all other groups, the risk increasing with age. As with other health factors, men who commit suicide are unlikely to have sought mental health care previously, though they are likely to have been seen by a primary care provider in the month prior to their death. Risk factors for suicide in older men include the presence of a psychiatric disorder, recently purchasing a firearm, deteriorating health, the presence of multiple medical problems, lack of someone to confide in, being unmarried, receiving disability or unemployment benefits, and living alone.

Two primary barriers for men in getting treatment for mental health problems are higher rates of perceived stigma and greater likelihood of seeking treatment via medical providers. While many medical providers may be well versed in prescribing antidepressants, many are often less familiar with behavioral and counseling interventions and are less comfortable assessing self-harm risk. In addition, many providers perceive symptoms of depression as normal symptoms of aging in older adults and, therefore, are less likely to accurately diagnose clients or offer treatment. There is also a high overlap between depressive symptoms and medical symptoms in older adults, such as vascular disorders and cognitive impairments. As with all older adult cohorts, treatment for depression in older men often requires an interdisciplinary approach, allowing for the ruling out and treatment of medical and mental health problems simultaneously.

Older Men of Color

The specific needs of older men of color in the United States is a generally underresearched topic, though the increasing representation of people of color within the overall U.S. population warrants more specialized focus. Often, people of color have fewer economic resources and face more discrimination than their Caucasian peers, which continue to affect individuals at the end of their lives. For example, the Latina/o community, the fastest-growing U.S. subgroup, is expected to reach 128 million people by 2050, representing 29% of the overall population. According to the CDC, the Latina/o community has one of the lowest education rates, with individuals being three times more likely to be impoverished. Many other specific groups of people of color are also seeing expansions in their populations, which will lead to more diversification in future generations.

People of color who are recent immigrants have additional considerations, as level of acculturation affects the specific needs of older men of color. Acculturation can act as a protective or a harmful factor, depending on the circumstances, though often less acculturated individuals are at a disadvantage in the United States. For example, Latino men who are less acculturated are more likely to value maschismo, a characteristic that includes high masculinity, which may affect how likely Latino men are to seek medical or mental health care. Some more traditional family circumstances, where multiple generations live together, can act as a protective factor for older people of color. Among Native Americans, older adults who live on rural reservations may experience health care limitations. As a result, elders in this community benefit from living with family members who can provide care at home. However, if acculturation levels differ between parents and children, older men may have difficulty in getting their care needs met.

Imbalances in rates of medical problems appear to abound in all people of color groups as compared with their Caucasian peers. Particularly among African American men, who have the shortest life expectancy in the United States (74.9 years), health problems such as diabetes, obesity, and heart disease are found to be prevalent at higher rates. Multiple factors account for the high rates of health problems in people of color groups, including exposure to discrimination, less access to healthy food, less leisure time, and increased chances of injury or toxic exposure in the workplace.

As with all male cohorts, access to and use of health care services is a barrier for many people of color. Some groups, such as African Americans and Native Americans, may harbor a distrust of Western health care due to the historic abuses their communities have suffered. Others may prefer to seek care through traditional medicine systems. Historical physicians' issues with communication and inadequate cultural competencies have resulted in changes to medical training programs, which are now focusing on developing greater knowledge and understanding of people of color. Some proponents have advocated for the need for more physicians of color, as it is believed that individuals from within these communities will be best suited to address the needs of these communities.

Data on rates of mental health problems for older men of color are mixed. Depending on the setting and the sample, some studies have found higher rates of depression among Hispanic and African American older adults, whereas other studies have found the rates in these groups to be lower than those found among Caucasian older adults. In general, gender differences in access to mental health care are found across ethnic/racial groups, with men in most groups being less likely to be screened for and receive mental health care. Often, mental health diagnoses go unrecognized among people of color, due to differences in symptomatic presentation, assessment of problems, and access to care. Men in most communities of color continue to utilize mental health and medical services less often than women.

Sexual Minority Men

Past research found that gay men may experience so-called accelerated aging, meaning that men in this group perceive themselves as being "old" at a younger age than their heterosexual peers and also reflecting the increased mortality rates secondary to the HIV/AIDS epidemic. In addition, the youth-focused culture of the nonheterosexual community is often cited as one of the primary causes for the perception of accelerated aging, according to theorists. Problems with increasing social isolation are often significant factors in the experience of older nonheterosexual men, due to their lacking status and a role within the larger sexual minority community.

However, recent research presents more varied results on the well-being of older, nonheterosexual men. Many studies have found that older nonheterosexual individuals are reporting increased success and happiness in later life. Other studies, however, show that this subset of the population continues to suffer from the lifelong effects of discrimination. As a result, nonheterosexual elders may find themselves with fewer resources in later years. Nonheterosexual men are also less likely to utilize preventive health services (e.g., yearly physical exams), leading to greater risk for health problems. In addition, numerous studies continue to show a higher lifetime prevalence of depression in men who have sex with men than in other groups. The 21st century has seen a rapid expansion in the recognition of and institution of legal rights for nonheterosexual individuals, which will likely result in social change and improved circumstances for this group.

Human Immunodeficiency Virus Status

Human immunodeficiency virus (HIV) infection rates remain higher for men than for women in the United States, with specific increases seen in older Caucasian men. In general, new HIV cases are on the rise in the older adult community, and older individuals are more likely to be diagnosed later in the disease process. Medical improvements have significantly reduced the risk for serious illness or early death for individuals who are HIV positive. However, there are now other complicating factors being seen for this cohort, particularly with regard to aging. Individuals living with HIV for several decades show earlier development of age-related diseases, including higher rates of cancer and cognitive problems. It is unclear if these health changes are the result of the HIV itself or the result of toxicity from long-term use of antiretroviral drugs. Research has focused on how HIV damages the ribonucleic acid, as well as the disease's effect on the central nervous system. HIV-associated neurocognitive disorders, ranging from mild cognitive impairments to dementia, are characterized by a unique set of cognitive and motor impairments. While combination antiretroviral therapy has proven effective in slowing or reversing some cognitive impairments, around 20% of individuals infected with HIV and receiving the therapy continue to experience some degree of cognitive dysfunction, though there have been reductions in the most severe forms of HIV-associated dementia.

Overall, the needs of aging men are as diverse as the population itself. Within the United States, though, there are some commonalities. While men continue to have shorter life spans than women, the aging gap is decreasing, and men's lives are lengthening. Across groups, men continue to underutilize health care and mental health resources. As a result, men face specific risks from chronic health problems, including HIV. There is also a significant problem in the United States with regard to depression and suicide in the older male community, which presents a unique public health crisis. Ongoing work is needed to educate physicians, reduce stigma, and increase health care resources for this population.

Maya Elace Pignatore

See also Aging and Mental Health; Depression and Men; Gender Socialization in Aging; Help-Seeking Behaviors and Men; Late Adulthood and Gender; Men's Health; Mental Health and Gender: Overview; Sexual Dysfunction; Suicide and Gender

Further Readings

Bartlik, B., & Goldstein, M. Z. (2001). Practical geriatrics: Men's sexual health after midlife. *Psychiatric Services, 52,* 291–306.

Blazer, D. G. (2000). Psychiatry and the oldest old. *American Journal of Psychiatry, 157,* 1915–1924.

Ferrini, A. F., & Ferrini R. L. (2008). *Health in later years.* New York, NY: McGraw-Hill.

Hahm, H. C., Lê Cook, B., Ault-Brutus, A., & Alegría, M. (2015). Intersection of race-ethnicity and gender in depression care: Screening, access, and minimally adequate treatment. *Psychiatric Services, 66,* 258–264.

Jeste, D. V., Savla, G. N., Thompson, W. K., Vahia, I. V., Glorioso, D. K., Martin, A. S., . . . Depp, C. A. (2013). Association between older age and more successful aging: Critical role of resilience and depression. *American Journal of Psychiatry, 170,* 188–196.

Sirey, J. A., Franklin, A. J., McKenzie, S. E., Ghosh, S., & Raue, P. J. (2014). Race, stigma, and mental health referrals among clients of aging services who screened positive for depression. *Psychiatric Services, 66,* 258–264. doi:10.1176/appi.ps.201200530

Menopause

Menopause marks the cessation of a woman's menstrual cycles and entails a natural decline in reproductive hormones. It is officially defined as occurring when 12 successive months have passed since the last menstrual period. Menopause occurs in all women and usually takes place in one's mid-40s or 50s; in the United States, the average age at which menopause occurs is 51. This entry reviews the physical symptoms and psychological impact of menopause and discusses its causes, postmenopause, and management of symptoms.

Symptoms

Although it is a natural life change and not a disease, menopause can cause various symptoms, many of which can be unpleasant and disruptive. Some symptoms of menopause include hot flashes and night sweats (both of which are classified as vasomotor symptoms), sleep disruption, and low energy levels.

The months or years immediately preceding menopause constitute a time termed *perimenopause.* During this time as well, many women experience symptoms that can prove uncomfortable and quite overwhelming. Such symptoms include the following: (a) mood changes, (b) irregular periods, (c) vaginal dryness, (d) hot flashes, (e) night sweats, (f) sleep problems, (g) slowed metabolism and subsequent weight gain, (h) thinning hair, (i) dry skin, and (j) breast changes such as loss of fullness.

As mentioned, perimenopause can last for years, entailing a long and uncomfortable transition phase. While some women menstruate every month until their menstrual period stops, this is very unusual. Far more commonly, women experience irregularity in their periods for months or years (constituting perimenopause) before having a year without menstruating. Notably, despite having irregular periods during menopause, pregnancy is possible.

With such a lack of stability, in addition to the other challenges of perimenopause and menopause, this stage in life and the changes it brings about can create not only physical discomfort but also emotional unrest and anxiety.

Psychological Impact

Indeed, in addition to the physical symptoms associated with perimenopause and menopause, this stage in life can be psychologically "loaded." Women may feel relieved about some aspects of moving into this juncture, such as no longer needing to worry about pregnancy or menstrual cycles. However, this end to fertility can also be a saddening change for some women. Indeed, this phase in a woman's life can trigger a sense of loss. For example, many report that they experience short-term memory loss, extreme mood swings, and problems in "thinking straight." In some women, menopause brings about various forms and degrees of emotional distress. The hot flashes and other symptoms may trigger anxiety.

However, this transition can also produce more positive psychological reactions. For instance, many women find that menopause marks the beginning of a new era in their lives; the ending of fears about unexpected and unwanted pregnancy may provide the woman with opportunities for positive changes toward self-fulfillment and greater autonomy.

The psychological states associated with menopause can also be somewhat mixed, in that other transitions often occur at this time in many women's lives. In other words, given the average age at which it occurs, menopause tends to coincide with other life changes that may carry psychological significance and can therefore include a great deal of peripherally related psychological adjustments. For example, for many women who have children, menopause coincides with the time when their children begin to move out of the house, leaving women of menopausal age with the proverbial "empty nest." This change in itself constitutes an emotionally significant shift in life circumstances. In addition, many women undergoing menopause are also faced with the new responsibility of caring for aging parents. Furthermore, some women at this age become grandparents, which may cause them to feel and be perceived as older women. This can be difficult in societies where the phenomenon of ageism, or discrimination against people in late life, is present. There may be an extreme sense of loss. This period also coincides with the death of parents, widowhood, or divorce. These other age-related life changes, which can be paired with both perimenopause and menopause, can make this physical transition a marker of a new era in various domains of life.

Causes

Most commonly, menopause occurs naturally as a result of a decline of reproductive hormones. Indeed, starting in the late 30s, women's ovaries begin to cease producing estrogen and progesterone, which are the hormones that regulate menstruation. Thus, women experience a decline in fertility around this age. Then, in the 40s, the menstrual periods may change in heaviness, frequency, and duration, until eventually they cease entirely.

However, several other factors can trigger menopause earlier than it would have naturally occurred. For example, surgeries where the ovaries are removed (total hysterectomy or bilateral oophorectomy) cause menopause without any perimenopause phase. Women in this situation will experience an abrupt end to their menstrual periods as well as a sudden surge in menopause symptoms such as hot flashes and sleep disturbances.

Partial hysterectomies, where only the uterus, but not the ovaries, is removed, may cause early menopause as well, but this is not always necessarily the case. This is due to the fact that the mechanism for menopause has to do with the functioning of the ovaries rather than that of the uterus. Although a woman whose uterus has been removed may no longer have periods, her ovaries may still release eggs and produce estrogen and progesterone.

Other factors that can induce premature menopause include chemotherapy and radiation therapy, as well as primary ovarian insufficiency. Primary ovarian insufficiency is a condition in which the ovaries fail to produce normal levels of reproductive hormones due to genetic factors or an autoimmune disease.

Postmenopause

After menopause, the risk for certain medical conditions increases due to changes in the body's hormone levels. Some examples of this are cardiovascular disease and osteoporosis. Postmenopausal women also become more prone to urinary incontinence as the tissues of the vagina and urethra lose elasticity. As a result women in the postmenopausal phase may experience urinary tract infections more often.

After menopause, women also often experience changes in their sexual functioning. These changes can be distressing in that vaginal dryness from decreased moisture production and loss of elasticity can cause discomfort and slight bleeding during sexual intercourse. These changes as well as decreased sensation may reduce the desire for sexual activity (libido). Application of local vaginal estrogen is often used to alleviate these symptoms.

Another example of common postmenopausal physical change is the heightened propensity for weight gain. During and after menopause, the metabolism tends to slow, causing many women to increase in weight during the transition and more easily thereafter. More exercise and more judicious eating often become necessary for the maintenance of a healthy weight.

The physical ramifications of menopause and the postmenopausal state constitute another reason why menopause can be a difficult time in women's lives. The changes enumerated herein are mostly uncomfortable and unfavorable to women and can be felt as ways in which the body is moving past its prime. Hence, this is a stage at which one is strongly advised to increase preventive care, such as mammography, colonoscopy, pelvic exams, and lipid screening, as well as other examinations based on one's history and one's family history.

Management

While perimenopause and menopause are not diseases and therefore do not require medical treatment, many women choose to seek palliative medical therapy for symptoms that prove disruptive to their lives or are otherwise uncomfortable.

One option for managing menopause symptoms is known as hormone replacement therapy (HRT), which here refers to the use of estrogen and progestin in menopausal women. HRT may be helpful for the treatment of menopausal symptoms such as hot flashes. HRT is also helpful in preventing bone loss and osteoporotic fracture and is often used for this purpose. However, some research shows that HRT use can increase the risk for strokes and blood clots and may increase the risk for breast cancer as well. There is a good deal of variation in the way in which menopausal women respond to HRT, which is thought to be a result of genetic variation in estrogen receptors. There are also some new indications that taking hormones after the age of 65 years is harmless for some women, as long as it is needed to meet their needs and the lowest possible doses are given. Their use may be appropriate when the woman is at high risk for bone fractures and has very bad reactions to other bone drugs.

Another treatment choice for menopause symptoms is the use of selective estrogen receptor modulators (SERMs). SERMs are a category of drugs that act selectively as agonists or antagonists (depending on the target issue) on the estrogen receptors throughout the body. SERMs are either synthetically produced or derived from a botanical source called phytoserms. SERMs are usually used primarily for the prevention of postmenopausal osteoporosis; however, many such modulators have been associated with an increase in hot flashes.

Alternative Therapies

A variety of alternative therapies, including natural supplements and Eastern remedies, are available for alleviation of menopause symptoms; however, the research on their effectiveness is mostly inconclusive.

Black cohosh, the extract of the root of the black cohosh plant, has been popularized as a natural remedy for menopause symptoms. For some women, black cohosh may help decrease the incidence and severity of hot flashes, but there is insufficient evidence to determine its effect more conclusively. It has also been linked to liver damage and other unwanted side effects.

In addition, ginseng, an Asian herb, has been used for relief during menopause. Some research has shown that 200 milligrams of ginseng a day can improve mood in women undergoing menopause. Further research also indicates that it can help improve sexual arousal in menopausal women. Some research also suggests, however, that ginseng can contribute to heart problems in some women.

Another natural treatment for menopause is found in hops, or the flower clusters of the *Humulus lupulus* plant. Limited research has been done on its effectiveness in this matter. However, some research on 8-PN, an estrogenic compound found in hops, concluded that the compound decreased the severity of hot flashes and other menopausal symptoms. Other research suggests that another hops derivative, xanthohumol, may have anti-inflammatory properties.

Vitamin E, found naturally in nuts, vegetable oils, and green leafy vegetables, has also been touted as an alternative to chemical treatments for menopause symptoms. Research has shown that vitamin E outperforms placebo in (minimally) reducing hot flashes in breast cancer patients. In addition, one clinical trial showed that women taking vitamin E experienced one less hot flash per day than those women who were on a placebo.

Research on several other popularized alternative therapies has disproved their effectiveness. For example, while dong quai (a Chinese herb) and primrose oil have been thought to be useful in alleviating menopause symptoms, research has shown that these supplements perform no better than placebos. While research on the effects of soy isoflavones on menopausal symptoms is promising, it is not yet conclusive. Further, it is unclear if acupuncture is effective in treating menopausal symptoms.

Elizabeth Midlarsky and Liat Segal

See also Ageism; Aging and Gender: Overview; Aging and Mental Health; Body Image and Aging; Middle Adulthood and Gender

Further Readings

Bielawska-Batorowicz, E. (2013). The psychology of the menopause: The experiences during the transition and individual conceptualization of menopause. In *Nutrition and diet in menopause* (pp. 333–345). New York, NY: Humana Press.

Cordingley, L., Hart, J., & Bundy, C. (2008). Psychology-based approaches to the menopause. *Menopause International, 14*(4), 184.

Formanek, R. (Ed.). (2013). *The meanings of menopause: Historical, medical, and cultural perspectives* [Kindle ed.]. Abingdon, England: Routledge.

Jafary, F., Farahbakhsh, K., Shafiabadi, A., & Delavar, A. (2011). Quality of life and menopause: Developing a theoretical model based on meaning in life, self-efficacy beliefs, and body image. *Aging & Mental Health, 15*(5), 630–637.

Mishra, G., & Kuh, D. (2006). Perceived change in quality of life during the menopause. *Social Science & Medicine, 62*(1), 93–102.

Vesco, K. K., Haney, E. M., Humphrey, L., Fu, R., & Nelson, H. D. (2007). Influence of menopause on mood: A systematic review of cohort studies. *Climacteric, 10*(6), 448–465.

Men's Friendships

Men's friendships take many forms, though there are patterns that have been identified as being uniquely associated with friendships among males. In the United States, young boys are likely to have emotionally and physically close relationships with other boys and with girls during the preschool years. Crying in front of other children; physically embracing, hugging, or helping nurture another boy who is having difficulty; or simply playing together without consciousness of whether their playmate is a boy or a girl is common. Thus, boys who spend time together, share interests, and are compatible in other ways bond without restrictions on how they act or express themselves.

As toddlers, boys are not necessarily aware of their sex, of being male, nor do they consider their behavior as "gendered"—meaning that they feel that they must perform in some way "as a boy." During the preschool years, cross-gender play and friendships emerge around shared interests. However, by preschool, boys are often discouraged from pursuing activities with girls; thus, cross-gender friendship opportunities may be limited, making opportunities to have friendships with girls less likely. At this stage, adults often sexualize boy-girl friendships, teasing the boy for having a "girlfriend." At the same time, parents and others are also likely to discourage physically and emotionally close relationships between boys. Boy play tends to be organized around performing a task in sports and skill building, rather than processing feelings with other boys.

Once boys reach elementary school age, what has been called the "boy code" sets in. Boys become increasingly conscious of their identity as a boy and aware of the expectations that come with it, so they distance themselves from both girls and any behavior associated with being like a girl. Thus, boys' interactions with other boys take on behaviors, particularly in public, that are aligned with being male. While public displays of intimacy among boys decrease with age, close friendships among adolescent boys often, secretly, include sharing private thoughts, dreams, fears, confusion, and hurts with their closest male friends. By high school, however, this is less likely to occur for fear of ridicule.

Friendships, particularly emotionally intimate friendships, are important for boys. Yet boys receive little public or institutional support for such friendships. They receive greater support for performance-based relationships—for instance, playing sports, playing computer games, or learning skills. Boys gain status among peers and the approval of adults when they are successful at performing. Thus, boys learn to limit their emotional expressiveness and distance themselves from public displays of neediness or desire, focusing on tasks and achievement.

The fear of being viewed as feminine, which is associated with homosexuality, influences boys', and later adult male, relationships. For heterosexual men, adult male same-sex relationships become organized around "manhood acts" that display the culturally desirable qualities of independence and stoicism. Meanwhile, gay and bisexual men may internalize similar negative messages about same-sex friendships and even romantic relationships.

Over their life span, males in the United States receive less physical touch and are less likely to express desire for or have emotionally close same-sex relationships than their female counterparts. Men's friendships are more likely to involve "shoulder-to-shoulder" relationships. For instance, it is common for heterosexual male friends to play or attend sports events or work on projects together; it is less common for heterosexual male friends to have "heart-to-heart" conversations or vulnerable interactions.

Even the vocabulary to express appreciation or affection among male friends reflects caution for fear of not appearing manly. For instance, young men are more likely to say, "Love you, man," to another male but unlikely to say, "I love you," even though the intent may be the same. Such caution in men's expressions reflects discomfort with same-sex emotional intimacy. Men in the United States are likely to rely more on females than on other males for physical touch and emotional support. This places expectations on women to do the emotional labor in their relationships with males.

The effect of isolation and resistance to same-sex emotional intimacy on males can be significant. A sense of emotional isolation has been shown to be related to males' experience of depression and addictions. This can also be associated with there being a greater likelihood for males than for females to commit suicide, to die from unnecessary risk taking, and to break rules—including getting expelled from school, excessive drinking and drug use, or committing crimes. Isolation, feelings of inadequacy, shame, and guilt are all common themes in the lives of men pursuing psychotherapy. Males are also less likely to pursue counseling or other help-seeking actions.

Emotional intimacy can be thought of as an exchange between two people wherein they experience being deeply connected. They come to trust that their deepest feelings will be understood and that they are safe from judgment or ridicule. Research suggests that such intimacy with male (or even female) friends is difficult for many males. However, males who do report having intimately close male friends are likely to have had emotionally close relationships with their fathers (or a father figure) as children. They are also more likely than adult males who do not have such friendships to say that they desire more close friends and would also like even deeper friendships with the friends they already have.

There are differences among males in terms of their friendships based on both culture and family influence. Some cultures and families allow the display of intimacy among males (e.g., experiencing physical touch, kissing on the cheeks when greeting, handholding). For example, in Middle Eastern countries, men are likely to have greater comfort with physical intimacy with other men. Males growing up or living in families and communities where sharing vulnerabilities is encouraged and shaming is not part of the "male code" are likely to have greater levels of emotional intimacy with the males in their lives.

Men's friendships are highly dependent on both a male's individual life experience and cultural expectations. Like all humans, males have a need for emotionally intimate relationships. Emotionally close same-sex relationships can serve to help males resist isolation and emotional dependency on females (particularly for heterosexual men) and can enhance the likelihood of their seeking help when they are vulnerable. This capacity can contribute to men becoming nurturing fathers, spouses, and emotionally intimate friends to others.

Robert Heasley

See also Cultural Gender Role Norms; Fraternities; Friendships in Adolescence; Gender Role Conflict; Masculinity Gender Norms; Men's Issues: Overview

Further Readings

Canada, G. (2010). *Fist, stick, knife, gun: A personal history of violence*. Boston, MA: Beacon Press.

Crane, B., Towne, A., & Crane-Seeber, J. (2013). The four boxes of gendered sexuality: A framework and lesson plan for teaching about the history and effects of gendered sexuality. *American Journal of Sexuality Education, 8*(4), 274–305. doi:10.1080/15546128.2013.854008

Garfield, R. (2015). *Breaking the male code: Unlocking the power of friendship*. New York, NY: Gotham.

Goleman, D. (2005). *Emotional intelligence: Why it can matter more than IQ*. New York, NY: Bantam Books.

Kimmel, M. (2011). *Manhood in America: A cultural history* (3rd ed.). New York, NY: Oxford University Press.

Kinndlon, M., & Thompson, M. (1999). *Raising Cain*. New York, NY: Ballantine.

Pollack, W. (1999). *Real boys: Rescuing our sons from the myths of boyhood*. New York, NY: Owl Books.

Real, T. (1998). *I don't want to talk about it: Overcoming the secret legacy of male depression*. New York, NY: Scribner.

Schrock, D., & Schwalbe, M. (2009). Men, masculinity, and manhood acts. *Annual Review of Sociology, 35*, 277–295.

Way, N. (2013). *Boys' friendships and the crisis of connection*. Cambridge, MA: Harvard University Press.

Men's Group Therapy

Many boys and men are involved in same-sex groups, such as sports teams, school-based friendships, and certain male-dominated job specialties like engineering and construction. Rarely, however, do men seek out male-only therapeutic experiences. Culturally, asking for help from a therapist can be perceived as shameful because many men are taught to deal with problems on their own. Even more difficult is revealing that vulnerability in front of other men in a group situation. The most common route to group therapy for men is often as a result of a crisis involving loss, trauma, addiction, depression, or severe illness. Another typical pathway is when group therapy is mandated by the authorities or significant others because of destructive or inappropriate behavior such as domestic violence. Men with positive experiences in previous therapeutic groups, such as Alcoholics Anonymous, may seek group therapy on their own for personal growth and support. This entry reviews the history of men's group therapy and discusses its themes and stages.

A Brief History

The first men's therapy groups in the early 1970s involved male soldiers who after returning from the Vietnam War with posttraumatic stress reactions participated in group treatment where veterans could talk about their experiences with one another. The group format was also attempted with gay men who were coming out and then as a response to the AIDS epidemic in the 1980s.

In recent years, men's groups have consisted of teenage boys, expectant fathers, recently divorced and separated men, individuals with substance abuse problems, prisoners and parolees, those involved in domestic violence, or those who have experienced childhood abuse, and these groups have been utilized to help the members cope with anger or with unemployment, or for personal growth.

Themes Addressed by Men's Therapy Groups

While a men's group may have a specific focus, it is inevitable that certain themes associated with masculinity will emerge. These include the following:

1. What does it mean to be a man? Often, the group will critique the damaging aspects of the masculine role as well as acknowledge what is positive about being a man. Examples include competitiveness, bravery, autonomy, and expressing vulnerability.

2. Most groups will reflect on how men differ in expectation and behavior when they are in public settings versus more private and intimate environments. Men often describe how they protect themselves through displays of strength and assertiveness while privately acknowledging their fears, insecurities, and uncertainties.

3. Health issues such as taking time for self-care and the physical and psychological consequences of aging are often discussed in men's groups.

4. Men wrestle with the messages they tell themselves, including the harsh internal criticism for not living up to ideal masculine scripts and the perceived expectations of others in their environment.
5. Discussion about purpose and meaning in life is often part and parcel of a men's group. It gives men time to reflect on their lives, rekindle passion, and remind themselves of what is most important. Because most men do not talk openly or deeply outside this setting, it is significant that universal truths about mortality, creativity, and finding purpose are at the center of the deepening group process.

The Stages and Structure of a Men's Therapy Group

While all groups go through stages, the men's group is unique in how it forms and moves through these stages. Because of the traditional male socialization, the early stages of group therapy are laden with trust concerns among the men. Discussion often remains at a superficial level until trust is established through self-disclosure and by receiving supportive responses. The middle stages of group therapy have an even more dynamic quality where interpersonal and internal conflicts can be explored in more depth. In the final stage, members not only consolidate their learning but also work through issues of loss that are often not acknowledged in men's lives.

Themed men's groups, such as a group for recently divorced men, often have a predetermined curriculum, a session limit, and a protocol that dictates the topics to be covered. Ongoing long-term men's groups can be more loosely structured to take into account the particular individuals and their reasons for being in the group.

Conclusion

Men's groups provide a safe place for men to explore what it means to be a man, to gain support from other men, to improve interpersonal skills, and to discover passion and meaning in life. For many men, it is a safe haven where they remove their "social masks" and let down their guard. After one man in the group shared about the recent death of his father, he commented,

> This is so different than talking about this to the people at work. I feel like I can talk about how much he meant to me, but also what I never got from him. I can feel the loss, shed some tears. I know you guys are not going to judge me.

While there will be heavy moments, the laughter and openness present in an experienced men's group attest to the comfort that men can obtain by being authentic and discussing genuine concerns in their lives.

Fredric Rabinowitz

See also Gender Dynamics in Group Therapy; Masculinity Gender Norms; Men's Friendships; Sexual Orientation Dynamics in Group Therapy

Further Readings

Andronico, M. P. (1996). *Men in groups*. Washington, DC: American Psychological Association.

Caplan, T., & Thomas, H. (1995). Safety and comfort, content and process: Facilitating open group work for men who batter. *Social Work With Groups, 18,* 33–51.

Murphey, C. M., & Shillingford, M. A. (2012). Supporting unemployed, middle-aged men: A psychoeducational group approach. *Journal of Employment Counseling, 49,* 86–96.

Nahan, D., & Lander, N. L. (2010). The effectiveness of gender role re-evaluation and non-gender focused group psychotherapy in the treatment of recently separated men. *International Journal of Men's Health, 9,* 102–125.

Rabinowitz, F. E. (2014). Counseling men in groups. In M. Englar-Carlson, M. P. Evans, & T. Duffey (Eds.), *A counselor's guide to working with men* (pp. 55–70). Alexandria, VA: American Counseling Association.

Rabinowitz, F. E. (2014). Innovative group therapy with men. In A. Rochlen & F. E. Rabinowitz (Eds.), *Breaking barriers in counseling men: Insights and innovations* (pp. 67–76). New York, NY: Routledge.

Yalom, I. D., & Leszcz, M. (2005). *The theory and practice of group psychotherapy*. New York, NY: Basic Books.

Men's Health

Men's health is a multifaceted phenomenon that involves the intersection of environmental, physiological, psychological, and sociocultural factors that shape the health transitions and trajectories of men. From the moment a male child is born, societal influences navigate the cultural and environmental socialization of how that child will experience health over his life course. Researchers who study men's health examine various risk and protective factors that contribute to the higher rates of both chronic illness and earlier death among men compared to women. It is important to identify these factors in efforts to mitigate the disparate effects of men's health outcomes. Researchers and health and human services professionals work collaboratively to provide healthy living conditions for men so that they—and the individuals who are in their communities and social networks—can live healthy, fruitful lives. This entry expounds on these issues. First, the unique experiences of men and how these experiences are influenced by multiple dimensions of health are described. Next, how the health of men influences the health of others is framed as a phenomenon based on gender roles that are manifested in the home and within one's community. Finally, how the health and well-being of men can be improved through the reduction and/or elimination of men's health disparities is discussed.

Dimensions of Men's Health

Examining the intersection of sex and gender with other aspects of men's identities and experiences is necessary to understand the varied dimensions of men's health. These dimensions include the social determinants of men's health that arise from men's positions in social systems and how this is affected by the distribution of resources, opportunities, privilege, and relationships. These socially defined and socially meaningful characteristics are interwoven and challenging to fully appreciate as factors that operate independently or additively. The World Health Organization defines social determinants as the conditions in which people are born, grow, live, work, and age. For men, how they manage their health and navigate various systems with which they have direct contact (e.g., health care, education, judicial) is directly influenced by the social determinants of their health. Some of the social determinants that influence health outcomes for men include employment and socioeconomic status, kinship and social support, and masculinities. In addition to system-level influences, these conditions also include various interpersonal and intrapersonal factors, such as the physical, mental, and emotional health of men.

Socioeconomic status is the most robust and consistent factor affecting health outcomes, whether measured by income, education, or occupation or measured during childhood, adolescence, or adulthood. For men in particular, socioeconomic status is an important determinant often used to define their worth, character, power, and success, as well as the likelihood that they will find (and sustain) a relationship with a significant other.

Research has suggested that a large network of *kinship and family support* (i.e., uncles, aunts, significant others) is essential to the functioning of a healthy home. In fact, kinship and support are found to be especially important for maintaining a sense of community and social support for issues surrounding the health of men. A large part of kinship and family support for men usually involves the role of spouses and significant others in helping men follow through with important health behaviors and decisions as they age, including getting routine checkups, adhering to medical treatment, and taking prescribed medications. Previous research has underscored the role of women in the completion of healthy behaviors and in continuity of help seeking by men.

Masculinities (used in the plural form here to illustrate the various definitions and ways in which men identify as "masculine" men) influence the pressing concerns of men as well as their decisions to use positive or negative coping strategies and resources to address their problems. Leading men's studies scholars have acknowledged the importance of understanding the multiple ways in which masculinities can be conceptualized beyond a sole focus on the sex differences between men and women. For example, there are advantages and disadvantages for men who engage in traditional gender roles. In this context, traditional gender norms refer to the idea that a man should be confident, dominant, strong, and stoic, and not exude feminine characteristics and behaviors. Men who are young, those who have lower educational levels, those with low family incomes, and men of color tend to endorse more traditional, dominant norms of masculinity than their counterparts. The endorsement of traditional gender norms by men is consistent across studies, and the endorsement of traditional norms of masculinity changes depending on the age and professional or nonprofessional status of men. Adherence to more traditional norms also affects health decisions and behaviors, as men who identify as traditional and demonstrate confidence, strength, and stoicism tend to avoid health care professionals and not discuss their health challenges and concerns with others for fear of appearing weak or not a "real man." Men who adhere to more traditional notions of masculinity also report poor physical and mental health compared with those who adhere to more progressive definitions of masculinity.

The Importance of Men's Health to the Health of Others

Adherence, or lack thereof, to traditional gender norms can also mean that the decisions that men make about their health will also influence the lives of those around them. This speaks to the importance of men's health to the health of others, which emerges at the intersection of a series of interwoven social formations that include historic, economic, political, linguistic, interpersonal, and psychological threads. The behaviors of some men, particularly those who engage in risky lifestyles (e.g., street life, crime), and other marginalized subgroups of men may result in psychosocial stressors associated with perceived gender norms in the context of their environments. These men may also prove to be less desirable partners, which leads to relationship disruption, resulting in high divorce rates, female-headed families, out-of-wedlock births, less commitment of men to relationships, and negative perceptions of men by the women in their lives. Under this type of gender-induced stress, many men will be limited in their ability to serve as responsible father figures, which may include providing love and social and financial support for their children and families. A study by the National Institute of Justice estimated that 16% of individuals in jail and prison had a mental illness, and an overwhelming number of those incarcerated are men. These kinds of numbers challenge the notion that rehabilitation is attainable, given the number of challenges that men in the judicial system may face prior to or immediately following their time spent incarcerated. Individuals who are substance users, unemployed, have lower incomes, and have fewer years of education are also at greater risk for incarceration. Oftentimes, when men rejoin society after incarceration, they lack the skills needed to secure unsubsidized employment, lack occupational skills, and/or have fewer skills to seek jobs or confront potential employers, who may be apprehensive about hiring an ex-offender.

When comparing the health outcomes of men with those of women, research suggests that men are more likely to be diagnosed with chronic illnesses, have a shorter life expectancy, and have an increased likelihood of experiencing a host of other unfavorable health conditions. Early work in the field of men's studies identified these occurrences as mere biological differences. However, research shows that this trend is not rooted in sex, as it is men's attitudes, perceptions, and behaviors toward health that ultimately shape their life's trajectory. It is important to consider these implications as men's health directly affects those around them, including their partners, children, and families. When men engage in poor lifestyle choices, their health is oftentimes compromised. If their conditions worsen, much of the caretaking responsibility falls on their partner or the other members of their family, who may be expected to resume regular familial and household duties as normal. Therefore, when men subscribe to unhealthy practices, their unhealthy characteristics are modeled early and are passed down to their children and the other youth in their families. This in turn creates a cyclical process of both complicated and compromised relationships among men, their health, and their responsibilities to themselves and others.

Health Disparities Among Men

Men's health disparities have become a topic of global proportions. Not only have health disparities captured the attention of the health care system, but they also have captured the attention of policymakers, religious leaders, the judicial system, and researchers alike. This growing interest in men's health disparities is largely due to the numerous sources that have documented the ways in which women fare better than men across a number of different health outcomes. Men's health disparities research has primarily focused on the extent to which social and cultural factors shape men's health practices and health outcomes. Beyond this lies an important gap in the literature regarding how to explain the differences in health among men. Focusing on men's health disparities enables a deeper understanding of how masculinities are related to health; how gender is constructed and embedded in social, economic, and political contexts and institutions; and how culture and subcultures influence how men develop their masculinities as well as how they respond and react to health challenges and concerns.

Some scholars have used the phrase *men's health movement* to describe the more recent attention on men's health disparities and the resources invested in men's health. This is primarily because the health of women and girls has been the priority for researchers and clinicians, leaving men to fend for themselves regarding matters involving their health. While the men's health movement has helped identify the disparities that exist between men and women, men's health disparities research considers how the health of men is determined by cultural, environmental, and economic factors associated with race, ethnicity, and other socially defined identities and group memberships. Because the social and cultural roles, expectations, and norms of those who are biologically male are fundamentally shaped by race, ethnicity, and gender, it is critical to examine how these socially defined characteristics shape men's health and influence the relationship between masculinities and men's health. Research on men's health has examined the challenges experienced by men of color and men who live in poverty (who have historically been invisible in research studies), though these men account for much of the sex difference in mortality globally. Although scholarly contributions to men's health disparities are growing, there continues to be a lack of discourse around concrete solutions that can be applied to reduce or eliminate differences in health outcomes among groups of men in the United States and abroad.

Oftentimes, the dream of an education, a decent job, a house, and a family becomes impossible to attain for some subgroups of men, particularly those who are members of marginalized communities. Although men within patriarchal societies experience unearned advantages based solely on their biological sex, the same privileges are not always afforded to men of color and men with socioeconomic disadvantages. Traditionally, women's health concerns have garnered most of the attention and remained at the forefront of many health initiatives, leaving some men and their health experiences in the margins. Not only are myriad barriers in place to limit the progress of these men, but research also shows that men from underserved populations experience increased rates of incarceration and unemployment, which also contribute to poor health outcomes and ultimately prevent them from living long, healthy lives. According to the World Health Organization, disparities in social determinants of health can be reduced if researchers and practitioners make a concerted effort to improve daily living conditions; tackle the inequitable distribution of power, money, and resources; and understand the problems and assess the impact of action. These efforts, tailored to subgroups of men, will help address and ultimately close the widening gap of health disparities among men.

Daphne C. Watkins and Janelle R. Goodwill

See also Health Issues and Gender: Overview; Hegemonic Masculinity; Male Privilege; Masculinities; Men's Studies

Further Readings

Crawshaw, P., & Smith, J. (2009). Men's health: Practice, policy, research and theory. *Critical Public Health, 19*(3–4), 261–267. doi:10.1080/09581590903302071

Creighton, G., & Oliffe, J. L. (2010). Theorising masculinities and men's health: A brief history with a view to practice. *Health Sociology Review, 19*(4), 409–418. doi:10.5172/hesr.2010.19.4.409

Griffith, D. M. (2012). An intersectional approach to men's health. *Journal of Men's Health, 9*(2), 106–112.

Griffith, D. M., Metzl, J. M., & Gunter, K. (2011). Considering intersections of race and gender in interventions that address U.S. men's health disparities. *Public Health, 125*(7), 417–423. doi:10.1016/j.puhe.2011.04.014

Lohan, M. (2007). How might we understand men's health better? Integrating explanations from critical studies on men and inequalities in health. *Social Science & Medicine, 65*(3), 493–504. doi:10.1016/j.socscimed.2007.04.020

Treadwell, H., & Braithwaite, K. (2005). Men's health: A myth or a possibility? *Journal of Men's Health & Gender, 2*(3), 382–386.

Treadwell, H. M., Young, A. M. W., & Rosenberg, M. T. (2012). Want of a place to stand: Social determinants and men's health. *Journal of Men's Health, 9*(2), 104–105.

Men's Issues: Overview

Men's issues is a broad interdisciplinary field that has included scholarship from a variety of areas of academic inquiry since the latter half of the 20th century. The entries presented in this section reflect topics that have historically and contemporarily been relevant to psychology, sociology, medicine, law, and other fields. This overview primarily reviews men's issues from a psychological perspective, including the origins of the psychology of men and masculinity and the formation of the Society for the Psychological Study of Men and Masculinity (SPSMM)—Division 51 of the American Psychological Association (APA). It also introduces several key concepts in the psychology of men and masculinity. These include a brief overview of the gender role socialization process that shapes men's psychological development, correlates of traditional conceptualizations of masculinity, and tools for the measurement of masculinity variables in empirical research.

History of Men's Issues in Psychology

Contemporary perspectives in the psychology of men and masculinity arose in reaction to earlier trends in gender research. In particular, Joseph Pleck, in 1981, summarized the paradigm that he identified as having dominated masculinity research since the 1930s, which he showed had not been clearly identified or defined by researchers during this period and had rested on numerous assertions that were unsupported or contradicted by the empirical literature. Pleck described this perspective as the gender role identity paradigm (GRIP). According to this perspective, the development of a secure gender identity congruent with one's assigned sex at birth—based on stereotyped attributes and traditional norms for men's and women's roles, respectively—was viewed as a potentially perilous but essential task in an individual's psychological adjustment. This process was characterized as stemming primarily from early relationships with one's same-sex parent, based on early psychoanalytic theories, particularly drive and ego psychology. A fundamental component of this paradigm for gender research was that masculinity and femininity constituted two fixed, diametric opposites. For men, fostering masculinity and rejecting femininity were therefore seen as closely intertwined and imperative tasks for achieving healthy psychological development. Men who displayed either feminine or insufficiently masculine (hypomasculine) personality traits were pathologized by early gender researchers as well as by clinicians.

Critiques From Feminist Psychology

This early psychology of gender, including the GRIP, has been identified by feminist scholars such as Janis Bohan as an essentialist approach. Used in this context, the term *essentialist* indicates that this perspective asserted that gender was constituted by personality traits located within the individual and derived from biology (as opposed to the social learning perspective that gender is defined by socialization processes, including the influence of ongoing social interaction). Thus, the first steps toward superseding the early perspectives on gender were initiated not by researchers specifically focused on men's issues but rather by the feminist psychologists and critics who began to turn their attention toward these bodies of research in the 1960s and 1970s. Feminist psychologists during this period began to highlight the androcentric bias in early gender research, which routinely identified the experiences of male research participants as normative while ignoring women's unique experiences. With the formation of multiple professional organizations dedicated to scholarship in this area (e.g., the Division of the Psychology of Women in the APA), attention was turned toward previously accepted perspectives, techniques, and methodologies. In her critical 1973 review of psychologists' attempts to measure masculinity and femininity (M and F) as a bipolar trait, the feminist psychologist Anne Constantinople highlighted the poor utility of the widely used MF scale for predicting mental health and psychopathology, challenging the notion that "deviant" MF scores (i.e., scores on the opposite end of the scale from the individual's own assigned sex) are indicative of poor psychological adjustment. By critiquing prior researchers' and psychometricians' assumptions of unidimensionality for MF scales despite evidence for multidimensionality, Constantinople further challenged the notion that masculinity and femininity reflect opposite ends of a fixed, bipolar spectrum.

Proposed solutions to the problems raised by Constantinople and other feminist critics of early gender research took diverse forms. For instance, for androgyny researchers such as Sandra Bem, masculinity and femininity were conceptualized as two separate, orthogonal attributes, each composed of distinct, socially desirable personality traits traditionally associated with either men or women. These traits were generally described as having been identified with a given gender more or less arbitrarily as a result of historical accident. Although this was in some respects a very progressive stance, Bem and other androgyny researchers such as Janet Spence retained critical elements of an essentialist conceptualization of gender by defining masculinity and femininity as being constituted by intrinsic personality traits—aspects of temperament implicitly connected to biology. Taking a more radical departure from earlier research paradigms, other feminist psychologists such as Anne Fausto-Sterling and Judith Butler rejected the essentialist explanations altogether, instead asserting that femininity was constructed socially by cultural forces rather than by existing within individual women. As the field of psychology began to recognize the socially constructed nature of femininity, the need to apply a similar lens to the construction of masculinity and men's norms became apparent. It was at this juncture that researchers began to discuss the emergence of a need for a new psychology of men and masculinity.

Masculinity as Roles and Ideology

One approach taken by researchers who responded to these insights was to begin studying masculinity in terms of normative social roles and gender ideologies. Gender ideologies refer to cultural beliefs about the roles and behaviors that are normative for individuals of a given gender. Rather than emphasizing intrinsic personality traits that have been historically associated with men and women, gender ideology researchers began to focus instead on the ways in which individuals endorse or fail to endorse beliefs about how men and women should think, feel, and behave. Psychologists interested in the emerging research area of men and masculinity thus began by identifying the norms that make up the traditional male role. In 1976, Robert Brannon was the first to explicitly compile a list of norms for traditional male role behavior. With the development of the Brannon Masculinity Scale, the first psychological measure of traditional masculinity ideology, along with the subsequent measures that followed, researchers were able to begin investigating the role that gender ideology played in shaping men's lives.

As research related to men's issues was gaining interest among psychologists, Pleck's 1981 book *The Myth of Masculinity* introduced the sex role strain paradigm, which Pleck would later retitle the gender role strain paradigm (GRSP). This new paradigm for understanding men's experiences was contrasted with the earlier GRIP and other essentialist ways of understanding or explaining gender. Pleck's theory employed social learning theory and the notion of masculinity ideologies and suggested that consequences for violating the traditional masculine norms often led men to overconform to them—resulting in dysfunctional behaviors and negative outcomes. As this theoretical perspective for research on men and masculinity gained popularity, research on gender role strain indicated that a number of negative outcomes were found to correlate with the endorsement of traditional masculine norms, including mental health diagnoses, substance abuse, engagement in violence, poor relationship satisfaction, and engagement in health risk behaviors. The GRSP has since come to dominate the literature on the psychology of men and masculinity as the most frequently used theoretical perspective in empirical research in this area.

History of Division 51

Formation of the Division

The formation of an organized division within the APA devoted to studying men's issues in the context of new paradigms for gender research did not follow spontaneously from the insights of early feminist critics. The process of establishing the SPSMM as Division 51 of the APA spanned well over a decade from the first attempts to form similar organizations during the 1980s. Building from these earlier efforts, Gary Brooks and Ronald Levant formed the Committee for the Psychological Study of Men and Masculinity (CPSMM) in 1990. In their statement of purpose, the CPSMM proposed to form an organization that would "bring together diverse psychologists doing work on men's issues, enlightened by the new psychology of men." This psychology is depicted as stemming directly from the psychological insights of women's studies and being rooted in a social-constructionist framework for understanding gender.

Following a successful meeting at the 1990 APA convention, leading to the development of an organizational structure for the committee as well as the establishment of a newsletter, efforts toward documenting the required show of interest among APA members were initiated in earnest. Still, the attainment of divisional status would not be arrived at without difficulty. Resistance to the notion of a division focused on men's issues could be found both within CPSMM itself and from other members within the APA. One concern hinged around the relationship that would exist between the proposed division and the existing division on the Psychology of Women (Division 35), with some expressing concern that a division on men's issues could become a vehicle for efforts inimical to the goals of feminist psychologists. However, the leadership of CPSMM worked collaboratively with members of Division 35, both prior to as well as during and after their candidacy for divisional status, and began to express more clearly the importance of establishing a division on men's issues that was specifically grounded in feminist values. While this stance may have resulted in resignations among some SPSMM members who aligned themselves with so-called men's rights groups, or other ideologies at odds with feminist psychology, by and large, its membership was united in asserting the need to work collaboratively with feminist scholars in seeking gender equality. It was not until the fall of 1995 that this process resolved into the vote for the SPSMM's inclusion in the APA, and after securing further approval from other APA divisions and the APA Council of Representatives, SPSMM became Division 51 of the APA in February 1997.

Psychology of Men and Masculinity and Division 51 Today

Since its formation, SPSMM has facilitated a considerable body of literature related to men's issues. One outlet for such scholarship has been Division 51's journal *Psychology of Men and Masculinity* (*PMM*), first published in 2000 under the editorship of David Lisak. In the years since its inception, *PMM* has moved from being a biannual publication to publishing four issues each year and has established itself as an important vehicle for research related to men's issues. It has also expanded its coverage statement to convey the journal's aims of including research examining populations of boys and men of greater diversity in terms of race, ethnicity, nationality, age, sexual identity, and gender identity groups, as well as employing more diverse qualitative and quantitative research methodologies; and it focused on health as well as mental health.

Another topic of note for the psychological study of men's issues is the diversity of theoretical research orientations that have been employed in *PMM* and in the psychology of men and masculinity literature as a whole. A content analysis conducted by Joel Wong and colleagues in 2010 concluded that in its first 8 years of publication, published research in *PMM* overwhelmingly made use of the GRSP and other theoretical frameworks closely associated with, and derived from, this model (i.e., gender role conflict theory, masculinity ideologies theory, and masculine gender role stress theory). This finding seems reflective of the prominent role that this theoretical orientation has maintained in the historical development and contemporary state of the psychological study of topics related to men's issues. It has also prompted calls from scholars in the field for a broadening of the research perspectives being employed by psychological researchers interested in men's issues.

Current Perspectives in Men's Issues

Gender Role Strain Paradigm

As noted earlier, the GRSP and associated theories are the most widely employed theoretical orientations for research in the psychology of men and masculinity. While not the first perspective to attempt to explain the role of masculinity in men's psychological lives, the GRSP played a foundational role in the psychological study of men's issues by paving the way for nonessentialist investigations of masculinity. Although Pleck did not employ social-constructionist language in his earliest incarnation of this perspective as the "male sex role identity paradigm," he would later clarify that he understood his model to be a social-constructionist perspective that simply predated the term. The GRSP and related perspectives are now understood as being philosophically grounded in the notion that masculinity may be differently constructed by or for men of divergent cultural and demographic backgrounds.

The GRSP has characteristically emphasized that traditional norms for masculine gender roles often result in a variety of negative consequences for men, their families, and society at large, including consequences related to physical health, social relationships, and psychological well-being. Pleck categorized the types of strain that may result from the often contradictory nature of traditional gender roles, and the processes of socialization into them, using three categories.

First, *discrepancy strain* refers to the experiences of individuals whose personal characteristics fail to meet their own internalized same-gender ideals. Men who experience a perceived discrepancy between their actual selves and the gender role standards that they have adopted may experience a variety of negative consequences, such as low self-esteem, as a result.

The second category of strain identified by Pleck is *trauma strain*. This refers to exceptionally harsh experiences of gender socialization, which may lead to long-term consequences for men. Trauma strain may include normative experiences of gender socialization but may be particularly salient for certain groups of men, such as men who are combat veterans or athletes. Trauma strain may also disproportionately affect men whose identities are marginalized by traditional conceptualizations of gender roles, such as men of color, gender minority men, and sexual minority men.

Pleck identified the third category of gender role strain as *dysfunction strain*. This type of strain occurs when the effort to meet social standards for masculinity results in negative consequences for individual men or for those who are affected by their behaviors. Dysfunction strain has been studied in terms of two primary constructs—traditional masculinity ideology and gender role conflict—which are discussed in greater detail later in this entry.

Multiple Masculinities

With the rejection of biological essentialism as an explanation for gender, the notion that masculinity is a universal construct that could be applied equally to all men across historical and cultural contexts has come under the scrutiny of scholars interested in men's issues. Whereas the GRSP and associated perspectives generally recognize that no one conceptualization of what it means to be a man is exhaustive of the possible meanings of masculinity, researchers under this paradigm have typically selected the traditional, dominant, White Western conceptualizations of masculinity that pervade our culture as the primary focus of their research. Researchers emphasizing a multiple-masculinities perspective add to this discussion by providing a deeper and more specific understanding of the unique ways in which various groups define masculinity, which may diverge from the dominant conceptualization of masculinity. Research that has been attentive to the notion of multiple masculinities has examined the different forms that masculinity ideology takes in men from different racial or ethnic groups, nationalities, and sexual orientations.

Further problematizing the notion of masculinity, scholarship under a multiple-masculinities perspective does not suggest that for each man one and only one conceptualization of masculinity will be salient. Multiple masculinities may play important roles not only in shaping understanding of the differences among groups of men but also in individual men's lives. Some men may identify with marginalized or minority groups or subcultures that prescribe specific sets of expectations for masculinity, while also being subject to expectations associated with the masculine norms dominant within the broader culture. Multiple masculinities may also be enacted by men who identify more closely with the dominant culture. Some early research in this vein suggested that even men who view their masculinity in terms of common components may carry these out in very different contexts—for example, by pursuing status via athletic versus academic or occupational competition. Other men who have been influenced by feminism in recent generations may reject facets of traditional masculinity.

The idea of a plurality of masculinities has been accepted widely in contemporary psychology of men and masculinity and may be viewed as compatible with a number of other conceptualizations of gender. Research using the GRSP, for instance, has found that masculinities may differ across groups in terms of the different weightings given to specific masculine norms. Other researchers may attempt to identify qualitatively distinct masculine norms among men with different sociocultural backgrounds.

Reference Group Identity Dependence Theory

The male reference group identity dependence (RGID) theory was first advanced by Jay Wade in 1998. This perspective suggests that men typically derive their gender role self-concept from reference groups composed of peers or other males with whom an individual man identifies. Reference groups may employ definitions of masculinity with varying degrees of similarity to that which dominates the broader culture. As such, RGID theory is by its nature compatible with a social-constructionist and multiple-masculinities perspective and seeks to explain variations in men's enactment of gender across groups.

Wade distinguishes among three categories of male RGID statuses, describing men's sense of relatedness to other groups of men. These statuses may be used to understand the relationships among men's personal gender role self-concepts.

First, men falling under the *no reference group* status display only a minimal sense of relatedness with any groups of other men. As such, men in this group are understood to be lacking clearly defined gender role self-concepts.

Second in Wade's conceptualization is the *reference group dependent* status. Men in this category identify with a particular male reference group to the exclusion of others. Consequently, such men would be anticipated to have a relatively well-defined and inflexible gender role self-concept that is understood in terms of the external characteristics of the relevant reference group.

Third, men in the *reference group independent* status identify themselves with men more generally, experiencing a sense of relatedness with men in general, rather than with men in a specific reference group or groups only. As the gender self-concept of an individual so categorized is not anticipated to be defined in relation to a narrowly limited perspective on masculinity, these men are expected to display a broader and more flexible understanding of their gender.

Research based on RGID theory has employed constructs and methodologies borrowed from multiple theoretical research orientations to support this system of categorizing men's relatedness to other groups of men. For instance, men categorized under the "reference group independent" status experience decreased gender role conflict as compared with other groups, while those in the "reference group dependent" status experience greater gender role conflict as well as being more likely to endorse traditional beliefs about appropriate roles for boys and men.

Important Constructs in Psychology of Men and Masculinity

Gender Role Socialization

Men acquire their patterns of gender salient behaviors, cognitions, and emotions as a result of an ongoing process of male gender role socialization, which may begin in infancy and continue into adulthood. Parents, teachers, and peers all tend to contribute to boys' socialization during early childhood. As a result, boys often come to internalize beliefs and acquire characteristics congruent with the masculinity ideology held by these influential groups. Early developmental research has documented differences in the styles of play typically encouraged for young boys and girls. Young boys, as compared with girls, are encouraged to engage in games involving larger groups, often divided into competing teams, in which attributes such as risk taking and assertiveness are valued. Male gender role socialization may also take the form of proscriptions against certain forms of behavior; for instance, boys may be taught that "boys don't cry" and discouraged from expressing vulnerable emotions. Rather than attributing observed gender differences to biological differences rooted in sex, scholarship on male gender role socialization leads us to the conclusion that powerful social forces affect the unique aspects of boys' and men's development.

Masculinity Ideology

One outcome of a patriarchal system is the formation of masculinity ideologies—systems of beliefs about the kinds of behaviors that ought to be deemed appropriate for boys and men. While the masculinity ideologies dominant across different cultures tend to share many similarities, variations in masculinity ideologies across groups also exist. The phrase *traditional masculinity ideology* refers specifically to the set of expectations for men's behavior that have been observed to be most pervasive among White people in the Western world.

In one recently developed measure designed to examine individual differences in traditional masculinity ideology, the Male Role Norms Inventory–Short Form, traditional masculinity ideology is conceptualized as having seven different dimensions: (1) avoidance of femininity, (2) aggression, (3) toughness, (4) negativity toward sexual minorities, (5) importance of sex, (6) self-reliance through mechanical skills, and (7) restrictive emotionality. Individual differences in this construct and its dimensions have been found to correlate with variables such as substance abuse, relationship satisfaction and social support, health-related behaviors, and psychosocial well-being.

Gender Role Conformity

Gender role conformity is distinct from the endorsement of traditional masculinity ideology in that it does not refer to men's beliefs about masculinity but rather to men's self-concept of their engagement in behaviors in conformity with the dominant set of masculine norms. While conformity to gender role norms is conceptually distinct and measured separately from masculinity ideology in psychological research, measures of these two constructs have been shown to correlate strongly. On average, men who endorse traditional masculinity ideology are more likely to report engaging in behaviors congruent with that ideology. However, for some individuals, the relationship between these constructs may differ. For instance, some men may endorse traditional beliefs about how men ought to act but not succeed in living up to these expectations for themselves. Furthermore, recent research has found that the dimensions of these two multidimensional constructs are distinctive.

Gender Role Conflict

Gender role conflict occurs when conformity to socialized gender roles results in negative consequences. Researchers interested in gender role conflict as it pertains to men and masculinity, such as James O'Neil, have most clearly emphasized the ways in which personal characteristics encouraged by male gender role socialization may lead to experiences of personal devaluations, restrictions, and violations for men or for others who are affected by their behavior. Of these, devaluations include criticisms experienced as a result of one's conformity or nonconformity to socialized gender roles, while restrictions refer to efforts to limit one's own behavior or another's behavior in order to conform more closely to those roles. Finally, violations refer to actions taken to harm oneself or others as a result of that individual's nonconformity to masculine roles. Research has uncovered significant associations between gender role conflict and a number of variables, including psychological and physical health variables, experiences of violence, oppression and abuse, and numerous demographic variables.

Future Directions in Men's Issues

Drawing from theoretical perspectives and constructs like those addressed herein, scholarship in the field of men's issues may have implications for a wide variety of areas of men's lives, as reflected by the breadth of entries included in this section. Future research will likely continue to develop constructs central to the relatively dominant research paradigms within the psychology of men and masculinity described in this overview. Researchers may also respond to calls from within the field to adopt more diverse research methodologies and perspectives. Some commentators within the psychology of men and masculinity have noted that research within this realm has tended to prioritize dominant conceptualizations of masculinity (e.g., traditional masculinity ideology) to the exclusion of others. New measures can be developed to further scholarship on nontraditional or nondominant masculinities, such as African American masculinity and gay masculinity. Research utilizing unique perspectives, such as objectification theory and positive psychology perspectives on men and masculinity, can also help provide a richer understanding of the experiences and consequences of men's socialization.

Ronald F. Levant and Stefan Jadajewski

See also Gender Role Strain Paradigm; Masculinities; Masculinity Gender Norms

Further Readings

Brooks, G. R., & Levant, R. F. (1999). A history of Division 51 (the Society for the Psychological Study of Men and Masculinity). In D. A. Dewsbury (Ed.), *Unification through division: Vol. 3. Histories of the divisions of the American Psychological Association* (pp. 197–220). Washington, DC: American Psychological Association.

Connell, R. W., & Messerschmidt, J. W. (2005). Hegemonic masculinity: Rethinking the concept. *Gender & Society, 19,* 829–859.

Levant, R. F. (2011). Research in the psychology of men and masculinity using the gender role strain paradigm as a framework. *American Psychologist, 66,* 765–776.

Pleck, J. H. (1995). The gender role strain paradigm: An update. In R. F. Levant & W. S. Pollack (Eds.), *A new psychology of men* (pp. 11–32). New York, NY: Basic Books.

Wong, Y. J., Steinfeldt, J. A., Speight, Q. L., & Hickman, S. L. (2010). Content analysis of *Psychology of Men and Masculinity* (2000–2008). *Psychology of Men and Masculinity, 11,* 170–181.

Websites

Society for the Psychological Study of Men and Masculinity (SPSMM): http://division51.net/

Men's Studies

Men's studies is an interdisciplinary field devoted to topics that involve men, masculinity, masculinities, feminism, pro-feminism, gender, justice, equity, and politics. Although not a relatively new field of study, men's studies has begun to grow and expand on academic campuses and in professional settings around the world. Men's studies was formed largely in response to, and as a critique of, an emerging men's rights movement, and as such, it has been taught in academic settings only since the 1970s. In many academic settings, men's studies is taught as a direct parallel to women's studies or as a part of a larger gender studies program. Thereby, faculty members in gender studies departments tend to be engaged in advocacy work associated with feminist politics or gender equality. The relationship between men's studies and feminism has been a topic of interest and debate since the beginning, yet feminism's connection to men's studies is clear as feminism often examines the diverse intersections of women's identities. Furthermore, men's studies, which according to some scholars was once a strictly pro-feminist discipline, has become more expansive and now includes multiple representatives who are now becoming more vocal about their various opinions as they concern the conditions of men and boys.

One of the most provocative aspects of men's studies is the use of the plural *masculinities* in scholarship and dialogue—referring to the multiple types of masculinity that can be understood and performed by men. Raewyn Connell was the first to propose the concept of a wide and varied interpretation of masculinity (i.e., masculinities) in her 1995 book *Masculinities*. The use of *masculinity* in the plural form helped frame the current academic field, which is frequently considered as men's studies or the critical study of masculinity. Also, there have been a series of criticisms of the separation between men's studies and gender studies. Likewise, scholars who study transgender studies have questioned the relationship between male biology and gender identity in men's studies and masculinity studies.

This entry looks back to the history of men's studies, discusses the work of the premier organization on men's studies, and looks ahead to the challenges and opportunities for change.

History of Men's Studies

Although there are a number of supporting and oppositional resources that document the origin of men's studies, many resources suggest that it emerged out of the pro-feminist movement of the 1970s. *Pro-feminist* is used to describe an individual who supports feminism, without implying that he or she is a member of the feminist movement. Historically, the term *pro-feminist* has been reserved for men who are active supporters of feminism as well as its efforts to bring about the political, economic, cultural, personal, and social equality of women and men. Thereby, pro-feminism not only benefits women, but it also benefits the men who support these women. During the early years of the pro-feminist movement, men were also actively involved in political activism, most often in the areas of gender equality, women's rights, and violence against women. The core beliefs of pro-feminism are aligned with gender equality in employment and life experiences, passion and commitment to positive change, and an inquisitive reaction to traditional gender roles and expressions.

Pro-feminist men generally believe that (a) society is shaped in such a way that women suffer inequalities and injustices while men experience various forms of power and privilege; (b) the current, hegemonic (i.e., dominant) model of manhood is oppressive to women and limits men themselves; and (c) men should take responsibility for their own behaviors and attitudes and work to change those of other men whose expansions of the definitions of manhood and gender equity are limited. Pro-feminist men typically also recognize the importance of other forms of injustice and other kinds of social relations. Pro-feminists assume that class, race, sexuality, age, and other factors are important influences on the relations between and among men and women. The work of pro-feminists of the past few decades has also made connections to intersectionality. This means that it is committed to serving as a multidisciplinary forum of men and women—irrespective of class background, ethnic origin, religious background, sexual orientation, or physical abilities—whose purpose is to promote a critical discussion of issues involving men and masculinities and to disseminate knowledge about men's lives to a broad audience.

The American Men's Studies Association

In the early 1980s, when the National Organization for Changing Men changed its name to the National Organization for Men Against Sexism, a group of pro-feminist men who were a part of the Men's Studies Task Group decided to break away and start a new organization called the Men's Studies Association. The Men's Studies Association was an explicitly pro-feminist group, and those who felt this was too constraining split away several years later to form the American Men's Studies Association (AMSA), which soon became the premier men's studies organization in the world. Early pioneers of the AMSA included Martin Acker, Shepherd Bliss, Harry Brod, Sam Femiano, Martin Fiebert, and Michael Messner.

Although the AMSA originated in 1991, the first official conference was held in Stony Point, New York, in 1993. Despite this, however, efforts by the AMSA's founding members predate the early 1990s, as many of them taught men's studies classes at various colleges across the United States during the 1970s and 1980s. The mission of the AMSA is to advance the critical study of men and masculinities by encouraging the development of teaching, research, and clinical practice in the field of men's studies. One of the distinguishing characteristics of the AMSA is its interdisciplinary nature, as several of the members come from all walks of life and various academic and professional disciplines. One could even argue that the AMSA is truly interdisciplinary in that it is a welcome space for all disciplines, professions, and persons, whether they be high school students, college students, engineers, attorneys, or professors at institutions of higher learning, who may specialize in history or the humanities, performing arts, social sciences, health sciences, or biological sciences, among other fields and disciplines.

For more than 20 years, the AMSA has held yearly conferences on the critical study of men and masculinities, as well as enriched its membership with educational opportunities, cutting-edge research, and opportunities for involvement and support in its own efforts to understand and expand the study of men and boys. In this way, the AMSA provides a forum for teachers, researchers, students, and practitioners to exchange information and gain support for their work on men and masculinities. The AMSA's reach has grown to include an international audience, meaning that AMSA members are from all over the world. At the yearly meetings every year, there is a growing representation of attendees from South America, Europe, Canada, and Asia. This is the irony of the "A" in the AMSA, as the organizational efforts began with the hope of spreading the mission across North America and now its members expand across the globe.

The goals of the AMSA are aligned with those of men's studies, as the organization was founded on many of the concepts derived during the pro-feminist movement. First and foremost, the AMSA strives to be inclusive of scholarly, clinical, and activist endeavors engaging men and masculinities as social-historical-cultural constructions. According to its website, the AMSA is reflexively embedded in the material and bodily realities of men's and women's lives. The AMSA considers itself an organization that is multidisciplinary in nature and committed to disseminating new knowledge about men and masculinities to a broad audience. Also, the AMSA actively seeks the participation and membership of all men and women irrespective of race, class, ethnicity, sexual orientation, physical abilities, nationality, or religious identity. Similarly, AMSA members are committed to excellence, inclusiveness, and ethical behavior in men's studies research, publication, teaching, and practice. They also strongly encourage student participation and membership, offering scholarship and mentoring opportunities for young scholars in the field. Finally, the AMSA values and encourages mutually empowering scholarly and professional relationships that are generative, empowering, and affirming in nature.

Challenges Experienced by Men and Opportunities for Change

There are many challenges associated with men's studies and with deepening the current knowledge on masculinities, but arguably, the most prominent challenge involves the lack of personal freedom associated with individual definitions of manhood and masculinities. Many topics stem from this challenge, such as men's ability to fully come into their own and express themselves and society's receptivity (or lack thereof) of these expressions. Another way to think about this is to acknowledge how society has a tight grip on how men and boys define manhood and that there is still much to do to loosen that grip and educate the world on the various possibilities associated with manhood and masculinities. This is an important aim of scholars who are committed to the critical study of men and masculinities.

There are also challenges associated with the multiple levels of identity associated with studying the living and working conditions of men and boys. Not only are men's studies scholars grappling with the gender identity of men, but they are also probing for a deeper understanding of the other identities that men experience (e.g., race, sexual orientation, religion, disability, age). These additional layers mean that truly understanding men and boys comes with additional challenges, especially if those in this field of study want to broaden their understanding of the study of men and boys for the purpose of improving their conditions and the conditions of their families. Some of these inquiries have brought together scholars from critical race theory and intersectionality as a way to deepen the critical study of men and masculinities.

Recent news outlets have highlighted society's issues with men and boys. These come at a time when threads of men's studies issues are unraveling more and more in pop culture, the media, and men's studies scholarship. Most poignantly, this generation has witnessed stories in the media about murders and suicides by men and boys, not to mention the policing of young men of color in urban areas, and domestic violence in professional sports. All the while, some audiences have questioned the position and role of men's studies in all of this, wondering if it is truly a viable field of study or if it is just a trendy topic that will be here today and gone tomorrow. As men's studies as a field of study approaches its fourth decade (and the AMSA approaches its third), men's studies scholars are growing more confident that it is here to stay. This is due, in part, to the persistence of the field's predecessors, as well as the new generation of scholars advocating for men's studies literature, research, and activism.

Despite all of the work of its predecessors, there is still so much work to be done with and for men. Previous efforts to understand men and masculinities are not enough because those who identify as scholars, advocates, and activists need to continue to evolve their efforts so that society can keep up with the evolution of men and boys. There are opportunities here for the next wave of men's studies scholars to be active participants in learning and building critical knowledge on men and masculinities. One of the biggest opportunities for men in the 21st century involves redefining manhood (not just for the men themselves but also for the world to see). Thus far, progress has been made with how men's studies leaders (as well as the men themselves) across the globe have started their own initiatives and campaigns around reshaping their definitions of the roles and expectations for men. But the work is not over yet.

Daphne C. Watkins

See also Hegemonic Masculinity; Masculinities

Further Readings

Brod, H. (1987). The case for men's studies. In H. Brod (Ed.), *The making of masculinities: The new men's studies* (pp. 39–62). Boston, MA: Allen & Unwin.

Cohen, J. W., & Suen, Y.-T. (2012). Taking stock: Exploring trends in the field of men's studies through a content analysis of the American Men's Studies Association (AMSA) annual conference programs 1993–2011. *Journal of Men's Studies, 20*(1), 73–83.

Connell, R. W. (1995). *Masculinities*. Sydney, New South Wales, Australia: Allen & Unwin.

Femiano, S. (1991). The next step: The American Men's Studies Association (AMSA). *Men's Studies Review, 8*(4), 3.

Kimmel, M., & Messner, M. (Eds.). (1992). *Men's lives* (2nd ed.). New York, NY: Macmillan.

Menstruation

To be physically, emotionally, and mentally healthy, a woman needs to be exposed to cyclical, normal levels of both estradiol and progesterone for 30 to 45 years of her menstruating life span. The consequence of these cyclic ovarian hormone levels is approximately monthly vaginal bleeding during which the endometrium (lining of the uterus) is shed. This is called menstruation, or a period. A menstrual cycle is normally 21 to 35 days long, including the first day of flow until the day before the next cycle begins. Humans are rather unique among female mammals in having obvious cyclical vaginal bleeding. Human cultures, however, have generally negative views about menstruation; this negativity is projected onto the half of all humans who intermittently, normally bleed. Currently, both men's and women's attitudes toward menstruation are complex and often contradictory. Although menstrual flow is still viewed negatively in the dominant, men-centered cultures of the world, for many women today it is a reassuring nonevent. What science and medicine know about normal cycles in prospectively studied random populations, however, continues to be sparse and incomplete. New evidence documents that clinically normal cycles may have silent ovulatory disturbances with absent or low progesterone levels. Increasing evidence indicates that normal ovulation with normal progesterone and estradiol levels is needed not only for fertility but also for lifelong bone, heart, and breast health.

Characteristics of the Normal Menstrual Cycle

Menarche, the first menstruation, occurs between the ages of 9 and 14 years—on average, at about 12.5 years of age in privileged societies and at older ages where food scarcity or war exist. The menarche age has decreased by about 2 years in the past century. Menstrual bleeding lasts for 3 to 5 days, during which time 20 to 60 milliliters or about 12 teaspoons of blood/fluid is lost.

The menstrual cycle is created by complex interactions among hypothalamic, pituitary, and ovarian hormones. Menstruating life has three phases: (1) maturational (menarche and about a decade thereafter), (2) mature (premenopause), and (3) involutional (perimenopause). The menstrual cycle is unique as an outward manifestation of endocrine secretions because, instead of coming from a gland, each egg is created by a single ovarian follicle, which then disappears. Also important is that during the maturational and mature reproductive phases, central adaptation allows for graded, protective modifications based on nutritional, thermal/physical, and social/emotional inputs from the internal and external environments.

The menstrual cycle may normally be 3 to 5 weeks long (21–35 days) but averages 28 days (or a lunar month). It has two hormonal phases: (1) the follicular phase and (2) the luteal phase. The follicular phase has low progesterone levels but rising estradiol levels, which reach a midcycle peak about 220% above its low levels during flow. The estradiol peak triggers a spike in the amount of luteinizing hormone, which stimulates ovulation (i.e., the release of an egg with subsequent progesterone). The follicular phase is variable from 10 to 25 days. The luteal phase begins when the luteinizing hormone peaks and ends the day before the next flow begins. It is dominated by a progesterone plateau (1,400% higher than in the follicular phase) with moderate estradiol levels. Normal luteal phases are 10 to 16 days long and quite variable.

Life Cycle Variations in Menstrual Cycles

In the year after menarche, cycles tend to be long; it is normal to experience oligomenorrhea (i.e., cycle lengths of more than 35 days) and may even be normal to have amenorrhea (i.e., skipping flow for 3 to 6 months). In early adolescents, the flow tends to be very light or extremely heavy (more than 80 milliliters). It is also common in young women for cycles to be irregular (varying by more than 1 week from cycle to cycle). Finally, with teen pregnancy implications, the first post-menarche-year cycles are usually anovulatory, or if ovulation develops, they are almost always short in luteal length.

In mature, premenopausal women, starting at about 20 to 25 years of age, cycles are predictable in length and flow, and cycle and phase lengths are usually normal. It is assumed that regular, normal-length cycles are ovulatory; however, recent population-based data for more than 3,000 Norwegian women between the ages of 20 and 49 years showed that at least 30% of the regular, normal-length cycles were anovulatory (as indicated by a cycle-timed serum progesterone level). Fertility is optimal between the ages of 20 and 30 years and associated with maximal health and survival of mothers and offspring. However, as women move toward perimenopause, cycle lengths first become shorter, flow tends to increase, and 25% of cycles have very heavy flow (>80 milliliters); normal ovulation and luteal phase lengths and fertility are markedly decreased.

Cultural Concepts of Menstrual Cycles

That adult women have vaginal bleeding with near-lunar cyclicity has, through centuries of male-dominated society, been viewed as an obscene and fearful horror. Anything that bleeds for several days a month and is paradoxically still healthy is not to be trusted! The mystery that is menstruation generates mistrust, which is visited on women. Across time, a few woman-centered cultures, however, have revered the menstruation-moon connection as a mythic, life-giving miracle. Science also says that normally ovulatory cycles are needed for spontaneous fertility and the survival of the human race. Although perhaps moderated by education and civilization, today these diverse negative and positive concepts coexist—menstruation as a threatening mystery and menstrual cycles providing a life-giving connection with past and future human life. Responses to menstruation are related to gender, sex, sexual orientation, generation, culture, and society. The purpose of this entry is to provide some current concepts and perspectives while conveying what is scientific and yet to be documented about menstrual cycles and ovulation.

Menstrual Taboo

Menstrual cycles are a taboo or as close as we come to one in today's "free" societies. Most women learn as girls that they must never mention menstruation. This lack of discussion is reinforced by both women's and men's negative reactions when it is mentioned. Most heterosexual women actively hide the fact that they are menstruating from everyone in their households, even from other women and perhaps especially from their sexual partners. Tampons are made as small and as absorbent as possible (at risk for threats, e.g., toxic shock syndrome) so that a woman without a pocket can hide one in her hand on the way to the washroom; a woman carrying a purse to the toilet gives away her secret. Television ads for sanitary products show blue fluid to illustrate absorbency—never would screens show red or blood-like fluid.

Men's Attitudes Toward Menstruation

Men appear to be mostly negative about menstruation, perhaps because bleeding women often refuse sex. Anthropologists describe many male-dominated cultures that exclude women from active society (food gathering, cooking, hunting, or fishing) while they are menstruating. Today, many educational jurisdictions do not allow hygiene or sex education in elementary schools, even if the classes are segregated by gender. These negatives are unlikely to be true of all men or all cultures, or of every generation and orientation.

Women's Attitudes Toward Menstrual Cycles

Few mothers have an open and unembarrassed talk about menstrual cycles with their preteen daughters. Younger women appear eager to suppress menstruation through long-cycle or continuous use of combined hormonal contraception, perhaps because advertising commonly presents it as a healthy, lifestyle choice (although scientific evidence of its safety, especially in teen women, is unproven). They less commonly seek options such as a 3-month, high-dose injection of the synthetic progestin medroxyprogesterone or a levonorgestrel-releasing intrauterine device (IUD; progestin IUD) for contraception, in the hope that these will stop the flow, but both are more likely to produce fewer bleeding days, and recovery of fertility is faster after removing the progestin IUD.

Despite accommodating and sometimes absorbing the negative menstrual cycle attitudes of the dominant culture, women today are increasingly declaring that menstruation is as much a part of who they are as breathing. Young women especially are refusing to leave menstruation hidden; some even make Internet announcements when they are having their period. There are worldwide movements to eliminate taxes from sanitary products and in support of the environment (300 pounds or a woman's lifetime of nondegrading sanitary products are dumped into landfills) to use durable silicone menstrual cups or washable cloth pads. Groups such as the international Society for Menstrual Cycle Research and the Centre for Menstrual Cycle and Ovulation Research promote acceptance of the menstrual cycle as a normal part of younger women's lives.

Negative Associations With Menstrual Cycles

Not only must men not trust a bleeding woman, but it is also culturally assumed that before her flow she will be transformed from the sexy, accommodating, and ideal female into a depressed, bitchy, and threatening woman. Premenstrual symptoms are very real for some women some of the time and increase in perimenopause; they are effectively decreased by multimodal, nonpharmaceutical strategies, and thus, it is not helpful to view them as a disease. Premenstrual syndrome or premenstrual dysphoric disorders continue to be enshrined as mental illness in psychiatric manuals. Yet 1-year prospective records in healthy, ovulatory, normal-weight women show no premenstrual increase in negative moods. Also, within-woman moderate exercise training decreases negative moods and physical premenstrual experiences in initially normally ovulatory, healthy women. Although depression is supposedly common premenstrually, rates of premenstrual suicide are not increased in those with premenstrual dysphoric disorder when compared with controls. Some counselors and researchers assess the time before flow as the only window each month during which society "allows" women to honestly express their feelings. Other evidence says that life circumstances and stressors are fundamental to experiencing negative premenstrual symptoms. Finally, premenstrual changes in mood, appetite, fluid retention, and breast size and tenderness are attributed to the neuroendocrine effects of changing ovarian hormones. Epidemiological data show that premenstrual breast tenderness, negative moods, and other symptoms increase in very early perimenopause, when menstruation is still regular but estradiol levels are higher and progesterone levels are lower. The lived reality of premenstrual symptoms involves a very complex, individual, life cycle, and culture-specific combination of physical, hormonal, and cultural factors.

Menstrual Cycle–Related Problems

As well as being irregular and unpredictable, cycles in the first postmenarche year may also start being associated with menstrual cramps (dysmenorrhea). This is a deep pelvic pain caused by hard uterine contractions from higher endometrial and uterine muscle production of prostaglandins. Typically, cramps are worse in those with early menarche, who are younger, who have not been pregnant, who are obese, or who are smokers.

Cramps improve over time in premenopausal women before worsening again in perimenopause. High prostaglandin levels not only increase uterine contractions but also have negative systemic effects such as nausea, dizziness, sleep disturbances, and fatigue. Cramps can be effectively prevented or treated by ibuprofen, the over-the-counter antiprostaglandin medication, taken early in high and frequent doses (400 milligrams initially, followed by 200 milligrams as soon as the cramps start to return).

Heavy flow is also common in adolescents and, like cramps, increases again in perimenopausal women—in both life phases, ovulatory disturbances and an estradiol imbalance with lower progesterone are common. Very heavy flow (80 milliliters, or more than 16 soaked normal-sized sanitary products per menstrual period) carries a high risk for potentially debilitating iron deficiency anemia (low blood count). It is significantly improved (by about 25% to 50%) by taking ibuprofen (200–400 milligrams with each of three meals a day). Other effective treatments require medical prescriptions including cyclic (14 days per cycle) or daily oral micronized progesterone in the luteal phase—equivalent to a dose of 300 milligrams at bedtime—or the progestin IUD.

Ovulatory disturbances (anovulation and short luteal phase cycles) appear to be the most subtle of the body's finely tuned adaptations to nutritional, social, emotional, or physical stress. New evidence suggests that silent anovulation may occur in 30% of clinically normal cycles. Only with prolonged and multiple stressors or in an adolescent soon after menarche do these common stressors cause disturbances of cycle length or flow as well as of ovulation, with the resulting diagnoses of hypothalamic oligomenorrhea or amenorrhea.

After hypothalamic (stress related) disturbances, the most prevalent problem causing cycle disturbances is polycystic ovary syndrome (PCOS, or anovulatory androgen excess [AAE]). Typically, PCOS/AAE presents in adolescence with persistent oligomenorrheic cycles more than 1 year postmenarche. Inconsistent ovulation is associated with tonically higher estradiol levels, often higher testosterone levels, clinical evidence of acne and unwanted facial hair, and commonly an increased waistline or weight gain. If untreated, women with PCOS/AAE may experience psychological problems (e.g., low health-related quality of life and self-esteem, depression), decreased fertility, obesity, and/or diabetes, as well as increased risks for endometrial and breast cancers. Usual treatment is combined hormonal contraception; metformin is added for obesity. Others suggest that cyclic oral micronized progesterone with spironolactone (an antiandrogen) with or without metformin is a more physiological approach. All agree that support is necessary to achieve a healthy lifestyle.

Jerilynn C. Prior

See also Depression and Women; Perimenopause; Puberty; Sexism, Psychological Consequences for Women

Further Readings

Bedford, J. L., Prior, J. C., & Barr, S. I. (2010). A prospective exploration of cognitive dietary restraint, subclinical ovulatory disturbances, cortisol and change in bone density over two years in healthy young women. *Journal of Clinical Endocrinology & Metabolism, 95,* 3291–3299.

Li, D., Hitchcock, C. L., Barr, S. I., Yu, T., & Prior, J. C. (2014). Negative spinal bone mineral density changes and subclinical ovulatory disturbances: Prospective data in healthy premenopausal women with regular menstrual cycles. *Epidemiologic Reviews, 36,* 137–147.

Munster, K., Schmidt, L., & Helm, P. (1992). Length and variation in the menstrual cycle: A cross-sectional study from a Danish county. *British Journal of Obstetrics and Gynaecology, 99,* 422–429.

Prior, J. C., Naess, M., Langhammer, A., & Forsmo, S. (2015). Ovulation prevalence in women with spontaneous normal-length menstrual cycles: A population-based cohort from HUNT3, Norway. *PLoS One, 10*(8), e0134473. doi:10.1371/journal.pone.0134473

van Hooff, M. H., Voorhorst, F. J., Kaptein, M. B., Hirasing, R. A., Koppenaal, C., & Schoemaker, J. (2000). Polycystic ovaries in adolescents and the relationship with menstrual cycle patterns, luteinizing hormone, androgens, and insulin. *Fertility and Sterility, 74,* 49–58.

Vollman, R. F. (1977). The menstrual cycle. In E. A. Friedman (Ed.), *Major problems in obstetrics and gynecology* (Vol 7, 1st ed., pp. 11–193). Toronto, Ontario, Canada: W. B. Saunders.

Mental Health and Gender: Overview

Mental health disorders are costly to treat in the United States. According to the Agency for Healthcare Research and Quality, the cost of treatment of mental health problems rose from $35.2 billion in 1996 to $57.5 billion in 2006. The National Institute of Mental Health notes that mental health problems are quite common throughout the United States, yet only about half the individuals who have a disorder receive treatment. There are many risks associated with mental health problems. These risks can be attributed to a variety of social and economic disparities.

Mental health problems can range from, for example, depressive disorders, such as major depressive disorder and postpartum depression, to anxiety disorders, such as agoraphobia and social anxiety disorder, to psychotic disorders, such as schizophrenia and delusional disorder. In the *Diagnostic and Statistical Manual of Mental Disorders* (*DSM*), the American Psychiatric Association outlines the criteria that are needed to diagnose these disorders. In 2013, 43.8 million adults had a mental illness, excluding problems related to substance or alcohol abuse.

Gender and Mental Health

Throughout the entries in this encyclopedia related to the role of gender and mental health, the authors document various disparities along gender lines. In general, experts agree that women in the United States are more likely to have a mental illness than men, approximately 23% and 14%, respectively.

The authors of the entries also document that rates of mental health problems in women and men vary not only by the type of mental health disorder but also by how the criteria for mental illness are conceptualized. For example, clinical and research publications have documented that the prevalence of depression may be underestimated in adult males, who may experience depression in the form of feelings of anger, substance abuse, and increased risk taking, as opposed to the general criteria for depression, which consists of mostly internalizing symptoms such as crying out of the blue, loss of energy, sleeping less or more than usual, and feelings of worthlessness. Whereas women are more likely to be diagnosed with depression, men are generally more likely to be diagnosed with a substance use disorder. Traditional criteria published in the *DSM* may not adequately capture the role of gender and gender norms in mental health disorders. For example, other authors note that when "gender-fair" criteria are used, prevalence rates differ in comparison with rates using traditional criteria. In the case of depression, men and women tend to have similar rates of depression when externalizing symptoms such as substance abuse are included. Therefore, it is important for counselors, psychologists, and general medical providers to be cognizant of the role of gender norms inherent in current diagnostic systems.

Other authors note that the prevalence of mental health disorders, when comparing women and men, also varies greatly by race, ethnicity, nationality, and culture. Therefore, it is important to attend to the nuanced aspects of racial and cultural issues and how these relate to mental health problems, treatment, and help seeking. In fact, in addition to the traditional mental health disorders outlined by the *DSM*, as noted earlier, the *DSM* also includes a list of "culture-bound syndromes" that describe a range of mental health problems that occur across the world, not just those based on constructs developed or relevant mostly for Western cultures, such as the United States. These, for example, include *ataque de nervios*, which represent diverse ways in which people may manifest or express distress, and neurasthenia, which consists of symptoms such as fatigue, dizziness, or headaches. The fifth edition of the *DSM* (*DSM-5*), published in 2013, is divided into three main sections. The first two sections (i.e., "DSM-5 Basics" and "Diagnostic Criteria and Codes") provide an introduction to the *DSM* and the criteria for traditional mental health problems (e.g., depression and anxiety) found mostly in Western cultures. The third section ("Emerging Measures and Models") includes information on how to conduct a cultural assessment (i.e., cultural-formulation interview) and on cultural concepts of distress (e.g., *ataque de nervios*). Therefore, to understand mental health and gender, it is also important to address how mental health affects cultural and racial groups differently and how at times these differences are also affected by gender.

Sexual Orientation and Gender Identity

Transgender and gender nonconforming people, as well as lesbian, gay, bisexual, or queer (LGBQ) individuals, may also be at higher risk of developing mental health problems. Research has supported that these disparities are due to additional stressors related to discrimination and stigma around gender identities and sexual orientations. It should also be noted that the fields of psychiatry, psychology, and other mental health fields have contributed to the marginalization and stigmatization of transgender and gender nonconforming people and LGBQ people throughout history. The first three versions of the *DSM* had initially categorized nonheterosexual sexual orientations as pathological, which encouraged physically invasive and harmful treatments and procedures for LGBQ people. While the sexual orientations of LGBQ people today are viewed as normal and healthy identities, there are still some mental health practitioners who may attempt to "convert" or change someone's sexual orientation to heterosexual. Despite this, research has consistently supported that these sexual orientation change efforts are not empirically supported and instead cause severe psychological distress for those who undergo these procedures.

Race, Ethnicity, and Culture

As noted, psychology researchers and other scholars have documented that the prevalence of mental health disorders varies greatly by race, ethnicity, nationality, and culture. Generally, racial and ethnic minority populations (e.g., Asian Americans and Pacific Islanders, African Americans, and Native Americans) tend to have higher rates of psychiatric disorders than their non-Hispanic White counterparts. For instance, in a nationally representative study of the National Survey of American Life, researchers showed that African Americans and Caribbean Blacks are more likely to have a chronic major depressive episode. African Americans are also more likely than non-Hispanic Whites to experience trauma as a result of being victims of violent crimes. Similarly, Asian Americans have been shown to have higher rates of depression than non-Hispanic Whites. Racial and ethnic minorities who identify as lesbian, gay, bisexual, transgender, or queer (LGBTQ) are also at higher risk of developing mental health problems, given their experiences with racism, sexism, heterosexism, and transphobia.

Whereas women in general tend to have higher rates of mental health problems, these differences also vary by race, ethnicity, and nationality. For example, some authors show that Asian American women may have higher suicide rates than their White and African American counterparts. When looking at differences by age, other differences also emerge. For instance, in the case of suicide risk, Latina adolescents are at higher risk than their non-Latina counterparts.

Social class and income are additional stressors that affect women's mental health, as well as their help-seeking behaviors. For example, studies have found that while cognitive behavioral therapy may be a common and effective treatment for individuals who are victims of intimate partner violence, this approach may not be effective for low-income African American women who have been victims of domestic abuse and have posttraumatic stress disorder.

Women of color experience additional stressors related to seeking help for mental health problems. For example, studies on the perception of mental health care providers who work in the areas of HIV prevention within urban communities and with women of color with severe mental illness (e.g., bipolar disorder, schizophrenia, major depression, substance use disorder) show that these women may have additional risks due to social norms and attitudes about sexuality. Others have shown that women of color also have to navigate issues of stigma and that treatment is also affected when there are differences between the mental health provider and the client with respect to gender roles and religion. As such, addressing the mental health of women needs to be comprehensive and inclusive of issues such as social class, income, and racial or ethnic backgrounds.

Influences of Sexism

Systemic sexism, or the societal notion that men are superior to women, also influences how mental health might manifest in the lives of women (and even men). Systemic sexism can manifest in many ways—ranging from how women are portrayed in the media to how women in many educational systems are not encouraged to reach their fullest academic potential. Systemic sexism can manifest through how women leaders in government are critiqued for their looks and are challenged on their intellect. Systemic sexism can also manifest in how the government and the criminal justice system handle violence against women.

The media perpetuates unrealistic body image expectations on women, setting the standards of beauty for girls and women across the United States. Girls and women are taught explicit and implicit messages about their bodies, as well as shown consistent examples of what ideal bodies should be. When girls and women are exposed to these pressures to be thin, beautiful, or sexy, they may develop feelings of low self-esteem—particularly those who are not able to reach or maintain these standards. Through constant exposure to the media messages about beauty, girls and women may develop an array of mental health issues, including eating disorders, body dysmorphic disorders, and depression.

Violence against women can also influence mental health issues, particularly with how violence is managed in the United States. Research has found that about one in every five women (or 20%) experiences a sexual assault in her lifetime and that women are more likely to be targeted for sexual violence than men. When women do experience violence, they often do not report the crime for fear that they will not be believed, that they will be blamed or slut shamed for the incident, or that they will be retraumatized by police officers. When women do report the incident but their assailants are not convicted of the charges, other women may lose faith in the justice system and not report the violent crimes they experience. As a result of these violence-related issues, women can develop an array of mental health issues. For example, survivors of sexual assault may develop symptoms of posttraumatic stress disorder, which may negatively affect their ability to concentrate, their performance at school or work, their friendships and romantic relationships, and their overall view of the world.

Gender Roles

All societies socialize individuals in the context of gender roles (e.g., girls wear pink, and boys wear blue). These gender roles often affect treatment for mental health problems. Some argue that the values and social norms associated with these roles are particularly salient among some racial and ethnic minority groups. For example, in some Latin American ethnic groups, gender-related social norms characterize women as being self-sacrificing for their families (also known as *marianismo*) and men as protectors and the sole providers for their families (also known as machismo or more recently as *cavallerismo*). Therefore, when in treatment, Latin American men and women may focus on familial issues irrespective of the reason why they are in treatment. For some providers, patients who focus on their family, as opposed to their "individual" reason for seeking treatment (e.g., depression or anxiety), may appear as the ones who are being resistant. As a result, within traditional talk therapies, grounded mostly in Western notions of individuality, providers may focus on helping a Latina become more assertive to take care of her "self" and a Latino become more democratic in sharing household responsibilities. Although these interventions may appear rational from a Western perspective, they dismiss the role of gender norms in the lives of Latin American men and women. Asian American women have other stressors related to stigma, shame, and "saving face" (i.e., preserving public appearance for the sake of their families and community), which create additional risk for mental health problems. They may also create obstacles to seeking traditional mental health services since the act of seeking treatment may bring shame to the women's families.

Gender roles also vary greatly within racial and ethnic groups. For instance, African American women tend to be characterized as self-reliant and responsible in caring for themselves and their families without support from others, as opposed to Latin and Asian American women, who are characterized as more interdependent. Gender roles of African American women have emerged as a coping mechanism against a history of slavery, abuse, and trauma, and some have designated this social norm as the Superwomen complex or the

Superwomen syndrome. While these characteristics may capture African American women's resilience and strength, they may also create additional stressors if not properly assessed by therapists and may also affect their help-seeking behaviors. For example, while African American women may go to treatment more often than their male counterparts, the pressure to be the "strong Black woman" may keep them away from traditional services.

Although women across all racial groups are affected by gender roles, it is well documented that mental health providers must attend to the variations in how these manifest. However, equally important, mental health providers ought not to overgeneralize these gender roles as being applicable to all women within their racial and ethnic minority groups. For example, not all African American women endorse the "strong Black woman" phenomenon, and not all Latinas adhere to *marianismo* gender roles. Therefore, mental health providers must first assess the role of gender roles in treatment and subsequently assess how they may serve as both protective factors and stressors in the lives of women.

Cultural Worldviews

Every culture has social norms and values that inform its view of the world. These social norms and values inform the meaning that people have about gender and how they navigate their relationships. As such, several authors note that gender is influenced not only by biology but also by where people live, who they interact with, and the culture in which they participate. The cultural worldview of the United States tends to be informed by Western values of individuality, democracy, self-expression, self-actualization, verbal communication, and differentiation from family. Therefore, Western notions of healing emphasize verbal expressions of one's feelings and emotional ailments and one's ability to focus on the self as a means toward healing and recovery. Individualist cultural values are woven throughout all Western psychological therapies (e.g., individual therapy, the importance of verbal communication in therapy, and the importance of helping one's "self" as a means to get better). Individual cultural values are often considered normal and appropriate for all clients. However, many cultural groups do not adhere to individual cultural values. In fact, many Americans identify with collectivist values and, instead, value interdependence, cooperation, family alliance and loyalty, and extended social support networks. Latin American, African American, and Asian American cultures are typically considered collectivist cultures, whereas Western or Euro-American cultures are typically considered individualist cultures.

Cultural worldviews may negatively affect treatment when clinicians or therapists do not adequately understand or assess them. For example, Asian American women who have been socialized within collectivist values to see "emotional control" as a sign of strength may be misunderstood by practitioners as hiding their emotions, as being unable to self-express, or as avoiding emotions. In this case, however, verbal expression of feelings may be culturally inappropriate and may result in additional stressors for Asian American women in treatment. Similarly, the Latin American culture is at times driven by strong family allegiance (*familism*), and therefore, the family may be present in therapy even when the focus of treatment is on the "individual." Therefore, practitioners need to adequately assess the need to "bring in the family" in individual therapy irrespective of whether the client is in individual treatment.

Cultural worldviews can cause significant stress for individuals when there is a pull to hold on to collectivist worldviews while at the same time endorse individualistic values. This tension has been documented to increase risk for mental health problems. As stated previously, Latina adolescents are at higher risk for suicide (approximately one in five Latino girls) than non-Latina adolescents. Recent statistics from the Centers for Disease Control and Prevention estimate that 26% of Latinas in Grades 9 to 12 seriously consider attempting suicide. Researchers have shown that some of these disparities may be due to the tension between obligation to family (collectivist worldviews) and adolescents' need for independence and autonomy (individualist worldviews).

Conflicting cultural worldviews affect all people. For example, research on the "Latino health paradox" shows that although Latino immigrants are healthy when they first arrive in the United States, Latinos who are born in the United States or those who have lived in the United States for longer periods of time report more substance use, binge drinking, and mental health problems. Racial and ethnic minorities who navigate two cultural worldviews (e.g., their heritage culture and the mainstream culture of the United States) often have to negotiate different, and at times conflicting, cultural demands (e.g., interdependence vs. autonomy values). Stressors related to adapting to different cultural worldviews and values may increase the risk for psychiatric disorders, such as depression and anxiety. Epidemiological studies have also shown that risk for mental health problems, including depression and anxiety, increases the longer some immigrant groups live in the United States. Yet many immigrant and racial ethnic minority women and men who live in the United States successfully navigate both cultures. Studies show that individuals who internalize two distinct cultural worldviews, said to be bicultural, may have better mental health outcomes, such as less acculturative stress, depression, and anxiety. Accordingly, it is important for mental health practitioners to assess the extent to which individuals adhere to cultural values and the way this also affects their gender expression and mental health concerns.

Silvia Lorena Mazzula

See also Anxiety Disorders and Gender; Depression and Gender; Mental Health Stigma and Gender; Substance Use and Gender; Suicide and Gender; Worldviews and Gender Research

Further Readings

Arredondo, P., Gallardo-Cooper, M., Delgado-Romero, E. A., & Zapata, A. L. (2014). *Culturally responsive counseling with Latinas/os*. Alexandria, VA: American Counseling Association.

Comas-Díaz, L., & Greene, B. (Eds.). (1994). *Women of color: Integrating ethnic and gender identities in psychotherapy*. New York, NY: Guilford Press.

Lundberg-Love, P. K., Nadal, K., & Paludi, M. A. (2011). *Women and mental disorders* (4 vols.). Santa Barbara, CA: ABC-CLIO.

Mazzula, S. L., & Rangel, R. (2011). Cultural consideration for mental health treatment with women of color. In P. Lundberg-Love, K. L. Nadal, & M. Paludi (Eds.), *Women and mental disorders: Vol. 4. Treatments and research* (pp. 75–91). Santa Barbara, CA: Praeger.

Miville, M. L. (2013). *Multicultural gender roles: Applications for mental health and education*. New York, NY: Wiley.

Prior, P. (1999). *Gender and mental health*. New York: New York University Press.

Rosenfield, S., & Mouzon, D. (2013). Gender and mental health. In C. S. Aneshensel, J. C. Phelan, & A. Bierman (Eds.), *Handbook of the sociology of mental health* (pp. 277–296). New York, NY: Springer.

Travis, C. B. (2014). *Women and health psychology: Vol. 1. Mental health issues*. New York, NY: Psychology Press.

Mental Health Stigma and Gender

Stigma refers to the linking of negative stereotypes (widely regarded beliefs about a group) to a label denoting membership in a marginalized group, such as "mentally ill." Common negative stereotypes about mental illness include beliefs of dangerousness, unpredictability, inability to recover, lack of intelligence, and weakness. Stigmatizing attitudes are believed to be acquired during childhood through general socialization processes. These attitudes may then be reinforced during adulthood through exposure to media presentations that emphasize negative stereotypes. Stigmatizing attitudes may also lead to exclusionary behaviors, including overt discrimination (e.g., in housing or employment) and social rejection behaviors. In addition to the challenges posed by discrimination and social rejection, people diagnosed with mental illness may also experience a decline in self-esteem and self-efficacy as a result of their awareness of their membership in a stigmatized group.

Gender is relevant to the issue of mental health stigma because there is evidence that gender roles and expectations may affect stigma in its various forms. Exploring the role of gender in mental health stigma remains vital to understanding the characteristics of people who endorse stigma along with the experience of those who are stigmatized. Doing so can foster the development of tailored interventions for antistigma campaigns and stigma interventions for people with mental illness. This entry compares and explores gender differences in the endorsement of mental health stigma and overviews the impact of gender on mental health self-stigma. Given the lack of existing literature on genders outside the male/female dichotomy, only male and female genders are covered in this entry.

Differences in the Degree of Mental Health Stigma by Gender

Gender has been examined in two ways with regard to mental health stigma. First, studies have explored the impact of gender as a predictor of mental health stigma. Second, studies have investigated differences in the degree of mental health stigma based on the gender of the stigma target (e.g., a person with mental illness).

While the majority of research finds that gender does not substantially influence the beliefs and attitudes toward people with mental illness, some research does provide evidence for gender differences in the endorsement of mental health stigma. Men and women tend to report similar attitudes about people with mental illness and desire for social distance. Despite overall findings indicating similar degrees of mental health stigma across genders, divergences do occur in particular areas related to mental health stigma.

Research shows that preferences in mental health treatment and models of mental illness do differ by gender: Women show a greater likelihood of accepting a psychosocial model of mental illness than men do, and hence, women recommend seeking psychological help (e.g., psychotherapist, psychologist) more frequently than men do. Indeed, research on mental health stigma with adolescents suggests that this preference to reach out for mental health support begins from an early age. One study of eighth graders revealed that boys, relative to girls, reported more mental health stigma and less mental health knowledge and girls were at least twice as likely to use mental health services. For boys, a common reported barrier to seeking out mental health services included anticipated parental disapproval of their decision to seek help. Furthermore, women tend not to find individuals with mental illness as blameworthy for their condition as men do, and they report a greater willingness to directly help people with mental illness. Although women may endorse more acceptance than men, some research reveals that women, relative to men, report greater anxiety when faced with individuals with mental illness. Finally, there is some support, although less, to suggest that women, relative to men, report more reservations about restricting the civil rights of people with mental illness (e.g., voting, driver's license).

In terms of males and females diagnosed with mental illness, minimal differences are described with regard to degree of mental health stigma. Some studies demonstrate that men with schizophrenia elicit more rejection from respondents than women with schizophrenia. In addition, some surveys indicate that men with mental illness are classified as more dangerous than women with mental illness. Furthermore, when gender norms are congruent with psychiatric disorders, such as female notions of enhanced expressivity and depression (i.e., gender congruent), people tend to hold harsher views, perceiving the mental illness as an exaggeration of gender-expected behaviors. In contrast, gender incongruent mental illnesses, such as men with depression, show the opposite effect whereby people are more likely to rate the men as having a true mental disorder.

Taken together, the pool of research evidence indicates that the endorsement of mental health stigma remains largely consistent among males and females; however, differences emerge in areas of mental illness conceptualization, blameworthiness, anxiety toward persons with mental illness, and help-seeking behavior. In addition, although people report similar levels of mental health stigma toward males and females with mental illnesses, the congruence between specific mental illnesses and gender expectations appears to influence the extent to which people report mental health stigma.

Explanations for Gender Differences in Degree of Stigma by Gender

There are a variety of theoretical explanations for the extent to which mental health stigma is influenced by gender. It is noteworthy that this body of literature finds more similarities across genders than differences. Given that society generally deems the endorsement of mental health stigma as socially acceptable, it could be expected that both men and women would adopt such stigma at similar rates.

The findings that women prefer psychosocial formulations of mental illness over men and that women perceive people with mental illness as less blameworthy suggest that women may give more weight to environmental factors in the expression of psychiatric distress. In line with this form of thinking, women may be more likely to ascribe to an interdependent and collectivistic framework than men, who may focus on individual attributes (i.e., rugged individualism) in the manifestation of mental illness. As direct evidence for this situational explanation, women do indeed seek out psychological help more often than their male counterparts.

Another hypothesized mechanism that may account for gender differences in terms of blameworthiness toward mental illness is the speculation that women show higher rates of empathy and lower rates of social dominance toward others. Reasons for this proposed difference are subject to debate (socially vs. biologically determined), and to date, no empirical research has examined these attributes in the context of mental health stigma. Another theory that has not gained much support posits that women also face prejudice in society, and as a result, they may empathize with other disenfranchised groups. This theory fails to find support when one considers the similar rates of mental health stigma endorsement among other groups experiencing prejudice, such as people of color.

With dangerousness, the confluence of male gender stereotypes and mental illness may explain the elevated rates of perceived dangerousness of men compared with women. That is, notions of men as more threatening, aggressive, and dominating than women may account for the higher reported rates of dangerousness in this group.

Differences in Perceptions of Stigma and Self-Stigma by Gender

Another important dimension of the stigma process relates to the impact of awareness of negative stereotypes on people diagnosed with mental illness themselves. *Perceived stigma* refers to the extent to which people with mental illness expect that others endorse stigma, while *self-* (or *internalized*) *stigma* refers to the process of applying negative stereotypes to oneself (e.g., "Because I have a mental illness, I am unpredictable."). Studies suggest that both perceived and self-stigma are associated with a wide range of psychosocial outcomes among people diagnosed with severe mental illness, including diminished self-esteem, hope, and self-efficacy and increased psychiatric symptoms and treatment nonadherence.

The overwhelming majority of studies do not reveal marked gender differences in mental health self-stigma or perceptions of mental health stigma. However, in studies with larger samples, some gender differences regarding self-stigma do emerge. In a study of self-stigma among more than 2,000 persons in 14 European countries, women with schizophrenia spectrum disorders were found to report slightly higher self-stigma scores on average than men with schizophrenia spectrum disorders; however, there was no difference between men and women diagnosed with affective disorders (including bipolar disorder). In contrast, in studies emerging from Australia on self-stigma and perceived stigma, although men and women endorsed similar levels of perceived stigma, men with anxiety and/or depressive disorders reported slightly more elevated levels of self-stigma. In research from Ethiopia examining self-stigma in approximately 420 psychiatric inpatients, compared with men, women reported significantly higher rates of alienation (i.e., feeling isolated from the world due to one's mental illness diagnosis), which is regarded as a core feature of self-stigma. Thus, factors such as culture and type of psychiatric diagnosis may interact with gender in affecting the extent to which one will demonstrate mental health self-stigma.

Explanations for Gender Differences in Perceptions of Stigma and Self-Stigma

Given the high societal prevalence of mental health stigma across both males and females, it is not surprising that the rates of perception of stigma and self-stigma largely do not differ along gender lines. Nonetheless, differing cultural attitudes may account for the gender differences in self-stigma reported in a few studies. It could be argued that culturally determined attitudes about gender, such as men showing emotion being regarded as a sign of weakness, may influence the rates of self-stigma. Paradoxically, research demonstrates that people show more acceptance and presumably less stigma toward people with a gender incongruent mental illness (i.e., males with depression), yet some studies suggest that it is men with depression, rather than women with depression, who experience higher rates of self-stigma. These explanations are speculative given that the literature has minimally explored the mechanisms underlying the differences, and lack thereof, in self-stigma and perceptions of stigma.

Future Directions

Further research is needed to understand the relationship between cultural factors, gender, and mental health stigma. Specifically, further research is needed to better understand the process by which culturally based gender role expectations increase or decrease the likelihood that one will endorse stigma and/or experience self-stigma. Another major gap in the knowledge base relates to the relationship between gender nonnormativity (including persons who are transgender or deviate from culturally prescribed gender roles in other ways) and mental health stigma. At present, research in the area of gender and mental health stigma has implicitly assumed that individuals who identify as male or female also identify with the cultural roles that are prescribed for those genders; however, a more nuanced approach would also include perceptions of gender roles and identification and examination of how this interacts with gender of origin to predict mental health stigma in its various forms.

Beth Vayshenker and Philip T. Yanos

See also Mental Health and Gender: Overview; Microaggressions; Stereotype Threat and Gender; Stigma of Aging

Further Readings

Angermeyer, M. C., & Dietrich, S. (2006). Public beliefs about and attitudes towards people with mental illness: A review of population studies. *Acta Psychiatrica Scandinavica, 113*(3), 163–179.

Chandra, A., & Minkovitz, C. S. (2006). Stigma starts early: Gender differences in teen willingness to use mental health services. *Journal of Adolescent Health, 38*(6), 754.e1–754.e8. doi:10.1016/j.jadohealth.2005.08.011

Holzinger, A., Floris, F., Schomerus, G., Carta, M. G., & Angermeyer, M. C. (2012). Gender differences in public beliefs and attitudes about mental disorder in western countries: A systematic review of population studies. *Epidemiology and Psychiatric Sciences, 21*(01), 73–85. doi:10.1017/S2045796011000552

Link, B. G., & Phelan, J. C. (2013). Labeling and stigma. In C. S. Aneshensel, J. C. Phelan, & A. Bierman (Eds.), *Handbook of the sociology of mental health* (2nd ed., pp. 525–541). Dordrecht, Netherlands: Springer.

Link, B. G., Yang, L. H., Phelan, J. C., & Collins, P. Y. (2004). Measuring mental illness stigma. *Schizophrenia Bulletin, 30*(3), 511–541.

Livingston, J. D., & Boyd, J. E. (2010). Correlates and consequences of internalized stigma for people living with mental illness: A systematic review and meta-analysis. *Social Science & Medicine, 71*(12), 2150–2161. doi:10.1016/j.socscimed.2010.09.030

Wirth, J. H., & Bodenhausen, G. V. (2009). The role of gender in mental-illness stigma: A national experiment. *Psychological Science, 20*(2), 169–173. doi:10.1111/j.1467-9280.2009.02282.x

Microaggressions

Microaggressions are defined as commonplace verbal and nonverbal slights that communicate denigrating or demeaning messages to people of color based on their racial group membership. In their 1978 seminal research, Chester M. Pierce, Jean V. Carew, Diane Pierce-Gonzales, and Deborah Willis coined the term *racial microaggressions*. Pierce and colleagues utilized content analysis to empirically investigate the covert, visual, verbal, and nonverbal messages transmitted about Black people through television commercials. Their findings illustrated that Black people were often entirely excluded from media programming. They also identified a preponderance of racially biased images and found that among the limited examples in which Black women and men were represented, they were represented with highly negative and stereotypical characteristics, such as subservient, working for a low wage, unintelligent, and unattractive. In addition, Black people were never shown in the context of a family unit or as leaders in managerial positions. In contrast, White women and men were repeatedly portrayed in positions of power and influence, with strong family ties and in a variety of situations. This narrow and reductive media representation of Black individuals established how racial microaggressions could be hidden within the context of seemingly harmless communication (e.g., television commercials). Pierce and colleagues demonstrated that subtle racist images and ideologies are often left unchallenged and increasingly perpetuate negative stereotypes and racial bias about Black people to large audiences.

In 2007, the taxonomy of microaggressions was extended to include the lived experiences of people of color, women, and LGBT individuals. Expounding on the original definition provided by Pierce and colleagues, researchers developed a conceptual framework stressing the everyday implications of microaggressions in the lives of people of color. Microaggression theory posits that members of marginalized groups encounter microaggressive environments across life domains, including at work, at school, in the media, and in the community. Indeed, microaggressions have been conceptualized as more threatening than overt bias and discrimination because of their pervasive nature, difficulty in detecting and proving, and seemingly innocuous exterior presentation.

Microaggressions may be conscious and deliberate, but research has focused on the subtle and unconscious exchanges that reveal that many well-intentioned individuals perpetuate discrimination without being aware of doing so or conscious of the negative impact. Although it is possible that anyone could be the perpetrator of microaggressions, the most harmful and threatening instances usually occur between those who hold power and those who are disempowered or marginalized. This entry discusses how microaggressions are communicated, the major forms microaggressions can take, and the various types of psychological dilemmas arising from experiences with microaggressions.

Communication of Microaggressions

Microaggressions can be communicated through verbal, nonverbal, or environmental channels. Verbal examples of gender microaggressions include negative statements made about women or gender nonconforming individuals, stereotypical gender norms, and assumptions of inferiority. For example, the statement "What a bitch! How dare she boss me around?" is an implicit message that women are not designed for leadership roles and have no authority or competency to direct and organize. Another example is "I believe the most qualified person should get the job and no other factors should be considered," in which the perceived message is that "race and gender do not matter and White, male privilege does not exist."

Nonverbal microaggressions can also foster tension or hostility. For example, awkward silences, failure to make eye contact, and closed body posture during dialogues about social injustice may be interpreted as "I do not want to talk about this" or "Social identity is not important." Other interpretations include "I am not listening" or "What you are saying is not important."

Perhaps the most insidious platform on which gender microaggressions fester are environmental, and they do not always originate from interpersonal exchanges and can often remain unchallenged. Environmental gender microaggressions are demonstrated through the media and in the educational, economic, societal, political, and professional arenas—symbolic representations that ridicule, ostracize, and threaten women. For instance, environmental microaggressions occur when women note the absence of other women or the lack of historical accounts that include robust diverse cultural experiences in the curriculum, at the workplace, and across professional and personal settings. The implied message is that "women are not valued; equal and diverse experiences are not valid." Verbal, nonverbal, and environmental gender microaggressions perpetuate gender-based disparities.

Forms of Microaggressions

Microaggression theory outlines three major forms: (1) microassaults, (2) microinsults, and (3) microinvalidations. Microassaults are frequently compared with the concept of sexism, because both consist of overt, charged, intentional discriminatory attacks or avoidant behaviors. Most perpetrators of microassaults intend to harm and insult others; to propagate an ethnocentric, patriarchal worldview; and to express the superiority and dominance of one group over another. Examples include sexist language, hate crimes, sexual objectification, and discriminatory treatment toward women and gender nonconforming individuals. For example, the sexist comments made by U.S. president Donald Trump during his presidential candidacy in 2016 typify gender-based microassaults. Trump, an entrepreneur and media personality, characterized women he did not like as "fat pigs," "dogs," "slobs," and "disgusting animals." When questioned about the aforementioned comments, he denied any wrongdoing.

The denial of individual sexism is a theme that has emerged in gender microaggression literature, which speaks of the tendency of enactors of gender microaggressions to respond defensively and deny individual culpability. Trump later insulted a female reporter's professionalism by referring to her as a "bimbo" and implying that her menstrual cycle was negatively affecting her mood and objectivity. Left unchallenged, such comments perpetuate negative assumptions and stereotypical notions of women as emotionally labile and unsuited for the workplace. Notably, many real-life enactors of microaggressions may not be as candid as Trump, even though they may endorse similar sexist ideologies, because many people maintain a veneer of politically correct gender equality in their public persona. Although microassaults may be hidden behind a cloak of anonymity (e.g., online bloggers with anonymous sexist posts), initiated by a loss of impulse control (e.g., sexist slurs spoken after alcohol or drug consumption), or limited to enclosed, private discussions (e.g., sexist jokes told among a group of friends and family), microassaults are often premeditated, deeply rooted aggressions.

In contrast to microassaults, microinsults and microinvalidations function as unconscious expressions of sexist ideals, making them more difficult to detect. Microinsults are characterized by covert expressions of ethnocentrism and patriarchy. Gender-based microinsults convey hidden offensive messages, while the perpetrators may remain unaware of the negative connotations reflected by their words and actions. Consider, for instance, an academic advisor expressing significant surprise and hesitation that a young Latina would like to pursue a law degree. In this example, the recipient may perceive the underlying message as "Latinas are not intelligent enough to succeed in law school," whereas the advisor may assume that his or her reaction was innocent and not influenced by race or gender. Another example is a coach who tells a boy, "Pick it up; you run like a girl"—the metacommunication here is that girls are "slow, weak, and not athletic."

Microinvalidations are defined as a type of communication that excludes, minimizes, or challenges the lived experiences of women. Similar to microinsults, perpetrators of microinvalidations often do not recognize the concealed messages in their behaviors during mixed-gender exchanges. When female employees are continually spoken over, interrupted, or left out of discussions during staff meetings, the outcome is to negate their contributions and to convey that women are not as valuable or competent as men. Another example of microinvalidations is when an Asian American student confides in a peer about how class participation is often overlooked or interrupted, only to be told that "it's not a big deal" or "it happens to all the quieter students." The experience may result in feelings of rejection and invalidation for the recipient.

In 2010, scholars such as Kevin Nadal began to synthesize the large and complex scholarship on everyday sexism; overt, covert, and subtle sexism; gender harassment; interpersonal objectification; and benevolent and hostile sexism. Eight gender microaggressions specific to women emerged: (1) sexual objectification, (2) assumptions of inferiority, (3) assumptions of traditional gender roles, (4) use of sexist language, (5) denial of individual sexism, (6) invisibility, (7) denial of the reality of sexism, and (8) environmental gender microaggressions.

Characteristics of Microaggression Exchanges

Microaggression theory describes four psychological dilemmas that arise from experiences with microaggressions: (1) the clash of realities, (2) the invisibility of unintentional bias, (3) the perceived minimal harm of microaggressions, and (4) the catch-22 dilemma of responding to microaggressions. This section further outlines these psychological dilemmas to provide greater insight about the internal processes of the recipients and the perpetrators during microaggressive exchanges.

Clash of Realities

Woman may experience encounters in the workplace, school, and other public settings as sexually charged and inhospitable to women and may view sexism as a contemporary threat to their life success. In contrast, many men may view sexism as a thing of the past that no longer compromises women's access and upward mobility. Gallup's annual research work and education survey, which originated in 1953, asks participants to state their preference for a male or female boss. In 2013, participants were more likely than in prior years to state that they did not have a preference, but when gender preference was identified, male bosses have been preferred every year since the inception of the survey. Although the reasons were not explicitly accessed, one hypothesis was that people are not exposed to female supervisors or women in leadership roles as compared with their male counterparts and, therefore, people are more likely to fear or shun what they do not know. Moreover, men and women may have very different perspectives and experiences with gender discrimination and biases. It follows that men's and women's contrasting worldviews and lived experiences facilitate different constructions about their reality.

A direct consequence of the subtle and ambiguous nature of gender microaggressions is that individual perception and interpretation of microaggressive experiences and the underlying messages foster conflict about the nature and existence of the microaggressions. For instance, one may believe that "sexism is a thing of the past; everyone is judged based solely on his or her own merit," but in reality, less than 5% of Fortune 500 companies are led by women. When there is a conflict between worldviews, it is likely that the reality of the perpetrator, who is usually from the dominant group, is validated rather than the reality of the victim, who is often from a marginalized group. As such, in the aftermath of the clash of realities, further gender microaggressions are perpetuated by invalidating the lived, antagonistic experiences of women.

The 2013 Gallup work and education poll also found that 4 out of 10 Americans believe that there are not more women in top executive positions or political posts because corporate America and the electorate are not ready for women leaders. Although there has been an increase in female leaders in Fortune 500 companies, female heads of state, and female legislators in the United States, women are still significantly underrepresented in leadership positions.

For decades, researchers have found that when people think of leaders, they tend to think of men. High-quality leaders are often perceived to possess characteristics, attitudes, and roles that are more commonly ascribed to masculine characteristics than to feminine ones. People often associate women with "taking care" and men with "taking charge," and many have never been exposed to females in management positions, which can perpetuate unconscious judgment, fear, and bias. This places female leaders in a "double bind" of having not only to demonstrate enough warmth to be viewed as feminine and avoid negative backlash (e.g., being referred to as a bitch and other negative appraisal by colleagues) but also to demonstrate enough assertion to be viewed as a capable leader.

Invisibility of Unintentional Bias

Given the nebulous nature of gender microaggressions, the behavior of the perpetrator is often overlooked or minimized as innocent, which can lead perpetrators to challenge the very existence of gender microaggressions. In reviewing the literature of gender microaggressions specific to women, themes emerge that underscore the difficulty that many men experience in accepting the notion of unearned privilege conferred systematically within society. Such a system serves to automatically demote and discourage women while elevating men. Environmental gender microaggressions or the institutional processes of gender discrimination within economic, academic, political, and social spectrums are often more recognizable to women, who are disadvantaged by the inequality, and invisible to men, who are often the benefactors. Men and women are socialized throughout their lives via subtle and not so subtle messages that reinforce masculinity and male dominance as normative, desirable, and supreme. These messages are transmitted through the media, teachers, administrators, employers, caretakers, and peers.

For example, boys and girls often track similarly in math and sciences at the start of elementary school; however, studies have shown that a marked gap between girls' and boys' performance begins in late elementary or middle school and then widens significantly through high school and college, with boys seemingly outperforming girls by a significant margin. Women have traditionally been and continue to be underrepresented in STEM (science, technology, engineering, and math) fields. Male dominance in computer science is one striking illustration; women earned only 18% of computer science bachelor degrees in 2012, according to the National Science Foundation. Scientific inquiry has ruled out that women are somehow innately less skilled at math or science; instead, multiple findings identify differential treatment and subsequent internalized expectations of poor competency as major contributions to this disparity. In other words, teachers are more likely to call on boys and to overlook female students who demonstrate aptitude or promise in these academic domains. Parents and caregivers are more likely to encourage their daughters to pursue other fields of study.

Because of such social conditioning, many people unknowingly perpetrate microaggressive acts without conscious recognition of the underlying gender bias. As previously noted, on the surface, gender microaggressions can appear as minor snubs or normal aspects of U.S. culture, concealing the underlying message of male dominance and gender oppression. For example, when a male supervisor assigns his female subordinate to plan the holiday party (e.g., "You are probably better at that kind of stuff than I am."), unbeknownst to the male supervisor, the inherent assumption could actually be perceived as a gender microaggression, the implied message being that women are ascribed traditional gender roles such as the party planner and the domestic sage while being overlooked for other opportunities to advance and lead within the work environment.

Many well-intentioned individuals do not believe themselves to be complicit in discriminatory behavior. Yet previous scholarship authenticates the existence of unconscious bias in well-meaning individuals who have been socially conditioned by a racist and sexist society. The majority of microaggressive acts are automatic, hidden, and culturally sanctioned expressions of gender bias, which may occur outside one's awareness. Often, the most accurate perception about whether a microaggression transpired likely resides within the disempowered victim rather than within the privileged perpetrator.

Perceived Minimal Harm of Microaggressions

Often, when perpetrators are confronted with their microaggressive behavior, they may assume that the victim has overreacted and is being overly sensitive. On the surface, the occurrence of a gender microaggression can appear seemingly minor, unintentional, rationalized as occurring for an alternative purpose, or even benign; however, these indignities and underlying messages communicate a gender-based hierarchy; establish White, male, Eurocentric values as the normative standard for comparison; and denigrate people of color and women. In addition, microaggressions often result in psychological distress, seriously impair relationships, and foster sociocultural inequities.

Unlike overt sexism, gender microaggressions can be "invisible" because they oftentimes go unnoticed and unchallenged. The damaging and isolating effects of gender microaggressions are exacerbated by the ambiguity and the subjectivity inherent in the experience. Targets of microaggressions spend substantial time and energy defending their integrity and self-worth against microaggressive attacks, which consequently distracts them from their ability to concentrate and focus. The accumulation of these subtle slights and unacknowledged sexism, harassment, and environmental bias promotes an oppressive climate that invalidates the contributions of women and perpetuates patriarchy. Microaggressions are traumatic stressors that are hostile and unwelcoming and that obstruct pathways of upward mobility for many women. Microaggressions are implicated as triggers in perpetuating well-documented systemic health, occupational, academic, and economic disparities.

Catch-22 Dilemma of Responding to Microaggressions

The targets of microaggressive communication may find themselves in a catch-22 situation, a situation in which they have to sacrifice something no matter what course of action is chosen. Although microaggressions may be a universal experience for many women, the experiences can elicit varied responses, including confusion, hesitancy, sadness, or anger. According to the catch-22 psychological dilemma of responding to microaggressions, there are a number of factors that influence how individuals respond to a perceived microaggression: (a) an appraisal of whether the action or event actually qualified as a microaggression, placing the burden of proof on the target of the microaggression; (b) evaluation of the intention of the perpetrator (i.e., Was it intentional or not?); and (c) assessment of the consequences of confronting or avoiding confrontation with the perpetrator of the microaggressive action. For the perpetrator, feelings of being misunderstood, reluctance to deal with feelings of anxiety when engaging in interracial dialogues, and defensiveness about the apparent racism often occur, which make it even more difficult for recipients to confront microaggressive actions.

For the recipients of the microaggressions, how they react may result in differential outcomes. Saying nothing and repressing one's affective reactions is common because the alternative of confronting a defensive perpetrator and having to prove that one's experience is valid can often be a daunting and dissatisfying challenge. However, when left unchallenged, the impact of microaggressions may fester and cause significant psychological and physical damage to the recipients. When women opt to stay silent, it can make the women who choose to speak out appear abnormal and adversarial. Regardless of the recipient's course of action, additional negative affective, cognitive, and behavioral reactions may occur, such as diminished self-worth, rejection and isolation, and systematic disadvantages. Empirical scholarship illustrating the scope and impact of microaggressions has grown during the past decade, and the demand for increased skills to decipher and combat microaggressive interactions persists.

Nicole L. Jackson

See also Gender Bias in Education; Gender Bias in Hiring Practices; Gender Bias in Research; Gender Bias in the *DSM*; Gender Discrimination; Gender-Biased Language in Research

Further Readings

Jones, M. L., & Galliher, R. V. (2014). Daily microaggressions and ethnic identification among Native American youth. *Journal of Cultural Diversity, 21,* 1–9.

Nadal, K. L. (2010). Gender microaggressions and women: Implications for mental health. In M. A. Paludi (Ed.), *Feminism and women's rights worldwide: Vol. 2. Mental and physical health* (pp. 155–175). Santa Barbara, CA: Praeger.

Nadal, K. L., Davidoff, K. C., Davis, L. S., & Wong, Y. (2014). Emotional, behavioral, and cognitive reactions to microaggressions: Transgender perspectives. *Psychology of Sexual Orientation & Gender Diversity, 1*(1), 72–81.

Nadal, K. L., Hamit, S., Lyons, O., Weinberg, A., & Corman, L. (2013). Gender microaggressions: Perceptions, processes, and coping mechanisms of women. *Psychology of Business Success, 1,* 193–220.

Pierce, C., Carew, J., Pierce-Gonzalez, D., & Willis, D. (1978). An experiment in racism: TV commercials. In C. Pierce (Ed.), *Television and education* (pp. 62–88). Beverly Hills, CA: Sage.

Sue, D. W. (2010). *Microaggressions in everyday life: Race, gender, and sexual orientation.* Hoboken, NJ: Wiley.

Sue, D. W., Capodilupo, C. M, Torino, G. C., Bucceri, J. M., Holder, A. M. B., Nadal, K. L., & Esquilin, M. (2007). Racial microaggressions in everyday life: Implications for clinical practice. *American Psychologist, 62,* 271–286.

Watkins, N. L., LaBarrie, T. L., & Appio, L. M. (2010). Black undergraduates' experiences with perceived racial microaggressions. In D. W. Sue (Ed.), *Microaggressions and marginality: Manifestations, dynamics and impact* (pp. 25–58). New York, NY: Wiley.

Middle Adulthood and Gender

Definitions of *middle adulthood* and *gender* vary widely throughout the relevant literature. For the purposes of this entry, *middle adulthood* is defined as a period in an individual's life that begins at the end of young adulthood (around age 40 years) and ends at the onset of the young-old stage (around age 65 years). Due to an increase in life expectancy in recent history, the upper limit of this age range continues to expand as many adults are now enjoying longer, healthier lives than ever before. For many, this is the happiest and most satisfying time of life, due to new levels of self-awareness and accomplishment of a host of difficult life tasks. The concept of gender as it relates to this entry is defined as individuals' gender ideology, or sense of where they fall on the continuums of both feminine and masculine qualities. Exploring the intersection of these two constructs is indeed pertinent to this encyclopedia, as will be discussed in this entry, due to the major reciprocal impact on each other. Middle adulthood, specifically, is a unique time in an individual's life, in which tremendous changes typically unfold in several important life areas. These changes in turn affect the individual's identity and gender ideology. This review explores this intersection by addressing changes in gender identity throughout the life span; life roles in middle adulthood, including work, relationships, and parenthood; the differences in the experience of gender in middle adulthood between cisgender men and women; and considerations for transgender and gender nonconforming (TGNC) people.

Changes in Gender Identity Throughout the Life Span

The concept of gender was once thought to be a true dichotomy based on possession of male or female secondary sex characteristics. It is now known that gender is far more complex and exists separately from an individual's sex. This conceptualization is thought of as a more accurate way to encapsulate a vast range of human experience, wherein secondary sex characteristics are not always aligned with one's gender. Whereas gender was once construed as static and fixed (e.g., you are either male or female), gender as a personal construct is now conceived as ever changing and shifting throughout the life span. It is also highly sensitive to the environment, comprising culture, family, and life experience. This is particularly crucial when looking at gender as it exists in middle adulthood, given that this is a unique time of life when many individuals are faced with novel situations that largely affect their gender ideology. A discussion of the specific changes during middle adulthood that affect gender follows.

By the time many individuals within Westernized cultures reach middle adulthood, they have likely achieved several major milestones while passing through previous life stages. Childhood, adolescence, and young adulthood all entail their own set of challenges and important accomplishments in both personal and professional lives. For many, successfully reaching certain milestones, such as graduating high school or college, accruing work experience, and establishing both peer and romantic relationships, is a critical goal. Accomplishment or failure to accomplish these milestones has important implications for the trajectory of an individual's life. From this framework, individuals who have achieved some or all of these milestones are likely to, in middle adulthood, be relatively established in whichever life path or career they chose to pursue at an earlier juncture. Such individuals might, for example, find themselves married, with children, and working in a stable, full-time job. Should this be the case, these individuals might have a sense of stability and belonging that simply had not existed before, as their lives were more focused on activities devoted to the achievement of these objectives.

Research in this area has demonstrated that when individuals attain this sense of stability, it is, not surprisingly, associated with a robust sense of well-being and satisfaction. This is achieved through accomplishing difficult goals, learning from mistakes, and establishing a strong sense of identity through life experience. Now, of course, this exact succession of events and accomplishments is by no means commonplace or guaranteed in modern society. It does, however, exemplify one way in which individuals at this stage of life may find themselves faced with not only a sense of stability but also a set of novel challenges, regardless of how many or which of the aforementioned milestones have been achieved.

In middle adulthood, a major portion of an individual's waking hours is devoted to work and professional activities, whether in one or multiple career paths and workplaces. According to gender theorists, individuals' ascription to a certain gender role or gender identity can have a great deal of impact on their chosen profession. This idea played out much more explicitly in time periods leading up to the late 20th century, when expectations for men and women were more clearly outlined by society at large. Consider, for example, the 1950s heterosexual married male who works full-time while his wife stays at home and cares for the children. A woman living in a society in which this is the norm might not even consider embarking on a professional career, and in some sense, her role in life has been predetermined. Subsequently, the expectation falls on the man to provide for his family, and he may pursue any range of professional activities. Given that the individuals within these circumscribed roles are acting in line with the expectations for their gender, it is likely that in turn their gender ideology will be reinforced through living out these roles. Acting out of line with these roles—for instance, if the husband were to stay at home while the wife worked full-time to support the family—would have the potential impact of shifting each spouse's gender ideology. The woman may feel more masculine and less feminine for acting in line with a traditionally male role, and vice versa for the man.

More recently, society has shifted away from this highly traditional model of expected work roles for men and women. No longer are individuals' career path, at least in theory, determined solely by their gender. Following the feminist movement in the 1960s and 1970s, women are now a major part of the workforce in Western society. Here is a case in which the change in expectations regarding gender roles has had a major impact on the workplace environment and, as such, has rearranged the lives of women in society. Whereas perhaps middle adulthood was once defined around the woman's role in the home, it is now more commonly centered on her professional career and development. Of course, there continue to be women who choose to stay at home to raise their families or do so out of necessity. However, the cultural notion that there is a choice undoubtedly changes the way in which women see their role in society and provides a setting for greater fluidity of gender ideology. For instance, women who stay at home might not see themselves as feminine simply because of this role. In the case of men who stay at home to raise children and care for the home while their wife is the sole breadwinner, they may not feel any less masculine based on this arrangement.

To what extent individuals ascribe to their gender ideology may, in turn, determine which career they choose, which itself can reinforce gender ideology. For instance, a woman who chooses to become a grade school teacher—a traditionally feminine career—may not consider other, less traditionally feminized options, such as engineering or mechanics. By overlooking these options, she may not have the opportunity to explore if they would be viable. Thus, in choosing to become a teacher, she contributes to the feminization of this particular professional activity. Given the previously described notion that many individuals in middle adulthood spend the majority of this life stage in one career field, it is probably unlikely that her sense of gender will change as a result of her professional work.

In terms of personal life and relationships, middle adulthood is in many cases associated with marriage or partnership, and parenthood. One particular theoretical construct highlights the important way in which gender and relationships in middle adulthood affect each other—*doing gender.*

The roles of marriage and parenthood entail a host of changes to an individual's practical, day-to-day responsibilities. In modern society, the division of household labor entails the assignment of chores, which are often themselves gendered. In the literature, it is noted that more feminized tasks usually involve routine, necessary activities such as laundry, cooking, and cleaning. For instance, in a traditional sense, the task of doing laundry is conceptualized as a feminine task. This is apparent in popular culture through advertisements that typically portray women involved in the task of doing laundry. Masculine chores typically involve less frequent tasks such as house maintenance and paying bills. In the concept of doing gender, it is the specific performance of activities that tends to reinforce individuals' sense of their own gender.

The division of household labor typically depends on couples' ascription to gender roles—that is, as either traditional or egalitarian or somewhere in between. The concept of doing gender relates that even if a couple is egalitarian in their gender ideology, it is through the act of gendered household activities and roles (e.g., parenting) that individuals in this life stage actually become more traditional in their gender ideology than they were in earlier life stages. For instance, a woman who identifies as mostly egalitarian in her gender ideology, and who is also tasked with cooking and doing laundry for her household, may eventually come to see herself as more traditional over time. Although this example is an oversimplification, it demonstrates the ways in which gender can be affected by activities at this stage of life, particularly given that middle age is a period of taking on new life roles and responsibilities.

Individuals in middle adulthood who are parents experience a transition in life roles as their children grow older and eventually leave the home. In this way, their gender ideology may also shift throughout this period as their roles and responsibilities change focus as well. For instance, a 50-year-old woman whose children have left the home may now shift her focus from managing her children's lives to focusing more on her career or starting other projects. This might make her feel more accomplished and empowered, and thus, her gender ideology may change as well, as she finds herself spending more time in less traditionally feminine tasks.

Men Versus Women: Differential Impact of Aging on Gender

There is some discussion in the literature on differences in fluidity of gender ideology throughout the life span between men and women. Generally, findings point to a higher degree of change among women, whereas men are thought to stay more constant. This may be attributed to several factors. First, in terms of personality, it is similarly thought that women experience a greater shift over the life span while men's personality is found to be more stable. Theorists here point to the role of a transactional model, whereby individuals become more competent with greater experience and changes in life roles or the environment. Given that women are more apt to experience greater personal change, particularly in the realm of parenthood, and the physical changes that experience entails, factors—such as personality and gender—that are fluid are thus more likely to shift over time. If women are from more traditional backgrounds and experience changes in work and professional life whereby they improve in competence, this can also have a reciprocal impact on emotional stability and gender; as they become more empowered, they may subscribe less to traditional female ideology.

TGNC People and Middle Adulthood

Very little is known about the life experiences of TGNC people in middle adulthood. Because TGNC research is limited in general, it is difficult to assert the common trends that may occur for TGNC people in their middle or late adult lives. Furthermore, because TGNC people of different generations may have faced different types of stigma or discrimination or may have struggled or not struggled with issues related to gender affirming medical procedures, there are potentially great disparities in the types of experiences of transgender people across the lifetime. Furthermore, because of violence toward TGNC people (e.g., hate assaults and murders of transgender women), health issues (e.g., many TGNC people are homeless or live in poverty, which prevents them from seeking medical attention), or mental health issues (e.g., some TGNC teenagers commit suicide because of the stigma experienced by their families or peers), the life span of TGNC people may be quite different from that of their cisgender counterparts. Future research can explore how middle adulthood affects TGNC subgroups, including TGNC people who transition or develop affirming gender identities at a young age, TGNC people who transition or develop affirming identities at later ages, and everyone along that spectrum. Furthermore, scholars may investigate how TGNC people may experience middle adulthood as a result of their professional activities, their romantic partnerships, and even parenthood.

Jennifer L. O'Brien

See also Aging and Gender: Overview; Doing Gender; Gender Development, Theories of; Gender Identity; Gender Role Behavior

Further Readings

Fan, P. L., & Marini, M. M. (2000). Influences on gender-role attitudes during the transition to adulthood. *Social Science Research, 29*(2), 258–283.

Lachman, M. E., & James, J. B. (Eds.). (1997). *Multiple paths of midlife development.* Chicago, IL: University of Chicago Press.

Parker, R., & Aldwin, C. M. (1997). Do aspects of gender identity change from early to middle adulthood? Disentangling age, cohort, and period effects. In M. E. Lachman & J. B. James (Eds.), *Multiple paths of midlife development* (pp. 67–107). Chicago, IL: University of Chicago Press.

Skultety, K. M., & Whitbourne, S. K. (2004). Gender differences in identity processes and self-esteem in middle and later adulthood. *Journal of Women & Aging, 16*(1–2), 175–188.

Stewart, A. J., & Ostrove, J. M. (1998). Women's personality in middle age: Gender, history, and midcourse corrections. *American Psychologist, 53*(11), 1185–1194.

West, C., & Zimmerman, D. H. (1987). Doing gender. *Gender & Society, 1*(2), 125–151.

Military and Gender

The U.S. Armed Forces comprise five branches: (1) the Army, (2) the Navy, (3) the Marine Corps, (4) the Air Force, and (5) the Coast Guard. The Army comprises the Regular Army, the Army National Guard, and the U.S. Army Reserve. As of 2015, there were approximately 1.4 million active duty and 820,000 reservist military personnel. The active duty forces are now more than 15% female. According to the U.S. Department of Veterans Affairs (VA), female veterans are the fastest-growing group of veterans. There are 19.6 million veterans in the United States, with 1.6 million of those veterans being women.

While the number of women in the service and transitioning to veteran status continues to rise, the culture of the military is largely male focused, presenting an increasing challenge to the structure, culture, and operations of the U.S. military. This entry outlines gender equality in the military, the experiences of transgender servicemen and servicewomen, and mental health gender differences in military personnel and veterans, including military sexual trauma.

Gender Integration and Equality in the Military

Women officially began serving in the U.S. Armed Forces in 1901. Prior to this time, women unofficially served as laundresses, cooks, hospital administrators, spies, and nurses; some served in the military disguised as men. Disguised as her deceased brother, Deborah Samson Gannett was one of the first American servicewomen. In 1782, she served for 17 months in the Revolutionary War. Also during the Revolutionary War, Margaret Corbin initially assisted the military with cooking and doing laundry but later fired her husband's cannon during the Battle at Fort Washington in 1776 when he was wounded; she was the first woman to receive a pension. Despite women's courageous service for more than two centuries of American history, several institutional policies have served as barriers to their full participation and advancement. However, over the past several years, the U.S. military has been experiencing a monumental cultural shift that is beginning to close the gender gap.

In January 2013, the Department of Defense's Direct Ground Combat Definition and Assignment Rule, which excluded women from holding direct ground combat assignments, was repealed. Since January 2016, the military must open all combat jobs to women or seek an exception. The expansion of roles for women will help mitigate the existing gender bias in earnings, promotions and career advancements, and future retirement benefits as women are not considered for the military's highest posts without combat experience. The main reason for this cultural shift was the change in how wars were fought during Operation Desert Storm (1990–1991), Operation Enduring Freedom (OEF; 2001–2014), and Operation Iraqi Freedom and Operation New Dawn (OIF/OND; 2003–2011). Unlike previous wars, these wars were not fought on traditional battlefields and with clear demarcation of enemy lines, largely due to technological innovations such as global positioning system units, scud missiles, and improvised explosive devices.

The modernization of weapons of warfare has placed everyone at risk, and thus, women have been serving in combat roles without the commensurate recognition; more than 800 women were wounded during the active phases of the Iraq and Afghanistan wars, and at least 130 women were killed. Monica Lin Brown, a U.S. Army combat medic stationed in Afghanistan, risked her life in 2007 to save fellow soldiers who were hit by an improvised explosive device by running through gunfire, using her own body to protect them, and treating them in extremely dangerous conditions; she became the second woman in history to receive the Silver Star, the United States' third highest medal for valor. This is just one of countless examples in which servicewomen have demonstrated their ability to perform both heroically and effectively in combat situations. Another historic moment in support of gender equality and a milestone advancement for military women occurred in January 2015, when the Army granted women the ability to participate in the first gender-integrated Army Ranger Course, one of the most grueling courses in the military.

While significant strides have been made to afford military servicewomen greater occupational equality, their successful, full integration into a male-dominated culture will not be without its challenges. Some of the long-standing gender-related issues in the military include sexism, sexual harassment and sexual trauma, gender stereotyping, the controversy related to gender neutral physical training standards, and gender imbalance in a hypermasculine environment, which can foster social isolation and alienation of servicewomen. Another group of U.S. military personnel who are at risk for discrimination and alienation are military servicemen and servicewomen who identify as transgender.

Transgender Servicemen and Servicewomen

In 2014, the Williams Institute estimated that there were more than 15,500 transgender people on active military duty or in the National Guard or Reserve services in the United States. These military servicewomen and servicemen are forced to work in secrecy because they will be discharged otherwise on the grounds that they are medically unfit. The "Don't Ask, Don't Tell" policy, which prohibited lesbian, gay, and bisexual people from serving openly in the U.S. military, was repealed in 2011; however, this did not include transgender military personnel. It appears that the military is taking small steps at reviewing the policy regarding involuntary separation of individuals who identify as transgender. For example, in February 2015, Defense Secretary Ashton Carter told U.S. military personnel that he was "very open-minded" about transgender troops serving openly in the military. A month later, the Army issued a directive that requires the decision for discharge based on disclosure of a transgender identity to be made by the service's top civilian for personnel matters as opposed to midlevel officers.

The Air Force issued a similar directive in June 2015, elevating the decision-making authority to the director. The Air Force has also eased its ban by announcing that transgender airmen and airwomen will not be discharged from active duty for identifying as transgender or for receiving a diagnosis of gender dysphoria—a mental health diagnosis in the *Diagnostic and Statistical Manual of Mental Disorders, Fifth Edition*—which refers to an incongruence between an individual's experienced or expressed gender and assigned gender at birth that causes clinically significant distress. Discharge from the Air Force will now be based on whether a serviceperson's gender dysphoria interferes with their ability to serve. Only days after the Air Force announcement, the American Medical Association approved a resolution against the ban prohibiting transgender people from serving in the military, stating that there is "no medically valid reason to exclude transgender individuals from service in the military of the United States."

Gender Differences and Mental Health Implications

Posttraumatic stress disorder (PTSD), the mental health diagnosis often associated with the military, is characterized by symptoms of avoidance, intrusive memories, hyperarousal, and negative changes in mood and cognition. Higher rates of PTSD have been found for those deployed in Iraq than for those deployed in Afghanistan, and some literature finds higher rates of PTSD in National Guard/Reservist than in other branches. The VA data estimate that 20% of OEF/OIF female veterans are diagnosed with PTSD. Their data show similar rates of PTSD for male veterans from recent combat. Similarly, the National Vietnam Veterans Readjustment Study showed similar rates of PTSD in males and females following the Vietnam-era service, with 27% of female veterans and 31% of male veterans experiencing PTSD at some point. These findings of men and women experiencing PTSD following service at similar rates is contrasted with the rates for the general population, where women are diagnosed with PTSD at a rate almost double that of men.

Although rates of PTSD are similar following OEF/OIF/OND combat, Army data showed that suicide rates for women tripled during deployment, unlike the rates for men. Rates of depression are also higher for deployed women than for deployed men, whereas alcohol abuse is higher for men than for women. This suggests that women and men may express their postdeployment stress in different ways despite similar rates of PTSD. In addition, health complications secondary to PTSD appear to be higher in female veterans than in male veterans. VA data show that 31% of female veterans experience comorbid physical and medical illness as compared with 24% of male veterans. There are also some characteristics of PTSD that have been found to differ depending on gender. One study found that women may be more distressed by the violence of war than men, as indicated by higher scores on measures of PTSD symptoms. Men tend to have more predominant emotional numbing associated with their PTSD than women, and men tend to self-medicate with alcohol more often than their female counterparts.

Transgender veterans have their own unique set of needs and challenges. Transgender veterans without severe mental health diagnoses have a completed suicide rate equal to veterans with serious psychiatric diagnoses such as schizophrenia or severe major depressive disorder. In addition, transgender veterans who completed suicide did so at a younger age. One study found that more than 60% of transgender veterans had experienced suicidal ideation as compared with 8% of the general population.

Military Sexual Trauma

At least 25% of female veterans have experienced military sexual trauma (MST) during their service history. One study reported that approximately 50% of women experienced unwanted sexual encounters during deployment overseas. It is important to consider that reports of MST are likely underestimations, given that these are the numbers of reported cases and women face significant barriers to reporting MST, including the threat of retaliation. Studies estimate that 20% of women who experience MST develop PTSD from the event. Research also indicates a higher rate of PTSD diagnosis in men than in women when rape was the identified traumatic event. MST is associated with additional mental health concerns, including substance use disorders, suicidal ideation, binge eating disorder, depression, and dyspareunia. Chronic pain, increased risk for infection, and decreased physical activity have also been linked to MST in women. It can also lead to avoidance of important gynecological screening tests that are essential for women in the prevention of, and detection of, illness.

Women are more likely to face psychosocial stressors during deployment, including general harassment, separation from family, and lack of social support. Following their military service, their stressors continue as female veterans are at a two to four times increased risk for homelessness compared with their nonveteran counterparts. Between 6% and 8% of all homeless veterans in 2009 and 2010 were women, and 45% of those female veterans had dependent minors.

Overall, female veterans present with a more complex psychiatric and medical picture and require integrated and high-quality health care. VA medical centers have made concerted efforts to meet the needs of their female veterans by offering gender-sensitive care with private waiting areas, and slowly services are expanding to offer women-specific services such as gynecology and mammography. However, female veterans are still 30% less likely to enroll in VA health care than male veterans.

Lauren D. Fisher and Amanda Spray

See also Gender Bias in Hiring Practices; Gender Equality; Gender Stereotypes; Military Sexual Trauma; Transgender People; Women and War

Further Readings

American Medical Association. (2015, June 8). *AMA adopts policies to improve health of nation on first day of voting at annual meeting*. Chicago, IL: Author. Retrieved from http://www.ama-assn.org/ama/pub/news/news/2015/2015-06-08-new-policies-annual-meeting.page

Burrelli, D. F. (2013, May 9). *Women in combat: Issues for Congress*. Washington, DC: Congressional Research Service.

Gates, G., & Herman, J. (2014, May). *Transgender military service in the United States*. Los Angeles, CA: Williams Institute.

Hourani, L., Williams, J., Bray, R., & Kandel, D. (2015). Gender differences in the expression of PTSD symptoms among active duty military personnel. *Journal of Anxiety Disorders, 29*, 101–108.

Robert, C. (2004). *Founding mothers: The women who raised our nation*. New York, NY: HarperCollins.

U.S. Government Accountability Office. (2009, July 16). *VA health care: Preliminary findings on VA's provision of health care services to women veterans*. Washington, DC: Author. Retrieved from http://www.gao.gov/new.items/d09899t.pdf

Websites

Military.com: http://www.military.com
Service Women's Action Network: http://servicewomen.org
TransMilitary: http://www.transmilitary.org
Women in the Army: http://www.army.mil/women/

Military Sexual Trauma

Military sexual trauma (MST) is defined as any experience of sexual harassment, rape, or sexual assault that occurs during one's military service period (Title 38 U.S. Code 1720D). Sexual harassment is characterized as recurrent, unsolicited verbal or physical contact of a sexual nature that is intimidating in nature. Examples of MST include unsolicited touch; inappropriate remarks about one's physical form; threats of a sexual nature; repeated, threatening comments about sexual behaviors; unwanted sexual advances; physically forced or psychologically pressured sexual activities; abuse of authority that renders the recipient in a disempowered position; and sexual activity without mutual consent of all involved parties (e.g., due to intoxication).

In the United States, a discrepancy exists between the incidence of MST, formal processed reports, and adjudication of cases. In 2010, approximately 108,000 incoming veterans receiving outpatient services via the Department of Veteran Affairs (VA) health care system screened positive for MST. The Department of Defense received 3,374 formal reports of new sexual assaults by active duty service members in 2012, and the actual number of unwanted sexual contact cases was estimated to be around 26,000. In 2011, only 240 of the 3,192 reported crimes from that same year went to trial. Less than 6% of the total reports resulted in a conviction by court martial. According to a 2012 Department of Defense Sexual Assault Prevention and Response Office (SAPRO) report, many of the convicted sexual assault perpetrators in 2011 were sanctioned by reduction in rank or placement in confinement. Monetary fines were far more commonplace than were military discharges. The aforementioned military sexual assault disciplinary procedures do not effectively eliminate or reduce the crimes that constitute sexual assault, as the report also noted that repeat offenders account for 90% of all assaults.

Many barriers to reporting MST and seeking help have been identified, including victim blaming; fear of retribution, including being overlooked for promotions or being discharged from the military; perpetrators being generally older and higher in rank, with more status and power; failure to fairly adjudicate cases; and a sexually hostile work culture, negative stigma associated with being identified as a survivor, or backlash against reporting crimes among service members (i.e., due to being perceived as disloyal to the unit). The hierarchical structure and the culture of impunity and retaliation inherent in military culture foster more negative aftereffects associated with MST, such as feelings of powerlessness, experiences of recurrent victimization, and the reinforcement of self-blame and guilt among survivors. According to a 2014 RAND Military Workplace study, 52% of women in the military who reported sexual assault perceived that they experienced professional or social retaliation as a result. This entry first discusses gender considerations with regard to MST and then focuses on the health outcomes and treatment of patients with MST.

Gender Considerations

Widespread myths about sexual assault that continue to persist are that men cannot be sexually assaulted and that only males are perpetrators of assault. In truth, both male and female service members are targets of MST. Notably, male veterans' experiences account for more than 50% of all incidents of MST. However, the higher number of male survivors should be understood within the context that males constitute approximately 85% of U.S. service members. Overall, 1 in 4 women and 1 in 100 men who were seen in the VA health care system in 2010 screened positive for a history of MST when asked about their experience of sexual trauma while in the military.

Rates of MST among female veterans who seek health care services within the VA health care system are estimated to be as high as 25%. Among female veteran survivors of MST, posttraumatic stress disorder (PTSD) is the most common MST-related diagnosis. PTSD is characterized by the following persistent symptoms subsequent to a traumatic experience: (a) intrusive thoughts, images, and nightmares; (b) negative, disproportionate cognitive and emotive reactions; (c) emotional numbing and disconnection from others; (d) avoidant behaviors related to trauma triggers; (e) hyperarousal; (f) sleep and concentration difficulties; (g) increase in risky behaviors; (h) irritability and poor distress tolerance; and/or (i) difficulty recalling trauma-related memories.

When the perpetrator of sexual assault is a woman, some may not take the assault seriously, which can result in male survivors feeling invisible, minimized, or confused about their own experience. Compared with their female counterparts, male sexual assault targets were more prone to emotional, physical, and social disturbances; were more likely to have experienced multiple incidents in a year, to have been assaulted during duty hours, and to have been assaulted by multiple offenders during one incident; and experienced more chronic difficulties coping. Male survivors are also more likely to report physical assault to a clinician and to omit details of a sexual nature involved in any assault. Heterosexual male veteran survivors of male-perpetrated MST are more likely to question their sexual identity, masculinity, and sexual orientation after an assault, especially if their body had a natural physiological response (i.e., erection or ejaculation) during the assault. Although this normal physiological reaction does not indicate consent and should not be interpreted as an indicator of latent sexual orientation, some heterosexual male survivors may fear being perceived as gay if they report the crime or seek health care services. Gay male survivors may internalize the assault as punishment for being gay, may feel unsafe to publicly disclose their sexual orientation and therefore avoid reporting the event or seeking treatment, and/or may find themselves repeat targets of various forms of unchallenged discrimination and abuse, given that historical military culture is entrenched in hypermasculinity, homophobia, and heteronormative bias.

The repeal of the Don't Ask, Don't Tell policy in 2011 lifted the prohibition of gay male and female military service members to serve openly in the U.S. military. In 2016, the ban on transgender service members, individuals whose gender identity and/or expression differs from that assigned at birth, serving in the armed services was lifted. Being perceived as gay, lesbian, or transgender had routinely been considered grounds for military discharge. It is estimated that thousands of transgender individuals serve their country every year and are at increased risk for violence, discrimination, and health care disparities. Consistent across gender identities and expression, all sexual assault survivors are vulnerable to physical and mental health outcomes that are far-reaching, insidious, and severe.

Health Outcomes and Treatments

Given the prevalence of MST and associated co-occurring negative psychological, physical, social, and occupational outcomes, the call for increased awareness, screening, and evidence-based treatment services to address the impact of sexual trauma has grown. Although not all service members who experience MST later develop clinical diagnoses, experiencing sexual trauma is a life-changing event that can result in significant shifts in one's self-concept, views of others, and notion of the world. Following a traumatic event like sexual trauma, reactions may include relief to be alive or out of immediate danger, shock, severe stress, fear, confusion, sadness, horror, anger, and recurring thoughts or images about what happened. The duration of intense physical or emotional reactions may vary widely, ranging from a few days to years. In the direct aftermath of traumatic experiences, common reactions include feeling hopeless about the future, feeling detached from others or disillusioned, difficulty with concentration or decision making, being jumpy or easily startled by sudden movements or noises, feeling constantly on guard or alert for potential threats, having nightmares or disorienting flashbacks of the event, and disruptions in occupational, academic, or social functioning.

A variety of negative physical, behavioral, cognitive, and emotional outcomes have been linked to trauma exposure:

> *Negative physical consequences* associated with sexual trauma may include upset stomach; rapid heart rate; edginess; respiratory issues; disordered sleep; chronic fatigue; decreased libido or severe, increased pelvic pain or menstrual problems; and recurrent headaches.
>
> *Common behavioral reactions* to trauma may be exemplified by failing to exercise; difficulty maintaining a balanced diet; neglecting to practice safe sex or take care of one's health; isolating from loved ones; avoiding public spaces or crowds; withdrawing from previously enjoyed activities; being more prone to tearfulness and engaging in angry outbursts or violence; binge drinking, smoking, and/or drug abuse; or avoiding activities, people, or places related to the assault.
>
> *Emotional responses* to trauma may include feeling nervous, abandoned, rejected, helpless, fearful, sad, shocked, emotionally numb, irritable, easily upset, or agitated, and a loss of intimacy or feeling detached from self and others.
>
> *Cognitive responses* to trauma often include general distrust toward others, especially authority figures, self-blame and negative views of self and the world, increased vigilance regarding safety and being on guard for any potential threats, a desire to be in constant control and attempts to overcontrol the environment, and negative self-esteem. Difficulties coping are often seen as personal weakness.

MST is a type of traumatic experience that can lead to or exacerbate mental health diagnoses such as PTSD, other anxiety disorders, depressive disorders, sleep and sexual problems, and substance abuse issues. Sexual trauma is more likely to result in symptoms of PTSD than are most other types of trauma, including military combat. Global initiatives to support posttraumatic growth, resilience, and positive change following a major life crisis such as MST have emerged to address this problem.

In 2005, the Department of Defense created the SAPRO, which was a central agency designed to implement organizational reform in sexual assault policy, prevention, staff training, and treatment resources in the U.S. military. SAPRO mandated that trained sexual assault response coordinators and victim advocates be available to facilitate appropriate and responsive care for active-duty sexual assault survivors. Free mental health services are offered for military service members coping with the aftermath of MST via in-person individual or group counseling, online, or by telephone sessions. The VA has designated an MST coordinator at every VA health care facility to promote effective treatment service options for veterans who screen positive for MST. Free, confidential, and recovery-focused health care services are also available for veterans. Effective treatments include inpatient, residential, and outpatient service options. For veterans who are uncomfortable in mixed-gender groups, gender specific programs are offered throughout the country. Veterans are also eligible to apply for disability compensation, which could result in monthly nontaxable compensation, free health care services via the VA health care system, a 10-point hiring preference for federal employment, and other benefits to address current problems that are related to their service period, including any difficulties associated with surviving MST.

Many trauma survivors recover utilizing their own personal, spiritual, and community support systems to make sense of their experiences and reactions. Trauma-related symptoms can naturally dissipate over time; however, some survivors benefit significantly from structured behavioral health treatment options such as trauma-focused psychotherapy and psychopharmacology. The recovery process can be long lasting and gradual. Research-supported treatment interventions include the following: (a) awareness about the body's natural response to trauma; (b) knowledge about how to cope with traumatic distress and recognizing the triggers; and (c) meaning making and skills to recalibrate one's threat response system.

Healing from trauma does not mean forgetting that the traumatic event occurred or avoiding anything that could remind one of the experience. Recovery is measured by less frequent or intense symptoms, greater self-confidence in one's ability to cope with memories and reactions to past trauma, emotional regulation, ability to manage daily stressors, social support, eliminating or reducing risky behaviors, self-care, and respect for one's own experience.

Nicole L. Jackson

See also Rape Culture; Sexual Assault; Sexual Assault, Survivors of

Further Readings

Burns, B., Grindlay, K., Holt, K., Manski, R., & Grossman, D. (2014). Military sexual trauma among US servicewomen during deployment: A qualitative study. *American Journal of Public Health, 104,* 345–349.

Holland, K., Caridad-Rabelo, V., & Cortina, L. (2014). Sexual assault training in the military: Evaluating efforts to end the "invisible war." *Society for Community Research and Action, 54,* 289–303.

Holland, K., Caridad-Rabelo, V., & Cortina, L. (2016). Collateral damage: Military sexual trauma and help-seeking barriers. *Psychology of Violence, 6*(2), 253–261. doi:10.1037/a0039467

Legal Information Institute. (1992). *Title 38 U.S. Code 1720D: Counseling and treatment for sexual trauma.* Ithaca, NY: Author. Retrieved from https://www.law.cornell.edu/uscode/text/38/1720D

The Sexual Assault Prevention and Response Office. (2015). *The Department of Defense fiscal year 2014 annual report on sexual assault in the military.* Washington, DC: Author. Retrieved from http://sapr.mil/index.php/reports

U.S. Department of Veteran Affairs. (2011). *Make the connection: The effects of military sexual trauma.* Washington, DC: Author. Retrieved from http://maketheconnection.net/conditions/military-sexual-trauma

Minority Stress

Epidemiological research consistently concludes that sexual and gender minority populations —lesbian, gay, bisexual, transgender, and queer (LGBTQ) individuals—have higher rates of mental and physical health problems than their heterosexual and cisgender peers. These health disparities are not likely to be caused by or inherent to sexual and gender minority identities in and of themselves. Instead, theory and research suggest that these health disparities are attributable to the fact that sexual and gender minority individuals are exposed to more social stress than their heterosexual peers because of stigma and prejudice directed toward them in society. In turn, excess exposure to social stress puts sexual and gender minority individuals at increased risk for negative health outcomes.

Rooted in heterosexist and cisgenderist social structures, these stigma-related stressors have been termed *minority stressors*, given that they result from the disadvantaged social status afforded to sexual and gender minority individuals. Integrating theories of stress, prejudice, and stigma, Ilan Meyer developed the minority stress theory in 2003, in the area of sexual orientation, to account for the ways in which exposure to minority stressors might lead to negative health outcomes among lesbians, gay men, and bisexual individuals. Minority stress theory has since been extended to account for the stressors experienced by gender minorities (i.e., transgender and gender nonconforming people).

Minority Stress Processes

The minority stress model specifies stress and coping processes. The stress processes are (1) stressful events and conditions, (2) expectations of rejection and discrimination (stigma), (3) concealment of one's identity, and (4) internalized stigma (internalized homophobia and transphobia). Ameliorating factors are (5) coping and social support. Together, these five countervailing effects either add to the stress burden that causes disease outcomes or ameliorate the negative impact of stress, having a salutogenic impact. Disease outcomes are hypothesized to be determined by the proportion of these countervailing effects causing adverse health outcomes (including mental and physical health problems that are known to be caused at least in part by stress) in sexual and gender minorities.

Stressful Events and Conditions

Prejudice Events

Prejudice events typically manifest in the form of interpersonal interactions, perpetrated by individuals either in violation of the law (e.g., perpetration of hate crimes) or within the law (e.g., lawful but discriminatory employment practices). There are numerous accounts of the excessive exposure of sexual and gender minority people to such prejudice events. Unlike the prejudice events perpetrated against racial and ethnic minority individuals, prejudice events experienced by sexual and gender minorities can occur at home and be perpetrated by family members. For example, some young people are kicked out of their homes to become homeless because of their family's rejection of their sexual or gender minority identities. The experience of prejudice events has been shown to negatively affect the health of sexual and gender minority persons, over and above the impact of other stressful life events that do not involve prejudice.

Everyday Discrimination

In addition to prejudice events, more minor incidents and chronic conditions can be considered prejudice-related stressors. Harassment (e.g., being called derogative names) and other instances of rejection and disrespect—sometimes called everyday discrimination or heterosexist daily hassles—are stressful even when they are not acute large events. Microaggressions, or everyday insults, such as receiving poorer service in stores or people acting as if they are afraid of someone because they are a sexual or gender minority person, can be included within this type of minority stress. Although minor in comparison with prejudice events, everyday discrimination experiences can accumulate, and even a minor insult, snub, or avoidance can have symbolic meaning and thus create pain and indignity beyond its seemingly low magnitude.

Nonevent Stress

Since the publication of Meyer's minority stress framework in 2003, there has been a call for increased attention to documenting additional forms of unique social stressors that are not easily conceptualized or operationalized within the five categories of minority stress and coping processes described earlier. Nonevents—or anticipated events or experiences that do not come to pass—can also have deleterious effects on mental health. Examples of nonevents include expected life course milestones that were frustrated, like a job promotion not received when expected. Family and relationship milestones, such as getting married, having children, and having grandchildren, are among the most widely expected events. Sexual and gender minority persons share these expectations for life course milestones, as do their families, friends, colleagues, and acquaintances; not achieving such aims can be a significant stressor and on its own stigmatizing. Although nonevents are an elusive construct to measure in research, preliminary data suggest that nonevent stress with regard to frustrated goal pursuit can be detrimental to mental health and psychological well-being.

Expectations of Rejection

Even in the absence of any apparent explicit event, prejudice and the potential rejection of the sexual and gender minority person are always implicit stressors. Like other minority group members, sexual and gender minority individuals learn to anticipate—indeed, expect—negative regard from members of the dominant culture. To ward off potential negative regard, discrimination, and violence, they must maintain vigilance. The greater one's perceived stigma, the greater the need for vigilance in interactions with heterosexual and cisgender peers. By definition, such vigilance is chronic in that it is repeatedly and continually evoked in the everyday lives of sexual and gender minorities.

Stigma Concealment

Concealing their sexual and gender minority identities is a way in which some people seek to avoid exposure to prejudice events and everyday discrimination. School, workplace, health care contexts, and even family are areas where concealment occurs. Concealment can be thought of as a "double-edged sword," in that keeping one's sexual or gender minority identity a secret can shield one from overt forms of minority stress but concealing does require a significant cognitive effort on the part of the individual, which is demanding and thus stressful. The isolating effects of concealing prevent sexual and gender minority individuals from living an authentic life and connecting with and benefiting from social support networks and communities of similar others.

For transgender and gender nonconforming individuals, gender nonaffirmation has been described as a related stressor; gender nonaffirmation refers to being unable to tell others that one is transgender and, regardless of telling others, not experiencing affirmation of one's gender identity (e.g., referring to a trans man by a female pronoun by way of negating his gender identity).

Internalized Stigma

Internalized stigma in the form of internalized homophobia (and by extension internalized transphobia) represents the ways in which sexual and gender minority individuals direct negative social attitudes toward the self. In its extreme forms, it can lead to the rejection of one's sexual orientation and gender identity. Internalized homophobia is further characterized by an intrapsychic conflict between experiences of same-sex affection or desire and feeling a need to be heterosexual. Internalized transphobia manifests in several ways, most notably a denial of authentic transgender feelings and self-imposed acceptance of one's sex assigned at birth. Theories of identity development suggest that internalized stigma is commonly experienced in the process of sexual and gender minority identity development, and overcoming internalized stigma is essential for the development of a healthy self-concept as a sexual and gender minority person. Research has shown that internalized homophobia and internalized transphobia can have a negative impact on mental health and psychological well-being.

Coping and Community Connectedness

Sexual and gender minority individuals attempt to cope with and counteract minority stress through a variety of means. Indeed, recent attention has shifted beyond documenting the experience of minority stress and its negative effects on health to a focus on sexual and gender minority individuals' experiences of resilience that stem from exposure to minority stress. As articulated in the original minority stress framework and recent adaptations, sexual and gender minority individuals engage in various individual and group-level coping mechanisms.

Like any person faced with the challenge of coping with general stress, sexual and gender minority individuals utilize a range of personal coping mechanisms, such as mastery and resources to withstand stressful experiences. However, there may also be components of sexual and gender minority identities that allow them to construct a positive sense of self in the face of devaluing social stigma. Indeed, a salient sexual or gender minority identity that is also positively valenced has been theorized to be protective against the negative impact of minority stress on health. In addition, such personal resources may allow for sexual and gender minority individuals to make meaning of their experiences of minority stress in ways that externalize (rather than internalize) the cause of the stress and derive personal growth from the challenge presented by minority stress.

In addition to such personal coping, group- or community-level coping resources can be especially beneficial in mitigating the negative effects of minority stress. Specifically, feeling part of a community of similar others may allow sexual minorities to make positive social comparisons with other people like them, instead of making negative comparisons, based on heterosexist stigma, with members of the out-group. For these reasons, connectedness to the LGBTQ community may play an ameliorative role in the relationship between minority stress (i.e., stigmatization, prejudice, and discrimination) and mental health. Developmentally, the process of establishing a connection to the LGBTQ community is thought to coincide with and be invaluable to sexual minority individuals' coming out processes and abatement of internalized stigma. The positive effects of community connectedness have been demonstrated in various studies regarding mental health and well-being, safer-sex practices, sexual risk, medication adherence among HIV-positive men who have sex with men, and coping with chronic sorrow among HIV-positive men and women.

Critiques of Minority Stress Theory

The minority stress framework is the most frequently cited in the literature on sexual minority populations, and it is being increasingly adapted in attempts to better understand the health of gender minorities. However, there are some critiques of the theory that should be considered. Prominent among these is the view that there has been so much positive change in the social environment of sexual and gender minorities—at least LGB youth—that they are no longer exposed to minority stress. This critique is valid because as a social theory, minority stress assumes certain stigmatizing social conditions; however, empirical findings to date do not support this critique. Even with the many advances in sexual minority rights and the increasing visibility of gender minority individuals in the media, news stories about the negative and sometimes tragic results of bullying school children because they are perceived to be sexual or gender minority individuals continue to be seen. Indeed, population-based studies continue to indicate that sexual and gender minority individuals continue to evidence higher rates of health problems relative to their heterosexual and cisgender peers, thus pointing to the continued relevance of the minority stress framework.

Future Directions

The growing body of research documenting the multitude of outcomes in which disparities exist between sexual and gender minority populations and their heterosexual and cisgender peers remains a concern for researchers, clinicians, and health advocates around the world. The development and employment of the minority stress framework have resulted in the specification of social stress mechanisms that potentially explain the health disparities and can therefore be targeted by emerging interventions. Despite these advancements, there is a great deal left to do in order to achieve the aims of sufficiently documenting, understanding, and addressing health disparities based on sexual orientation and gender identity. Thus, the continued employment of the minority stress framework can give rise to additional research and interventions that stand to benefit sexual and gender minority individuals' lives.

David M. Frost and Ilan H. Meyer

See also Dual Minority Status; Mental Health and Gender: Overview; Mental Health Stigma and Gender; Microaggressions; Racial Discrimination, Gender-Based; Racial Discrimination, Sexual Orientation–Based

Further Readings

Bockting, W. O., Miner, M. H., Swinburne Romine, R. E., Hamilton, A., & Coleman, E. (2013). Stigma, mental health, and resilience in an online sample of the US transgender population. *American Journal of Public Health, 103*(5), 943–951.

Frost, D., Lehavot, K., & Meyer, I. (2015). Minority stress and physical health among sexual minority individuals. *Journal of Behavioral Medicine, 1*(38), 1–8.

Hendricks, M. L., & Testa, R. J. (2012). A conceptual framework for clinical work with transgender and gender nonconforming clients: An adaptation of the minority stress model. *Professional Psychology: Research and Practice, 43*(5), 460–467.

Meyer, I. H. (2003). Prejudice, social stress, and mental health in lesbian, gay, and bisexual populations: Conceptual issues and research evidence. *Psychological Bulletin, 129*(5), 674–697.

Meyer, I. H. (2015). Resilience in the study of minority stress and health of sexual and gender minorities. *Psychology of Sexual Orientation & Gender Diversity, 2*(3), 209–213. doi:10.1037/sgd0000132

Meyer, I. H., & Frost, D. M. (2013). Minority stress and the health of sexual minorities. In C. J. Patterson & A. R. D'augelli (Eds.), *Handbook of psychology and sexual orientation* (pp. 252–266). New York, NY: Oxford University Press.

Nadal, K. L., Issa, M. A., Leon, J., Meterko, V., Wideman, M., & Wong, Y. (2011). Sexual orientation microaggressions: "Death by a thousand cuts" for lesbian, gay, and bisexual youth. *Journal of LGBT Youth, 8*(3), 234–259.

Sue, D. W., Capodilupo, C. M., Torino, G. C., Bucceri, J. M., Holder, A., Nadal, K. L., & Esquilin, M. (2007). Racial microaggressions in everyday life: Implications for clinical practice. *American Psychologist, 62*(4), 271–286.

Misogyny

Misogyny is defined as hatred, bias, or prejudice toward women. The definition previously focused exclusively on hatred, but the definition was expanded in the early 2000s to incorporate bias and prejudice. The definition shifted as a way to acknowledge the systemic, institutional, and at times unconscious biases that exist in individuals and in society against women. Underlying misogyny is a belief that women are inferior and men should be in positions of power as it relates to them. Misogyny is different from sexism in that sexism focuses on bias toward either sex and misogyny is particularly focused on bias toward women. Misogyny is necessary to study as it affects all people. The following is a discussion of misogyny as it relates to microaggressions, the socialization of misogyny, and the impact misogyny has on individuals.

Socialization of Misogyny

Misogyny is learned through socialization. American author bell hooks points out that in Western culture, misogyny is embedded in a culture that includes racism, capitalism, income inequality, and gender inequality. As part of the culture of misogyny, misogynistic views are translated through different venues. Two examples of methods that socialize misogyny include segregated sports and media representations of women.

Sports that are segregated (e.g., basketball, baseball, hockey, football) traditionally adhere to a masculinity that denigrates women, viewing them as inferior in terms of athletic prowess and leadership ability. This culture begins early, with derogatory terms such as *sissy* or insults such as "you throw like a girl." Boys are encouraged by their fathers and by society to become invested in sports from a young age.

Another method of enabling misogyny is through media; a common example is music. It is important to acknowledge that music, even of a similar type, is not homogeneous, and there is wide diversity within all genres of music. At various historical times, there has been an emphasis on misogynistic messages, such as treating women as objects, within rock music in the 1980s and within rap music in the 2000s. There is evidence that repeated exposure to misogynistic messaging may increase misogynistic beliefs. There is also evidence to support that those who hold misogynistic views are more likely to seek out media portrayals that confirm their bias.

Another example of a form of media that has misogynistic foundations is heterosexual pornographic content. In many of these films, women are treated as objects and often degraded aggressively. The interpersonal violence (in the form of shoving, spanking, or manipulating someone into sexual practices) depicted in these films are often performed by men on women. A meta-analysis in the 2010s indicates a relationship between watching pornography and believing rape myths (e.g., a woman can resist a man if she does not want to have sex; men are entitled to have sex if a woman has implied she would sleep with him). In addition, viewing pornography is correlated with viewing women as sexual objects (e.g., statements such as attractive women should expect sexual advances). Viewing of pornographic material appears to change the way in which women are perceived; this finding is true for both males and females.

Misogyny is so pervasive in U.S. society that it is socially acceptable and even encouraged among heterosexual male peers. For instance, if a heterosexual man makes demeaning comments to his friends that he plans on having sex with a woman he meets at a public space (e.g., a party, a bar), his friends may respond with laughter and encouragement. Comments may even be made to describe women as "fresh meat" or a "piece of ass"—implying that women are property, animals, or are allowed to be consumed.

Similarly, misogyny can also facilitate a rape culture, in that men may view their sexual needs as justification to assault women. In some sexual assault scenarios, a woman may be intoxicated (or drugged) and unable to give consent to engage in sex with a man; however, the man may believe that she is interested and take advantage of her. His friends may even encourage the behavior and suggest that she was "asking" to engage in sex. Such misogynistic assumptions that males are entitled to sex with a woman can result in sexual misconduct.

Derald Wing Sue and colleagues have discussed how the expression of bias or hate has become subtler in Western contexts. They propose that as equal rights become more available, and overt hatred and bias less acceptable in society, these beliefs are hidden, even to oneself. These biased views will come out in often small, unconscious ways—otherwise known as microaggressions. An example of a microaggression as it relates to misogyny is the focusing on a woman's professional attire as a way to classify how competent she is. Another example includes presuming that a woman in a high-power position did not achieve her successes but is rather a product of tokenism or gained power by performing sexual favors.

Another aspect of microaggression theory and misogyny is the understanding that misogyny has a cumulative effect on a woman's sense of self and comfort within the world. If a microaggressive event occurs once, it may be dismissed or attributed to a person's rudeness. However, when microaggressions occur over time, they can take a psychological toll on the recipient. Furthermore, sometimes women (and other marginalized groups) may not acknowledge microaggressions or seek retribution, due to their fears of repercussion. For instance, if a woman is sexually assaulted, the assaulter (as well as attorneys, police officers, judges, and society members) may blame her for the attack. Victim blaming, which implies that a woman is at fault for being sexually mistreated, is a form of misogyny.

Psychological Effects of Misogyny

Misogyny is present in multiple cultures and communities. It is present in communities of men, of gay men, of men of color, of women, and of transgender individuals. It is important to examine the ways in which the intersection of multiple identities affects one's experience of misogyny. There is some evidence that indicates that misogynistic views (e.g., victim blaming) are moderated through culture. For some cultures where traditional gender roles are encouraged, misogyny may be a part of the patriarchal structure of society. There is also evidence that more identification with an ethnic identity may mediate misogynistic behaviors, although there is debate in the field about the impact of ethnic identity. It is important to acknowledge that misogyny exists in many cultures, but the way in which it is taught and communicated is through cultural means. This concept is important to acknowledge when thinking about methods to decrease misogyny.

Within a culture, the way misogyny is present is connected to one's social positioning within that society. For example, a White heterosexual male may reveal misogyny by discussing a woman of color dressing revealingly as an invitation for sexual advances and believe that any rebukes are her playing hard to get. A gay male may be annoyed by Lesbian Nights at gay bars, believing that women should have their own space and that the bar he frequents should be a gay male bar. While gay men may be misogynistic, the literature also indicates that misogyny and homophobia are linked as dual ways in which masculinity is policed and an "other" is constructed. Women and gay men are frequently seen as "less than." It has been argued by some that misogyny is at the root of homophobia, as it is an expression of distaste for men acting effeminately.

Heterosexual men are also affected and troubled by misogyny. Starting in the 1970s, there has been an increase in men's rights groups in the Western world. These groups focus on the way in which men are perceived to have lost something. This perceived loss is often an expression of masculinity that is rooted in a romanticized and idealized historical masculinity and concurrently a loss in males' ability to be nurturing providers. Within U.S. culture, misogyny is often based on the idea that men have lost something and are being mistreated by a system that does not allow them to act like men.

While misogyny affects all women, it is important to acknowledge the differential impact on women who have multiple marginalized identities (e.g., race, socioeconomic status, sexual orientation). The type of misogyny that a middle-class White woman may experience might be a very different form of misogyny from that experienced by a Black, low-income, queer identified woman. There is evidence that interethnic conflict can exacerbate misogynistic views toward women of a group one is not a member of.

There is also empirical evidence that women who have been sexually harassed in the workplace have higher experiences of fear, negative mood, and poorer job performances. Seeing a female coworker sexually harassed can lead to bystander stress, a phenomenon that lowers work satisfaction. In addition to these effects that occur to women who are sexually harassed, people (both men and women) who witnessed such treatment also have lower levels of job satisfaction and describe reduced health satisfaction.

Overall, misogyny affects everyone within a culture. Author bell hooks discusses how feminism is for everyone, because by men (and women) perpetuating misogyny, everyone is less fully human.

Matthew LeRoy

See also Rape Culture; Sexism; Sexism, Psychological Consequences for Men; Sexism, Psychological Consequences for Women; Sexual Assault; Slut Shaming

Further Readings

Anderson, E. (2008). "I used to think women were weak": Orthodox masculinity, gender segregation, and sport. *Sociological Forum, 23*(2), 257–279. doi:10.1111/j.1573-7861.2008.00058.x

hooks, b. (2000). *Feminism is for everybody: Passionate politics*. Cambridge MA: South End Press.

Johnson, C., & Samdahl, D. (2005). "The night they took over": Misogyny in a country-western gay bar. *Leisure Sciences, 27,* 331–348. doi:10.1080/014900400590962443

Katz, J. (2006). *The macho paradox: Why some men hurt women and how all men can help*. Naperville, IL: Sourcebooks.

Koo, K., Stephens, K., Lindgren, K., & George, W. (2012). Misogyny, acculturation, and ethnic identity: Relation to rape-supportive attitudes in Asian American college men. *Archives of Sexual Behavior, 41*(4), 1005–1114. doi:10.1007/s10508-011-9729-1

Murthi, M. (2009). Who is to blame? Rape of Hindu-Muslim women in interethnic violence in India. *Psychology of Women Quarterly, 33,* 453–462.

Rollmann, H. (2013). Patriarchy and higher education: Organizing around masculinities and misogyny on Canadian campuses. *Culture, Society & Masculinities, 5*(2), 179–192. doi:10.3149/csm.0502.179

Sue, D. W. (2010). *Microaggressions in everyday life: Race, gender, and sexual orientation*. Hoboken, NJ: Wiley.

Motherhood

Motherhood is a historically and culturally located social role defined by the relationship between a woman and her children. These relationships may or may not be biologically based. Psychology has historically focused heavily on the influence of mothers on their children. Mothers were seen as the main socialization agents of children and thus blamed for their children's emotional or behavioral problems. More recently, there has been a focus on understanding motherhood as a personal identity and as a constructed set of relationships, both experienced in a particular social context. This entry provides an overview of the psychological aspects related to motherhood, including beliefs about and representations of motherhood, the transition to motherhood, and the ways in which diverse mothers challenge the notion of one universal motherhood experience. It is important to note that motherhood, like womanhood, is an ever-evolving construct. Who is included under the umbrella of "mother," and how they are expected to behave, is subject to sometimes fierce debate and critical examination.

The Motherhood Mandate

Also known as compulsory motherhood, the motherhood mandate refers to the widespread belief that women should (and should want to) bear and raise children. It assumes that women are inherently nurturing and that being a mother is a natural and inevitable expression of femininity and womanhood. The psychological costs of these ideologies can be high. For example, women who experience fertility challenges may feel that they are not "real" women. For others, the inability to meet the standards of motherhood once they do have children can also result in feelings of failure and inadequacy. These broader ideologies also often reflect the assumption that the ideal mother is White, married, middle class, heterosexual, and does not work outside the home.

The mandate is reflected in gendered toys, activities, and cultural messages to which girls, adolescents, and women are exposed. While it may be the case that the increased availability of reproductive technologies (e.g., egg and embryo donation and surrogacy) have made it possible for more women (usually those with economic resources) to become mothers, and have disrupted the notion that bearing children is "natural," little research has examined their effects on the cultural mandate for women to have children.

Those who challenge these ideologies are not arguing that women should not have children, or that the experience of motherhood is not a positive personal experience. Rather, they argue that these beliefs have negative effects on women's well-being and that motherhood should not be considered the sole or main source of sense of self and satisfaction for women. Furthermore, they argue that motherhood cannot be understood solely as an individual psychological experience but must also be thought of in relation to structures and institutions that perpetuate specific and limited views of what motherhood means. Not inconsistent with this, some psychologists have argued that motherhood can be a source of deep personal satisfaction and sense of self.

Representations of Motherhood

As with other representations of women, cultural representations of motherhood are often binary and have often been used to marginalize those who fail to acceptably embody them. "Good" mothers are viewed as caring and warm and focused on their children's needs above their own. "Bad" mothers (whose ranks often include stepmothers, as well as poor women, women of color, and working women) are considered to be cold, distant, unable to properly care for their children, or to prioritize their own needs above those of their children. Women who violate some aspects of ideal motherhood, by working, for example, may be viewed as less nurturing than women who do not violate these norms. Working mothers often also face stereotyping at work, where they may be viewed as more emotionally warm but less competent and less committed to their careers. Finally, women who chose not to or are unable to have children are believed to be selfish, unwomanly, and unhappy; research does not confirm these stereotypes.

Transition to Motherhood

Research has focused primarily on the transition to motherhood after being pregnant and giving birth (often called biological motherhood). However, there is also some research examining transitions to motherhood after adoption. Increasingly, there is the recognition that, for many women, the transition to motherhood (both adoptive and biological) can be characterized by negative, as well as positive, emotions. In addition to postpartum depression, it is common for women to experience nonclinical levels of negative emotions, including sadness, anxiety, and even anger. These negative emotions may dissipate over time, although there is increasing discussion of the ways in which motherhood can be stressful, given the inherent demands children make combined with the intensive social pressure mothers face in relation to raising well-adjusted children, balancing multiple family and work demands, and acknowledging only positive feelings about their roles.

Diversity of Motherhood Experiences

Understanding the ways in which women's social locations affect their experiences of motherhood is central to developing a rigorous social science of motherhood. More research is needed on diverse mothers and experiences of motherhood, including those of women of color, women with disabilities, sexual and gender minorities (including trans and gender variant people), and immigrant women.

Experiences of motherhood are inflected by race and class in significant ways. For example, some representations of women of color challenge their suitability to be mothers and thereby create different sets of expectations that mothers of color must meet. Others have argued that while movements for White and middle-class mothers have focused on challenging ideologies such as compulsory motherhood, women of color have had to fight for the right to bear and raise their own children.

Furthermore, because of changing social norms, and advances in reproductive technology, sexual minority women are increasingly becoming visible in their roles as mothers, and women are becoming mothers at later ages than ever before. The research on same-sex parents, including women, has focused more on the well-being of children in such families than on the experiences of women themselves. However, the limited evidence available indicates that lesbian mothers are similar to their heterosexual counterparts, though somewhat less conventional in their approach to child rearing. Similarly, psychologists are only now starting to study older women's experiences of motherhood. Again, there is limited research but some indication that the transition to motherhood may be characterized by less negative emotional experiences for older women, who tend to be more psychologically mature.

Nicola Curtin

See also Assisted Reproduction and Alternative Families; Gender Socialization in Women; Gender Stereotypes; Parenting Styles, Gender Differences in; Postpartum Depression

Further Readings

Cuddy, A. J., Fiske, S. T., & Glick, P. (2004). When professionals become mothers, warmth doesn't cut the ice. *Journal of Social Issues, 60*(4), 701–718.

De Marneffe, D. (2009). *Maternal desire: On children, love, and the inner life.* New York, NY: Little, Brown.

Rich, A. (1995). *Of woman born: Motherhood as experience and institution.* New York, NY: W. W. Norton.

Thurer, S. (1994). *The myths of motherhood: How culture reinvents the good mother.* Boston, MA: Houghton Mifflin Harcourt.

Multiculturalism and Gender: Overview

Given the increasing diversification of the United States, the study of multicultural issues in psychology has become an important aspect of the field. Paul Pedersen, a leading multicultural psychologist, states that multiculturalism is the "fourth force" in psychology, meaning that it is important for psychologists to recognize the ways in which culture and context affect the development of human behavior. Just like psychoanalysis, behaviorism, and humanism (the first, second, and third forces, respectively), multiculturalism has shifted the way in which psychologists study and understand human behavior. Multicultural psychology embraces an inclusive and broad definition of culture, which includes dimensions of race/ethnicity, gender, sexual orientation, socioeconomic status, religion/spirituality, age, language, ability/disability, and other aspects of culture.

This entry is focused on highlighting current research and scholarship that encompasses the broader topic of multiculturalism and gender. This overview section is organized into several subsections, with the first being a brief history of the field of multicultural psychology. Then, it provides a brief review of the literature in the following areas: (a) race/ethnicity and gender, (b) social class and gender, and (c) sexual orientation, gender identity, and gender. This is a selected review that does not encompass all of the multicultural identities that intersect with gender. It reviews recent research and scholarship in multicultural psychology, with special attention to the impact of discrimination on health, because there is a large body of research in this area. This overview also applies an intersectional lens and highlights intersecting identities.

Brief History of Multicultural Psychology

Over the past several decades, there has been a history of psychologists working on incorporating multiculturalism into the field. In the 1960s and 1970s, psychology was beginning to be criticized for the lack of attention to issues of race, ethnicity, gender, class, and sexual orientation. There is a body of research that has focused on these issues and has challenged the extent to which existing psychological theories did not adequately address the psychological development and behavior of people of color; women; lesbian, gay, bisexual, transgender, and queer (LGBTQ) people; and other marginalized groups. In particular, several racial/ethnic minority and feminist psychologists challenged the field regarding the ways in which scientific racism and sexism have been reflected in the research and assumptions made about human behavior, which led to a variety of theories and diagnostic assessments that pathologized individuals who did not conform to the White heterosexual male middle-class standard.

In Robert V. Guthrie's 1998 book *Even the Rat Was White: A Historical View of Psychology*, he highlighted the history of scientific racism in the field of psychology. According to Guthrie, in the early 1900s, the study of "ethnical psychology" was the study of the minds of other races and peoples, which was grounded in the assumption of White racial superiority and the desire for White European scientists to lend scientific credence to these perspectives. Guthrie also asserted that the Stanford-Binet intelligence test, which was developed in 1916 with a sample of White children in

California, was biased to reflect White middle-class culture, which in turn used its findings to conclude that African Americans and other racial/ethnic groups were intellectually inferior.

African American psychologists Kenneth and Mamie Clark conducted one of the earliest significant psychological studies on race and ethnicity in 1939. Their study of African American children's preferences for White dolls over Black dolls helped inform the 1954 Supreme Court decision of *Brown v. Board of Education* to desegregate public schools, citing the psychological harm of discrimination on children.

Under the backdrop of the 1960s' civil rights movement, many racial/ethnic minority psychologists shed light on the scientific racism in the field of psychology. For example, in 1968, Joe White and other prominent psychologists confronted the American Psychological Association (APA) about the lack of attention to issues affecting African Americans in the field. As a result, in 1968, the Association of Black Psychologists was formed as an organization focused on self-determination and improving the mental health and well-being of the African American community. The Association of Psychologists por la Raza was established in 1969, which later joined with other Hispanic/Latin American psychological groups to become the National Latina/o Psychological Association in 1979. In addition, the Asian American Psychological Association was founded in 1972, and the Society of Indian Psychologists was formed in 1975. These separate multicultural organizations are known as the Ethnic Minority Psychological Associations (EMPAs) and have pushed for inclusion of multicultural issues within APA. In 2013, these EMPAs—Association of Black Psychologists, National Latina/o Psychological Association, Asian American Psychological Association, and Society of Indian Psychologists—along with the APA formed The Alliance of National Psychological Associations for Racial and Ethnic Equity (otherwise known as the "Alliance"). The Alliance was created to encourage the sharing of information and resources, the promotion of culturally inclusive models of psychology, and the call for political action, cultural diversity, and social justice. Each group of the Alliance is an equal partner, and the presidents and higher leaders of each organization serve as representatives of each. Accordingly, each group has the opportunity to meet with the executive leadership of the other organizations (including the APA) in order to advocate for common interests related to racial justice.

As a result of the women's movement, women psychologists critiqued the field for its exclusion of women in psychological research and the ways in which women had been pathologized in clinical diagnosis and practice. At the APA convention in 1969, a group of women psychologists discussed issues related to discrimination in academia, sexist practices in the field, and the oppression of women in psychological theory and research. As a result of these meetings, a group of feminist psychologists founded the Association for Women in Psychology. Similarly to the EMPAs, Women in Psychology wanted to create an organization separate from the APA due to the lack of attention being paid to their concerns in APA leadership at the time.

Thus, there has been a long history of psychologists fighting for multiculturalism in the discipline. Over time, the results of the advocacy of these multicultural organizations was the establishment of several divisions of APA focused on race/ethnicity, gender, and sexual orientation issues, including the APA Divisions 35 (Society for the Psychology of Women), 44 (Society for the Psychological Study of Lesbian, Gay, Bisexual, and Transgender Issues), and 45 (Society for the Psychological Study of Culture, Ethnicity, and Race). Throughout the push for greater attention to multiculturalism, diversity, and inclusion was an active effort by several prominent counseling psychologists focused on multicultural issues in counseling practice. In 1999, the Society of Counseling Psychology (APA Division 17), in addition to Divisions 35, 44, and 45, established the National Multicultural Conference and Summit, which has been a biennial conference focused on bringing together psychologists focused on theory, research, and practice in the field of multicultural psychology.

Within the past 15 years, the field of psychology has made strides in highlighting the importance of multicultural issues in the study of human behavior by developing a set of multicultural guidelines. With influence from many of the aforementioned organizations, in 2002, the APA developed a set of guidelines on multicultural education, training, research, practice, and organizational change for psychologists. This set of guidelines applied a narrow definition of multiculturalism, which focused on race and ethnicity. Thus, these guidelines focused on racial and ethnic minority groups in the United States, including Asian American, Black/African American, Latin American/Hispanic, Native American/American Indian, and multiracial/biracial individuals. These multicultural guidelines were largely based on the multicultural competencies proposed by Derald Wing Sue, Patricia Arredondo, and Roderick McDavis in 1992. Although these multicultural guidelines are not intended to be a mandatory code of behavior for interacting and working with racial/ethnic minority groups, they are intended to provide a suggested set of standards for psychologists who conduct research, teach, and practice in the field.

The set of six APA multicultural guidelines are the following: (1) awareness of one's own biases, attitudes, or beliefs that can affect work with racial/ethnic minority groups; (2) recognition of the importance of cultural sensitivity and knowledge of racial/ethnic groups; (3) the importance of multiculturalism and diversity in education in psychology; (4) culturally sensitive and ethical psychological research; (5) the use of culturally appropriate clinical skills and practices; and (6) culturally informed organizational change.

In 2000, the APA developed the *Guidelines for Psychotherapy With Lesbian, Gay, and Bisexual (LGB) Clients*, which included a set of 16 guidelines focused on an understanding that homosexuality and bisexuality are not forms of mental illness, an appreciation and awareness of LGB relationships and families, issues of diversity within LGB individuals, and education and training around LGB issues. In 2007, the APA created the *Guidelines for Psychological Practice With Girls and Women*, which focused on encouraging psychologists to increase their awareness of the impact of gender role socialization, stereotyping, and oppression on the life experiences of women and girls; the importance of professional responsibility and culturally sensitive clinical practice; and practice applications. In 2015, the APA developed the *Guidelines for Psychological Practice With Transgender and Gender Nonconforming People*, which includes guidelines for assisting psychologists in providing culturally competent clinical practice to transgender and gender nonconforming individuals.

Taken together, these guidelines have advanced multiculturalism and culturally competent research, education, training, and clinical practice with racial/ethnic minority groups, women, and LGBTQ individuals. Next, this overview briefly highlights research and scholarship in the areas of race/ethnicity and gender, social class and gender, and LGBTQ issues and gender.

Race/Ethnicity and Gender

Race is defined as a socially constructed category whereby individuals are assigned to certain groups based on their physical characteristics, such as skin color, hair type, and facial features. Ethnicity refers to the cultural values and traditions such as religion, familial structure, and language. Research demonstrates that race/ethnicity and gender are intertwined and influence one's experiences with racial discrimination, as many racial categorizations and assumptions are gendered in nature. The social construction and expectations of gender roles for men and women vary greatly based on race. Historically, research on race and gender focused on separating and teasing apart the experiences of racism and sexism. However, recently, psychologists have begun to increase their attention to the simultaneous experience of multiple social identities, using an intersectional framework. Intersectionality is the analysis of multiple interlocking systems of oppression and identities. Although the concept of *intersectionality* has increased recently in the field of psychology, Kimberlé Crenshaw, a critical race and feminist legal scholar, originally coined the term in 1989.

Drawing on intersectionality theory, psychology researchers have begun to assess the simultaneous experience of both gender and race discrimination. Previous research has found that women and men of color experience gendered racism (i.e., intersection of racism and sexism) in various environments such as work, school, and service work settings. In addition, researchers have found that greater experiences of gendered racism are related to greater psychological distress. However, some studies have found that social identity (racial or gender identity) and coping styles can buffer individuals against the negative effects of stress associated with gendered racism. Although much of the extant literature on gendered racism has focused on women, recent studies have begun to explore the experiences of men of color. For example, some studies have explored the impact of gender roles and masculinity on the racial discrimination experienced by men of color. More research is needed to explore the intersections of race/ethnicity and gender on the lived experiences of individuals from various backgrounds.

Social Class and Gender

Social class is typically examined using indirect measures—including income level, occupation, education, numerical formulas for socioeconomic status (SES), and attitudes and beliefs about social class. Social class researchers argue that it is important to study social class stratification rather than solely focusing on limited financial means. Social class stratification theory is focused on understanding social class in the context of the societal hierarchy that ranks people in poverty on the bottom and limits access to resources and assets compared with individuals with greater financial resources. Social class also intersects with other social identities, such as gender.

Gender plays a prominent role in shaping the influence of social class and socioeconomic status on overall well-being. According to the 2014 American Community Survey, women working full-time in the United States typically were paid 79% of what men were paid. Not only are women making less on the dollar than their male counterparts, but women are overrepresented in lower-paying jobs, with one in six women in low-wage jobs. Racial differences in financial wealth also intersect with gender. Women of color are paid less on the dollar than their White female counterparts. According to a 2010 U.S. Bureau of Labor Report, women of color make 66 cents on the dollar, compared with the 77 cents on the dollar that White women make in the workforce. Less than half (48%) of the women in low-wage jobs are women of color, and African American and Latina women are at greater risk of experiencing chronic poverty in their lifetime.

Research on social class and health outcomes has suggested that those who live in poverty experience poorer mental and physical health. In a study that evaluated the impact of social class on health from childhood to later adulthood, results indicated gender differences in predictors of health. These results suggested that education level, another aspect of SES, was a stronger predictor of better health in adulthood for women, while higher income for men predicted better health later in life. Although education was a buffer against poorer health later in life for women, this study also reported that women had fewer opportunities for upward mobility. Studies have suggested that complex factors within SES such as material status, child adversity, and social connectedness could help further explain health outcomes.

Some multicultural researchers have argued for more research to be conducted on social class that focuses on issues such as classism (i.e., attitudes, behaviors, and policies that perpetuate the low status of poor people). More research is needed to explore the psychological impact of poverty on poor and working-class people, many of whom are women and people of color.

LGBTQ Issues and Gender

In 1973, the American Psychiatric Association made the decision to remove homosexuality from its list of mental disorders. Following suit, in 1975, the APA adopted a similar resolution to no longer view homosexuality as pathology and to encourage psychologists to remove the stigma of sexual orientation. One of the earliest studies to debunk the assumption that homosexuality and bisexuality were mental illnesses was conducted by Evelyn Hooker in 1957. She explored the differences between heterosexual and homosexual men on projective tests and found no significant differences. Thus, her research paved the way for future psychological research that found LGBTQ individuals to be well adjusted compared with heterosexual individuals. Over the next few decades, a large body of research found that there were very few significant differences between heterosexual and LGBTQ individuals. Of the studies that found differences, research indicated that minority status stress and discrimination influenced the health outcomes of LGBTQ individuals rather than any inherent differences due to sexual orientation.

There has been a large body of research to suggest that heterosexism negatively affects the health and well-being of LGBTQ individuals. In addition, some studies have explored within-group differences among LGBTQ individuals as it relates to discrimination. For example, research indicates that some bisexual individuals feel like they experience increased discrimination within the LGBTQ community. In addition, research on LGBTQ people of color has found that individuals often experience racism within the LGBTQ community, heterosexism within their ethnic and racial community, and discrimination within romantic and close relationships. Lesbian, bisexual, and transgender women also report greater experiences of objectification, hypersexualization, and exoticization than their male counterparts.

Transgender individuals experience unique forms of discrimination both within the LGBTQ community as well as in society at large. One of the most common forms of discrimination faced by transgender individuals is prejudicial attitudes and assumptions about transgender identity such as binary gender norms. For example, many people often make assumptions about the sexuality of transgender individuals and do not realize that sexual orientation and gender identity are distinct yet interrelated constructs. Research indicates that transgender women are at greatest risk for discrimination and criminalization from law enforcement. Two of the primary forms of structural discrimination experienced by transgender women include treatment within the prison system and maltreatment from police and law enforcement officers. For example, transgender women are often stopped, searched, and arrested for suspicion of being sex workers. This mistreatment from law enforcement often reduces the likelihood that transgender women report harassment and assault cases to the police, which leads to underreported criminal cases for this population. Some of the unique microaggression experiences of transgender individuals include exoticism, generalizing transgender experience, transphobia, endorsement of binary gender roles, and denial of privacy to the body. More research is needed to explore the unique experiences of transgender people of color who are at greater risk of experiencing violent hate crimes compared with other LGBTQ individuals.

In sum, the history of multicultural and feminist psychology has pushed the field to apply an intersectional and inclusive definition of culture, which includes dimensions of race/ethnicity, gender, sexual orientation, SES, religion/spirituality, age, language, ability/disability, and other aspects of culture. There has been significant advancement in the research, training, and clinical work focused on intersecting and marginalized populations in the field of psychology.

Jioni A. Lewis, Cecile A. Gadson, and Marlene Williams

See also Arab Americans and Gender; Asian Americans and Gender; Black Americans and Gender; Intersectional Identities; Latina/o Americans and Gender; Minority Stress; Native Americans and Gender; Pacific Islanders and Gender; White/European Americans and Gender

Further Readings

American Psychological Association. (2000). Guidelines for psychotherapy with lesbian, gay, and bisexual clients. *American Psychologist, 55*(12), 1440–1451.

American Psychological Association. (2002). *Guidelines on multicultural education, training, research, practice, and organizational change for psychologists.* Washington, DC: Author. Retrieved from http://www.apa.org/pi/oema/resources/policy/multicultural-guideline.pdf

American Psychological Association. (2007). Guidelines for psychological practice with girls and women. *American Psychologist, 62*(9), 949–979.

American Psychological Association. (2015). Guidelines for psychological practice with transgender and gender nonconforming people. *American Psychologist, 70*(19), 832–864.

Enns, C. Z. (2004). *Feminist theories and feminist psychotherapies: Origins, themes, and diversity* (2nd ed.). Binghamton, NY: Haworth Press.

Helgeson, V. S. (2012). *The psychology of gender* (4th ed.). Upper Saddle River, NJ: Pearson Education.

Mio, J. S., Barker, L. A., & Domenech Rodriguez, M. M. (2016). *Multicultural psychology: Understanding diverse communities* (4th ed.). Oxford, England: Oxford University Press.

Nadal, K. L. (2013). *That's so gay! Microaggressions and the lesbian, gay, bisexual, and transgender community.* Washington, DC: American Psychological Association.

Ponterotto, J., Casas, J. M., Suzuki, L. A., & Alexander, C. M. (2010). *Handbook of multicultural counseling* (3rd ed.). Thousand Oaks, CA: Sage.

Sue, D. W., & Sue, D. (2013). *Counseling the culturally diverse: Theory and practice* (6th ed.). Hoboken, NJ: Wiley.

Multiracial People and Gender

The number of multiracial people in the United States continues to grow. This entry briefly introduces the complexity of multiracial and gender identity development issues that multiracial individuals face. The entry then discusses nuances in the intersection of race and gender in identity development as well as factors that might influence an individual's experience. Finally, the entry calls for a more sophisticated understanding of multiracial people and gender psychology.

Multiracial People in the United States

In the year 2000, for the first time in contemporary U.S. history, people were able to identify themselves on the U.S. Census questionnaire as multiracial or mixed race. As a result, 7 million people identified as multiracial. Multiracial people are individuals who identify with mixed ancestry of two or more races (e.g., biracial, Hapa, Mestizo, Mexipino, Amerasian, and Afroasian). As of 2010, more than 9 million people (about 3% of the U.S. population) identified as multiracial. Although this may appear as a small percentage, it is projected that by 2050, one in five Americans will identify as multiracial, making the number approximately 16.2 million.

The racial makeup of the multiracial population is also diverse. According to the 2010 U.S. Census, most multiracial people are biracial (93.1%), with the Black/White subgroup as the most common combination (20.4% among all combinations), followed by White/Other Race (19.3%), White/Asian (18%), and White/Native American (15.9%). Only 20% of multiracial people identified as exclusively non-White. This means that the majority of multiracial people are of partly White racial backgrounds.

Almost half (4.2 million) of the multiracial people are youths—which designates them as the fastest growing racial group of youths in the United States. Furthermore, multiracial identity is becoming more visible through individuals within popular culture, such as mixed-race athletes, artists, activists, models, and musicians. For example, in 2008, Barack Obama, who is of both White and African descent, was elected as the first multiracial president of the United States.

Despite the growing population and increasing visibility of multiracial individuals, there continues to be little understanding on the experiences of multiracial people. This lack of understanding is partly related to the long-standing history of racial segregation in the United States and historical laws banning interracial marriages, which were in place until 1967. Other factors that contribute to the lack of understanding of multiracial people include the large variability in racial makeup of multiracial people and the complexity of combining more than one racial identity. Scholars' opinions differ on whether or not to regard race and ethnicity as distinct concepts, since both are socially structured concepts related to privilege and power; the terms *race* and *ethnicity* are used interchangeably throughout this entry.

Multiracial Identity Development

Identity development is a lifelong dynamic process centered on the question "Who am I?" Individuals' identity formation is a complex process, shaped by individual characteristics, social interactions, and historical, sociocultural, and political contexts. Among the various formed identities, racial identity is important and salient for most multiracial people, especially in the context of how race is socially structured in the United States.

As most multiracial people are biracial from both minority and White heritages, it is relevant to understand racial development from both standpoints. The Minority Identity Development Model and Helm's White Racial Identity Development Model have been two of the most influential racial identity development models to explain the process of racial identity development for both ethnic minorities and Whites, respectively. The Minority Identity Development Model consists of five stages, depicting a process that ethnic minority individuals go through, from identification with the dominant cultural values to resolved discomfort and acceptance of one's ethnic minority identity. Helm's White Racial Identity Development Model involves six stages, whereby a White person might change from being oblivious to racism (e.g., "I don't see color") to understanding racism and White privilege (i.e., advantages due to being White, such as being less likely to be stopped by the police while driving) in society and one's life, both on intellectual and personal levels. Both the Minority Identity Development Model and Helm's White Racial Identity Development Model involve a process whereby one becomes more aware and accepting of one's racial identity, as well as being aware of the reality of racism in U.S. society.

For multiracial people, multiracial identity development can be more complicated due to their multiracial backgrounds, experiences in their schools and communities, and sociopolitical factors. Because of one's multiple ethnic heritages, choice of group affiliation as well as integration of heritages (acceptance of and confidence in one's multiple ethnic heritages) become important aspects in the process of racial identity development.

Historically, racial categories in the United States have been used to create separation and hierarchy. White individuals were perceived to be superior, more intelligent, and biologically advantaged, whereas Blacks were viewed as less civilized and less capable. Historically, such ideas attempted to justify slavery and racial segregation laws. Rigid lines have been drawn between White and non-White groups; as a result, race has been perceived as something absolute and inflexible. Even nowadays, opportunities and resources for individuals are affected by racial categories. For example, compared with Asians and Whites, Black and Hispanic individuals are more disadvantaged in the education system, are more likely to be suspended from school, and experience prejudicial attitudes when applying for jobs and housing.

The increasing numbers of multiracial families since 1970 challenged this idea of race being absolute. For decades, multiracial people were portrayed as fundamentally flawed and wounded because they were the product of conflicting racial combinations. Yet in reality, multiracial people are psychologically and physically healthy on average, with potentially more linguistic assets and cultural resources.

Although individuals were finally able to identify as multiracial in the 2000 U.S. Census, the dichotomous understanding of race is still prevalent. Multiracial people often feel pressured by others to identify solely as one race, making it difficult for them to embrace their multiracial identities. For example, a biracial Latina/White woman might constantly experience people commenting that she "passes" as White and may say things to her such as "You don't look like a Latina," when she discloses her Latina background. These experiences may lead this biracial Latina/White woman to believe that she cannot be both races and that there is something wrong with her being half-Latina.

Like the identity development models previously described, multiracial people progress toward integration of their multiracial identities—a stage when one accepts and connects with one's multiple ethnic heritages. However, considering the sociopolitical context surrounding multiracial identities, integration can be difficult for multiracial individuals to achieve. Many multiracial adolescents report that they think of themselves as belonging to only one racial group as a result of how they were raised, pressure received from friends and family to identify with only one race, and being perceived negatively when identified as multiracial. On the other hand, many multiracial people indicate a reverse process: They stop identifying as multiracial after engaging in environments with more pressure to identify with only one race.

These processes demonstrate how the integration of multiracial identities often involves social learning with parents, friends, and other cultural and environmental influences. Because of the nature of this social learning, racial identity development for multiracial people is often fluid, subjective, and context based.

Intersection of Multiracial and Gender Identities

Gender, like race, is a complex concept. At birth, babies are assigned to either the male or the female sex categories based solely on their biological characteristics, which is the "sex" of the child. Gender identity refers to how one identifies oneself, which may or may not align with one's sex. One may think of oneself as a boy/man, a girl/woman, both, neither, or something in between. *Cisgender* is a gender identity term that refers to individuals whose gender identity is congruent with their sex assigned at birth, whereas *transgender* is a gender identity term that refers to individuals whose gender identity is incongruent with their sex assigned at birth.

Humans learn how to behave accordingly with their assigned sex from a young age. Children learn gender role behaviors—that is, doing "things that boys/girls do." The process of learning the social expectations and attitudes associated with one's gender, also called gender socialization, occurs largely in social relationships via observation, as well as from reinforcement and feedback of one's behaviors (e.g., "boys don't cry"). Meanwhile, messages about gender from social media outlets may also be an influential force in gender role learning for children and adults.

As described herein, gender socialization is socially and culturally rooted; what it means to be a man or a woman can vary among different cultures, ethnic groups, and social classes. For example, compared with White women, Asian women are perceived to be more feminine, and society commonly stereotypes Asian women as being submissive, compliant, and domestic. Those cultural expectations may be "internalized"—a process of embedding others' beliefs and attitudes into one's own, causing minority members to act more according to others' stereotypes.

The picture becomes more complex when gender and multiple ethnic backgrounds are considered simultaneously. For example, school teachers may have assumed that a biracial, Asian/Latino boy would be good at math and quiet when they initially saw the boy's Asian father. However, when teachers only met the boy's Latina mother, they assumed that the boy would be athletic and outgoing. This is solely one example of how others might commonly acknowledge only one racial/ethnic identity and interact with persons based on these assumptions.

Another theme in multiracial people's race and gender identity is their experience of trying to blend in yet commonly being viewed as "other" by both racial/ethnic groups. For example, a Black/White man may feel the need to act "extra masculine" in order to fit in with his Black male friends and "talk smart" in order to break the stereotype of Black men and be accepted by his White male peers. Despite the high stress and flexibility involved in such navigation, he may still be considered as not belonging to either ethnic group, resulting in further marginalization of racial/ethnic identities.

For multiracial women, they experience both gender and racial disadvantages. Because of their mixed racial status, multiracial women are often objectified and labeled as "exotic." For instance, a biracial White/Black woman may often receive compliments about her "olive skin tone" by others instead of being praised for traits not associated with looks (e.g., being hardworking or intelligent). These messages about body and sexuality certainly influence multiracial women's idea about their body and what it means to be a multiracial woman. Multiracial women may develop more disordered eating behaviors and have more self-objectification behaviors through treating oneself as an object to be looked at and evaluated on the basis of appearance.

Factors Shaping Multiracial Identity and Gender Development

Various factors can shape one's development of racial and gender identity, including social interactions with others, socioeconomic status, family function, racial makeup of neighborhood and school, and sociopolitical environment. Multiracial people indicated that their treatment by others largely depends on their perceived physical features. For example, many White/Black men are primarily perceived to be solely Black, whereas some White/Asian women may be perceived as White as a result of their skin tone. Other multiracial individuals encounter the question of "What are you?" if they look "racially ambiguous."

Regardless of the specific types of perceptions of others, multiracial people often experience discrimination and microaggressions in various ways. Discrimination refers to unfair treatment against a certain group, whereas microaggression refers to the delivery of often unintended or well-intended comments or expressions regarding one's group membership that are subtle and often stereotype based. Multiracial people commonly experience being subjected to racial slurs and jokes, poor service in restaurants and businesses, and unfair treatment by law enforcement. Examples of microaggressions include a biracial Black/White woman receiving compliments on how articulate she is and an Asian/White man being asked for help to solve a math problem. While these comments may be well intended, the underlying assumptions are that women with darker skin tone are uneducated and less verbal and all mixed-Asian men are good at math. These comments are often automatic, as microaggressions come from our unconscious bias, yet they cause long-term negative effects for people who receive them on a daily basis, such as frustration, stress, and self-esteem issues.

Discrimination and microaggressions can come from both White and minority groups, placing multiracial individuals in a more vulnerable position. For instance, biracial Black/White women sometimes receive hostility from Black females based on the perception that they receive more attention from men due to their lighter skin tone. Events of discrimination, microaggressions, and criticism tend to have more impact on minority women than men, as women are more likely to internalize these messages and blame themselves for the unfair treatment. Despite the gender effect in receiving others' treatment, events of discrimination and microaggressions can create stress and adverse mental and physical health outcomes. Multiracial transgender people often experience double rejection from their desired gender group as well as from their ethnic heritage groups.

Social interactions in one's family, school, and community environment may either reinforce or stigmatize multiracial identity. When the family accepts the multiracial and gender identity of the youth, the person is more likely to develop acceptance and confidence in one's identity. When parents provide multiracial youths with information and resources related to their multiple racial identities, children have advantageous access to larger knowledge and broadened cultural education. They are also likely to develop an enhanced sense of self, greater intergroup tolerance, flexibility, language facility, and the ability to see multiple perspectives. For multiracial transgender people, when family members accept their transgender identity, they are likely to have improved mental health outcomes. However, it is important to recognize that family acceptance alone should not dismiss the impact of sociocultural factors on mental health outcomes. For instance, even with family acceptance of transgender identity, multiracial transgender people still attempt suicide at alarmingly high rates.

Meanwhile, when family members have conflicts or lack understanding of their multiracial children, microaggressions toward one's multiracial identity may also occur, such as denial of one's multiracial identity by one side of the family. Not having discussions about race can also cause confusion for multiracial youths. For multiracial people who grow up with a single parent, they may experience lack of knowledge and understanding about the other parent's cultural heritage, often resulting in a lengthened integration process of multiple ethnic heritages.

Besides family factors, school and community environment also affect one's racial and gender identity development. Biracial people who grow up in a predominately White, more conservative neighborhood, compared with a neighborhood with more diversity, may experience more pressure to identify and associate with only one racial group. For example, an Asian/White girl growing up in a White neighborhood may experience a longer multiple racial identity integration process due to a lack of Asian friends. Her gender learning may be similar to that of her White female peers outside the family context. The racial and gender development of this individual would be very different if the environment was more diverse, with more freedom to incorporate fully her racial heritages and gender socializations with both Asian and White communities.

For any multiracial individuals, their identity is context based, meaning that they may choose to exhibit certain parts of their identity based on social context or what they feel others may perceive as favorable. For example, an Indian/White biracial teen may answer his classmates' question about where he is from by only acknowledging his Indian heritage in an attempt to resolve people's curiosity and avoid further questions.

Due to the diversity in the racial makeup of multiracial people, as well as environmental and sociopolitical factors with each multiracial group, there is a lack of multiracial community. Multiracial people often shift their identity with different racial groups, yet they struggle to find peers and role models who are also multiracial and share similar experiences. Lack of community support further reinforces the difficulty in claiming to be multiracial.

Finally, it is worth noting that there is very limited knowledge on multiracial people's racial and gender identity development and important factors involved, paralleling the societal exclusion and overlook of multiracial people. This calls for a more nuanced and complex conceptualization in this domain.

Shufang Sun, Laura Minero, and Stephanie Budge

See also Biculturalism and Gender; Cultural Gender Role Norms; Microaggressions; Multiculturalism and Gender: Overview; Multiracial People and Transgender Identity; Race and Gender

Further Readings

Downing, K., Nichols, D., & Webster, K. (2005). *Multiracial America: A resource guide on the history and literature of interracial issues*. Lanham, MD: Scarecrow Press.

Helms, J. E. (1990). *Black and White racial identity: Theory, research, and practice*. New York, NY: Greenwood Press.

Kang, S. K., & Bodenhausen, G. V. (2015). Multiple identities in social perception and interaction: Challenges and opportunities. *Annual Review of Psychology, 66*, 547–574.

LeMaster, B. (2013). Telling multiracial tales: An autoethnography of coming out home. *Qualitative Inquiry, 20*(1), 51–60. doi:10.1177/1077800413508532

Miville, M. L. (2013). *Multicultural gender roles: Applications for mental health and education*. Hoboken, NJ: Wiley.

Miville, M. L., Constantine, M. G., Baysden, M. F., & So-Lloyd, G. (2005). Chameleon changes: An exploration of racial identity themes of multiracial people. *Journal of Counseling Psychology, 52*(4), 507.

Rockquemore, K. A. (2002). Negotiating the color line: The gendered process of racial identity construction among Black/White biracial women. *Women's Studies, 16*(4), 485–503.

Rockquemore, K. A., Brunsma, D. L., & Delgado, D. J. (2009). Racing to theory or retheorizing race? Understanding the struggle to build a multiracial identity theory. *Journal of Social Issues, 65*(1), 13–34.

Root, M. P. P. (Ed.). (1996). *The multiracial experience: Racial borders as the new frontier in race relations*. Thousand Oaks, CA: Sage.

Wehrly, B., Kenney, K. R., & Kenney, M. E. (1999). *Multicultural aspects of counseling series 12: Counseling multiracial families*. Thousand Oaks, CA: Sage. doi:10.4135/9781452231969

Multiracial People and Sexual Orientation

Race and sexual orientation are important factors for understanding individuals' identity development and psychological well-being. Although attention has been paid to people of color and sexual orientation in general, limited empirical research has focused on multiracial people and sexual orientation. This entry examines current understandings of the intersections of multiracial identity and sexual orientation identity and particularly how sexual orientation affects multiracial people's everyday lives.

Historical Contexts of Mixed-Race People

At the foundation of multiracial people and sexual orientation are the concepts of race and sexuality. Although traditionally examined independently, researchers and theorists have started to use more intersectional approaches, particularly in examining how race and gender, or race and sexual orientation, influence individuals' identities and experiences. When examining multiple identities, previous research has focused mainly on lesbian, gay, bisexual, transgender, and queer (LGBTQ) people of color, as well as men or women of color, often in comparison with the experiences of White LGBTQ people (or White men and women). However, the experiences of multiracial people, or those individuals who identify with more than one racial background or identify exclusively as "multiracial," have been overlooked in the literature on sexual orientation identity.

While many people may assume that multiracial people are a generally newer or smaller population, racial mixing has occurred throughout history. Furthermore, contrary to popular belief, the 2000 U.S. Census was not the first time when multiracial Americans were enumerated. As early as 1850, Census forms counted multiracial individuals in categories such as "mulatto" and "quadroon" appearing at different points in the history of the U.S. Census. Moreover, the population of multiracial people continues to grow, with the number of Americans identifying with more than one racial group in 2010 reaching more than 9 million, growing more than a third since the

2000 Census. Much of this growth has been attributed to increases in interracial marriages and subsequent birthing of multiracial offspring; in fact, according to the U.S. Census, multiracial youth are the fastest growing demographic in the United States. The growth in multiracial identification can also be attributed to changing social contexts that now make a multiracial identity less stigmatized as notions of the "one-drop rule," or laws of hypodescent (meaning mixed heritage offspring must hold the monoracial identity of the "lower"-status parent), are increasingly being viewed as antiquated. Individuals of mixed ancestry who previously identified monoracially (i.e., with only one racial group) now feel greater freedom to identify in multiple ways, including as multiracial.

These changes in social contexts are also reflected in how multiracial identity has been theorized over time. Initially viewed from a problem-based approach (i.e., being biracial is a problem and doomed to a tragic ending), theorizing moved to a more equivalent approach (i.e., biracial people experience their racial identities similarly to monoracial people of color), and then through a variant approach (i.e., biracial people have a unique experience with their racial identity). Recent theorizing reflects the importance of the environment and context, representing an ecological approach to multiracial identity.

Similar changes in social contexts can be seen with sexual orientation. Much progress has been made fighting for equal rights for LGBTQ individuals within the United States and across the globe. Although there have been many issues affecting LGBTQ people in the United States over the years, one of the more popular civil rights issues since the turn of the 21st century has been the concept of marriage equality. Through the years, as more states in the United States legalized same-sex marriage, the public opinion of marriage equality switched from majority of Americans being unfavorable to majority of Americans being favorable. In June 2015, through *Obergefell v. Hodges*, the U.S. Supreme Court ruled that marriage was a federal right for same-sex couples across the United States.

At the intersection of multiraciality and sexual orientation are the connections proponents of marriage equality have made to the 1967 U.S. Supreme Court case *Loving v. Virginia*, which struck down the remaining antimiscegenation laws. During that time, public opinion held that "traditional" marriage was only acceptable between spouses of the same racial group, often stating that interracial couples were going against Christian teachings and that multiracial children would be psychologically damaged or "confused."

Forty years after the Supreme Court decision in *Loving v. Virginia*, a majority of Americans are in support of interracial marriages, and research has consistently found that multiracial children are as psychologically healthy as monoracial children in the United States. In the 2000s, antagonists of same-sex marriage made similar arguments as those who were anti-interracial marriage, asserting that "traditional" marriage was only acceptable between a man and a woman, that LGBTQ people were immoral abominations according to Christian teachings, and that the children of same-sex couples would be psychologically damaged or "confused." Similarly, research has found that children of same-sex couples are as psychologically healthy as children of heterosexual couples, while also finding that divorce rates are much lower in same-sex couples than in heterosexual couples.

Multiraciality and Sexual Orientation

Multiracial people do not represent a monolithic group. People included in the "multiracial" racial category identify their race in numerous ways. In addition to multiracial or mixed race, some individuals identify as monoracial (i.e., one racial group), with multiple monoracial groups (e.g., Black and Asian yet not multiracial), with groups in which they do not share ancestry (e.g., a mixed race person of Asian and White heritage who identifies more as Latino/a because of how they look), without a racial group (e.g., opting out of racially identifying altogether), or in a more situational or fluid manner. Part of this diversity in identification has to do with the many factors that influence one's choice of racial identity. Charmaine Wijeyesinghe developed an eight-factor model of multiracial identity, in which each of the factors was influential for a multiracial person's choice of racial identity: (1) racial ancestry, (2) early experience and socialization, (3) physical appearance, (4) other social identities (e.g., gender, sexual orientation), (5) religion, (6) cultural attachment, (7) political awareness and orientation, and (8) social and historical context. While some might put preference or prioritize certain factors over others (e.g., physical appearance), it is important to maintain that individuals should be allowed to decide which factors to consider when making their choice of racial identity.

Other social identities, like sexual orientation, influence multiracial identity in a variety of ways. Theoretically, if multiracial people have a strong view of the socially constructed nature of race and/or tend to identify situationally and fluidly, then they might also be more likely to see sexual orientation as something socially constructed, situational, and more fluid. Such openness might mean that individuals who identify as non-monoracial or multiracial might be more open to also identifying as nonheterosexual.

Contemplating multiple identities helps us understand not only how different identities influence one another but also how the systems of oppression attached to such identities might overlap or inform one another. Debate exists about the types of oppression faced by multiracial people, with some arguing that multiracial people only face the racism associated with one of their monoracial identities of color. For instance, a Black and White biracial person who experiences racial discrimination might be presumed to only experience anti-Black racism. Others argue that multiracial people face a unique system of oppression, termed *monoracism*, in that they experience discrimination due to the fact that they do not fit monoracial categories. Marc Johnston and Kevin Nadal described monoracism manifesting in multiracial people's everyday lives in the form of multiracial microaggressions, or the subtle, everyday, often unintentional insults, put-downs, or invalidations of multiracial people's racial realities. Examples of a multiracial microaggression include the ubiquitous "What are you?" types of questions that multiracial people receive about their racial background. The perpetrator of the microaggression (the one asking the question) unintentionally upholds a monoracial system of racial categorizing by trying to put the multiracial person into racial boxes.

The theorizing of monoracism has been built on other identities and forms of oppression where individuals do not fit society's norms. For instance, bisexual individuals may face prejudice and discrimination like lesbians and gay males due to homophobia, but they may also face discrimination by lesbians and gay men who do not understand or believe in bisexuality. This biphobia may share some similar social forces with monoracism in that the underlying rationale is a distrust of people who are not easily categorized by sexual orientation or race, respectively.

Some might argue that multiraciality and sexual orientation are similar identities in that they might be viewed as "invisible" identities when compared with others such as race and gender. Within a heterosexist society, the norms prevail where the immediate assumption is that one is heterosexual. This is why the coming out process has been focused in terms of LGB identity development. Because it is an invisible identity, one must disclose a nonheterosexual identity. Similarly, depending on how one looks or behaves, a multiracial person's mixed background may not be apparent and the individual may have to disclose a multiracial identity, or come out of the closet as multiracial.

Clinical psychologist Vivienne Cass developed one of the first stage models of gay and lesbian identity formation, which provided the foundation for future models on sexual orientation development. Through a series of six stages, an individual may come to terms with his or her sexual orientation since each stage features a successive commitment to one's sexual identity, moving from "identity confusion" to "identity synthesis." Cass's model has been critiqued similarly to other stage-based models in that there is a perceived end of development or a preferred outcome. It also does not incorporate bisexual identity. Other researchers have proposed models containing more interactive and nonsequential processes, additionally incorporating more explicitly the environment and the context influencing development. Some recent work by education researcher Alissa King has helped pave the way for rethinking multiraciality and bisexuality by exploring the identity development of women who identify as both multiracial/biracial and pansexual/bisexual.

In most instances, multiracial people are identifying in ways that solidify both race and sexual orientation as more fluid than usually conceptualized. Perhaps because multiracial people can often see the socially constructed nature of race, they can see that sexual orientation is also socially constructed, and therefore, they might feel more freedom in identifying outside of just a gay/straight binary.

Future Directions

Considering the increased growth and prominence of multiracial people as well as the increasing acceptance of LGB identities, as seen in the increased support for marriage equality, more attention must be given in the research on the intersections of multiracial identity and sexual orientation. Several areas of inquiry are ripe for future research directions. Empirical investigations of the extent to which multiracial identity allows one to see the socially constructed nature of both race and sexual orientation would offer leads into whether this increases the likelihood of identifying as nonheterosexual. The forms of oppression individuals face could be examined to see how they are mediated by sexual orientation. Gender differences exist, but it is unclear the extent to which sexual orientation matters for multiracial persons experiencing racism and/or monoracism. One form of microaggression multiracial people face occurs through the objectification or exoticization of multiracial individuals. While gender differences likely exist (e.g., multiracial women have been reported to be exoticized more than multiracial men), it is unclear to what extent such differences occur within heterosexual or LGB relationships. Further research is needed to better understand the dynamics of sexual orientation among multiracial people.

Marc P. Johnston-Guerrero

See also Biculturalism and Sexual Orientation; Microaggressions; Multiracial People and Gender; Sexual Orientation Identity

Further Readings

Johnston, M. P., & Nadal, K. L. (2010). Multiracial microaggressions: Exposing monoracism in everyday life and clinical practice. In D. W. Sue (Ed.), *Microaggressions and marginality: Manifestation, dynamics and impact* (pp. 123–144). New York, NY: Wiley.

Kich, G. K. (1996). In the margins of sex and race: Difference, marginality, and flexibility. In M. P. P. Root (Ed.), *The multiracial experience: Racial borders as the new frontier* (pp. 263–275). Thousand Oaks, CA: Sage.

King, A. R. (2011). Are we coming of age? A critique of Collins's proposed model of biracial-bisexual identity development. *Journal of Bisexuality, 11*(1), 98–120.

Loving v. Virginia, 388 U.S. 1 (1967).

Obergefell v. Hodges, 576 U.S. ___ (2015).

Rockquemore, K. A., Brunsma, D. L., & Delgado, D. J. (2009). Racing to theory or retheorizing race? Understanding the struggle to build a multiracial identity theory. *Journal of Social Issues, 65*(1), 13–34.

Root, M. P. P. (1990). Resolving "other" status: Identity development of biracial individuals. *Women & Therapy, 9*(1–2), 185–205.

Wijeyesinghe, C. L. (2001). Racial identity in multiracial people: An alternative paradigm. In C. L. Wijeyesinghe & B. W. Jackson III (Eds.), *New perspectives on racial identity development: A theoretical and practical anthology* (pp. 129–152). New York: New York University Press.

Multiracial People and Transgender Identity

Individuals who identify as multiracial and transgender or other gender nonconforming may experience both challenges and opportunities in navigating racial and gender identity development within cultures and societies that prefer simple social categorization. While race and gender are distinct social constructs, multiracial people who identify as transgender (throughout this entry, the term *transgender* is used to include individuals who identify as gender nonconforming) may experience discomfort and tension regarding both their racial and gender identity development processes, especially in response to confusion, denial, and rejection from others. However, intersections of racial and gender identities may also serve as opportunities for resilience and liberation as multiracial transgender individuals develop unique coping strategies, strengths, and social support systems.

This entry briefly introduces available theoretical and research literature regarding multiracial and transgender issues. While research on multiracial transgender issues is limited, this entry synthesizes available literature on both multiracial and transgender issues. This entry therefore includes a review of some challenges and opportunities that may arise for multiracial transgender individuals as they navigate identity development, identity intersections, identity ambiguity, identity conflict or denial, identity fluidity, and identity expression. Implications for medical, mental health, and community service agencies are also discussed.

Identity Development

Identity development for people who identify as multiracial and transgender often occurs both internally and externally. Multiracial transgender individuals internally discern and clarify their identities over the course of their lifetimes, often in response to personal interpretations of interpersonal, sociopolitical, cultural, and spiritual experiences. Multiracial transgender people may shift over time from passively accepting societal labels to actively exploring and defining their own identities. This may include identifying differently in various contexts, and it may include identifying differently over the course of one's life span.

While in the midst of discerning their own multiracial transgender identities, multiracial transgender persons may find that their identity development process is disturbed by the beliefs, biases, and expectations of others. In her *Bill of Rights for Racially Mixed People*, Maria P. P. Root affirmed the needs and rights of multiracial persons to not have to justify their existence to others, to not keep the races separate within themselves, to identify differently than strangers expect, to identify differently than how their parents identify them, and to identify differently than their siblings. With regard to transgender identity development, Aaron H. Devor discussed the importance of witnessing and mirroring in his stage model of transsexual identity formation. Like their cisgender counterparts, transgender individuals benefit from validation of their own selves and particularly their gender identity or expression by objective witnesses around them (e.g., friends, family, coworkers). When transgender individuals' gender identity or expression is not witnessed and reinforced—but is instead continually challenged by society—they may experience significant conflict and feel compelled to profoundly alter the self seen by others.

Identity Intersections

Identity development for individuals with multiple marginalized identities often occurs within the context of other identities. For example, the expression of one's gender identity may be influenced by the gender role expectations of one's race, ethnicity, and culture (e.g., cultural expectations of males within one's culture may affect one's willingness to transgress traditional male gender roles). One's racial identity development process may conversely be affected by societal gender role stereotypes (e.g., African American and Latino male identified individuals may experience more discrimination based on stereotypical expectations of criminality than their female identified counterparts). Multiracial transgender individuals may therefore develop their racial and gender identities within the context of other aspects of their identity (e.g., racial/ethnic identities, gender identity or gender assigned at birth, sexual orientation, socioeconomic status, religion, disability). Indeed, Karen Maeda Allman described race, gender, and sexuality as "a sort of unstable triad," adding that a shift in one construct creates movement in the other two constructs. She noted that transgressing racial boundaries as a multiracial person not only challenges notions of racial purity but also reveals racialized ideas about traditional gender roles.

In addition, the beliefs and expectations of others may affect the identity development process for multiracial transgender individuals. For example, research indicates that one's socioeconomic status and perceived gender can affect how one's race is interpreted by others (e.g., a person who demonstrates higher socioeconomic status is more likely to be perceived as White; women receiving welfare are more likely to be perceived as African American than men receiving welfare). As noted earlier, multiracial transgender persons benefit from validation of intersecting identities by objective witnesses. When such validation is not forthcoming, the process of understanding one's multiracial transgender identity can be disturbed by the negative beliefs, biases, and expectations of others. Multiple marginalized identities can result in greater stigmatization when multiracial transgender individuals experience the additive stressors of both racism and transphobia.

Identity Ambiguity

Multiracial transgender individuals may experience underlying tension regarding their multiracial and transgender identities, especially during the early stages of identity development as they first learn to grapple with ambiguity. Identifying with different racial and gender identities in various social contexts can initially feel exhausting and result in increased risk for depressed mood and decreased psychological well-being.

Multiracial transgender persons may also experience confusion, rejection, and even hostility from cultures and societies that prefer simple, discrete categorizations of the social world. Individuals who identify as multiracial and transgender may challenge these unrealistic notions of simplicity with identities that are ambiguous and complex. Hasty attempts to categorize multiracial transgender persons are often fraught with bias. For example, U.S. legal traditions have followed the principle of hypodescent in racial categorization, assigning individuals of multiracial heritage to a monoracial identity assumed to be socially subordinate (e.g., a Latino/White person would be considered a Latino). The principle of hypodescent does not allow multiracial individuals to access more socially privileged identities, and it conserves resources for the dominant group. Multiracial transgender individuals may also experience bias with regard to their gender identity and expression when others attempt to "gender police" the actions of gender nonconforming persons (e.g., transgender individuals being verbally and/or physically harassed for using gender specific rest rooms and locker rooms). At times, multiracial transgender persons may even feel that the ambiguity of their identities prevents them from being fully accepted within their own minority communities.

Identity Conflict or Denial

When multiracial transgender individuals experience identity conflict and are denied their identities by others, they may experience higher levels of medical and mental health issues due to acculturative stress and discrimination. Multiracial persons who also identify as gender nonconforming may be pressured to "choose" only one race and identify with the gender and sex assigned at birth. Multiracial transgender individuals may experience identity denial in which others categorize them solely according to minority group membership and the gender and sex assigned at birth.

Identity Fluidity

While multiracial transgender persons may face challenges in their identity development process, they may also discover opportunities for resilience and liberation in the fluidity and adaptation of their identities. Multiracial transgender individuals who choose to align gender expression with their gender identities and/or pursue various transition options (e.g., hormones only, partial gender reassignment surgery, full gender reassignment surgery) may experience liberation in fully accepting and celebrating their gender identities.

Individuals who identify as multiracial and transgender may also "code switch" and emphasize different aspects of their racial identities depending on the social context. While code switching can initially feel tiring and even disorienting, it can also help buffer against stereotype threat and even violence. Multiracial transgender persons may also discover the benefits of code switching once the practice becomes more familiar and routine. Identifying with various cultures and identities may help multiracial transgender persons enjoy more opportunities for personal fulfillment and community building. A study by the Pew Research Center found that the majority (59%) of multiracial individuals felt that their racial heritages made them more open to other cultures.

Identity Expression

While disclosure of marginalized identities can expose multiracial transgender individuals to discrimination and even violence, identity expression at least in some social contexts can also provide opportunities for resilience and liberation. Multiracial transgender persons may learn multiple ways to represent their group identities in various social situations. Learning how to successfully integrate multiple racial identities and one's transgender identity (or chosen gender identity) can result in significant improvements in overall health and well-being. Self-determination (and the right to shift over time, as needed) in defining one's racial and gender identities is crucial for healthy multiracial transgender identity development, self-acceptance, resilience, and liberation. In fact, multiracial transgender individuals may discover freedom in being nonprototypical in the disadvantaged groups, and they may experience a sense of liberty in rejecting stereotypes and redefining themselves.

Implications for Medical, Mental Health, and Community Service Agencies

Multiracial transgender persons may experience both challenges and opportunities in navigating complex, intersecting, or ambiguous social identities. Race and gender are social constructs with real-world consequences, and persons who identify as multiracial and transgender are at risk for negative educational, occupational, medical, and mental health outcomes due to multiple and intersecting experiences of marginalization. Multiracial transgender individuals often experience discrimination and even violence from cultures and societies that reject ambiguity and prefer simple social categorization. Medical, mental health, and community service agencies that specialize in treating transgender and racial minority populations are still very limited, especially outside major metropolitan areas.

Providers and advocates working with multiracial transgender individuals should seek comprehensive and ongoing training about best practices for treatment and advocacy. Such training includes a review of both the challenges and the strengths of multiracial transgender populations. The intersections, ambiguity, and fluidity associated with a complex identity development process also provide unique opportunities for healing, resilience, and liberation through identity expression. A strengths-based approach to working with multiracial transgender persons should appreciate the complexity inherent in identity adaptiveness, encourage multiple opportunities for need fulfillment, and promote autonomy in defining and accepting one's multiracial transgender identities.

Kirstyn Y. S. Chun

See also Gender Nonconformity and Transgender Issues: Overview; Multiculturalism and Gender: Overview; Multiracial People and Gender

Further Readings

American Counseling Association. (2010). Competencies for counseling with transgender clients. *Journal of LGBT Issues in Counseling, 4,* 135–139. doi:10.1080/15538605.2010.524839

American Psychological Association. (2011). *Answers to your questions about transgender people, gender identity, and gender expression.* Washington, DC: Author. Retrieved from http://www.apa.org/topics/lgbt/transgender.aspx

Devor, A. H. (2004). Witnessing and mirroring: A fourteen stage model of transsexual identity formation. *Journal of Gay & Lesbian Psychotherapy, 8*(1–2), 41–67. doi:10.1300/J236v08n01_05

Kang, S. K., & Bodenhausen, G. V. (2015). Multiple identities in social perception and interaction: Challenges and opportunities. *Annual Review of Psychology, 66,* 547–574. doi:10.1146/annurev-psych-010814-015025

Maeda Allman, K. (1996). (Un)natural boundaries: Mixed race, gender, and sexuality. In M. P. P. Root (Ed.), *The multiracial experience: Racial borders as the new frontier* (pp. 277–290). Thousand Oaks, CA: Sage.

Pew Research Center. (2015). *Multiracial in America: Proud, diverse, and growing in numbers.* Washington, DC: Author. Retrieved from http://www.pewsocialtrends.org/files/2015/06/2015-06-11_multiracial-in-america_final-updated.pdf

Remedios, J. D., & Chasteen, A. L. (2013). Finally, someone who "gets" me! Multiracial people value others' accuracy about their race. *Cultural Diversity & Ethnic Minority Psychology, 19,* 453–460. doi:10.1037/a0032249

Root, M. P. P. (Ed.). (1996). *The multiracial experience: Racial borders as the new frontier.* Thousand Oaks, CA: Sage.

Sanchez, D. T., Shih, M., & Garcia, J. A. (2009). Juggling multiple racial identities: Malleable racial identification and psychological well-being. *Cultural Diversity & Ethnic Minority Psychology, 15,* 243–254. doi:10.1037/a0014373

Singh, A., & Chun, K. Y. S. (2012). Multiracial/multiethnic queer and transgender clients: Intersections of identity and resilience. In S. H. Dworkin & M. Pope (Eds.), *Casebook for counseling lesbian, gay, bisexual, and transgender persons and their families* (pp. 197–209). Alexandria, VA: American Counseling Association.

Websites

Children's National Health System, Gender and Sexuality Development Program: http://childrensnational.org/gendervariance

Family Acceptance Project: http://familyproject.sfsu.edu/

Gender Spectrum: https://www.genderspectrum.org/

Lambda Legal: http://lambdalegal.org

National Center for Transgender Equality: http://transequality.org/

National LGBTQ Task Force: http://www.thetaskforce.org/

Sylvia Rivera Law Project: http://srlp.org/

Transgender Law Center: http://transgenderlawcenter.org/

Narcissistic Personality Disorder and Gender

Narcissism is a multifaceted personality trait characterized by inflated self-concept, extremely high self-esteem, a preoccupation with the self and one's own interests, and unrealistically positive beliefs about one's abilities, appearance, and status. In short, narcissism is an obsession with the self in positive terms. Although the term is used in popular culture to refer to any instance in which a person seems vain, entitled, self-absorbed, or arrogant, in the psychological literature, the term is often used much more precisely. Individuals who display excessive levels of vanity, entitlement, grandiose self-concept, and arrogance may have what is known as narcissistic personality disorder (NPD), which is a personality style in which the person's entire life is characterized and even defined by narcissistic tendencies. Narcissism and NPD can be experienced and expressed by both genders, but men tend to display higher levels of both than women. As discussed in this entry, this prevalence of narcissism in men is particularly concerning in light of the relationships between narcissism and sexual violence.

Historical Considerations

Among psychological disorders, narcissism and NPD have a long history. In ancient Greek mythology, Narcissus was a beautiful and vain hunter who scorned love from others, whom he found to be inferior and undesirable. As punishment for his pride, Narcissus was led to a river by the goddess Nemesis, where he fell in love with his own reflection. Realizing that he would never be loved by someone as fair as his own reflection, Narcissus ended his own life. Although it is just a myth, this irrational and fanatical self-love formed the basis for what is now known as narcissism and NPD. A seemingly obsessive affection for the self, to the extent of harming external relationships and ultimately creating misery, is the hallmark of extreme narcissism.

In the late 19th and early 20th centuries, various psychotherapists speculated about the nature of narcissism. Most notable among these speculations were those of Sigmund Freud, who characterized the excessive self-love of the narcissist as a developmental arrest that was primarily erotic in nature. Rather than conceptualizing narcissism as a disorder of the total self, Freud characterized it as the state in which one is only sexually attracted to the self. Although such an attraction would clearly fall under aspects of what is now known as narcissism, subsequent researchers revised and expanded Freud's conceptions substantially.

Moving beyond Freud's work, throughout the 20th century, the concept of narcissism was refined, and the notion of a narcissistic personality or NPD was developed. From the 1950s to the 1980s, Otto Kernberg and Heinz Kohut became seminal figures in the understanding of narcissism. Although their theories diverged slightly, they both conceptualized narcissism as a pervasive personality disorder characterized by an inflated self-view and entitled demands of others. Similarly, both Kohut and Kernberg described narcissism as an important part of early-childhood development (e.g., the self-absorbed infant/toddler), which, under ideal circumstances, eventually subsided into an adaptive and accurate self-image. It was their work that ultimately led to the inclusion of the NPD diagnosis in the third edition of the American Psychiatric Association's *Diagnostic and Statistical Manual of Mental Disorders* (*DSM-III*).

Narcissism

Having given some historical context to the notion of narcissism, it is appropriate to describe the present conceptualizations of this personality trait. Although narcissism may be nuanced in very specific ways, it generally entails a range of self-absorbed and prideful attitudes, such as grandiosity, vanity, entitlement, exploitativeness, leadership, and authority. Grandiosity refers to that aspect of narcissism that is characterized by an inflated self-view as someone special, amazing, or better than others. Vanity refers to the aspect of narcissism characterized by inflated views of one's physical beauty or attractiveness. Entitlement is characterized by attitudes of deservingness and demandingness in most life domains. Exploitativeness refers to the narcissistic individual's tendency to abuse or manipulate others to enhance self-image. Leadership refers to a perceived innate ability to be in charge and be recognized for having superb interpersonal skills. Finally, authority refers to the tendency of narcissistic individuals to demand positions of authority and dominance over others.

Flowing from this general understanding of narcissism, NPD is the net result of narcissism so elevated that it pervades all aspects of a person's life. According to the *Diagnostic and Statistical Manual of Mental Disorders, Fifth Edition* (*DSM-5*), published in 2013, NPD is characterized by arrogant behaviors and attitudes, feelings of envy of others, feelings of being the target of envy from others, exploitative tendencies in relationships, an inflated sense of entitlement, a pervasive need for admiration, a perception of the self as special and unique, elitist tendencies precluding associating with individuals deemed inferior to the narcissist, an obsession with fantasies or hypothetical scenarios in which the narcissist is admired and envied, and an inflated sense of self-importance. Notably, to warrant a diagnosis of NPD, these tendencies must be so inflated as to cause problems in the narcissist's life. Although many individuals might display some of the previously described attributes, it is the collection of these tendencies in high concentration that may lead to significant impairment. When such impairment occurs, a diagnosis of NPD is appropriate.

Narcissism and Gender

Although narcissism theoretically extends to both genders, a large body of research strongly suggests that narcissism tends to be expressed more by men than by women. Although those differences are subtle, they are reliable. In a meta-analytic review (a type of review combining the results of several studies) of more than 350 studies involving more than 470,000 people, Emily Grijalva and colleagues found that men consistently display slightly higher levels of narcissism than women. Similarly, the *DSM-5* cites that up to 75% of individuals diagnosed with NPD are male. These figures are confirmed by the results of a nationally representative survey. Results of the second wave of the National Epidemiologic Survey on Alcohol and Related Conditions, a nationally representative survey that provides information on a range of mental health concerns in the United States, found that the lifetime prevalence (how many people have had this diagnosis at some point in their lives) of NPD was 7.7% for men but only 4.8% for women.

Despite the body of research suggesting that narcissism and NPD are more commonly seen in men, there has been some disagreement among psychologists regarding the reasons for these differences. At present, there are at least two contrasting views explaining these differences. Primarily, as many psychologists contend, narcissism may simply be higher in men than in women. It is possible that men, for either genetic or societal reasons, are more likely to display excessively positive self-concept and grandiosity. Alternatively, some psychologists speculate that the reason for the seeming difference in narcissism levels between men and women is the gendered bias in present understanding and diagnosis of narcissism and NPD. These psychologists would contend that narcissism, as presently described in diagnostic and academic literatures, is a reflection of male traits in a patriarchal society, such as that seen in the United States. For example, narcissistic tendencies, such as a preoccupation with leadership, excessive entitlement, a propensity toward dominance in social settings, and feelings of superiority, could arguably be seen as a by-product of patriarchal values that tell men to behave like strong and bold leaders while telling women to be submissive and demure. If this is the case, then narcissism would be more commonly observed in men, whereas other disorders or traits (e.g., borderline personality disorder, histrionic personality disorder) may be more traditionally feminine.

In sum, although narcissism and NPD are certainly experienced and expressed by women, compelling research indicates that these constructs and diagnoses are much more common in men, although these differences may be the result of gender biases in diagnosis and assessment of narcissism.

Narcissism and Gender-Relevant Behaviors

Moving beyond gender differences in narcissism and NPD, both narcissism and NPD may also have impacts on gender-relevant behaviors, many of which are very concerning. For example, a great deal of research has found that narcissism, particularly in the form of excessive entitlement, is associated with exploitative tendencies in romantic relationships. Both men and women who are narcissists tend to be emotionally abusive and manipulative in their romantic relationships and tend to be more likely to cheat on their partners.

Regarding gender specific differences, men who are narcissistic tend to display a wide range of sexist behaviors and attitudes. Most notably, men who are high in trait narcissism tend to also be very high in attitudes of hostile sexism, which is characterized by a mistrust of women and beliefs that women are manipulative and controlling. By contrast, women who are high in trait entitlement, a facet of narcissism, tend to display higher levels of benevolent sexism, which is characterized by notions of women as fair, pure, and deserving of special treatment. Collectively, these differing associations between narcissism and sexism suggest that both men and women who are narcissist are likely to endorse gender specific attitudes that they find personally advantageous.

Moving beyond attitudes alone, narcissistic tendencies in men are also known risk factors for sexual violence. A plethora of studies have found that men who are high in trait narcissism, particularly in the form of excessive entitlement, are more likely to be aggressive and violent when provoked or insulted. However, a number of studies have also found that excessive entitlement is predictive of more accepting attitudes toward rape and sexual violence and a greater personal likelihood of raping a woman. No such associations have been found for women who are high in trait narcissism.

Joshua B. Grubbs

See also Ambivalent Sexism; Gender Socialization in Men; Gender-Based Violence; Personality Disorders and Gender Bias; Rape Culture

Further Readings

Baumeister, R. F., Catanese, K. R., & Wallace, H. M. (2002). Conquest by force: A narcissistic reactance theory of rape and sexual coercion. *Review of General Psychology, 6,* 92–135.

Bushman, B. J., Bonacci, A. M., Van Dijk, M., & Baumeister, R. F. (2003). Narcissism, sexual refusal, and aggression: Testing a narcissistic reactance model of sexual coercion. *Journal of Personality and Social Psychology, 84,* 1027–1040.

Campbell, W. K., & Miller, J. D. (Eds.). (2011). *The handbook of narcissism and narcissistic personality disorder: Theoretical approaches, empirical findings, and treatments.* Hoboken, NJ. Wiley.

Emmons, R. A. (1987). Narcissism: Theory and measurement. *Journal of Personality and Social Psychology, 52,* 11–17.

Grijalva, E., Newman, D. A., Tay, L., Donnellan, M. B., Harms, P. D., Robins, R. W., & Yan, T. (2014). Gender differences in narcissism: A meta-analytic review. *Psychological Bulletin, 141,* 261–310.

Grubbs, J. B., Exline, J. J., & Twenge, J. M. (2014). Psychological entitlement and ambivalent sexism: Understanding the role of entitlement in predicting two forms of sexism. *Sex Roles, 70*(5/6), 209–220.

Hammond, M. D., Sibley, C. G., & Overall, N. C. (2013). The allure of sexism: Psychological entitlement fosters women's endorsement of benevolent sexism over time. *Social Psychological and Personality Science, 5,* 422–429.

Hartung, C. M., & Widiger, T. A. (1998). Gender differences in the diagnosis of mental disorders: Conclusions and controversies of the *DSM–IV. Psychological Bulletin, 123,* 260–278.

Keiller, S. W. (2010). Male narcissism and attitudes toward heterosexual women and men, lesbian women, and gay men: Hostility toward heterosexual women most of all. *Sex Roles, 63*(7/8), 530–541.

Stinson, F. S., Dawson, D. A., Goldstein, R. B., Chou, S. P., Huang, B., Smith, S. M., . . . Grant, B. F. (2008). Prevalence, correlates, disability, and comorbidity of *DSM-IV* narcissistic personality disorder: Results from the Wave 2 National Epidemiologic Survey on Alcohol and Related Conditions. *Journal of Clinical Psychiatry, 69,* 1033–1045.

Native Americans and Gender

Native Americans are indigenous to the lands now known as the United States and have experienced a 400-year history of oppression and prejudice. Many of the historical stereotypic images and racist attitudes persist, affecting the psychological well-being of Native Americans. This entry addresses some of the major psychological aspects of gender for Native Americans, including gendered stereotypes and related consequences, gender roles within tribal populations, and sexual and gender identity.

There are many terms commonly used to label American Indians, and as there is no single preferred term, this entry uses the terms *(American) Indian*, *Native (American)*, *Tribal*, and *Indigenous* interchangeably. Indigenous people may identify with any of these terms, but most prefer to identify with their tribe or clan first and foremost. As of the 2010 Census, more than 5 million people self-identify as American Indian or Alaskan Native in the United States.

Overview of Native Americans

As of 2014, there are more than 566 federally recognized tribes in the United States. There exists tremendous diversity across tribal nations as each tribe has its own cultural beliefs, values, and norms, including those around gender-related issues. There are more than 250 Native languages spoken by tribes who live in incredibly diverse lands across the country, and there is great variability in governing structure and traditional practices. Yet tribes across the United States share a common history as a result of being subjected to the same legal and political agendas from the federal government.

Federally recognized tribes are sovereign nations within the United States with the inherent right to make their own laws and policies. Although this power is limited and overseen by the federal government, it allows for governance over tribal members. One of these aspects of governance is determining who is eligible to be members of the tribe.

There are many different definitions used to determine "who is Indian," including social, legal, and individual constructions. Most federal and tribal legal definitions are based on ancestry, blood quantum, tribal membership, or a combination of these. Through self-governance, each tribe defines who is eligible for membership, which is at least partially based on lineage of tribal descent. Some tribes consider the residency within tribal lands or require maintained contact with the tribe, and other tribes require lineage from a particular parent, such as matrilineal or patrilineal ancestry, to be eligible for enrollment. Clanship within a tribe may also be based on parental clanship, often only from either the maternal or the paternal side. This can result in the loss of clan membership for some individuals. For example, if clanship is based on the maternal membership and the mother is not a tribal descendant but the father is, the result is that the child is not eligible for enrollment and likely not recognized by the tribal or federal government. Such rules may affect family formation and suitable romantic partners if a relationship would result in exclusion from clan or tribal membership.

The U.S. Census solely requires an individual to identify as American Indian. Thus, one's individual cultural identity is often based on much more than the legal definition and usually includes factors such as knowledge of tribal history, culture, religion, language, kinship, and a sense of connectedness. Development of identity, coupled with a sense of connection and belonging, is fundamental in addressing one's psychological needs. Identity conflicts can arise when internal and external expectations of one's roles do not match. For Native Americans, these conflicts may arise in many ways, but one prominent way is by not being "recognized" as Native, either through legal barriers to membership or through not meeting the majority culture's expectations of a Native American. Expectations of what it means to be Indian tend to be rooted in historical and stereotypical notions, not in contemporary society.

Gendered Stereotypes

American Indians are affected by a combination of racial and gender stereotypes. This is particularly troublesome for American Indians, as stereotypes are often all most people know about American Indians. Most members of the general U.S. population struggle to name contemporary American Indians because American Indians are not represented in popular culture and media as members of the current society. For many people, American Indians exist only as a memory of a group of people represented (usually inaccurately) in movies, television, and history books. The broad strokes of these stereotypes tend to be highly gendered and affect not only the way others treat American Indians but also the way American Indians view themselves, their own identity, and possibilities for their future, such as family, education, and careers.

American Indian Men: Noble Savage or Warrior

Beliefs about American Indian men are informed by the mythological quality of depictions from the past, and thus, they are often seen either as a brutish warrior or as noble but still savage. In general, American Indian men tend to be thought of as stoic and unemotional or very aggressive and violent, even murderous. The more romanticized option is that of the noble savage, who is "noble" enough to listen quietly before reacting, and with guidance from the colonizing culture, may be "savable." But this man is still portrayed as a savage and, thus, must still be feared. These types of portrayals are what ignite identity conflict, as adolescents in schools cannot see how they can fit with these images. There are some representations of contemporary Native American men, but they remain stereotypical and harmful, such as being lazy and a drunk.

American Indian Women: Princess or Squaw

American Indian women tend to be represented as either an Indian princess or the squaw. The Indian princess tends to be seen as virginal and pure and is often portrayed as a helper to White men. Often characterized as holding the position of daughter of the chief of the tribe, she was thought to have some influence over the political process of the tribe and was thus charged with helping the tribe to understand the White man's ways. In historical depictions, all other Indian women are seen as a "squaw" (a term so negative that it is often referred to as the "S" word within Indigenous communities), or the drudge or slave. These Native women are dehumanized in an effort to rationalize their role. Bea Medicine coined this as the Prostitute-Princess syndrome. In reality, tribes did not have royalty positions within the social structure, and thus, there were no "princesses." In addition, Indigenous women have always held important roles in their tribes and societies, but this is not and never has been portrayed in the mainstream media. These representations limit the possible aspirations of American Indian females.

Impacts of Stereotypes

Views of American Indians are rooted in historical stereotypes and typically ignore any role for Native Americans in contemporary society. That is to say, for many people, American Indians are an extinct group, one whose totality is described in history books and other media only. These stereotypes are different for American Indians compared with other racial and ethnic groups in the United States as they are still rooted in the past and lead to more overt racism. These aspects have a significant psychological impact on American Indians. Mascots are one of the few common representations of Indigenous peoples in the United States, and they represent another illustration of the limited stereotypical historical roles of American Indians in our current society. Mascots influence the way

American Indians are viewed by others and the ways in which American Indians see themselves. When exposed to American Indian mascots, Native American youth tend to hold less achievement-related views of the self, thus affecting what "dreams" they pursue. These stereotypical images result in negative psychological consequences for Native youth, such as lowered self-esteem. In contrast, European Americans show increased self-esteem when exposed to American Indian stereotypes.

Overall, these dated stereotypes result in biased treatment and perception of Native Americans by others in society. The majority of stereotypes of American Indians result in diminished societal roles and less societal value. When others buy into these stereotypes, it leads to further ramifications for American Indians. For example, it may be difficult for Native men to gain employment if they are seen as unreliable (drunk and lazy). The stereotypes of Native women can lead to experiences of degradation and can be a catalyst for violence. Beyond the legal complications of the jurisdictional maze for addressing violence against American Indian women, those who are victims of crime tend to be valued less than White women. In addition, the majority of violence against Indian women is intergroup (perpetrated by non-Indians). This devaluation is seen throughout the fabric of the United States, including the high number of places with the term *squaw* in the title.

Gender Roles

Tribes vary considerably in their approach to gender roles. A number of North American tribes are based on egalitarian systems of reciprocity in which separate, complementary, and similarly identified tasks are mutually assigned to each sex. Some tribes are patrilineal, patrilocal, patrifocal, and patriarchal, whereas others are matrilineal, matrilocal, matrifocal, and matriarchal. In matrilineal tribes, property and ownership are passed down to later generations through the maternal side of the family. Some tribes include tribal roles in this ownership, such that the women of the tribe name who serve in what roles, including decisions about which male members would serve in particular roles, such as chief.

Generally, the roles of women in traditional Native families were well grounded in their spirituality, extended kin, and tribe. Women identified themselves as communal beings, pursuing balance within their natural, spiritual, and social spheres. Historically, women have valued motherhood and the ability to raise healthy families, while spiritually, women were identified as extensions of the Spirit Mother, representing the life force of their people. Socially, women were the conduits of cultural knowledge and caretakers of their families (e.g., children, relatives). The roles of traditional Native American women were revered and considered to be privileged within Indigenous communities.

Traditionally, Native American men also held honored positions within their families and communities. In many cases, their privileged roles were integral to the providing for and protection of their kinship networks. Regarding the traditional Native American family system, men took on expected duties aligned with being grandfathers, fathers, husbands, sons, brothers, and uncles. Historically, these duties for men and women were reinforced through ceremonial, ritual, and spiritual practices.

Well-established Native researchers were among the first to situate the discussion of contemporary gender roles through the lens of a feminist Native American cultural perspective. From this viewpoint, traditional Native American social systems and ways of life have been fractured as a result of colonization and expansion with an overarching theme of male dominance.

Sexual and Gender Identity

As already discussed, tribal traditions vary with respect to the expectations of gender roles. However, these differences are further pronounced when considering the variations of gender and sexual identity. Gender identification in precolonial Native American tribes appeared to focus on an individual's participation in gender specific ceremonies and tasks, rather than on sexual identity or choice of sexual partners. Transitions from female to male gender roles could be prompted and validated by a girl's interest in traditionally male tasks or her refusal to participate in traditionally female-oriented tasks. For example, families in one tribe that had all daughters but desired a son would encourage the child with the most inclination to become "like a man" to participate in the puberty initiation ceremonies and customs for boys instead of girls. In another tribe, cross-gender females would adhere to the male custom of nose piercing rather than having their chins tattooed like other women.

Research has demonstrated the existence of institutionalized, alternative female roles, in addition to roles that have been held as traditional. Women in Plains tribes have historically been identified as virtuous, hardworking wives. Some support exists that endorses stereotypical roles within this tribe, such as those of the "manly hearted women," the chief wives, and the important religious role of the Sun Dance woman. These alternative roles indicated freedom to express masculine traits or participate in male-associated occupations, with or without dressing as men or assuming masculine social roles.

An ethnographic contextual framework should be considered when examining the process by which Native lesbians, gay males, bisexuals, and transgendered individuals begin to identify themselves. Lakota (Sioux) utilize the term *winkte* ("gay male"), and the term is referred to in Dine (Navajo) as *n* to indicate the status of these individuals. In the past, the Lakota term *berdache* represented what many Plains tribes considered to be a socially constructed sexual "abnormality." It should be noted that this term does not reflect the cultural variance that contributed to the forms and functions of the berdache role. Some perceive the term as rather offensive because anthropological researchers tended to include Native American homosexuals, transvestites, hermaphrodites, and transgendered individuals in the same socially constructed category. Ultimately, the term was developed through a rather imperialistic and colonial discourse. Gender identity labels, and naming from an Indigenous perspective, are important among Native American LGBT individuals. In fact, there is an agreed-on label, *neizh manitoog*, which means "two spirit," that might be more representative of Native American LGBT community members who do not ascribe to U.S. socially constructed labels aligned with gender identity/sexual identity. *Two spirit* extends beyond the binary often associated with typical gender terms.

Tribal Response to Same-Sex Marriage

Tribal communities' perspectives vary with regard to support of gender nonconformity. There are tribes in which homophobia is not typically endorsed and other tribes in which homophobia is congruent with the influence of outside organized religions (e.g., Christianity or Catholicism). Third and fourth genders (what may be most closely represented by the terms *transgender* and *gender nonconforming individuals*) and same-sex marriage have been consistent parts of some tribal societies. Support for cross-gender roles within some tribal societies is demonstrated with privileges and honor for individuals who tend to have gender role flexibility.

In 2015, the U.S. Supreme Court provided legal recognition for same-sex marriages in all 50 states. Because tribes are sovereign nations and have a government-to-government relationship, they do not have to comply with this policy change within their membership on tribal lands. Tribes are split on the stance of same-sex marriage. Most tribes do not currently have gender language in their marriage policies, leaving support for same-sex marriages ambiguous. Some tribes have reinforced their definitions of marriage as being between a man and a woman, and a few tribes have passed marriage acts banning same-sex marriage. As of 2015, 11 tribes oppose the legalization of same-sex marriage and 10 tribes support it. Native American LGBT advocates are considering challenging the tribes that do not recognize same-sex marriages under the Indian Civil Rights Act of 1968 and extension of the Bill of Rights to tribal members. This approach is contentious as it may further limit tribal sovereignty and give more power to the federal government.

Native American Trans Experiences

Although some tribal societies have considered the legal implications of same-sex marriages, few have established protective measures for Native American transgendered or gender nonconforming individuals. Bias and discrimination experienced by these individuals permeate all aspects of their lives. In fact, recent studies demonstrate that transgender Native Americans experience bigotry at some of the worst rates. For example, according to a 2012 study, during a 6-month time frame, based on a sample of 350 Native American transgender and gender nonconforming participants, approximately 86% reported harassment, 51% reported physical assault, and 21% reported sexual assault during grades K–12. Suicide rates for transgender Native Americans reached 56%, in comparison with 41% of all study participants. These findings provide insight into the importance of recognizing that Two-Spirit, trans, and gender nonconforming American Indians are significantly ostracized members of both tribal communities and the majority culture. In addition, it would be appropriate for clinicians to consider culturally relevant, trauma-informed, and transgender informed guidelines for treatment. Furthermore, tribal councils might consider consulting the aforementioned research and similar studies in an effort to develop informative policies and tribal codes that could be more supportive of trans individuals' experiences. There are likely regional differences that can inform policy development and implementation within tribal communities (e.g., urban vs. rural areas) and influence access to supportive resources for Native American LBGT community members.

Gender influences the psychology of Native Americans in numerous ways, such as gendered stereotypes and the impacts of stereotypes in the treatment of American Indians and Indigenous people's self-identity. This identity may include gender-based roles and sexual and gender identity as they relate to feelings of connectedness and belonging to tribal communities. These topics are important to keep in mind in the development of American Indians' psychological well-being as well as for clinical providers to consider within the contexts of assessment, diagnosis, and culturally appropriate interventions.

Melissa Tehee and Julii M. Green

See also Cultural Gender Role Norms; Gender Nonconformity and Transgender Issues: Overview; Matriarchy; Multiculturalism and Gender: Overview; Sexual Orientation: Overview; Spirituality and Gender; Women of Color and Discrimination; Worldviews and Gender Research

Further Readings

Fryberg, S. A., Markus, H. R., Oyserman, D., & Stone, J. M. (2008). Of warrior chiefs and Indian princesses: The psychological consequences of American Indian mascots. *Basic and Applied Social Psychology, 30*(3), 208–218.

Garcia Rodriquez, V. (2015, April). Native American tribes split on same-sex marriage. *Christian Examiner.* Retrieved from http://www.christianexaminer.com/article/native.american.reservations.split.on.same.sex.marriage/48715.htm

Indian Country Media Network Staff. (2012, October). *Study: Transgender Native Americans experience discrimination at worst rates.* Verona, NY: Author. Retrieved from http://indiancountrytodaymedianetwork.com/2012/10/12/study-transgender-native-americans-experience-discrimination-worst-rates-139388

LaFromboise, T. D., Heyle, A. M., & Ozer, E. J. (1990). Changing and diverse roles of women in American Indian cultures. *Sex Roles, 22*(7/8), 455–476.

Medicine, B. (2002). Directions in gender research in American Indian societies: Two spirits and other categories. *Online Readings in Psychology and Culture, 3*(1). doi:10.9707/2307-0919.1024

Red Horse, J. (1997). Traditional American Indian family systems. *Family Systems & Health, 15,* 243–250.

Towle, E., & Morgan, L. (2002). Romancing the transgender Native: Rethinking the use of "third gender" concept. *GLQ, 8*(4), 469–497.

Wexler, L. (2009). The importance of identity, history, and culture in the wellbeing of Indigenous youth. *Journal of the History of Childhood and Youth, 2*(2), 267–276.

White, J., Godfrey, J., & Iron Mocassin, B. (2006). American Indian fathering in the Dakota Nation: Use of Akicita as a fatherhood standard. *Fathering, 4*(1), 49–69.

Native Americans and Sexual Orientation

See Two-Spirited People

Native Americans and Transgender Identity

In Native culture, the term *two spirit* refers to someone who is an embodiment of feminine and masculine qualities. Traditionally, Native Americans accepted those with variation in gender identities and expressions, whereas Western cultures adhered to a binary view of gender as male and female. Two-spirit people were often highly respected in spiritual, medicinal, caregiving, and economic roles within their culture. As a result of the colonization of Native people and the acculturation of Christian beliefs, the two-spirit people were silenced but since have been somewhat re-acculturated into Native culture.

Traditional Native Culture

The first record of two-spirit people was reported during European expeditions to North America. Álvar Nunez Cabeza de Vaca, a conquistador who explored what is now Texas and the southwest in 1528 to 1536, noted that he saw men married to men and men who appeared "womanish." He seemed to be disturbed by their female appearance and behaviors, but Cabeza de Vaca also observed that they were armed with bows and arrows, which according to European culture was the domain of men. Cabeza de Vaca lived among Native Americans for many years as a slave and performed work that was common for Native women. Cabeza de Vaca, who was described as very masculine, acknowledged that his gender role was female, as defined by Native culture. He accepted other roles of Native women, such as a trader, and never took part in Native male roles such as hunting.

Cabeza de Vaca had heard prior to his expedition of Native men who appear as women and engage in feminine social and sexual roles. European culture called two-spirit people *berdache*, which is a French term for a passive man in a homosexual relationship or "kept boy." In modern Native culture, *berdache* is controversial and considered pejorative. Within Native culture, two-spirit people were given roles that others could not hold. For example, because they possessed the feminine and masculine spirits, they were considered the negotiators or mediators of their tribal nation.

Will Roscoe, a Native American activist and writer, notes that 160 tribal nations in the United States acknowledged two-spirit people, who were described as man-woman (male bodied with feminine traits, or third gender) in their native languages. Woman-man (female bodied with male traits, or fourth gender) two-spirit people were recognized in fewer tribal nations than man-woman. Notably, man-woman two-spirit people tended to move between genders, whereas woman-man two-spirit people tended to remain men in their gender expression and roles.

Among tribal nations, gender and sexual variations were accepted because of the contributions made by these individuals. In some tribal nations, even more than four genders were recognized. In these tribal nations, specific words were used to describe these variations in gender. For instance, in the Navajo Nation, *nadleehi* ("male bodied") is the term used for someone who is two spirited. These words differ depending on the tribal nation. In the Lakota Nation, it is *winkte* ("male bodied"), *lha'mana* ("male bodied") and *katotse* ("female bodied") in the Zuni Nation, and *agokwa* ("male bodied") and *okitcitakwe* ("female bodied") in the Ojibwe Nation. The term *two spirit* is a modern term that captures the essence of the male-female characteristics that may be embodied within an individual.

It is important to note, however, that modern-day homosexuality did not exist in Native culture. Gender was not linked to biological sex but according to the gender roles with which one aligns oneself. Thus, a woman-man may marry a woman and a man-woman may marry a man and be biologically in a same-sex relationship, but in Native culture their relationship would be based on gender, not sex. Thus, their relationships would be considered with people of the other genders (i.e., male gender and third gender).

In most Western cultures, gender is assigned at birth based on visible biological sex, not on whether traits or preferred behaviors correspond to gender identity. Therefore, if a man is more inclined to female gender traits and behaviors, he may still be considered a man in his culture because of his assigned gender at birth. This gender biological association poses difficulty in a culture, such as in historical European countries, for people whose gender identity does not match their assigned gender at birth. People who have gender/biological sex incongruity are considered transgender in modern-day language. Thereby, the binary gender construct of historical European countries is still being imposed on modern-day U.S. culture, that one must fit into male or female categories. The gender binary may change due to more and more people identifying as gender nonconforming and challenging the gender binary social construct.

How two-spirit people were identified varied in Native culture. Some two-spirit people were instructed through spiritual or supernatural dreams to take on the roles of the other gender, others were identified as two spirit by the gendered tools they were inclined to during childhood, and some chose the other gender as their path. The most recognized two spirit in Native American history was We'wha of the Zuni Nation. We'wha was a skilled weaver and proficient in the Zuni religion. In the 1880s, We'wha spent much time in Washington, D.C., as a representative of the Zuni Nation. She interacted with government officials, demonstrated weaving techniques, and worked with anthropologists at the Smithsonian. In fact, We'wha, who was dubbed a "princess" by newspapers, was believed by those she encountered to be a biological woman even though she was 6 feet tall. Because of the cultural difference in expectations of gender, Europeans and American settlers described berdaches as male whores who were denigrated by others within their tribal nation. Some report that berdaches were among the Native men in battle who engaged in female roles and provided sex to the warriors. In addition, German missionaries reported seeing female-bodied berdaches among the Delaware Nation hunting and forgoing the typical work and lifestyle of Native women.

Colonization of Native Culture

Two-spirit Native Americans were silenced with the colonization of the "New World." Explorers often were disgusted at what they perceived as gender and sexual indiscretions and used this to justify the brutality toward and dehumanization of Native people. For example, Peter Martyr's account of Balboa's 1513 expedition to Panama speaks to the disdain for the gender and sexual variation he saw in Native culture. Martyr reported that Balboa turned his dogs free on 40 Native men to be eaten alive because they were dressed as women or having sexual relationships. Because of his rigid perception of gender as binary and sexuality as procreation-based intimacy, he used this "savage behavior" as a justification for brutality, which more broadly translated to European settlers colonizing Native Americans into the White, Christian, heteronormative way of life.

Through the colonization process, Native Americans were exposed to the Christian view of gender crossing and same-sex relations as deviant behavior. Passive sodomy, or anal sex, was considered effeminate by Europeans and was sometimes used to de-masculinize slaves or those captured during war. Thus, European settlers looked to assimilate Native Americans into their perception of what it means to be European American men and women. After the establishment of the Americas, the newly established U.S. government focused on acculturating Native Americans into European American culture.

From 1880 to 1930, Native American children were forced to attend boarding schools in various parts of the United States to learn subjects and values deemed appropriate by the dominant White culture. Many of these children were separated from their families by hundreds and thousands of miles. Boarding school Native children were forced to speak English, dress in European American clothing, and attend Christian churches. They also were punished harshly for speaking their Native language or engaging in Native traditions. Native children died from poor nutrition and harsh conditions, including hard labor for White families during the summer; the reported incidents of child physical and sexual abuse highlight the suffering experienced at these boarding schools.

The first boarding school was established in Carlisle, Pennsylvania, in 1879; it was called the Carlisle Indian Industrial School. Boys were educated in vocational areas and girls in domestic tasks that followed the patriarchal, gendered stratification of European American culture. Through this acculturation process, two-spirit people were silenced. European American acculturation and Christian teachings taught Native children that sexual and gender variation went against the "order of nature and God."

With the European American acculturation and forced movement onto reservations, the negative direct and indirect effects of "civilizing" Native Americans have been reported in two-spirit people. Teresa Evans-Campbell and colleagues reported that Native American two-spirit people who attended boarding school had higher levels of alcohol and drug use and more suicide attempts than two-spirit people who did not attend boarding school. In addition, those who were raised by someone who attended boarding school reported higher levels of anxiety, posttraumatic stress symptoms, and suicidal ideation than those who were not raised by someone who attended boarding school. Researchers and practitioners suggest that the experiences in Native American boarding schools have lasting effects that are intergenerationally transferred to others. These negative effects, coupled with the forced abandonment of Native culture and decreased acceptance of two-spirit people in Native culture, lead to marginalization from both the Native and the European American cultures.

Contemporary Two-Spirit People

Since the Spanish exploration and the European American acculturation of Native Americans began, Native two-spirit people have endured many obstacles, including racism, heterosexism, and transphobia. Efforts have been made to repair some of the damage that was inflicted on Native Americans, although it is likely that true reparations will never cover the losses and suffering they and their culture experienced. Overall, the lack of knowledge surrounding the two-spirit people in Native culture remains. However, tribal nations have recently recognized or continue to recognize the significance of two-spirit people within their communities.

In the past 150 years, the two-spirit communities have been oppressed within the Native and European American communities. Not only has the acculturation of Native people into European American lifestyles been influential in this oppression, but acculturation over generations has created a Native culture that became unaccepting of gender variance. However, not all tribal nations followed this intolerant path. Sabine Lang explained that some two-spirit people went underground and were only known, and in some cases were unknown, to their tribal nation, whereas some tribal nations follow the traditional third- and fourth-gender designation and encourage people to follow their chosen gender.

Following one's gender path in modern-day America is difficult for Native people due to capitalism and the loss of specific male and female gender roles within their Native culture. However, it is common for two-spirit people to choose occupations that are largely taken up by people of the other gender. Occupational examples for man-woman two spirits include nursing and social work, and firefighting and construction work may be chosen occupations for woman-man two spirits. The construction of identity according to gender typically occurs on reservations where third and fourth genders are accepted or tolerated. Two-spirit people who may or may not live on reservations may refer to themselves using terminology that is more common in mainstream America, such as *gay* or *lesbian*, which focuses on same-sex or same-gender relationships.

Homophobia on and off reservations is an issue resulting from influences of acculturation from White, Christian, European American culture. However, it is noted that there are gay and lesbian couples living on reservations without incident. It appears that these relationships are not openly discussed with others in the community, but notably, these couples seem to be accepted within the community, and they purposely do not set themselves apart from others to maintain Native solidarity and connectedness. On some reservations, however, there are reports of gay and lesbian people being thrown off the reservation and disowned by their tribal nation because of their sexual identity.

Because of the oppression faced by two-spirit people related to race and gender and/or sexual identity, issues related to mental and physical health are of concern. Jane Simoni and colleagues reported that Native American two-spirit men have higher levels of victimization and lifetime HIV risk-taking behaviors than heterosexual Native American men. Other researchers have found that two-spirit women tend to be more vulnerable to childhood and adulthood sexual abuse or assault than their other-race peers. In addition, Native two-spirit people are more likely to report anxiety and posttraumatic stress than Native heterosexual people. There is no doubt that oppression has consequences for physical and mental health outcomes in Native American two-spirit people.

Violence committed against two-spirit or transgender people also is a concern in modern society. In 2001, Fred Martinez, a two-spirit teen, was brutally murdered by an 18-year-old in the town of Cortez, Colorado. After his death, more education surrounding two-spirit people emerged from various organizations in the western states, and more non-Native communities were educated about the two-spirit people. In May 2011, an Independent Lens film aired on PBS (Public Broadcasting Service) that told the story of Fred Martinez and two-spirit people in Native culture. In addition, two-spirit organizations have been surfacing to embrace two-spirit Native people and their families. Two such organizations are the East Coast Two-Spirit Society and Northwest Two-Spirit Society. These organizations provide educational programming and advocacy for two-spirit people.

Through two-spirit organizations in North America, Native people are slowly reclaiming acceptance of the nonbinary expressions of gender they once had in their tribal nations. In fact, it was in 1990 in Winnipeg, Canada, that the term *two spirit* was coined and adopted at the intertribal Native American/First Nations gay and lesbian conference. The term *two spirit* was adopted to distance themselves from European American and White terms that inaccurately described them as berdache and gay or lesbian. The efforts of Native American two-spirit organizations are making strides in bringing reverence and honor back to two-spirit Native Americans within their Native culture.

Catherine J. Massey

See also Colonialism and Gender; Native Americans and Gender; Two-Spirited People

Further Readings

Morgensen, S. L. (2011). *Spaces between us: Queer settler colonialism and Indigenous decolonization.* Minneapolis: University of Minnesota Press.

Roscoe, W. (2000). *Changing ones.* New York, NY: Palgrave Macmillan.

Slater, S., & Yarbrough, F. A. (Eds.). (2012). *Gender and sexuality in Indigenous North America, 1400–1850.* Columbia: University of South Carolina Press.

Nature Versus Nurture

The nature versus nurture debate is one that has long been present in many subfields within psychology—particularly in developmental psychology. For example, developmental psychologists have debated whether nature (a person's biological inheritance, especially his or her genes) or nurture (a person's environmental and social experiences) is responsible for intellectual ability, musical skill, and even height and weight. This debate includes gender and focuses on the question of whether nature or nurture has a greater impact on, for example, a person's gender development, gender performance, and gender identity. It is important to note that the focus of this entry is on gender, which is usually defined as a social and cultural construct (i.e., the roles and performances expected of people based on their gender identity), and not on sex, which is viewed as a biological construct (i.e., a person's chromosomes, gonads, hormones, genitalia, and secondary sex characteristics, which determine classification as male or female).

The easiest and most basic answer to the nature versus nurture debate is that it is not nature *or* nurture that influences a person's psychology, including his or her gender, but rather nature *and* nurture, working together and influencing each other. Although it might seem obvious to assume that nurture (or the environment) influences a person's gender and nature (or genetics) influences a person's sex, it is important to understand how nature and nurture interact with each other in various ways and on various levels to influence a person's gender. The environment and a person's biological characteristics interact in many different areas, such as genetics and epigenetics, puberty and hormones, culture, socialization, and adult role preparation. These areas of interaction between nature and nurture are discussed in the following paragraphs. This entry concludes with a discussion on thinking about gender as a complex interaction between biological and environmental influences.

Genetics and Epigenetics

Genes and Chromosomes

In addition to genitalia, chromosomes differentiate, and are sometimes used to denote, biological sex. Typically, biological females have two of the same type of sex chromosomes (XX), and biological males have two different sex chromosomes

(XY). These chromosomes not only determine biological sex but are also linked to genes that influence other aspects of a person's genotype (e.g., his or her genetic makeup) and phenotype (e.g., the way his or her genes are expressed after interacting with the environment). For example, the genes related to issues such as certain types of color blindness and muscular dystrophy are typically found only in males. These genes and chromosomes, which would fall under the nature side of the debate, affect biological sex rather than gender. Even though there are phenotypical issues related to these genes and chromosomes, such as the sex-linked issues mentioned earlier, few would claim that these genes play a significant or solitary role in determining a person's gender. Instead, any effect that sex chromosomes might have on an individual's gender will be greatly influenced by the interactions between the person's genes and the environment.

Epigenetics

One way in which a person's phenotype can be influenced by his or her environment is explained by the emerging science of epigenetics. Epigenetics refers to the way in which environmental variables influence the expression of genetic material. In other words, genes can be "activated" or not, and can be understood differently by other cells, depending on what has happened or is happening in a person's environment. Epigenetic research mostly focuses on issues related to disease and disorders, such as cancer. However, some research has indicated that epigenetic influences can affect gene imprinting, which refers to when certain genes are activated or not in sperm and ova. These influences are then replicated when cells begin to divide after conception—possibly leading to differences in brain structure based on sex. Interestingly, these epigenetic influences seem to lead to differences in sex-based hormones (e.g., testosterone), which may be one of the stronger influences on sex differences in the brain. It is important to keep in mind, though, that these epigenetically influenced sex differences do not necessarily lead to differences in gender identity, the performance of gender roles, or gender differences in cognitive or neurological ability. As stated earlier, any epigenetic-based impact on a person's gender will be influenced by an interaction with that person's social, cultural, and physical environment.

Puberty and Hormones

Puberty

Many of the physical characteristics that are associated with males and females develop and become apparent through the process of puberty. Most people, at least in Western societies, tend to begin puberty in early adolescence. The changes that occur during puberty include growth spurts, the development of primary sex characteristics (i.e., parts of the body necessary for reproduction, e.g., the penis and vulva) and secondary sex characteristics (e.g., breasts or facial hair), menarche (i.e., a female's first menstruation), and shifts in the body's fat-to-muscle ratio. Although many societies associate these physical and biological changes with gender, this is not necessarily the case. An individual's gender identity could very well stem from the reproductive aspects of his or her postpuberty body. However, while many people develop a gender identity that matches with society's expectation for their biological sex, this is not always the case—and when it is the case, it is a result of socialization processes (described later in this entry) as well as any biological influences.

Hormones

The onset of puberty is triggered by the release of hormones specific to the development of gonads in both males and females. Specifically, gonadotropin-releasing hormone is released by the hypothalamus, and it motivates the pituitary gland to release two important gonadotropins—follicle-stimulating hormone and luteinizing hormone. These two gonadotropins then influence the sex glands (i.e., ovaries in females and testes in males) to release sex hormones, the best known being estradiol (a type of estrogen) and testosterone. While both sex hormones are present in both females and males, the levels are drastically different. For example, during puberty the amount of estrogen in females increases more than 5 times, and the amount of testosterone in males increases more than 15 times. Although the increased amounts of these sex hormones play a major role in the process of puberty and the development of sex characteristics in both sexes, they have also been linked to different behavior patterns. For example, increased amounts of testosterone have been associated with higher levels of aggression and risk taking—even in domains such as financial decision making. Because testosterone levels tend to be higher in postpubescent males than in females, it seems logical that we tend to observe higher levels of aggression and risk taking in men than in women. However, as with the other biological influences discussed earlier, social and cultural expectations and socialization will influence how the sex hormones affect a person's behavior.

Culture, Socialization, and Role Preparation

The biologically based aspects of sex likely have an impact on an individual's gender identity and performance of gender roles. However, any influence that biology has on a person's gender is manifested through a complex interaction with various social, cultural, environmental, and other contextual factors. The way a person's culture defines gender and gender roles, how those roles and expectations are communicated, and how they are socialized all have a strong influence on that person's gender.

Nonbinary Gender

Perhaps the best evidence for the cultural and social construction of gender is the fact that many cultures do not define gender in a binary fashion. In other words, these cultures do not expect that biological sex will map onto gender in a precise or exact manner, and they might in fact have more than two categories that are acceptable as gender identities. One of the best known of these situations comes from various American Indian cultures. Sometimes referred to as people with two spirits (and previously referred to as *berdache*, though this term is considered pejorative and has fallen out of favor), these individuals often did not take on themselves the gender identity or roles usually assigned to their sex, nor did they take on all of the roles assigned to the opposite sex. Instead, they identified (and were often identified by their kin and tribe) as a third (and, in some instances, fourth) gender category. These individuals often wear specific clothing and participate in behaviors designated as appropriate for their gender. The existence of cultures such as these and others that do not define gender in a binary way is strong evidence for the social and cultural influence on a person's gender identity and performance of gender roles, underscoring how people's biological sex is not synonymous with their gender.

Gender Intensification Hypothesis

One way in which people are socialized, or shaped, to exhibit culturally appropriate gendered behavior is explained by the gender intensification hypothesis, as proposed by John P. Hill and Mary Ellen Lynch. They argue that as children begin the process of puberty and become adolescents, other members of their society and cultural group increase the intensification and pressure used to socialize the adolescent into culturally appropriate gendered behavior. This increased and intensified expectation that adolescents engage in culturally defined appropriate gender behavior can take various forms, such as withdrawing girls from formal schooling, expecting boys to begin working to help support the family, or demanding that boys and girls wear specific clothing and refrain from interacting with members of the opposite sex. This intensification of expectations is usually accompanied by punishments for violations of appropriate gender behavior. The punishment can be emotional, physical, or social but is often successful in socializing the adolescent to behave in culturally acceptable ways. The gender intensification hypothesis provides an excellent example of how culture and society interact with biology to create expectations for behavior deemed gender appropriate. While both biology and intensified cultural expectations may influence a person's gender identity and the performance of gender roles, neither factor functions in isolation.

Flexibility in Socialization

In addition to gender roles and expectations being socialized, and that socialization intensifying in adolescence, the sexes are socialized differently. For example, in most cultures, males are provided more flexibility and freedom as they develop into what their cultures define as men, whereas females are usually more restricted once they begin puberty and start developing into what their culture defines as a woman. Much of the decision about this level of restrictiveness is based on the biological sex of the child, which leads to differential treatment as adolescents, thus influencing gender identity and the performance of gender roles.

One example of the ways in which males and females are socialized differently into culturally appropriate gender roles is the *rite of passage*. A rite of passage is usually a formalized ceremony that a culture uses to mark a person's transition from childhood to adulthood. Rites of passage vary from culture to culture, but they are often different for males and females and are usually based on the person's biological sex. For instance, in some cultures, girls and boys are circumcised (or genitally mutilated) on reaching puberty, or they are expected to engage in other gender appropriate behaviors, such as hunting, exploring, herding, dancing, or construction. The different rites of passage required for males and females, and the different levels of flexibility allowed as adolescents develop into adults, provide further evidence that nurture, via cultural and social expectations, interacts with biology to influence a person's gender.

It is clear that the debate about whether nature or nurture is responsible for a person's gender suggests an incorrect dichotomy. Instead, an individual's gender is the result of a complex and intricate interaction between nature *and* nurture, with neither playing a solitary role. As discussed herein, genetics, epigenetics, hormones, cultural expectations, the intensification of socialization, and the amount of flexibility (or lack thereof) allowed to adolescents all interact to influence the development of a person's gender. This process always happens within a cultural and social context and often (though not always) leads to gender identities and performances of gender roles that have been deemed acceptable and appropriate by the person's culture.

Brien K. Ashdown

See also Adolescence and Gender: Overview; Cross-Cultural Differences in Gender; Gender Identity; Gender Roles: Overview; Puberty

Further Readings

Callender, C., Kochems, L. M., Bleibtreu-Ehrenberg, G., Broch, H. B., Brown, J. K., Datan, N., . . . Strathern, A. (1983). The North American berdache. *Current Anthropology, 24*(4), 443–470.

Chung, W. C., & Auger, A. P. (2013). Gender differences in neurodevelopment and epigenetics. *Pfügers Archiv—European Journal of Physiology, 465,* 573–584. doi:10.1007/s00424-013-1258-4

Hill, J. P., & Lynch, M. E. (1983). The intensification of gender-related role expectations during early adolescence. In J. Brooks-Gunn & A. C. Petersen (Eds.), *Girls at puberty: Biological and psychosocial perspectives* (pp. 201–228). New York, NY: Plenum Press.

Sapienza, P., Zingales, L., & Maestrpieri, D. (2009). Gender differences in financial risk aversion and career choices are affected by testosterone. *Proceedings of the National Academy of Sciences, 106,* 15268–15273. doi:10.1073/pnas.0907352106

Neofeminism

Neofeminism describes a body of feminist legal scholarship and ideas (emerging roughly in the late 1990s) that is concerned with gender justice but critical of many tenets of mainstream or second-wave feminism (the popular feminist theories of the 1960s through mid-1980s). There are a variety of second-wave feminist theories espousing heterodox views of the female condition and how to achieve equality, but three particular theories predominate: (1) liberal feminism, (2) cultural feminism, and (3) dominance feminism. Since the 1970s, feminist legal theorists have often identified with one of these three camps and debated which best describes and addresses women's subordination. Since the mid-1990s, a new generation of legal scholars has focused on how second-wave feminism more generally affects law and policy, for better or worse, and the problems common to the second-wave theories, despite and perhaps owing to their contradictory natures. Neofeminist legal scholars are principally concerned with the subordination of women but critical of feminism's tendency to essentialize the female (and male) experience; turn a blind eye to race, class, and other marginalized statuses; and rely on authoritarian criminal policies. The term *neofeminism* is deliberately political and intended to help revitalize a feminism that many view as dead, outmoded, or ideologically captured by the right.

This entry explores *neofeminism*, both as a descriptive term and as a call to political and scholarly action. It first outlines the dominant theories of second-wave feminism. Next, it describes neofeminists' identification and critique of the second-wave orthodoxies. Third, the essay illustrates the operation of neofeminist theory in domestic violence law and policy and explores how neofeminist analysis might similarly inform the current (post-2013) campus sexual assault discussion.

Second-Wave Feminism

The term *second-wave feminism* describes the collective feminist theories that emerged during the women's and equal rights movements of the 1960s through the mid-1980s. During that quarter-century period, feminist theory, including feminist legal theory, ranged from purely liberal philosophy concerned with equal opportunity to radical theory conceiving male supremacy as a perfect structural system of oppression. This part concentrates on the theories that dominate legal scholars' analyses of second-wave feminism—liberal, cultural, and dominance.

Liberal feminism is the theory of "women's lib" and the equal rights era, exemplified by Betty Freidan's (1971) *The Feminine Mystique*. Liberal feminism decries the relegation of women to the realm of bored housewife-dom and insists that women should have equal opportunity to compete against men in the workplace. However, liberal feminism does not address the deep structures and culture that constrain women's choices, despite equal opportunity, and holds little tolerance for reforms that address women's unique status. For example, when it comes to pregnant women in the workplace, liberal feminists call primarily for nondiscrimination (treating pregnant women like men). They justify pregnancy leave by arguing that such leave is analogous to disability leave granted to men (treating pregnant women like injured men). Liberal feminism embraces individual rights, choice, and consent (as in rape law). Moreover, liberal feminism, like liberalism in general, largely accepts the public-private distinction and concerns itself more with whether women have the opportunity to engage in public economic life than with regulating private family labor.

The basic premise of cultural (or relational) feminism is that women have a different culture, ethic, language, and even epistemology from men, which involves prioritizing relationships over competition and being caring rather than dominating. Cultural feminism grew out of sociologist Carol Gilligan's (1982) qualitative studies of women, described in her foundational book *In a Different Voice*. From this, feminist legal theorists normatively argued that law and policy, rather than prioritizing competing on men's terms outside the home, should value and regulate domestic labor and reconfigure the workplace to be more "maternalist." Law professor Robin West, for example, has posited a feminist, maternalist (and humanist) moral theory that prioritizes caring and communitarianism. The second wave of feminism is, in many ways, characterized by the clash between liberal feminists, who viewed cultural feminism as embracing gender stereotypes and separate spheres, and cultural feminists, who viewed liberal feminism as glorifying the inherently male workplace and relegating domestic labor to a hidden, subordinate, unregulated realm.

In the late 1970s, a group of feminists began publicizing the sexual subordination of women through workplace sexual harassment, rape, prostitution, and pornography and formulating a forceful response. The primary figures of dominance or radical feminism were Andrea Dworkin, who popularized the theory through political activism, and Catharine MacKinnon, who penned law reform proposals and legal scholarship. Among dominance feminism's many achievements were anti–sexual harassment laws and an unimplemented but culturally significant antipornography ordinance. Dominance feminism, as MacKinnon articulates it, departs significantly from both liberal and cultural feminism. She argues that given rampant, deeply embedded male supremacy, liberal feminism's call for equal rights and opportunities will simply reaffirm women's subordination. Dominance feminism regards cultural feminism as "false consciousness," asserting that it affirms woman's moral and epistemic conditions, which are necessarily products of oppression.

For dominance feminists, the key to understanding women's subordination is recognizing the ways in which social, legal, political, and cultural structures permit men to dominate women and reforming those structures to reverse the power balance. Dominance feminists identify sex as the primary tool of male supremacy and sexual oppression as constitutive of female identity. Thus, a priority of dominance feminism is eradicating sexual subordination, if not much of sex, even by authoritarian and violent state regulation.

The Critique of Second-Wave Feminism

The 1990s witnessed the dawn of a significant internal critique of second-wave feminism. Incorporating critical theories such as Marxist feminism, queer theory, critical race theory, and critical race feminism, progressive feminist scholars began to document and resist some of the principles and policies (collectively called *orthodoxies*) of mainstream feminist theory. This part of the entry describes those efforts.

The most frequently critiqued aspect of second-wave feminism is its presumption that there is an essential female experience. In liberal feminism, women desire liberation through nondomestic work. Cultural feminists, by contrast, hold that women are predisposed toward domesticity. The unifying female conditions in dominance feminism are sexual subordination and false consciousness. According to critics, second-wave feminist camps are locked in an intractable battle over which group has correctly described women's innate condition, when, in fact, women's experiences intersect and diverge depending on the individual and the context. Queer and critical race theorists reject second-wave feminism's assumption of a singular female experience and highlight the diversity in women's socioeconomic status, interest in sex and reproduction, domesticity, and view of state power, among others.

Critics also object to second-wave feminism's reductive views of good and bad. In liberal feminism, bad is housewife-dom and good is the workplace. Cultural feminists regard the primary problem as the uncaring culture of men and the solution as the caring culture of women. Dominance feminists see dominating men as the source of all evil and thus advocate eradicating male sexual, economic, and social privilege through any means necessary. To collapse the world of female subordination to such flattened dichotomies, these theories espoused hackneyed visions of women and men. More even than essentializing women, second-wave feminism essentialized men. For second wavers, especially dominance feminists, men occupied the role of enemy number one—the sole entity responsible for female subordination. In turn, despite the recognition of the deeply embedded and hidden nature of patriarchy, second-wave feminists tended to describe male dominance in hyperbolic terms and focus on the criminal or sexually outrageous behavior of bad men.

Attributing women's inequality to (bad) men naturally led to proposals for the state to control male behavior. But second-wave activism in the 1970s and 1980s coincided with other phenomena in U.S. law and society such as long-standing puritanical views of sex, the media-driven repulsion for deviant sexuality, and a burgeoning war on crime. Within this climate, second-wave law reform often manifested as prohibitive laws (i.e., sexual harassment law) and criminalization (i.e., tougher punishment for rape and domestic violence) rather than distributive reforms and economic programs. Dominance feminists openly embraced the authority of the state, whereas liberals repressed their wariness of state action when it came to punishment of "true" criminals. Even cultural feminists were willing to reject caring, nonviolence, and cooperation in their proposals for how the state should treat male offenders. In light of modern-day mass incarceration, the racist and masculinist nature of police power, and the rise of criminal law as a main governance institution (what Bernard Harcourt terms *neoliberal penality*), many critical feminists now query whether second-wave feminism's faith in criminal law and the state was ultimately misplaced.

Finally, neofeminists have highlighted and critiqued second-wave feminism's wholesale rejection of privacy. Dominance feminism is clear in its condemnation of any argument that unequal gender relationships or male-dominating behaviors should be immune from government regulation because they are private. Cultural feminism abandons the glorification of domesticity when it involves direct violence and coercion. Liberals tolerate selective impositions on privacy to enforce prevailing notions of sexuality and domestic order, even within their privacy-protecting philosophy. In response, feminist critics have objected to the second-wave's relentless focus on criminalizing sex, asserting that it comes dangerously close to morality policing. In addition, scholars highlight the negative consequences attendant on feminism opening the family home's door to the police and the regulatory state.

Neofeminism in Action

Neofeminist analysis is apparent in current feminist legal scholarship on domestic violence. Second-wave feminist theorizing on domestic violence from the 1970s through the 1990s often characterized the social problem of domestic violence as a product of criminal underenforcement. Domestic violence reformers regularly called for increased arrests, prosecution, and incarceration of male abusers regardless of the wishes and sometimes interests of victim. Domestic violence reformers discounted the voices of nonprosecutorial victims by characterizing them as coercively controlled, perpetually threatened, or, worse, psychologically defective. The feminist intervention proved incredibly generative, with every state modifying its statutory regime to encourage or mandate arrest and many prosecutor's offices adopting no-drop policies.

Neofeminist scholars pushed back against domestic violence reform, contending that it has not uniformly improved the lives of marginalized women but has, instead, granted enormous authority to the penal system and re-envisioned feminism's relation to the state. Neofeminist writings expose domestic violence reform's adoption and reification of essentialist characterizations of abused women and abusers. Reform has objectified women as totally controlled, incapable of meaningful choice, and invariably served by harsh prosecution. It conceived of batterers as empowered, culpable, evil, and deterred only by harsh punishment. These reductionist views of domestic violence victims and perpetrators, according to neofeminist critics, are often inaccurate and create racial disparities. Critics assert that reform discourse renders invisible minority women victims, who are viewed as passive and weak, and renders hypervisible minority men, who are considered inherently violent.

Relatedly, neofeminist scholars express concern that the prosecutorial/separation model marginalizes the experiences of minority, immigrant, and poor women who do not favor incarceration of and separation from domestic partners. They note that abuse victims often engage in complicated calculi, balancing the harm of battering against the social, emotional, and pecuniary benefits of staying with the partner, taking into account the possibility of temporary relief through selective utilization of criminal and civil processes. Neofeminists caution against an unreflective embrace of criminal law and maintain that when a woman's choice not to prosecute is preceded by a subordinating factor, such as poverty, immigrant status, or lack of child support, the solution is not to force prosecution but to help alleviate the subordinating conditions. Indeed, criminalization presumes that domestic violence is a product of individual evil men and not of women's structural inequality or certain men's racial and economic marginalization. As a result, society's general condemnation of domestic violence has not translated into social welfare. Finally, domestic violence reform's explosion of the public/private distinction may have produced consequences that feminists did not anticipate and might not want. Experts like Jeannie Suk note that the misdemeanor domestic violence system empowers the government to reorder nearly all aspects of the disordered home. In the end, as the domestic violence story illustrates, the neofeminist perspective sheds a skeptical light on feminist law reform proposals that define women as victims and call for increased criminalization within the penal state.

Neofeminists can add a voice to the campus sexual assault conversation that tempers a wave of feminist activism likely to produce harsh prohibitive laws and cultural norms that are difficult to reverse. Beginning in late 2013, media outlets and the government began to publicize and address an "epidemic" of campus sexual assault. Since then, increased administrative and university regulatory policy has been generated. Universities are "modernizing" their disciplinary systems to adopt expansive definitions of rape (sex without affirmative consent), ratchet down due process, and express a zero-tolerance attitude toward rapists and anyone who enables "rape culture."

These events appear to be propelled by a revitalized brand of feminism, which famed second-wave feminist Susan Brownmiller calls the fourth wave of feminism but others have termed *trauma feminism*. Several empirical contentions animate trauma feminism, including that a substantial percentage of women have experienced trauma, that such trauma is primarily related to sex, that trauma is constitutive of women's identity, and that women are perpetually at risk for emotional distress when trauma is "triggered." Like cultural feminism, trauma feminism posits a uniquely emotional women's experience, yet this experience is not to be celebrated but regarded as unfortunate and avoidable. Trauma feminism thus shares space with dominance feminism in regarding the female condition as one of subordination. Unlike dominance feminism, however, trauma feminism's main prescription is not reversing the gender hierarchy through punitive intervention, although it certainly endorses punishment of traumatizers. Rather, trauma feminism calls foremost for therapy, self-care, identifying triggers, creating social practices for trauma avoidance (i.e., bystander intervention), and reporting.

Neofeminism might provide a critical perspective on campus sexual assault policy that is lacking. Although fully maintaining that rape is terrible and that women disproportionately suffer from botched sex, a neofeminist might question trauma feminism's essentialist assumptions, cultural messages, and punitive proposals. A neofeminist framework would create space for feminist scholars to question some of the dogmas of campus rape reform without running the risk of being cast as an anti-feminist in league with sexist rapists. With this space opened up, feminists might critically interrogate the messages that campus rape reform sends about college sexual encounters and young women's relation to sexuality. Feminists might question the desirability of constructing drunk sex as a gendered traumatic event and pushing this construction on female students who are still forming their senses of self, politics, and sexuality. Feminists might attempt to predict or trace the distributional effects of punitive reform by analyzing the winners and losers, the role of race, the effects on speech (particularly alternative, sex-positive, leftist speech), and whether such reform liberates young women or instills a new chastity.

Aya Gruber

See also Critical Race Feminism; Feminism: Overview; First-Wave Feminism; Second-Wave Feminism

Further Readings

Brownmiller, S. (1975). *Against our will.* New York, NY: Simon & Schuster.

Friedan, B. (1971). *The feminine mystique.* New York, NY: W. W. Norton.

Gilligan, C. (1982). *In a different voice.* Cambridge, MA: Harvard University Press.

Gruber, A. (2007). The feminist war on crime. *Iowa Law Review, 42,* 741–833.

Gruber, A. (2013). Neofeminism. *Houston Law Review, 50,* 1325–1390.

Halley, J. E. (2006). *Split decisions: How and why to take a break from feminism.* Princeton, NJ: Princeton University Press.

Harris, A. (1990). Race and essentialism in feminist legal theory. *Stanford Law Review, 42,* 581–616.

MacKinnon, C. A. (1989). *Toward a feminist theory of the state.* Cambridge, MA: Harvard University Press.

Suk, J. (2009). *At home in the law: How the domestic violence revolution is transforming privacy.* New Haven, CT: Yale University Press.

West, R. (1988). Jurisprudence and gender. *University of Chicago Law Review, 55,* 1–72.

NEUROFEMINISM

Psychologist Cordelia Fine coined the term *neurosexism* to describe contemporary sex difference research in neuroscience and psychology. According to Fine (2008), neurosexism "cloaks old-fashioned sexism in the respectable and authoritative language of neuroscience" (p. 69). Feminist criticisms of this research can therefore be described as neurofeminism; just as feminism as a social movement arose in response to sexism, and attempts to identify and overcome sexist beliefs and practices, neurofeminism can be understood as providing a similar antidote to neurosexist research. Neurofeminist work includes both critical work that examines neuroscience research and also empirical neuroscience research that challenges the underlying assumptions of sexist research and/or offers an explicitly feminist alternative.

Neurosexist Research

Feminist scholars in both the sciences and the humanities have produced a large literature criticizing research on sex/gender differences in the brain. In some cases, the primary problem has been that the research is androcentric (male centered); it considers women only in terms of their differences from men or, more commonly, ignores women altogether. Until recently, this has been common practice in the biomedical sciences, where, for example, both human and animal research investigating physiological processes has used only male subjects. This decision has been justified on the basis of two contradictory assumptions: first, that hormone cycles in females will complicate research studies or confound their results and, second, that the knowledge of male physiology obtained from these studies can be readily applied to understanding female physiology.

The cognitive and behavioral sciences, unlike the biomedical sciences, have a long history of including both women and men and, frequently, of searching for differences between them. The primary focus of feminist critique here has been that the research has often been sexist rather than androcentric; its comparisons of women and men have tended to reflect, and to reinforce, gender stereotypes. In the early days of psychology, the sexism of this science was often explicit. For example, during the late 19th century, scientists sought to find sex differences in the brain (mainly differences in the size of the whole brain or of some part of it) that would explain women's inferior intelligence and their resulting inability to benefit from higher education or to participate in politics. Despite failing to find such a difference, these scientists never considered the possibility that the intelligence difference they were trying to explain did not actually exist.

Contemporary research does not tend to be explicitly sexist; however, it is still frequently influenced by sexist assumptions. For example, it is more common to talk about the different strengths and abilities of women and men than to assert the superiority of male characteristics. Yet the strengths assigned to each sex reflect gender stereotypes: Men have superior visuospatial and mathematical skills (explaining why they are better suited to careers in engineering and computer science), whereas women are better at communication and more able to read others' emotions (and therefore are better qualified to work in the "caring" professions). A variation on this approach suggests that, because of their neural differences, women and men have different interests and therefore develop these gendered abilities, neatly avoiding the suggestion that women are incapable of developing "masculine" skills. But because sex differences in interests are still seen as a natural (and normal) result of differences in the brain, and because our society still values engineers more highly than kindergarten teachers, feminists have argued that the overt sexism of earlier research has merely become more subtle.

Criticisms of Neurosexist Research

A number of different criticisms have been raised against research that investigates (and purports to find) neural or cognitive differences between women and men. First, feminist critics have argued that it is debatable whether there really *are* differences. For example, a number of studies have been published that report sex/gender differences in the size and/or shape of the corpus callosum, a thick band of fibers that connects the two cerebral hemispheres of the brain, but a meta-analysis of this research concluded that there were no differences. Moreover, even if the research does support the claim that a specific anatomical, physiological, or behavioral difference exists, this may be the result of publication bias: Studies that show a statistically significant result are more likely to be published than those with null results.

A second line of criticism addresses the interpretation of neural differences. Even if researchers show that there is a structural or functional difference in the brains of women versus men, the behavioral significance of these differences is not yet clear. Given that, in general, there is great variability in brain size, shape, and function, it has been suggested that there are many ways in which a group of research participants (or of brains) could be divided into two groups and compared, and that some of these comparisons are quite likely to reach statistical significance. Sex is perceived by many researchers as a logical way to divide a group of research subjects, so researchers are quite likely to conduct an analysis that compares women and men, even in studies that do not have the primary aim of examining sex differences. A subset of these studies will actually find sex differences, but this does not mean that the importance of these differences for understanding cognition is readily understood. For example, one major difference (on average) between women's and men's brains is their size; women's brains, like their bodies, tend to be smaller. Thus, it has been suggested that the apparent differences between the sexes may actually reflect a difference in size—larger brains require different "wiring" to connect areas of the brain, and therefore, there will also be some differences in the way the brain functions to perform cognitive tasks.

A third source of controversy has to do with the cause of the structural or functional differences. One influential explanation for sex differences in the brain is furnished by brain organization theory. According to this theory, during fetal development, the brain is exposed to sex hormones that permanently influence (or organize) the brain. Because male and female fetuses are exposed to different levels of these hormones, their brains end up having structural (and therefore functional) differences. Initially, the theory posited that what was most important was the amount of testosterone to which the developing brain was exposed; testosterone "masculinized" the brain. The female brain, exposed only to low levels of testosterone, was the "default" pattern. Thus, males who, for some reason, had lower levels of testosterone exposure during development would have a "female" brain, and females exposed to higher than normal levels of fetal testosterone would have a more "male" brain. More recently, the theory has been revised to acknowledge that "female" sex hormones also influence the brain, but by and large, the theory has not changed over the 60-plus years of its existence.

According to brain organization theory, sex differences in brain structure lead to functional differences, which in turn lead to sex differences in behavior, abilities, and characteristics. The theory has therefore been criticized for promoting a very strict form of biological determinism: Sex differences in chromosomes lead to the production of different levels of sex hormones, which lead to sex differences in the brain, which, in turn, lead to sex differences in behavior. Feminists have pointed out that, on this account, there is no significant room for sex differences in experience, especially in early socialization, to play a role in brain development or to explain any existing behavioral or character differences between women and men. Moreover, even if it is the case that fetal hormone levels affect the developing brain differently in male and female fetuses, it is not inevitable that there will be corresponding differences in cognition and behavior. Geert J. de Vries has suggested that the observed anatomical differences between women's and men's brains actually serve to *prevent* behavioral differences by compensating for the effects of differential exposure to hormones during fetal development.

Rebecca Jordan-Young has published an extensive criticism of the empirical evidence given in support of brain organization theory, arguing that what looks at first, and from a distance, like an impressive and sizable collection of solid evidence for the theory turns out on closer inspection to be much more equivocal in its support. Moreover, later studies drawing on the overarching framework of brain organization theory took the earlier studies as confirming evidence in support of their own conclusions, despite important differences in variables such as the behaviors measured, the operational definitions used to define the behaviors, and even the species being studied (e.g., human, rodent). Jordan-Young concludes that the theory is actually not very well supported.

Jordan-Young's work also exemplifies another important characteristic of much feminist criticism of sexist neuroscience research: It frequently involves close examination of the research, including the kinds of hypotheses that are tested, the experimental methods and statistical analyses used, and the conclusions that are drawn on the basis of the data. This kind of fine-grained analysis has identified a number of problems that recur in various eras and areas of research. These problems include using dubious methods for measuring differences (and the switch to different methods when the original ones do not uncover the expected results), drawing conclusions that are not supported by the evidence, relying on gender stereotypes to both motivate the research and bridge the gap between the evidence and conclusions, and using this deeply flawed research to justify sexist social practices.

Alternative Feminist Approach

Many of the critics engaged in this kind of analysis are themselves neuroscientists or psychologists, or scholars in the humanities with training in the sciences, a point that their own critics may fail to recognize. In fact, some feminist neuroscientists are beginning to develop an alternative, explicitly feminist neuroscience. These researchers may draw on feminist theory in designing their experiments or may deliberately challenge the sexist aspects of existing research that have been identified by previous feminist critics. For example, they may start from the assumption that (contra the dominant framework of biological determinism) experience can cause important differences in brain structure and function. This approach not only allows early socialization to play an important role in the development both of the brain and of gender, it also emphasizes neural plasticity, the ongoing responsiveness of the brain to experience.

A feminist approach to neuroscience does not simply deny that there are differences between women and men; rather, it aims to understand why the narrative of natural and immutable sex differences has been so compelling and how it has influenced science. It also aims to provide an alternative to both the androcentrism that has characterized biomedical research, by ensuring that physiological differences between women and men are taken into account, and the sexism found in much research on sex differences, by seeking to understand how the social environment shapes both neuroscience and the brains it studies.

Robyn Bluhm

See also Androcentrism; Feminism: Overview; First-Wave Feminism; Neofeminism; Second-Wave Feminism

Further Readings

Bleier, R. (1984). *Science and gender: A critique of biology and its theories on women.* Oxford, England: Pergamon Press.

Cahill, L. (2014). Equal ≠ the same: Sex differences in the human brain. *Cerebrum.* Retrieved August 8, 2015, from http://www.dana.org/Cerebrum/2014/Equal_%E2%89%A0_The_Same__Sex_Differences_in_the_Human_Brain/

de Vries, G. J. (2004). Minireview: Sex differences in adult and developing brains: Compensation, compensation, compensation. *Endocrinology, 145*(3), 1063–1068.

Einstein, G. (2012). Situated neurosciences: Exploring biologies of diversity. In R. Bluhm, H. L. Maibom, & A. J. Jacobson (Eds.), *Neurofeminism: Issues at the intersection of feminist theory and cognitive science* (pp. 145–174). Houndslow, England: Palgrave Macmillan.

Fausto-Sterling, A. (1992). *Myths of gender: Biological theories about men and women* (Rev. ed.). New York, NY: Basic Books.

Fine, C. (2010). *Delusions of gender: How minds, society, and neurosexism create difference.* New York, NY: W. W. Norton.

Jordan-Young, R. M. (2011). *Brain storm: The flaws in the science of sex difference.* Cambridge, MA: Harvard University Press.

Shields, S. (1975). Functionalism, Darwinism, and the psychology of women. *American Psychologist, 30*(7), 739–754.

Van Anders, S. M. (2013). Beyond masculinity: Testosterone, gender/sex, and human social behavior in a comparative context. *Frontiers in Neuroendocrinology, 34*(3), 198–210.

Neurosexism

Neurosexism is defined as the assumption that behavioral differences between males and females stem from variations in brain development rather than from socialization. Neurosexism uses neuroscientific research to legitimize gender stereotypes and roles despite improper application or lack of scientific research. These sex differences are theorized to originate from early stages in fetal development during the growth of the brain, creating predispositions for behavior and abilities. Typical female behavior (e.g., greater emotional perception) is explained by the introduction of hormones in early fetal development, allowing areas of the brain associated with stereotypical female behavior to develop normally, such as areas related to emotion. However, typical male behavior (e.g., greater math ability) is explained by hormones like testosterone inhibiting the development of areas associated with female abilities, allowing greater development in areas of the brain associated with male abilities. Neurosexism has negative consequences because it creates a perceived predisposition of ability among males and females that can inhibit development. This entry describes the research supporting and criticizing neurosexism's claims, as well as the negative consequences of neurosexism for individuals and society.

Brief History

The basis of neurosexism stems from the organizational-activational hypothesis, which posits that the hormones responsible for shaping genitalia during fetal development also affect brain development. During fetal development, the gonads remain unisex until the sixth week of gestation, when hormones are released that trigger the gonads to develop into male or female genitalia. The introduction of these hormones creates a cascade of changes that affect fetal development, such as inhibiting the growth of female mullarian ducts in males. This surge of hormones has been used by many researchers as the basis of neurological sex differences.

One of the major advocates for sex differences in brain development is Simon Baron-Cohen, who argues that male and female brains differ by their capacity to systemize (organizational skills) or empathize (ability to identify with emotions). Baron-Cohen theorizes that there are three main brain types that stem from fetal development: (1) brains that are better at systemizing (characteristic of males), (2) brains that are better at empathizing (characteristic of females), or (3) brains that are balanced between the two. Other major proponents of neurological sex differences, such as Norman Geschwind and Louann Brizendine, theorize that fetal development inhibits brain growth depending on sex, allowing the development of areas specific to stereotypical abilities.

Hardwired Biological Sex Differences

Theories of fetal development describe how differences between males and females are hardwired such that the sexes have different brains, which explains the differences in societal gender roles and gendered behavior. The two most prevalent arguments of hardwiring come from (1) research on the role of testosterone in prenatal development and (2) the use of neuroimaging to study sex differences in the brain.

The Role of Testosterone

A prevalent theory behind neurosexism involves the role of testosterone during fetal development. Researchers believe that there is a testosterone surge during fetal development that initiates differences in brain development between males and females. Some theorize that increases in testosterone alter areas of the brain responsible for communication and the observation and processing of emotions, such that increased testosterone in males during fetal development inhibits the growth of these areas so that there is less potential for development of these functions. These differences early in fetal development create predispositions for males and females to develop differently, regardless of how the child is socialized later.

Research has tried to establish fetal testosterone as a predictor of sex differences early in development and has shown that testosterone measured in amniotic fluid after birth is related to parents' self-reports of their child's ability to systemize or empathize. Results of these studies show that as testosterone increases in the amniotic fluid, systemizing increases, reflecting male development. Conversely, as testosterone decreases in the amniotic fluid, empathizing increases, reflecting female development. However, evidence for this model is sparse, and it is subject to much criticism. The validity of these measures has been called into question, citing that the systemizing and empathy quotients are not actually measuring what is intended. Amniotic testosterone is a biological, objective measure, whereas parents' self-reported observations of their child's behavior is subjective. Parents' responses may be distorted by stereotypes of what behavior is expected of male and female infants and children. Thus, these studies cannot disentangle biological from social influences on gender differences in behavior. In addition, replication of these studies has found inconsistent results.

Research examining congenital adrenal hyperplasia (CAH) has established the importance of fetal hormones such as testosterone. During fetal development, high levels of testosterone in female fetuses disrupt normal development. As a consequence, many female newborns with CAH are physically indistinguishable from males. Research examining females with CAH has found that they are more systematic and show less attention to detail than females without CAH, similar to stereotypical males. In addition, females with CAH tend to prefer male-oriented activities (e.g., sports) compared with females without CAH. These findings support the organizational-activational hypothesis of how hormones affect behavior and establish that increases in fetal testosterone do play an important role in development.

Brain Imaging

Advances in neuroscience methodology have allowed researchers to examine the structural and functional properties of the brain using magnetic resonance imaging and functional magnetic resonance imaging, respectively. Research has specifically examined the impact of testosterone on fetal brain development. One theory proposed that high levels of fetal testosterone inhibit the physical growth of the left hemisphere, making it smaller than the right hemisphere. This inhibition would then allow the right hemisphere to be dominant over the left, strengthening traditional attributes associated with the right hemisphere, such as artistic and musical abilities. However, some meta-analyses, or large studies combining the results from previous research, have not found these effects and indicate that primarily only studies with small sample sizes have shown significant sex differences in hemisphere sizes. The corpus callosum, the part of the brain responsible for connecting the two hemispheres, has been observed to be larger in females than in males. It is theorized that this larger connection between the two hemispheres of the brain creates an increase in communication between the two hemispheres, enabling more efficient processing of language and communication. However, recent research has established that differences in corpus callosum size may be explained by the total size of the brain rather than biological sex. Individuals with smaller-sized brains have larger corpora callosa than individuals with larger brains, regardless of sex.

To test theories of sex differences in language processing, brain imaging studies have been conducted using language tasks. This research has found that females show activation in both brain hemispheres compared with males, who typically only show activation in the left hemisphere. Additional research has compared spatial skills between males and females and has shown that males show more activation in both hemispheres compared with females, the opposite of what is found in language tasks. Thus, activation of both hemispheres is linked with stronger abilities in that domain—language (empathizing) for females and spatial skills (systemizing) for males.

Because emotional processing is argued to show sex differences, brain imaging research has also examined activation in the amygdala, a part of the brain associated with emotional responses and emotional learning. Females showed increased activation in both hemispheres compared with males in response to the stimuli, as well as showing increased activation in the amygdala. Although this research supports the concept of neurological sex differences, attempts to replicate these findings have been inconsistent, with many studies finding no differences in lateral activation between the sexes.

Brain Plasticity, Culture, and Socialization

A major criticism of the neurosexist view of hardwired biological sex differences is the claim that such developmental differences are permanent, are innate, and affect subsequent behavior. This view fails to recognize the very social nature of humans, that our brains are greatly influenced by our social and cultural environments. Recent research on neuronal plasticity documents changes in neuronal characteristics in response to external experiences that result in physical changes within the brain. These changes include growth in dendritic branching, greater synaptic connections, increased neuronal responsiveness, changes in gene expression, and changes in gray and white matter volume. For example, research shows that reading a book or taking a course changes the physical and functional properties of the brain. The evidence for neuronal plasticity is in stark contrast to the view of the structure and properties of the brain as innate and fixed and that sex differences in brain development predestine men and women to different roles in society.

Several of the so-called sex differences found in neurosexist research can be reduced or eliminated with learning. For example, males' oft-touted spatial skills advantage can be eliminated by training females with tools such as building blocks and video game play. Similarly, encouraging boys to create different imaginary social situations using action figures or dolls can reduce gender differences in emotional expressivity. This example highlights the role of early-childhood socialization in gender differences in skills, namely play with toys. A large body of research documents gender differences in play and preference for toys, which is strongly tied to socialization. That is, parents, peers, caregivers, teachers, and other important figures in children's lives enforce gender stereotypes by offering their approval or disapproval of children's toy preference. The media and those profiting from the sale of toys market their products to boys and girls by using colors (e.g., blue and pink) and other symbols to cue children to learn which toys are allegedly gender appropriate. As a consequence, many girls choose to play with dolls and toy houses, role-playing washing dishes, preparing meals, having tea, and engaging in other stereotypically domestic activities. In contrast, boys are encouraged to engage in physical and hands-on activities such as building castles with blocks, designing racetracks for toy cars, and building robots from scratch. These gendered play behaviors support the development of gender stereotyped skills and traits, such as emotion expressivity and language development in females from caring for dolls and interacting with friends in games of fantasy. Boys develop spatial skills from building and manipulating objects, a skill linked to success in science, technology, engineering, and mathematics (STEM) fields; this is one potential explanation for the underrepresentation of females in such fields. Thus, even if hormones influence fetal development, as proposed by the organizational-activational hypothesis, these differences can be greatly influenced through socialization and cultural influences throughout childhood and adulthood.

Consequences of Neurosexism

Neurosexism is problematic because it misuses scientific research for political or ideological purposes by perpetuating gender stereotypes and gender roles. The development and life potential of males and females can be hindered by these restricted roles, by conveying that girls and boys should conform to the seemingly appropriate gender stereotyped behaviors. When developing one's identity in adolescence, gender stereotypes can limit what is viewed as achievable. For example, boys may enjoy caretaking but may steer away from the helping professions because of negative experiences when expressing gender inconsistent preferences. Likewise, girls may have interests in math and science but shy away from STEM careers due to discouragement from role models.

Gender stereotypes not only limit self-development and self-actualization, they also affect social relationships. Research shows that men and women will adopt stereotypical roles in mixed-gender interactions when they are led to believe that others hold traditional views of gender roles. Popular ideas such as "men are from Mars, women are from Venus" actually promote unhealthy behavior patterns, such as being emotionally withdrawn in romantic relationships. Although stereotypic gender roles may be acceptable and even preferred among some individuals, they ultimately limit our growth as social beings and our lifelong trajectories.

In addition to affecting our preferences, relationships, and social roles, gender stereotypes can affect achievement. For example, stereotype threat, or the fear of confirming a negative stereotype about one's group, can limit achievement in gender stereotyped domains. Hundreds of lab experiments and field studies show that when women take math tests, activation of stereotype threat may lower their score on the test despite their actual ability. Lower performance in a domain discourages individuals from pursuing careers in that domain. Thus, the current gender gap in STEM fields may be due in part to the effects of gender stereotypes on achievement via stereotype threat. In sum, neurosexist research reinforces cultural stereotypes that have harmful long-term consequences for human development beyond the uterus.

Bettina J. Casad and Zachary W. Petzel

See also Gender Stereotypes; Stereotype Threat and Gender; Stereotype Threat in Education

Further Readings

Fine, C. (2010). *Delusions of gender: How our minds, society, and neurosexism create difference.* New York, NY: W. W. Norton.

Fine, C. (2013). Neurosexism in functional neuroimaging: From scanner to pseudo-science to psyche. In M. K. Ryan & N. R. Branscombe (Eds.), *The SAGE handbook of gender and psychology* (pp. 45–61). Thousand Oaks, CA: Sage.

Nonbinary Gender

See Gender Nonconforming People

Obsessive-Compulsive Disorder and Gender

Obsessive-compulsive disorder (OCD) is diagnosed based on an individual's experience of persistent and recursive thoughts and repetitive behaviors. Individuals diagnosed with OCD can have either obsessions or compulsions, but most people have both. Obsessions are thoughts that are intrusive to one's awareness and that generate anxiety, whereas compulsions are actions performed repeatedly and focused on alleviating the anxiety generated by the undesired preoccupations. Some common obsessions are concerns about contamination, hoarding, grooming, religion, or physical issues. Compulsions that are prevalent include checking, ordering, counting, and washing. The interplay of obsessions and compulsions can create debilitating consequences in people's relationships, careers, families, and ability to live independently.

Within the *Diagnostic and Statistical Manual of Mental Disorders, Fifth Edition* (*DSM-5*), OCD is clustered with related disorders including hoarding disorder, trichotillomania (the recurrent pulling or plucking of body hair), excoriation disorder (skin picking), and body dysmorphic disorder (BDD). Prevalence rates in the United States (1.1%) are comparable with those in international populations. Overall, OCD prevalence is equitably distributed across genders, which is not reflected in the other OCD-related disorders. Gender variance in prevalence does exist in BDD, trichotillomania, and excoriation disorder. One gender-related difference for OCD is that women tend to be diagnosed more often in adulthood, whereas men are more likely to be diagnosed in childhood. One potential explanation for this gender-related difference in age of onset is the increased male risk for perinatal brain trauma and neurological soft signs.

OCD has a multifaceted etiology, with environmental and genetic factors contributing to its emergence. Risk factors include neurobiological, family-based history, history of sexual or physical abuse, autoimmune neuropsychiatric disorders, and psychological attribution patterns. OCD has a high rate of comorbidity with other mental health disorders, which confounds the diagnostic and clinical trajectory. More than 60% of individuals diagnosed with OCD have also been diagnosed with either an anxiety disorder or a depressive or bipolar disorder. Approximately one third of individuals diagnosed with OCD have a tic disorder. This particular dual diagnosis is most prevalent in men who had early onset of OCD symptomatology. Rates of comorbidity are higher than would be expected compared with the general population's prevalence rate for schizophrenia, eating disorders, Tourette's disorder, BDD, trichotillomania, and excoriation disorder.

Obsessive-Compulsive and Related Disorders

The *DSM-5* groups OCD in with several diagnoses collectively termed "Obsessive-Compulsive and Related Disorders. These disorders all feature obsessive thoughts and/or compulsive behaviors as essential diagnostic factors. Diagnostic validators are shown to frequently overlap, and the symptomatology of the disorders is often intersecting. There is increasing evidence demonstrating the clinical utility of viewing the range of disorders as a possible spectrum, separate but not unrelated to anxiety disorders.

Clinically significant distress and impairment due to preoccupation with defects in physical appearance is the primary diagnostic criteria of BDD. In BDD, the perceived flaws are distorted or exaggerated but are not seen as significant by others, specifically the diagnosing clinician. BDD diagnoses are slightly more common in women than in men, with 2.5% of women in the United States having received a BDD diagnosis at one point in their life compared with 2.2% of men. There are major gendered differences in the manifestations of the disorders. Men are more likely to be diagnosed due to preoccupation with their genital size, and muscle dysmorphia, a rare subset, is almost exclusively diagnosed in men. Women with BDD diagnoses present with significantly higher rates of comorbidity, specifically with eating disorders.

As BDD is defined as a preoccupation with an imagined defect in appearance, there are cultural expectations regarding beauty interacting with such a diagnostic classification. Both men and women, though it is especially salient and potent for women, are bombarded with societal messages of beauty and desirability that can require excessive body modifications through hair removal, dieting, and/or size reduction exercise. Cultural prescriptions for body size and appearance can dictate the resources women invest in time-consuming behaviors that are potentially consistent with the construct of compulsions in the diagnostic criteria for OCD and BDD. Furthermore, obsessions about body shape and appearance can be coupled with compulsive behaviors such as restrictive dieting and cosmetic procedures. Such preoccupying thoughts and compulsive behaviors can be indistinguishable from the clinically salient features of BDD, which may complicate the appropriate diagnosing of BDD. The thoughts and behaviors associated with cultural expectations of beauty can be considered normative for women, but the same manifestation in men may be construed as pathological based on the intersectionality of gender-based socialization and gender scripts. Gender scripts are socially constructed expectations about what males and females do and how they should be.

Trichotillomania and excoriation are variations of body-focused repetitive behaviors (BFRB). Both disorders are diagnosed by body-focused compulsions that lead to impairment in social, occupational, or physiological functioning. Trichotillomania is 10 times more common in women than in men. Excoriation first appeared in the *DSM-5*. General awareness, understanding, and research are scant, but preliminary empirical and anecdotal research shows a similar gender distribution with trichotillomania. The high prevalence in women suggests that gender-related differences in standards of beauty and the societal yoking of female self-esteem to physical attractiveness may be exacerbating the symptom dimensions in women.

The affective, cognitive, and physical symptoms of BFRBs can all contribute to occupational and social impairment. Unlike BDD, physical evidence of trichotillomania and excoriation is commonly present and observable to outsiders. Distress over the physical manifestations of the disorders, such as hair loss, scarring, and lesions, can have deleterious effects on both self-image and economic stability related to employment. Individuals who experience BFRB are often situated outside the boundaries of normative beauty standards, compounding social and relational isolation.

Sociocultural and Environmental Factors

Gender-related differences have been identified in the context of sociocultural and environmental factors. For women, pregnancy and sexual assault can exacerbate OCD symptoms and can generate symptoms misdiagnosed as OCD, respectively. OCD also negatively affects sexual functioning for women. For men, OCD symptoms tend to be more severe in chronicity and manifestation. Such heightened severity has a more negative impact on functioning, thereby disrupting quality of life.

During peripartum, women are at increased risk of developing OCD symptoms, which can preclude the development of healthy attachment between mother and infant. For women who are pregnant or postpartum, symptoms tend to focus on cleaning, hurting the infant, checking on the child, or avoidance of the baby. The anxiety that is evoked during peripartum and postpartum can generate shame and guilt for women, thereby exacerbating the OCD symptomatology. If not treated appropriately, women can experience long-term negative consequences on their ability to bond with their child and to navigate the establishment of a parental identity.

Sexual functioning in women can be negatively affected by OCD. Experiencing the symptoms of OCD can correlate to anorgasmia and avoidance of sexual experiences. The impact of OCD on sexual functioning can negatively affect overall quality of life and intimate relationships. Even though women diagnosed with OCD are more likely than men diagnosed with OCD to be partnered and to have children, the potential impact of symptoms on sexual functioning can damage healthy intimate partnerships.

It is important to understand that sexual trauma can contribute to the development of obsessions with cleanliness and sanitation. It is common for people to experience feelings of being unclean for months after a sexual assault. The perceived uncleanliness can generate compulsive cleaning behaviors that disrupt the individual's functioning. Such manifestation of persistent thoughts and behaviors can be misconstrued as OCD, and this is especially important for understanding the experience of women, who represent 97% of all sexual assault survivors in the United States. In addition to the potential for misdiagnosis, sexual assault can also be a risk factor for the development of OCD. Careful attention needs to be given to how women survivors of sexual assault are experiencing the impact of their trauma and how emergent symptoms could or could not be reflective of OCD.

Researchers consistently conclude that men report a more significant impact of OCD symptomatology on their global functioning and are more likely to seek help to alleviate symptom severity. Interestingly, men diagnosed with OCD are less likely to be married and have children than their matched-age counterparts. The heightened severity and chronicity of OCD in males has been correlated to the increased risk for early onset and the increased likelihood of genetic and neurobiological correlates to etiology for men.

Gender-Related Differences in Symptomology and Comorbidity

Gender-related differences in symptomatology and comorbidity have been well documented in the literature. One gender-related difference that is present in men diagnosed with OCD is that they are more likely to have experienced perinatal trauma and to be dually diagnosed with substance abuse, social phobia, and tic disorders. After onset, men are more likely than women to experience hypomanic episodes. They are also more likely to experience religious or sexual-oriented obsessions and symmetry or organizing compulsions. In addition, aggression is more prevalent in the obsessions of men with OCD.

Women are more likely to have a history of eating disorders and depression than their male counterparts. Comorbidity with impulse control disorders is also higher compared with men. Once OCD symptomatology has emerged, women are more likely to develop panic attacks than men. Women are also more likely to evidence contamination obsessions and the correlated compulsion of cleaning.

The scope of extant research into OCD and gender is primarily limited to the symptoms and manifestations of those diagnosed with the disorders. There is limited research into the role bias plays in the assessment and treatment of OCD and related disorders. There are significant gender differences in help seeking for psychological concerns across the spectrum. Women are more likely to seek help and disclose mental health challenges by speaking to primary health care providers, whereas men are more likely to seek out mental health practitioners. Several studies demonstrate that women describing symptoms of OCD are more likely to be diagnosed with general depression and anxiety when treated by their primary care provider. This may be a result of some gaps in the knowledge and training required to conduct differential diagnoses. Diagnosis may also be influenced by unexamined practitioner biases surrounding gender roles and expectations. Although it is impossible to determine the causation, the significance of gender bias in both the manifestation and the diagnosis of OCD and related disorders demands critical examination.

Nicole R. Hill and Cara A. Levine

See also Anxiety Disorders and Gender; Bipolar Disorder and Gender; Body Dysmorphic Disorder and Gender; Depression and Gender; Dual Diagnosis and Gender

Further Readings

American Psychiatric Association. (2013). *Diagnostic and statistical manual of mental disorders* (5th ed.). Arlington, VA: Author.

Berrie, B. (2007). *Beauty bias: Discrimination and social power.* Westport, CT: Praeger.

Labad, J., Menchon, J. M., Alonso, P., Segalas, C., Jimenez, S., Jaurrieta, N., . . . Vallejo, J. (2008). Gender differences in obsessive-compulsive symptom dimensions. *Depression and Anxiety, 25,* 832–838. doi:10.1002/da.20332

Lochner, C., & Stein, D. J. (2001). Gender in obsessive-compulsive disorder and obsessive-compulsive spectrum disorders. *Archives of Women's Mental Health,* 4(1), 19–26.

Lundberg-Love, P. K., & Waits, B. (2010). Women and sexual violence: Emotional, physical, behavioral, and organizational responses. In M. A. Paludi (Ed.), *Feminism and women's rights worldwide* (Vol. 2, pp. 41–64). Santa Barbara, CA: Praeger.

Mathis, M. A., Alvarenga, P. D., Funaro, G., Torresan, R. C., Moraes, I., Torres, A. R., . . . Hounie, A. G. (2011). Gender differences in obsessive-compulsive disorder: A literature review. *Revista Brasileira de Psiquiatria, 33*(4), 390–399.

Orgasm, Psychological Issues Relating to

Orgasm has long troubled psychological researchers with its elusive, hard to measure, difficult to understand, and power-laden qualities. Although researchers often define sexual satisfaction based on orgasm, how people interpret sexual satisfaction and how they experience or enact orgasm remain infinitely complex. For example, studies have suggested that it is nearly impossible for physiological or biological researchers to definitively determine in the laboratory when someone has had an orgasm. Orgasms are a composite of physiological responses (e.g., contractions of the anal sphincter, shortness of breath, flushing of cheeks, pupil dilation) rather than a singular (and measurable) incident. As such, orgasms are experienced differently from person to person and from incident to incident. Some orgasms may feel intense and prolonged, whereas others fizzle out or feel like a warm sensation. Some produce body shaking and proclamations of joy, whereas others lull people to sleep. If researchers cannot meaningfully determine what an orgasm is, identifying its meaning becomes equally, if not more, difficult.

The evolutionary reasons for cisgender women's orgasms have also eluded researchers, with several book-length works that have addressed the subject and have concluded that women's orgasms have no specific function that aids in reproduction. They do not, as previously believed, facilitate sperm to move toward the egg, nor do they help in conception. They do not allow women to choose more appropriate mates, and they do not prepare the egg for implantation. Scientific biases (or researchers seeing what they want to see) are clearly evident in the scientific and psychological literature on women's orgasms. Orgasms for women may indeed exist only as a tool to experience pleasure and not as a tool for maximizing reproductive capacities, raising questions about the role of orgasmic pleasure in sexual and social life.

Researchers who have attempted to study the phenomenon with heterosexual women have also had difficulty in understanding the social scripts of orgasm. Following the sexual revolution, orgasm has become a much sought after goal of many sexual exchanges, prompting some feminist and socialist critics to argue that women have been thrown into an "orgasm frenzy," whereby "good sex" is only defined by the occurrence of orgasm. Whereas women's orgasms were largely absent in public discourses about sex prior to the sexual revolution, the period after the sexual revolution emphasized orgasm as a clear expectation for women. This goal-directed sex has led to new norms whereby men and women have become more interested in how to "give" and "get" orgasms. Some have even argued that orgasms operate within a sexual economy as a visible product of sex and that both men and women are expected to orgasm during sexual encounters, even though intercourse only reliably leads to orgasm for men and not for women.

Researchers who study the concept of "faking" orgasms have consistently found that more than 50% of women have faked orgasm during heterosexual sex, whereas a small percentage of men have occasionally faked orgasm (though because of the production of semen, faking orgasm is far more difficult and logistically complex for men than for women). As many as 20% of heterosexual women fake orgasm regularly or every time they have sex, suggesting that faking orgasms is not only commonplace but also pervasive in many women's sexual lives. The reasons for women faking orgasm have included the following: wanting to make a (male) partner feel confident, ending the sexual encounter, feeling sexually "normal," feeling pressured to engage in penile-vaginal intercourse more than they wanted to, being physically exhausted, avoidance of conflict with a partner, and feeling pressure to perform. The high incidence of women faking orgasm also suggests that communication issues and gender and power imbalances may pervade contemporary sexual scripts. Same-sex couples too reported faking orgasm, suggesting that while women in heterosexual relationships faked orgasm more often than those in same-sex relationships, women across sexual identities reported faking orgasm at least some of the time.

Gender imbalances also pervade the psychological studies of orgasm, as researchers have found consistently that heterosexual men feel entitled to orgasm more often than do women. Although orgasm has been constructed as a goal of many sexual encounters, far more men than women experienced orgasm regularly (e.g., 69% vs. 95% for a person's "last sexual encounter"). Nonintercourse behaviors such as cunnilingus, manual sex, and phone sex reliably led to orgasm more often for women than did intercourse itself. Still, many social scripts emphasize the centrality of intercourse at the expense of other sexual behaviors, just as women's sexual pleasure is deprioritized compared with men's sexual pleasure, raising questions about who gets the "fair deal" during sexual exchanges.

Sexual orientation also influences the experience of orgasm, as well as the social scripts attached. First, while there are no significant differences in the number of orgasms that heterosexual men, gay men, and bisexual men have during sexual activity, it has been found that lesbian women are likely to experience orgasm at much higher frequencies than heterosexual women and bisexual women. For gay and bisexual men, it has been found that orgasm frequently occurs during sexual encounters but is more likely to happen during sex with a relationship partner (e.g., husband, boyfriend) than during sex with a nonrelationship partner (e.g., casual dating partner, friend, acquaintance).

Some sex therapies are starting to address the benefits of non-goal-directed sex and non-orgasm-directed sex, finding that when the pressure to orgasm is removed, people can orgasm far more easily and reliably. Furthermore, the sex toy industry has started to recognize the value and marketability of products that are not shaped like phalluses, as products like vibrating tongues and clitoral suction devices have entered the high-end vibrator market. Overall, the social imperative to prioritize orgasm and to perform as if sexually excited, regardless of a woman's true feelings, has defined much of women's sexual lives, creating enormous complexity around interpretations of what orgasms mean and how to produce them.

Furthermore, while people are starting to understand and challenge the social meanings of orgasm, scientific and social knowledge about orgasm is still in its infancy. For instance, there are no known studies on the phenomenon of orgasm as it relates to transgender or gender nonconforming people. Future research on these people's experiences with sex and orgasm is especially important as one study had indicated that transgender experiences and orgasm are two of the five least discussed sexuality education topics in medical training. Furthermore, understanding orgasm as it relates to race, ethnicity, and religion would be important in considering how cultural factors may influence the experience of, and the social script in talking about, orgasm.

Breanne Fahs

See also Pornography and Gender; Sex Education; Sexual Desire; Sexuality and Women

Further Readings

Armstrong, E. A., England, P., & Fogarty, A. C. K. (2012). Accounting for women's orgasm and sexual enjoyment in college hookups and relationships. *American Sociological Review, 77*(3), 435–462.

Cacchioni, T. (2007). Heterosexuality and "the labour of love": A contribution to recent debates on female sexual dysfunction. *Sexualities, 10*(3), 299–320.

Fahs, B. (2014). Coming to power: Women's fake orgasms and best orgasm experiences illuminate the failures of (hetero)sex and the pleasures of connection. *Culture, Health & Sexuality, 16*(8), 974–988. doi:10.1080/13691058.2014.924557

Frith, H. (2015). *Orgasmic bodies.* London, England: Palgrave.

Jackson, S., & Scott, S. (2001). Embodying orgasm: Gendered power relations and sexual pleasure. *Women & Therapy, 24*(1/2), 99–110.

Jagose, A. (2012). *Orgasmology.* Durham, NC: Duke University Press.

Pacific Islanders and Gender

Pacific Islanders are persons with indigenous origins to the subregions of the Pacific known as Polynesia (e.g., Tonga, Sāmoa, Hawai'i, and Aotearoa New Zealand), Melanesia (e.g., Fiji, Papua New Guinea, and Vanuatu), and Micronesia (e.g., Marshall Islands, Guam, and Palau). Their ancestors first migrated into the Pacific more than 4,000 years ago from Southeast Asia. They settled and thrived on many of the 25,000 islands and atolls spread across these subregions that span both the northern and southern hemispheres of the Pacific. The Pacific region comprises 180 million square kilometers of ocean, islands, and atolls, with more than 1,500 languages spoken across different island groups, nations, and territories. This entry is an overview of Pacific Islanders and gender. It is important to recognize the sociocultural diversity of Pacific Islanders on issues related to gender discussed in this entry, which cannot be adequately covered here.

Gender Roles and Expectations

Prior to Western contact (before the late 1700s), gender roles and expectations varied between and within the Pacific subregions. For example, gender roles (e.g., division of labor) and expectations (e.g., acceptable behaviors) in the Polynesian islands collectively known as Hawaii were clearly delineated and strictly enforced, as illustrated by the prohibition (*kapu*) of women from eating certain types of food (e.g., those associated with male deities) and the separation of men and women in the act of eating and other activities. The consequences of violation of these prohibitions were often severe. Men occupied most key leadership positions, with a few exceptions, in which they served as *Ali'i Nui* (island and district chiefs) and *Kahuna* (priests and professional experts). These gender demarcations were often ascribed to spiritual or religious explanations linked to ancient ancestors who were deified. Contrast Hawaii with Palau in Micronesia, where gender role differentiation was less distinct and enforced. Although men were part of the traditional governing councils in ancient Palau, senior women also served on these councils, selected the male titleholders, and allocated wealth and property within family groups.

It is difficult to describe precontact Pacific societies as fully patriarchal because women in many places did hold high ranks and leadership positions. In precontact Hawaii, women could be *Ali'i* ("royalty") and wield a high degree of power. There were also numerous female deities who were revered by both men and women and who embodied behaviors typically associated with both feminine (e.g., nurturing) and masculine (e.g., aggression) traits, such as Pele, the goddess of volcanoes and creator of islands in Polynesia, or Ligobubfanu in Chuuk, Micronesia. In most parts of the Pacific, women were generally well regarded and often exalted because they gave life through childbirth.

The rigid gender roles seen in some precontact Pacific societies might have been a response to the demands of a growing population and a means of managing finite resources. It is also speculated that women were kept from certain activities (e.g., ceremonies and political affairs) to protect them from possible harm. This is reflected in the division of labor on islands like Pukapuka, a coral atoll in the Cook Islands, where women worked primarily in the interior of the island tending to the taro fields while men worked on the periphery and encircling dry land. In Sāmoa, men and women fished within the reef, while only men ventured out into the deep ocean. For the most part, the division of labor in activities of daily living was similar across Pacific groups, in which men engaged in hunting, fishing, building of houses and canoes, and tool making and women engaged in child care, certain food gathering and preparation, and the making of materials needed for daily living (e.g., *tapa* for clothing).

In general, precontact Pacific societies are described as being patrilineal (i.e., a clan system in which a person's membership is determined through his or her paternal lineage), matrilineal (i.e., a clan system in which a person's membership is determined through his or her maternal lineage), or ambilineal, which is a combination of both. Ambilineal was typical of Polynesian societies, such as in Sāmoa, Hawaii, and Aotearoa. Matrilineal was typical of Micronesian societies, such as in Palau and Yap. A strictly patrilineal clan system was perhaps less common but practiced in some Pacific Island societies, such as in Tikopia of the Solomon Islands. Because a person's inheritance of property, rank, and family titles was determined by these clan systems, they reflect the differential degree of power and influence men and women had across various Pacific Island societies.

With colonization of the Pacific by European countries (e.g., Great Britain, Germany, and Spain) and the United States in the 1800s, and their introduction of Christianity (e.g., Calvinism and Catholicism) and laws based on Christian morality, traditional gender roles were altered. In places where women held some degree of power in society, their influence on matters of politics and wealth distribution diminished as male leadership was emphasized. In the Solomon Islands, women viewed the emphasis placed on the nuclear family over the extended family system by foreigners as a loss of their traditional autonomy. In island societies with stricter gender roles, women could now engage in activities once reserved for men, but they were expected to be subservient to their husband. There was a pacification of men by removing them from their traditional role as warriors and other activities that threatened the settlers' aspirations. They were expected to be the primary, if not only, "breadwinner" in their household. Christian notions of marriage, monogamy, family, and sexual and gender specific behaviors altered traditional gender roles and expectations, such that they also reflected the Victorian notions of acceptable masculine and feminine attitudes and behaviors.

By the 21st century, subsistence living in many Pacific societies had given way to wage labor for both men and women. There is less distinction in gender roles and expectations in the division of labor because both men and women often need to engage in wage labor in order to make a living. Although leadership roles and certain professions are still dominated by men in most Pacific societies, both men and women debatably have similar educational and career opportunities. In family and community affairs, some of these societies have become more matriarchal (i.e., a female-dominated social system) in nature as women have taken on many of the roles once assigned to men, such as roles in the managing of family affairs and resources. Notwithstanding, many Pacific Islanders have maintained aspects of their traditional gender roles; canoe building and house building remain predominately activities done by men, while clothes making and child care are predominately assigned to be the role of women. Where traditional ceremonies continue to be practiced (e.g., *'ava* ceremony in Sāmoa and *Pōwhiri* welcoming ceremony in Aotearoa New Zealand), men still preside over these practices as they have done in the past.

Gender Identity and Development

In precontact Pacific societies, there was less of the gender binary (i.e., the social dichotomy to enforce the ideals of masculinity and femininity related to one's biological sex and gender identity) seen in many Western cultures in which ideals of masculinity and femininity were less strictly dichotomized. For example, a person was often admired for his or her ability to exhibit both masculine (e.g., assertive) and feminine (e.g., nurturing) traits regardless of biological sex. The physical distance among gender, even men, was often close and intimate in social settings. However, there were elaborate rituals to usher a child into adulthood based on the biologically assigned sex.

Many precontact Pacific societies performed elaborate rituals to facilitate the gender identity development of a prepubescent or pubescent boy. In Hawaii, a boy of 6 or 7 years of age would undergo *kā i mua* ("to thrust forward into the men's eating house"), in which he is separated from his mother and other women to join the ranks of men. It signified the start of his formal development into manhood. The *hale mua*, or the eating and ritual house of the men, is where he learned his occupation (e.g., fishing and farming), expectations of manhood (e.g., serving the community and chief), and the ceremonies necessary to protect his family and community. Male deities were emphasized in the learning of these rituals and served as the ancestral role models for masculine attitudes and behaviors, such as prudence, aggression, and compassion. Pubescent males in the Sepik River region of Papua New Guinea underwent extreme and elaborate initiation rites, such as intense scarification and brutal treatment by older men. Throughout the Pacific, practices similar to those in Hawaii and Papua New Guinea existed, but the degree of gender separation and to which they endured ritualistic privation varied. Many of these rituals can still be found among many tribes in Papua New Guinea and the outer islands of Micronesia.

Women in precontact Pacific societies also had rituals to facilitate and celebrate their passage into puberty and womanhood. In some Polynesian societies, puberty rituals for girls involved secluding them from others while they were instructed on feminine virtues, kept sedentary and out of direct sunlight, and fed large quantity of foods to make them more sexually desirable. In Tahiti, this kind of ritual was called the *ha'apori* ("to make fat"), and it was for both boys and girls. The girl's first menstruation was celebrated by a communal feast in many areas of Polynesia and tattooing in some areas of Melanesia. In Sāmoa, a female-specific tattoo, called *malu*, was applied in the years following puberty. Women with *malu* were expected to perform key ceremonial tasks and represent their families and villages on official occasions. Some of these practices, such as the applying of the *malu*, are being reintroduced.

In precontact Pacific, the concept of the third gender, or transgender, in which a person would personify both masculine and feminine qualities or identify with the gender not typically associated with his or her biologically assigned sex, was common. Examples include *māhū* in Hawaii and Tahiti, *fa'afafine* in Sāmoa, *fakaleitī* in Tonga, and *whakawahine* in Aotearoa New Zealand—all of which traditionally described a biological male at birth who identifies with being both male and female. They often had romantic and sexual relations with men who did not identify as either *māhū* or *fa'afafine* and did not consider themselves to be homosexual. For *māhū*, it was also the gender identity assigned to hermaphrodites (i.e., persons who have both reproductive organs typically assigned to male and female sexes). In ancient Hawaii, *māhū* were believed to possess healing powers and could be a *Kahuna* ("priest") or even an *Ali'i*. A person could self-identify with being *māhū* or *fa'afafine* at an older age of development or be socialized from birth into this gender. The latter sometimes occurred when the female role was needed in a particular household or village.

Gender identification and its development among Pacific Islanders also changed with the introduction of Western and Christian morals. Rituals that once provided a psychological, social, and spiritual entry into manhood or womanhood were abandoned for Western notions of childhood and adulthood, with no distinct rites of passage. Being a man or a woman became more closely tied to one's biological sex, according to Western notions of masculinity and femininity. The third gender became immoral, and persons who identified as *māhū* or *fakaleitī* were often alienated and discriminated against by the settler society, and this discriminatory attitude was adopted and perpetuated by many Pacific Islanders themselves.

By the 21st century, gender identification and development in Pacific Islander societies had become more similar to that of many European and North American societies. The influence of Christianity in defining acceptable masculine and feminine attitudes and behaviors has given way to the influence of Western ideals espoused by the media. With the loss of traditional notions of masculinity and gender roles, some Pacific Islander men struggle to find their role and value within their families and communities, and some even express their gender identity through exaggerated masculine attitudes and behaviors, such as public posturing and homophobia. Due to the marginalization of women in many areas of society, many Pacific Islander women are part of the feminist movement in the Pacific to promote women's rights and gender equality. Persons who identify as *māhū* or *fa'afafine* openly celebrate their gender identity and have redefined their role in society and contribute significantly to their communities. For example, members of the Society of Fa'afafine in American Samoa (SOFIA), a well-respected non-profit community organization, hold important positions in churches, villages, and government offices through years of *tautua*, or service to their community.

Gender Stereotypes and Discrimination

The image of the exotic and half-naked Pacific Island female hula dancer or the loincloth-donning, muscular Pacific Island male warrior has been extensively used to promote their islands as the ideal tourist destination or as mascots for sports teams. These portrayals have resulted in the sexualization (i.e., regarding a person as a sex object whose worth is based on physical attractiveness and sexiness) of many Pacific Islanders. Girls and women are the most affected by these portrayals, leading to a narrow and unrealistic expectation of them by foreigners. Their sexualization by the media and popular culture can be detrimental to the gender identity and sexual development of young girls (e.g., more body dissatisfaction and depression) and can contribute to sexist attitudes and a tolerance of sexual violence.

Pacific Islander men have increasingly become sexualized and objectified by the media. They are often portrayed as the muscular native warrior in tourism and other types of advertisements. For example, at the Opening Ceremonies of the 2016 Olympic Games in Rio, Pita Nikolas Taufatofua from Tonga made waves when he marched shirtless—displaying his muscular physique. While Taufatofua could explain the cultural meanings behind his clothing and his use of coconut oil, many experts viewed his treatment in mainstream and social media outlets as exoticization. The increase in and success of Polynesian men in American football and in rugby in countries like New Zealand and Australia have led to misconceptions and stereotypes of Pacific Islander men being naturally large in stature, aggressive, and athletically gifted. These unrealistic and narrow expectations are being placed on many young Pacific Islander men, which can negatively affect their sense of self-worth and perceived career opportunities when they do not conform to these stereotypes. Studies with Sāmoan youth find that, while young women are using their customary roles to take advantage of educational opportunities, young men seek non-academic means of achieving and maintaining prestige, such as through sports.

Although there is a greater acceptance for gender variations in Pacific societies, such as *fa'afafine* and *fakaleitī*, than in most Western societies, discrimination and negative stereotypes against persons who identify with being transgender do exist. They are often mistakenly identified as homosexual, despite the fact that many do not view themselves that way. Because a majority are males by biological assignment whose appearance and behaviors are associated with the female gender, they are often shunned or ridiculed for being different. They are often and erroneously placed in the category of transvestite or sexually deviant. Studies in Hawaii show that Native Hawaiians who identify as *māhū* report frequent discrimination and are more likely to drop out of high school and be homeless than other Native Hawaiians.

Gender Relations and Inequality

A 2014 brief released by the Economic and Social Commission for Asia and the Pacific of the United Nations reported that the violence against women in many Pacific Island countries was extremely high. Women between the ages of 15 and 49 years who experienced physical and/or sexual violence from a partner or family member in the previous 12 months ranged from 41% in Sāmoa to as high as 68% in Kiribati, which is considerably higher than the global average of 33%. Awareness and the reporting of domestic violence against women are extremely low in many areas of the Pacific, particularly in rural areas.

Political representation by women in the national parliaments of many Pacific Island countries is extremely low at an average of 4.7%, compared with the world average of 22%. In 2013, the Economic and Social Commission for Asia and the Pacific reported no women members of parliament in Fiji, Vanuatu, the Federated States of Micronesia, Nauru, and Palau. Two seats were held by women in the Solomon Islands, while three seats each were held in the Marshall Islands and Papua New Guinea. Kiribati and Tuvalu had the highest number of seats held by women—nine and seven, respectively. After amending its constitution, Sāmoa committed 10% of parliament seats for women. From 1975 to 2010, the Kingdom of Tonga elected only seven women as members of parliament. In the Cook Islands, the number of elected women parliamentarians in 2014 was four—the highest ever in the country's history.

Gender and Psychosocial Issues

Historical trauma is the emotional harm caused by traumatic experiences spanning over a person's life and across generations. It is a type of psychosocial trauma experienced by indigenous peoples because of displacement from their ancestral lands, banning of their native language and practices, compulsory acculturation strategies, and discriminatory treatment. These discriminatory acts have led to substantial disadvantages for Pacific Islanders in education, housing, and employment in their own island communities. The emotional response to past and present injustices has ranged from moral outrage to despondency, which can be transmitted from one generation to the next. The adverse ramifications for both Pacific Islander men and women have been higher rates of emotional distress and suicide, substance use and abuse, and family and partner discord and violence.

Pacific Islander men compared with men of other ethnic groups have disproportionately higher rates of substance use and abuse, violence toward partner and family members, and incarceration. Most disturbing are their higher rates of suicide, especially among those between the ages of 15 and 24 years, when compared with males of other groups and Pacific Islander females. Comparisons of Pacific Islander men and women show suicide ratios of 6:2 in Guam, 23:2 in Chuuk, and 3:1 in Hawaii. Across Micronesia, suicide ratio of Pacific Islander men to women is 23:2. Although Native Hawaiian youth of ages 10 to 15 years constitute 27% of their age range in Hawaii, they make up 50% of completed suicide cases. There is a suicide epidemic in many parts of the Pacific, making it one of the leading causes of death in places like Guam, Chuuk, Fiji, and Sāmoa.

Although the suicide rates for Pacific Islander women are substantially lower than those for their male counterparts, their rates are higher than those of women of other ethnic groups. Pacific Islander women compared with their male counterparts and women of other groups also have higher rates of psychological disorders. In Hawaii, for example, Native Hawaiian adolescent females, Grades 9 to 12, have roughly 10% more depression and anxiety disorders than Native Hawaiian adolescent males and other females of the same grade levels. A similar gender pattern of higher psychological distress in women is also found in adult Pacific Islanders. These higher rates of psychological distress among Pacific Islander women than among Pacific Islander men are reflected in their comparable, if not higher, rates of cigarette smoking and other substance use in many parts of the Pacific.

There is a dearth of information regarding the psychological status of Pacific Islanders who identify with the third gender. A few studies of people who identify as *māhū*, for example, find substantially higher rates of high school dropouts, homelessness, tobacco and illicit drug use, and risky sexual behaviors than in those who do not identify as such, suggesting high rates of psychological distress in this population. Studies of other transgender communities find an association between discrimination and psychological distress.

The psychological issues experienced by Pacific Islanders are associated with threats to their cultural identity and the loss of their cultural practices and modes of living. In some parts of the Pacific, there is evidence that the cultural discord and racism experienced by Pacific Islanders are associated with their higher rates of depression, suicidal behaviors, and substance use and abuse across all ages and genders. Pacific Islander men, however, are believed to have fared the worst in response to the loss of their traditional gender roles and status in society and struggle to acculturate into the mainstream society. They are more likely to be undereducated and have limited job opportunities than Pacific Islander women. Many Pacific Islander women have had to assume the role of provider for the family while also managing the household and child care. There are movements by Pacific Islander men in many parts of the Pacific to develop positive male role models and end the violence toward women and children and to engage other men in community and family affairs. For Pacific Islanders of all genders, a strong cultural identity and a return to their traditional Pacific values and practices may hold the key to a healthy and vibrant future.

Joseph Keawe'aimoku Kaholokula, Nia Aitaoto, and Kamuela Werner

See also Gender Identity; Gender Roles: Overview; Gender Socialization in Men; Gender Socialization in Women; Transgender People

Further Readings

Jolly, M., & Macintyre, M. (Eds.). (1989). *Family and gender in the Pacific: Domestic contradictions and the colonial impact.* New York, NY: Cambridge University Press.

Mikaere, A. (2003). *The balance destroyed: Consequences for Maori women of the colonisation of Tikanga Maori.* Auckland, New Zealand: University of Auckland.

Poasa, K. (1992). The Samoan fa'afafine: One case study and discussion of transsexualism. *Journal of Psychology & Human Sexuality, 5,* 69–81. doi:10.1080/0314909 7809508656

Tengan, T. P. K. (2008). *Native men remade: Gender and nation in contemporary Hawai'i.* Durham, NC: Duke University Press.

Pacific Islanders and Sexual Orientation

When examining the experiences of Pacific Islanders, it is crucial to recognize how myriad methodologies, strategies of resistance, and theoretical interventions span a large window of time—ranging from the perpetuation of cultural erasure and forced assimilation to the reclamation of indigenous epistemology and practices. Therefore, in attempting to articulate a succinct picture of sexual diversity among Pacific Islanders, it is important to acknowledge the effects of temporality, colonization, and sovereignty on gender identity and sexuality. While acknowledging the use and misuse of these tools and the parameters of the current literature, an immediate objective is to highlight indigenous Pacific Islander perspectives on sexualities in accompaniment with the Western notion of linear time (e.g., prior to colonization, during colonization, and postcolonization). In this entry, historical identity dimensions are considered as a means of clarifying sexual social constructions that beget patterned living, regulation, collective acceptance, colonization/oppression, and reclamation. To understand Pacific Islanders and sexuality, it is important to examine (a) the indigenous perspectives of sexualities and gender identities among Pacific Islanders prior to Western contact; (b) the impacts of colonization and cultural genocide, both of which contribute to indigenous conceptions of religion, gender roles, and sexual relating; and (c) indigenous perspectives, traditions, and practices that encompass resistance strategies of consciousness raising, advocacy, and indigeneity reclamation.

Before delving into the literature on Pacific Islander identities and sexualities, it is important to first highlight the limitations of such an undertaking. Shared ownership of human suffering among indigenous women and men reflects collectivity and a certain degree of cohesiveness. However, the transgenerational effects of colonization, historical trauma, and varying historical relationships with Western/European societies present markedly different consequences for Pacific Islanders, all of whom perform, embody, and conceptualize their identities in unique ways. Integral to the vast landscape of identity politics is the art form of self-construction, actualization, and, thus, self-identification. Furthermore, it is necessary to remember that identity is contingent on how one is perceived in a given locality. Equally important variables with determinative value include physiognomy, cultural practices, style of dress, and beliefs. While these concrete and abstract factors have substantial predictive value, particularly in how people self-identify, they do not guarantee uniformity across Pacific Islander groups. Put differently, subjective interpretation of history relative to identity markers has significance for group membership *and* difference. Sexuality and gender are drawn into this process, both of which have implications for conceptualizing sexual orientation.

Continuing with the theme of group or shared experience, it is important to create spaces for human diversity and incorporate multiple voices across and within Pacific Islander communities. While the term *Pacific Islander* is beneficial for organization, it is important to be aware of limitations when using this framework: overgeneralizations across cultural and ethnic groups, overreliance on a Western system of language and meaning making, and disregard for the complexities of individual and collective needs, distinct histories, and the worldviews within these cultures. Sexuality is a fluid and multifaceted concept that has private and public meaning interrelated with gender and culture. All of these demographic-related variables are theoretically based on social behavior and context; therefore, from an indigenous perspective, one needs to be mindful of presenting emic experiential knowledge about sexuality.

This entry should be viewed as a snapshot of Pacific Islander identities and sexualities, and it should be noted that this phenomenon is dynamic, ever-changing, and nuanced within each culture. Examples are provided as illustrative rather than as all-encompassing. This assertion is relevant to indigenous communities in that it does not account for the diversity within cultures and it presupposes that women and men from this background confer an allegiance to the U.S. revolution of lesbian, gay, bisexual, transgender, and queer (LGBTQ) agendas. The LGBTQ movement in the United States may have varying degrees of influence on Pacific Islander cultures, and therefore, it is important not to impose or critique indigenous cultural perspectives through this lens, as it may perpetuate a colonial stance toward indigenous communities.

Moving forward, the term *Pacific Islanders* typically refers to the indigenous people of the islands in the Pacific Ocean, encompassing three areas: (1) Polynesian, (2) Micronesian, and (3) Melanesian. Based on a literature review of Pacific Islanders and sexuality, the majority of sexuality-themed research has focused on the Polynesian triangle, which encompasses Hawaii, Rapa Nui (Easter Island), and Aotearoa. The indigenous peoples of these islands include (but are not limited to) Native Hawaiians, Sāmoans, Tongans, Fijians, Tahitians, and Māoris. Given the voyaging and exploration of the early Polynesians within this triangle, these indigenous groups share commonalities in language, values, traditions, and family practices. However, it should be noted that each community has its own unique history of origin, migration trajectory, and interfacing with colonization and Western entities.

Precolonization and Indigenous Perspectives

The cultures of Pacific Islanders prior to Western contact were and remain very rich, each with its own language, cultural customs, and art, along with indigenous epistemologies, including conceptualizations about gender and sexuality. *Sexual orientation* may be considered a term imported by Western colonizers and may not reflect the conceptualization of sexuality and sexual diversity among Pacific Islander peoples prior to Western contact. Indigenous understandings of gender and sexuality have been examined across multiple disciplines, including anthropology, psychology, social work, history, and cultural studies. Additionally, indigenous knowledge has often been transmitted in the oral tradition; thus, evidence of sexual diversity is drawn from traditional storytelling and chants passed down across generations. The written word about traditional Pacific Island cultures was typically written by colonizers, entrepreneurs, and missionaries and, therefore, was embedded through their contextual lens of Christianity and the sexual norms and morals of the Victorian era. Indigenous perspectives prior to European Christian contact can be found through historical evidence, including oral accounts, artwork, and genealogical histories.

The family (referred to as *'ohana* in Hawaiian and *aiga* in Sāmoan) and the cultural community provided processes of socialization to pass on the knowledge, traditions, and practices of gender roles and sexuality. The communal living arrangements among Pacific Islanders created an open perspective about sexuality as children were exposed to sexual activity/intercourse, menstruation, and childbirth. Physical preparation for sexual activity began in puberty, and extended kin (e.g., grandparents) assisted by providing education on sexual activity to grandchildren. This education was segregated by gender. Sexual activity was not only for procreation but also for pleasure and fulfillment. Sexuality and sexual activity were considered natural and to be enjoyed. Boundaries and restrictions did exist, such as taboos against sexual relations among family members and times when sex could not occur (e.g., during menstruation). Homosexual practices in traditional Pacific Islander cultures were not cultural violations, and given the living arrangements, opportunities arose for these relationships for both men and women.

Cultural perspectives on sexual diversity, including same-sex sexuality among Pacific Islanders prior to Western contact, reflect an acknowledgment of nonheterosexual relationships, with varying degrees of cultural and communal acceptance. Evidence of sexual diversity as recognized, accepted, and celebrated can be seen in oral accounts and artworks from precolonial times among the Māori people and the Native Hawaiians. Māori carvings depict same-sex relationships and a diversity of multiple relationships, indicating an accepting and tolerant view of same-sex relationships in pre-European Māori society. In Ancient Hawaii, Hawaiian men could increase their power, status, and *mana* ("spiritual power") to the level of a high chief by having a male lover, or *'aikane*. It was socially recognized and accepted that the *Ali'i,* high chiefs and chieftesses, had bisexual relationships. In New Zealand, documentation has been found of a preordained minister having same-sex relations with Māori men and cohabiting with a Māori man for 2 years. This relationship and living arrangement appeared to have been condoned and accepted by the local Māori community.

Indigenous language terms also indicate the acknowledgment of varying sexual and transgender orientations and gender identities among Pacific Islanders. Indigenous words, such as *fa'afafine* and *fakaleitī* illustrate this phenomenon and the intersection of gender identity, sexuality, and culture in the Tongan and Sāmoan communities. The terms *fa'afafine* and *fakaleitī* refer to the biological sex of men who psychologically and behaviorally identify as women, commonly referred to today as *transgendered.* Some scholars assert that the *fa'afafine* and *fakaleitī* in traditional (e.g., precontact) Polynesian culture were considered high-profile members of society prior to Christianity, while other scholars suggest that these terms are postcontact and postcolonial. In traditional society, the *fa'afafine* and *fakaleitī* were able to transcend certain traditional gender norms and shaped some traditional views of homosexuality differently than Western notions.

Colonization, Gender, and Sexuality

The history of colonization among the Pacific Islands is well documented, including the landing of Captain James Cook on the Hawaiian Islands in 1778 and the missionaries' arrivals in Tonga in 1822 and in Sāmoa in 1830. Colonization and the influence of Christianity have greatly affected the perceptions and scholarship on sexuality and sexual orientation among Pacific Islanders. The process of settler colonialism involved the depopulation of the indigenous peoples, the taking of land rights from the inhabitants of the islands, and the colonizers becoming the authority over the indigenous peoples. In addition, missionaries and their teaching of Christian doctrine significantly limited sexual relations for both women and men, thereby reducing sexual diversity and eradicating indigenous views of sexuality among Pacific Islanders. Foreigners had preconceived notions about the indigenous peoples of the Pacific Islands, viewing the islands as an idyllic Eden and its native peoples as uncivilized, sexualized, and infantilized, and in need of salvation. The influence of settler colonialism and heteronormativity can be seen in the English common law imported to many Pacific Islands, including Tonga, Sāmoa, Australia, and New Zealand. These laws were intended to regulate individual identity and sexual coupling. Gender was dichotomized as male or female, with a determinative structure used for the process of legitimizing heteronormative relationships. Sexual identity and social behavior became the basis for determining one's eligibility to marry, as this was the normative and highly valued way of life, one that included benefits in legal proceedings.

Colonial powers also disrupted ancestral epistemologies transmitted via communicative, word-of-mouth means, including attempts at outlawing indigenous languages, traditions, customs, and behaviors. These acts led to a decentering of native peoples and their customs and reshaping personhood and sexuality in the image of the oppressor/

colonizer. In this regard, the controlling of bodies is also reflective of authority over knowledge production, the dispensing of narrow views of sexuality and conduct, and Christian ideologies of marriage. Additionally, Christian codes of behavior were imposed, ultimately confining sexuality, sexual identity, and sexual behavior to the private bedroom and between a husband and a wife. The sole function of the two-person, opposite-gender, monogamous relationship was procreation. The migration of missionaries with Christianity and their message had a profound impact on the self-perceptions and sexuality of Pacific Islanders, and its influence can be seen postcolonially.

Decolonization and Centering Indigenous Voices

The notions of gender and sexuality are in flux and changing over time given the globalization and the influence of the Western world and the reclaiming of indigenous identities, land, government, cultures, and practices. The process of decolonization and the reclaiming of indigenous epistemologies are a complex activity. In both Hawaii and Aotearoa, indigenous men and women are engaged in struggles for decolonization, self-determination, land, *mana*, and healing as a people. Many of these struggles have been notably gendered, just as gender relations have become increasingly politicized. Postcolonial thought pushes the boundaries of dichotomous thinking that is embedded with notions of gender, race, social positioning, and sexuality. In conjunction with this process is the reclamation of indigenous epistemologies that shape the way in which sexuality and gender identity are defined, conceptualized, and placed in context among indigenous Pacific Islanders. This can be clearly seen in the reclaiming and revitalization of indigenous languages. For example, the Māori term *takatapui* has been reclaimed and used to describe people who might otherwise be described as gay, lesbian, transgender, bisexual, and intersexual. The use of indigenous language to reclaim sexual diversity and connect with one's ancestors is a phenomenon that is seen among Pacific Islander communities, including Native Hawaiian, Sāmoan, Tongan, and Māori. This reclaiming through language indicates the uncovering of ancestral knowledge to help in shaping and changing perceptions of gender identity and sexuality in the present and future.

Healing and restoration need to occur, and the oppression and subjugation related to historical trauma, cultural genocide, and forced assimilation still deeply affect Pacific Islander indigenous identity, connection to place and land, and sexuality. Racism, gender oppression, heteronormativity, and homophobia are part of the imperialist history of the Pacific Islands and thus affect sexuality and notions of sexual orientation. Reengagement of indigenous ways of knowing to piece together Pacific Islander histories is a substantial part of the political resistance to disrupting the subjectivity/personhood of sexuality in the image of the oppressor and breaking down narrow views of sexuality and conduct. As scholarships among Pacific Islanders engage in methodologies incorporating decolonization, critical race theory, indigenous/native studies, and queer theory to examine, understand, and reconceptualize sexuality, collective action is occurring to recenter sexuality and identity within the context of indigenous conceptions of personhood and agency. Spaces and *hui* (the Māori word for gatherings) where knowledge can be shared and voices formerly oppressed can be heard and validated are being created within and across Pacific Islander communities. Additionally, connections are being made with other indigenous peoples, including Native Americans, across the globe to collectively share perspectives and experiential knowledge about gender and sexual diversity. These gatherings have culminated in publications advancing theory and research while also creating spaces for affirmation, validation, and inclusion for indigenous peoples who identify as gay, lesbian, bisexual, transgender, queer, and two spirit, which refer to gender variant individuals in some indigenous communities in North America. Pacific Islander scholars are creating distinctive knowledge and engaging in complex methodologies, theories, and research to understand indigenous ways of understanding sexuality. Current scholarship by Pacific Islanders is recentering indigenous knowledge systems with the use of indigenous language terms as part of a reflexive process in making, reshaping, and co-constructing gender identity and sexual diversity.

Laurie "Lali" McCubbin and Marvice D. Marcus

See also Asian Americans and Gender; Asian Americans and Sexual Orientation; Pacific Islanders and Gender

Further Readings

Aspin, C. (2011). Exploring Takatapui identity within the Māori community: Implications for health and well-being. In Q. Driskill, C. Inley, B. J. Gilley, & S. L. Morgensen (Eds.), *Queer indigenous studies: Critical interventions in theory, politics and literature* (pp. 113–122). Tucson: University of Arizona.

Aspin, C., & Hutchings, J. (2007). Reclaiming the past to inform the future: Contemporary views of Māori Sexuality. *Culture, Health & Sexuality, 9*(4), 415–427.

Driskill, Q., Fingley, C., Gilley, B., & Morgensen, S. (2011). *Queer indigenous studies: Critical interventions in theory, politics and literature*. Tucson: University of Arizona.

Farran, S. (2010). Pacific perspectives: Fa'afafine and Fakaleiti in Samoa and Tonga: People between worlds. *Liverpool Law Review, 31,* 13–38.

Hall, L. K. C., & Kauanui, J. K. (1994). Same-sex sexuality in Pacific literature. *Amerasia Journal, 20*(1), 75–81.

Mokuau, N. (1986). Human sexuality of Native Hawaiians and Samoans. In L. Lister (Ed.), *Human sexuality, ethnoculture, and social work* (pp. 67–80). New York, NY: Haworth Press.

Rifkin, M. (2011). *When did Indians become straight? Kinship, the history of sexuality and Native sovereignty*. New York, NY: Oxford University Press.

Smith, A. (2011). Queer theory and native studies: The heteronomativity of settler colonialism. *GLQ: A Journal of Lesbian and Gay Studies, 16*(1–2), 41–68.

Tengan, T. K. (2002). (En)gendering colonialism: Masculinities in Hawai'i and Aotearoa. *Cultural Values, 6,* 239–256.

Panic Disorder and Gender

Panic disorder (PD) is characterized by a fear of panic-related sensations that leads to significant anxiety about the occurrence of future panic attacks and/or avoidance of situations that could trigger further attacks. Similar to other anxiety disorders, PD is substantially more common in women. In addition, there is some evidence of differences in the presentations and consequences of PD among men and women. This entry explores the environmental, biological, and psychological reasons underlying such sex differences. In addition, it examines the role that gender characteristics play in the development of PD. The entry concludes by discussing the implications of such gender and sex differences for the treatment of this disorder.

Prevalence

As with other anxiety disorders, epidemiological studies consistently show PD to be more common among women than among men. The most recent estimate from the United States reported that 4.5% of adult females and 2.2% of adult males have met the diagnostic criteria for PD in the past 12 months, while lifetime prevalence rates are estimated to be 7.1% for females and 4.0% for males. Notably, the difference in the prevalence of panic attacks among men and women appears to be smaller than for PD, though the cause of such a pattern is unclear. One epidemiological study in the United States found that women were 2.3 times more likely than men to have a lifetime diagnosis of PD but only 1.4 times more likely to have a lifetime history of panic attacks.

A number of factors that contribute to differential rates of all anxiety disorders among men and women likely contribute to the greater likelihood of women having PD. For instance, socialized gender norms reinforce traits such as independence, bravery, and self-efficacy among males, which can serve as protective factors against the onset of anxiety disorders. The female gender role, however, is associated with characteristics such as interdependence, expectations of protection, and emotional expressiveness. Implicit and explicit expectations to conform to such a stereotyped gender role can lead to the development of avoidance behaviors, low confidence in the ability to cope with distress, and other characteristics that increase the risk of developing anxiety disorders. Furthermore, biological factors such as increased hormone fluctuations among women can lead to greater levels of anxiety, and some evidence exists suggesting that traits underlying fear and anxiety are more heritable among men than among women.

Nonetheless, several characteristics specific to the nature of PD may also play a role in the increased prevalence of the disorder among women.

Specifically, beliefs about the consequences of physical sensations of anxiety, differential physiological reactivity in response to panic-like physical symptoms, and the exacerbation of such symptoms due to hormonal changes associated with the menstrual cycle all appear to contribute to the increased risk of developing panic attacks and PD among females.

Anxiety Sensitivity and Panic in Women

Regarding beliefs about the consequences of anxiety, research has demonstrated that women have greater concerns about the physical consequences of anxiety (a characteristic especially relevant to the etiology of PD), while men are more concerned about the social consequences. Accordingly, women with PD endorse greater fears of suffocating, passing out, and choking to death during panic attacks. One study examining panic-relevant cognitions compared anxiety sensitivity (AS; i.e., fear about the consequences of anxiety) and courage (a stereotypically masculine trait) as potential mechanisms that might explain greater phobic avoidance of panic-relevant situations among women. Greater levels of AS in women were found to fully account for the differences in phobic avoidance, while no differences in courage were detected between males and females. Thus, it appears that sex differences in the interpretation of physical sensations of anxiety may explain the higher incidence of panic attacks and PD among women.

This notion is also supported by research examining the differential response to the CO_2 challenge, a procedure in which participants are asked to breathe in carbon dioxide–enriched air in order to induce physical sensations of anxiety and panic (e.g., increased heart rate, shortness of breath, lightheadedness). Studies have shown that even in healthy samples, women report greater subjective anxiety and avoidance, more severe physical panic symptoms, and larger increases in heart rate in response to the CO_2 challenge than men, even when controlling for variables such as neuroticism, AS, and recent panic attack history. Women with PD have also been shown to exhibit a greater "nocebo" response (i.e., an adverse response to something that should not produce a harmful effect) when blindly taking either a sugar pill or sodium lactate, a substance designed to induce a panic attack. Women who took a sugar pill thinking that they might be taking sodium lactate exhibited greater anxiety about developing panic symptoms than their male counterparts (whereas there were no differences between men and women who took sodium lactate), likely due to greater sensitivity to the possibility of physical symptoms of panic. Such elevated levels of sensitivity to anxiety, and in particular to the physical symptoms and consequences of anxiety, seem then to play an important role in the greater likelihood of women developing PD.

The Menstrual Cycle and PD

Another likely cause for increased rates of PD among women is related to the physiological and psychological effects of sex-specific hormonal changes resulting from the menstrual cycle and, in particular, the premenstrual phase. Research has demonstrated that during the premenstrual phase, anxiety symptoms are exacerbated even in healthy samples, and panic attacks occur more frequently among those with a history of panic. Acute stressors are particularly liable to trigger panic-like symptoms during this phase, as women who undergo the CO_2 challenge during their premenstrual phase exhibit greater physiological reactivity and panic symptoms than women in the follicular phase of their cycle. The strength of this effect also depends on the severity of premenstrual symptoms, as greater premenstrual distress predicts more panic symptoms and skin conductance in response to the CO_2 challenge, as well as a greater likelihood of panic attacks in response to sodium lactate ingestion. In the most extreme cases, premenstrual distress can lead to a level of sensitivity to physical anxiety symptoms comparable with that of full-blown PD, for women diagnosed with premenstrual dysphoric disorder show similar panic responses to CO_2 challenge procedures as those diagnosed with PD.

While the exact hormonal mechanism through which premenstrual symptoms lead to heightened panic sensitivity is not known, preliminary evidence suggests that the fall of progesterone levels during the premenstrual phase is primarily responsible. Animal models have shown that withdrawal of progesterone and its metabolite allopregnanolone increases anxiety behaviors in the context of an aversive stimulus. In essence, the menstrual cycle leads to periodic instances of heightened vulnerability to anxiety, which in the proper psychological context can set the stage for a panic attack. Importantly, the beliefs discussed previously regarding the potential harm of physical symptoms of anxiety appear to interact with these hormonal changes. Women with high AS in their premenstrual phase have been shown to demonstrate greater levels of panic symptoms in response to the CO_2 challenge than women with high AS in the follicular phase and women with low AS in either the premenstrual or the follicular phase. Thus, a trait like AS, which tends to be stronger in females, amplifies the impact of sex-specific hormonal changes associated with the menstrual cycle, leading to an increased likelihood of making the catastrophic interpretations of physical anxiety symptoms that are central to PD.

Genetic Influences

A growing body of research has sought to identify sex-specific genetic influences on the prevalence of PD in men and women. Curiously, many of the genetic polymorphisms that have been found to interact with sex in predicting the presence of PD have been specific to males, despite the greater presence of PD in females. One exception is a variant of the glutamate decarboxylase 1 gene, which was found to be associated with a significantly greater likelihood of PD among females in a sample of 531 individuals with PD matched with healthy controls. Further research is needed, however, to confirm this association and to test its specificity toward PD, as variants of the glutamate decarboxylase 1 gene have been implicated in a number of different psychiatric disorders. With regard to genes specific to male PD, a coding polymorphism of the neuropeptide S receptor gene was found to be related to PD in males but not in females, a result that was not found in individuals with schizophrenia or attention-deficit/hyperactivity disorder. In addition, two separate studies found that the angiotensin-1-converting enzyme was found more frequently in males with PD than in females with PD and healthy controls. Other genes that have been found to have sex-specific interactions in patients with panic are polymorphisms of brain-derived neurotrophic factor and catechol-O-methyltransferase, neither of which have been found to predict the presence of PD itself but were associated with characteristics such as neuroticism and state anxiety, most strongly among males with PD. While this research offers promising new directions for further understanding the causes of sex differences in PD, more research is needed to replicate these findings and examine the potential mechanisms through which these genes may have their effect.

Nature and Impact of PD in Men and Women

Beyond the causes of discrepant prevalence rates of PD among men and women, a number of differences have been found in the presentation and impact of the disorder in males and in females. For instance, women are more likely to experience shortness of breath, feeling faint, and feeling smothered during panic attacks, whereas men report more pain in the stomach and sweating. Perhaps related to increased concern about the physical consequences of anxiety, female PD patients report greater impairment in physical functioning as a result of the disorder. Women with PD have also been found to report more impairments in family functioning and other interpersonal problems. Given that women have higher rates of most psychiatric disorders, it is unsurprising that women with PD are at greater risk of having comorbid Axis I disorders, in particular agoraphobia, generalized anxiety disorder, specific phobia, or somatization disorders. Men, on the other hand, are more likely to have an alcohol use disorder. Differences in likelihood of comorbid personality disorders have been found as well, with women being more likely to have histrionic or dependent personality disorders and men being more likely to have schizoid or borderline personality disorder. On the whole, these findings reflect an overall greater burden of illness among women with PD than among men with PD, a pattern that mirrors findings from large-scale epidemiological studies of other anxiety disorders.

Treatment

Evidence of differential treatment response among men and women with PD is limited, but a recent trial of more than 1,000 patients with mixed anxiety disorders did show some differences in outcomes. Patients were randomly assigned to receive collaborative care, in which they received cognitive behavioral therapy, medication, both or neither, or treatment as usual, and only women showed superior treatment response from collaborative care. Furthermore, women receiving cognitive behavioral therapy attended more therapy sessions, completed more exposures, and were rated as more committed by their therapists. In a separate study that pooled data from four placebo-controlled sertraline trials for PD, women demonstrated equivalent improvement on most outcome measures, but they did show greater reductions in panic attack frequency and time spent worrying about panic attacks posttreatment. Thus, there is preliminary evidence that women with PD respond better to certain types of treatment than men, but more research is needed before firm conclusions can be made.

Additionally, when taking long-term outcomes into account, a different picture of symptom outcome emerges for women. Longitudinal studies have shown that women are just as likely as men to experience remission from PD but they are three times more likely to relapse following a period of remission (64% of women relapse vs. 21% of men). Hormone fluctuations resulting from the menstrual cycle may be partly responsible for such a discrepancy as the increased anxiety in response to panic-related stressors during the premenstrual phase appears to be a high-risk period in which symptoms may return. Accordingly, it may serve patients well in the treatment of this disorder to acknowledge the specific vulnerability that the menstrual cycle creates for women with a history of panic.

Joseph K. Carpenter, Teresa M. Bolzenkötter, and Stefan G. Hofmann

See also Agoraphobia and Gender; Anxiety Disorders and Gender; Cultural Gender Role Norms; Gender Roles: Overview; Gender Socialization in Women; Mental Health and Gender: Overview

Further Readings

Bunaciu, L., Feldner, M. T., Babson, K. A., Zvolensky, M. J., & Eifert, G. H. (2012). Biological sex and panic-relevant anxious reactivity to abrupt increases in bodily arousal as a function of biological challenge intensity. *Journal of Behavior Therapy and Experimental Psychiatry, 43,* 526–531.

Foot, M., & Koszycki, D. (2004). Gender differences in anxiety-related traits in patients with panic disorder. *Depression and Anxiety, 20,* 123–130.

McLean, C. P., Asnaani, A., Litz, B. T., & Hofmann, S. G. (2011). Gender differences in anxiety disorders: Prevalence, course of illness, comorbidity and burden of illness. *Journal of Psychiatric Research, 45,* 1027–1035.

Nillni, Y. I., Toufexis, D. J., & Rohan, K. J. (2011). Anxiety sensitivity, the menstrual cycle, and panic disorder: A putative neuroendocrine and psychological interaction. *Clinical Psychology Review, 31,* 1183–1191.

Schmidt, N. B., & Koselka, M. (2000). Gender differences in patients with panic disorder: Evaluating cognitive mediation of phobic avoidance. *Cognitive Therapy and Research, 24,* 533–550.

Pansexuality

The term *pansexual* is used as a label for a sexual orientation that means attraction to people regardless of their gender or sex. Pansexuality is sometimes considered its own category but is also sometimes considered to be a subcategory of bisexuality. More recently, the term has been used to be more inclusive of genders and sexes that are not exclusively cisgender or binary. Thus, pansexuality can include attractions to transgender people, intersex, genderqueer, nonbinary gender identities, as well as cisgender people (i.e., people whose gender identity conforms with their sex assigned at birth). Unlike the term *bisexual*, which connotes a binary attraction to both men and women, *pansexual* is considered a more inclusive term and is gaining popularity. *Pansexual* is also used in communities as a descriptor for events that aim to be inclusive of all genders and sexualities. This entry provides an overview of the etymology, history, theory, and present-day use of the term *pansexual.*

Etymology

The term *pansexual* is derived from the Greek prefix "*pan-*" meaning "all" or "every." "Pansexualism" is a concept credited to Sigmund Freud and dates back to 1917, and it refers to sexual instincts being the primary influence for all human activity. Contrary to *bisexual*, which utilizes the prefix "bi-"—meaning "two"—pansexuality opens up attractions that go beyond the gender binary.

History and Origins of Sexual Identities

Sexual identity is conceptualized as how a person understands to whom they are romantically and sexually attracted. In the 21st century, sexual identities such as heterosexual, homosexual, and bisexual are commonly used and understood by most people. However, these identities are relatively new in human history. Philosopher Michel Foucault argued that modern-day understanding of binary sexual identities such as heterosexual and homosexual arose from the medicalization of sexuality in the 19th century, when medical professionals began labeling certain sexual behaviors as "perversions" and those engaging in these practices had new labels such as "homosexual." According to Foucault, this new categorization gave birth to awareness of sexual identity as a construct. Prior to this time, men may have engaged with other men sexually, but these acts did not have a label.

While Foucault wrote about homosexuality, most of his work was focused on men. The term *lesbian* was derived from the home of the poet Sappho on the Greek isle of Lesbos and dates back to the 6th century BCE; the term *lesbian* appeared in medical dictionaries in the late 19th century. Unlike homosexual men, who were defined by their sexual acts with other men, lesbians were viewed as women who rejected traditional and expected gender roles and as having a mental illness. Later, the *Diagnostic and Statistical Manual of Mental Disorders*, second edition (*DSM-II*), published in 1968, would diagnose all homosexual men and women as having a mental illness because of their homosexual attractions.

The term *bisexual* was also used by Freud to describe those who had both masculine and feminine psychological traits. The earliest recording of the use of the term as a sexual orientation can be seen in the work of Richard von Kraft-Ebing in the late 1800s. Alfred Kinsey identified as bisexual, and his research conducted between the 1940s and 1950s showed that 28% of women and 46% of men experienced sexual attractions to both sexes. The earliest known bisexual organization, the Sexual Freedom League, was founded in 1967 in San Francisco. Since then, bisexuality has continued to gain visibility. Some have written about this identity being illegitimate or merely a "transition" stage between heterosexuality and homosexuality. Indeed, many stereotypes about bisexuality exist, with gays and lesbians believing that bisexual individuals are really straight and performing for their partner's excitement or wanting to do something exotic or different and heterosexuals believing that bisexual individuals are just unwilling to admit that they are gay or lesbian. Other stereotypes of bisexuality include being diseased, hypersexual, and deviant. As a result of these prejudicial stereotypes, bisexual people often feel invisible and rejected from both heterosexual and gay and lesbian communities.

While sexual orientations, gender identities, and relationship styles other than heterosexual man and woman and monogamy are emerging and progress is being made in terms of societal acceptance, there is a common assumption of both monosexuality (i.e., people are only attracted to either a woman or a man) and monogamy (i.e., people only want and strive for one significant romantic relationship). Heteronormativity, or the belief that heterosexuality is the only natural, normal type of sexual orientation or relationship style, may be influenced and reinforced by the assumption of monosexuality and discrimination of anyone who is not heterosexual or monogamous. However, recent research, informed by queer and feminist critiques, has demonstrated that a number of people identify with nonbinary sexual orientations.

A nonbinary sexual identity is characterized by greater inclusivity than identities that are focused on men, women, or both. However, empirical research on such identities is limited. Indeed, most of the research on sexual identity focuses on lesbian and gay identities, with limited research on bisexual identity and even less on nonbinary identities. *Queer* and *pansexual* are both newer and more commonly used terms that are only recently being included in research. *Queer* is a term that, while used as a derogatory term toward gay and lesbian individuals starting around the late 19th century, was reclaimed in the 1980s by those who wanted to reject traditional gender and sexuality norms. It is a sexual orientation and political identity under the LGBT (lesbian, gay, bisexual, and transgender) umbrella that embrace nonconformity of gender and sexuality. Younger adults tend to use the term *queer* more than older adults, who still view it as a derogatory term, with some regional differences.

In recent scholarship, some social scientists have examined these newer, more fluid and inclusive sexual and gender identities by borrowing theories of racial and ethnic identities that embrace multiple identities. Broadening conceptualizations of gender and sexuality inevitably go hand in hand. The increase in the visibility of trans* identities (and now genderqueer and other nonbinary gender identities) calls into question sexual identities that are binary and brings awareness and visibility to identities that go beyond the binary. Indeed, research on adults born after 1980 demonstrates that this new generation understands sexual identity as being more fluid and more broadly defined, and thus, they are less interested in using labels to encompass their sexuality.

Borderland theory follows the creation of identities that do not subscribe to cultural norms, create their own subcultures within those identities, and challenge the dominant paradigm. Unlike most theories on identity that aim to cultivate understanding by homogenizing identities, these borderland identities, by their very nature, are heterogeneous. For example, the term *queer* may be preferred over *bisexual* because of the innate problem many individuals and their partners, including transgender and gender nonconforming (TGNC) individuals and cisgender people, have in fitting into specific label categories. Queer identity is often intentionally ambiguous. Pansexuality, like queer, is another borderland identity that challenges existing paradigms and social norms, taking it a step further by going beyond any binary.

Present-Day Use

Pansexual Pride

The pansexual pride flag emerged on the Internet in 2010. It includes three horizontal colored stripes starting top to bottom with pink, yellow, and blue. The pink stripe on the top signifies female gender identity, regardless of sex assigned at birth. The yellow stripe in the middle signifies those whose gender identity includes no gender, both genders, or a third gender, such as androgynous, agendered, genderqueer, transgender (nonbinary), intersex, bigendered, or gender fluid. Finally, the blue stripe on the bottom signifies male gender identity, regardless of sex assigned at birth. This flag was created to distinguish the pansexual community from the bisexual community. Unlike other pride flags, the pansexual pride flag does not credit its creation to any one person.

Overlapping Identities

Polyamory refers to the practice of engaging in multiple intimate romantic relationships simultaneously and encompasses those who identify as polyamorous, nonmonogamous, and having open relationships. Some literature has shown an overlap between those who identify as pansexual and those who identify as polyamorous and/or BDSM—the practice of bondage and discipline, dominance and submission, sadism, and masochism, sometimes referred to as *kink* or *leather*. BDSM organizations date back to post–World War II, when homosexual men and women who returned from war landed in major cities such as New York, San Francisco, Chicago, and Los Angeles. These organizations were predominantly gay or lesbian. Some theorists postulate that heterosexuals began getting involved in these communities after the Internet became accessible to the public and people could explore fantasy and role-play in an online setting. Despite the existence of the pansexual identity as early as the 1980s, there is some evidence that this identity became more visible and popular with the establishment of BDSM communities.

The term *pansexual* has also been used by more contemporary BDSM communities to form alliances across sexual orientation groups, with the intention of making this subculture more inclusive. Perhaps because leather, BDSM, and kink are still considered somewhat taboo, though they are gaining more acceptance, there is greater solidarity in these communities and greater acceptance of sexual identity diversity. As with the intentional ambiguity in the pansexual identity, BDSM blurs the lines and definitions of what is considered to be sex, erotic, or intimate. However, while the term *pansexual* is commonly used in BDSM communities, some LGB people may find pansexual events off-putting when heterosexual men are present and may experience heteronormative attitudes. While the aim of a pansexual identity is one of welcoming all, regardless of biological sex or gender identity, discrimination and microaggressions can still occur in such environments.

Future Directions

Pansexuality is a term used with the intention of being inclusive of TGNC individuals and transcending the gender and sexual binaries that exist in historical as well as contemporary culture. While some TGNC people identify as gay, lesbian, or straight, these individuals and their partners may be particularly drawn to the identities queer and pansexual. As the visibility of TGNC people and nonbinary genders and sexualities grows, binary identities may become less common, and people may feel more able to explore their own sexual and gender fluidity. Indeed, current scholarship suggests that sexuality and gender may be more fluid than was previously thought. Furthermore, it has been acknowledged that gender is largely a social construct, yet it is still common for people to be forced to select male or female and heterosexual or homosexual identities in many domains. As pansexuality gains visibility, this concept has the potential to promote awareness of gender and sexual fluidity that can emulate that of multiculturalism and other forms of diverse identities.

Kimberly F. Balsam and Arielle Webb

See also Bisexuality; Genderqueer; Homosexuality; Queer

Further Readings

Callis, A. S. (2014). Bisexual, pansexual, queer: Non-binary identities and the sexual borderlands. *Sexualities, 17,* 63–80. doi:10.1177/1363460713511094

Diamond, L. M. (2008). *Sexual fluidity.* New York, NY: Wiley.

Elizabeth, A. (2013). Challenging the binary: Sexual identity that is not duality. *Journal of Bisexuality, 13,* 329–337.

Galupo, M. P., Davis, K. S., Grynkiewicz, A. L., & Mitchell, R. C. (2014). Conceptualization of sexual orientation identity among sexual minorities: Patterns across sexual and gender identity. *Journal of Bisexuality, 14,* 433–456.

Galupo, M. P., Mitchell, R. C., Grynkiewicz, A. L., & Davis, K. S. (2014). Sexual minority reflections on the Kinsey Scale and the Klein Sexual Orientation Grid: Conceptualization and measurement. *Journal of Bisexuality, 14,* 404–432.

Lenius, S. (2011). A reflection on bisexuals and BDSM: Bisexual people in a pansexual community—ten years later (and a preview of the next sexual revolution). *Journal of Bisexuality, 11,* 420–425. doi:10.1080/15299716.2011.620466

Parental Expectations

Parental expectation refers to a strong belief or anticipation by parents that their children will meet certain standards, milestones, or achievements. Parents are often a consistent and stable presence throughout a child's life, as opposed to other perceived caretakers (e.g., teachers, extended family members) who play a more transient role. Consequently, the role of a parent has been found to be of significance in a child's social, affective, behavioral, and cognitive development. Comprehension of the impact of parental expectations on children's development, therefore, is of great importance. This entry examines parental expectations research with regard to sex and the manner in which these factors are related to psychological well-being, education and achievement, and financial investment.

Heteronormative Family Model

Historically, a heteronormative family model has been the most salient depiction of family in the United States, where parents have often been defined as a mother and a father who are married and reside with their biological children. This model includes viewing males as the financial provider and females as caregivers and predominantly responsible for the maintenance of household duties. As a result, women may feel the need to have part-time rather than full-time employment, which results in lower income but allows more flexibility to permit them to fulfill these duties, thus strengthening the role of men as breadwinners. However, research shows that these roles are socially, not biologically, constructed; mothers are capable of providing financially, while fathers can form the same quality of attachment with their children and execute caregiving and household duties just as effectively as mothers do. Despite research to the contrary, parents' gender roles, relationship status, and sexual orientation are sometimes viewed as negatively affecting their children's development. For example, many studies have shown that children from gay and lesbian parents or from varying family models have comparable healthy development. Thus, given the role parents play in child development through the process of modeling, children from nonheteronormative family models have exposure to various gender roles that may be more flexible (e.g., fathers as caregivers) in their conceptualization of family and gender representation.

Numerous studies have shown that parents have different views of their children and treat them differently based on their sex. By the age of 3 years, children are influenced by their parents to engage in play that is deemed sexually appropriate. Reinforcement and punishment for suitable play are also administered differently based on a child's sex. As children transition into adolescence, boys perform chores deemed to be masculine, such as taking out the trash and mowing the lawn, whereas daughters participate in kitchen and child care chores, which are viewed as feminine. It also appears that parents have expectations that their sons should have increased independence whereas the autonomy of their daughters, in some cases, is encouraged to a lesser extent.

Parents seem to have differing expectations of the gender roles their children will assume based on their own sex. Fathers in particular are more invested in the compliance of their sons to heteronormative gender roles, which includes their attitudes, behaviors, sexual orientation, and gender expression. Studies suggest that fathers prefer that their children identify as heterosexual and view themselves as responsible for passing down masculine values (e.g., being a breadwinner) and the development of their heterosexual identity. While parental expectations have no impact on children's sexual orientation, they can influence heteronormative gender roles and expression. To illustrate this point, children model their behavior on their parents and report imagining themselves in similar roles (e.g., if mothers are observed as contributing to the family financially, they will imagine fulfilling a similar role).

Psychological Impact of Expectations

Parents have a principal role in their children's affective, behavioral, and cognitive development through various mechanisms such as their childrearing practices (e.g., authoritative and authoritarian parenting styles), expectations, involvement (e.g., time spent with children on certain activities, interaction, and supervision), investment (e.g., financial resources), and socialization. Research demonstrates that the socialization process teaches children how to operate in their environment in a manner that is socially acceptable. In essence, parent-child relationships serve as a means of generational transmission, for example, of financial benefits or disadvantages, and creation of a positive or negative image of oneself.

Societally, there is more preference for the expression of stereotyped masculine behaviors and attitudes (even in girls as "tomboys") as opposed to feminine traits, particularly by male children. Children can thrive in non–gender conforming roles; however, it is their relationships with peers, teachers, and parents that can negatively affect their well-being. Lack of acceptance by teachers and parents or bullying by peers with regard to one's gender identity may have great adverse psychological and emotional effects for school-age children, manifesting in depression, anxiety, self-injurious behavior, and low self-esteem.

Expectations parents have about their children range from hopes about their emotional well-being, to academic performance and career success, to relationship success. These expectations are mediated by parents' socioeconomic status (SES), education level, family constellation and structure (e.g., number and birth order of children), and the race and the sex of the child. Expectations have been found to have negative and positive effects on children. If expectations are viewed positively, they can increase motivation and encouragement, thus decreasing distress levels and positively affecting performance. However, if perceived as negative, expectations can elicit a desire for perfectionism, feelings of pressure, and unattainable standards that are experienced as a burden by the child. As an example, parental expectations have been identified as one of the factors that contribute to substantially high psychological distress levels (e.g., anxiety and depressive symptoms) in college populations. Young adults are cognizant of and affected by parental expectations. For instance, in one study, the meaning derived from these expectations was correlated to the presence of bulimic symptoms. Negative views of high expectations can elicit use of bulimic actions to cope with the presence of negative affect.

Education and Achievement

As one might imagine, there are also racial, ethnic, and gendered differences in parents' aspirations related to education and achievement. Parental expectations are used as a vehicle to pass down educational values and help in developing their children's educational goals. Academic achievement at the elementary, middle, and high school levels has been positively correlated with parental expectations to a greater extent than parental supervision and involvement, SES, race, and family structure.

There is some evidence of decreased levels of achievement and expectations in single-parent homes compared with in two-parent homes, which display particularly higher math and science achievement. Parents with significantly elevated expectations seem to encourage higher academic achievement and tend to increase their level of involvement. Parents with raised educational expectations are also more likely to have some level of postsecondary education. This demonstrates the need for children to meet their parents' high educational expectations and manage how these expectations can be internalized as their own.

Sex differences have also been detected in choosing to attend a college and the type of college chosen. Females have demonstrated a decreased interest in science, technology, engineering, and mathematics fields, which may be an important factor in college admittance. Some research provides evidence that females receive a lower level of familial support to pursue a college education and, instead, may encounter higher expectations to get married, which may not include a career outside the home. Parents have been found to be a helpful influence in career decision making for young adults compared with peers. Fathers in particular were found to have substantial influence on career-related decisions, especially of their male children. Parental expectations have an impact on the aforementioned sex differences, but peer and academic counselors and teachers also influence these sex-based variations to a certain extent.

In addition to peer, teacher, and parental influence on education and achievement, racial and ethnic differences are also an important consideration. Studies suggest that due to increased levels of societal racial discrimination, African American youth reported higher expectations from parents but the children experienced it as a display of acceptance and emotional support. These expectations have been understood as a necessary means of equipping the children to successfully navigate the majority culture. Further evidence of this was found when SES was controlled for. African American parents had higher expectations of their children to attend college than their White counterparts. Some studies found that African American males reported increased autonomy and overprotection and lower levels of discipline and rules from African American mothers as opposed to their female counterparts. However, in one study, maternal love and acceptance did not vary based on sex. In another example, Asian American parents displayed higher expectations of their children across the United States. Some postulate that Asian cultures emphasize the importance of family and compliance toward elders (including parents) throughout one's life, which may explain the elevated expectations. Furthermore, Chinese parents expect their sons (particularly their firstborn sons) to have higher income levels and educational achievement and to earn the bulk of the family's household income due to the son's ability to carry on the family name.

Financial Investment

The level of financial investment (as demonstrated by the allocation of financial resources) is an important component in parental expectations research. Financial investment seems to be informed by the sex, birth order, and health of children, as well as by the social class of parents. Recent studies demonstrated a difference in spending based on sex in families with only male children versus families with only female children. For example, only-son families seemed to allocate fewer resources to clothing but instead spent more money on housing.

Parents may harbor beliefs about what their children require with regard to their development. Beliefs about how resources are allotted are informed by parents' education level and SES. Parents who identify as middle class may find it beneficial and necessary to increase their children's social, educational, and athletic activities due to those activities being viewed as an essential part of middle-class culture. Some racial minorities live in areas with minimal resources, which affects the parents' ability to invest in their children, thus affecting their expectations. With regard to career expectations, middle-class parents prepare their children for their career, whereas lower-SES parents expect that their children will naturally cultivate such career aspirations.

Parental expectations are informed by beliefs about which child will provide the biggest return on their investment in the future; this view is consistent with the idea of children as human capital. Thus, if educating women is viewed as less valuable than educating males, with limited resources available, allocation of resources toward education is affected. A recent Ghanaian-based study on the role of parental expectation in student enrollment indicated that children are viewed as resources for increasing household income by working outside the home and taking care of household duties including taking care of younger siblings. Therefore, decisions about which children attend school are based on the age and sex of the children, the probability of the children obtaining a good job, the sex of the parent, and numerous other factors. Results indicated that male-dominated households showed a preference in enrolling male children in school, and female-dominated households showed no such preference. However, female-headed households seemed to use age of the female children as a gauge for whether female children would be enrolled in school. Given that female-led households typically had fewer resources than their male counterparts, as female children become older, it was viewed that they could be used as a source of income through performing child care or house cleaning duties to earn an income, which may be more beneficial to the household than enrolling them in school. Additionally, in a study conducted on parental spending and expectation, results indicated that parental expectations had a causal relationship on school spending for their children.

Implications

As highlighted throughout this entry, there exists a complex relationship between parental expectations and developmental outcomes among children. From psychological well-being to educational attainment, parental expectations have a great impact on child development and a child's future success. Additional research is highly warranted in assisting parents in gaining awareness and regulation of these expectations. Interventions that increase parental awareness and regulation of their expectations would be valuable to their child's growth.

Batsirai Bvunzawabaya

See also Education and Gender: Overview; Gender Bias in Education; Gender Roles: Overview; Parental Messages About Gender; Parenting Styles, Gender Differences in

Further Readings

Ahiakpor, F., & Swaray, R. (2015). Parental expectations and school enrolment decisions: Evidence from rural Ghana. *Review of Development Economics, 19*(1), 132–142. doi:10.1111/rode.12122

Bardone-Cone, A. M., Harney, M. B., & Boyd, C. A. (2012). What if high expectations feel good? Perceived parental expectations, their meanings, and bulimic symptoms in Black and White college women. *Eating Behaviors, 13,* 170–173. doi:10.1016/j.eatbeh.2012.01.005

Found, A., & Sam, D. (2013). Gender, sibling position and parental expectations: A study of Chinese college students. *Journal of Family Studies, 19*(3), 285–296.

Froiland, J. M., & Davison, M. L. (2013). Parental expectations and school relationships as contributors to adolescents' positive outcomes. *Social Psychology Education, 17,* 1–17. doi:10.1007/s11218-013-9237-3

Fulcher, M. (2014). Gender and sexual orientation in the family: Implications for the Child Welfare System. *Washington and Lee Journal of Civil Rights and Social Justice, 21,* 94–116.

Hao, L., & Yeung, W. J. (2015). Parental spending on school-age children: Structural stratification and parental expectation. *Demography, 52,* 835–860. doi:10.1007/s13524-015-0386-1

Schmitt-Wilson, S. (2013). Social class and expectations of rural adolescents: The role of parental expectations. *Career Development Quarterly, 61,* 226–239. doi:10.1002/j.2161-0045.2013.00051.x

Trask-Tate, A. J., & Cunningham, M. (2010). Planning ahead: The relationship among school support, parental involvement, and future academic expectations in African American adolescents. *Journal of Negro Education, 79*(2), 137–150.

Parental Messages About Gender

Very early on in children's lives, they are exposed to countless messages regarding gender-based societal expectations. This can include both direct and indirect messages about acceptable and unacceptable behaviors for boys and girls, stereotypes around levels of emotionality, expectations on typical appearances for each sex (e.g., girls have long hair, boys have short hair), and even sex-based beliefs about ability. Although children are bombarded with these subtle and not so subtle communications from all around their environment, parents are one of the primary and powerful sources of these messages and cues. This entry first reviews some gender-based beliefs and stereotypes before exploring parental messages on gender and how those and societal norms influence children.

Gender-Based Beliefs and Stereotypes

Research suggests that generally people hold gender-based stereotypes about even very young children and infants. In several classic studies, the participants who were asked to observe a child generally reported divergent judgments depending on whether they were told that the child was a boy or a girl. For instance, in one study, the adults described an upset infant as "afraid" when they were told that the baby they were watching was a girl, while those who were told that they were watching a boy described that very same child as "angry." In another classic study of Baby X, the researchers provided individuals an opportunity to interact with a 3-month-old baby and found that the participants were more likely to provide the child with a doll (as opposed to a football or teething ring) when they were told that the baby is a girl. When they were not told the sex of the child, women were more likely to give a doll while men were more likely to give a teething ring.

Parents have also been shown to hold such stereotypes even about their own children. For example, in one study that examined mothers' perceptions regarding their infant children's crawling abilities, the mothers were shown to overestimate their sons' abilities and underestimate their daughters' skills in navigating a new crawling task. Actual measures of those babies' capabilities showed no differences. One study found that even within 24 hours after birth, the parents of boys and girls described their children's characteristics differently even if there were no measurable or observable differences.

Research suggests that stereotypes around gender perpetuate as children grow older. Parents of elementary school–age boys have reported higher expectations and estimations of competence in comparison with parents of girls; parents of high schoolers have also reported traditional stereotypes around their children's future careers. Findings of studies that examine whether such stereotypes are linked to actual competencies in girls and boys have been mixed.

Parental Messages and Gender Socialization

Beliefs, expectations, and stereotypes around gender can be communicated to children in many ways. Researchers have long been interested in how parents differentially socialize their sons and daughters and have found numerous differences in the ways parents treat their children across gender lines.

Parents of young children are especially influential given that they have the capacity to organize children's time, choose the contexts and activities children can access, and, to some extent, even choose the companions with whom their children can interact. One area of research has examined parents' and nonparental adults' stereotypes and preferences regarding children's toys. Parents and nonparents alike have been shown to be aware of stereotypes around gender appropriateness of toys (e.g., dolls for girls, toy trucks for boys). In various studies, researchers have shown a prevalence of gender stereotyped toys in girls' and boys' rooms. Parents have also been shown to react more positively when their children play with traditionally gender stereotyped toys, although this gender stereotyping appears to be stronger for boys than for girls. These subtle cues are not lost on children. Children whose parents report stronger gender stereotypes and sex typing have been shown to have stronger preferences for sex-typed toys. And even at preschool age, children predict that their parents would approve of their playing with gender stereotyped toys and disapprove of their playing with gender-crossed toys.

With regard to messages about children and adolescents' sex-typed social behaviors, there is evidence that suggests that parents also communicate messages that reflect divergent expectations. Parents have been shown to react differently to children's prosocial behaviors. In one self-report study, boys and girls did not appear to have any measurable differences in levels of prosocial behaviors; nonetheless, the fathers of the boys were less likely to respond favorably (e.g., express affection) to their sons' prosocial behaviors toward peers or to encourage these types of actions. They were more likely to encourage and respond favorably to their daughters' display of prosocial behaviors. Such gender differences may be related to later prosocial outcomes, though this was not directly examined in this study. Related research suggests that parents differentially assign tasks to boys and girls at home—with girls more likely to be given traditionally feminine domestic tasks (e.g., cooking) versus traditionally more masculine tasks (e.g., mowing the lawn).

Effects of Gender Messages on Children

Parental messages about gender can come in different forms—from the color of clothing infants are immediately dressed in to parents' reactions to behaviors and choices of activities, to the types of toys that parents buy, to direct communication of approval and disapproval of how boys and girls are expected to act. The effects of these messages on gender stereotypes persist as children grow older. Research has found that exposure to traditional gender messages is highly associated with adults' endorsement of the traditional view of gender. Likewise, exposure to egalitarian parental messages is related to endorsement of egalitarian views. Intergenerational transmission of parenting suggests that parents' own experiences as children will most likely influence their own parental beliefs and child-rearing practices. In line with this assertion, children who are reared in traditional values, for example, will also teach traditional messages about gender when they become parents themselves. The values and assumptions of that particular perspective then perpetuate.

Aileen Garcia and Maria Rosario T. de Guzman

See also Gender Role Behavior; Gender Role Socialization; Gender Socialization in Adolescence; Gender Socialization in Childhood; Parental Expectations

Further Readings

Campenni, N. E. (1999). Gender stereotyping of children's toys: A comparison of parents and nonparents. *Sex Roles, 40*(1–2), 121–138. doi:10.1023/A:1018886518834

Epstein, M., & Ward, L. M. (2011). Exploring parent-adolescent communication about gender: Results from adolescent and emerging adult samples. *Sex Roles, 65*(1–2), 108–118.

Hastings, P. D., McShane, K. E., Parker, R., & Ladha, F. (1997). Ready to make nice: Parental socialization of young sons' and daughters' prosocial behaviors with peers. *Journal of Genetic Psychology, 168*(2), 177–200.

Witt, S. D. (1997). Parental influence on children's socialization to gender roles. *Adolescence, 32*(126), 253–259.

Parental Stressors

Parental stress is part of the parenting experience for both mothers and fathers. It arises when parenting demands exceed the expected and actual resources available to mothers and fathers that permit them to succeed in the parental role. Comparisons of mothers' and fathers' parental stress have found similarities and differences. In understanding these findings, it is important to consider that parenthood is often associated with a greater number of changes in mothers' than in fathers' lives because mothers are frequently children's primary caregivers. Mothers and fathers have different opportunities to observe and interact with their children, and form different relationships with them, and so may have different experiences and outcomes of parental stress. This entry focuses on the determinants and effects of parental stress and how they vary in fathers and mothers, as well as interventions to reduce parental stress.

Levels and Domains of Parental Stress

Overall, mothers may experience more parental stress than fathers. This is consistent with women generally experiencing more chronic and daily stressors than men. Mothers and fathers may experience parental stress in different domains. Mothers may experience higher stress related to their perceived incompetence in parenting and to role restriction (i.e., having reduced time and opportunity for their own interests and activities), whereas fathers may experience higher stress related to the social isolation brought on by parenthood.

Determinants of Parental Stress

There are two main theories of the sources of parental stress. One is that parental stress arises from the dynamics of the parent, the child, and the qualities of their dyadic relationship. The other is that parental stress is due to daily hassles—that is, the mild to moderate stressors typically occurring in households with young or adolescent children. The two theories offer complementary perspectives on the causes of parental stress, and ample evidence supports them both. The *Parenting Stress Index* by Richard Abidin is the most widely used measure for quantifying parental stress levels. Beyond these two general theories, the literature shows that, in addition to gender, parents' demographic, psychological, and personality characteristics, as well as children's characteristics, all influence the levels of parental stress. Furthermore, different factors influence parental stress, including mothers' and fathers' family, community, and cultural contexts.

Low education and income are associated with parental stress in fathers and mothers, but especially in fathers. Poor relationship quality between parents and poor parental health are also associated with more parental stress in mothers and fathers. Mothers and fathers report lower parental stress when the father shares in child care activities. LGBTQ (lesbian, gay, bisexual, transgender, and queer) parents face additional parental stress compared with their heterosexual and cisgender counterparts, often in the form of overt discrimination or microaggressions, due to the marginalization of LGBTQ people in the general society.

A predictor of parental stress is the child having a disabling or chronic health condition or behavioral problems. A commonly used framework for examining parental stress when children have health problems is the Double ABCX Model. In this model, parental stress is an imbalance in demands or stressors (aA factor) and capabilities or resources (bB factor). The parents' appraisal (cC factor) of the imbalance influences its impact. When the parent is unable to balance demands and capabilities, crises (xX) occur.

In families with a child with an intellectual disability, mothers' and fathers' stress was due primarily to appraising the situation as catastrophic. Among mothers, this appraisal derived from the child's behavioral problems, but among fathers, it derived from the child's lack of social acceptance. In families having a child with autism spectrum disorder, on the whole, mothers experience greater levels of parental stress than fathers. Although, in these families, both parents report higher stress in relation to their children's more severe symptoms, such as externalizing behaviors, mothers are affected by the children's emotional dysregulation and poor social skills to a greater degree than fathers. In studies of developmentally delayed and typically developing children, bidirectional relationships were found between parenting stress and child behavior problems for both mothers and fathers.

Another predictor of parental stress is stepparenting. Stepmothers have especially high parental stress; it is even higher than that of other at-risk groups, such as parents of children with behavioral disorders. Stepparent stress is attributed to lack of boundaries and role clarity, familial and societal expectations, and tense family relationships. The combination of less traditional views about gendered family roles and higher dyadic adjustment in the marriage (more satisfaction, cohesion, consensus, and affection) may be associated with less parenting stress for stepparents.

Effects of Parental Stress

It is clear that high parental stress is associated with negative consequences for mothers and fathers, such as dissatisfaction with being a parent, psychological symptoms, and physical health problems. Chronic stressors, including those associated with parenthood, wear down the cardiovascular, immune, and gastrointestinal systems. It is still unclear whether parental stress is a stronger predictor of poor mental and physical health among mothers or among fathers.

High parental stress is also associated with negative consequences for children, such as lower levels of health-related behaviors, including poorer sleep and nutrition, and fewer medical checkups and safety practices. It negatively affects parenting behavior and the quality of parent-child interactions. Specifically, parents who experience more stress are less warm and sensitive, more withdrawn in their interactions with their children, and less likely to use effective supervision, monitoring, and discipline strategies. Parental stress negatively influences the parent-child relationship and predicts poorer social-emotional and cognitive outcomes for children and adolescents. Indeed, high levels of parental stress may interrupt important developmental processes related to cognitive and social skills in young children. The little research available suggests that associations of parental stress with poorer parent-child communication are equally strong between mothers and fathers. In addition, mothers' and fathers' parent-child communication is mainly affected by their own parental stress level rather than by the other parent's parental stress level.

Interventions to Reduce Parental Stress

Few research trials have examined interventions to reduce parental stress. Among children with disabilities, standard service models such as respite care and case management, and psychoeducational and cognitive behavioral group interventions help reduce parental stress. However, these approaches have been studied much more among mothers than among fathers. Mindfulness practices and peer-mentor models, combined with advances in telemedicine and smart technology for intervention delivery, hold promise for effective parental stress reduction. It is important for researchers and health care professionals to consider gender differences when preparing and delivering intervention programs aimed at reducing parental stress. The management of high stress levels may require a multifaceted approach, incorporating parents' access to social support, services for their children, and parenting training. Mothers may be in greater possession or need of some of these help resources than fathers, given their generally higher levels of parental stress and general stress. Finally, family leave laws, which vary by state within the United States and by country, can reduce parental stress by offering paid and unpaid leave to protect employees' jobs.

Christine Timko and Christina Garrison-Diehn

See also Fatherhood; Motherhood; Parenting Styles, Gender Differences in

Further Readings

Abidin, R. R. (1992). Presidential address: The determinants of parenting behavior. *Journal of Clinical Child Psychology, 21*(4), 407–412.

Crnic, K. A., & Greenberg, M. T. (1990). Minor parenting stresses with young children. *Child Development, 61*(5), 1628–1637.

Deater-Deckard, K. (2004). *Parenting stress.* New Haven, CT: Yale University Press.

McCubbin, H. I., & Patterson, J. M. (1983). The family stress process: The double ABCX model of adjustment and adaptation. *Marriage & Family Review, 6*(1–2), 7–37.

Parenting Styles, Gender Differences in

In the field of psychology, parenting style refers to a combination of attitudes, values, beliefs, and the general approach that a parent takes to child rearing and socialization. This general approach creates an emotional environment in which the child is raised, which research suggests is linked to a host of well-being outcomes in both childhood and adulthood. In this entry, the types and dimensions of parenting styles in traditional, two-parent, heteronormative families are reviewed, including an examination of differences in the styles of mothers and fathers. The effects of parenting styles are also examined, and future directions for research on this topic are suggested.

Types and Dimensions of Parenting Styles

Perhaps one of the most prominent theorists to tackle the issue of parenting styles is Diana Baumrind, who, in 1966, developed a typology of parenting styles that classified parents based on the level of control they exercise over their children. Parents who imposed high levels of control were classified as having an authoritarian parenting style. Some of the outcomes associated with this style are children who are anxious, are withdrawn, and have poor self-esteem and coping skills. Those who exercise a moderate level of control are said to employ the authoritative style, and this is associated with children who have a good level of self-esteem, are self-controlled, and have good social skills. Parents who exercise inappropriately less or no control are categorized as permissive. Children who are reared in this style are described to be defiant, lack self-control, and be more likely to engage in risky behaviors later in life.

In 1983, this initial conceptualization of parenting styles was reconceptualized by psychologists Eleanor Maccoby and John Martin to be made up of two dimensions—responsiveness and demandingness. Responsiveness refers to the parent's warmth, acceptance, and sensitivity toward the child, whereas demandingness refers to the parent's assertion of rules, standards, and expectations of child behavior. This led to the split of the originally conceptualized permissive type into permissive indulgent and permissive indifferent or neglectful. Authoritarian parents are described to be high in demandingness but low in responsiveness, the authoritative parenting style is high in both demandingness and responsiveness, the permissive indulgent style is low in demandingness and high in responsiveness, and the permissive indifferent style is low in both demandingness and responsiveness. This typology is more commonly used in today's literature.

Of the typology, the more commonly studied types are the authoritative and authoritarian parenting styles. Needless to say, the authoritative parenting style is viewed as undisputedly the best approach to parenting. A mother or a father who displays a combination of reasonable demands, firm control, and sensitivity toward the child's needs serves as a good role model. This helps the child internalize the importance and rationality of the demands, in turn making the child more confident, independent, and behave more prosocially. On the other hand, the authoritarian parenting style has been the most controversial of the four styles. It is characterized by punitiveness, power assertion, and absolute standards. Because all of these are not sensitive and fair to the child, most studies have recognized that this style—regardless of whether it is the mother or the father who employs it—is detrimental to optimum development. However, some research claimed that the authoritarian parenting style is not always disagreeable and that the meanings and the effects of each parenting style vary across cultures. Certainly, the negative child outcomes consistently associated with an authoritarian parenting style in Western cultures are not always present in some Eastern cultures. In fact, in Chinese samples, researchers have found that this style is associated with higher academic achievement, determination, and obedience—values that are highly desirable in Asian children.

Regardless of culture, parenting style occurs in a context, and before discussing gender differences in parenting style, it is essential to understand the mechanisms by which parenting style influences child outcomes. Compared with parenting practices, parenting style is not goal defined. Rather, parenting style influences the effect of parenting practices by providing the emotional climate in which the parent's behavior is expressed. For example, a parent who has a goal of having the child excel in school may impose a television ban on weeknights. Imposing a television ban is the parenting practice, but how this rule is implemented and communicated to the child is influenced by the parenting style. A parent who calmly talks to the child about the reasons for the rule and who allows verbal give-and-take should the child have questions or thoughts about the demand is more likely to be effective than a parent who is aggressive and believes that an adult should not be questioned. It is possible then that a mother and a father with the same parenting goals and practices may not have the same effect on the child if they employ different parenting styles.

Mother and Father Differences

Through gender socialization, males and females learn the social expectations associated with one's sex. Role theory explains why differences in parenting between mothers and fathers may emerge. Because they learn different roles, men and women are expected to behave differently. Society expects the mother's role to be that of a caregiver, so early on, girls are taught to be caring and to provide warmth. The father's role, on the other hand, is characterized to be that of a financial provider and disciplinarian. Boys are socialized to be serious and stern, and that to show warmth and sensitivity is a sign of weakness. As such, fathers traditionally have little involvement and responsibility in the child-rearing front. As they act out their gender roles, a traditional mother is assumed to be more nurturing than controlling, whereas the opposite is expected of a traditional father. With this assumption, it was first suggested that a combination of an indulgent mother and an authoritative or authoritarian father is the most prevalent in conventional households. This claim, however, has not been consistently supported by research.

Empirical studies conducted in various cultures have indeed shown that gender is a significant predictor of the use of certain parenting styles. However, because parenting is not solely determined by gender and parenting styles are influenced by factors outside the parent-child and husband-wife dyads and the family itself, different studies have revealed a range of patterns. For instance, Australian mothers were found to use the authoritative and permissive styles more than Australian fathers did. In a sample of Singaporean parents, results showed that mothers and fathers are more authoritative than authoritarian, but mothers are more authoritative than fathers. A U.S.-based study comprising mostly White adolescents reported that mothers were rated higher in the authoritative and permissive subscales compared with fathers. European American fathers, on the other hand, were found to be more permissive compared with mothers. A combination of an authoritative father and a neglectful mother has also been reported to exist in parent-adolescent relationships. Evidently, these studies are not unifying or conclusive in terms of the specific effects of the parent's gender on parenting style. Nevertheless, it is clear from these findings that mothers and fathers do differ in their parenting styles.

Effects of Parenting Styles

The various effects of parenting styles on child outcomes have been established by research. In addition to that, existing literature has consistently revealed that one's parenting style may also influence the style the other parent will adopt. Mothers can affect fathers' parenting approach as much as fathers can influence mothers. For instance, the compensation effect states that when a parent adopts a less desirable parenting style, the other parent uses a more ideal approach of parenting to buffer the negative consequences of the ineffective parenting style. A study has found that the positive effects of authoritative parenting seemingly counterweigh the harmful effects associated with an authoritarian, indulgent, or neglectful parenting style, particularly when it is the mother who is authoritative. In contrast, the same research reported that having an authoritative father does not outweigh the negative influence of a neglectful mother. This finding also shows how the same parenting style employed by a mother and a father may have a different effect on the same child.

There are also cases wherein the two parents have the same parenting style. The evolutionary perspective of mate selection states that people are wired to marry someone who is similar to them. An indulgent and laid-back woman is likely to attract an indulgent and laid-back man, most likely resulting in a household with two indulgent parents. Additionally, as mothers' and fathers' parenting styles interact with each other, it is also plausible that two parents with different approaches at the start may end up using similar parenting styles as a product of socialization. Related to this are studies that found that congruency and consistency across two parents are beneficial for children. Note, however, that this is only true for the authoritative parenting style. Having an authoritarian or neglectful parent is not optimal for a child, and having two of either exacerbates these parenting styles' harmful consequences on child development.

Future Directions

Although the literature on parenting has grown in the past two decades, most of these have solely focused on mothers. Studies that did include fathers either only examined fathers or looked at mothers and fathers as a single source of data as though they were one and the same. To this day, studies including both parents and exploring the degree of their similarities and differences remain sparse as is the research on parenting styles of same-sex couples or LGBTQ single parents. Knowing from empirical data that mothers and fathers do parent differently, it is important to investigate mothers and fathers comparatively instead of aggregating them, as this may conceal unique patterns or important distinctions between them. Previous research has also suggested that parents may use different styles depending on the sex of their children. This is another central point that deserves further investigation. In addition to this, as family dynamics change and the roles of mothers and fathers become more flexible, examining changes in adopted parenting styles across gender and time is also an interesting line of inquiry.

Aileen Garcia and Maria Rosario T. de Guzman

See also Gender Role Behavior; Gender Role Socialization; Gender Socialization in Adolescence; Parental Expectations; Parental Messages About Gender

Further Readings

Baumrind, D. (1966). Effects of authoritative parental control on child behavior. *Child Development, 37*(4), 887–907.

Conrade, G., & Ho, R. (2001). Differential parenting styles for fathers and mothers: Differential treatment for sons and daughters. *Australian Journal of Psychology, 53*(1), 29–35.

Darling, N., & Steinberg, L. (1993). Parenting style as context: An integrative model. *Psychological Bulletin, 13*(3), 487–496.

Maccoby, E. E., & Martin, J. A. (1983). Socialization in the context of the family: Parent-child interaction. In P. H. Mussen (Series Ed.) & E. M. Hetherington (Vol. Ed.), *Handbook of child psychology: Vol. 4. Socialization, personality, and social development* (4th ed., pp. 1–101). New York, NY: Wiley.

McKinney, C., & Renk, K. (2008). Differential parenting between mothers and fathers: Implications for late adolescents. *Journal of Family Issues, 29*(6), 806–827.

Simons, L. G., & Conger, R. D. (2007). Linking mother-father differences in parenting to a typology of family parenting styles and adolescent outcomes. *Journal of Family Issues, 28*(2), 212–241. doi:10.1177/01925X06294593

Passing

In 1929, Nella Larsen published a novella called *Passing*, which was about a light-skinned woman of color whose skin tone allowed her to be perceived as a White woman and enjoy the associated rights and privileges thereof. The term *passing* was later used by sociologist Erving Goffman in his 1963 work *Stigma: Notes on the Management of Spoiled Identity*. Goffman conceptualized passing as the process of managing information in an attempt to avoid the stigma associated with a potentially concealable stigmatized identity and to enjoy the benefits of being viewed as what he called *normal*. As an example, lesbian, gay, bisexual, transgender, and queer (LGBTQ) individuals who present as heterosexual and cisgender are described as passing successfully in society. This entry further explains the meaning of and reasons for passing as described by Goffman. The process of passing is also reviewed. Finally, the advantages and disadvantages of passing are discussed.

Goffman identified three sources of stigmatized identity: (1) physical abnormalities, (2) character weaknesses, and (3) ethnic or cultural variations. Because sexual orientation and gender identity have the potential to be concealed, they are what Goffman referred to as discreditable, meaning that their discovery would lead to the individual being discredited or shamed. Goffman made specific mention of homosexuality as an indication of character weakness and suggested that homosexual individuals might endeavor to conceal their invisible or ambiguous identities. Goffman's statements about so-called physical abnormalities suggest that he would have also viewed transgender individuals as engaging in some level of passing by virtue of the societally dictated covering of genitalia.

Meanwhile, identities that are immediately visible, such as those marked by certain physical characteristics, are not concealable and therefore provide little to no opportunity for passing as "normal." Modern technologies, particularly developments in plastic surgery and prostheses, have expanded the realm of passable identities well beyond what was passable at the time of Goffman's writing. The Internet also affords a new opportunity for individuals to conceal previously unconcealable identities. This phenomenon has garnered a specific label—*catfishing*—and is looked on negatively by individuals who feel as though they have been duped by the presentation of a false persona via social media.

Being out as an LGBTQ individual with full acceptance and support appears to be ideal for maximizing positive affect and minimizing guilt and shame; however, in the sociopolitical climate of the 21st century, this experience remains the exception rather than the rule. While the term *passing* has been part of the common lexicon for many years, this is an underdeveloped area of research. It is apparent that, at least for some individuals, actively concealing sexual orientation or gender identity is a difficult and cognitively demanding task, yet it is not clear whether it is more stressful for individuals to be open in society as LGBTQ individuals or to pass as heterosexual and cisgender.

The Process of Passing

Individuals vary in the degree to which they disclose their sexual orientation or gender identity in different contexts. As Goffman noted, an individual may aim to conceal an identity from certain sectors of the population (e.g., law enforcement) but not from others (e.g., similarly identified individuals). Research on LGBTQ experiences indicates that many individuals hide their sexual orientations from family members and that managing sexual orientation in the workplace is also a serious concern for many individuals. Research indicates that two means of passing are predominant: enacting a false heterosexual identity or evading the topic of sexuality altogether.

Goffman notes that individuals may pass with or without the intention to do so, and it seems that some LGBTQ individuals exhibit stronger indicators of queerness than others. A small body of experimental research indicates that gay men and lesbian women may be distinguishable from heterosexuals in their appearance, mannerisms, and speech patterns. Furthermore, research suggests that gay men and lesbians are often unsuccessful in attempts to disguise their sexual identities.

Advantages of Passing

Due to the prevalence of homophobic and transphobic attitudes and behaviors, passing appears to offer some advantages to LGBTQ individuals. Many LGBTQ individuals are fearful about openly expressing their identities due to the potential for violent victimization or other harassment. Experiencing sexual orientation–based discrimination appears to be associated with lower self-esteem, depression, and posttraumatic stress. Perceived discrimination among LGBTQ teens has been linked to a variety of negative psychological and behavioral outcomes, including depressive symptoms, suicidal ideation, and self-harm. Perceived discrimination among gay men has been linked to negative physical and behavioral outcomes, including substance abuse, workplace absenteeism, and weakened immune response in those affected by HIV. Avoiding these experiences is a major motivation for passing. It has been suggested that passing is an adaptive mechanism that empowers LGBTQ individuals to protect themselves in environments that are not fully inclusive of LGBTQ identities.

Disadvantages of Passing

Research on concealment suggests that individuals who hide their "true" selves experience a sense of inauthenticity that is connected to feelings of immorality and shame. Goffman stated that intimate relationships put further pressure on individuals to expose their concealed identities and that those who conceal their stigmatized identities may experience guilt about doing so. Efforts to conceal one's sexual orientation and/or gender identity are also a potential source of significant stress. Passing is an ongoing process that requires self-regulatory effort for many individuals. The further one's "true self" deviates from dominant gender norms, the more likely it is that passing will be stressful and effortful. Furthermore, it has been argued that passing constitutes a form of self-repression by LGBTQ individuals, in that they are silencing themselves to abide by heteronormative dictates.

Lindsey S. Davis

See also Gender Conformity; Gender Expression; Hate Crimes Toward LGBTQ People; Heteronormativity; Heterosexism; Homophobia; Transphobia

Further Readings

Goffman, E. (1963). *Stigma: Notes on the management of spoiled identity*. Englewood Cliffs, NJ: Prentice Hall.

Harrison, K., & Cooley, D. R. (Eds.). (2012). *Passing/out: Sexual identity veiled and revealed*. Burlington, VT: Ashgate.

Kanuha, V. K. (1999). The social process of passing to manage stigma: Acts of internalized oppression or acts of resistance? *Journal of Sociology & Social Welfare, 26*, 27–46.

Pathologizing Gender Identity

Gender is a fundamental concept that helps people categorize those with whom they interact. Assumptions that are made about a person's gender can lead to problematic interactions that serve to alienate people, especially those who have a gender diverse identity. This entry discusses assumptions about gender, gender norms, and the diagnostic considerations of gender.

Gender Norms

Gender is enforced in a number of ways. The result of that enforcement often leads to difficulties for people regardless of their gender identity or expression. In this section, we will explore the ways in which gender enforcement affects cisgender women, transgender and gender nonconforming (TGNC) people, and cisgender men.

Women and Girls

Women and girls constantly hear messages about how to behave, what they should like, and whether their behavior and actions are consistent with someone else's belief about what it means to be feminine. Granted, women and girls are given much more latitude in how they express their gender. Still, there are limits, and women and girls are quickly reminded when they are perceived to have stepped outside those limits.

With regard to one's body, women and girls are reminded that if they are not thin enough then they are not attractive. This message has led to disordered eating and self-esteem concerns for women and girls. Interestingly, women who are portrayed in popular advertising report that the thin ideal creates body image issues for the models. This double-bind message is confusing for women and girls and only further complicates the ways in which they view themselves and how they relate to others.

Another area of normed behavior for women and girls relates to emotional expression. It is safe to say that women and girls are provided a significant range of emotions that are deemed to be appropriate. This might include happiness, sadness, anxiety, grief, confusion, compassion, longing, fear, and uncertainty, to name a few. Having the latitude to express this broad range of emotions allows women to express themselves in a variety of ways. Just as there are "positive" emotions that a woman can express, so are there "negative" emotions. For example, a woman who is assertive with others is often referred to as a bitch. In this way, women are discouraged from letting their voices be heard by others.

Even though research has shown that women and girls have the aptitude for math and science (and other academic subjects), there still remains a gap in the numbers of women and girls who pursue these academic topics. Some women and girls are even cautioned that they cannot show others that they are smart. A smart woman is seen by others as a threat. This is one of the ways in which women are told that they must behave in a prescriptive manner instead of being encouraged to be themselves.

TGNC People

From early in life, children hear messages about the kinds of toys they can play with, the color of clothing that is acceptable to wear, and the types of friends they can bring home for a play date. All of these messages, while well intentioned, set the stage for gender nonconforming children to experience psychological conflicts related to gender.

Enforcing the ways in which children and adolescents express their gender can create a variety of challenges for young people. The fact that U.S. society adheres to the gender binary only further enforces gender norms. From which restroom a person can use to the decisions about what to wear to work or school, messages about gender only serve to silence TGNC people.

Most problematic for TGNC people is the insistence that one should be either a boy/male or a girl/female and one cannot move between these polar locations. Given that TGNC people have existed throughout history and across cultures, it is curious that, as a society, we continue to enforce this norm.

Men

In some ways, men are considered the norm. However, there are also clear expectations as to how men are expected to behave, emote, and express their gender. Men and boys are often told to "act like a man." The assumption here is that by not acting like a man, they are acting like a woman. This assumption is problematic for men and for women. For men, the expectations about mannerisms include a very narrow range of options. The same is true for how a man expresses his gender. Unless it is Halloween, one is unlikely to see a man in a dress or skirt. It is acceptable, though, for women to wear pants even in professional settings, provided they are women's pants.

Diagnosis

There are two basic concerns related to diagnosis. The first is about how men or women are overrepresented in various mental health diagnostic categories. The second concern is related to the fact that gender dysphoria (GD) is listed as a mental health disorder.

Overrepresented Diagnoses

There are several diagnoses in which either men or women are overrepresented. It is unclear whether this is due to true differences in prevalence between men and women or the ways in which the behavior of men and women is pathologized and therefore deemed to be a clinical concern. As an example, women are more likely to be diagnosed with depression. In fact, the diagnostic criteria are more descriptive of behaviors and emotional experiences that are more typical of women than they are of men. Does this mean that men do not experience depression? Or, rather, is it that men's expression of depression is incorrectly depicted in the *Diagnostic and Statistical Manual of Mental Disorder, Fifth Edition* (*DSM-5*).

Similarly, boys are more likely to be diagnosed with attention-deficit/hyperactive disorder (ADHD) than are girls. Going back to the ways in which boys and girls are expected to behave, according to gender norms, girls are unlikely to behave in a manner that might be deemed to be hyperactive. The fact that so many children and adolescents are being treated for ADHD has become problematic. Teachers and parents are very quick to label a child as hyperactive if the child fails to sit at the desk or pay attention to directions.

Women and girls are more likely to be diagnosed with mental health disorders that are thought to be especially damaging. For example, it is primarily women and girls who are diagnosed with histrionic or borderline personality disorders. Neither of these disorders are considered to paint women in a flattering light. Until recently, borderline personality disorders were considered to be untreatable. Fortunately, that has changed, and women are able to get treatment for this serious clinical concern.

The same might be said for oppositional defiant disorder and boys. Like ADHD, the disorder seems to pathologize behaviors that are more typical of boys. Another problematic diagnosis is transvestic disorder. This disorder is almost exclusively diagnosed in men—specifically in men who wear women's clothing. This draws us back to earlier discussions of what is and is not an "appropriate" expression of gender. Women can wear pants, but men are not allowed to wear dresses.

Pathologizing Gender

Until the *DSM-5* was published in 2013, transgender people were often diagnosed with gender identity disorder. Many TGNC people found this diagnosis disturbing because what was deemed to be problematic was a person's identity. The *DSM-5* introduced the diagnosis of GD. For some people, receiving this diagnosis provides an answer to questions they have had about their gender. For others, the diagnosis is unnecessarily pathologizing. Some

TGNC activists have maintained that any diagnosis related to gender identity is problematic. Other people insist that having a diagnosis is necessary, as there are people who will not be able to access care without a diagnosis. Typically, this includes people who are incarcerated or are living in poverty. There is not sufficient space in this entry to address the complexity of the controversy about diagnosis. Some believe that the GD diagnosis addresses some of the concerns that were present in the gender identity disorder diagnosis. This includes removal of the sexual orientation specifiers, the addition of an exit clause (meaning that if there is no clinical concern then a person is not diagnosable), and the development of criteria specific to children. Finally, the fact that GD was removed from the section of the *DSM-5* that included sexual concerns and paraphilic disorders was welcomed by many.

lore m. dickey

See also Anti-Trans Bias in the *DSM*; Criminalization of Gender Nonconformity; Doing Gender; Gender Dysphoria; Gender Nonconforming Behaviors; Mental Health Stigma and Gender

Further Readings

American Psychiatric Association. (2013). *Diagnostic and statistical manual of mental disorders* (5th ed.). Washington, DC: Author.

Substance Abuse Mental Health Services Administration. (2015). *Ending conversion therapy: Supporting and affirming LGBTQ youth*. Rockville, MD: Author. Retrieved from https://blog.samhsa.gov/2016/03/28/ending-conversion-therapy-supporting-and-affirming-lgbtq-youth/#.WIXq0NJ961s

Winters, K. (2008). *Gender madness in American psychiatry: Essays from the struggle for dignity.* Dillon, CO: GID Reform Advocates.

World Professional Association for Transgender Health. (2010). *WPATH de-psychopathologisation statement.* Retrieved from http://www.cpath.ca/wp-content/uploads/2010/05/WPATHpatho0510.pdf

Patriarchy

Patriarchy refers to the symbols and ideas that systematically privilege masculinity over femininity and are embedded in structural, institutional, and discursive practices. Patriarchy operates to stratify society, resulting in male advantages across a variety of social systems—such as the economy, politics, the family, and religion. Key to this definition is that patriarchy operates systematically. While patriarchy does affect interpersonal relationships, it is not an individual-level phenomenon. What this means is that neither does patriarchy ensure a privileged position to every individual male nor does it suggest that every male oppresses women. Instead, it refers to the overall patterning of behavior and how institutions are organized.

To clarify this point, the development of this term as referring to structural arrangements will be discussed first. Following this, the entry will explore what is meant by patriarchy systematically stratifying society. The entry will then address if the United States is a patriarchy and how patriarchy affects men, before concluding with critiques of the concept.

Development of the Term

In the late 1960s to 1970s, radical feminists introduced the term *patriarchy* to refer to male domination in social institutions. Using it to replace terms such as *male chauvinism* and *sexism*, which suggest an individual-level struggle between men and women, radical feminists sought to highlight the structural realities of male domination that go beyond beliefs and common practices. The reason they felt the need for a change in terminology is best explained through comparing the assumptions of liberal feminism with those of the radical movement.

Liberal Feminism

In the United States, liberal feminism dates back to the American Revolution. Many of the early writings of this movement predate this, coming out of England after the Industrial Revolution. Derived from Enlightenment thinking, liberal feminists held that human beings are essentially rational. As such, equality between men and women could be accomplished through educating the population that beliefs about women's inferiority are misguided. They held that changes could be accomplished legitimately through reforming the current system and supported electoral, judicial, and legislative actions to create these changes.

Radical Feminism

A major critique of liberal feminism is that it failed to understand how deeply rooted male privilege is within society. Recognizing that it was not simply a set of beliefs about male superiority that shape practices (e.g., unequal pay), radical feminists argued that male privilege gave shape to our current social systems. As such, it is impossible to work from within these structures and make changes through reform. Instead, there needs to be a revolution to supplant these structures with egalitarian ones. Differentiating themselves from other feminists (e.g., socialist or Marxist) of the time, radical feminists would argue that patriarchy was a system of stratification that is separate from race- and class-based systems and existed prior to these other stratification systems. Gender inequality, they would argue, served as the model for how other stratification systems would develop.

Patriarchy as Systematic Stratification

What does it mean when one says that patriarchy systematically stratifies society? The best way to answer this question is to think of patriarchy as a taken-for-granted assumption that is at the core of societal beliefs. A key component is the idea that it is "taken for granted," meaning that it is so fundamental that it seems natural and, as such, is left to operate largely unchallenged and invisibly. Indeed, part of what is radical about radical feminists is that to point out such an ingrained part of our society and to name it a dysfunction, as something that needs to be eradicated, is a radical act in itself. Operating as patriarchy does—as a belief at the core of our very society—when anything is created in society, patriarchy becomes a part of how this new thing operates. It does this through an associated set of symbols and ideas (through a discourse) that defines what is valued and associates that with masculinity, and what is devalued and associates that with femininity. Institutions (e.g., the family, economy, politics, and religion) and everyday interactions (from how we arrange our relationships, to conversations, to sexual relations) are ruled by our shared understanding of and complicity with these discourses.

In terms of discourse, patriarchy includes an underlying understanding of the nature of social objects. The essential elements of this understanding highlight dichotomies such as reason/emotion, culture/nature, independent/dependent, and public/private. In each of these pairs, the first is associated with the male and is valued, while the second is associated with the female and is devalued. Feminists have applied these dichotomies to instructions to explain structural and lived arrangements.

For example, in terms of economic institutions, feminists argue that the public versus private dichotomy began in the 17th century with capitalism. Referred to as a "doctrine of separate spheres" and associated with the "cult of true womanhood," the household (private) was understood as the appropriate place for women, where they could take care of the home and children as it was their special ability to nurture (nature and emotion). They should be kept separate from the public and cultural sphere of men, who could rule society best due to their rational nature. It was then men's duty to protect women (dependence). As work continued to be separated from the home after the Industrial Revolution, the resulting ideology that men belonged in the workforce and women at home would shape many policies, practices, and expectations for behavior that still exist today. For example, research on the pay gap in 2013 (women working full-time year-round made, on average, 78% of what men did) points to concepts such as a "family wage" (i.e., men earn more than women because they are assumed to be supporting the family and women's wages are extra) to explain the continuing discrimination.

Beyond the economy, feminism illustrates how these dichotomies shape the overall cultural arrangements. For example, feminists such as Susan Brownmiller in *Against Our Will* (1975) argued that the United States has a "rape culture" whereby violence against women is a normalized and accepted method of policing a woman's behavior to keep her restricted to a private sphere. According to this perspective, when a woman steps outside her rightful place in society, she is no longer worthy of a male's protection, and violence is an effective means to punish her to serve as a warning to other females. This can be seen in how women are blamed for their own attacks when they go out into public places late at night without a male's protection.

Furthermore, daily experiences, no matter how mundane, are also shaped by these dichotomies. Long after radical feminism declined in the 1980s, feminists have written cultural analyses with the intent of explicating how fundamental patriarchy affects our social arrangements. For example, feminists in 2015 spent a considerable amount of time discussing "man sprawl" on public transport (i.e., men sitting with their legs far apart, taking up unnecessary space) and arguing that it is evidence of men's sense of entitlement to public spaces.

The United States as a Patriarchy

Allan Johnson argued that a society is patriarchal to the extent that it is male dominated, male identified, and male centered. *Male dominated* refers to who has positions of authority. Men dominate leadership in many institutions, such as the economy, politics, and religion. For example, in 2015, only 23 women were CEOs of Standard & Poor's (S&P) 500 companies, and only 14% of all leadership positions were held by women. Women were sworn into Congress in record-breaking numbers in 2015 but still made up only 20% of its elected officials. Similarly, they made up only 24.8% of statewide elected officials (including governors) and 18.4% of mayors across all U.S. cities.

Male identified refers to the extent to which characteristics associated with males are deemed more desirable than characteristics associated with females and are assumed to be the norm. As previously discussed, the idea of a male is associated with valued concepts such as rational, in opposition to the devalued female association with emotion. Feminists who point this out in daily life will show images of male figures being used to stand for a generic person.

Finally, *male centered* is the extent to which society focuses on the contributions of men. This is true across many domains. Men are more likely than women to be the focus of television shows or movies. The majority of children's books have males as the central character. Men even tend to dominate conversations by speaking more often and for longer periods of time.

Patriarchy as a Problem for Men

Much of the mainstream pushback against the concept of patriarchy is based on a fundamental misunderstanding of what patriarchy is. Discussed as the oppression of women and privileging of men, people often hear this and believe it to be men as individuals being oppressive toward individual women. Indeed, some feminists would take this stance. However, the correct meaning of *patriarchy* reflects how social structural arrangements privilege men (as a class of person) over women. In short, men are not the problem; society is.

Michael Kimmel writes extensively about what living in a patriarchy requires of, and costs, men. While masculinity and its associated discourses are privileged (i.e., seen as more competent or worthy), men and boys are under constant social pressure to prove that they meet the requirements of masculinity. To do so, they must repudiate anything associated with femininity. This can include everything from how they function as a father to the emotions they are culturally expected to experience and express. Kimmel argues that men and boys are charged with policing each other, resulting in relationships primarily composed of competition. Everything becomes part of this competition—wealth, power, and even women. Heterosexuality is compulsory, and homosexuality is associated with femininity and is thus to be avoided, even by association. When men step outside the boundary, they can be sanctioned through violence from other men. The fear of being seen as less than masculine is so complete that men and boys may remain silent rather than speak out against homophobia, racism, and sexism.

Critiques of Patriarchy

The nature of patriarchy is such that everyone who lives within a system defined by patriarchy is ruled by it. This includes both men and women. Furthermore, because patriarchy is at the very core of our society, both women and men accept it as natural and right, making it largely invisible. Therefore, it should be no surprise that the biggest opponents of claims that patriarchy exists and/or is problematic include both women and men.

There are several anti-feminist groups run by women that are for women. For example, the

Independent Women's Forum and Concerned Women for America argue that inequality between men and women no longer exists. There are similar groups for men. For example, some men's rights activists groups, which developed partly in response to radical feminist movements, argue that the United States is not a patriarchy and say that either it is already a matriarchy (where femininity is privileged) or feminists are working toward that goal. To be clear, many men's rights groups instead focus on positive social change for men, such as custody rights and the high rate of sexual assault on male children.

Feminists have also critiqued the concept of patriarchy. Marxist feminists, for example, reject the notion that patriarchy is the fundamental arrangement of society and instead point to how capitalism structures women's oppression. They point to the example of the "cult of true womanhood" as illustrating how the shift from an agricultural-based economy to an industrial one is what fundamentally defined woman's roles in society. Black feminist thought also critiqued the radical feminist notion of patriarchy for its emphasis on the oppression of women by male-centered systems while ignoring other types of stratification. These feminists would note that patriarchy, while real, does not explain how White women can oppress Black women. Instead, it is necessary to understand how different systems (usually race, class, and sex—or what bell hooks refers to as White supremacist capitalist patriarchy) form interlocking sets of oppression.

Bridget K. Diamond-Welch

See also Androcentrism; Anti-Feminist Backlash; Feminism: Overview; Feminism and Men; Second-Wave Feminism; Third-Wave Feminism

Further Readings

Brownmiller, S. (1975). *Against our will: Men, women, and rape.* New York, NY: Simon & Schuster.

Figes, E. (1971). *Patriarchal attitudes.* Greenwich, CT: Fawcett.

hooks, b. (2000). *Feminist theory: From margin to center.* Cambridge, MA: South End Press.

Johnson, A. (2014). *The gender knot: Unraveling our patriarchal legacy* (3rd ed.). Philadelphia, PA: Temple University Press.

Kimmel, M. (2008). *Guyland: The perilous world where boys become men.* New York, NY: HarperCollins.

Lerner, G. (1986). *The creation of patriarchy.* New York, NY: Oxford University Press.

Mann, S. A. (2012). *Doing feminist theory: From modernity to postmodernity.* Oxford, England: Oxford University Press.

Walby, S. (1990). *Theorizing patriarchy.* Oxford, England: Basil Blackwell.

PEDOPHILIA AND GENDER

Pedophilia is considered a *paraphilia*—an abnormal or unnatural attraction. In the case of pedophilia, this is sexual attraction toward children. This includes fantasies, sexual urges, or behaviors that involve sexual activity with a prepubescent child. Although this definition includes sexual activity with a child, not all pedophiles commit sexual offenses against children, and these individuals are able to desist from offending. Conversely, not all individuals who sexually offend against children are pedophiles and may not be sexually attracted to children. Studies have estimated that the prevalence of pedophilia among men who commit sexual offenses against children is around 50%. Given that most research and theory in this area examines pedophiles who have committed sexual offenses, this entry will mainly focus on this group.

The topic of pedophilia and gender encompasses two main areas: (1) the gender of pedophiles and (2) the erotic gender preference of pedophiles. Although the majority of pedophiles and child sex offenders are male, it is becoming increasingly apparent that females may also perpetrate sexual offenses against children and/or may be pedophiles. The second issue relates to pedophilic individuals' erotic gender preference (i.e., whether they are sexually attracted to female children, male children, or both genders). Related to this is victim preference—whether pedophilic sexual offenders commit their offenses against female children, male children, or both genders.

This entry discusses the gender of pedophiles, how the genders differ in their attraction toward children, and the motivations to offend in the case of pedophilic sex offenders. Included in this examination will be the development of gender preference in these individuals.

Prevalence of Pedophilia and Sexual Offenses Against Children

The true prevalence of pedophilia is very difficult to calculate. This is primarily due to the significant underreporting of sexual offenses in general. Furthermore, nonoffending pedophiles are not necessarily likely to come to the attention of law enforcement. Prevalence in the general population is not known, but it is estimated to be lower than 5% in men. The prevalence of pedophilia in females is estimated to be much lower. It is thought that females may account for 0.4% to 5% of convicted sexual offenses. Of course, this figure may include nonpedophilic sex offenders and conversely does not account for pedophilic females who do not commit offenses.

As mentioned, sexual offenses frequently go undetected, and this is especially true when the victims are children. Child sex offenders (of either gender) will go to great lengths to conceal their offending, and this often includes persuading victims to remain silent. However, there are also various gender-related issues in relation to the recording of sexual offenses. For example, male victims are much less likely to report abuse compared with female victims. This is especially true if the offender is female. In fact, sexual offenses committed by females are much less likely to be reported by either gender victim than offenses committed by male offenders.

Gender of Pedophiles and Pedophilic Sexual Offenders

Much of the literature on sex offenses focuses on adult males who have offended against children, therefore including pedophiles who have sexually offended against children. However, the distinction between pedophilic and nonpedophilic child sex offenders is not often made in such research. The focus on female pedophiles and sexual offenders is relatively new. A large proportion of the research conducted with female sex offenders utilizes adolescent samples, whereas research with males covers all age groups. This raises an interesting question about the levels of pedophilia among sex-offending females, given that adolescent offenders may not be old enough to be diagnosed as pedophiles.

Male Pedophiles

As the majority of sexual offenses against children are perpetrated by men, it is reasonable to assume that pedophilia is more common in men than in women, and this is reflected in the number of diagnoses made. As discussed previously, it is very difficult to estimate the true prevalence of pedophilia, as most of the data come from samples of men convicted of sexual offenses; not all child sex offenders are pedophiles, and not all pedophiles commit sexual offenses against children, which makes it difficult to estimate the true prevalence. Furthermore, no epidemiological survey relating to sexual attraction to prepubescent children has been conducted. Because what is learned about pedophilia largely comes from studies of convicted offenders, not a lot is known about men who are sexually attracted to children but do not offend. Consequently, there are numerous theories related to the etiology of sexually offending against children, which have been tested empirically, but not so many that are devoted specifically to the development of pedophilia. Three main theories, however, explain (1) the conditioning of sexual arousal, (2) child sexual abuse, and (3) neurodevelopmental causes. These theories are discussed in greater detail later in this entry.

Female Pedophiles

Until relatively recently, female pedophiles and sexual offenders were assumed to be characteristically similar to their male counterparts. However, recent research has highlighted the fact that female sex offenders are in fact different from male offenders, with different motivations, psychological characteristics, and offense patterns. However, like male sex offenders, there is no one type that characterizes them, and as such, female pedophiles and sex offenders are a heterogeneous group. Researchers have attempted to create typologies of female sex offenders that describe the differences between these women. Frequently included in these typologies is the pedophilic female sex offender, who is sexually attracted to prepubescent children. This type of offender is often called "the predisposed offender" and is typically a woman with her own extensive abuse history who tends to abuse younger children and is therefore likely to be pedophilic. Another common type of female sex offender is the "teacher-lover," who is described as someone who falls in love with her adolescent victim and believes him to be her equal and an active participant in their sexual "relationships." Although these types of offenders typically hold a sexual attraction for their victim, the fact that the victim is usually an adolescent, and therefore pubescent, means that these offenders are unlikely to be pedophiles; instead, they may be hebephiles (i.e., adults with a sexual interest in early-pubescent individuals). A third type of female sexual offender is the "male-coerced offender," who is pressured, forced, or manipulated into facilitating sexual abuse by her male partner. This type does not necessarily take part in the actual abuse but has a major role in the facilitation of the abuse. These women may be less likely to be pedophilic given that they were coerced into their offenses, but case studies have revealed that following the offenses, these women may develop a sexual attraction to prepubescent children.

Gender Differences in Pedophiles and Child Sex Offenders

Theorists and researchers have uncovered several major gender differences in pedophiles and child sex offenders. Generally, female pedophiles and child sex offenders have more extensive abuse histories than their male counterparts. Often, the abuse experienced by these women includes severe and sustained sexual victimization. Male pedophiles and child sex offenders may also have a background of sexual victimization, but the prevalence is estimated to be around 30% for men compared with around 70% for women. Possibly related to this, female child sex offenders tend to have significantly greater mental health problems than male offenders. In terms of victim preference, female child sex offenders are more likely to offend against children who are related or known to them, compared with male offenders. Finally, female offenders are a lot more likely to co-offend with a male partner, whereas male offenders almost exclusively offend alone.

Gender Identity and Erotic Gender Preference of Pedophiles and Child Sex Offenders

Most of the research and theory in this area relate to male pedophiles and child sexual offenders. Clinical observations have revealed gender identity disturbances in male pedophiles, with individuals commonly experiencing precarious perceptions of themselves as sexual beings. This can also influence erotic gender preference. It is thought that these issues stem from a difficulty in integrating typical masculine and feminine characteristics. It is hypothesized that in the case of male pedophiles, this is heavily influenced by individuals' relationships with their parents and early sexual experiences, including sexual trauma.

Erotic gender preference refers to an individual's sexual arousal to a preferred gender. It is often assumed that most male pedophiles are homosexual, but in fact, this is not the case. While some male pedophiles do have an erotic preference for male children, they might also be attracted to adult females. Furthermore, some pedophile sex offenders have both male and female victims. Several studies have examined erotic gender preference in pedophiles. In most of these studies, plethysmography (an instrument that measures blood volume) is used to measure penile erectile response in order to test erotic gender differentiation in samples of pedophilic sex offenders, rapists (individuals who sexually offend against adult women), and nonoffender controls. Results have generally shown that pedophilic sex offenders are less differentiated in their gender preference than men who offended against adults. In other words, rapists almost exclusively showed arousal to females, whereas pedophiles were more likely to show arousal to both genders. This lack of differentiation in arousal to gender is known as *gender crossover* when discussing offenders who have victims of both genders. A large body of research has found evidence for gender crossover in male pedophilic child sex offenders, but little is known about the phenomenon in female child sex offenders, whether pedophilic or nonpedophilic.

Various studies have attempted to ascertain the origins of erotic gender preference in pedophilic male child sex offenders. Studies that have examined adolescent males who have sexually offended against both children and adults have found that individuals who offend against male children are more likely to have been sexually abused themselves, compared with those who offend against adult females. This seems to be the case even if an individual offends against both male and female children, so the presence of at least one male victim is associated with the offender's own sexual victimization. Conversely, adolescent sex offenders who only offended against female peers or adult females had a much smaller likelihood of having been victimized. Interestingly, erotic preferences for male victims in male child sex offenders are associated with a greater number of offenses, and a greater number of victims, than those who offend against females.

Theorists have posed several explanations for these findings, most of which involve the development of sexual orientation and sexual attraction, making these explanations more relevant to pedophilic child sex offenders. One theory is that individuals may have experienced sexual arousal during their own abuse and, consequently, masturbate to fantasies of the abuse. This could then condition their own sexual arousal to cues of young boys. A second theory posits that if a male child is abused by a male perpetrator (as is most prevalent), then this may lead him to question his own sexuality, particularly if he experienced sexual arousal during the abuse. Therefore, offending against a male child may represent an attempt at regaining a sense of control and mastery over homosexual conflicts. A third explanation involves social learning theory and posits that a male adolescent offender may be modeling the behavior of the male who victimized him when he is offending against his own victim.

Due to the scarcity of research relating to female sexual offenders in general, not much is known about erotic gender preference in female pedophiles and sex offenders. However, several studies have shown that female child sex offenders are more likely to victimize female children than male children. However, the origins of this preference are not clear.

Emily Blake

See also Cycles of Abuse; Female Sex Offenders; Gender Identity; Measuring Sexual Orientation; Sexual Abuse; Sexual Assault; Sexual Offenders

Further Readings

Freund, K. (1969). Erotic preference in pedophilia. *Behaviour Research and Therapy, 5*, 339–348.

Gannon, T. A., & Cortoni, F. (2010). *Female sexual offenders: Theory, assessment and treatment.* Hoboken, NJ: Wiley.

Marshall, W. L., Laws, D. R., & Barbaree, H. E. (1990). *Handbook of sexual assault: Issues, theories, and treatment of the offender*. New York, NY: Plenum Press.

Seto, M. C. (2008). *Pedophilia and sexual offending against children.* Washington, DC: American Psychological Association.

Seto, M. C. (2009). Pedophilia. *Annual Review of Clinical Psychology, 5*, 391–407.

Peer Pressure in Adolescence

The developmental period of adolescence (ages 12–18 years) marks a transition between childhood and adulthood. It involves biological changes related to puberty, cognitive and psychological maturation, and transitions in social relationships. Adolescence is a critical period for establishing one's identity and autonomy from parents, with peer relationships playing a key role in this process. Feedback from peers and perceived social status among peers become important determinants of adolescents' identity and self-evaluations. The mere presence of peers makes adolescents behave more recklessly (e.g., driving too fast) and intensifies problem behaviors that emerge in adolescence (e.g., delinquency and alcohol use). Peers become a powerful source of influence in adolescence, a phenomenon often called "peer pressure" in everyday language. However, peers rarely exert explicit "pressure" to make adolescents behave in certain ways. Instead, peer influences on adolescents' behavior work in more subtle ways. This entry reviews the peer context in adolescence, the methods used to study peer influence, the reasons for adolescents' greater susceptibility to peer influences, how peer influence works, the factors that affect susceptibility to peer influence, and what steps can be taken to reduce negative peer influence.

Peer Context in Adolescence

In Western cultures, peers represent the most salient social reference group for adolescents. Compared with children, adolescents spend less time with their families and more time with their peers, in both face-to-face and digital communications (e.g., texting, social media). With more developed cognitive and social skills, interactions with peers become more complex, and friendships grow in closeness and intimacy. Biological maturation drives increasing interest in romantic relationships. Predominantly same-sex peer interactions of childhood give way to mixed-sex peer groups and the later emergence of dyadic romantic relationships. Feedback from peers and perceived social status among peers (i.e., popularity) shape how youth view and evaluate themselves, more so than at any other point in people's lives. Adolescents are influenced by different types of peers—close friends, friendship groups (cliques), romantic partners, siblings, acquaintances, and even the larger peer group including unfamiliar peers.

How Scientists Study Peer Influence

Most studies of peer influence have used one of three methodologies: (1) asking youth about their susceptibility to peer influence, (2) inferring peer influence by linking peer behavior with changes in adolescents' behavior, and (3) measuring peer influence directly in the lab.

Self-report studies ask youth directly how susceptible or resistant they are to peer influences (e.g., "I give into peer pressure easily"; "Some people think it's more important to be an individual than to fit in with the crowd, but other people think it is more important to fit in with the crowd than to stand out as an individual—which sort of person are you most like?"). Alternatively, studies present participants with hypothetical scenarios and ask them how they would act (e.g., "A friend asks you to smoke a cigarette, but you really don't want to. What would you do?"). Although people are not always accurate reporters of their own behavior, self-reports of susceptibility to peer pressure have been validated against other measures of personality characteristics (e.g., impulsivity), changes in behavior (e.g., youth who report being more susceptible show greater increase in antisocial behavior over time if they have antisocial friends), and brain functioning (e.g., lower inhibition and connectivity from the prefrontal cortex to other brain areas are seen in those who report being more susceptible). In studies comparing different age groups, self-reported susceptibility to peer influence typically decreases from the ages of 14 to 18 years, with little change before the age of 14 and after the age of 18 years.

Inferential studies attempt to measure peer influence as it occurs naturally among friends and peer groups by inferring it from changes in behavior. We have long known that people are similar to their friends in attitudes and behaviors (called homophily) and that this similarity can result from the selection of similar peers for friends, friends influencing one another over time, or both. Many studies have tried to disentangle the roles of peer selection and peer influence by measuring the characteristics of adolescents and their friends over time and testing whether friends' attitudes and behaviors predict changes in adolescents' attitudes or behaviors.

In general, these studies support robust peer selection effects, particularly for behaviors and attitudes that are more common in the age group (e.g., sexual attitudes and aggressive behavior rather than sexual behaviors or alcohol use among younger adolescents). In addition, these studies provide considerable support for peer influences on alcohol use, smoking, and other drug use; disruptive, aggressive, and delinquent behavior; risky sexual behavior; risky driving; and related attitudes. More recent work shows that peers also influence adolescents' depressive symptoms, nonsuicidal self-injury, body image concerns, disordered eating, weight control behaviors (e.g., dieting), food intake, and physical activity. Although most studies have focused on undesirable behaviors, peer influences also extend to positive behaviors such as academic motivation, scholastic achievement, and prosocial behavior.

A common limitation of these studies is using adolescents' reports of their friends' behavior, which tend to be biased by the adolescents' own behavior (i.e., we typically perceive our friends to be more similar to us than they are). Although some argue that teens' perceptions of peer behavior are more influential than the actual behavior of the peers, a number of studies have supported peer influence using measures independent of the target teens, such as friends' reports of their own behavior or ratings from teachers or peers. Although most inferential studies have focused on adolescence, peer influence has been demonstrated for younger and older age groups as well, from children as young as kindergarten to young adults.

Lab studies allow for a direct assessment of peer influences, either through observations of peer interactions or through manipulation of different peer conditions. In observation studies, youth may be asked to bring a friend to the lab and discuss specific topics together. Their conversations are typically videotaped and later coded for instances of peer influence. For example, one study conceptualized the inability to maintain one's viewpoint in a discussion with a friend as a direct measure of susceptibility and linked it with more problem behaviors outside the lab.

Lab experimental studies manipulate peer presence or peer behavior through the use of peer confederates or computer programs. For instance, peer rejection is often manipulated with the "Cyberball" game, where participants play a ball game on the computer with other players who are believed to be real. After a few throws, the other players stop throwing the ball to the participants, inducing a feeling of rejection. Studies consistently find that rejection has more negative effects on mood in adolescents compared with adults. Other experimental studies require participants to make decisions under different peer conditions. These studies find that the mere presence of peers (real or believed, known or unknown) leads to more risky and impulsive decisions made by adolescents compared with being alone, whereas the presence of peers makes no difference in adults' decision making. Another variation involves making decisions before and after receiving information about peers' decisions or peers' evaluations of their own or other players' decisions. Again, adolescents show greater conformity with their peers' behavior or opinions compared with other age groups, particularly adults. Another example of experimental studies are those conducted in the "bar lab" (i.e., a lab equipped to look like a bar), showing how confederate peers' drinking affects youth alcohol use in naturalistic situations.

Why Are Teens More Susceptible?

Individuals of all ages are influenced by other people to some degree. However, early adolescents (ages 12–14 years) are more influenced by their peers than any other age group, and their susceptibility gradually decreases as they mature into adulthood. Developmental neuroscience points to the role of puberty-triggered maturation in brain areas responsible for social cognitions (thinking about and understanding other people's behavior), which makes early adolescents more self-conscious, as well as more aware of and concerned about others' opinions. Coupled with developmental changes in the brain reward system, adolescents become highly sensitive to social rewards, particularly those involving peers. Being accepted and admired by peers assumes increasing importance, and just being with other peers becomes more rewarding than ever before or after. Peer presence also primes the brain reward system to be more sensitive to other immediate rewards, such as the thrill of doing something risky (e.g., shoplifting, speeding) or the pleasures of alcohol or drugs. With the continued maturation of the prefrontal cortex through adolescence and young adulthood, youth become better able to regulate their behavior, and sensitivity to peers decreases. After about the age of 20 years, the mere presence of peers no longer has the same effect on brain functioning and risk taking as it did in the teen years.

Mechanisms of Peer Influence

As described by social learning theories, peers influence youth primarily through modeling and reinforcement. Adolescents often imitate behaviors exhibited and valued by peers to conform to perceived social norms in the peer group, and in turn, these behaviors are reinforced through peers' positive feedback. Thomas Dishion and colleagues described this process for antisocial behavior as "deviancy training" (e.g., a friend smiling or laughing in response to a rule-breaking talk). They found that youth who engaged in more deviancy training during their lab visit with a friend took part in more alcohol and drug use, as well as delinquent and risky sexual behavior later on. On the other hand, adolescents who do not conform to peer norms risk social punishment of being ridiculed or excluded. For example, gender-atypical behavior and perceived nonnormative sexual orientation are often punished with homophobic name-calling, exclusion from group activities, and other forms of maltreatment. This peer pressure is effective in reducing gender-atypical behavior but contributes to low self-esteem, depression, and other negative outcomes in sexual minority youth. Similarly, youth who do not conform to peer norms for appearance (e.g., racial/ethnic minority youth in mostly White schools, overweight and obese youth) are more likely to become targets of peer teasing and exclusion, with negative effects on their identity and adjustment. Peers also influence youth through the provision of opportunities for certain types of behavior, such as offering cigarettes or inviting youth to parties where alcohol and drugs are available. Corumination is a mechanism specific to peer influences on emotional problems. It involves repeatedly discussing and rehashing problems with a friend, which improves the quality of the friendship but also makes the youth more depressed and anxious.

Factors Affecting Susceptibility

The amount of peer influence varies across teens and situations. For instance, boys, White youth, and more acculturated immigrant youth (in the United States) tend to be more susceptible to negative peer influences. Additionally, adolescents who start puberty earlier and have poorer self-regulation, flexibility, and social skills; more conduct problems and social anxiety; and a history of peer rejection are more susceptible. Likewise, youth who receive less support, appropriate discipline, and monitoring from their parents are influenced by their peers more. Genetic vulnerabilities to problem behaviors (e.g., substance use or aggression) also increase youths' susceptibility to peer influences on these behaviors, and neural correlates of greater susceptibility include lower connectivity in brain regions related to perceptions of others and decision making.

Some peers are more influential than others, particularly those who are well liked and popular. Students are also more likely to emulate the behavior of peers from the "crowd" with whom they identify (e.g., jocks, nerds). Similarly, friendship groups or dyads may develop their own norms for behavior. In summary, peers who are admired and valued by a teen will be more influential. Other-sex friends also exert some unique influences; for instance, girls who are friends with more boys are more likely to start smoking, but boys whose friends include more girls will drink less alcohol. Finally, characteristics of the peer relationships also make a difference. Youth are more influenced by peers with whom they have closer and more positive relationships, although lower friendship quality was also related to greater peer influences in some studies, perhaps driven by the motivation to improve the friendship.

Reducing Negative Peer Influence

Peer influence on problem behaviors is more likely to occur when youth hang out together without structured activities and adult supervision. A particular concern has been raised about the settings that group antisocial youth together for interventions (e.g., in schools or juvenile corrections), which may enable deviancy training during less structured moments. Opportunities for negative peer influence can be reduced by involving teens in structured and adult-supervised activities and minimizing unstructured and unsupervised time with peers (e.g., afternoons at a friend's house without the parents present). Academic, treatment, and correction settings can reduce deviancy training by training leaders in behavior management and supervision skills and promoting prosocial norms in peer groups or by providing services and interventions in ways that avoid grouping high-risk youth together (e.g., individual or family-centered interventions). At the community and policy levels, laws and their enforcement may reduce peer influences on some high-risk behaviors, such as youth substance use and risky driving (e.g., raising the age for buying cigarettes, no texting and driving, limiting the number of passengers for teen drivers). Finally, helping children and adolescents develop stronger self-regulation and self-control skills may reduce their susceptibility to peer influences, and correcting misperceptions about risky and problem behaviors being highly prevalent and valued by peers may decrease adolescents' willingness to engage in these behaviors.

Sylvie Mrug

See also Bullying in Adolescence; Friendships in Adolescence; Identity Formation in Adolescence

Further Readings

Albert, D., Chein, J., & Steinberg, L. (2013). The teenage brain: Peer influences on adolescent decision making. *Current Directions in Psychological Science, 22,* 114–120.

Brechwald, W. A., & Prinstein, M. J. (2011). Beyond homophily: A decade of advances in understanding peer influence processes. *Journal of Research on Adolescence, 21,* 166–179.

Dishion, T. J., & Tipsord, J. M. (2011). Peer contagion in child and adolescent social and emotional development. *Annual Review of Psychology, 62,* 189–214.

Larsen, H., Engels, R. C. M. E., Granic, I., & Huizink, A. C. (2013). Does stress increase imitation of drinking behavior? An experimental study in a (semi-) naturalistic context. *Alcoholism: Clinical & Experimental Research, 37,* 477–483.

Leung, R. K., Toumbourou, J. W., & Hemphill, S. A. (2014). The effect of peer influence and selection processes on adolescent alcohol use: A systematic review of longitudinal studies. *Health Psychology Review, 8,* 426–457.

Steglich, C., Snijders, T. A. B., & Pearson, M. (2010). Dynamic networks and behavior: Separating selection from influence. *Sociological Methodology, 40,* 329–393.

Steinberg, L. (2014). *Age of opportunity: Lessons learned from the new science of adolescence.* New York, NY: Houghton Mifflin Harcourt.

Perimenopause

Perimenopause is a woman's normal life phase that occurs between the ages of 35 and 58 years and lasts for 2 to 10 years. It can be considered the physiological transition between premenopausal regular, fertile menstrual cycles and menopause, when fertility and menstruation have ended. Variability is the only predictable characteristic of perimenopause. For many years, perimenopause and menopause (the life phase that begins 1 year after a woman's final menstrual flow) have both been considered to be characterized by estrogen deficiency, aging, and health risks. Perimenopause and menopause are often still viewed as a single entity, perhaps because they share increased risks for hot flushes/flashes and night sweats (called vasomotor symptoms [VMS]) as well as, to some degree, decreased sexual interest/vaginal dryness. Otherwise, perimenopause and menopause are very different. In perimenopause, estrogen levels are extremely variable but average 30% higher than in menstruating younger women; in menopause, estrogen levels are stable and low. During perimenopause, new experiences/symptoms occur of which the onset of VMS is archetypal, previous patterns of menstrual cycles and flow are changed, and fertility is decreased. About 20% of women will be highly symptomatic, many will have a hysterectomy due to heavy flow, some will be unable to work, some go through relationship turmoil, and others develop obesity, high blood pressure, or diabetes. The purpose of this entry is to describe common changes in perimenopausal menstrual cycles, ovarian hormones, and experiences as well as the role perimenopause plays in cultural concepts and in society. Finally, this entry reviews various approaches to decreasing the unpleasant experiences of perimenopause and improving midlife women's quality of life.

The Timeline of Perimenopause

Clarifying the Meaning of Menopause

There are three different meanings of the word *menopause* in use today. The first definition of *menopause*, which is the epidemiological and now general scientifically accepted use of the word, is a woman's normal life phase that begins 1 year after the final menstruation. Note that this is a statistical definition, since 90% of women will have no further flow, but 10% may bleed normally again. It is also age related, so if a woman is 45 years or younger, she has a 20% chance of further bleeding despite a year without flow. Laypeople (both men and women) and media sources tend to use the word *menopause* to mean both perimenopause and menopause. The third, and usually gynecological, use of the term *menopause* is literally the final episode of menstruation. This definition is problematic to operationalize since it cannot be known to have actually been the final flow until a year has passed without a further episode of bleeding.

Often, within a single scientific article, authors use the term *menopause* to mean each of these three different definitions. This highlights the cultural as well as scientific confusion surrounding women's reproductive aging.

The Start of Perimenopause

According to the latest international consensus, the early menopause transition stage begins when women develop irregular menstrual cycles, defined as cycle lengths that are persistent in being more than 7 days different in length in consecutive cycles. A woman with a regular, 25-day menstrual period who is waking with night sweats several times a night, has started sleeping poorly, is having very heavy menstruation, and has sore breasts before her period is still considered premenopausal. After all, her cycles are regular, so she must be premenopausal. If her follicle-stimulating hormone level taken early in the cycle is somewhat variable, she might be in the late reproductive stage. And should she seem frustrated when seeking explanations and help, her physician may diagnose anxiety and prescribe sleeping pills.

In contrast, some believe that when a midlife woman develops characteristic symptoms (e.g., night sweats, new sleep problems, heavy flow, new premenstrual breast tenderness/swelling, or new or worsened migraines) and changed experiences (e.g., shorter cycles), she is in very early perimenopause. Such a symptomatic woman is very likely to have the higher estrogen and lower progesterone levels that characterize perimenopause. Prospective daily records of changing experiences, cycles, and hormone levels are needed to determine which of these approaches is correct.

The Duration of Perimenopause

The duration of perimenopause or the menopausal transition varies widely and may last for more than 10 years. We know little about the predictors of a longer or shorter perimenopause. However, it appears that the younger a woman is when she notices changing experiences or irregular flow, the longer her perimenopause is likely to be. For example, if a woman is in her mid-30s at her first night sweat, she may still be menstruating irregularly in her late 40s. If a woman starts having skipped cycles in her mid-50s, she may become menopausal by her late 50s. Similarly, if VMS start when a woman is still having regular menstrual cycles, they may last longer than 14 years. However, if VMS start in the 50s, they may end in only a few years. Although the age at menopause is related to heredity and is decreased 1 to 2 years by moderate to heavy cigarette use, there are almost no data, except having had a tubal ligation or perhaps a hysterectomy, that predict a younger age at the onset of perimenopause.

Phases of Perimenopause

Once experts began to realize that there were differing cycle patterns and experiences across perimenopause or the menopause transition, they began efforts to classify the stages of reproductive aging. This led to various ways of describing the stages or phases of perimenopause. It is important at this point to realize that there is not an orderly progression from one phase to the next; women may go back a phase or two or even appear to skip one. We have already discussed the controversies around the onset of perimenopause. Two phases on which all agree are the early and late menopause transition. The early menopause transition (also called early perimenopause) begins with the onset of irregular cycles (defined as >7-day cycle-by-cycle length variability). This phase lasts until a woman experiences her first skipped cycle. The late menopause transition begins when a woman has been without flow for a full cycle (experienced as 60+ days between episodes of flow), and this lasts for 1 to 3 years. The final menstrual flow is considered by current consensus to be the end of the menopausal transition. It is followed by postmenopause. However, others consider very late perimenopause to be the phase from what turns out to be the last flow until a further year has passed without more flow.

Sociocultural Concepts of Perimenopause

In the dominant culture, estrogen is viewed as "what makes a girl, a girl," as well as sexy, fertile, and accommodating. Perimenopause and menopause are both considered to be life phases during which women experience estrogen deficiency or deprivation. Thus, both life phases are associated with frigidity, aging/illness, and becoming difficult or undesirable. That estrogen levels are not low in perimenopause has not penetrated common understanding. Given these negative social expectations, a woman may dread her first night sweat, assume that after perimenopause she will never be interested in sex again, and feel that she is becoming old (with all its negative connotations in a youth-focused culture). This leads to enormous efforts by many women to deny any of the known changes of perimenopause. Also, some seek to maintain the illusion of youthfulness with clothing, hair dying, and styling, refusing to admit their age. This denial, in turn, causes women to lack the information, social support, and health care that would assist them through a potentially highly symptomatic as well as socially stressful time of life. How strongly a woman adopts culturally negative concepts about perimenopause/aging is likely to influence her physical and psychological experiences of perimenopause.

There are also common but hushed notions that at perimenopause women become crazy. Stories circulate of women being hospitalized for depression, psychosis, or attempted suicide. Early research showed that perimenopausal women were at increased risk for depression if they had previously been depressed and were not exercising regularly. Sufficient prospective population-based data are not available to either confirm or deny that more women in perimenopause than premenopausal or menopausal women develop depression.

Common Symptoms of Perimenopause

Vasomotor Symptoms

Almost 80% of the perimenopausal women surveyed in the United States experience night sweats or hot flushes/flashes (VMS) at some time during the long course of perimenopause. Nine percent of them report severe VMS (50 per week of moderate to severe intensity). Note that menopausal VMS occur in 69% of menopausal women, of whom 7% experience severe VMS. Night sweats (but not daytime flushes/flashes) and sore breasts are reported to significantly cluster around flow in women with regular menstruation. Research suggests that VMS are most frequent and problematic in the late menopause transition and in very late perimenopause. However, it may be that very early perimenopausal night sweats are more problematic and are associated with disturbed sleep and quality of life, perhaps because they also frequently cause an aura of very intense anxiety, nausea, or dizziness. Women have reported that they have more frequent VMS (in the daytime as well as during sleep) in late compared with very early perimenopause but that they were bothered less by them.

Combined hormonal contraception is a usual medical prescription for VMS in menstruating women. However, only one randomized controlled trial has been conducted in perimenopause; it showed no significant benefit over placebo (which typically decreases VMS by 20% to 50%). There is also a concern about the safety of combined hormonal contraception in perimenopause because the supraphysiological synthetic estrogen levels in this therapy may not suppress endogenous and often very high estradiol levels. It is inconvenient that VMS are more frequent and more commonly severe in perimenopause, yet there is currently no effective, safe, and evidence-based therapy. Oral micronized progesterone has been shown to be clinically effective.

Very Heavy Menstruation

Heavy menstrual bleeding (menorrhagia, defined as flow of more than 80 ml/period, associated with cramps and anemia) occurs in about 25% of very early/early perimenopausal women. Because of the confusion over diagnoses discussed earlier in this entry, the association with perimenopause is often not perceived. Heavy flow is commonly attributed to uterine fibroids (although there is little evidence that they are causal rather than coexistent). A case-control study showed that midlife women with heavy flow have very high estradiol levels; endometrial biopsies also do not show evidence of ovulation/progesterone. Thus, both fibroids and heavy flow that increase in perimenopause may be caused by the higher estradiol/lower progesterone levels of this life phase.

Hysterectomy or ablation of the endometrium (uterine lining) is the most common treatment for heavy flow. Menorrhagia and current approaches to its treatment cause major physical, occupational, and emotional disruption for perimenopausal women. There is strong evidence that the over-the-counter antiprostaglandin, ibuprofen in moderate, intermittent doses of 200 to 400 mg with breakfast, lunch, and dinner on every heavy-flow day decreases bleeding by 25% to 50%. All women need to know that ibuprofen decreases heavy flow, but especially in perimenopausal women. Given that heavy flow improves over time, nonsurgical therapies make sense. Evidence-based, effective, and safe nonsurgical approaches to heavy flow include daily full-dose oral micronized progesterone (300 mg at bedtime daily for 3 months) or insertion of the levonorgestrel-releasing intrauterine device.

Decreased Libido and Vaginal Dryness

Women in perimenopause often report that they are less interested in sex; some women even report aversion to any nonintercourse intimacy. The reasons for this change are not clear. Since vaginal dryness results from decreased sexual activity and the lack of interest-related arousal, it is not surprising that perimenopausal women report vaginal dryness. Because vaginal dryness is commonly attributed to low estrogen levels, this symptom causes yet another confusion between perimenopause and menopause despite their very different estradiol levels.

Jerilynn C. Prior

See also Aging and Gender: Overview; Menopause; Menstruation

Further Readings

Prior, J. C. (Ed.). (2005). *Estrogen's storm season: Stories of perimenopause.* Vancouver, British Columbia, Canada: Centre for Menstrual Cycle and Ovulation Research.

Swan, A., Prior, J., & Zala, L. (2006). *Transitions through the perimenopausal years: Demystifying your journey.* Bloomington, IN: Trafford.

Perpetrators of Violence

That men commit the most violence is one of the most robust findings across both the psychological and criminological literatures. However, it would be erroneous to assume that women commit negligible amounts of violent crime and inaccurate to assume that their motives for, pathways to, and targets of violence are the same as men's. The literature on female-perpetrated violence is still largely underdeveloped compared with the body of literature on male-perpetrated violence. This is likely due to the significant discrepancy in the rates of violence. According to the Federal Bureau of Investigation, males were responsible for 79.9% of all violent crimes committed in 2013, a base rate that remained generally consistent over the preceding decade. Nevertheless, females were responsible for approximately one fifth of the officially documented acts of aggression. Thus, identifying the ways in which female perpetrators of violence differ from males is critical for effective prevention and treatment efforts. The following sections focus on key areas of difference between adult males and females who commit acts of violence, including contributing factors, manifestation, risk assessment, recidivism, and treatment.

Factors Contributing to Aggression

Extant models formulated to explain general offending and violence have derived largely from male samples; however, researchers have demonstrated the utility of these models among women, albeit with some inconsistency in results and disagreement among researchers. Terrie Moffit's seminal research elucidating the developmental trajectories of criminal behavior in young males remains a robust model for explaining the onset and persistence of criminal behavior. Subsequent research has consistently supported the two trajectories identified for general offending behavior among males: (1) those who start early and continue to offend throughout their lives and (2) those who start in adolescence and desist by early adulthood. These offenders are referred to as life-course-persistent offenders and adolescence-limited offenders, respectively. Though these models were originally developed to explain general antisocial behavior, they have also been used to explain violent offending. Although some researchers have identified similar childhood- and adolescent-onset pathways to antisocial behavior in females, inconsistency in the research literature continues to prompt discourse on trajectories of female violence. According to some research, like their male counterparts, female life-course-persistent offenders tend to demonstrate earlier onset, longer duration of criminal career, and more violent offenses compared with those who begin offending in adolescence or adulthood. Other researchers found that females begin perpetrating violence earlier, peak, and stop sooner than males. Still other authors proposed a unique, late-onset pathway among females, in which antisocial behavior begins in either late adolescence or early adulthood. Overall, evidence regarding the age of onset and offset of violent behavior and factors related to desistance among females is largely discordant. These variable findings may be explained by a number of methodological factors, including sampling differences, duration of follow-up, and discrepant definitions of violence, including the conflation of violent offending with more general criminal behavior.

Factors contributing to the onset of violence point to differential relationships between male and female offenders. Some factors contributing to violence are gender specific, some are gender universal, and still others are relevant for both genders, although their relative strength or proposed mechanism of action is moderated by gender. Prostitution and other forms of sex work are examples of gender specific risk factors that have been consistently related to increased risk for aggression among females. Multiple studies have indicated the universality of other risk factors, including the use of substances and mental illness. Males and females classified as life-course-persistent offenders tend to exhibit neurocognitive deficits (e.g., low intellectual ability and reading difficulties), a difficult childhood temperament, and childhood hyperactivity. Additionally, these offenders were purportedly raised in high-risk social settings characterized by low socioeconomic status, insufficient parenting practices (e.g., minimal parental supervision), and poor interpersonal relations. Those classified as adolescence-limited offenders theoretically experienced less adversity in these domains. Although findings have been inconsistent, some research suggests that there is increased risk among females, compared with males, due to poor parenting practices and conflictual parental relations witnessed as children. Gang membership has also been identified as a risk factor for male and female violence, although sex differences are still present as male gang members are involved in more frequent and more serious violence compared with female gang members.

The experience of childhood abuse and/or neglect is also a universal risk factor for violence, although it is proposed to operate through different mechanisms as a function of sex. Compared with women who did not experience childhood maltreatment, researchers postulated, those women who did experience childhood maltreatment went on to display higher rates of internalizing symptomology such as depression, which precipitated substance use and later engendered violence. The pathway for adult female violence as it arises from childhood maltreatment would therefore be indirect. Among men, it was hypothesized that early-childhood maltreatment prompted early aggressive behavior, which then led to violent offending as adults, suggesting a more direct influence of early-childhood maltreatment among men. A sample of approximately 1,500 abused or neglected children and matched controls were followed from the late 1960s to the 1980s to test these pathways. Structural equation modeling indicated that for women, childhood maltreatment was indirectly related to violent offending in adulthood. Specifically, women with histories of childhood maltreatment and parental substance use were likely to engage in problematic drinking, which then predicted arrests in adulthood for violent offenses. Interestingly, some women demonstrated early aggression independent of maltreatment, which then predicted drinking problems, which contributed to adult violence. Among males, child abuse and neglect were directly related to violent offending as adults. However, an indirect relationship was also identified, such that childhood maltreatment among males was predictive of early aggression, which predicted drinking problems and arrests for violent offenses as adults.

Manifestations of Aggression

Studies consistently indicate that males are more physically and sexually aggressive, commit more physically and sexually violent offenses, and have a higher recidivism rate for violent offenses than females. Regarding the targets of violence, females are more often violent to those close to them, including romantic partners, children, and other family members, whereas males are more likely to offend outside the home. This trend is seen in fatal violence as well. The majority of male-perpetrated homicide is inflicted on persons with whom they have no or limited acquaintance, whereas female-perpetrated homicide is much more commonly targeted toward intimate partners and family members. Men are also much more likely to use a firearm in the commission of a homicide than women. Regarding murder within the home, males and females appear to kill their own children at comparable rates. However, females are much more likely to commit filicide when the child is young, while fathers tend to kill older children. Regarding neonaticide (the murder of a child within the first 24 hours of life), the perpetrators are overwhelmingly the mothers.

Violence in correctional settings appears to mirror the trends seen in the community among individuals without mental illness. Among a sample of 202,532 (12.22% female, n = 24,765) inmates admitted to federal prisons between 1991 and 1998, males were disproportionately responsible for violence and serious violence in particular. Comparable rates of violence among male and female inmates were demonstrated only for less serious (i.e., less injurious) acts of violence.

Research suggests that the gender differences in the risk for aggression and violence are attenuated among individuals with mental illness both in the community and in inpatient treatment settings. Regarding inpatient violence, findings indicate that females commit as many or more violent acts in the hospital as males. Staff members tend to be more frequently victimized by female patients, although the risk for injury appears equivalent regardless of the gender of the patient. Risk for injury to other targets (e.g., other patients) appears to follow the same pattern as in the community, where male perpetrators commit more severe violence. In the community, among a sample of 1,136 discharged psychiatric patients (41.3% female, n = 469), males perpetrated more violent crimes after a single year of follow-up; however, differences in rates of violence disappeared over a 4-year follow-up period. As with individuals without mental illness, violence by females was likely to be less severe with respect to injury. Also, discharged patients displayed the same pattern regarding the targets of violence. Females were much more likely to be violent toward a family member, while males were significantly more likely to be violent toward friends, acquaintances, or strangers.

Intimate Partner Violence

One area in which rates of violence perpetration are comparable between sexes is intimate partner violence. Research has indicated that females and males engage in comparable rates of physical aggression within intimate relationships, though the severity of the violence appears to be moderated by sex. Men tend to perpetrate more severe forms of violence against their partners; however, less severe violence (i.e., that which does not warrant medical attention) is often reciprocal and committed at equivalent rates. Men also tend to commit more sexual aggression and stalking in the context of intimate relationships. Specifically, men tend to use physically threatening forms of stalking patterns, such as approaching an ex-lover, while women are more likely to engage in verbally aggressive stalking (e.g., leaving unwanted phone calls). Women, however, tend to commit more relational aggression within intimate relationships. Relational aggression is defined as any behavior that damages a relationship directly or indirectly and can include not only physical violence but also nonphysical aggression. Findings suggest that in early childhood and adolescence, peer-directed relational aggression is more common among females, although the rates for males and females tend to equalize in young adulthood.

Research findings suggest that intimate partner violence is often related to problematic or high levels of anger for males and females. For males who commit intimate partner violence, research suggests that their problems with anger and hostility present as a more generalized characteristic or predisposition than for men who commit other assaultive behaviors. Additionally, the relationship between the interpersonal and affective traits of psychopathy (e.g., lack of remorse, grandiose sense of self-worth, callous indifference) and intimate partner violence tends to be stronger in males than in females. Thus, the presence of psychopathic symptomatology generally exacerbates intimate partner violence perpetration in men but does not predict intimate partner violence as well in females. For female perpetrators of intimate partner violence, specifically among those who are violent only in the context of the intimate relationship, self-defense is often cited as a central motivating factor for violence. This reactive use of violence appears to be typical of women who are violent only with their partners, whereas women who are violent in other relationships are more likely to use violence instrumentally—to gain power or control. Substance use appears to elevate the risk for intimate partner violence regardless of gender.

Assessment of Violence Risk and Violent Recidivism

Effectively assessing risk for violence and violent recidivism among offenders is difficult due to problems associated with low base rates. Additionally, disentangling the specific features of male and female risk for violence and violent recidivism is exacerbated by the fact that researchers have typically assumed a gender neutral approach to risk assessment. In a recent review of 12 measures of violence risk, only the Historical-Clinical-Risk Management-20 (HCR-20) was reliably and significantly associated with violence among female offenders. The Psychopathy Checklist-Revised (PCL-R) showed significant associations with female violence as well but exhibited greater variability in relation to female violence across studies and was not designed for assessing risk for violence. In contrast, nine of the most frequently used violence risk assessment tools appear to function adequately as measures of violence risk for males but demonstrate variable effectiveness among females. Specifically, the PCL-R and the Psychopathy Checklist: Screening Version (PCL:SV) obtained larger effect sizes when predicting violence among females, while the effect sizes for men and women when predicting violence using the HCR-20 were comparable, and men obtained far larger effect sizes than females on the Offender Group Reconviction Scale and Risk Matrix 2000 for violence. Overall, it appears that the HCR-20 is uniquely suited to assess risk for violence among females. It is critical to note that this particular meta-analysis reflects the compilation of data from multiple countries, correctional and psychiatric samples, and institutional and community settings, and that even those scales considered to be the "best" in the field demonstrated only moderate accuracy.

Given the inability of most tools to reliably predict female violence and the consistent perpetration of roughly 20% of violence by females, gender specific risk assessment tools are clearly needed. There currently exists only one such tool designed for use with females, the Female Additional Manual (FAM), which is used in conjunction with the HCR-20. Research on the FAM is still in its infancy, but it has demonstrated preliminary efficacy in predicting inpatient violence among a small sample of female forensic patients.

Going beyond the efficacy of particular measures of violence risk, a number of empirically validated static (e.g., history of violence) and dynamic (e.g., presence of violent attitude or ideation) risk factors have been linked with violent recidivism. Many of the same static factors are relevant for the prediction of male and female recidivism (e.g., history of trauma and use of substances). However, some risk factors, particularly dynamic risk factors (e.g., violent ideation), demonstrate less robust relationships to violent recidivism in female samples as compared with male samples. The FAM includes several static and dynamic risk factors shown to be relevant to the assessment of female violence risk that are not represented in the more male-oriented risk assessments, including suicidal and self-injurious behavior, prostitution, parenting difficulties, low self-esteem, and problematic relationships.

As mentioned previously, mental illness is related to violence and violent recidivism for males and females, though some differential relationships exist. In female samples, posttraumatic stress disorder is a common disorder among those who engage in and experience intimate partner violence. However, posttraumatic stress disorder in this population may also be associated with the experience of physical and sexual assault, a risk factor in its own right. Mood disorders appear to increase the likelihood that a female will commit aggression within a domestic relationship, although they demonstrate a weaker association with other types of violence. Psychotic disorders are frequently associated with violence among males, though less consistency has been demonstrated in female samples. Substance use and substance use disorders are frequently cited as risk factors for violence and violent recidivism among males and females. To the extent that men are diagnosed more frequently with co-occurring substance use disorders, the increased rate of offending by males may be partly explained by this diagnostic discrepancy. Several personality disorders appear to be linked with an increased risk for violence. Among males, the risk for violent recidivism is greater among those diagnosed with antisocial personality disorder and psychopathy. Among females who perpetrate violence, narcissistic and borderline personality disorders, in addition to antisocial personality disorder and psychopathy, are linked with violence.

Specific psychiatric symptoms have also been associated with violence and recidivism in female samples. Suicidal ideation, past suicide attempts, and hopelessness have been linked specifically with female violence and recidivism. In addition, women who commit violence are more likely to have attempted suicide than violent men. Emotional instability, low frustration tolerance, impulsivity, as well as antagonistic, egoistic, and competitive attitudes are also related to female violence. Similarly, impulsivity, lack of insight, anger, and egocentric, distrustful, and hostile attitudes are related to male violence. However, incarcerated women consistently exhibit higher levels of anger than men in the same setting and are more easily provoked to act aggressively and more likely to be repetitively violent. Furthermore, hostile attribution bias, selective attention to aggressive cues, and external blame attribution have also been linked to female violence. The association between these cognitive processing deficits and violence is more prominent in female than in male samples.

A 2010 meta-analysis indicated that extensive criminal histories and shorter sentence lengths were related to a greater likelihood of violent recidivism among men. Alternatively, longer sentences were predictive of violent recidivism among females, although no relationship between criminal history and recidivism was found. The relationship between longer sentences and violent recidivism among female offenders may be related to the notion of double deviance, which refers to the loss of community ties as a function of long imprisonment and the concurrent violation of the culturally feminine expectation of passivity and gentleness. Lengthy incarceration experiences likely increase stigmatization of female offenders, which then increases their risk for violent recidivism, according to this perspective.

Treatment and Management of Violent Offenders

Strategies for managing violence vary as a function of the setting, and as such, this section focuses on those interventions used in clinical settings and those used in correctional settings.

In clinical inpatient settings, strategies for managing violence committed by both males and females include physical interventions (e.g., restraint), active control techniques (e.g., seclusion, emergency medication), and interpersonal techniques (e.g., de-escalation). Although techniques such as seclusion and restraint are used regardless of the gender of patients, some studies have found that the majority of restrained or secluded patients are male, and according to some studies, males are restrained for a longer duration than women. It is difficult to ascertain if the physical interventions and active control techniques truly decrease violence. For example, patients often act aggressively in the context of being restrained, such that it is unclear whether this behavior is caused by or results from the attempted restraint. There exists a growing consensus that it is countertherapeutic to use seclusion and restraint as control measures for patients regardless of gender. Improved trauma-informed training for staff, changes in policy, and increased oversight in inpatient facilities have led to significant reductions in seclusion and restraint rates. Other enacted efforts intended to reduce rates of seclusion and restraint include less restrictive rules and language, increased patient involvement in treatment planning, and improved patient-staff communication. However, due to a lack of well-controlled studies, it is unclear whether these measures have served to decrease violence as well.

Cognitive behavioral approaches are often used with male and female offenders to reduce aggression. Multifaceted treatment is designed to address aggression as well as the antecedents of aggression, such as anger and violent attitudes. Teaching and using coping skills and generating prosocial alternatives to anger help produce meaningful reductions in anger. Treatment goals include the development of insight into the antecedents and outcomes of violent behaviors, empathy for victims, and taking responsibility for actions. Additional treatment foci include correcting social cognitive deficits using interpersonal interactions and treating the sequelae from past abuse. Research evaluating the outcomes of treatment in female samples is limited, though cognitive behavioral interventions have demonstrated efficacy in decreasing the likelihood of violent recidivism in male offenders and perpetrators of intimate partner violence. However, these effects are diminished in males with diagnosed antisocial and borderline personality disorders. Techniques found in dialectical behavior therapy, initially developed to treat patients exhibiting self-injurious behaviors in the context of borderline personality disorder, are incorporated to address the emotional dysregulation that often characterizes violent female offenders. Dialectical behavior therapy techniques have also been applied to male samples and have resulted in decreased anger and aggression in males with borderline personality disorder.

In correctional settings, the risk-needs-responsivity model is used to guide treatment interventions aimed at reducing future violent behavior regardless of the offender's gender. According to this model, the focus and intensity of treatment are determined by the level of violence risk and presence of dynamic risk factors (e.g., antisocial cognitions or interpersonal factors). Empirically supported treatments (e.g., cognitive behavioral approaches) that engage offenders and affect behavioral change and the offender's responsivity to treatment influence not only the type of treatment chosen but also the techniques used. Research has indicated that treatment addressing dynamic risk factors is effective in decreasing the likelihood of violence. Using cognitive behavioral, motivational interviewing, and relapse prevention techniques, research has shown that in male samples positive treatment change is negatively correlated with violent recidivism, even in high-risk offender samples. A wide variety of treatment programs have been developed that incorporate varying levels of structure and specificity. Research shows that when applied to female offenders, specifically those who are designated as high risk, the risk-needs-responsivity model can be similarly effective in reducing risk for recidivism, though the effect on violent recidivism specifically is unclear.

Although a gendered perspective of violence risk is empirically supported across multiple studies, few gender specific risk reduction interventions exist. Most programs were initially designed for men and modified to address female-specific factors. For instance, emotion control therapy is an adapted female-specific intervention. Offered as a group-based intervention, sessions focus on emotional disturbance and regulation followed by individual sessions addressing trauma and anger replacement. Due to limited research and methodological problems (e.g., the inclusion of both violent and nonviolent offenders in treatment groups), data regarding the efficacy of this program and others like it are not presented. Beyond Violence is the first violence prevention intervention designed to treat females convicted of violent offenses. This program aims to reduce violent recidivism by focusing on female-specific issues of mental health, substance abuse, trauma history, and anger regulation. Preliminary research purported that Beyond Violence results in greater reduction of symptoms associated with violence (e.g., anger) than treatment as usual; however, research on its violence reduction ability is currently limited, and thus, statements regarding its efficacy cannot be made at this time.

Future Directions

With regard to violence risk assessment and treatment intervention, the field has been compelled to generate extensive research, and with its completion, results may prompt revision of practice and potentially theory as it relates to female violence. Thus, the field continues to grow as new research informs previous theory, and constant attention is necessary. Notably absent from the foregoing discussion is any notion of how these findings might apply to transgendered individuals. It is not clear which body of literature regarding pathways to violence, manifestation of violence, risk factors for violent recidivism, or treatment intervention is most applicable and consistent with their lived experience or whether these literatures are inapplicable.

Hali Griswold, Melanie Schneider, Ashley DeBlasi, and Debbie Green

See also Violence Against Women Act; Violence and Gender: Overview

Further Readings

Chesney-Lind, M., & Pasko, L. (2012). *The female offender: Girls, women, and crime*. Thousand Oaks, CA: Sage.

Moffitt, T. E. (2001). *Sex differences in antisocial behaviour: Conduct disorder, delinquency, and violence in the Dunedin Longitudinal Study*. Cambridge, England: Cambridge University Press.

Odgers, C. L., Moffitt, T. E., Broadbent, J. M., Dickson, N., Hancox, R. J., Harrington, H., . . . Caspi, A. (2008). Female and male antisocial trajectories: From childhood origins to adult outcomes. *Development and Psychopathology, 20*(2), 673–716.

Personality Disorders and Gender Bias

Personality disorders are psychiatric disorders outlined in the *Diagnostic and Statistical Manual of Mental Disorders* (*DSM*), published by the American Psychiatric Association (APA). According to the *DSM*, personality disorders are defined as having a maladaptive, inflexible pattern of behavior, cognition, and intrapsychic experience, causing significant distress or disability and impairment in self- and interpersonal functioning. While there have been variations of the types of personality disorders throughout the different revisions of the *DSM*, the *DSM-5* lists 10 distinct personality disorders, grouped into three clusters. Cluster A is characterized by odd, bizarre, and eccentric traits; diagnoses include paranoid personality disorder, schizoid personality disorder, and schizotypal personality disorder. Cluster B is characterized by dramatic or erratic traits; diagnoses include antisocial personality disorder, borderline personality disorder, histrionic personality disorder, and narcissistic personality disorder. Cluster C is characterized by anxious or fearful traits; examples include avoidant personality disorder, dependent personality disorder, and obsessive-compulsive personality disorder.

Gender bias can be defined as a prejudiced attitude toward males or females. Thus, gender bias in personality disorders occurs when there is a discrepancy in how males and females are diagnosed with personality disorders. Gender bias in personality disorders is significant because it can result in misdiagnosis and misdirected clinical treatment, which in the very least leads to no change in progress or in the worst scenario harm to the client/patient. Gender bias in personality disorders has been a topic of debate among clinicians and researchers alike. Critics have postulated that gender bias stems from a variety of factors: (a) gender stereotypes within cultures, (b) genetics, (c) sampling errors, (d) criterion bias (defining criteria for the disorders), and (e) assessment bias (bias in how diagnostic criteria are applied). This entry examines cultural, diagnostic criteria, assessment, and clinician biases as they relate to personality disorders and gender bias.

Cultural Bias

Some critics propose that personality disorders are culture-bound syndromes explaining the difference in prevalence rates in genders that reflect the biases and value judgments a society places on each gender. For example, although there has been a progressive movement, the United States is still considered a patriarchal society that emphasizes individualism and determination, which are encapsulated in masculinity. All these values may be reflected in the preponderance of narcissistic personality disorder in men. On the other hand, women are viewed as emotionally expressive, without control of their emotions, and as clingy or interdependent. Women are seen as weak, irrational, and otherwise inferior. Hence, women are more frequently diagnosed with borderline and dependent personality disorders. Thus, some critics argue that gender role socialization promotes an inherent gender bias in how a society views symptom expression in different genders. This means that society may play a large role in the emergence of a personality disorder in addition to individual factors.

The *DSM* is based on the medical model in which illnesses are defined along with their symptoms and outcomes. It is the dominant group in a society that holds the power to decide what behaviors and attitudes are deemed sick, deviant, or abnormal and thus labeled as an illness. Thus, gender, a social construct, can similarly hold powerful influence over what symptoms are considered to be of an illness. Gender's effects can be seen in diagnosis, clinician-patient relations, and treatment.

Some argue that personality disorder criteria are unfairly pathological of stereotypical characteristics of women. Feminist critics believe that there are feminine characteristics that are pathologized in the *DSM* due to the inherent historical sexism and the fact that the individuals largely responsible for identifying disorders and their symptoms have historically been men. Specifically, they believe that certain personality disorders such as histrionic and dependent disorders contain common traits associated with women that are used to pathologize women.

Specific to racial and ethnic populations, there have been some studies that have illuminated the potential biases of specific personality disorders, particularly borderline personality disorder (BPD). Some studies have found that African Americans tend to score lower than White Americans on BPD overall but that clinicians score higher on affective intensity and emotional dysregulation, as well as on thoughts of interpersonal aggression, than White patients. Similarly, some studies have found that Latinos, especially Latina women, score higher on BPD than White and Black patients, with higher scores on intense anger, affective instability, and unstable relationships. Despite these findings, researchers are critical of therapist competence and cultural bias in diagnoses. When not culturally competent, clinicians may potentially score people of color as more aggressive or emotionally unstable, when other factors (e.g., clinicians' racial biases, clients' struggles with discrimination and acculturation) may influence these perceptions.

Diagnostic Criteria Bias

It is possible that there is a difference in symptom expression by gender just as there are differences in ethnic or other cultural expressions; however, the *DSM* should be efficient in being able to diagnose regardless. What some experts say may be happening is a polarization of two extremes: (1) a systematic overpathologizing or (2) an underrepresentation of mental illness in gender. Another explanation is that perhaps the symptoms of the personality disorders are not complete—they do not provide a complete symptomology for both genders. For example, there are more women than men who are diagnosed with BPD. This may be due to the possibility that the current diagnostic criteria do not capture the symptoms expressed by men who have the disorder but only capture the symptoms expressed by women. Some regard this gender bias as being rooted in the inherent sexism found in society.

Some have postulated that there is an inherent bias in the diagnostic criteria themselves. Others argue that the issue is not with the diagnostic criteria but with the assessment and diagnosis by the clinician. In other words, the interpretation and assessment of the diagnostic criteria made by clinicians may be at fault. These results have been mixed, but in general, attention has been placed on both the assessment and the diagnostic criteria.

Assessment Bias

Research shows that clinicians do not apply diagnoses of certain personality disorders equally to men and women. This can be due to a combination of assessment instruments being inherently biased and clinician bias. If instruments are created and normed on specific samples that are not representative of the whole population, then they are biased and will not capture those individuals who do not fit into the expression of the disorder in other groups (i.e., gender). Some critics say that there is no bias in the instruments used but rather in the way clinicians utilize them and interpret them. Others have evidence contrary to the fact, finding that some items of some of the assessment instruments are more easily applicable to men than to women, and vice versa.

Clinician Bias

In the field of psychology, trying to understand the mechanisms behind mental health is a complex task that requires certain knowledge, skill, and capacity to unpack the multiple layers of an individual and their context. Similar to what medical doctors do in medicine, psychologists or clinicians utilize their knowledge, skill set, and resources to diagnose and treat their patients while doing no harm. However, a main difference is that the internal psychological workings of each patient are quite strikingly different due to the patterns of relationships and contextual influences, including ethnicity, sexual orientation, religion, race, and gender. Needless to say, there are many unknowns.

Clinicians are required to attend to and emphasize certain information while de-emphasizing and/or ignoring other information in order to make an accurate clinical diagnosis.

Due to these factors, many critics believe that the brunt of the responsibility rests on the shoulders of clinicians to accurately determine who fulfills the diagnostic criteria for which mental disorders. In terms of gender bias, many researchers have found that clients with identical symptoms are diagnosed differently depending on gender and have attributed this to clinician bias. More specifically, this bias has been speculated to be evident not only of the attitudes and beliefs of clinicians but also of their decision-making processes and skill capacity.

Self-Awareness

Attitudes and beliefs about certain groups, whether regarding ethnicity, race, sexual orientation, religious affiliation, or gender, among others, are sources of bias. When in training, students of psychology are taught that they have biases that they must become aware of to limit their influence on their assessment, diagnosis, and treatment of clients. Bias is unavoidable, and all humans are dependent on individual and environmental factors. Yet they can be problematic if there is a lack of awareness of them when interacting with patients.

Bias can operate on two levels: (1) implicit (or an unconscious bias) and (2) explicit (conscious bias). Personal identities and cultural backgrounds influence what types of attitudes and beliefs clinicians and trainees have regarding certain groups. Clinicians' worldview is a huge influential force in how they interact with and think about their clients. Everyone has implicit bias whereby they make automatic assumptions based on very little information when meeting a man or a woman. Essentially, everyone carries a gender schema (a framework regarding a specific concept) of how men and women should behave. This is based on an individual's history, what they have been taught, and what they have adopted into their schemas.

These automatic assumptions many times are based on the stereotypes that people are exposed to. They cannot be avoided, but what can be avoided is acting on them. Many experts in the field of psychology have emphasized that clinicians' self-awareness of their own biases, assumptions, and stereotypes is vital to being culturally sensitive and accurate in diagnosing as well as in understanding clients. This is also a way to lower the gender bias while assessing and diagnosing, particularly with personality disorders. Researchers and scholars alike have recommended that clinicians should explore their biases on a range of notions, including stereotypes of personality disorders and what relationship gender plays, if any, in their assumptions.

Biases can also come from emotional reactions that may or may not be from implicit bias. Sometimes, clients may remind clinicians of someone they like or highly despise, or they may experience countertransference (letting their emotions onto their client), which may interfere with their ability to accurately diagnose and appropriately treat the client. This type of bias can influence the diagnosis of personality disorders and has also been raised by critics as another explanation for gender bias. For example, a clinician can come across a client who reminds them of another client who they have diagnosed with BPD, and they automatically focus on that diagnosis without taking into consideration other pertinent information that may point to a different diagnosis. For example, the presentations of BPD and posttraumatic stress disorder can sometimes be very similar.

Knowledge and Skills

Scholars in the field have emphasized the importance of trainees and clinicians to be active consumers of research in order to understand and determine what information is relevant and credible to their practice of psychology. This holds for diagnosing personality disorders as well. The APA, the scientific and professional organization of psychologists in the United States, has provided evidence that knowledge, self-reflection, consultation, and education should be continued to ensure best practice while minimizing the effects of bias in the assessment and treatment of clients. The APA encourages clinicians to be aware of their attitudes and beliefs as well as their clinical limitations.

Clinicians who focus narrowly on pathology and ignore or dismiss other information from the cultural context of a client may be disregarding pertinent information that is essential to the differential diagnosis. These clinicians will rely more on their implicit bias than those who are more open, self-aware, and introspective. The skills of perspective taking, perception, and attention to nuanced information are complex and require self-monitoring and practice. Thus, scholars recommend increasing self-awareness, knowledge, and skills to minimize gender bias when diagnosing personality disorders.

Rebecca Rangel Campon

See also Antisocial Personality Disorder and Gender; Borderline Personality Disorder and Gender; Gender Bias in the *DSM*; Histrionic Personality Disorder and Gender; Panic Disorder and Gender; Schizoid Personality Disorder and Gender; Schizophrenia and Gender

Further Readings

Caplan, P. J., & Cosgrove, L. (Eds.). (2004). *Bias in psychiatric diagnosis*. Lanham, MD: Jason Aronson.

Jane, J. S., Oltmanns, T. F., South, S. C., & Turkheimer, E. (2007). Gender bias in diagnostic criteria for personality disorders: An item response theory analysis. *Journal of Abnormal Psychology, 116*(1), 166–175.

Jani, S., Johnson, R. S., Banu, S., & Shah, A. (2016). Cross-cultural bias in the diagnosis of borderline personality disorder. *Bulletin of the Menninger Clinic, 80,* 146–165.

Widiger, T. A., & Spitzer, R. (1991). Sex bias in the diagnosis of personality disorders: Conceptual and methodological issues. *Clinical Psychology Review, 11,* 1–22.

Physical Abuse

Physical abuse can begin as early as the prenatal period and might continue through older adulthood. Acts of physical abuse have been related to negative physical and psychological outcomes. Official records monitor physically abusive acts with gender neutral labels such as victim and perpetrator, even when the abuse becomes an act of homicide. The U.S. Department of Justice categorizes crimes by type, such as violent crime, property crime, and drugs and crime, not by the gender of the victim or the perpetrator. Any mention of gender has been embedded briefly within a complex report. This practice has implied that gender neutrality is the gold standard for understanding physical abuse and other forms of violence.

While both males and females can be the victims, perpetrators, or victim-perpetrators of physical abuse, significant gender differences have been found across the life span. In preschool, young boys have been found to engage in antisocial and aggressive behavior at twice the rate as young girls. As adults, males and females often have different motivations for aggression. Male aggression has been found to be more severe and more often lethal than female aggression. This entry provides a gendered analysis of physical abuse across the life span. It explains the view that gender neutrality impedes efforts to heal those who are already victims or perpetrators of abuse and can misdirect prevention efforts.

Contexts of Physical Abuse

Physical abuse occurs within the context of a relationship. Whatever the age, the abuse is most likely caused by an intimate other. When a child is the identified victim, the perpetrators are usually one or both parents. During their first year of life, almost 20% of children are victims of physical abuse. Fathers and mothers physically abuse their children at close to equal rates if acts of aggression are considered in isolation from the context in which they occur.

One context that has been ignored in official statistics has been the amount of time a mother or father spent with a child who was abused. Traditional gender roles have made the mothering role more central to a woman's identity than the fathering role for a man. Most children (64%) under 18 years of age live with two married parents, and two thirds (61%) of the time both parents are working. When this is not the case, one study by Jonathan Vespa and colleagues found that 31% of the time the father is working and the mother is at home. However, even when both parents are working, statistics indicate that only 32% of working fathers indicated being a regular source of care for their children. When not living with both parents, children are more likely to live alone with their mother (12%) than with their father (2%). This pattern is stable across different ethnic and racial groups. African American children are most likely to live only with their mothers (29%), followed by Latino American children (18%).

Thus, whether the sole parent in the home, a married stay-at-home parent, or a working parent, as expected within the context of traditional gender roles, mothers generally spend more time with children than fathers; yet fathers are still physically abusing their children at equal rates to mothers. In addition, the intensity of abusive acts differs between mothers and fathers. When a child is killed as a result of abuse, it is most likely at the hands of the father or male partner of the mother and the child is most often male. If the amount of time a parent spends with a child is considered as a context for understanding violence statistics, it would indicate that men are committing more acts of child abuse and more severe acts of abuse than women.

Poverty of the family has been found to increase the risk for physical abuse in the home. Women-headed households are poorer than male-headed households. One in two children living only with their mother live below the poverty line, thus increasing their risk for maltreatment. Despite fathers having higher income levels than mothers, they physically abuse their children at equal rates to mothers. If level of income is considered as a context for understanding child abuse statistics, men are committing more acts of child abuse than women.

Gendered Analysis Across the Life Span

Physical abuse in childhood has been found to have a greater impact on young boys than on young girls on whether they will commit later acts of violence. Abused boys are also found to be more likely to engage in dating violence and engage in both violent and nonviolent criminal violence than abused girls and nonabused boys. They are also more likely to abuse an intimate partner as an adult. Longitudinal studies show less violent outcomes for girls who were physically abused than for boys who were physically abused; however, some girls who were abused have become extremely violent adults.

Males and females perpetrate acts of physical abuse against intimate partners at roughly equal rates. However, examining context reveals significant gendered effects. Males who adhere closely to traditional gender roles, and are perpetrators of violence, are more likely to be violent toward an intimate partner when they perceive any loss of power within the relationship. When they are victims, they put the need to appear autonomous and strong ahead of their safety. Male perpetrators of intimate partner violence are also three times as likely as females to also abuse their children. When women are the perpetrators, they use violence as a last resort. As victims, women who adhere closely to gender role stereotypes put love and the desire for connection ahead of their own safety.

In addition, the meaning and impact of the acts of violence differ for males and females. Mary Beth Phelan and colleagues found that the intensity of abusive acts is greater for male perpetrators than for female perpetrators; males cause more injuries and more severe injuries, and are more likely to kill their partners than females. Seventy percent of female victims reported "being very frightened" of their violent male, in comparison with 85% of male victims reporting "no fear." This fear disempowers women and puts men in the position of control and authority in the relationship. In addition, fear and lack of power among women victims of intimate partner violence result in worse long-term outcomes; physical abuse is more strongly associated with posttraumatic stress and depression for women than for men.

Just as male perpetrators of physical child abuse are more likely to kill their victims than females, male perpetrators of intimate partner violence are also more lethal. One in 3 women is killed by a male partner in the United States, while 1 in 20 males is killed by a female partner. Since the mid-1980s, rates of males being killed by an intimate partner have decreased, while the rates have increased for female victims. Two possible causes for this difference in lethality have been raised. One is that women kill their partners only as a last resort for escaping the relationship. The second is that it reflects the traditional resources offered predominately to female victims—shelters and protection-from-abuse orders. These resources give women a respite from violent relationships and thus might decrease risk for male-victim homicide. On the other hand, traditional gender roles dictate that men should have power and control in relationships with women. Intervention steps that equalize the power between victim and perpetrator or are perceived to be taking some power away from a man, such as shelters or protection-from-abuse orders, can be perceived as a threat. Thus, men might use lethal methods to maintain power and control over their partner.

Rates of intimate partner violence vary by race and ethnicity. The Centers for Disease Control and Prevention's 2011 National Intimate Partner and Sexual Violence Survey indicated that American Indian men and women, multiracial men and women, and Black men and women are most likely to be physically victimized by an intimate partner. However, women of a specific race are consistently more likely to be victimized in comparison with men of the same race. While women are sometimes the perpetrators, the pattern of increased rates of female victimization is stable across races and ethnicities.

Power and the abuse of power in intimate couples have been explored as the dynamics that might fuel violence rather than gender roles per se. If traditional gender roles are the most important context for understanding violence, then the relationships between same-sex intimate partners would show less violence. Instead, violence within same-sex intimate relationships occurs at twice the rate for both physical and sexual abuse. Victimized lesbian women report having less authority and control within their same-sex relationship than heterosexual women. Thus, understanding the dynamics of power within interpersonal relationships might be key to preventing and intervening in acts of violence.

U.S. Census data adjusting for greater longevity in women found that older adult women are abused at higher rates than older adult males. Women older than 60 years have an estimated rate of 18.4% of physical abuse. One out of 10 elderly adults experiences some form of abuse, but only a small fraction of cases are reported. Most reports are made by professionals, and those working with older adults have usually not received training in recognizing the warning signs of violence in this population. As a result, they might not differentiate signs of physical abuse from signs of injuries brought on by decreased mobility. Physical abuse of older adults consists of both continued intimate partner violence from their younger years as well as abuse that started only later in life. As in all forms of physical abuse, the vast majority of perpetrators are family members. Older adult victims are hesitant to report physical abuse to the authorities due to fear of retaliation or to protect another family member. As with abuse in younger years, perpetrators use coercive strategies to maintain power and control over their victim. The decline in physical and executive functioning that some older adults experience increases their vulnerability to physical abuse.

When older adults are physically abused, they are also likely to be verbally abused and to have the perpetrator intentionally isolate them from others; this type of co-occurrence is also found in younger intimate partners. Both prospective and retrospective studies have found that co-occurrence of types of violence is the normative experience for victims, whether the target population is older adults, adults, or children. In addition, when historical exposure to violence was examined, most individuals were repeatedly involved in maltreatment either as perpetrators or victims, or as both a victim and a perpetrator.

Intervention and Prevention Efforts

Acts of physical abuse, viewed in insolation of context, will lead to failed intervention and prevention efforts. These acts occur within relationships at the hands of intimate others whether in childhood, adulthood, or older adulthood. Thus, these relationships, and the desire to maintain them, must be considered in all intervention and prevention efforts. Gender roles have a powerful impact on acts of maltreatment; men and women have been found to have different motivations for engaging in violence, to use different levels of severity, and to seek different relationship goals. These differences must be taken into account in intervention and prevention efforts. In addition, accurate assessment of individuals' historical exposure to violence must be carried out to provide more comprehensive and effective interventions. In conclusion, a multitiered effort is needed. At the individual level, accurate assessment of each person's violence history in terms of co-occurrence, polyvictimization, and polyperpetration is critical to understanding their motivations and skills deficits. At the relationship level, it is important to understand how individuals seek to meet their needs for nurturance and autonomy, particularly the role that power and control have played. At the societal level, sexism and social support for the pursuit of power within intimate relationships must end. Instead, society needs to support the development of egalitarian relationships, encourage men to make their role as fathers more primary to their identity, and provide education about child development and positive parenting techniques. Finally, social initiatives that reduce poverty will reduce violence across the life span.

Pearl Susan Berman and Marissa Perrone

See also Acquaintance Rape; Cycles of Abuse; Gender-Based Violence; Violence and Gender: Overview

Further Readings

Centers for Disease Control and Prevention. (2014). *Prevalence and characteristics of sexual violence, stalking, and intimate partner violence victimization: National Intimate Partner and Sexual Violence Survey, United States, 2011*. Atlanta, GA: Author. Retrieved from http://www.cdc.gov/mmwr/preview/mmwrhtml/ss6308a1.htm?scid=ss6308a1_e

Hamby, S., & Grych, J. (2013). *The web of violence: Exploring connections among different forms of interpersonal violence and abuse* (Springer Briefs in Sociology). New York, NY: Springer.

National Center on Elder Abuse, Administration on Aging. (2015). *Elder abuse: The size of the problem*. Alhambra, CA: Author.

Phelan, M. B., Hamberger, L., Guse, C., Edwards, S., Walczak, S., & Zossel, A. (2005). Domestic violence among male and female patients seeking emergency medical services. *Violence and Victims, 20,* 187–206. doi:10.1891/vivi.2005.20.2.187

U.S. Department of Health and Human Services, Administration for Children & Families, Administration for Children, Youth, & Families, Children's Bureau, Office on Child Abuse & Neglect. (2015). *The Child Abuse Prevention and Treatment Act (CAPTA) 2003*. Washington, DC: Author. Retrieved from http://www.acf.hhs.gov/programs/cb/resource/capta2003

Vespa, J., Lewis, J. M., & Kreider, R. M. (2013). *America's families and living arrangements: 2012* (Current Population Reports No. P20-570). Washington, DC: U.S. Census Bureau.

Physical Assault, Female Survivors of

A female survivor of physical assault is a self-identified female who has experienced physical aggression directed toward herself resulting in psychological or physical harm, including loss of life. This entry adds to the current volume by detailing what physical assault means, a framework to understand females' experience of physical assault, and the history of the documentation of physical assault against females, which includes the rates, risk factors, and consequences of intimate partner relationships. This entry ends with a brief overview on the strength and resilience of female survivors of this form of violence.

Understanding Physical Assault

Physical assault is one type of violence that can take many forms. It can be self-directed (e.g., self-injurious behaviors), experienced collectively (e.g., a community dealing with organized crime), and also happen within interpersonal relationships (e.g., intimate partner violence [IPV]). Physical assault includes the use of physical violence toward another person, such as, but not limited to, pushing/shoving, slapping, kicking, punching, pulling hair, restraint, utilizing a weapon against someone, such as stabbing with a knife or whipping with a belt, and so on. For females, physical violence occurring in the context of a current or former relationship or partnership (e.g., life partner and spouse), that is, IPV, is the most common form of violence. Additionally, females are disproportionately affected by intimate partner homicide, which is physical violence that results in loss of life. This entry focuses on understanding physical assault in the context of IPV.

Understanding IPV Against Females

Since the women's rights movement brought attention to the issue of violence occurring in the context of intimate partners, many frameworks emerged in an attempt to understand and intervene in the issue. Early frameworks included focusing on individual psychopathologies and personality characteristics of victims as reasons for violence, blaming violence of women on intimacy issues within the relationship, while others promoted the understanding of social pressures and their influence on the family. However, the dominant perspective has been that of the feminist perspective that understands violence against women as a manifestation of what occurs in the patriarchal system—that is, a system where male privilege keeps women subordinate to men. The traditional first-wave feminist perspective was critiqued for being too limited by only focusing on gender. This perspective ignored other factors for which women are oppressed (e.g., race, class, sexual orientation). In response, over the past two decades, the intersectional perspective has emerged for understanding violence experienced by women within a complex system of other forms of oppression (e.g., race, class, sexual orientation, able-bodiedness). That is, violence against women can also be based in racism, classism, heterosexism, ableism, and so on, and the unique intersections of these factors. For example, while all women are at risk for violence, a Latina lesbian woman may experience different risk factors and different forms of violence, and may be judged differently than a White heterosexual woman when she attempts to seek help.

As with experiences of oppression, discrimination, and classism that occur within the social sphere, intersectionists posit that physical violence is the manifestation of power and control within a partnership. That is, much like in the social sphere, where violence is used to oppress certain groups or communities by those who hold (dominant) power, the manifestation in an intimate partner relationship is the use of violence to control and coerce based on various factors of power held by one partner over the other (e.g., gender, class, ethnicity, education). This is important to understand as violence against women cannot be understood outside the context of the larger societal system of power and control.

History of Documenting IPV

IPV has been noted as a global issue since 1979, when the surgeon general of the United States stated that violence and the impact of violence could no longer be ignored. Since that time, the World Health Organization (WHO) has taken the lead in documenting rates across the world, starting with the 2005 WHO Multi-country Study on Women's Health and Domestic Violence Against Women: Initial Results on Prevalence, Health Outcomes and Women's Responses. The most recent report distributed by the WHO is the 2014 global status report on violence prevention. The WHO has been at the initial forefront in documenting prevalence rates of violence against women and has moved toward predicting risk factors, with an emphasis on preventing violence against women worldwide.

Within the United States, national reporting of violence against women dates back to 1975, with Murray A. Straus's study titled National Family Violence Survey; 10 years later, in 1985, it was conducted again and continued to document the rates of violence against women. Since that time, numerous studies have emerged, including the 1992 National Alcohol and Family Life Survey, the 1992–1993 National Crime and Victimization Survey, the 1995–1996 National Violence Against Women Survey, the 1997 Women's Experience With Violence National Study, the 1998 Commonwealth Fund of Women's Health, the Centers for Disease Control and Prevention's (CDC) 1996 Behavioral Risk Factor Surveillance System, the CDC's 2010 National Intimate Partner and Sexual Violence Survey, a longitudinal study by the Bureau of Justice Statistics called the National Crime Victimization Survey of Intimate Partner Violence (1993–2010), another Bureau of Justice Statistics study called the Nonfatal Domestic Violence (2003–2012), and the CDC's Mobility and Mortality Weekly Report, which featured its 2011 "Prevalence and Characteristics of Sexual Violence, Stalking, and Intimate Partner Violence Victimization." Efforts to document violence against women both within the United States and globally have heightened the awareness of this issue and documented the need for resources to combat it.

Rates of IPV

IPV is an issue for women across the world. Global studies indicate that one in three females has experienced IPV in her lifetime. When looking at rates across global regions, rates of violence for females are slightly higher than for males in African, eastern Mediterranean, and Southeast Asian regions. Although these rates must be considered through the lens of their limitations, such as their differences in methodologies (e.g., data drawn from police reports vs. data drawn from death records), this information does provide insight into the reality of violence experienced by women across the globe. In fact, global studies also indicate that while general homicides are experienced mostly by men, women disproportionately experience homicide within the context of an intimate relationship. Thus, women are most likely to be killed by an intimate partner than a stranger or other associate. Similarly, within the United States, of the female victims of homicide who knew their murderer, more than half of them were murdered by their partners (e.g., spouse, common law spouse, boyfriend, or girlfriend).

Disparities exist in which groups are more likely to be affected by IPV. Black females are disproportionately affected by intimate partner homicide as they are murdered at a rate that is two and a half times the rate of White females. Understanding of nonfatal IPV within the United States is growing, although it remains limited. Nevertheless, large-scale studies provide detailed information regarding physical violence for various subcategories of women (e.g., race/ethnicity, LGBTQ identity). Current surveys note that 32% of women in the United States have experienced physical aggression by a partner and 24% of women in the United States have experienced severe physical violence (e.g., being hurt by choking) by a partner in their lifetime. By ethnicity, 35.2% of Hispanic, 41% of Black, 45.9% of American Indian or Alaskan Native, and 50.4% of multiracial women have experienced physical violence from a partner in their lifetime. Regarding foreign-born status, studies indicate that women who are born within the United States experience a higher rate of physical violence by a partner compared with those born outside the United States. Studies examining the occurrence of IPV in immigration populations are beginning to document immigrant-specific tactics of control, in addition to unique barriers to accessing services for immigrant survivors. Another growing area is that of IPV among sexual minorities. Current data indicate that 40.4% of lesbians and 56.9% of bisexual women have experienced physical violence by a partner in their lifetime. Rates are higher among these groups compared with heterosexual women (32.3%).

Risk Factors and Consequences

Research on the experience of violence over the life span has helped us understand that experiencing violence or witnessing violence early on in life (including childhood) is a risk factor for future victimization. We also know that women rarely experience only one form of violence. Although this entry is limited to physical assault experienced by women in the context of intimate partner relationships, to understand violence against women, it is necessary to address other forms of trauma as they are all intimately connected (e.g., childhood abuse, neglect and trauma, sexual violence, and emotional, economic, and collective trauma). In fact, within the United States, one in five female victims of IPV experienced IPV for the first time between the ages of 11 and 17 years. Moreover, 47.1% were between the ages of 18 and 24 years when they experienced physical violence by a partner for the first time. Previous experience of any form of violence is a risk factor for experiencing physical violence in a relationship later in life. Additionally, research has indicated various risk factors for intimate partner homicide, including recent legal or physical separation, stalking, previous experience of strangulation, the partner's accessibility to a firearm, partners with a history of alcohol/substance abuse, abuse during pregnancy, forced sex, and controlling behavior.

The field of public health has brought a tremendous amount of attention to the nonfatal consequences of physical violence experienced by women. Women who have experienced physical violence are likely to endure physical health and mental health consequences across the life span more than women who have never experienced violence. Women who have experienced IPV are more likely to acquire HIV and other sexually transmitted diseases, have a low-birth-weight baby, and suffer from brain and other neurological injuries. In addition, IPV is linked to gastrointestinal issues as well as immune and endocrine system issues. Women who have experienced IPV are also more likely to experience posttraumatic stress disorder, depression, and suicide attempts as well as partake in high-risk behaviors such as alcohol/drug abuse and risky sexual behaviors (which put them at risk for other illnesses, e.g., cancer). Importantly, a women's cumulative experience of violence influences adverse health outcomes. Thus, it is important to understand the history of violence, as noted in the previous paragraph. The experience of physical violence by women has a lasting impact on their physical and mental health.

Resilience and Strength

Traditionally, the field of IPV has been dominated by a deficit-focused lens in understanding survivors of violence. However, over the past decade, practitioners have urged researchers to explore the strength and resilience demonstrated by survivors. The knowledge base is increasing about protective strategies and resilience demonstrated by women survivors of violence. Women survivors, whether currently in an intimate relationship or not, demonstrate profound ways of coping and problem solving. Many women draw on spirituality as a coping source, while others engage in formal (e.g., shelters and hospitals) and informal (e.g., friends and family) help-seeking behavior. Other strategies include forgiveness, mobilizing resources, carefully planning their activities, being proactive and protecting their children (e.g., teaching children to call the police), communicating with their children to prevent intergenerational transmission of violence, and avoiding situations of violence (e.g., by walking away or de-escalating the situation). Survivors also engage in self-care strategies during (or after) abusive situations, such as exercising, engaging in hobbies, or studying for school or self-enhancement. Despite the very difficult circumstances that women survivors who experience violence endure, their narrative is also filled with strength, resilience, and coping that can inform the knowledge base about healing from trauma and personal as well as collective growth.

Josephine Serrata

See also Cycles of Abuse; Sexual Assault, Female Survivors of; Violence and Gender: Overview

Further Readings

Breiding, M. J., Chen, J., & Black, M. C. (2014). *Intimate partner violence in the United States 2010*. Atlanta, GA: Centers for Disease Control and Prevention, National Center for Injury Prevention and Control.

Hamby, S. (2013). *Battered women's protective strategies: Stronger than you know*. New York, NY: Oxford University Press.

Sokoloff, N. J. (Ed.). (2005). *Domestic violence at the margins: Readings on race, class, gender, and culture*. New Brunswick, NJ: Rutgers University Press.

World Health Organization. (2014). *Global status report on violence prevention 2014*. Geneva, Switzerland: Author. Retrieved from http://www.who.int/violence_injury_prevention/violence/status_report/2014/en/

Physical Assault, Male Survivors of

Physical assault against males has been a neglected research area. Much of society still focuses on males as perpetrators of physical assault and fails to acknowledge that men are victims as well. Until recently, the research focus on survivors of physical assault has been primarily on females. However, scholars are starting to shift a portion of their attention to male survivors of physical assault, as rates of physical assault against males are greater than once believed. Physical assault against males comes in different forms, including hitting, biting, punching, stabbing, burning, and scratching. Physical assault may also involve more than one perpetrator, and oftentimes, physical assault occurs alongside sexual assault. Even though the relationship that the perpetrator has to the male victim can vary, such as a nonacquaintance or a nondomestic partner, physical assault against males perpetrated by romantic partners has become increasingly studied in recent years. This entry examines the prevalence, predictors, and impacts of physical assault against males with regard to romantic relationships, as well as the public's response to physical assault against males. This entry concludes with the media's impact on how society views physical assault against males.

Prevalence of Physical Assault Against Males

Determining the prevalence of males who have survived physical assault can be difficult, as many male survivors are hesitant to report their experiences. Many men keep their experiences of physical assault private, as, historically, violence against men has rarely been treated as a serious issue. The prevalence of physical assault against males is likely higher than what is reported. Males are typically the dominant partner in the relationship; therefore, admitting to physical assault may be seen as emasculating. Additionally, males are oftentimes hesitant to report physical assault for fear that they will not be believed, as society focuses most efforts on violence against women. Males in both homosexual and heterosexual relationships are reluctant to report being physically assaulted.

Data from the 2010 National Intimate Partner and Sexual Violence Survey report that more than 13% of males in the United States have experienced severe physical assault by a partner at some point in their lifetime. Severe physical assault includes being beaten, hit with a fist or a hard object, or slammed against something. In addition, more than 25% of men have been pushed, shoved, or slapped at some point in their lifetime. Prevalence rates are highest among Native American and African American populations, with 45.3% and 36.8%, respectively, experiencing physical assault in their lifetime. However, because of the disproportional racial breakdown in the United States, the majority of men who experience physical assault are Caucasian, with more than 21 million reporting physical assault in their lifetime. Additionally, physical assault against males occurs throughout the life span. Physical assault against males occurs in childhood until late adulthood. Young males who experience physical assault are more likely to experience physical assault as adults. Because of these high prevalence rates, more research is being conducted on physical assault against males. As a result, researchers are finding that males are just as likely as females to be physically assaulted by their partners. However, due to the differences in physical force between male and female perpetrators, female victims suffer higher rates of severe injuries and death than male victims. Most male survivors of physical assault are victimized by female partners; however, many male survivors of physical assault are victimized by male partners.

Predictors of Physical Assault Against Males

Historically, physical assault committed by females against males has been viewed as self-defense. Women have typically been viewed as the victims of physical assault, and men have been viewed as the main aggressors. However, evidence shows that few females perpetrate physical assault as a form of self-defense. Scholars now argue that physical assault is not a gender issue but a human issue, as there are no gender-based predictors for physical assault at the individual or microsystem levels of the ecological system. Males are physically assaulted by their partners for the same reasons that females are assaulted by their partners. Because violence oftentimes accompanies stress, males who are unemployed and live in low-income neighborhoods are at an increased risk of being physically assaulted by their partner. Alcohol and substance use, mental health problems, and personality traits of impulsivity, neuroticism, and disagreeableness place men at higher risk for physical assault. Additionally, relationship issues such as jealousy, conflict, and communication difficulties can be predictors for physical assault. Even though most instances of physical assault against males are not in self-defense, many cases of physical assault qualify as reciprocal assault, where both partners voluntarily perpetrate the violence during a specific instance.

Impacts of Physical Assault on Male Survivors

Compared with men who have not been physically assaulted, male survivors of physical assault experience higher rates of difficulty sleeping, chronic pain, and recurrent headaches. They also report having poorer physical and mental health. In addition, male survivors tend to be fearful and concerned for their safety and report needing medical care as a result of physical injuries. It is common for male survivors to visit emergency rooms for burns, cuts, and other wounds as a result of a weapon, such as a knife or gun, having been used against them. The more severe the physical assault, the greater the levels of stress and depression male survivors face. Furthermore, many male survivors miss work or school as a result of the impacts of physical assault.

Public's Response to Physical Assault Against Males

The perceptions of male victims of physical assault are often misconstrued. Stereotypical gender roles are that men are strong and aggressive while women are submissive and nurturing. Scholars have explained that the views of how men and women act in relationships can affect how society views males as victims of physical assault. Because men are stereotypically strong and masculine, being a victim to physical assault may cause society to question their masculinity. Male survivors frequently report that they were told that the physical assault they experienced was their fault or that they should have just defended themselves against their partner. There is oftentimes a double standard of physical assault against men, as certain individuals may not view violence against men as a crime whereas violence against women is viewed as a crime.

The stereotypes against men often affect the ways in which local authorities respond to physical assault against males. Law enforcement is less likely to assume that the male is the victim of physical assault in a heterosexual relationship. Research has discovered that even if law enforcement does respond to a situation, it may not take action against a female perpetrator. Because males are typically larger and stronger than females, it is oftentimes not believed that a female could cause physical harm to a male. Physical assault perpetrated by females can also be viewed as self-defense, and as a result, the public can have a hard time believing that the violence was originally coming from the female. Injury or a sign of injury is not necessary for an action to be considered physical assault. Therefore, the lack of physical evidence can negatively affect the help male survivors get from the community and professionals, such as law enforcement or nurses.

Many males do not leave relationships in which physical assault is occurring for many of the same reasons why women do not leave violent relationships. Many men do not think that their friends, family, or society will believe them. They may also feel ashamed and think that the physical assault they have experienced or are experiencing was their fault. In addition, many males may not be aware of resources that can help them. The stereotypes against men also cause male victims to be hesitant about seeking help. Males are less likely than females to seek out services for physical assault, such as mental health providers or domestic violence shelters, as a result of the stigma they face for being a male victim. Even if a male does seek out services, there are few resources available to help men who have been physically assaulted. More services and resources exist for female victims of physical assault than male victims of physical assault. The lack of resources for males may stem from society failing to recognize that physical assault against males is an issue. Many domestic violence shelters are willing and able to offer services to males, such as counseling services. However, very few shelters exist in the United States to house male survivors of physical assault. With the lack of shelter space for males, many males have nowhere to go to escape the physical assault they are experiencing.

Media's Influence on Perceptions of Physical Assault Against Males

Society's perceptions of physical assault against males can influence whether or not a male survivor seeks help, as well as the services he may receive. The media can have a significant influence on society's perceptions of physical assault against males. Singers are notoriously known for including physical assault in their music. Male singers are often accused of singing about assaulting females; however, scholars have recently pointed out that it is not often acknowledged how many female artists sing about assaulting or retaliating against their male partners. Music videos even frequently show women physically assaulting their male partners.

It has recently been suggested that there is a double standard in the media with regard to physical assault against men. Family-centered sitcoms have made light of women kicking or hitting their male partners. These actions are oftentimes justified in these shows as the male character deserving the physical assault. However, sitcoms rarely show men assaulting their female partners, and if they do, it is portrayed in a negative way. Even cartoon shows depict wives chasing their husbands around the house while swinging objects at their heads. In addition, reality television shows often depict both male and female victims of physical assault. However, scholars point out that these reality television shows usually only offer assault hotlines at the end of episodes where violence against women has occurred. Scholars have indicated that making light of physical assault against males in the media can discourage males from reporting their incidences of victimization. The media can also encourage society to think that physical assault against males is justifiable.

Ultimately, the awareness of physical assault against males is minimal. Instances of physical assault against males are not well documented or responded to by society. This topic needs additional attention, specifically with regard to how gender stereotypes affect male survivors' experiences, the resources available to male survivors, and the reported instances of physical assault against males.

Sarah Taylor and Yan Xia

See also Gender Stereotypes; Gender-Based Violence in the Media; Gendered Stereotyped Behaviors in Men; Intimate Partner Violence; Measuring Gender Roles; Sexual Assault, Male Survivors of; Violence and Gender: Overview

Further Readings

Barber, C. F. (2008). Domestic violence against men. *Nursing Standard, 22*(51), 35–39.

Cook, P. W. (2009). *Abused men: The hidden side of domestic violence* (2nd ed.). Westport, CT: Praeger.

Graham-Kevan, N. (2007). The re-emergence of male victims. *International Journal of Men's Health, 6*(1), 3–6.

Hines, D. A., & Douglas, E. M. (2009). Women's use of intimate partner violence against men: Prevalence, implications, and consequences. *Journal of Aggression, Maltreatment & Trauma, 18*(6), 572–586.

Seelau, S., & Seelau, E. (2005). Gender-role stereotypes and perceptions of heterosexual, gay and lesbian domestic violence. *Journal of Family Violence, 20*(6), 363–371.

Physical Assault, Transgender Survivors of

Regarding physical assault of transgender and gender nonconforming individuals, researchers have debated the prevalence rates of physical assault, particularly in assessing whether physical assaults are related to the victim's transgender and gender nonconforming identity. Most crime victimization statistics are collected by law enforcement or agencies funded by the federal government, who have not given victims the option to state their gender identity (if they identify as transgender) or gender history (if they were assigned a sex at birth that is different from their gender identity). That makes it impossible to know how many people reporting having been physically assaulted are transgender or gender nonbinary. Therefore, accounts of physical assault are generally limited to media reports of cases that reach the attention of a reporter who deems it worth reporting, as well as convenience surveys that rely on self-reporting by those who may have access to the studies. As discussed in this entry, both methods have serious limitations and do not allow for generalizing about the whole transgender community or determining accurate prevalence rates.

Murders

The type of physical violence that gains the most media attention is murder. Both the websites associated with the Transgender Day of Remembrance and the annual hate crime and intimate partner violence reports of the National Coalition of Anti-Violence Programs (NCAVP) collect such media reports. The past two NCAVP hate crime reports (2014 and 2015) collectively listed murders of 24 transgender people in the United States, all of whom were trans women. All but two were also people of color. The Transgender Day of Remembrance website lists nearly 1,000 such deaths worldwide, stretching back to 1970. Here, too, the vast majority of victims had a female gender identity and were people of color.

Murders associated with intimate partner violence have a much different profile. The past two NCAVP reports (2014 and 2013) indicate that only 4 of the 42 reported intimate partner violence fatalities were of trans women. It should be noted that while no deaths of transmasculine people were reported in these 2 years, this could in part result from the media's focus on trans women.

It is also important to note that murders that observers may classify as hate crimes may actually be the result of non-gender-related street crime or interpersonal conflicts unrelated to the victim's gender identity or expression. Many reported deaths are never definitively solved, and early published reports are seldom updated when an investigation reveals something other than an anti-transgender motive.

Physical Assault

Motives for physical assault of transgender individuals are a little clearer than those for murder. The 2011 seminal National Transgender Discrimination Study (NTDS) asked its 6,400 respondents to report only those assaults that they felt were motivated by their gender identity or expression. The results showed a stunning amount of physical violence experienced by transgender people because of their transgender identity or history in a large array of settings:

- 35% in Grades K–12 (including 5% assaulted by teachers)
- 25% of those who tried to access a homeless shelter
- 16% while incarcerated
- 8% in public accommodations (e.g., stores, restaurants, hotels)
- 7% at work
- 6% while interacting with the police
- 3% when presenting identification that did not match their identity or expression
- 1% while trying to access a rape crisis center or domestic violence program

A common site of physical assault for transgender people is at home. Nineteen percent of NTDS respondents said that they had experienced domestic violence at the hands of a family member because they were transgender.

Sexual Assault

Of violence against transgender people, sexual assault is one of the most documented crimes, with multiple local and national surveys showing that at least 50% of transgender people have experienced sexual assault. Like other sexual assault survivors, the vast majority of transgender survivors experience their first sexual assault as children, with most reporting that they were assaulted more than once. FORGE's 2004 (n = 256) survey of transgender sexual assault survivors found that 42% thought that their assault or assaults had been motivated at least in part by their gender identity or expression. Twenty-nine percent were sure that was not the motivation, with the balance being unsure if gender was a motivator in the assault.

The NTDS asked its respondents to report only sexual assaults that the survivors thought were motivated by their gender expression or identity. The survey found sexual assault rates of

- 22% of those trying to access a homeless shelter,
- 15% while incarcerated,
- 12% in Grades K–12 (including 3% sexually assaulted by a teacher or school staff), and
- 6% at work (if the worker was undocumented, the rate skyrocketed to 19%).

Polyvictimization

A transgender person who has experienced one type of physical assault or violence is highly likely to be victimized in at least one other way. A 2011 FORGE study asked 1,005 transgender people if they had experienced sexual assault as a child or as an adult, dating violence, intimate partner violence, stalking, or a hate crime. Between 64% and 88% of those who reported that they had experienced one type of violence also reported having experienced one or more other types.

Rate Disparities

Transgender people of color tend to report higher rates of physical assault than their White peers. For example, while the NTDS reported an overall rate of transgender-related family violence of 19%, the figures were far higher for racial minorities: 45% for American Indians, 36% for Asian Americans, 35% for both African Americans and Latino/as, and 31% for multiracial respondents. While 6% of the NTDS respondents who had interacted with the police reported physical assault and 2% reported sexual assault by the police, those numbers rose to 15% and 8%, respectively, if the respondent was also African American.

With the exception of hate-motivated murders, violence disparities between transmasculine and transfeminine individuals tend to depend on how the questions are asked. Most of the time when the NTDS asked about the various types of violence respondents had experienced because of their gender identity or expression, trans women reported experiencing somewhat more violence than trans men. In sharp contrast, when FORGE asked transgender individuals if they had experienced different types of violence without asking them about the motives of those who had attacked them, transmasculine individuals reported that they had experienced more violence in every category except hate crimes: (a) child sexual assault: 50% female-to-male (FTM) versus 48% male-to-female (MTF) individuals, (b) adult sexual assault: 31% FTM versus 28% MTF, (c) dating violence: 23% FTM versus 6% MTF, (d) intimate partner violence: 36% FTM versus 29% MTF, (e) stalking: 18% FTM versus 17% MTF, and (f) hate violence: 29% FTM versus 30% MTF. It is possible that the differences might be traced to trans women being more likely than trans men to assume that they were attacked because of their transgender status or history, but testing this theory would require much more research.

Health Disparities

Experiencing physical violence greatly increases a transgender person's chances of also having a range of mental and physical health conditions. Forty-one percent of the NTDS respondents reported having made at least one suicide attempt (compared with 4.6% of the general public), but those rates went up to 61% for physical assault survivors, 64% for sexual assault survivors, and 65% for those who had experienced family violence. The evidence for linkages to other health disparities is indirect but still compelling. The U.S. Centers for Disease Control and Prevention's Adverse Childhood Experiences Study has found that adults who experienced trauma such as child sexual abuse were far more likely to later develop diseases such as heart disease, cancer, autoimmune diseases, fibromyalgia, and depression. Recognizing that at least 50% of transgender individuals have experienced sexual assault in childhood, it is highly likely that the Adverse Childhood Experiences Study data of health disparities apply to transgender survivors as well as nontransgender survivors.

A 2011 study of 2,560 older sexual and gender minorities, *The Aging and Health Report: Disparities and Resilience Among Lesbian, Gay, Bisexual, and Transgender Older Adults*, found that while the nontransgender lesbian, gay, and bisexual older adults had experienced a lifetime average of four experiences of verbal and/or physical violence, the transgender older respondents had experienced a lifetime average closer to six. The transgender elders were also far more likely than their nontransgender peers to report suicidal ideation (71% vs. 36%), diabetes (26% vs. 14%), asthma (33% vs. 15%), and obesity (40% vs. 25%). They were also far more likely to smoke (15% vs. 9%) and have drinking binges (20% vs. 10%).

Barriers to Physical Care

Transgender people face many barriers to accessing physical health care. Two common issues facing new victims of physical assault seeking or receiving physical care are (1) whether or not they will seek medical services and (2) whether they want to report or keep open the possibility of pursuing legal action against their attacker. Both have trans-specific complications.

Most transgender people who seek medical care may not have a choice in disclosing their transgender identity or history. The majority of transgender individuals' cannot afford to or do not wish to have gender-related surgery, and their unclothed bodies may be perceived by others to be incongruous with their gender identity. Others may be outed because their health insurance card has a name or gender designator different from their gender identity or expression. In addition, most physicians have had no formal training in caring for transgender patients and may refuse to care for or may act inappropriately toward transgender individuals as a result. Fear of being maltreated in a health care setting may well lead to an injured transgender victim deciding not to seek medical care at all. NTDS respondents reported a great many problems in health care settings: 19% had been refused care, 28% had experienced harassment, and 2% had experienced more violence. Transmasculine people were more likely to postpone both preventive (48% FTM vs. 24% MTF) and illness/injury (42% FTM vs. 24% MTF) care due to fears of discrimination and/or inability to afford care.

Issues in Reporting to Law Enforcement

Only 35% of NTDS respondents said that they would feel "comfortable" asking for police help if they needed it; 46% said that they would feel "uncomfortable." This concern is largely based on previous law enforcement interactions (their own or their peers'): 54% of respondents had interacted with the police as a transgender or gender nonconforming person, and one fifth (22%) said that the police had responded with "harassment." Twenty percent were denied service, 6% reported being physically assaulted by police, and 2% reported being sexually assaulted by officers. When the transgender person was also Black, all the police victimization rates were higher.

Choosing not to report a crime to the police has more ramifications than simply closing out the possibility of prosecuting the attacker. In most states, people cannot access Victim Compensation—funds to cover medical and mental health care, reimburse lost wages, and replace items stolen or destroyed in the attack—if they have not filed a police report on the incident. Thus, transgender victims may have less access to healing services than nontransgender victims due to concerns about police misconduct.

Current Efforts and Future Directions

There have been many recent improvements that should both reduce assaults against transgender people and increase victims' access to appropriate and respectful help. The first federal law to explicitly address transgender people was the Matthew Shepard & James Byrd, Jr., Hate Crimes Prevention Act of 2009, which added sexual orientation and gender identity to the list of offender motivations that could result in a federal hate crimes charge. In its 2013 Violence Against Women Act Reauthorization, Congress also responded to widespread complaints about discrimination by domestic violence and sexual assault programs by requiring them to serve transgender and LGB survivors equally. These laws have been augmented by the funding of nationwide training and technical assistance focused on helping victim service providers serve transgender victims of violence better. Finally, rapidly increasing public awareness of transgender people should reduce assaults motivated by fear of the unknown.

Michael Munson and Loree Cook-Daniels

See also Hate Crimes Toward LGBTQ People; Sexual Assault; Sexual Assault, Survivors of; Transgender Day of Remembrance; Transgender People and Resilience; Transgender People and Violence; Transphobia

Further Readings

Ahmed, O., & Jindasurat, C. (2014). *Lesbian, gay, bisexual, transgender, queer, and HIV-affected hate violence in 2013: A report from the National Coalition of Anti-Violence Programs.* New York, NY: National Coalition of Anti-Violence Programs.

Ahmed, O., & Jindasurat, C. (2015). *Lesbian, gay, bisexual, transgender, queer, and HIV-affected hate violence in 2014: A report from the National Coalition of Anti-Violence Programs.* New York, NY: National Coalition of Anti-Violence Programs.

Cook-Daniels, L., & Munson, M. (2008). Sexual violence, elder abuse, and sexuality of transgender adults age 50+: Results of three surveys. *Journal of GLBT Family Studies, 6*(2), 142–177.

Fredriksen-Goldsen, K. I., Kim, H. J., Emlet, C. A., Muraco, A., Erosheva, E. A., Hoy-Ellis, C. P., & Goldsen, J. (2011). *The aging and health report: Disparities and resilience among lesbian, gay, bisexual and transgender older adults.* Seattle: University of Washington.

Grant, J. M., Mottet, L. A., Tanis, J., Harrison, J., Herman, J. L., & Keisling, M. (2011). *Injustice at every turn: A report of the national transgender discrimination study.* Washington, DC: National Center for Transgender Equality and National LGBTQ Task Force.

U.S. Centers for Disease Control and Prevention. (n.d.). *Adverse childhood experiences.* Atlanta, GA: Author. Retrieved from http://www.cdc.gov/violenceprevention/acestudy/

Pornography and Gender

Social scientists use the term *pornography* to refer to media that depict nudity or graphic sexual acts designed to arouse consumers. Studies of adolescents and adults from a wide variety of countries are increasingly finding that large numbers of individuals consume pornography. Social-scientific research on pornography and gender has primarily addressed two questions: (1) Does pornography portray men and women in power-imbalanced and stereotypical roles? (2) Are individuals who consume pornography more likely to possess gendered behavioral scripts than individuals who do not consume pornography or who less frequently consume pornography? This entry summarizes findings from research on these questions. In addition, it presents findings and directions for future research with regard to the experiences of lesbian, gay, bisexual, transgender, and racial minority consumers of pornography. First, however, it is important to consider why exposure to pornography can affect viewers' ideas about appropriate and desirable sexual and social behavior.

Behavioral Script Theory

Behavioral scripts encompass procedures for human social behavior. They specify who should interact with whom, how people should interact, and what consequences should arise as a result of different interaction patterns. Behavioral scripting occurs when observers integrate the behaviors of others into their own social repertories. The concept of behavioral scripting provides a theoretical foundation for the hypothesis that pornography is a socializing agent. From media, such as pornography, individuals can be told directly (e.g., through verbal statements) or deduce (e.g., from observing which patterns of behavior are common or rewarded) how men and women should behave. Because pornography shows men and women interacting in social as well as sexual spheres, pornography may affect scripts related to nonsexual social interactions in addition to sexual interactions. Furthermore, through a psychological process known as higher-order scripting, individuals can abstract underlying principles about the nature of gender and gender roles from one type of context (e.g., sexual) and apply it to another (e.g., social). For example, from seeing frequent depictions of women acting subserviently and deferentially to men during sex, a viewer may conclude that men are more dominant than women and that women will acquiesce to men's requests in business or other competitive settings.

Gendered Portrayals in Pornography

Three categories of gender stereotypes and power imbalances are often observed in content analyses of pornography. First, women are targets of aggressive acts more than men, and men are the perpetrators of aggressive acts more than women. In a study of aggression in best-selling videos, women were the targets approximately 95% of the time, and men were the perpetrators 70% of the time. Another study of best-selling videos found that women were the targets of aggression even when scenes were directed by women, suggesting an overall norm of female victimization in popular pornography. Second, women are frequently depicted in ways that suggest that they are objects for males' sexual pleasure. Women's physical characteristics receive extensive description and focus, physically unattractive women are disparaged, women are portrayed as easily sexually accessible, and men are shown using women as instruments for their sexual gratification. Third, men tend to appear in more powerful social roles. Studies of videos and websites have found, for example, that men were cast as bosses, businessmen, or other professionals, while women were cast as housewives, clerical staff, or students.

Pornography Consumption and Consumers' Behavioral Scripts

Aggressive Scripts

A diverse body of studies coalesce around the conclusion that increased pornography consumption is associated with an increased probability of holding attitudes supportive of violence and engaging in aggressive behavior. Quantitative syntheses (meta-analyses) of laboratory experiments have found an overall positive association between manipulated pornography exposure and both attitudes supportive of violence and the likelihood of engaging in aggressive acts. A recent meta-analysis of self-reported pornography exposure and attitudes supportive of violence also found an overall positive correlation. No meta-analysis has yet been conducted on self-reported pornography exposure and sexually aggressive behavior in general population samples, but cross-sectional surveys in Canada, Italy, Sweden, and the United States and longitudinal surveys in Brazil, China, and the United States have found significant linkages.

Objectification Scripts

Early experimental research suggested that pornography exposure could affect viewers' objectification scripts. For instance, an experimental study published in the early 1980s found that exposure to conventional pornography over the course of several weeks increased men's agreement with statements such as "Pickups should expect to put out" and "A man should find them, fool them, fuck them, and forget them." Studies published in the past decade with adolescents and young adults align with the findings of early experimental research. A cross-sectional survey with college students in the United States found that higher levels of pornography consumption were predictive of concurrence with declarations such as "The best thing about women is their bodies." Likewise, a cross-sectional survey with college students in Japan found that more frequent exposure predicted stronger agreement that "attractive women should expect sexual advances." Longitudinal survey results echo these findings. A three-wave longitudinal survey of Dutch adolescents indicated that prior pornography exposure was a consistent correlate of later notions of women as sex objects (e.g., perceiving that "there is nothing wrong with boys being interested in a women only if she is pretty"). A three-wave longitudinal survey of Belgian adolescents showed that pornography consumption was a prospective correlate of placing a higher priority on women's breasts, buttocks, and belly.

Social Role Scripts

Behavioral script theory would predict weaker associations between pornography consumption and viewers' nonsexual social role scripts than between pornography and their sexual aggression and objectification–related scripts for two reasons. First, the graphic depiction of sexual acts is pornography's focus; general social role scenes are less prevalent or serve as contextual preludes for sexual encounters. As frequency of exposure increases the likelihood of behavioral scripting, viewers' sexual scripts are more likely to be affected than their nonsexual scripts. Second, in the absence of depictions of nonsexual social roles, consumers must extrapolate and infer rules and principles from sexual interactions for their general social role scripts to become more gendered postexposure. Such abstract modeling effects are less likely to occur because they require a more active cognitive process. Nevertheless, several studies have distinguished individuals' social role perceptions along gendered lines as a function of their pornography consumption.

Early experimental studies found that prolonged exposure to pornography decreased support for the women's liberation movement and increased the view that wives should yield to their husbands in conflict situations. A recent experimental study indicated that exposure to pornography could lead to heightened agreement with views such as "Many women are actually seeking special favors, such as hiring policies that favor them over men, under the guise of asking for equality" and "Feminists are making unreasonable demands of men." The results of a cross-sectional survey study showed that exposure to pornography with themes of dominance was associated with more conservative attitudes toward women (e.g., in terms of their vocational roles, marital relationships, and freedom and independence). Longitudinal research with adolescents has found that earlier pornography consumption predicts more subsequent regressive gender role perceptions, for example, that girls should not play competitive sports. Longitudinal research with adults has found that prior pornography consumption can correlate with more later agreement with statements such as "It is much better for everyone involved if the man is the achiever outside the home and the woman takes care of the home and family" and "Most men are better suited emotionally for politics than are most women."

Selective Exposure

From a media effects perspective, associations between pornography consumption and gendered perspectives on sociality found in naturalistic studies are due to behavioral scripting processes. An oft-stated alternative explanation for correlations between themes in pornography and correspondent behavioral scripts among consumers is selective exposure. The selective-exposure argument maintains that the congruence between consumers' attitudes and behaviors and pornographic content is due to consumers seeking out sexual media that affirm their preexisting scripts.

Only studies that sample the same participants on more than one occasion can test this alternative explanation. If selective exposure is responsible for associations between pornography consumption and gendered attitudes and behaviors, any correlation found between prior pornography consumption and later attitudes or behaviors in longitudinal research will become nonsignificant when earlier indices of the attitude or behavior are included in the analysis. This is because from a selective exposure standpoint, the variability common to the predictor and the criterion is due to earlier levels of the criterion. To illustrate, if in a two-wave panel study, the association between prior pornography consumption and a later gendered attitude becomes null after the time-one measure of the attitude is controlled, there is evidence to support the selective exposure hypothesis. Conversely, if the association maintains its significance, the behavioral scripting hypothesis is supported.

Longitudinal research does not support selective exposure as a viable explanation for the associations between pornography consumption and gendered attitudes and behaviors in naturalistic studies. Prospective associations between pornography consumption and aggressive scripts, objectification scripts, and social role scripts have been maintained after earlier measurements of these variables were included as covariates.

Individual Differences

Research on pornography consumption and gender has been more interested in exploring whether there are overall associations than in testing for moderating individual differences. Given the diversity in human thought and action, however, it stands to reason that the effects of exposure vary across individuals. There are data that support this supposition, although much more research is needed before definitive and precise conclusions can be made about which characteristics of viewers make them more likely to adopt pornographic depictions of gender as their own.

Probably the most conclusive finding to date is that an effect of pornography on sexually aggressive behavior is most likely for men who have a hostile approach to masculinity (e.g., see male-female relationships as inherently adversarial) and an impersonal view of sex. The importance of these individual differences in enhancing sexual aggression risk has been indicated in multiple studies.

A few studies have found stronger associations between pornography consumption and gendered beliefs among older consumers. Because older individuals tend to have more gendered beliefs than younger individuals, they may be more influenced by stereotypical and traditional social role portrayals in pornography.

Most studies suggest that the gendered scripts in pornography affect females. There are longitudinal studies in each of the three areas reviewed in this entry—(1) aggressive scripts, (2) objectification scripts, and (3) social role scripts—that have found prospective associations for females in addition to males. It is also the case, however, that the effects of individual differences on reactions to pornography may differ for men and women. Results of a recent pornography experiment, for example, suggested that the moderating effect of personality on consumers' sexist attitudes and attitudes supportive of violence may differ for men and women. Studies are needed that test three-way interactions between pornography exposure, consumers' self-identified gender, and other individual differences.

Areas in Need of Inquiry

Much of the pornography literature focuses on depictions of White performers engaging in heterosexual acts. However, ready access to pornography on the Internet has circumvented past social norms, which made the consumption of alternative forms of pornography more difficult. As such, academic research has recently begun to examine gay and lesbian pornography. Issues of race and how it intersects with other concerns in pornography have also been broached.

A public health framework dominates much of the empirical literature on pornography depicting MSM (men who have sex with men). Of particular concern is the frequency of bareback sex (unprotected), which researchers warn could lead to the development of risky sexual scripts. Cross-sectional survey data from a variety of sources suggest an association between pornography consumption and engaging in risky sexual behaviors for MSM. One study found that 34% of online gay pornography depicted unprotected anal intercourse while 36% of videos contained protected anal sex; while the difference between these two frequencies was not significant, researchers did find videos depicting unprotected anal intercourse to have greater viewership. Another study comparing gay pornography with straight pornography found no significant differences in the frequency of aggressive acts. While there are little longitudinal or experimental data to account for the effects of gay pornography, some cross-sectional survey data suggest that as much as 99% of men who identify as gay had consumed pornography in the past 3 months.

The majority of pornography depicting lesbian sex is consumed by and produced for heterosexual men. As such, most pornography depicting females engaging in various sexual acts with other females mirrors the aforementioned violence of traditionally heterosexual pornography. In a sample of popular adult videos, researchers found that female aggressors targeted other females in 17% of the scenes. While studies examining the impact of pornography on women's attitudes about sexual or social roles demonstrate significant effects, as mentioned previously, many of these studies do not differentiate between heterosexual consumers and lesbian consumers.

Empirical studies of pornography depicting transgender individuals or consumed by transgender individuals are difficult to locate. Research is needed on the content, use, and effects of pornography for transgender people and other marginalized groups. Furthermore, experimental and longitudinal data are particularly lacking with regard to gay and lesbian pornography. While the body of pornography literature continues to grow, a more diverse perspective is needed.

While there is a dearth of research related to issues of race and ethnicity in pornography, some important research has been conducted. Cross-sectional data suggest that White men and women consume less pornography than individuals who identify as non-White, but a theoretical explanation for this finding is absent. Qualitative interview data suggest that low-income, urban-dwelling Black and Hispanic youth report experiencing a greater pressure to imitate pornography, as well as a preference for pornography featuring actors of the same race. Content analyses of online pornography and traditional adult videos indicate that interracial pornography, often with a White male and a non-White female, is more common than pornography depicting two members of a non-White race. Further research is necessary to determine what, if any, impact this phenomenon has on navigating the intersections between race and gender roles.

Paul J. Wright and Stephen R. Stewart

See also Anti-Feminist Backlash; Body Objectification; Gender Role Behavior; Masculinity Ideology and Norms; Media and Gender

Further Readings

Hald, G. M., Malamuth, N., & Yuen, C. (2010). Pornography and attitudes supporting violence against women: Revisiting the relationship in nonexperimental studies. *Aggressive Behavior, 36,* 14–20.

Linz, D., & Malamuth, N. (1993). *Pornography.* Newbury Park, CA: Sage.

Mulac, A., Jansma, L., & Linz, D. (2002). Men's behavior toward women after viewing sexually-explicit films: Degradation makes a difference. *Communication Monographs, 69,* 311–328.

Mundorf, N., Allen, M., D'Alessio, D., & Emmers-Sommer, T. M. (2007). Effects of sexually explicit media. In R. W. Preiss, B. M. Gayle, N. Burrell, M. Allen, & J. Bryant (Eds.), *Mass media effects research: Advances through meta-analysis* (pp. 181–198). New York, NY: Lawrence Erlbaum.

Peter, J., & Valkenburg, P. M. (2009). Adolescents' exposure to sexually explicit Internet material and notions of women as sex objects: Assessing causality and underlying processes. *Journal of Communication, 59,* 407–433.

Sun, C., Bridges, A., Wosnitzer, R., Scharrer, E., & Liberman, R. (2008). A comparison of male and female directors in popular pornography: What happens when women are at the helm? *Psychology of Women Quarterly, 32,* 312–325.

Wright, P. J., & Bae, S. (2014). A national prospective study of pornography consumption and gendered attitudes toward women. *Sexuality & Culture, 19*(3), 444–463.

Postpartum Depression

Postpartum depression (PPD) refers to depressive episodes that occur during the period following the birth of a child. PPD is one of the most common complications following childbirth. In addition to the distress and impairment experienced by women with PPD, it is associated with increased risk to other members of the family, especially the infant. This entry provides a review of the symptoms and diagnostic criteria for PPD, its prevalence, issues in screening, risk factors, and consequences. It concludes with an overview of the available interventions for PPD.

Symptoms and Diagnosis

Like other depressive episodes, PPD is characterized by depressed mood or loss of interest, in addition to other related symptoms. Cognitive symptoms of PPD include feelings of worthlessness or excessive/inappropriate guilt, diminished ability to think/concentrate, difficulty making decisions, and recurrent thoughts of death or suicide. Somatic symptoms include significant changes to appetite/weight, sleep disturbances, psychomotor agitation/retardation, and fatigue or loss of energy. To meet the diagnostic criteria for major depressive disorder according to the *Diagnostic and Statistical Manual of Mental Disorders, Fifth Edition* (*DSM-5*), women must experience at least five symptoms (one of which must be depressed mood or loss of interest) for at least 2 weeks; the symptoms must cause distress or impair a woman's ability to function. Comorbid symptoms of anxiety, such as excessive worry about the infant, are also common.

The *DSM-5* does not treat PPD as a separate diagnostic entity. Postpartum women meeting the criteria for a depressive disorder can receive a diagnosis with the specifier "with peripartum onset" if the episode begins during pregnancy or the first 4 weeks postpartum. Other classification systems, including the World Health Organization's *International Statistical Classification of Diseases and Related Health Problems*, similarly apply the same criteria used to classify nonpostpartum depressive episodes to postpartum depressive episodes.

There is no standard definition for the time frame following childbirth that constitutes the postpartum period. While the *DSM-5* limits the peripartum onset specifier to episodes beginning during pregnancy or the first 4 weeks postpartum, in research and clinical settings, the term is commonly used to refer to episodes occurring during the first 12 months postpartum. Additionally, there is no consensus regarding the use of the term *postpartum depression*. Whereas some authors reserve the term for episodes of depression with onset during the postpartum period, others use it to describe depressive episodes that begin before or during pregnancy and continue through the postpartum period. These differences in the way the term has been defined across studies can lead to challenges in interpreting and synthesizing research.

One challenge of diagnosing PPD is that some symptoms of depression are also normal and common postpartum experiences. For example, breast-feeding women often experience significant increases in appetite, which can be a symptom of depression. It can be difficult to determine whether sleep disturbances are a symptom of depression or related to infant waking. Research comparing the structure of symptoms in postpartum women with nonchildbearing women has found that the same symptoms that characterize non-postpartum episodes characterize postpartum depressive episodes. Despite the fact that many somatic changes are normal during the postpartum period, these symptoms remain reliable indicators of depressive episodes. In clinical practice, however, assessment of symptoms of depression should be guided by an understanding of normal postpartum experiences. For example, rather than asking a woman if she wakes frequently in the night, the clinician may assess whether a woman has difficulty falling asleep while others are caring for the infant or wakes in the middle of the night while the baby continues to sleep.

It is important to differentiate PPD from other psychiatric disorders, as well as from nondisordered emotional responses to childbirth. Most women experience some degree of the "baby blues," which is characterized by symptoms including anxiety, labile mood, and crying spells. Typically, the baby blues are mild and resolve without intervention. The baby blues can be differentiated from PPD by the low severity of the symptoms and their transience. PPD should also be distinguished from postpartum psychosis, which is characterized by serious alternations in perception and cognition. Postpartum psychotic episodes can occur in the context of a variety of psychiatric illnesses, including bipolar disorder, schizophrenia, and other psychotic disorders. Postpartum psychosis is rare, effecting approximately 1 in 1,000 women. Both the severity of symptoms and the presence of psychotic symptoms such as hallucinations, delusions, or disorganized thoughts distinguish postpartum psychosis from PPD. Finally, other psychiatric illnesses may also have their onset during the postpartum period, including anxiety disorders, obsessive-compulsive disorder, and posttraumatic stress disorder. While the term *postpartum depression* is commonly used to refer to any emotional disturbance during the postpartum period, evaluation of psychiatric symptoms in this population should consider the full range of potential diagnoses.

Prevalence

PPD is relatively common. Reviews suggest that between 10% and 20% of North American and European women experience a major or minor depressive episode during the first year postpartum. Prevalence estimates vary widely across studies and are influenced by many methodological factors, including the method of ascertainment (e.g., self-report vs. interview), the criteria used to define PPD (e.g., elevated symptoms vs. clinical diagnosis), the time frame used to define the postpartum period, and the population sampled in a given study.

There are striking differences between countries in the reported prevalence of PPD, with some countries (e.g., Malaysia, Singapore) reporting very low rates of PPD and others (e.g., South Korea, Taiwan) reporting rates approaching 50%. These differences may reflect the inadequacy of current screening and diagnostic measures in different cultural contexts. While descriptions of PPD are similar across cultures, it is primarily in Western cultures that these experiences are conceptualized as an illness. Cultural practices related to the postpartum period, such as the Chinese tradition of "doing the month" or *la cuarentena* in Mexico and other Latin American countries, may be protective against PPD.

Research investigating whether the postpartum period is associated with increased risk for depression has been mixed. Overall, research suggests that prevalence rates are comparable between postpartum women and nonchildbearing women of reproductive age. However, there appears to be a slight elevation in risk for depression during the early postpartum period, particularly the first 4 weeks. This time period is also associated with increased risk for other psychiatric illnesses (e.g., manic and psychotic episodes).

Screening

Screening is an important tool for identifying women experiencing or at risk for depression during the postpartum period. The American College of Obstetricians and Gynecologists recommends that clinicians screen patients for symptoms of anxiety and depression using a standardized, validated tool at least once during the perinatal period. Self-report measures specifically designed to assess postpartum depressive symptoms include the Edinburgh Post-Natal Depression Scale and the Postpartum Depression Screening Scale. Screening tools for depression in the general population, such as the Beck Depression Inventory and the Patient Health Questionnaire 9, can also be used with postpartum women. Screening is most effective when provided in concert with further evaluation, referral, and treatment options.

Risk Factors and Causal Mechanisms

Several systematic reviews have synthesized the sizable literature addressing risk factors for PPD. Overall, these reviews find that risk factors for PPD are comparable with those for depression in the general population. The strongest risk factor for PPD is a personal history of depression, especially depression during pregnancy. Social characteristics such as inadequate social support and psychological characteristics such as neuroticism and a negative attributional style are moderately to strongly correlated with postpartum depressive symptoms. Sociodemographic characteristics such as marital status and socioeconomic status are weakly associated with PPD. Other characteristics such as obstetric complications, infant health, and infant temperament are also associated with PPD.

While it is often assumed that hormones play a causal role in the development of PPD, research findings in this area have been mixed. Levels of estrogen and progesterone are elevated during pregnancy and decrease rapidly and dramatically after delivery. However, while all women experience this rapid hormonal shift, not all women develop PPD. Moreover, most research does not find that levels of estrogen or progesterone differ between depressed and nondepressed postpartum women.

Some research suggests that women with PPD may constitute two distinct groups: one group for which childbirth is a nonspecific stressor (who may also be at risk for depressive episodes unrelated to childbearing) and a second group that is particularly vulnerable to depression in the context of childbearing. Several sources of evidence converge to suggest that a subset of women may be specifically vulnerable to PPD. One study found that women whose first depressive episode occurred during the postpartum period were at significantly greater risk for subsequent postpartum depressive episodes but not for subsequent depressive episodes unrelated to childbearing. Another study found stronger sibling concordance rates for early-postpartum depressive episodes (especially following first pregnancies) compared with depressive episodes occurring later in the postpartum period. Finally, there is direct experimental evidence that some women with PPD experience a recurrence of depressive symptoms when hormone levels are manipulated to mimic the changes that accompany pregnancy and childbirth, while women without a history of PPD do not experience changes in mood when exposed to the same hormonal manipulation.

Consequences

PPD is associated with a range of adverse outcomes not only for women but for their families as well. According to the World Health Organization, depression is one of the leading causes of disability worldwide. Beyond the emotional suffering associated with the symptoms of depression, moderate to severe depression can lead to poor functioning in contexts such as work, school, and family life. Women with PPD often experience a decreased sense of self-efficacy, especially their confidence in the maternal role. They may also exhibit objective difficulties in parenting. For example, women with PPD may be less likely to adequately address the health and safety needs of their children (e.g., attendance at well-child visits, appropriate use of car seats). Women with PPD show decreased responsiveness in interactions with their infants. They are also more likely to experience impaired bonding with their infants, and in rare but serious cases, PPD is associated with increased risk for child abuse and neglect.

Children of depressed mothers are at increased risk for adverse behavioral, cognitive, and emotional outcomes. Children of mothers with PPD are at increased risk for both internalizing and externalizing disorders. PPD is also associated with impaired cognitive and language ability in childhood and adolescence. The timing, severity, and chronicity of maternal depressive symptoms are important determinants of the long-term effects of PPD on child outcomes.

Treatment and Prevention

There are many treatment options for women experiencing PPD. While many women express a preference for nonpharmacological treatment options, antidepressants remain the most commonly utilized treatment for PPD. The ability to receive a prescription from a primary care physician or obstetrician may make medication more accessible for many women. Practical barriers to treatment, such as a need for child care and transportation, may also make pharmacological management more feasible for many women. Overall, evidence suggests that antidepressant use during the postpartum period is safe and effective, even for women who choose to breast-feed. Reviews of the safety of antidepressants in breast-feeding women suggest that nortriptyline, paroxetine, and sertraline may have the most favorable safety profiles.

Several types of psychotherapy are effective treatments for PPD, including nondirective counseling, cognitive behavioral therapy, interpersonal psychotherapy, and psychodynamic therapy. Therapy can be administered individually or in groups, in a range of settings ranging from the home to primary care settings, to traditional outpatient clinics, and by a range of professionals (e.g., nurses and home visitors). Internet-based interventions are becoming more widely utilized and appear to have comparable efficacy with traditional face-to-face therapy. There is growing interest in the use of complementary and alternative therapies for PPD, including hormonal treatments, herbal supplements, and exercise-based interventions, such as yoga.

PPD can also be effectively prevented with a variety of approaches, including educational programs, psychotherapy, social support programs, and medication. Most women are engaged in the health care system through pregnancy and the early postpartum period, which provides opportunities for screening and referral for intervention. Integrating mental health care into existing services for pregnant and postpartum women, such as obstetric clinics and childbirth education classes, presents a promising avenue for dissemination of effective prevention programs.

Laura E. Sockol

See also Depression and Women; Mental Health and Gender: Overview; Motherhood; Pregnancy

Further Readings

Milgrom, J., & Gemmill, A. W. (2015). *Identifying perinatal depression and anxiety: Evidence-based practice in screening, psychosocial assessment and management.* Chichester, England: Wiley-Blackwell.

O'Hara, M. W., & McCabe, J. E. (2013). Postpartum depression: Current status and future directions. *Annual Review of Clinical Psychology, 9,* 379–407.

Ross, L. E., Dennis, C.-L., Blackmore, E. R., & Stewart, D. E. (2005). *Postpartum depression: A guide for front-line health and social services providers.* Toronto, Ontario, Canada: Centre for Addiction and Mental Health.

Stone, S. D., & Menken, A. E. (2008). *Perinatal and postpartum mood disorders: Perspectives and treatment guide for the healthcare practitioner.* New York, NY: Springer.

Posttraumatic Stress Disorder and Gender

The ongoing battle with posttraumatic stress disorder (PTSD) is an individual and a public health concern. In his work examining the burden of PTSD on the individual and society, Ronald Kessler identified the following burdens: (a) medical costs, (b) occupational impairment, (c) functional ability impairment, (d) treatment costs, and (e) psychological burden. To begin addressing this issue, accurate research, diagnosing, and treatment are necessary. As part of its effort to update the research and diagnostic criteria of all psychiatric disorders, the American Psychiatric Association's *Diagnostic and Statistical Manual of Mental Disorders, Fifth Edition* (*DSM-5*), includes information about PTSD. Symptoms of PTSD include direct exposure to a trauma, the experiencing of an intrusive symptom such as distress or flashbacks, the evasion of stimuli linked to the event, having negative thoughts or mood associated with a trauma, and having significant transformation in arousal and reactivity, such as concentration issues or sleep disturbances. Furthermore, the duration of symptoms is at least 1 month, it causes anxiety or distress in important areas of functioning, and these symptoms are not induced by substances or other medical conditions.

The aforementioned symptomology of PTSD is complicated in terms of general understanding as well as diagnosing. When practitioners treat persons diagnosed with PTSD, they must also be aware of the various diversity variables of every person. Multicultural psychology is concerned with the practitioner being able to identify the various diversity variables, appreciate and accept those differences, identify how they perceive themselves in the world, and have the ability to work with diverse individuals. One very important diversity variable is gender. The role of gender in any research is important; however, it is important to note that many research studies that examine gender are actually examining differences in sex. Although the terms are often used reciprocally, *gender* refers to behaviors and roles in society, whereas *sex* refers to the biological and physiological characteristics (male or female). Therefore, it is important to proceed with caution when reviewing articles regarding gender as many do not include gender-related variables, simply a comparison between males and females. This entry includes sex and gender considerations on the following: (a) a comparison and contrast of trauma and PTSD, (b) an overview of the various risk factors, (c) a review of the types of trauma, (d) an exploration of the comorbid link of alcohol use disorders and PTSD, (e) the identification of the importance of social support, and (f) an analysis of the future directions of gender and PTSD.

Trauma Versus PTSD

The American Psychological Association has defined trauma as when an individual has an emotional response, such as shock or denial, after being exposed to a terrible event. Trauma is the primary component of PTSD. If the exposure to a trauma is absent, a clinician would not consider a diagnosis of PTSD even if the person is exhibiting symptoms (besides trauma exposure) similar to the aforementioned criteria for PTSD. Simple exposure to a traumatic event does not equate to a diagnosis of PTSD. However, the clinician must consider the diagnosis of PTSD and review all the criteria to accurately diagnose the disorder or to rule it out. It has been well established in the trauma literature that lifetime exposure to a trauma is high, with men being exposed to traumatic events more often. It has also been well documented that although men tend to be exposed to more traumatic events, women are approximately twice as likely to be diagnosed with PTSD.

Risk Factors

As part of their research examining a variety of variables (age, prior trauma exposure, anxiety, depression, social support, negative affectivity, and dissociation) on PTSD and sex, Dorte Christiansen and Ask Elklit included the mediation hypothesis. The mediation hypothesis identifies that the sex differences in PTSD are related to risk factors during the time prior to the trauma, during the trauma, and after the trauma. These time frames can be broken up into pretraumatic, peritraumatic, and posttraumatic risk factors. Pretraumatic risk factors include the characteristics of an individual before the onset of a traumatic event, whereas peritraumatic risk factors include the details of the event coupled with the individual's response during or immediately after exposure to the traumatic event. Last, posttraumatic risk factors are the characteristics that are present after exposure to the traumatic event that play a role in the development of a diagnosis of PTSD. The pretraumatic, peritraumatic, and posttraumatic risk factors identified in the following sections are not meant to fully account for the individual sex differences in PTSD; they are meant to document the factors generally associated with each sex. Given the occurrence of diagnosed PTSD significantly favoring females, the combination of these risk factors may explain this phenomenon as opposed to examining the differences individually.

Pretraumatic Risk Factors

As previously stated, men tend to be exposed to more traumas; this is a significant pretraumatic risk factor. In their literature review on PTSD, trauma exposure, and sex differences, David Tolin and Edna Foa identified that females are exposed to more sexual trauma. Although not gender specific, when comparing the general population with individuals who are incarcerated, there are significantly higher rates of exposure to trauma among incarcerated individuals. Numerous other researchers have identified higher levels of pretraumatic risk factors for females when compared with their male counterparts, including depression, neuroticism, and anxiety sensitivity.

Peritraumatic Risk Factors

Although not gender specific, helplessness, extreme fear, and horror have been identified by researchers as peritraumatic experiences. Furthermore, dissociation, panic, and tonic immobility are all peritraumatic reactions. Tonic immobility is the profound motor inhibition that occurs when an individual experiences an inescapable threat. In their review of the literature surrounding sex differences and tonic immobility, Christiansen and Maj Hansen hypothesized that females would have more reports of tonic immobility than males.

Posttraumatic Risk Factors

Researchers have identified lack of posttraumatic social support and negative support as significant risk factors for developing PTSD. Negative thoughts have also been well documented as a predictor for psychiatric disorders, including PTSD. In terms of sex differences, negative social support and negative thoughts were more endorsed by females than by males.

Trauma Type and Onset

Norma Breslau identified that the type of trauma experienced by females and males seems to be different. In her epidemiological research, she identified that females, in general, tend to be exposed to more interpersonal forms of trauma, such as molestation, intimate partner violence, child abuse, or sexual assault, whereas males tend to be exposed to disasters, fires, and other events that are not interpersonal in nature. Given this information, females tend to be more exposed to interpersonal trauma (IPT). IPT occurs when an individual is exposed to a traumatic event in which the individual is assaulted or otherwise harmed by another individual. Furthermore, IPT typically increases the risk of being diagnosed with PTSD when compared with traumatic experiences that are non-interpersonal in nature. In addition to this research, Michelle Lilly and Christine Valdez examined IPT and gender in relation to PTSD. They too were able to identify that gender alone did not account for the high levels of diagnosed PTSD among females. In their research, they identified that the timing of the IPT exposure, revictimization, and continued exposure significantly affects PTSD symptomatology and severity more strongly than the gender variables. Although gender is an important variable, it can be reasonably concluded that the type of trauma experienced can have a significant impact on the prognosis of PTSD.

Alcohol Use Disorders and PTSD

The causal link between alcohol use disorders and PTSD has been well established and well documented in the research. The comorbidity of alcohol use disorders and PTSD can be viewed from two lenses: (1) individuals with PTSD manage its symptoms with alcohol use and (2) individuals with drinking problems can have PTSD. There are two motives for drinking that have been linked to PTSD: (1) drinking to cope and (2) drinking for enhancement. In the former, an individual consumes alcohol to reduce negative feelings. This is essentially linked to the idea of self-medication. In the latter, an individual consumes alcohol to increase an internal positive state. Data from the National Epidemiologic Survey on Alcohol and Related Conditions found that men were twice as likely to drink alcohol to cope with PTSD symptoms as women. When reviewing the current literature on PTSD, motives for drinking alcohol, gender differences, and increases in PTSD symptoms were more likely to be associated with drinking-to-cope motives for men than for women. Furthermore, both motives—coping and enhancement—were more likely to be linked to greater alcohol use in men as compared with women. In one study, when examining gender differences, drinking motives, and PTSD symptom severity, researchers found that men and women who reported higher levels of PTSD symptom severity also had greater motives to consume alcohol to cope. Although not all individuals with severe PTSD symptoms consume alcohol to cope, this is clinically important, as there is a significant positive relationship between these two variables.

Social Support and PTSD

Bernice Andrews, Chris Brewin, and Suzanna Rose were the first to hypothesize and conduct research that supported the idea that women's higher risk for the development of PTSD may involve specific gender differences in social support following a traumatic exposure. Based on the current research on this topic, the general consensus is that women tend to perceive greater positive social support as well as benefit more from it than men; this is strongly tied to their well-being. To minimize risk for the development of PTSD in women, social support can be included pretrauma so that in the event a trauma is experienced, women will already have social support in place.

Future Directions

The current research by Christiansen and Hansen combining pretraumatic, peritraumatic, and posttraumatic risk factors to explain sex differences among those diagnosed with PTSD is significant; identifying these sex differences can begin to explain the gender gap in PTSD. Future research can build on the work of these authors. Given that women benefit from social support posttrauma, future research can identify components of social support that females value and aim to implement these pretrauma so that the support already exists if a potential trauma arises.

Greg Bohall

See also Mental Health and Gender: Overview; Posttraumatic Stress Disorder and Gender Differences in Children; Posttraumatic Stress Disorder and Gender Violence; Vicarious Trauma

Further Readings

Christiansen, D. M., & Hansen, M. (2015). Accounting for sex differences in PTSD: A multi-variable mediation model. *European Journal of Psychotraumatology, 6,* 26068. doi:10.3402/ejpt.v6.26068

Friedman, M. J., Keane, T. M., & Resick, P. A. (Eds.). (2014). *Handbook of PTSD: Science and practice* (2nd ed.). New York, NY: Guilford Press.

Lehavot, K., Stappenbeck, C. A., Luterek, J. A., Kaysen, D., & Simpson, S. L. (2014). Gender differences in relationships among PTSD severity, drinking motives, and alcohol use in a comorbid alcohol dependence and PTSD sample. *Psychology of Addictive Behaviors, 28*(1), 42–52. doi:10.1037/a0032266

Lilly, M. M., & Valdez, C. E. (2012). Interpersonal trauma and PTSD: The roles of gender and a lifespan perspective in predicting risk. *Psychological Trauma: Theory, Research, Practice, and Policy, 4*(1), 140–144. doi:10.1037/a0022947

Olff, M., Langeland, W., Draijer, N., & Gersons, B. P. R. (2007). Gender differences in posttraumatic stress disorder. *Psychological Bulletin, 133,* 183–204. doi:10.1037/0033-2909.133.2.183

Tolin, D. F., & Foa, E. B. (2008). Sex differences in trauma and posttraumatic stress disorder: A quantitative review of 25 years of research. *Psychological Trauma: Theory, Research, Practice, and Policy, 5*(1), 37–85. doi:10.1037/1942-9681.S.1.37

Valdez, C. E., & Lilly, M. M. (2014). Biological sex, gender role, and criterion A2: Rethinking the "gender" gap in PTSD. *Psychological Trauma: Theory, Research, Practice, and Policy, 6*(1), 34–40. doi:10.1037/a0031466

Posttraumatic Stress Disorder and Gender Differences in Children

Posttraumatic stress disorder, or PTSD, was first introduced in 1980 by the American Psychiatric Association. Prior to that time, other diagnoses were used to label this specific condition. PTSD had historically been applied to understand reactions to war or combat experiences. It was then broadened to be applied to natural disasters and other traumatic events. Today, it is understood that PTSD can result from a variety of traumas and traumatic situations, singular experiences, or ongoing experiences at any point during life. PTSD can occur at any age and can affect young children who have experienced a trauma. Boys and girls have similar reactions to trauma, and there are minimal gender differences with regard to rates of PTSD. Differences between boys and girls who have PTSD often result from the culture's response to the child's symptoms. Stigma and other differences in how trauma and the symptoms of PTSD are understood by the culture can affect the child's expression of the disorder, as well as correct diagnosis and treatment of the disorder. This entry focuses on how PTSD affects boys and girls differently, first examining the incidence and causes and then reviewing the risk factors and various types of treatments. The social stigma associated with PTSD is then discussed.

Incidence and Causes

PTSD is a mental health condition that is triggered by witnessing or experiencing a terrifying or life-threatening event. A small proportion of children who experience a trauma will develop PTSD. Symptoms of PTSD vary but can include nightmares, reliving the event through intrusive thoughts or flashbacks, avoidance of situations that trigger a reminder of the event, anger, anxiety, numbness, and feelings of shame. Children may experience all of these symptoms, as well as other behaviors such as reenactments of the trauma through play or direct actions. According to the National Center for PTSD, it is estimated that about 14% to 43% of boys and 15% to 43% of girls experience at least one form of trauma. Boys are more likely than girls to be sexually abused by strangers or those in positions of authority, with the average age of the victim being 17 years. Of those boys who have experienced some form of trauma, 1% to 6% develop PTSD, whereas of girls who have had a trauma, 3% to 15% develop PTSD.

The development of PTSD is higher depending on the type of trauma experienced. Children and teens can develop PTSD after being sexually or physically abused; from experiencing domestic violence, early or forceful marriages, or a natural disaster; or witnessing violent crime. As with adults, not all traumas lead to PTSD. Without the development of PTSD, psychological and other consequences may occur from the trauma. Traumas may result in no psychological pathology; other conditions that can result from traumas may be an acute stress response or adjustment disorder. PTSD refers to a distinct condition or cluster of symptoms that cause impairment in functioning.

There are multiple screens and assessments that assist professionals in diagnosing PTSD in children. However, correct diagnosis can be difficult because the professional is tasked with inferring whether or not the symptoms are due to a trauma and also because symptoms may mimic the symptoms of many other disorders. Therefore, diagnosis and treatment by professionals trained in childhood trauma is optimal.

Traumas that occur in childhood can affect people throughout their lives in a variety of ways. In younger children, PTSD may present differently than in teens or adults. Younger children often display symptoms of trauma through play or other behaviors, given their lack of sophisticated language to describe their inner experience. They may be fearful of being left alone, of leaving caregivers, or of sleeping. Children may be fearful of death or may fear the death of a loved one. Children may also blame themselves for the trauma. Although teens may display symptoms of PTSD similar to adults, they may also "act out" in school or other settings. Teens may experience irritability, agitation, or aggression, which may lead to behavioral and/or academic problems in school or potential problems with the law. Traumas that occur in childhood may also affect functioning into and throughout adulthood.

Risk Factors

Although specific risk factors for developing PTSD exist, such as early exposure to trauma, ongoing trauma, existing anxiety or depression, a family history of PTSD, and others, it is challenging to draw direct connections between specific events and PTSD given the high variability among individuals and the multiple variables that can affect the development of this disorder. Girls are often acknowledged to be at a higher risk of becoming victims of specific types of crimes that are linked to trauma and thus linked to the development of PTSD. Girls have higher reported incidences of sexual abuse than boys. One study revealed that one in four girls is sexually abused before the age of 18 years, compared with one in six boys. The abuser is often an adult male, although abuse can be by siblings or peers. The abuser is also often a family member. For girls, interpersonal trauma is more of a risk factor for developing PTSD, in part because it is often ongoing and because girls sometimes blame themselves for being victimized. One of the hypothesized reasons why girls experience higher rates of PTSD than boys is the types of traumas they experience. In terms of populations of girls, among trafficked and sexually exploited girls, injuries and sexual violence were associated with higher levels of PTSD. Although the incidence of childhood sexual abuse is higher among girls than among boys, the long-term consequences of abuse are similar for boys and girls, with adults of both sexes experiencing problems with behavior and mental and social functioning.

Types of Treatments

Determining the appropriate treatment depends on the child's developmental level, the nature of the trauma, and the environment. Very young children may engage in child-parent psychotherapy to address issues related to attachment and their bond. Regardless of the age of the child, including the parent or caregiver in the treatment of the child is usually recommended. There are no known gender differences in terms of the effectiveness of various treatments, and all treatments could be offered to children regardless of gender or type of trauma.

Crisis Interventions

Crisis interventions can be provided by mental health professionals in the community and in hospital settings. When violence occurs within a school or within a school's community, these teams of professionals often visit the school to speak with the students and teachers. These interventions are intended to provide immediate assistance with coping with a recent trauma. Outside of school, the teams may work with the child and the family. This may include providing support, relaxation and self-care techniques, education, and referrals for mental health treatment.

Medication

Antidepressants such as selective serotonin reuptake inhibitors have been used to treat symptoms of PTSD. Other antianxiety medications and medications that help with sleep have also been used to treat symptoms. It is typically recommended that children who are receiving medication for symptoms of PTSD also receive some form of counseling or psychotherapy to assist with coping with and recovering from the event or trauma.

Types of Therapies

Cognitive behavioral therapy is an evidence-based therapy that has proven to be effective in treating anxiety disorders and symptoms of PTSD. This treatment often includes a collaborative relationship between the therapist and the client. Understanding how maladaptive thoughts and behaviors contribute to symptoms through various forms of reinforcement is a key component of treatment.

Eye movement desensitization and reprocessing is a treatment with some empirical backing and involves combining eye movements with desensitization. Therapists who provided this treatment are specifically trained. The goal of this treatment is to reduce the symptoms associated with PTSD or a trauma.

Prolonged exposure can be applied independently or as a component of other treatments that involve desensitization. This involves a methodical and planned exposure to aspects associated with the trauma in vivo, through mental imagery, or through other means. The goal of this is to reduce the negative response to anxiety-provoking stimuli. Research has shown that adolescent girls who have PTSD due to sexual abuse benefited more from prolonged exposure therapy than from supportive counseling.

Play or art therapy can be useful for children of all ages but is used especially with children who lack the capacity to verbally reflect or express themselves. This may involve a person trained in play or art therapy or a clinician who utilizes play or art as an avenue for expression and working through the trauma. Many times, children can reenact the trauma through play or drawing. This is often a recommended approach for younger children, as it is less intrusive and will not place the child at risk of feeling fear or being retraumatized by direct questioning about or discussion of an event.

Meditation has been shown to be useful for some in reducing symptoms of anxiety. Meditation has many benefits but, more recently, has been recommended for use by trained professionals in hospital and other mental health settings.

Support groups are made up of peers with a leader to guide the group. These may include similar-age boys who have experienced similar types of traumas. Support groups exist for survivors of various traumas, such as incest, rape, domestic violence, and others. These are often useful for facilitating support from others, reducing experiences of shame, and improving the capacity to connect with others around a traumatic event. These can be found in schools, hospitals, and community settings.

Stigma and Social Norms

Social stigma exists for victims of abuse and for those who experience any form of mental illness. Although boys and girls may have similar responses to traumas and may experience similar amounts of trauma throughout their lives, cultural stigmas may affect their experience of symptoms and may also affect society's response to them.

For example, boys who are abused by a female often experience invalidation by society regarding their experience. This invalidation can be received through the direct response of authority figures or through the media, which often creates jokes or makes light of women abusing boys. Research tells us that boys who are abused by females are more likely to develop a variety of issues later in life than boys who are not abused by females. Compared with those with no history of sexual abuse, young males who were sexually abused are five times more likely to cause teen pregnancy, three times more likely to have multiple sexual partners, and two times more likely to have unprotected sex.

A myth or fear exists among some adult men that being abused by a male causes them to become gay or bisexual. Although this is not true, boys may experience a specific type of shame as a result of this type of trauma. Social and gender expectations also lead boys and men to believe that they should not experience psychological symptoms as a result of a trauma, because they are expected to be able to cope independently without any ongoing psychological or behavioral consequences. This type of stigma may prevent boys from reaching out for help or receiving the appropriate help and support from family or professionals. There has been varying evidence showing that bullying may be a form of complex, or repeated, trauma and may result in higher incidences of PTSD. Although bullying occurs with both boys and girls, boys may be at risk to minimize the impact that bullying is having on them, which could serve as a barrier to effective diagnosis and treatment.

Symptoms of PTSD may be misunderstood given the presentation of the disorder in some teenage boys. Anger, anxiety, and avoidance are common symptoms of PTSD but may be viewed as aggression or oppositional behavior, particularly within school settings. Boys who develop PTSD from witnessing violence within their home or their community may reenact the violence with their peers, which may lead them to contact with the justice system. There are disproportionately high rates of teenage boys with PTSD in juvenile justice centers. According to a study conducted by the U.S. Department of Justice's Office of Juvenile Justice and Delinquency Prevention, 92.5% of youth had experienced at least one trauma, 84% had experienced more than one trauma, and 56.8% had been exposed to trauma six or more times. Witnessing violence was the most common source of trauma, and more than 1 in 10 detainees had PTSD in the year prior to the interview. Despite the challenges of identifying the cause of PTSD on incarceration, as incarceration in and of itself may be experienced as a trauma, correct diagnosis and treatment of the disorder are essential to an accurate understanding of the symptoms or behaviors.

For girls, PTSD that occurred as a result of dating violence may be questioned by society. Many girls have experienced "victim blaming" when reporting abuse. When PTSD is the result of abuse, girls and boys may experience personal shame and guilt around the abuse itself as well as the symptoms of the disorder. Shame is a common response to experiencing abuse by a family member or others close to the family, especially because children often blame themselves and lack the capacity to properly understand that they were not responsible for the abuse.

Girls within urban settings who experience ongoing exposure to community and domestic violence have reported high levels of symptoms of PTSD. This may be referred to as "complex trauma" because of the exposure to multiple traumatic events. Not all experiences of trauma or abuse will lead to PTSD, however, and there is no steady body of research regarding gender differences in the development of the disorder.

The term *rape culture* has been applied to understand the impact of objectifying and aggressive lyrics in songs, movies, and advertising, as well as the cultural norms or views regarding women, which lead to violence against girls and women, challenges with reporting violence, and barriers to receiving proper responses to violence. This may prevent appropriate identification or treatment of the disorder. All members of society, including girls and boys, women and men, are affected by cultural norms that may color their reactions to violence against girls and women and the acceptance of the consequences of that violence.

Pamela LiVecchi

See also Bullying in Adolescence; Bullying in Childhood; Posttraumatic Stress Disorder and Gender; Posttraumatic Stress Disorder and Gender Violence

Further Readings

Alisic, E., Zalta, A. K., Van Wesel, F., Larsen, S. E., Hafstad, G. S., Hassanpour, K., & Smid, G. E. (2014). Rates of post-traumatic stress disorder in trauma-exposed children and adolescents: Meta-analysis. *British Journal of Psychiatry, 204*(5), 335–340.

Dube, S., Anda, R., Whitfield, C., Brown, D., Felitti, V., Dong, M., & Giles, W. (2005). Long-term consequences of childhood sexual abuse by gender of victim. *American Journal of Preventative Medicine, 28*(5), 430–438.

Foa, E., McLean, C., Capaldi, S., & Rosenfield, D. (2013). Prolonged exposure vs. supportive counseling for sexual abuse–related PTSD in adolescent girls: A randomized clinical trial. *JAMA, 310*(24), 2650–2657.

Homma, Y., Wang, N., Saewyc, E., & Kishor, N. (2012). The relationship between sexual abuse and risky sexual behavior among adolescent boys: A meta-analysis. *Journal of Adolescent Health, 51*(1), 18–24.

Horowitz, K., Weine, S., & Jekel, J. (1995). PTSD symptoms in urban adolescent girls: Compounded community trauma. *Journal of the American Academy of Child and Adolescent Psychiatry, 34*(10), 1353–1361.

Hossain, M., Zimmerman, C., Abas, M., Light, M., & Watts, C. (2010). The relationship of trauma to mental disorders among trafficked and sexually exploited girls and women. *American Journal of Public Health, 100*(12), 2442–2449.

Sharf, A., Kimonis, E. R., & Howard, A. (2014). Negative life events and posttraumatic stress disorder among incarcerated boys with callous-unemotional traits. *Journal of Psychopathology and Behavioral Assessment, 36*(3), 401–414.

Websites

National Center for PTSD: http://www.ptsd.va.gov/public/types/violence/men-sexual-trauma.asp

Ready to Achieve Mentoring Program: http://ramp.iel.org/support-for-ramp

Posttraumatic Stress Disorder and Gender Violence

Posttraumatic stress disorder (PTSD) is a mental health condition occurring after a traumatic event characterized by symptoms of reexperiencing, avoidance, emotional numbing, dysphoria, and hyperarousal. Traumatic events are stressful events that an individual perceives to be life threatening or that threaten one's physical integrity. Gender violence is a type of traumatic event defined as physical, sexual, or emotional abuse and/or human rights violations; it affects women and girls more frequently than men due to patriarchal social norms and power differences. Examples of gender violence include child abuse, sexual assault, intimate partner violence, sexual harassment, stalking, human trafficking, and honor violence. While only 8% of the general population report PTSD, between 20% and 63% of victims of gender violence report PTSD. This entry begins with a description of PTSD, followed by a discussion of theories of PTSD development, and conditions subsumed under the PTSD diagnosis. The entry continues with possible causes for the increased rates of PTSD in gender violence victims and supported treatments for PTSD due to gender violence.

Posttraumatic Stress Disorder

PTSD is a psychological disorder that can develop after a traumatic event. According to the *Diagnostic and Statistical Manual of Mental Disorders, Fifth Edition* (*DSM-5*), published by the American Psychiatric Association, a diagnosis of PTSD requires (a) exposure to a traumatic event, (b) intrusive symptoms of reexperiencing the trauma, (c) active avoidance of reminders of the trauma, (d) emotional numbing and dysphoria, and (e) increased arousal and reactivity to reminders of the trauma. Dissociation may also occur. The symptoms must occur for at least a month and cause significant distress and impairment in daily functioning. PTSD was first added to the third edition of the *DSM* in 1980 in response to pressures from war veterans and gender violence survivors. The defining features of PTSD have not substantially changed since its inclusion in the *DSM*; however, more recent editions have introduced other trauma-related disorders (e.g., acute stress disorder, disinhibited social engagement disorder) and redefined others as trauma associated (e.g., reactive attachment disorder). The *International Statistical Classification of Diseases and Related Health Problems* (*ICD*), published by the World Health Organization, also includes PTSD as a diagnosis; the symptoms included in the *ICD* are not substantially different from those included in the *DSM*.

Risk factors for PTSD include pretrauma emotional problems, demographic and cultural characteristics, lack of social support, and biological predispositions. Trauma-specific factors, such as the type and severity of trauma, relationship to the perpetrator, injury, and perceived life threat can also increase PTSD risk. Dissociation, negative appraisals, maladaptive coping, poor emotional control, and interpersonal losses also increase PTSD risk. People with PTSD are almost twice as likely as people without PTSD to report an additional mental health problem, most often depression, anxiety, dissociation, and borderline personality disorder.

PTSD is thought to develop through multiple mechanisms. Conditioning theories propose that classical conditioning leads to the increased fear of PTSD, while operant conditioning leads to chronic avoidance of reminders of the trauma. Emotional processing theories suggest that trauma leads to pathological fear structures that are primarily emotional and not integrated in normal memory systems. These fear structures are easily triggered by reminders of the trauma. Cognitive theories suppose that maladaptive appraisals of the characteristics of a traumatic event and the victim's response to the event can lead to fragmented memories and poor trauma narratives, which increase negative emotional outcomes. Schema theories posit that traumatic events challenge the basic assumptions we have of ourselves and the world, leading to schemas in which victims are guilty and the world is an unsafe place.

Gender Violence and the PTSD Diagnosis

A number of gender violence–associated conditions have been subsumed under the diagnosis of PTSD. The first is rape trauma syndrome (RTS). Developed by Ann Burgess and Lynda Holmstrom, it is a group of physical, behavioral, and emotional reactions often reported after sexual assault. Burgess and Holmstrom proposed that these symptoms happen in two phases: (1) the acute stage, which occurs during or immediately following the rape, followed by (2) the chronic phase of recovery. Mary Koss and Mary Harvey later elaborated on RTS to include four phases: (1) the anticipatory stage, occurring immediately before the assault, when victims attempt to respond with fight, flight, or freeze; (2) the impact stage, which includes the assault itself and the immediate aftermath and may involve dissociation, extreme emotions, and acute stress; (3) the reconstitution stage, which can last for years and includes actions on the part of the victim to return to normal living, which may include denial, symptom development, and attempts to make meaning from the event; and (4) the resolution stage, in which the rape has been assimilated into normal memory systems.

The second condition is battered woman syndrome (BWS). BWS, developed by Lenore E. Walker, is a model of how intimate partner violence (IPV) can lead to serious impairment in emotional and psychological functioning in the victim. BWS can occur when a woman experiences repeated episodes of IPV from a spouse or cohabitating partner. According to Walker, IPV follows a cycle of violence. The first phase occurs when the perpetrator becomes more irritable, tense, and on edge, and tension in the relationship grows. The perpetrator may engage in mild to moderate emotional abuse and mild physical abuse. In the second phase, the perpetrator engages in acute violence, usually causing significant physical damage to the victim. The victim may attempt to placate the perpetrator or defend herself, but that may lead to more severe violence. In the third phase, often called the "honeymoon" phase, the perpetrator apologizes and shows remorse, usually promising change.

Walker posited that there are four characteristics of BWS: (1) the victim believes that the IPV is her fault, (2) the victim fears for her life and the lives of dependent others (e.g., children, elderly parents), (3) the victim struggles to put the responsibility for the IPV on the perpetrator, and (4) the victim believes that the perpetrator is all-knowing and inescapable. Psychological symptoms associated with BWS include intrusive thoughts, hyperarousal, avoidance and numbing, maladaptive interpersonal relationships, sexual dysfunction, and body image or somatic problems. The victim often stays in the violent relationship because of the power and control the perpetrator has over the victim in the form of physical threats, emotional abuse, economic abuse, and the use of privilege and attachment to the children. Victims also stay because they are afraid to leave, they believe that they can keep the violence from recurring, they have low self-esteem, and the perpetrator is kind and loving during the honeymoon phase.

Other conditions subsumed under PTSD refer to the negative effects of child abuse. Battered child syndrome (BCS), coined in 1962 by C. Henry Kempe and Frederic Silverman, describes the psychological injuries sustained by children abused by caregivers. Symptoms associated with BCS are consistent with those of a PTSD diagnosis. While BCS initially referred only to the negative psychological effects of childhood physical abuse, work by David Finkelhor and Angela Browne showed that childhood sexual abuse could lead to traumatic sexualization of a child in addition to PTSD-like symptoms.

Gender Violence and PTSD Development and Treatment

A large body of literature has shown that victims of gender violence have an increased risk of developing PTSD as compared with most other trauma victims. Symptoms tend to be more severe and debilitating and last longer than PTSD symptoms due to other trauma types. Revictimization is common in gender violence; victims of multiple types of violent events often suffer from even poorer outcomes. Trauma with agency, or a belief that one could have changed the outcome, seems to lead to worse outcomes due to increased self-blame. Jennifer Freyd suggested that gender violence may lead to more severe symptoms because the victim is betrayed by a trusted other; Ronnie Janoff-Bulman stated that this betrayal can lead to crushed assumptions about safety, power, control, and self-esteem. Gender violence also involves a violation of the sanctity of the self, which may lead to greater PTSD symptoms. The physical and emotional toll of gender violence may lead to increased emotion regulation difficulties, fear, maladaptive learned behaviors, and increased cognitive load. Gender violence is associated with increased prevalence of a number of comorbid conditions associated with PTSD, such as major depressive disorder, borderline personality disorder, panic disorder and other anxiety disorders, dissociative disorders, sexual dysfunction, and eating disorders—these other mental health problems can increase the risk for PTSD development and maintenance.

It is important to consider how victim gender can increase the risk for PTSD. Most research consistently shows that women experience a lifetime prevalence rate of PTSD that is twice that of men. While men are at greater risk of experiencing trauma, women and girls are at a much greater risk of experiencing gender violence. Women are more likely to be injured, receive medical treatment, be hospitalized, and lose time from work than men due to gender violence, which leads women to perceive gender violence as more traumatic than do men. Gender-related hormones and differences in brain development in language- and emotion-processing areas may influence biological stress responses. Women and men may interpret traumatic events differently due to gender role socialization, social learning of maladaptive responses, accessibility of emotions and emotion regulation ability, and differences in coping. The acceptability of gender violence and social norms that promote victim blaming and female purity may also inordinately affect women's risk for PTSD. Multiple experts have also shown that female gender and the experience of gender violence interact to lead to an even heightened risk for PTSD.

When gender violence is severe and prolonged (e.g., child abuse), it is considered by experts as a complex trauma. Victims of complex trauma often experience a complicated and more severe form of PTSD (called complex PTSD, developmental trauma disorder, or disorder of extreme stress not otherwise specified) classified by a higher degree of emotional numbing and dissociation. In addition, victims with complex PTSD also experience emotion regulation problems, attention deficits, poor self-worth, chronic guilt, poor interpersonal functioning, medical or psychosomatic problems, chronic hopelessness, self-injury, and increased suicidality. Victims of complex trauma are also more likely to experience comorbid conditions of borderline personality disorder and dissociative disorders.

Treatment for PTSD due to gender violence can take many forms. Support groups and one-on-one victim advocacy can help empower victims and provide them internal and external resources. There are also a plethora of evidence-based treatments for PTSD due to gender violence, including prolonged exposure, cognitive processing therapy, trauma-focused cognitive behavioral therapy, eye movement desensitization and reprocessing, narrative exposure therapy, brief eclectic psychotherapy for PTSD, skills training in affective and interpersonal regulation, acceptance and commitment therapy, dialectical behavior therapy, and emotion-focused treatment of complex trauma. Couples, family, and group therapy can also improve outcomes.

Melanie D. Hetzel-Riggin

See also Acceptance and Commitment Therapy; Acquaintance Rape; Borderline Personality Disorder and Gender; Bullying, Gender-Based; Gender-Based Violence; Posttraumatic Stress Disorder and Gender; Posttraumatic Stress Disorder and Gender Differences in Children; Violence and Gender: Overview; Women's Group Therapy

Further Readings

American Psychiatric Association. (2013). *The diagnostic and statistical manual of mental disorders* (5th ed.). Washington, DC: Author.

Burgess, A., & Holmstrom, L. (1974). Rape trauma syndrome. *American Journal of Psychiatry, 131,* 981–986.

Courtois, C. A. (2004). Complex trauma, complex reactions: Assessment and treatment. *Psychotherapy: Theory, Research, Practice, Training, 31*(4), 412–425.

DePrince, A. P., & Freyd, J. J. (2002). The intersection of gender and betrayal in trauma. In R. Kimerling, P. Ouimette, & J. Wolfe (Eds.), *Gender and PTSD* (pp. 98–113). New York, NY: Guilford Press.

Finkelhor, D. (1984). *Child sexual abuse: New theory and research.* New York, NY: Free Press.

Friedman, M. J., Keane, T. M., & Resick, P. A. (2014). *The handbook of PTSD: Science and practice* (2nd ed.). New York, NY: Guilford Press.

Herman, J. L. (1992). *Trauma and recovery: The aftermath of violence from domestic to political terror.* New York, NY: Basic Books.

Janoff-Bulman, R. (1992). *Shattered assumptions: Towards a new psychology of trauma.* New York, NY: Free Press.

Koss, M., & Harvey, M. (1991). *The rape victim: Clinical and community interventions.* Newbury Park, CA: Sage.

Schnyder, U., & Cloitre, M. (2015). *Evidence based treatments for trauma-related psychological disorders: A practical guide for clinicians.* New York, NY: Springer.

Walker, L. E. A. (2009). *The battered women syndrome* (3rd ed.). New York, NY: Springer.

Power-Control and Gender

Power-control theory was developed to explain minor forms of juvenile delinquency based on the association between power differentials in the workplace and parental control efforts in the home. Its main focus was to show that males are involved in relatively more delinquency than females when they are raised in homes in which the father exercises greater power than the mother. This entry outlines power-control theory and describes how it has been used to explain gender differences in delinquency and religiousness.

Outline of Power-Control Theory

Power and control are two central concepts in the social and behavioral sciences. Power involves the ability of people (or groups) to achieve their desires even when others are resistant. Control refers to activities that regulate the behaviors of individuals or groups. John Hagan combined these two concepts to develop a power-control theory of gender and delinquency. The main rationale for power-control theory was to link power in the workplace with control in the family to understand gender differences in delinquent behavior. Power-control theory has been used to explain the mechanisms underlying two common empirical observations: (1) the tendency of males to be more involved in delinquent behavior than females and (2) the greater religiousness of females relative to males.

The theory begins with the assumption that social classes are distinguished by power and control relations manifest in the workplace. In particular, there are four general workforce classes:

1. *Employers*: Owners who control workers by hiring and paying them
2. *Managers*: Who have some control over workers
3. *Workers*: Who take the orders and do most of the day-to-day labor
4. *Surplus population*: Who are unemployed or outside the workforce

Power-control theory assumes that parents in positions of power at work tend to have the most power in the home. For instance, in patriarchal families (i.e., where the father works outside the home in a position of power and the mother is not employed), it is still likely for the father to have more power. Conversely, in egalitarian families (i.e., in which both parents work outside the home), similar positions of authority may be presumed. In other types of family (e.g., same-sex couples, working mothers and stay-at-home fathers), there may be similar power-control dynamics; however, gender dynamics may also influence how the power manifests. The distribution of power among parents affects how they control children's behaviors. In patriarchal families, mothers provide most of the control efforts, and daughters are controlled more than sons. In egalitarian families, the control efforts are much more uniform. This relative degree of control has important implications for delinquency and its presumed antecedent, risk preferences. Daughters in patriarchal homes are controlled more than their brothers, so they are socialized to avoid risks. Sons are socialized to have relatively more power and are less controlled; thus, they are apt to prefer risks. Youth who prefer to take risks are more likely to get involved in delinquent behavior. Thus, males from patriarchal homes should be relatively more involved than females in delinquency; males and females in egalitarian homes should be similarly involved in delinquency.

Power-control theory further posits that there are two types of maternal control: (1) *relational* (e.g., affectionate ties) and (2) *instrumental* (e.g., supervision). Males in patriarchal families experience relatively fewer instrumental control efforts; they thus tend to become involved in physical aggression. Females in patriarchal families are exposed to more relational controls; they tend toward relational aggression and depression. Moreover, in patriarchal families, parents are inclined to accept traditional gender roles, whereas in more egalitarian homes, mothers are assumed to expose children to progressive gender roles, thus affecting their risk preferences.

Power-control theory has also been used to explain gender differences in religiousness. Males tend to be less religious than females because they have greater risk preferences, and this is especially pronounced in patriarchal families. Thus, although previous work on gender differences in religiousness posited that females are socialized to be more religious than males, power-control theory provides a description of how socialization affects this gender difference.

Studies of Power-Control and Gender

The evidence supporting power-control theory is mixed. Hagan's research on minor forms of delinquency has supported most of its main propositions. For example, he found that the difference in male-female delinquency is greatest in patriarchal families. In addition, mothers in patriarchal families are more accepting of traditional gender roles, and this may lead to relatively greater involvement of their male children in delinquency. Research also suggests that risk-taking preferences help explain male-female differences in religiousness.

Several studies have found little difference in male-female delinquency in patriarchal versus egalitarian homes, thus casting doubt on the validity of power-control theory. Nonetheless, some studies have shown that males and females in patriarchal and egalitarian families think about offending differently. Females in patriarchal families are more likely to think that they will get caught if they engage in illegal acts, whereas females in egalitarian families report relatively less potential embarrassment if caught. This likely reflects differences in how they have been socialized to calculate risks.

Limitations of Power-Control Theory

Even though power-control theory has not been generally successful in explaining gender differences in behaviors, it may be useful if elaborated. For instance, research should consider other sources of family control beyond affection and supervision. There may also be racial/ethnic differences in how power-control operates. Greater attention to actual, rather than perceived, child-rearing practices and spousal roles in the home is needed. Under what conditions do workplace variations in power translate into power and control differentials in the home? Diverse family structures, such as single-parent and same-sex parent families, should also be considered in greater detail.

John P. Hoffmann

See also Gender Socialization in Adolescence; Motherhood

Further Readings

Blackwell, B. S. (2000). Perceived sanction threats, gender, and crime: A test and elaboration of power-control theory. *Criminology, 38,* 439–488.

Collett, J. L., & Lizardo, O. (2009). A power-control theory of gender and religiosity. *Journal for the Scientific Study of Religion, 48,* 213–231.

De Coster, S. (2012). Mothers' work and family roles, gender ideologies, distress, and parenting. *Sociological Quarterly, 53,* 585–609.
Fenstermaker, S., & West, C. (Eds.). (2002). *Doing gender, doing difference: Inequality, power, and institutional change.* New York, NY: Routledge.
Hagan, J. (1989). *Structural criminology.* New Brunswick, NJ: Rutgers University Press.
Hagan, J., McCarthy, B., & Foster, H. (2002). A gendered theory of delinquency and despair in the life course. *Acta Sociologica, 45,* 37–46.
Miller, A. S., & Hoffmann, J. P. (1995). Risk and religion: An explanation of gender differences in religiosity. *Journal for the Scientific Study of Religion, 34,* 63–75.
Naffine, N. (1997). *Feminism and criminology.* Malden, MA: Polity Press.

Websites

FORGE: http://www.forge-forward.org

PREGNANCY

Pregnancy is a temporary bodily state referencing embryonic and fetal development occurring within the body. A human pregnancy ending in vaginal or cesarean birth typically lasts just over 9 months. Although commonly understood as a biological condition, all pregnancies occur within and in relation to psychological and social contexts, which in turn influence biological fetal development. These contexts idealize, and even fetishize, certain pregnant bodies, while vilifying pregnancy in others. This entry focuses on contexts specific to North America, which include stratified reproduction, pregnancy issues that can affect perinatal psychology and mental health, and biomedicalization, biosocialities, and socially constructed expectations.

Pregnancy is saturated with (cis)gendered and heteronormative assumptions and meanings. For example, pregnancy (and subsequent childbirth) is often viewed as a formative, appropriate, and typical developmental milestone for cisgender, heterosexual women and is frequently understood as a marker of "true womanliness," while those who decide not to become pregnant may be stigmatized as immature, selfish, or lacking physically and/or emotionally. Although pregnancy is a common experience shared by many cisgender women, not all cisgender women experience or want pregnancy, and not all pregnancies are among cisgender women. Nonetheless, the needs and experiences of family planning and pregnancy among transgender and gender nonconforming individuals remain insufficiently understood and frequently stigmatized.

Stratified Reproduction

The concept of "stratified reproduction" recognizes that political, social, and economic structures bolster and encourage the reproductive goals of some groups (i.e., White, heterosexual, monogamously coupled/married, able-bodied, cisgender women) while disadvantaging and discouraging those of others.

Stress has been demonstrated to take an important role in birth outcomes, including preterm birth and infant mortality. Mounting evidence suggests that experiences of racism and heightened stress, independent from socioeconomic status, contribute to the significant racial disparities in the United States, where Black infants face higher rates of preterm birth, low birth weight, and infant mortality than White infants. Access to fertility services is also racially and ethnically affected, with White cisgender women receiving more assistance than people of color, despite the higher rates of infertility among racially marginalized groups. Such disparities are only partially influenced by socioeconomic status and health care coverage.

Additive effects of multiple marginalized social locations exist, with infertility services being less accessible to cisgender women who identify as both racial and sexual minorities. Yet sexual minorities may be slowly gaining more access to services, possibly due to decreasing income disparities, burgeoning reproductive technologies, and growing social acceptance. The 2015 federal legalization of same-sex marriage within the United States, for instance, may lead to an increase in insurance coverage for fertility services for married sexual minorities, further supporting pregnancy among married gay, queer, lesbian, and bisexual cisgender women and men. However, pregnancy is still frequently assumed to result from heterosexual relationships, and stigmatization and feelings of erasure still exist. This may be particularly true for masculine lesbian, bisexual, and queer identified individuals.

Pregnancy rates among unmarried individuals are complex and are reflective of specific demographic information as well as fluctuations in recent years. For instance, while rates of pregnancy resulting in birth among unmarried individuals aged 15 to 44 years steadily increased by 2008, corresponding to a rise of abstinence-only sex education, they then began to decline through 2013. Such declines were seen mostly among unmarried teenage individuals. This decline tends to be uniform among individuals, regardless of racial and ethnic identification. The literature frequently associates pregnancies outside marriage with adverse pregnancy outcomes, often collapsing cohabitating pregnant individuals and noncohabitating pregnant individuals as unmarried. Little to no research exists on family planning and pregnancy among polyamorous relationship/kinship formations.

Pregnancy among teenagers is often associated with effects on socioeconomic status and mental distress. Approximately 6% of cisgender girls between 15 and 19 years of age will become pregnant; racialized and classed representations of teenage mothers exist. Teen pregnancy is often considered a social problem, and teenage mothers are considered a marginalized population; yet some qualitative research exists exploring the ways in which teenagers resist being deemed potentially "irresponsible" mothers. Pregnancies among individuals 34 years and older are increasingly common due to pervasive demographic shifts toward becoming pregnant later in life, and they are facilitated through improvements in, and increased use of, reproductive technologies. Medical advancements aside, miscarriages and birthing complications are more common among older pregnant individuals. Age, however, is inversely related to the rate of unintended pregnancy. Unintended pregnancies, which make up approximately half of all pregnancies in the United States, are more prevalent among cisgender women living in poverty and/or identifying as racial minorities and are associated with higher risks for depression after childbirth.

Individuals with mobility and intellectual disability can (and desire to) become pregnant. Pregnant individuals with mobility-related disabilities often face stigma, including assumptions of parenting incompetency, surprise around sexual activity, and hostility. Juxtaposing disability and the right to become pregnant is the controversial discussion of pregnancy termination of disabled or potentially disabled children, which is opposed by some disability rights advocates, including some advocates who are otherwise "pro-choice." This is particularly salient given the burgeoning reprogenetic diagnostics.

Perinatal Psychology and Mental Health

Up to 50% of pregnant individuals endure intimate partner violence (IPV); IPV data, however, can vary depending on how IPV type and severity are qualified. IPV has been associated with mental distress during pregnancy, with higher rates of severe depression experienced in conjunction with IPV. Mental distress is prevalent during pregnancy, with up to approximately one fifth of pregnant individuals experiencing depression. Stress, specifically relationship stress, is especially linked to depression during pregnancy. Although few concrete estimations of anxiety among pregnant cisgender women exist, the data suggest that general anxiety and anxiety regarding one's pregnancy do occur. Treating mental distress during pregnancy with psychotropic medications is controversial. Few long-term data on the effects of fetal exposure to medication exist, despite the increased risk for postpartum depression among individuals who experience prenatal depression. Pregnant individuals may feel caught in the fray of socially derived maternal expectations, feeling forced to endure or avoid certain interventions in order to "appropriately" care for the welfare of their fetus.

In the United States, one in three cisgender women will have an abortion in their lifetime. Although the emotional experience of abortion is complex and varied, researchers find that relief is the most commonly reported emotion. When mental health risks are viewed in context, the risks associated with termination of an unwanted pregnancy are no different from the risks associated with delivery. However, experiences of grief and psychological distress, such as depression and anxiety, are frequently associated with the loss, stillbirth, or termination of a desired pregnancy.

One's reaction can be influenced by myriad factors such as social support networks, existing children, and a previous history of mental distress.

Pregnancy is often considered a time when weight gain is accepted. However, body image can be complicated by other factors such as whether one is perceived as pregnant by others or "just fat," the likelihood of losing "baby weight" postpartum, the manner in which weight is gained (e.g., being "all baby" versus gaining weight in other areas of the body), as well as other non-weight-related physical changes. Furthermore, body image among nonpregnant cisgender women, gender nonconforming people, and transgender individuals is often experienced in nuanced ways depending on age, race, and ethnicity, adding additional complexity to understanding whether pregnancy might be considered a "body-positive" experience.

Biomedicalization, Biosocialities, and Socially Constructed Expectations

Many of the biomedical technologies utilized to become pregnant (e.g., in vitro fertilization) or during pregnancy (e.g., three-dimensional sonograms, amniocentesis, noninvasive genetic testing) are vastly influencing modern pregnancies. Barbara Katz Rothman coined the term *the tentative pregnancy* to capture how the modern-day, technology-driven pregnancy has become fraught. Burgeoning social medias, virtual information spaces, and smartphone applications create additional and constant ways for individuals to gain knowledge about pregnancy as well as new platforms in which individuals can be encouraged to engage with their pregnancies in specific ways (e.g., online pregnancy support groups and "mommy blogs," lists of foods to consume/avoid, fetal growth trackers, weight calculators, and globalized third-party reproduction exchanges).

Biomedicalization theory often focuses on the extent to which cisgender feminine bodies become a site for biomedicine and new social media, highlighting the ways in which individuals and institutions monitor, control, and modify the body, as well as the accessibility of such technologies among various populations. Feminist scholars have long explored concepts of intensive mothering and mothering mandates in which cisgender women are directly responsible for the needs, and perhaps desires, of their infant/child—placing extraordinary pressure on emotional, financial, and intellectual resources; this theory has been extended to pregnant individuals in relation to their fetuses. Such medical and social trends offer ostensible opportunities for reimagining how pregnancy happens, who becomes pregnant, as well as enhanced care for pregnant individuals and their fetuses—along with additional ways to monitor and survey pregnant bodies and added pressures to "do pregnancy right" and in the least risky way.

Jessica A. Joseph and Lisa R. Rubin

See also Egg Donation; Pregnancy Discrimination

Further Readings

Blanchfield, B. V., & Patterson, C. J. (2015). Racial and sexual minority women's receipt of medical assistance to become pregnant. *Health Psychology, 34*(6), 571–579. doi:10.1037/hea0000124

Iezzoni, L. I., Wint, A. J., Smeltzer, S. C., & Ecker, J. L. (2015). "How did that happen?" Public responses to women with mobility disability during pregnancy. *Disability and Health Journal, 8*(3), 380–387. doi:10.1016/j.dhjo.2015.02.002

McCormack, K. (2005). Stratified reproduction and poor women's resistance. *Gender & Society, 19*(5), 660–679. doi:10.1177/0891243205278010

Riggs, D. W. (2013). Transgender men's self-representations of bearing children post transition. In F. J. Green & M. Friedman (Eds.), *Chasing rainbows: Exploring gender fluid parenting practices* (pp. 62–73). Bradford, Ontario, Canada: Demeter Press.

Rothman, B. K. (2014). Pregnancy, birth and risk: An introduction. *Health, Risk & Society, 16*(1), 1–6. doi:10.1080/13698575.2013.876191

Pregnancy Discrimination

Pregnancy discrimination refers to the unfair treatment of women due to their pregnancy. Examples of pregnancy discrimination in the workplace include refusal to hire or promote pregnant women, denial of insurance coverage for pregnancy-related conditions, or terminating the contract of a pregnant employee. Such blatant discrimination is now illegal in most instances in the United States, but more subtle discrimination continues to occur. Discrimination is related to attitudes toward women, stereotypic beliefs about gender and gender roles, and other social-cognitive processes. This entry introduces the U.S. laws and workplace regulations designed to prevent pregnancy discrimination and the social-cognitive processes that underlie discrimination. The entry concludes with recent examples of discrimination and a discussion of how it affects the psychology of women and women's career progress.

U.S. Laws Designed to Prevent Pregnancy Discrimination

Title VII of the Civil Rights Act of 1964 prohibits discrimination based on race, color, religion, sex, and national origin. Government agencies at all levels, employment agencies, labor unions, and companies with at least 15 employees are required to abide by Title VII. The law is enforced by the Equal Employment Opportunity Commission, which distributes guidelines for employers. The guidelines include a warning not to ask job applicants questions about their reproductive or family status (e.g., Are you pregnant? Do you plan to have children? If you took a maternity leave, would you return to your job?). The Pregnancy Discrimination Act of 1978 is an amendment to Title VII, which was passed to make clear that employers may not discriminate against women with regard to pregnancy, childbirth, or related medical conditions. The Pregnancy Discrimination Act requires employers to treat pregnant women in the same way in which they would treat other employees or applicants with the same abilities or limitations, to hold open a job for a woman who takes pregnancy-related leave of absence for the same amount of time they would hold a job for someone who takes a disability leave, to cover pregnancy and childbirth expenses in insurance plans, and to apply the rules in the same way regardless of the pregnant woman's marital status. The Family and Medical Leave Act of 1993 standardized the amount of maternity leave (up to 12 weeks), extended the ability to take a leave for other family situations (e.g., adoption, elder care, major illness in the family), and allowed men access to family leave. The Family and Medical Leave Act applies only to companies with 50 or more employees, and the leave is not paid, which limits the number of employees who can take advantage of this benefit.

Social Cognition About Pregnant Women

Social cognition refers to thoughts, beliefs, attitudes, and role expectations that occur below the level of conscious awareness but influence people's behavior. Pregnancy is a powerful reminder of a woman's gender and the social role expectations for mothers (e.g., nurturing, kind, selfless). However, the role of mother and the role of worker are unlikely to require the same traits and behaviors, which can result in workplace discrimination if a pregnant woman is assumed not to be a good fit for a job. The stereotype content model has demonstrated the existence of four groups based on judgments along dimensions of warmth and competence: (1) admired (warm and competent), (2) hated (cold and incompetent), (3) envied (cold and competent), and (4) pitied (warm and incompetent). Pregnant women are among the pitied groups; everyone likes them, but they are seen as less capable than nonpregnant women. This view of pregnancy is similar to benevolent sexism, which refers to positive but restrictive attitudes toward women. Benevolent sexists believe that women are delicate creatures, who should be respected, assisted with difficult tasks, and treated gently. The sight of a pregnant woman may trigger benevolent sexism in others who want to help her (whether she needs help or not) and who treat her in a patronizing manner (e.g., patting her arm, calling her "dear" or "honey"). These processes are likely to underlie the demonstrations of bias against pregnant women in job interviews and performance appraisals. Men show a stronger bias than women do, and they are more likely to express concerns about pregnant women's stereotypic irrationality, emotionality, and limitations.

Effects of Pregnancy Discrimination on Women

Social cognition can lead employers and coworkers to see a pregnant woman's role and abilities as incompatible with those of a worker, especially a manager or other authority figure. Some faith-based institutions are not covered by federal anti-discrimination laws, and unmarried pregnant women have been fired from jobs as teachers at religious schools as recently as 2015. In 2013, in New York City, a pregnant police officer signed up to take an exam required for promotion to sergeant. She went into labor on the date of the exam, but her request for a makeup date (available for emergency situations) was denied. Pregnant professional and managerial women report that their views are taken less seriously than before they became pregnant and that coworkers speak to them more slowly and frequently ask them if they are "okay." Pregnant blue-collar workers have been told to go on disability leave early in their pregnancies when their bosses decide that it is "too complicated to accommodate" their condition. Thus, pregnancy discrimination has costs for women in terms of salary, opportunities for advancement, and respect on the job. These costs can be difficult to recoup and are added to the burdens experienced by mothers in the workplace, variously referred to as "the maternal wall," "the family wage gap," "the mommy gap," and "the motherhood penalty." Women cannot achieve equity in the workplace if they are required (as men are not) to choose between parenthood and employment or must suffer from discrimination in pay and opportunity if they try to combine these two important roles.

Joan C. Chrisler

See also Gender Equality; Motherhood; Pregnancy

Further Readings

Hebl, M. R., King, E. B., Glick, P., Singletary, S. L., & Kazama, S. (2007). Hostile and benevolent reactions toward pregnant women: Complementary interpersonal punishments and rewards that maintain traditional roles. *Journal of Applied Psychology, 92,* 1499–1511.

Masser, B., Grass, K., & Nesic, M. (2007). We like you, but we don't want you: The impact of pregnancy in the workplace. *Sex Roles, 57,* 703–712.

Swarns, R. L. (2015, August 10). Pregnant officer denied chance to take sergeant's exam fights back. *New York Times,* p. A13.

Pretend Play

Pretend play is a type of imaginary and dramatic play in which a child uses one object to represent another. The transformation of reality into symbolic representations of a child's world marks a developmental milestone. When a child takes a wooden block and imagines that it is a boat sailing across a sea, the child is engaging in pretend play and entering the world of make-believe. Pretend play is a vehicle for children to make meaning of and work to organize their experiences. During pretend play, play objects function as symbols for something the child has experienced, and they tend to evidence unconscious content. The child's unconscious is expressed symbolically through the play itself. Because of the manifestation of the unconscious in pretend play, children can experience abreaction in which past stressful events and feelings can be relived and eventually resolved through gaining mastery over the negative incidents. Pretend play, then, showcases a child's inner experience in a concrete manner.

Pretend play engages creativity and imagination through role-play, play scripts, imagined scenarios, and dress-up. Fantasy play encourages children to explore possibilities and to experience roles that they may not be able to engage in until they are adults. Examples of pretend play include playing doctor, dressing up, feeding and burping a baby doll, playing grocery store, using a pen as a magic wand, and playing school. Children's self-expression through play empowers them to establish a representation of the world from their perspective. Self-driven pretend play enables children to convert emotionally significant experiences that may seem unmanageable in reality to adaptable events through symbolic representation of self-expression. The symbolic function of play offers children an environment to master the ability to remember, picture, and replicate objects in their minds that are not immediately in front of them. For example, when children see a helicopter lifting a child to the hospital, they may play out mental images of the event at a later time by flying a helicopter to the rescue or using another item to represent the event. This entry reviews the developmental milestones and benefits of pretend play and examines the impact of culture as well as trauma on pretend play.

Developmental Milestones and Benefits of Pretend Play

From the earliest moments, infants are engaging in contact with the world and others. These early preverbal periods of child play involve children engaging with caregivers by copying and exaggerating facial and body expressions. As expressive language develops, toddlers between 18 and 24 months of age begin to play pretend by acting out adult actions, such as putting on shoes, carrying purses, using keys, preparing pretend food items, talking on the phone, and typing on a computer. As these play behaviors evolve, 2-year-old children will engage in adult play by caring for a baby doll, pretending to sleep, driving a pretend vehicle, and acting out the daily routines to establish an understanding of these roles in their lives. As children develop into more complex thinkers, they are able to establish imaginary thinking patterns in order to create imaginative play behaviors. For example, 3-year-olds may use a brush to represent a baby bottle rather than needing the literal item to serve this function.

Older children are less reliant on concrete props for pretend play and can engage in imaginative play that is not based on real-life experiences. Younger children fully engage all senses in pretend play by involving their entire bodies, as the child will pretend to be flying by running around a room with arms outstretched, making engine sounds. As children develop, they use less of their entire bodies in pretend play. Older children will use smaller figures to represent an action by handholding items and constructing, building, and manipulating the item rather than becoming the item, such as being the horse. Play offers children an opportunity to engage with their environment and practice behaviors in order to organize and adapt information into their self-identity and role in the world.

Pretend play has significant socio-emotional, cognitive, and language-developmental benefits. Children are interacting with potential future social and emotional roles when engaged in pretend play. Nurturing a baby doll, playing veterinarian, and driving a car are all examples of how a child is experimenting with adult roles. Increased empathy, emotional regulation, and self-esteem are additional socio-emotional outcomes of engaging in pretend play. On a cognitive level, pretend play stimulates multiple facets of brain development and encourages integration of executive functioning, language, emotionality, and sensorimotor skills. Pretend play engages three cognitive dimensions: (1) object transformation, (2) object attribution, and (3) symbolic objectification. As these cognitive skills develop, children enhance their problem-solving abilities and their ability to generate multiple and different play scenarios and scripts. Regarding language development, pretend play encourages children to imitate language they have heard from caregivers and others and increases their complexity of language usage. Overall, engagement in pretend play augments children's creativity and flexibility as they investigate different roles, styles, communication patterns, and the like.

Culture and Pretend Play

Pretend play reflects the cultural identities into which the child is being socialized, as well as serving to teach roles and shape development. Whereas all children regardless of culture engage in pretend play, the type and themes of play can vary across cultures. For example, American children may engage in pretend play that reflects typical gender roles in their culture. The gender roles enacted by children in Arab countries may be very different from those of American children. Also, children growing up in poverty evidence less pretend play. Therefore, the themes and prevalence of pretend play can provide insight into how children are assimilating cultural identities and how they are learning about cultural mores and expectations.

Impact of Trauma on Pretend Play

When a child endures early-childhood trauma by natural disasters or human-made events such as neglect or physical, mental, or sexual abuse, long-term impairment in psychological, social, academic, emotional, and mental consequences may occur. Unresolved early traumatic experiences affect brain development, leading to altered neurodevelopmental processes that result in compromising children's ability to self-regulate emotions. In pretend play, children are observed to demonstrate chronic fear by hiding figures/toys, pushing toys off shelves rather than engaging with the play materials, and feeling too insecure to engage in play with others. Children may play out as the aggressor in play situations by having all the toys attacked by the animals, monster, or plane. Some children may decrease their use of pretend play as they exhibit less spontaneity and imagination. Trauma can decrease the developmental benefits typically associated with pretend play by disrupting the process of pretend play.

Nicole R. Hill and Torey Portrie-Bethke

See also Child Play; Sociodramatic Play/Role-Play

Further Readings

Berk, L. E., Mann, T. D., & Ogan, A. T. (2006). Make-believe play: Wellspring for development of self-regulation. In D. Singer, R. M. Golinkoff, & K. Hirsh-Pasek (Eds.), *Play=learning: How play motivates and enhances children's cognitive and social-emotional growth* (pp. 145–168). New York, NY: Oxford University Press.

Hoffmann, J., & Russ, S. (2012). Pretend play, creativity, and emotion regulation in children. *Psychology of Aesthetics, Creativity, and the Arts, 6*(2), 175–184. doi:10.1037/a0026299

Lillard, A. S., Lerner, M. D., Hopkins, E. J., Dore, R. A., Smith, E. D., & Palmquist, C. M. (2013). The impact of pretend play on children's development: A review of the evidence. *Psychological Bulletin, 139*(1), 1–34. doi:10.1037/a0029321

Russ, S. W., & Dillon, J. A. (2011). Changes in children's pretend play over two decades. *Creativity Research Journal, 23*(4), 330–338. doi:10.1080/10400419.2011.621824

Psychoanalytic Approaches and Gender

Psychoanalytic theory, beginning with Sigmund Freud's classical psychoanalysis, has had a long-standing and somewhat controversial history with the concept of gender. Freud's original conceptualizations of gender development continue to be critiqued and revised by several of the more contemporary psychoanalytic schools of thought. This entry includes a brief overview of the universal elements in psychoanalytic theory and the foundations of Freud's concept of gender. It then reviews post-Freudian contributions and critiques offered by feminist psychoanalytic theory and the object relations and relational psychoanalytic schools of thought, and it concludes with future directions for the field.

Core Elements Across Psychoanalytic Approaches

Modern psychoanalytic theory stems from Freud, the originator of the classical psychoanalytic method. Freud coined the term *psychodynamic* to describe the ongoing conflict or tension between opposing forces within the psyche or the internal world. Freud believed that an individual's internal life consists of the management and balancing of these conflicts. *Psychoanalysis* is the term for both his theory and his clinical method and is often interchanged with the term *psychodynamic*. As this entry will outline, the term *classical psychoanalysis* is used to denote Freud's original theory, which represents but one of many psychoanalytic schools of thought.

There are various theoretical schools of thought under the psychoanalytic umbrella, classical psychoanalysis being one of them. What are the core elements that define psychoanalytic approaches to gender? Briefly stated, all psychoanalytic theories place an emphasis on the unconscious parts of an individual's personality. The unconscious is believed to contain our earliest and most primitive instincts, such as sex and aggression, as well as any material that is kept from conscious awareness. Gender, according to psychoanalytic theories, may often be influenced by unconscious processes in the individual. The second core element of psychoanalytic approaches to gender is the importance of early life experiences. Certain schools of theory place stronger emphasis on this than on others, but overall, psychoanalytic approaches take into account the formative experiences in the development of the self and gender expression. Psychoanalytic theory posits that adult behavior is influenced by events and relationships that affect the individual as a child or as an infant. It is believed that early life experiences play a large role in shaping one's gendered self and identity.

Classical Psychoanalytic Views of Gender

From its classical Freudian beginnings, psychoanalytic theories have been interested in issues of gender, identities, and sexualities. Despite developing a rather complex theoretical framework for this topic, Freud actually never used the terms *gender* or *gender identity*. This point may be of interest when considering the relative newness of the modern-day definitions of gender. Within Freud's historical context of early-20th-century Vienna, it was not taken for granted that gender and sex refer to fundamentally different realities. According to the classical psychoanalytic approach, gender arises from biology and, specifically, the child's growing awareness of the anatomical differences between the male and female bodies.

Childhood events and interactions are believed to play a significant role in adult functioning according to classical Freudian theory. Freud believed that the first 5 years of an individual's life contained the power to create a lasting impact on the rest of one's life. As Freud altered his theory over the years, he surmised that the primary influence on personality development, including one's gender identity, was the internal conflict surrounding one's sex drive during the foundational years of childhood.

According to Freud, each stage of development relates to an area of the body. Each bodily area is the predominant erogenous zone during the psychosexual conflict between one's instinctual gratification and the potential punishment from society for fulfilling that gratification: oral, anal, and phallic. Gender development and identity stems from the phallic stage, usually occurring between the ages of 3 and 6 years.

Around the age of 3 years, the child's genitalia become the predominant erogenous zone as both male and female children begin to explore their own bodies. Freud believed that both male and female children begin with the shared assumption that each has a penis. Pathways of gender identity and development then begin to diverge, according to Freud. At first, the boy may initially see the girl's clitoris as a smaller version of his own penis but then comes to believe that the littler girl has been castrated, her penis being cut off from her body. This gives rise to the boy's own fear of castration. The girl also comes to realize her own lack of a penis; this then leads to initial feelings of disappointment. According to Freud, this first awareness of anatomical differences becomes the seeds of the rivalry between the sexes.

This phallic stage of development sets the stage for Freud's signifying moment of male psychosocial development: the Oedipus complex. In simplest terms, each child is assumed to develop incestuous sexual feelings for the parent of the opposite sex. Alongside this process, the child then wishes to overtake and displace the same-sex parent. In accordance with Freud's internal conflict model, the male child feels a loving wish for his mother and a hostile fantasy toward his own father. This fantasy of violence toward his father produces a fear that the father will retaliate against the child in the form of castration. For Freud, resolution of these strong childhood conflicts is evidenced in the child's identification with the same-sex parent. It is through the boy's identification with his father that he then develops his own gendered identity. Freud sees resolution of this Oedipal conflict as the key to successful psychosexual development.

Carl Jung, an early follower of Freud, contributed to the classical psychoanalytic understanding of female gender identity. For a female child, gender identity begins with the realization that she has no penis. This signals the onset of what Jung called the Electra complex. Jung and neo-Freudians theorized that a girl then believes that she has been castrated, after noticing that little boys still have their own penises. According to classical psychoanalytic theory, this leads to the female child blaming her mother. Freud coined the term *penis envy* to describe the process of the female's recognition that she has no penis, which then results in feelings of powerlessness and shame. According to this theory, the girl then strongly desires a penis of her own but realizes that she cannot will this piece of anatomy into being. She then starts to desire her father, who she realizes possesses a penis, and develops jealousy and hostile fantasies toward her mother, thus mirroring the Oedipus complex in boys. Resolution of this complex results via similar same-gender identification mechanisms, and the young girl relinquishes her fantasy for a penis and begins to internalize and to identify with her own mother. Classical psychoanalytic theory posits that at this point, the young girl represses her desire for a penis and develops a female gendered identity.

Freud himself acknowledged that his theory of psychosexual development focused more on male identity than on female identity. It is important to note the historical and sociocultural context of Freud's theoretical contributions. At the time of his writings, both Freud and his female patients were part of a post-Victorian-era, Caucasian-dominant European society that greatly devalued women in comparison with men. Today, most contemporary psychoanalysts and analytically inclined psychotherapists view the Oedipal complex much more broadly than Freud. As the following sections will show, Freud's articulation of different psychological development for girls and boys has produced a multitude of reactions and rebuttals from within contemporary psychoanalytic schools of thought.

Horney's Feminist Critique

Over time, many of Freud's original psychoanalytic ideas about gender development have been challenged and revised by numerous feminist, queer, and postmodern psychoanalytic theorists. Arguably, the most noteworthy and influential critique of Freud's Oedipus complex came from Karen Horney, an early Freudian disciple who eventually parted ways with the classical school of psychoanalysis. Horney may be seen as the first feminist and sociocultural critique of Freud's model of gender identity and development. Horney countered Freud by arguing that women did not feel inadequate because they lacked a penis. According to Horney, if women, in general, appeared to envy men, it was primarily due to the fact that Western European culture was biased against women. Out of this bias arose unfair treatment of women by men; penis envy then represented a woman's symbolic desire to be treated equally. Horney also placed the focus on men's own areas of unconscious desire. According to her theory, men were also envious of women, specifically of their reproductive capacity. In response to Freud's penis envy, Horney coined the term *womb envy* to denote the male individual's desire to obtain the anatomical part he was born without. She suggested that it is primarily men's anxiety about feminine power that causes them to belittle and demean women.

Furthermore, Horney disagreed with Freud's assertion that the Oedipus complex is the result of anatomical differences between the sexes and also that it is the core psychological contribution to gender development and identity. She was the first feminist voice to critique Freud's grand theoretical premise and argued that relationships, especially those between parents and their children, are what hold the most influence on the child's developing gender identity. Horney's critique helped pave the way for future generations of psychoanalytic theorists to continue to explore the important sociocultural influences on gender. Horney believed that in dismissing these influences, Freud made a far-reaching theoretical error.

Post-Freudian Psychoanalytic Contributions: Object Relations and Relational Theory

Many psychoanalytic theorists since Horney have continued to critique and revise Freud's original ideas about gender. Their approaches have focused on the expansion of two primary areas when looking at gender from a psychoanalytic lens: (1) the impact of interpersonal relationships and (2) the cultural and societal influences on gender development and identity. Two post-Freudian psychoanalytic approaches that have worked to reformulate some of Freud's original ideas about gender are the object relations and the relational schools of thought. Object relations theory focuses on early development in the child, including infancy, while emphasizing the impact and internalization of key relationships for the child, especially the relationship with the mother. The relational psychoanalytic theorists utilize a social-constructionist approach while emphasizing the importance of interpersonal relationships over Freud's theory of instincts and drives. Each of these psychoanalytic approaches broadens Freud's original ideas about gender while delving deeper into the meanings of the child's relationships, real and internalized or symbolic, which work to define and enrich what it means to be a gendered individual in the context of one's society.

With their focus on infancy and early development, object relations theorists claim that, contrary to Freud's Oedipal-centered theory, the child's sense of gender is established by ages 1 to 2 years and has little to do with an understanding of sexuality. In many ways, object relations theory changed the focus from Freud's emphasis on the male child's relationship with his father to the role of the mother and her relationship with both male and female children.

Much of object relations theory arises from the assumption that children are raised by mothers or female caregivers. According to this set of theorists, female children internalize their mother's role and hence grow to feel a sense of connection and similarity with their mothers. Boys, on the other hand, grow to feel a sense of difference and danger due to dependence on a mothering figure whose sex is different from their own. In most traditional and modern cultures, men have been more esteemed and powerful than women. As children grow and becomes aware of their own gender, they also internalize the gendered inequalities of their society. Object relations theory provides the framework for understanding these ways in which a child may internalize and identify or de-identify with the gender roles and concepts in a particular culture at a particular time.

In her observational study, psychodynamic theoretician Margaret Mahler noted that boys and girls show developmental differences by 21 months of age. Mahler noted that girls appeared more involved with the mother and their relationship, even if this relationship was characterized by ambivalence. In contrast, boys demonstrated repeated tendencies to part from the mother and seek out external stimuli and engagement. Object relations theorists cite this study to demonstrate that inherent, and likely culturally influenced, differences exist between males and females at the pre-Oedipal stage, or before 3 years of age.

Beginning in the 1980s, American relational psychoanalytic approaches to gender have ushered in contemporary questions and viewpoints. Relational theorists such as Virginia Goldner, Jessica Benjamin, Adrienne Harris, and Ken Corbett have worked to deconstruct the binary masculine/feminine poles of gender and place concepts such as gender identity and gender roles within a much more nuanced and complex relational system, one influenced by cultures and changing societies. Modern relational theory posits that gender does not need to be developed from identification with the same-sex parent. Paradox and fluidity, mobility and discontinuity of self-identities may coexist. Relational theorists note that gender is produced by a complex psyche-body-cultural field and is open to multiple influences and meanings. According to modern relational theorists, the Oedipal complex can no longer be taken literally. The Freudian theory of instinct and drive has given way to theoretical contributions on the specific and individual meanings of relationships within an individual's unique psychical setting. Relational theory, overall, seeks to break psychoanalytic theory from its classical and more narrowly defined framework. It posits that we can no longer presume that fathers enable their sons to embody masculinity nor view a daughter's femininity as something solely internalized by her mother. In short, gender is an evolving concept for relational theorists, one that is now changing with the world around it.

Once thought of as revolutionary within various fields of psychoanalytic theory, relational approaches to gender have gained significant attention in the 2000s. Relational theory asks one to acknowledge the cocreation of realities and identities between individuals and their family, peers, societies, and cultures. In accordance with this school of thought, gender is seen to be constructed via a complex accumulation of exchanges, both conscious and unconscious, between the child and their parents, body, genitals, society, and social identities. These exchanges, or communications between self and other, work to form a gendered relational system, or matrix, in which an individual is both a participant and an observer.

Relational psychoanalytic approaches to gender within the therapeutic situation include the exploration of the cocreated dyad between a patient and a therapist. How does the gender of each individual contribute to the evolving dynamics of the clinical work and relationship? What conscious and unconscious representations or symbols of gender may become activated between the patient and the therapist, and how are things such as power, identity, and role related to or unrelated to the gendered selves in the therapeutic room? As gender is explored from a more developmental and historical position in therapy, it is also addressed in the here and now as it interacts with these relational elements between the therapist and the patient. From this perspective, gender, like the definition of the self in relational psychoanalytic theory, is seen as a process, not as a fixed and unchanging entity.

Future Directions

As can be seen, each school of psychoanalytic thought has to do with inner energies that motivate, dominate, and control people's behavior. These energies are based on past experiences and present reality. Broadly defined, psychoanalytic approaches to gender each retain the classical Freudian focus on the unconscious but broaden their frameworks to examine external relational, social, and cultural forces.

Contemporary psychoanalytic approaches to gender have come a long way since the early Freudian ideas of the Oedipal complex. With each developing school of thought, psychoanalytic theories have diversified, made space for Freudian dissent, and grown in complexity and understanding of the sociocultural influences on gender. With the growing visibility and heightened cultural awareness of transgendered and gender nonconforming individuals, psychoanalytic approaches may play a role in enhancing the close examination of the multiple facets of gendered identity as the psyche and body transition across formerly defined gender lines. The future theorists within psychoanalytic schools of thought may benefit from continued exploration into the definitions, limitations, boundaries, and meanings of gender in an ever-changing gendered world.

Jeremy J. Eggleston

See also Gender Development, Theories of; Gender Socialization in Men; Psychosexual Development

Further Readings

Borden, W. (2009). *Contemporary psychodynamic theory and practice*. Chicago, IL: Lyceum Books.

Chodorow, N. (1990). *Feminism and psychoanalytic theory*. New Haven, CT: Yale University Press.

Freud, S. (1956). *On sexuality*. London, England: Penguin.

Gozlan, O. (2008). The accident of gender. *Psychoanalytic Review, 95*(4), 541–570.

Jordan, J. (1997). A relational perspective for understanding women's development. In J. Jordan (Ed.), *Women's growth in diversity* (pp. 9–24). New York, NY: Guilford Press.

Layton, L. (2013). *Who's that girl? Who's that boy? Clinical practice meets postmodern gender theory* (Vol. 2). London, England: Routledge.

Masling, J., Bornstein, R. F., Fishman, I., & Davila, J. (2002). Can Freud explain women as well as men? A meta-analytic review of gender differences in psychoanalytic research. *Psychoanalytic Psychology, 19,* 328–347.

Mitchell, S. A. (2000). *Relationality: From attachment to intersubjectivity*. Hillsdale, NJ: Analytic Press.

Saari, C. (2002). Culture, sexuality and impingement. In *The environment: Its role in psychosocial functioning and psychotherapy* (pp. 92–105). New York, NY: Columbia University Press.

Wachtel, P. (2011). *Therapeutic communication: Knowing what to say when* (2nd ed.). New York, NY: Guilford Press.

Walker, M., & Rosen, W. B. (2004). *How connections heal: Stories from relational-cultural therapy*. New York, NY: Guilford Press.

Psychoanalytic Feminism

Psychoanalytic feminism is an interdisciplinary knowledge practice. It draws on the theorizations of sex and gender as found in psychoanalysis, feminist, and queer bodies of thought, as well as a critical understanding of their intersection. Given that psychoanalysis focuses on the internal, personal, and intersubjective (and feminism on action, thought, and the social), psychoanalytic feminism is necessarily a hybrid endeavor. It sees categories of mind in their cultural and historical contexts while viewing the social as both infused with and infusing the psyche; at their nexus are hierarchical structures and processes that have been theorized as crucial to the deployment and maintenance of patriarchal and class institutions (e.g., hegemony and interpellation).

At the same time, the practices of psychoanalytic feminism are found in two principal discursive sites, the seminar room and the consulting room, with the lecture hall only recently becoming a location where the two meet, exchange views, and change each other. It is safe to say that psychoanalytic feminism as practiced in the clinic has drawn more on psychoanalytic feminism as practiced in the halls of academe, rather than the other way around. This disparity is unsurprising, if all feminist theorists have the same formation in scholarship as pursued in graduate training, only those feminists who train in psychotherapy will know how psychoanalysis and feminism play out in the clinic. Indeed, it is fair to say that, in a certain sense, psychoanalytic feminists dwelling in the academy may, along with their cultural and queer studies colleagues, know the book of psychoanalysis—Sigmund Freud (and Jacques Lacan)—better than many clinicians, who, in contrast, know psychoanalytic theory as it is lived in the consulting room. This entry first investigates the intellectual and conceptual origins of psychoanalytic feminism. Next, the entry studies the field's two key terms, *gender* and *sexuality*. The developing implications of gender are then explored, as is how gender is stabilized by other binaries and how recent studies on psychoanalytic feminism view gender as a multilayered concept.

Intellectual and Conceptual Genealogy

Like many contemporary theoretical practices, psychoanalytic feminism is best understood through its intellectual and conceptual genealogies. Feminist theory, it is fair to say, commenced as a sociology. "One is not born, but rather becomes a woman," said Simone de Beauvoir. And in the charged and changing atmosphere of the 1960s, that becoming was construed as a social and cultural process. You are who you are because of the culture you inhabit and how it affects your behavior, mind, actions, and beliefs. Not too long into the second wave (around 1980), though, it became clear that although social theory anatomizes the conditions of daily working and civic life, it does not unravel the personal and interpersonal tangles of domestic intimacy with which it had been women's traditional cultural business to traffic. Social theory and, with it, early second-wave feminist theory lead right up to the bedroom door, to the hearth of family and psyche. Then they stop, defeated by the messy intangibles of domestic life, the same untidy interiority that constitutes the meeting of minds called psychoanalysis.

With this recognition, though, feminist thought began to shift from its venerable dismissal of Freud to the critical reinterpretation of certain Freudian and, especially, Lacanian ideas. Crucial contributions came from anthropology (Gayle Rubin), philosophy (Judith Butler, Elizabeth Grosz), literary theory (Jane Gallop, Teresa de Lauretis), Francophone psychoanalysis (Julia Kristeva, Luce Irigaray, Helene Cixous), and Anglophone and leftist social thought (Juliet Mitchell, Jacqueline Rose, Lynne Segal). At the same time, North American feminists who either were trained as psychologists (Dorothy Dinnerstein, Jean Baker Miller) or had gone through the academy and wound up in clinical training (Jessica Benjamin, Nancy Chodorow, Muriel Dimen, Jane Flax, Virginia Goldner, Adrienne Harris) were developing that other branch of psychoanalytic feminism, the one at home in the consulting room, and were adding their ideas to the corpus.

Sexuality and Gender

Psychoanalytic feminism has two key terms—*sexuality* and *gender*—with distinct conceptual and lexical histories and power in psychoanalytic theory, in feminism, and in the culture at large. Although sexuality became articulated as a unique aspect of individual psychology in the late 19th century, and the concept of gender (though not yet the term itself) emerged as a site of critical awareness with de Beauvoir's *The Second Sex*, it was not until John Money's empirical work on intersex (then "hermaphroditic") children in the 1950s that gender and sexuality were formally conceived as separate and distinct categories of analysis and experience. The term *gender* comes even later to psychoanalysis.

While the phenomenon it now denotes was obviously central in and to Freud's thinking, the word itself is not to be found in the *Standard Edition* or in *The Language of Psychoanalysis* (Jean Laplanche and Jean-Bertrand Pontalis), a canonical reference work of psychoanalytic concepts. That is to say, although one might discern gender phenomenology as implicit in these foundational or authoritative works, it is neither conceptualized nor named and hence not theorized. Indeed, gender did not emerge as a psychoanalytic category in its own right until Robert Stoller, elaborating and extending Money's research into the clinical domain, conceptualized it as a central dimension of self-organization, a move that launched the field of empirically grounded, psychoanalytic gender studies.

Many works demonstrate the centrality of psychoanalytic feminism in academic thought. Given that there is much less said about the history and scope of psychoanalytic feminism's clinical branch (see, e.g., Dimen and Goldner's anthology of abridged essays, *Gender in Psychoanalytic Space*), the remainder of this entry will focus on it.

With the advent of psychoanalytic feminism, Dinnerstein, Chodorow, and Benjamin complicated psychoanalytic gender theory by conceptualizing gender as an analytic and social category, not merely a psychological one. Following this move, the psychoanalytic study of gender became increasingly multidisciplinary, as cultural, philosophical, literary/linguistic, and sociopolitical theories intersected with those being developed in clinical psychoanalysis. It has become a major challenge and source of enrichment to hold the tension between "theoretical gender," as it has been constructed in the academy, and the "psychological gender" of lived experience that is theorized in the clinic.

Around 1990, psychoanalytic feminism took a sharp left turn, consequent on Judith Butler's now canonical critique of gender, a shift that welded psychoanalysis, feminism, queer studies, and philosophy into a new paradigm. Her *Gender Trouble* conceptualized gender as a culturally instituted, normative ideal that sexes the body and genders the mind in compliance with the hegemonic principle of gender polarity. Throughout history and across cultures, gender categories (male/female, masculine/feminine) are universally construed as mutually exclusive positions of subjectivity. In a dialectical move that would influence all future thinking in psychoanalytic feminism, Butler demonstrated that gender actually creates subjectivity itself: One becomes "intelligible," she showed, only "through becoming gendered." Consequently, sexual and gender identities that "fail to conform to norms of cultural intelligibility" appear as "developmental failures or logical impossibilities."

Gender's Pathogenic Implications

One of the core projects and accomplishments of psychoanalytic feminism has been to articulate the pathogenic implications of this regulatory regime. Chodorow's early work focused these questions by situating gender in the object-relational matrix of mothering rather than in the phallic discourse of the sexual instincts. Beginning with the obvious, but untheorized, fact that women are children's primary caregivers ("every infant's first love, first witness and first boss" [Dinnerstein]), Chodorow considered the implications of the (only) "women mother" (the first two words of her text). She showed how this culturally mandated kinship arrangement produced and reproduced genders crippled by pathology, such that masculinity was defined by the "not me" experience of difference (from mother and mother's femininity), whereas femininity could never escape its origins in the "part of me" sameness with mother.

Benjamin's initial contributions addressed the problem of gender domination. She argued that psychoanalysis took "women's subordination to men for granted, [making it] invisible" and went on to show how psychoanalytic theory could be used to make a special kind of sense of this ubiquitous phenomenon. Arguing that the polarity of masculinity/femininity was established and reproduced in each individual mind by the pathogenic action of splitting, Benjamin also showed how the gender binary serves as a template for other binaries, especially master and slave, subject and object. Goldner subsequently argued that the either/or structure of the gender paradigm was, in effect, a universal pathogenic situation that induces a traumatically compliant false-self system, which results in a multitude of symptoms and innumerable forms of suffering, unrecognized as such.

Gender Constitutes and Is Stabilized by Other Binaries

A postmodern discipline, psychoanalytic feminism locks in on feminist theory's defining move: deconstructing the monolithic, transhistorical category of gender itself. Work in cultural studies and queer theory added momentum, establishing gender not as a ubiquitous principle of polarity unmoored from the conditions of its making but actually constituted and stabilized by other human oppositions, especially those of race (Black vs. White) and sexuality, including gay rights.

Deconstructing the notion of gender as a pregiven, timeless cultural imperative, postmodern psychoanalytic feminist clinicians began to shift the question from "Gender, what is it?" to

"Gender, is it?" Instead of an essence or "thing in itself," Dimen argued, gender was "less a determinative category than a force field [of dualisms] . . . consisting not of essences, but of shifting relations among multiple contrasts." After Lacan, Harris called gender a "necessary fiction"; Benjamin, following Karl Marx, called it a "real appearance"; and Goldner characterized it as a paradoxical "false truth." Each of these metaphors condenses the art of the double take, making the point that while gender is neither an identity nor an essence at the core of a person, it is still a core experience that comes to constitute entity. The challenge is to neither essentialize gender nor dematerialize it.

Gender Clinically

This tension is especially important to maintain when theorizing the paradox of transsex and transgender identities, which simultaneously critiques and reinscribes traditional gender polarities. It is especially crucial to hold the complexity of such contradictions in the treatment situation, as argued by Ruth Stein, Chodorow, Jack Drescher, and Avgi Saketopoulou. More recently, the theoretical focus of psychoanalytic gender studies has shifted from deconstructing gender to "reassembling" it (Harris) in ways that do not re-essentialize it. In some of these approaches, gender is being reformulated as an intersubjectively constituted "compromise formation" (Goldner, Harris); in others, the emphasis is on psychic representations of gendered embodiment (Donna Bassin, Dianne Elise). But all contemporary perspectives emphasize that gender is a multilayered, dynamically inflected "personal idiom" (Christopher Bollas), and theoreticians of varying persuasions have come together around the idea that psychological gender is assembled from the gender tropes that family, culture, and historical period make available.

In this theoretical turn, gender has become a "symbolic resource" (John Gagnon) that not only acts "on" us but also is available "to" us, which shifts our question yet again, from "How does gender work?" to "How is gender worked?" Finally, it is important to note that psychoanalytic feminism, at least on the clinical side, already has heirs that are taking its theorizations of gender and sexuality in new directions. Especially noteworthy is the work of Ken Corbett (e.g., *Boyhoods*; *A Murder Over a Girl*). Newer on the scene are the psychoanalytic feminist revisions of sexuality, perversion, and cyber reality in the work of Stephen Hartman and of sexuality, perversion, and transsexuality in the work of Saketopoulou. The authors in the anthology *With Culture in Mind* (Dimen) can rightly be said to have been inspired by what psychoanalytic feminism has shown psychoanalysis: It needs the social. And finally, the trajectory of psychoanalytic feminism's clinical practice is both tracked and evolving in the journal *Studies in Gender and Sexuality: Psychoanalysis, Cultural Studies, Treatment, Research*.

Muriel Dimen

See also Psychoanalytic Approaches and Gender; Psychodynamic Feminism

Further Readings

Benjamin, J. (1988). *The bonds of love*. New York, NY: Pantheon Books.

Chodorow, N. (1978). *The reproduction of mothering*. Berkeley: University of California Press.

Dimen, M., & Goldner, V. (Eds.). (2002). *Gender in psychoanalytic space*. New York, NY: Other Press.

Flax, J. (1990). *Thinking fragments: Psychoanalysis, feminism, and postmodernism in the contemporary West*. Berkeley: University of California Press.

Mitchell, J. (1974). *Psychoanalysis and feminism*. New York, NY: Pantheon Books.

Wright, E. (Ed.). (1992). *Feminism and psychoanalysis: A critical dictionary*. Oxford, England: Blackwell.

Psychoanalytic Theories of Gender Development

See Psychodynamic Theories of Gender Development

Psychodynamic Approaches and Gender

Ever since its inception as a formal metapsychological theory and psychotherapeutic practice in the late 19th century, psychoanalysis has concerned itself with the development of the human personality and the role that gender plays in its formation. The earliest pioneering psychoanalysts considered a person's gender identification and expression to be among the foundational components of their existence and sought to explain its formation in terms of familial dynamics, sociocultural influences, and generative tension between conscious and unconscious mental processes. As psychoanalysis itself has seen its boundaries expand to include a growing number of related but distinct schools of thought, so too have various theorists and clinicians from these schools offered an increasing variety of analytic definitions of gender, challenging earlier formations and offering new theories adapted to contemporary understandings of human life. This entry reviews several of the major psychoanalytic conceptualizations of gender formation and identity and examines their efforts to critique, expand, and adapt psychoanalytic depictions of gender in and through the 20th and early 21st centuries.

Early Psychoanalytic Perspectives on Gender: Freud

Austrian neurologist Sigmund Freud, the founder of psychoanalysis, put forth the first psychoanalytic conceptualizations of gender development and expression, advancing a wide-ranging and multidimensional depiction of gender that incorporated anatomical, interpersonal, and sociocultural elements. Freud posited a theory of psychosexual development in which he asserted that every infant is born with a "libido," an instinctual and motivating energy that seeks expression and satisfaction through different parts of the body, or "erogenous zones," in early life. In the first year of life, the infant's erogenous zone is its mouth (i.e., the "oral stage" of development), leading children to experience the world and seek libidinal satisfaction through biting, swallowing, and sucking that which they encounter in the environment. These activities also serve as the primary means through which to engage with parents or primary caregivers. In approximately the second year of life, the infant's erogenous zone becomes the anus (i.e., the "anal stage"), initiating a period in which the retention and expulsion of feces become the primary means of libidinal gratification. In these early stages, Freud asserted that children make no distinction between permissible and impermissible gratifying objects, and they will seek libidinal satisfaction from any person or object they encounter regardless of their sex or gender because they are unaware of the social norms that would otherwise discourage them from any type of libido-gratifying relationships. In relation to other human beings, infants may freely seek gratification from men and women alike, an example of the infant's inherently bisexual disposition. Freud termed this infantile characteristic *polymorphous perversity*, and he argued that a vestige of that early disposition followed children into their adult lives and relationships.

In Freud's view, it was in the third psychosexual stage, beginning at roughly age 3 years, that the young child's genitals become the primary site of libidinal satisfaction (i.e., the "phallic stage"), a monumental shift that triggers a child's first recognition of the difference between the male and female sexes and their respective meanings. Freud argued that it was at this time that a boy may feel an urge to obtain phallic gratification by having sexual relations with his mother, a state of affairs that Freud termed the *Oedipus complex*. The boy's urge parallels his discovery and exploration of his own genitalia and his recognition of the dramatically dissimilar genitalia that his mother possesses. Though he desires sexual communion with his mother, he cannot consummate his urge for fear that his father, his primary competitor for his mother, will discover his desire and castrate him as punishment for it (i.e., "castration anxiety"). To protect himself from this terrifying outcome, the boy must unconsciously repress his sexual urges toward his mother and identify with his father, seeking to be like him in an effort to protect himself from the paternal wrath that would otherwise result from their maternal rivalry. Later in life, the boy will also unconsciously displace his sexual desire for his mother onto permissible and attainable sexual objects (i.e., a heterosexual man's attraction to other women), allowing him a safe and socially acceptable outlet for his phallic urges. In Freud's view, a boy's successful negotiation of the Oedipal period not only established the form and function of his conscious and unconscious mind but also served as the foundation for his gender identity as a heterosexual man, as well as his understanding of the ineluctable differences between men and women in the sexual and interpersonal realms.

Freud argued that a girl experiences a related but different set of conflicts during the phallic stage. He asserted that girls experience strong sexual desires toward their mothers at this time as well. However, Freud insisted that it is in their sexual preoccupation with the mother that girls discover that they lack a penis and thus cannot obtain sexual gratification from their mothers as a result. Freud termed a girl's desire to possess a penis, along with the power and opportunity it represents, as *penis envy*. In this phase, a girl views (and believes that she is viewed by) her mother as a competitor for her father's sexual affections. Thus, a girl may manage her impermissible, incestual desire by employing the unconscious defense mechanism of displacement to direct her libidinal desires toward more appropriate sexual objects, that is, toward men, just as boys do toward women. In Freud's estimation, it is as a result of the Oedipal conflict that girls and boys develop their gender identities as heterosexual women and men and, therefore, come to understand the meaning and significance of their and others' sexual features and behavior.

In addition to this distinctly physiological and interpersonal depiction of gender development, Freud also argued that larger sociocultural factors significantly influence not only how gender is defined but also the manner in which particular gender identities are allowed to be expressed and embodied in specific cultures. He posited that cultural factors exert a powerful influence on the conscious and unconscious formation of the mind, shaping how individuals are permitted to relate to others and to themselves. In his view, these social norms delimit the possible ways in which people can identify and express love for others. Drawing on his earlier theory of polymorphous perversity, Freud asserted that an infant's indiscriminate "bisexual" attraction to caregivers becomes increasingly impermissible with age and that the sociocultural environment requires the adaptation of libidinal desires to a rigidly heterosexual genital love. This pattern, he argued, reflected the longstanding reinforcement of a culturally prescribed image of human happiness and health that paradoxically contributed to the unhappiness and distress it was designed to assuage. Culture, in Freud's view, frequently inhibits the freedom individuals would otherwise have to explore their sexual desires and gender affiliations on their own.

Challenging Freud: Horney and the Feminist Psychoanalysts

Many criticisms against Freud's depiction of gender development and performance arose from theorists both within and outside the psychoanalytic realm in the mid- and late 20th century. Karen Horney, a German-born American psychoanalyst and one of the founding mothers of feminist psychology, disagreed with Freud's assertion that the Oedipal conflict was the major determining factor in the sexuality and gender identity of women. In contrast, she argued that early psychoanalytic ideas regarding gender reflected Freud's misunderstanding of female development and the Victorian-era patriarchal worldview, implicit in much of his writings.

While she remained adherent to many of Freud's metapsychological and psychotherapeutic ideas, Horney challenged his ideas on sexuality and gender by offering a wider-ranging sociocultural understanding of the roots of gender roles and identities in Western culture. Thus, she asserted that although penis envy may have been experienced by a small number of women, it was just as likely that men would experience "womb envy," longing to be equipped with the anatomical features that allow women to bear children. In Horney's view, this hypothesized envy may be partly responsible for men's unconscious motivation to create, achieve, and dominate in the world. She argued that men's persistent pursuit of accomplishment reflected their deep insecurities about the value of their existence: Whereas women are socially valuable by virtue of their inherent ability to carry, bear, and raise children, men are only conferred such value according to what they achieve in the world. This value system, Horney argued, inhibited the extent to which men and women could pursue contrasexual identity possibilities (e.g., men identifying themselves as nurturing parents, women seeking success in the workplace). Additionally, she argued that the early psychoanalytic views of gender contributed to rigid and deleterious definitions of masculinity as synonymous with production, creativity, and aggression and femininity as synonymous with passivity, family devotion, and dependence. In a final analysis, Horney asserted that men and women alike have approximately equal desires to be successful, productive, and nurturing and that society should foster individuals' adoption of these various personality traits, no matter their gender. Horney's ideas in this area greatly influenced a long lineage of psychoanalysts and psychologists intent on reworking, amending, or discarding classical psychoanalytic conceptions of gender and sexuality (e.g., Nancy Chodorow, Adrianne Harris, and Lynne Layton, all of whom have studied the unconscious manner in which gender role definitions are patterned and reproduced in contemporary society).

Freud and many of his psychoanalytic followers continue to be honored as among the first to systematically study the physiological, psychological, interpersonal, and societal dimensions of sexuality and gender, both in early childhood and in adult development. Psychoanalytic ideas continue to spur many clinical and theoretical inquiries into the nature of sexuality and gender in human life.

The Archetypal Psychoanalytic Viewpoint: Jung and the Post-Jungians

The Swiss psychiatrist Carl Jung, a longtime colleague and eventual critic of Freud, was a renowned psychological and cultural scholar and a founder of analytical psychology. Like Freud, he was cognizant of gender's complex and multifaceted nature. However, unlike his former mentor, he adopted a far less physiological and biologically deterministic view of sexuality and gender. Instead, Jung proffered a depiction of gender and identity formation based largely on his elaborate understanding of the depth and breadth of the unconscious mind. Specifically, he argued that a person's gender was heavily influenced by the universal patterns (i.e., "archetypes") of masculinity and femininity found emanating from the collective unconscious—a hypothesized realm of psychological patterns and structures common to all people throughout human history.

Jung observed in his male therapy patients a repressed type of creativity and a loving self-regard that he took to be associated with femininity. He identified this inhibited feminine aspect of the male psyche as *anima*, the Latin word for "soul," and suggested that it existed as an archetypal feminine presence in every man's mind. Conversely, Jung also observed in his female patients a similar kind of archetypal pattern characterized by yearnings for achievement, power, and influence. He associated this pattern with masculinity and termed it *animus*, an archetypal image experienced by women in all places and times. The anima was thought to be the archetypal image of vigor and relatedness from which Eros (or "love") originated, while the animus was understood to represent the solidity and rational thought from which assertiveness and cohesion emanated. In Jung's view, the archetypal presence of the anima and animus in a person's conscious and unconscious mind offers individuals the opportunity to cultivate and deepen their inferior (i.e., underdeveloped) relationships with the contrasexual characteristics of the opposing gender. Jung asserted that the individual can strive toward unity by seeking integration of the anima and animus qualities into their lives, thereby constructing a bridge between the conscious ego and the archetypal self that resides in the psyche. The anima and animus are understood to hold potential for both positive and negative aspects of human experience, resulting in a creative and dynamic tension that stimulates self-understanding and individuation.

Reformulating Jung: Mythological, Feminist, and Archetypal Challenges

In the second half of the 20th century, many critics of Jung emerged, noting that he advanced an essentialist interpretation of gender that implicitly reinforced a masculine/feminine gender binary and rigidly foreclosed on other gender identification and performance possibilities. A wave of feminist Jungian scholars have questioned the stereotypical nature of anima and animus, the rigid definitions of masculinity and femininity that Jung advanced, and called for the elimination of the kind of reductive gender formulations put forth in Jung's work on gender and sexuality.

In an effort to incorporate Jungian concepts into a more progressive gender discourse, a group of scholars have attempted to create new conceptions of gender based in part on Jung's extensive mythological studies, using mythology as a means through which to advance new ideas regarding gender identification and expression. By utilizing mythological inquiry alongside classical Jungian theory, scholars such as Christine Downing, Marion Woodman, and Sylvia Brinton-Perera introduced new ways of accessing the archetypal and imaginal aspects of the psyche, and the manner in which mythological motifs can deepen our collective understanding of an ever-broadening spectrum of gender possibilities. Frequently, these scholars have turned toward goddess mythology and the dynamic richness of divine feminine mythological expressions to expand the canon of gendered archetypes from which individuation narratives could be drawn. The turn toward mythology and the expansion of qualities linked to gendered archetypes has offered an approach for deepening men's and women's relationship to their interiorly felt gendered identities, while simultaneously undermining the pathological gender stereotypes that inhibit authentic gender expression. For example, Woodman's position emphasizes the separation of the feminine from gender and suggests that myths such as that of the pregnant virgin are relevant to all genders and speak to the outcast parts of the human psyche in all of us. Such scholarly efforts have led to an increasing panoply of mythologically and archetypally oriented conceptualizations of gender, many of which are made psychologically relevant with the aid of Jungian theory.

James Hillman, a Jungian scholar, phenomenologist, and founder of archetypal psychology, investigated Jung's anima as a phenomenological notion or emergent subjective experience. Like the feminists and mythologists, he challenged Jung's binaried position of anima and animus and removed the confining image of contrasexuality as a goal a person strives to achieve. In an effort to entirely reformulate an understanding of animus and anima, he argued that the anima is an archetypal structure of consciousness for all people and is primarily valuable as a way of accessing the generative and creative powers of the unconscious. Rather than viewing ego-centered consciousness as a means of developing these powers and achieving psychic wholeness, Hillman contended that the archetypal manifestation of the anima in life could displace the centrality of the ego, a beneficial shift capable of moving a person toward the unknowable and thereby expanding and deepening their capacity for growth, connection, responsibility, and individuation (i.e., soul making). Hillman profoundly reworked the traditional Jungian conceptualization of anima, and many scholars inspired by his effort have continued to challenge the fixed nature of archetypes. Thus, they have moved toward an understanding of archetypal images unhindered by dogmatic cultural assumptions regarding stereotyped gender categories.

In the late 20th and early 21st centuries, post-Jungian theorists have dialogued regarding the phenomena of gender construction as well as the archetypal nature of gender as part of implicit identity. Much of their work has centered on the concept of the subtle body, defined as the confluence and synergistic composition of a person's psychic and physical desires. The subtle body is viewed as a place where both gender and sexuality can be viewed as an emergent process without fixed views or expectation. This concept encourages individuals' exploration and expansion of their interiorly felt relationship to their gender and sexuality. Within this worldview, gender becomes an emergent phenomenon resounding from the archetypal unconscious and existing outside the culturally biased and rigid gender stereotypes that predominate in many cultures. Such contributions indicate that the Jungian tradition has contributed to a deconstructivist and postmodern approach to exploring gender construction, specifically encouraging an understanding of gender in terms of archetypal images, inner life, and the interplay between personal and collective experience.

Lacanian Perspectives on Gender

Jacques Lacan, a French psychoanalyst, served as another influential figure in shaping gender discourse in the second half of the 20th century. Perhaps more than any other psychoanalyst since Freud, Lacan's ideas have reverberated in areas far beyond the psychoanalytic domain. Initially, he repudiated Freud's argument regarding the innate configuration of gender identity and development in biological and relational terms, suggesting instead that an individual learns and develops sexual and gender identity through language, identifications with unconscious structures, and signifying symbols pervasive in culture. These points have inspired numerous scholars, including feminist theorists, to advance radical reformulations of gender and sexuality based not on biological determinism, but on language, social norms, and other unconscious processes. Additionally, Lacan's conceptualizations of "desire" and "jouissance" have been central to feminist theorizing regarding gender and sexuality. In his view, desire is a social experience of unconscious phenomena that is based not on need, demand, or instinct but rather on a longing that expresses repressed and unconscious symbols and images, the majority of which are marginalized by mainstream social restrictions. Many feminist scholars have embraced this depiction of desire as an essential component of women's embodied experience. Conversely, jouissance refers to an overflow of joy or enjoyment that leads to resisting social prohibitions and rules, an idea that Lacan utilized to highlight the limited extent to which women's sexual desire and experience are understood in late-20th-century socioculture. These and other Lacanian concepts (e.g., sexuation, the "Other") have shaped feminist discourse regarding gender performance and sexuality; scholastic inquiries regarding women's experiences in literature, film, and historical accounts; and an emergent body of literature critiquing the structures of language and culture through which rigid notions of gender and sexuality are prescribed. Although Lacan has been critiqued in his continued emphasis on the "father" figure as essential to the development of identity, his work stands as a powerful counterpoint to earlier psychoanalytic efforts, and an expansion of psychoanalytic conceptualizations of gender and sexuality into the wider world of gender discourse.

Jeffrey Grant, Shanna E. Butler, and Oksana Yakushko

See also Psychoanalytic Approaches and Gender; Psychoanalytic Feminism; Psychodynamic Feminism; Psychodynamic Theories of Gender Development; Psychosexual Development

Further Readings

Chodorow, N. (1978). *The reproduction of mothering: Psychoanalysis and the sociology of gender*. Berkeley: University of California Press.

Downing, C. (1992). *Women's mysteries: Towards a poetics of gender*. New York, NY: Crossroad.

Evans, D. (2006). *An introductory dictionary of Lacanian psychoanalysis*. New York, NY: Routledge.

Freud, S. (1976). The interpretation of dreams. In J. Strachey (Ed. & Trans.), *The standard edition of the complete psychological works of Sigmund Freud* (Vol. 4, pp. 1–626). London, England: Hogarth Press. (Original work published 1900)

Freud, S. (1976). Three essays on the theory of sexuality. In J. Strachey (Ed. & Trans.), *The standard edition of the complete psychological works of Sigmund Freud* (Vol. 7, pp. 135–248). London, England: Hogarth Press. (Original work published 1905)

Horney, K. (1967). *Feminine psychology*. New York, NY: W. W. Norton.

Jung, C. (1959). *Aion: Researches into the phenomenology of the self* (R. F. C. Hull, Trans.; The Collected Works of C. G. Jung, Vol. 9, Pt. II, H. Read, M. Fordham, G. Adler, & W. McGuire, Eds.). New York, NY: Bollinger Foundation.

Lacan, J. (1981). *The four fundamental concepts of psychoanalysis* (J. Miller, Ed., & A. Sheridan, Trans.). New York, NY: W. W. Norton. (Original work published 1973)

Rowland, S. (2002). *Jung: A feminist revision*. Cambridge, MA: Polity Press.

Woodman, M. (1985). *The pregnant virgin: A process of psychological transformation*. Toronto, Ontario, Canada: Inner City Books.

Psychodynamic Feminism

Psychodynamic feminism is an approach through which psychologists address intrapsychic distress, power differentials, and systemic injustices, both within the therapeutic dyad and on an institutional level. At its core, it is a therapy that has its philosophical roots in the second and third waves of feminism in the United States and in psychoanalysis; as such, it is a therapy that seeks to articulate the unique experiences of an individual while at the same time contextualizing those experiences within a sociopolitical, cultural, and economic framework. Not simply a treatment for women, it has evolved since its inception in the late 1960s to be a theoretical and clinical approach that addresses sexism, heterosexism, ableism, racism, classism, and other injustices based on power differentials. This entry reviews the history of psychodynamic feminism and the theories and practices on which feminist therapists base their work.

History

In the early 1970s, psychology, as an area of academic interest, remained rooted in behaviorism and focused on the empiricism that sought to classify and measure human behavior. Counseling psychology programs were, in contrast, based more in humanist, developmental, and psychodynamic theories. In fact, psychodynamic and humanistic theories were predominant in clinical practice. For many female practitioners, however, these theories did not adequately address the systemic injustices that women were facing. Psychodynamic theory had, at its roots, psychoanalytic theory, which implicitly reinforced the view of women as inferior (i.e., Sigmund Freud's theory about development that included penis envy). While there were some female psychoanalysts who were reckoning with his early theory and rethinking femininity and female psychic development, psychoanalytic theory and, by extension, psychodynamic theory were both predominately masculine and masculinized. With the backdrop of increased focus on women's rights as well as ongoing political and economic unrest, psychodynamic practitioners became interested in drawing from various theories and ideas. Class theory, feminism, gender theory, and the nascent theories of intersubjectivity infused the practice of psychotherapy. Psychologists and social workers began to question the assumptions made about mental health. Phyllis Chesler's 1972 book, *Women and Madness*, paved the way for practitioners to further question how women were so frequently, and wrongly, pathologized. Inherent to this process was the close examination of the structures that exert their force on an individual, be they economic, political, cultural, or social. In this way, psychodynamic therapy, which in the late 1960s was still upholding patriarchal views of women and gender roles, became infused with a revolutionary spirit.

This process of contextualizing the mental health of an individual meant a de facto questioning of the ways in which these structures were operating within the mental health care system and the practice of psychology and psychiatry. For many of the early feminist psychologists, this meant speaking up in class or in clinics that consisted largely of men, and White men at that. In fact, psychodynamic feminism grew out of precisely those experiences that these female practitioners acquired. Tired of feeling as if their voices were not being heard and that the very structures in which they found themselves working were actively trying to silence them, they began to practice and theorize differently. Initially, these women formed consciousness-raising groups in which they began to notice themes emerge. From these meetings, feminist psychologists began to develop theory and change practice.

Since the 1970s, psychodynamic feminism has broadened to include in its questioning not only issues of gender inequality but also issues of all systemic injustices. In 1990, the Feminist Therapy Institute created a code of ethics that delineates the central tenets of feminist therapy. Revised in 1999, the code of ethics articulates the following five ethical guidelines: (1) cultural diversities and oppressions, (2) power differentials, (3) overlapping relationships, (4) therapist accountability, and (5) social change. In creating this code, feminist therapists sought to explicate a vision of therapy that privileges a person's subjective experience within the context in which they live and empowers that person in the process. While the code seemed revolutionary at the time, many of the guidelines have been incorporated into standard practice in clinical psychology (e.g., obtaining written informed consent).

The trajectory of feminist therapy mirrors that of feminist thought since the 1960s. After an initial decade of focusing on the ways in which men and women were similar and equal, the 1980s ushered in a period of highlighting the specific strengths of women and how they differed from those of men. In the 1990s, feminist therapists began to question the construct of gender and the ways in which the patriarchal structures create distress not only for women but also for men. In the 2000s, feminist therapy shifted again to include a more multicultural and global lens.

Theory

At its foundation, feminist therapy seeks to address the ways in which power is exerted over and wielded by certain individuals. It is an ever-expanding practice that broadens to include the voices of those who have previously gone unheard. To meet those varied voices, various modalities are employed. In fact, by the 2000s, it was not possible to point to one single modality in feminist psychotherapy. Rather, feminist therapists are often integrative in terms of technique while being guided by an underlying belief that it is their responsibility to engage individuals (and families and couples) in a process that allows them to notice where and how they can feel more empowered. Feminist psychodynamic therapy addresses power differentials at the same time that it focuses on an individual's history and course of development. Using the relationship as a microcosm by which to understand the ways in which someone is received outside the consulting room, a psychodynamic feminist invites the person in therapy to look not only at their own dynamics and the ways in which those are shaped by personal history and institutional biases but also at the dynamics between the therapist and the person in therapy.

Generally, feminist therapists conceptualize their clients along four axes: (1) the somatic, (2) the intrapersonal/intrapsychic, (3) the intrapersonal/social contextual, and (4) the spiritual/existential. Along these axes, feelings of disempowerment or distress can be felt anywhere. An individual may feel empowered somatically (accepting of body, in contact with the body) but not in the social-contextual realm (feeling incapable of forming relationships). As a feminist therapist, one is always helping a person move closer to feelings of empowerment. As a feminist psychodynamic therapist, one is looking at the internal dynamics and the ways in which those are affected by external forces.

While traditional modalities privilege individuation and autonomy, feminist therapy maintains the importance of connectedness, mutuality, and interdependence. In this way, it is a practice that actively works to subvert the patriarchal structures and ideals that shape our values and experiences. Feminist therapists recognize that part of the power of the patriarchy is the ways in which people get lulled into submission. They also recognize that the therapeutic relationship can be a safe place for an individual to search for and find sources of empowerment.

Practice

In its practice, feminist psychodynamic therapy seeks to value the experiences of all people. It initially emerged from the subjective experiences of predominately White, middle-class female psychologists in a predominately (White) male field of psychology. Their firsthand experiences of being discriminated against because of gender (tacitly, at times, and institutionally quite often) provided insight into the ways in which White male experience had been viewed as the norm, and influenced their practice of psychology.

A central tenet in feminist psychodynamic therapy is that the person in therapy is an expert on their own experience. This works to destabilize previously held notions of the therapist as expert and therefore the holder of power. Transparency on the therapist's side about the process of therapy further chips away at expectations about power. By articulating their views and opinions and by engaging with the person in therapy to elicit their views and opinions about what it means to be healthy or "better," the feminist therapist works collaboratively to create an atmosphere that allows the client to feel empowered. Many feminist therapists have initial paperwork that articulates and highlights the collaborative nature of the relationship. In this way, a feminist therapist is, from the beginning, offering an individual access to information that may otherwise be obscured.

Contextualizing emotional distress is another central tenet of psychodynamic feminism. This means that not only are feminist therapists looking at the immediate context surrounding an individual (e.g., family, work, friends), but they are also looking at the sociopolitical impact on an individual. Furthermore, a feminist therapist will challenge certain assumptions about what it means to be mentally ill. A mother of three who comes into therapy describing feelings of depression will be met by a therapist who will not only look at the biological and psychological etiology of her depression but also help her examine the various ways in which she is feeling disempowered. Has she given up a career? Does she have any time for herself? Is her husband expecting that she take responsibility for all the child care? Is an employer demanding that she come in early (thereby creating a situation in which the mother cannot take her kids to school)? Additionally, a feminist therapist will look explicitly at how the institutions with which this mother comes into contact are disempowering her.

Feminist therapy has at its foundation activism and social justice. For the feminist therapist, not only is the personal political but also the political is personal. While the immediate aim in any individual therapy may be to facilitate the health (as collaboratively defined in the feminist therapeutic process) of the person in therapy, feminist therapy is also aimed at analyzing the structures of power outside the consultation room. As articulated in the code of ethics, a feminist therapist will engage in practices that facilitate social and political change. In the 1970s, 1980s, and 1990s, for instance, the standard of psychological care for gay men and women was to counsel them out of their "perverted" behaviors and "help" them become straight. Feminist therapists (among others) worked to challenge the underlying assumption that homosexuality is in any way deviant.

In the consultation room, a feminist therapist will allow herself to express the ways in which the person in therapy affects her. This may include judicious use of self-disclosure, allowing oneself to be visibly moved in a session, or the relating of ways in which a therapist's thought process has been affected by the client. At the root of this practice is the emphasis on the egalitarian nature of the therapeutic relationship in feminist therapy. By allowing a person in therapy to see the ways in which they can make an impact, the therapist is disproving the prevailing notion of the therapist as an expert and the person in therapy as someone to be passively changed. Additionally, this provides the person in therapy an embodied experience of being impactful.

Leigh Lyndon

See also Anorexia and Gender; Consciousness Raising Groups; Humanistic Approaches and Gender; Internalized Heterosexism; Psychodynamic Theories of Gender Development; Second-Wave Feminism; Third-Wave Feminism

Further Readings

Ballou, M., & Brown, L. S. (Eds.). (2002). *Rethinking mental health and disorder: Feminist perspectives.* New York, NY: Guilford Press.

Ballou, M., Hill, M., & West, C. (Eds.). (2008). *Feminist therapy theory and practice.* New York, NY: Springer.

Bograd, M. (Ed.). (1991). *Feminist approaches for men in family therapy.* New York, NY: Haworth Press.

Brown, L. S. (1994). *Subversive dialogues: Theory in feminist practice.* New York, NY: Basic Books.

Brown, L. S. (2010). *Feminist therapy.* Washington, DC: American Psychological Association.

Chesler, P. (1972). *Women and madness.* Garden City, NY: Doubleday.

Chodorow, N. (1989). *Feminism and psychoanalytic theory.* New Haven, CT: Yale University Press.

Chrisler, J. C., & Howard, D. (Eds.). (1992). *New directions in feminist psychology: Practice, theory and research.* New York, NY: Springer.

Enns, C. Z. (2004). *Feminist theories and feminist psychotherapies: Origins, themes and variations.* Binghamton, NY: Haworth Press.

Feminist Therapy Institute. (2000). *Feminist therapy institute code of ethics.* Denver, CO: Author.

Greene, B. (1992). Still here: A perspective on psychotherapy with African American women. In J. C. Chrisler & D. Howard (Eds.), *New directions in feminist psychology: Practice, theory, and research* (pp. 13–25). New York, NY: Springer.

Rawlings, E. I., & Carter, D. K. (1977). *Psychology for women: Treatment toward equality.* Springfield, IL: Charles C Thomas.

Psychodynamic Theories of Gender Development

Early psychodynamic theory of gender development has had a formidable impact on what is believed to be "normal" versus "abnormal" gender development. This entry begins by defining gender and then examines the trajectory of psychodynamic thought on gender development from Sigmund Freud to his followers, to the equal rights activists of the 1960s–1980s, and, finally, to more current psychodynamic discourse on gender development.

Definition of Gender

Sex refers to anatomical differences, while gender refers to the social, cultural, and emotional meaning assigned to those anatomical differences. In other words, gender is affected by the historical time frame; one's culture, social class, ethnicity, early attachments, and religious, spiritual, and political factors; the constitution into which one is born; and one's status of power versus powerlessness. There have been studies suggesting that regardless of the sex of a child, when one dresses the child in pink and says, "It's a girl," the infant will be handled in a very deliberate and delicate manner, whereas if the infant is dressed in blue and identified as a boy, the infant will be handled in a more rough-and-tumble way. As such, it has been argued by scholars such as Joan Berzoff that gender is a socially constructed phenomenon determined by social expectations of roles and behaviors.

Psychodynamic Theory

Psychodynamic theory suggests an understanding of human behavior as resulting from unconscious processes and/or conflicts. However controversial, Freud's ideas about human development, and in particular gender development, have had a profound impact on the field. Since Freud, many psychoanalysts have built on, and in many cases challenged, Freud's ideas. In relation to gender development, Freud postulated five phases of psychosexual development that are part of his psychosexual drive theory.

Freud postulated that children move through these five phases, which he identified as the (1) oral, (2) anal, (3) phallic, (4) latent, and (5) genital phases. According to Freud, the successful resolution of these phases results in finding mutual fulfillment with a partner of the opposite sex. Libido, the force that moves the developing child through these phases, has been defined as an instinct, drive, or "sexual energy" that works as a buildup of tension, followed by a release—pleasure. These buildups and releases are organized around the five psychosexual stages.

Freud's Psychosexual Stages

The Oral Phase (Birth to 18 Months)

Libido is first experienced around the mouth. Babies experience and find pleasure in their new world by putting objects into the mouth. Since babies are reliant on adults to feed them, this is an important stage in the development of trust and experiencing the world as a safe or unsafe, needs-fulfilling or needs-unfulfilling place. Thus, if not satisfactorily resolved, the baby's experiences of this phase of life could result in lingering issues around trust and dependence. For example, lack of resolution of this psychosexual stage may result in compulsive overeating or substance abuse in later life. It is generally assumed that children do not become aware of gender differences until the age of 3 years or, according to Freud, until the third psychosexual stage.

The Anal Phase (18 Months to 3 Years)

During this phase, the developing child is working on the task of potty training, and much of their psychic energy is organized around fecal activities. Lack of resolution of this stage can result in what Freud called anal-retentive or anal-explosive personality traits. These attributes were made famous in *The Odd Couple*—first a 1965 Broadway show, then a 1968 film, and later a television sitcom (1970–1975)—which told the story of two roommates, one fastidiously neat and the other tremendously messy. In addition to neatness and messiness, lack of resolution of these issues can be manifest in difficulty managing finances or managing the daily tasks of maintaining a home.

The Phallic Phase (3–6 Years)

The phallic stage, in particular, is where many have taken issue with Freudian theory. Freud suggested that boys entering the phallic stage have a wish to kill off their fathers and marry, possess, or be with their mothers. This stage is aptly named the Oedipus stage. As little boys come to the realization that this is not possible, they resolve to separate from their mothers and identify with their fathers, and perhaps grow up to marry women with the traits of their mothers. This is also the period when Freud suggested that boys develop castration anxiety as a result of these wishes. This is a pivotal developmental period, wherein boys develop a sense of autonomy and as such are not as cathected to their mothers. For Freud, girls, on the other hand, go through a similar process, wishing to kill off their mothers and marry their fathers.

This has been called the Electra complex. According to Freud, this resolution is never complete. Similar to boys, girls realize that they cannot kill off their mothers and marry their fathers; thus, they identify with the mother and hence never achieve the level of autonomy that boys experience and remain inferior to them. Freud believed that it is during this stage that girls develop "penis envy" and experience themselves as failed boys. It is in the resolution of this stage, through a process of identifying with the same-sex parent, that gender development is solidified.

The Latent Phase (6–12 Years)

In the fourth stage, the latent stage, Freud believed that the libido was quiet to make space for school-age children to focus on the development of new skills and on building peer group competencies. Libidinal energies are decathected from parents and instead cathected onto school-age peers, as together they strive to develop new skills and abilities. This phase is thought to be a time of increased moral development and repression of the earlier Oedipal impulses.

The Genital Phase (Puberty Through Adulthood)

Stage 5, in many respects, revisits Stage 3. If the latter is resolved satisfactorily, the teenager turns their attention to a partner other than the parent and learns to give and take in a mutually satisfactory relationship. The young adult person is now capable of achieving the three factors of a healthy adult life—the ability to (1) work, (2) play, and (3) love.

Although Freud is known to have expressed that his analysis of women might be incomplete, it remains the model by which other theories are measured. Nonetheless, many have responded to his assertions and developed theories that offer alternative models of development.

Freud's Followers

Karen Horney (1885–1952)

Horney did not take a radically different stance from Freud's conceptualization. She did, however, take issue on two discrete points. First, she reenvisioned the notion of penis envy. Rather than seeing this phenomenon as envy of an anatomical part, she perceived women's envy of men as symbolic. She believed that what women envied were the unearned advantages men experienced in society. Second, Horney suggested that men have envy of women—in particular of their ability to reproduce. She coined the phrase "womb envy" and suggested that this may explain male contempt of women and misogynous or violent behaviors.

Additionally, she did not believe that the development of masculinity and femininity was inherently biological; rather, she saw development as a factor of the limitations on women's rights at the time.

Erik Erikson (1902–1994)

Erikson, a disciple of Freud, built on Freud's theories. Incorporating a more considered social/societal dimension to his psychoanalytic origins, one of his major contributions to the psychoanalytic discourse was his development of what he understood to be the psychosocial phases of development: trust versus mistrust (0–1½ years), autonomy versus shame (1½–3 years), initiative versus guilt (3–5 years), industry versus inferiority (5–12 years), ego identity versus role confusion (12–18 years), intimacy versus isolation (18–40 years), generativity versus stagnation (40–65 years), and ego integrity versus despair (65+ years).

Erikson was interested in gender development and believed that gender differences were largely biologically determined. He looked at children's play and observed the gender differences with which children were born. His contribution to the thinking about gender development revolved around the idea that symbolically girls' play emphasized connecting and relating while boys' play was more about erecting tall buildings with toys, both a phallic notion and a symbol of reaching outward rather than inward. Play that emphasized connecting and relating prepared girls to grow into mothers, caregivers, nurses, teachers, and other nurturers, while boys' play prepared men for broader and less prescribed opportunities.

Contemporary Psychodynamic Theorists

Nancy Chodorow (1944–)

Chodorow, a more contemporary psychoanalyst, carefully examined children's experience of the pre-Oedipal stage of development. She was taken with the notion that early in their development, both boys and girls identify with their mothers. Thus, when the realization occurs for boys that they are different from their mothers, they have to separate and find another model with whom to identify. At this stage, boys identify with their fathers, who have not generally been their primary caretakers and nurturers. This is experienced as a loss, and Chodorow supposed that this may promote feelings of boys' anger at girls and women. In fact, Chodorow sees this loss, or possibly perceived rejection, as a potential cause of sexism.

Carole Gilligan (1936–)

Gilligan is best known for her work that resulted in the book *In a Different Voice*, which was first published in 1982. In observing children's play, Gilligan noted that boys play games that have clear and unchanging rules. Thus, boys can play these structured games with boys they do not like. Girls, on the other hand, often play highly imaginative games with fluid rules and thus can engage in these activities only with other girls for whom they have an affinity. If a boy does not appreciate the call in a game, he can cry, sit it out, and return when he is ready—rules are intact. Girls will more readily modify the direction of a game to accommodate a peer who is upset about the rules. It has been argued that this childhood play prepares men for the world of business while preparing women for motherhood and/or fields that require nurturing and empathy, such as teaching, social work, or nursing.

Another critical concept in gender development is that of male versus female moral development. Gilligan was a student of Lawrence Kohlberg, who presented a justice-based model of moral development. Gilligan disagreed and proposed a different model of moral development—a model of care. In the justice model, autonomous individuals set out to determine which party is right and which is wrong, and the "wrong" party is ousted (literally or figuratively). In the care model, it is understood that each party in a dispute has a perspective and that there may be a place for compromise or for solving problems creatively. When provided with dilemmas, girls are more likely to think through solutions from a care model, while boys are more likely to problem solve from a justice orientation. As Gilligan argues, the idea is not that one orientation is better than the other but that both are equally valid and that to integrate these two models as a society will yield a more fully realized moral development for men and women.

Women From the Stone Center for Female Development

Jean Baker Miller, Janet Surrey, Irene Striver, and Judith Jordan, through meeting and working together, ultimately founded the Stone Center at Wellesley College. Out of this collaboration came many scholarly articles reenvisioning, sharpening, and developing existing theory on gender development. Perhaps the most well known is relational cultural theory, key tenets of which include the notion that people grow through and toward relationship throughout their lifetimes, that movement toward mutuality characterizes mature functioning rather than separation and autonomy, and that mutual empathy and mutual empowerment fuel what Miller called growth-fostering relationships. Building on self-in-relation theory, which recognizes that women do not strive for autonomy and independence in the same manner as men but rather for relational interdependence, relational cultural theory recognizes that different cultures look at the notions of self, other, and interdependence in distinctive ways.

Concepts such as interdependence and autonomy are reexamined on an ongoing basis out of the Stone Center, and concepts have evolved from celebrating differences (e.g., men as autonomous and women as interrelational) to recognizing that women achieve autonomy in a different but equally valid way.

Current Discourse on Gender Development

Irene Fast (1928–)

Fast suggests that between 18 and 24 months, girls become acutely aware of their gender identity. Furthermore, she believes, as did Freud, that they experience this as a loss or a "less than" situation. Fast diverges from Freud by endorsing a perspective that recognizes the importance of mothers and fathers in children's development, above and beyond biological explanations. She posits what she describes as a "differentiation" paradigm. Fast sees three stages in early gender development that coincide with those of Freud: (1) one prior to awareness of sex difference, (2) one in which children are aware of the difference between the sexes, and, finally, (3) the Oedipal phase, wherein children consolidate their sex and gender orientation. The differentiation model, unlike Freudian theory, posits that the third stage and Oedipal period is a time when young children are consolidating their gender identity.

Fast states that parents become the measure by which children determine what is male and what is female. From her point of view, it is through the relations with their parents that children are able to consolidate their ideas of what it means to be male or female. Fast sees girl and boy development following a similar trajectory, unlike Freud, who saw these trajectories as quite divergent.

Diane Ehrensaft (1946–)

Transgender youth are at high risk for suicide. For most children who are different in appearance, attitudes, activities, or behaviors from the dominant culture, there is a family that is different in the same way and thus can provide support, skills, and coping mechanisms for dealing with the challenges of being somehow in the minority. For gay, bisexual, and transgender youth, often the very families that are needed to provide that acceptance and support are the ones behaving in a rejecting or even violent way.

Current discourse on the topic of gender development focuses on moving away from a binary system of looking at gender toward a more fluid framework. Ehrensaft's work is paving the way for scholars to explore and identify ways of raising healthy gender nonconforming children. Ehrensaft points out that rather than "coming out," gender nonconforming youth often "come to." In other words, rather than hiding their self-identity and coming out as teens or adults, these children often come to their parents at very young ages and report that they are "a boy" or "a girl" regardless of their anatomy. One of Ehrensaft's arguments is that rather than parents being somehow responsible for the gender development of a child, children affect the development of families when they "come to" their parents about their gender identity. Ehrensaft has provided a new set of terms for the way in which families typically respond: *the transforming family*, *the transphobic family*, and *the transporting family*.

For Ehrensaft, transformers work through the feelings, often including loss, that are engendered by the child's disclosure. They may struggle with their own ability to accept and understand the child, but their love for and attachment to their child wins out, and they ultimately embrace the child for the authentic self of the child. Transphobic families cannot get past their own fantasies of who their child was or who they wanted their child to be. They hold onto the anger and do not provide support and a holding environment for the child. Transporters are families that want to accept and be there for their child without working through the inevitable feelings of confusion, loss, fear, and so on. As Ehrensaft sees it, these families may be at most risk for pathology.

Concluding Thoughts

A great many valuable insights have been put forth by those who have challenged and/or elaborated on Freud's initial ideas. In letters to his friend and colleague, Wilhelm Fliess, Freud considered the concept of bisexuality. He suggested three types of bisexuality: (1) physical, (2) sexual (erotic), and (3) mental. He suggested a far more complex view of sexuality and gender than is typically interpreted, including that gender in any human being is a result of multicausal factors, both innate and acquired. Freud recognized his own conceptual limitations in understanding female gender development; however, he provided a strong and enduring framework from which to develop our understanding of gender development.

Debra Kram-Fernandez

See also Psychoanalytic Approaches and Gender; Psychoanalytic Feminism; Psychodynamic Approaches and Gender; Psychodynamic Feminism; Psychosexual Development

Further Readings

Auschincloss, E., & Samberg, E. (2012). *Psychoanalytic terms and concepts*. New York, NY: American Psychoanalytic Association.

Berzoff, J., Flanagan, L. M., & Hertz, P. (2002). *Inside out and outside in: Psychodynamic clinical theory and practice in contemporary multicultural contexts.* New York, NY: Rowman & Littlefield.

Brannon, L. (2011). *Gender: Psychological perspectives.* Boston, MA: Allyn & Bacon.

Brill, A. A. (Ed.). (1938). Three contributions to the theory of sex. In A. A. Brill (Ed. & Trans.), *The basic writings of Sigmund Freud* (pp. 551–629). New York, NY: Random House. (Original work published 1905)

Ehrensaft, D. (2012). Boys will be girls, girls will be boys. *Psychoanalytic Psychology, 28*(4), 528–548.

Fast, I. (1990). Aspects of early gender development: Toward a reformulation. *Psychoanalytic Psychology, 7*(3), 105–117.

Gilligan, C. (1982). *In a different voice.* Cambridge, MA: Harvard University Press.

Markus, H. R., & Kitayama, S. (1991). Culture and the self: Implications for cognition, emotion and motivation. *Psychological Review, 98*(2), 224–253.

Robesin, J., & Biringen, Z. (1995). Gender and emerging autonomy in development. *Psychoanalytic Inquiry, 15,* 60–74.

Psychological Abuse

This entry focuses on psychological abuse, which has alternatively been called psychological maltreatment, and a host of other related terms that may be conceptually similar (e.g., nonphysical abuse) or dimensions of a broader construct (e.g., verbal abuse, emotional abuse). Broadly defined, psychological abuse, in the context of intimate relationships, can be defined as any psychological behavior (i.e., not physical aggression) that is harmful or intended to be harmful to the well-being of a partner. But given that emotional pain and lack of cooperation are present to some degree in all relationships, a critical question is "When does negative behavior in relationships constitute a pattern of maltreatment or abuse?" It may be productive to think of psychological abuse as existing on a continuum. On one end of the continuum are isolated or occasional hurtful behaviors that may occur in any relationship (e.g., withdrawing attention or affection for a short time or speaking harshly in anger). At the other end of the continuum are pervasive, patterned, and severe behaviors that can resemble the isolation, fear, domination, and degradation that constitute the torture and brainwashing techniques used on political prisoners. Some have argued that the term *psychological abuse* should be reserved for this more severe end of the continuum and the terms *psychological aggression* or *psychological maltreatment* should be used as broader terms to identify the entire continuum. In the context of relationships in which violence has occurred, the extreme end of the continuum has also been labeled *coercive control* and *intimate terrorism* by some scholars. This entry examines an early model of psychological abuse, the Power and Control Wheel. The impact of psychological abuse is then considered, and various categories of psychological abuse are summarized. Measurement of psychological abuse is then explored, followed by a section on emerging issues in the continued study of psychological abuse.

Power and Control Wheel

One of the earliest and most enduring models of psychological abuse is the Power and Control Wheel, developed by the Duluth Abuse Intervention Project. The Wheel depicts eight forms of psychological abuse: (1) coercion, (2) intimidation, (3) emotional abuse, (4) isolation, (5) minimization/blame/denial, (6) misuse of children, (7) abuse of male privilege, and (8) economic abuse. The Power and Control Wheel exemplifies three important aspects of how the concept of psychological maltreatment has been developed. First, the Wheel was created in the context of understanding domestic violence (i.e., violence against intimate partners). Scientific measurement of psychological abuse also developed primarily in the context of domestic violence, and early measurement efforts drew on samples of battered women and the men who perpetrated abuse toward them.

The Power and Control Wheel has an explicit gender perspective—it describes particular aspects of the ways in which men use maltreatment against women in the context of intimate relationships. The literature has since expanded to also measure maltreatment of men by women and abuse in same-gendered relationships. However, the question of how gender informs our understanding of psychological abuse remains. Numerous studies have demonstrated that both men and women perpetrate maltreatment in same-gendered and different-gendered relationships. Studies drawing samples from the general population and high school and university student samples show men and women reporting psychological abuse at comparable rates. However, gender remains a significant factor in understanding the nature of psychological abuse and its impact on those involved.

The Power and Control Wheel also contains an implicit theory of how tactics of psychological abuse, physical abuse, and sexual assault form a constellation of tactics that a partner can use to exert power and control over another. Research demonstrates that psychological abuse generally precedes physical abuse and physical abuse is almost always accompanied by psychological abuse within a relationship. It is important to note that both psychological abuse and physical abuse can be motivated by an intent to establish dominance and control over an intimate partner and, in that way, can be considered functionally equivalent. Another reason why it may be misleading to draw a strict distinction between psychological and physical abuse is that both cause emotional harm. For example, a man who slaps his partner in front of his children may cause not only physical pain but also emotional harm because the woman he slapped may feel humiliated, demeaned, and fearful for the safety of her children. This emotional harm may be the most damaging aspect of the abusive behavior.

Impact of Psychological Abuse

Research finds that psychological abuse is in itself harmful and may even be more harmful than any physical abuse that might also occur in a relationship, as has been reported by victims of physical maltreatment. A number of studies have examined the effects of psychological maltreatment on numerous dimensions of psychological and physical well-being. Psychological maltreatment consistently predicts psychological symptoms and disorders (e.g., anxiety, depression, suicidal ideation, self-esteem), relationship satisfaction (problems), and physical functioning (e.g., migraines, gastrointestinal problems, pelvic pain, and chronic disease). Psychological abuse appears to account for some problems at least as powerfully as physical abuse. For example, even when controlling for the impact of physical abuse, psychological abuse has been demonstrated to be a significant predictor of posttraumatic stress disorder and alcohol abuse. Because of the impact of psychological abuse, interventions for domestic violence perpetrators focus not only on ending physical and sexual violence but also on the reduction or elimination of psychological abuse.

While research clearly demonstrates the impact of psychological abuse on women, there are very few studies that examine the impact of psychological abuse on men. When compared directly, women report more severe effects of psychological abuse than do men. Some studies have shown that psychological abuse of men by women does not significantly predict depression or posttraumatic stress disorder symptoms. However, given the very small number of studies in this area, it is important to continue this research and to view this gender difference in impact as inconclusive currently.

Categories of Psychological Abuse

Numerous classification systems have been devised to describe the dimensions of psychological abuse. One recent study identified 17 categories of psychological aggression. While not exhaustive, the following categories of abusive behavior exemplify some of the forms psychological abuse can take.

Creation of Fear

The most extreme form of creation of fear involves terroristic threats, such as threats to kill a partner, children, or family and friends, as well as threats to permanently disfigure a partner. On the other hand, physical threats can be implied by a frightening look or posture or even by an agitated mood that could signal the possibility of physical harm.

Isolation

Isolating behavior can take many forms, such as prohibiting friends and family from visiting or forbidding activities or visits outside the home. Isolation can take more subtle forms, such as putting down friends or being rude or threatening to people who come over, making it uncomfortable for a partner to maintain relationships with others.

Isolation can include controlling the flow of information, including restricting the use of cell phones and computers.

Monopolization

Monopolization refers to behaviors that make the abuser the psychological center of the victim's perceptions. An abusive man may be intrusive by interrupting his partner's activities: for example, by harassing his partner at work or constantly phoning or texting them. A partner can disrupt or deprive private time. An abusive partner might monitor their partner constantly and demand an account for how they use their time.

Economic Abuse

Forms of economic abuse include denying access to money to pay for household items, denying a partner a checking account or credit, and excluding partners from important financial decisions. An economic abuser may intentionally incur debts in their partner's name. By controlling financial resources, an abusive partner can limit the autonomy of their partner.

Degradation/Humiliation

Degrading behaviors serve to diminish the victim's sense of competence and self-esteem. Common forms of humiliation and degradation include insults, name-calling, put-downs, and criticism of someone's abilities. These may happen in private or in front of others. Examples of extreme degrading behavior include forcing a partner to perform sexual acts in front of other people or to eat from a bowl on the floor, or making them beg for something essential like food or going to the bathroom.

Psychological Destabilization

Destabilizing can leave a victim unclear as to the validity of their own perceptions. Forms of destabilization include lying, manipulation, and other deliberate attempts to confuse the victim. In the context of domestic violence, the abuser may deny their violent actions or blame their partner for the abusive behavior. Destabilizing acts include hiding possessions and denying knowledge of their whereabouts, or moving things or changing things and then denying the difference in the environment. Pervasive use of destabilization combined with other forms of maltreatment may shake a victim's confidence in their own perception of reality and trust in their own judgment.

Emotional Withholding/Withdrawal

Psychological abuse may take the form of withdrawing positive behaviors generally expected in a relationship. Withdrawal may be complete, by leaving the relationship for long periods of time with no explanation. Partners may remain physically present but maintain complete silence or otherwise ignore their partner. Abuse might take the form of insensitivity to a partner's emotional needs or by not showing appreciation for the efforts or accomplishments of one's partner.

Measurement

Attempts to measure psychological abuse encounter numerous difficulties. A wide range of actions, including many that are commonplace and take place in nonabusive relationships, may nonetheless be abusive in some contexts and combinations. A growing number of instruments have been developed and subjected to scientific scrutiny. Many measures of psychological abuse grew out of efforts to study intimate partner violence. A number of these were developed to be gender specific, like the Psychological Maltreatment of Women Inventory. Other measures, like the Measure of Psychologically Abusive Behaviors, are gender neutral or gender inclusive—that is, the same items are used to measure men's and women's use of psychological abuse, within both same-sex and different-sex relationships. A recently developed instrument of psychological abuse, the Controlling and Abusive Tactics measure, drew items from samples of both male and female perpetrators of intimate partner violence in an effort to create a gender inclusive instrument. This yielded some items that were thought to primarily characterize female-to-male and male-to-female psychological abuse. While the final measure shares a common pool of items, the Controlling and Abusive Tactics developers noted that their statistical analyses demonstrated the need to separately analyze male and female responses and to devise gender specific scoring methods. This supports the view that gender should continue to be a factor in exploring and understanding psychological abuse.

Emerging Issues

Digital media, or the use of Internet and cell phones, have created a new context for psychological abuse in intimate relationships. People use digital media, such as social media and texting, to search for, communicate with, and end romantic relationships. Although digital media can increase intimacy and feelings of closeness in relationships, they can also be used to harass, control, threaten, and coerce a partner. Therefore, researchers have begun to study how these media could be used to harm dating partners. Most researchers conceptualize these harmful digital behaviors—described with terms such as *digital dating abuse*, *electronic aggression*, and *cyber dating abuse*—as a new context for the psychological abuse behaviors previously recognized, rather than a new phenomenon.

All behaviors typically associated with psychological abuse (e.g., calling a partner mean names, blaming a partner for your problems, controlling who your partner spends time with) can now be perpetrated by using digital forms of communication. However, the unique characteristics of digital media communication warrant special attention as the study and prevention of psychological abuse moves forward. Digital media have changed the tactics and impacts of psychological abuse because romantic partners now have unprecedented access to communicating with their partners and to information about their partners' whereabouts and activities, and can make previously private dating interactions public to their entire social network. New digital behaviors such as pressuring a romantic partner for password access to social media accounts and pressuring a partner to send a sexually explicit photo using digital media can be considered under the umbrella of psychological abuse. Furthermore, the constant connection provided by digital media and the public nature of digital communication may worsen the consequences of digital forms of psychological abuse.

Research on digital forms of psychological abuse and the incorporation of digital media into psychological abuse prevention efforts is newly emerging. Studies find that, similar to off-line psychological abuse, digital psychological abuse is common among adolescents and college students and both girls and boys are victims. Research should continue to investigate the role of digital media in psychological abuse to assess its impact on both youth and adults.

Future research is needed not only to continue to devise increasingly sophisticated methods for measuring psychological abuse but also to better understand its development and how best to prevent it.

Richard M. Tolman and Lauren A. Reed

See also Cycles of Abuse; Physical Abuse

Further Readings

Domestic Abuse Intervention Project. (n.d.). *Power and control.* Duluth, MN: Author. Retrieved from http://www.theduluthmodel.org/pdf/PowerandControl.pdf

Hamel, J., Jones, D. N., Dutton, D. G., & Graham-Kevan, N. (2015). The CAT: A gender-inclusive measure of controlling and abusive tactics. *Violence and Victims, 30*(4), 547–580.

Lawrence, E., Orengo-Aguayo, R., Langer, A., & Brock, R. L. (2012). The impact and consequences of partner abuse on partners. *Partner Abuse, 3*(4), 406–428.

Reed, L. A., Tolman, R. M., & Ward, L. M. (2016). Snooping and sexting: Digital media as a context and tool for dating violence among college students. *Violence Against Women, 22*(13), 1556–1576.

Rogers, M. J., & Follingstad, D. (2011). Gender differences in reporting psychological abuse in a national sample. *Journal of Aggression, Maltreatment & Trauma, 20*(5), 471–502.

Tolman, R. M. (1999). The validation of the Psychological Maltreatment of Women Inventory. *Violence and Victims, 14*(1), 25–37.

Psychological Measurements, Gender Bias in

Mental health professionals use psychological measurements, also called psychological tests, as a means to investigate, standardize, and compare individuals' cognitive, emotional, and behavioral processes. Each test typically consists of one or more scales that evaluate factors such as abilities, symptoms, traits, states, and attitudes. The use of psychological tests is generally conducted within the context of a broader psychological assessment, which also commonly includes a clinical interview and behavioral observations, in addition to other sources of information. While psychological measurements are not required elements of an assessment, they are often utilized to supplement the evaluator's opinion.

Psychological tests are commonly divided into two broad categories: (1) cognitive abilities/achievement and (2) personality/psychopathology. Cognitive assessment refers to an evaluation of how an individual thinks and includes the measurement of general intellectual functioning as well as more specific domains of cognition including learning, memory, attention, language functioning, visual spatial functioning, executive functioning, and motor functioning. Personality assessment includes the evaluation of an individual's personality traits and symptoms of psychopathology—in other words, how individuals view themselves and the world and how they feel and behave on a regular basis. Other types of assessment include educational assessment, which typically involves an evaluation of academic skills and achievement; diagnostic assessment, which assesses for a specific set of signs and symptoms in an effort to determine if the individual meets the criteria for a particular diagnosis; and forensic assessment, which involves the evaluation of an individual's functioning as it is relevant to certain legal questions.

As psychological measures assess abstract concepts such as intelligence or extroversion, they can be prone to social and demographic biases. A biased test systematically overestimates or underestimates the variable the test is intended to measure. Gender bias in assessment can result from multiple sources. Entire tests or specific items can be biased if the test is used for both men and women, despite the use of a gender-based model for the tested construct. A test is also considered biased if the same responses are interpreted differently based on the gender of the test taker. Bias can additionally result when the characteristics, opinions, or personal biases of the individual administering the assessment have a direct effect on how the assessment is conducted and how the results are interpreted based on the gender of the individual being evaluated. Empirical research regarding gender differences and biases in assessment has focused largely on the assessment tests themselves and is often based on a binary conceptualization of gender (i.e., men vs. women). However, there is little if any research regarding gender bias in assessment as it applies to a more dimensional view of gender identity. This entry reviews the types of psychological measurements, how they are scored with respect to gender, as well as gender differences and potential biases within each assessment category. It concludes with future directions in relevant research.

Psychometrics and Gender

The basic elements of psychological measurement theory, or psychometrics, were developed in the mid-20th century. As many psychological tests were designed for comparison purposes, standard scores and normative data are often used, particularly in educational and intelligence measures. A standardized score allows one to compare an individual score with a normative mean and discover information such as a relative percentile rank for that individual. For instance, a score of 100 on many tests of intelligence indicates that the test taker scored higher than 50% of the normative sample. The normative data can be based on national, international, or developmental population groups. Some normative data sets have subgroups, including gender, race, socioeconomic status, and geographic region. Subgroups are only useful if there are substantial differences between the subgroups on the variables measured by the test.

For the purposes of test interpretation, when gender is considered, it is often considered as a dichotomous concept based on biological sex. Psychological measurements typically use one of two strategies to address gender: (1) gender specific data or (2) unisex normative data. The gender specific strategy assumes that there is a meaningful interpretive difference between raw scores for men and for women and therefore provides normative subgroups in the form of separate normative data based on gender. Therefore, women are compared only with other women, and men are compared only with other men. The unisex strategy does not account for gender and, therefore, combines men and women in the normative data. The unisex strategy assumes that the tested construct is free of gender bias.

Although the gender specific strategy was popularly used with psychological tests throughout the 20th century, the strategy faced both practical and empirical challenges in the 1990s. The practical challenge arose when interpretations of the 1991 Civil Rights Act and the Americans with Disabilities Act indicated that the use of demographic norms (e.g., gender) was a form of discrimination. The empirical challenge arose as cumulating research supported only minor gender differences in cognitive assessment and often lacked support for gender differences in personality assessment. In fact, some researchers have suggested that the use of gendered normative data could obscure actual personality trait differences. In reaction, many popular personality assessments created or revised since the 1990s have utilized unisex normative data.

Stereotype Threat

Even when the psychological tests are valid, social expectations can produce gender differences in individuals' performance. Numerous studies have focused on stereotype threat, which is the idea that individuals adhere to stereotypes when those stereotypes are implicitly triggered. For example, women perform worse on tasks relating to math and science abilities when they believe that men are better in these areas. Simply referring to a test as a math test can provoke gender differences, which disappear when the same test is referred to as a test of problem solving. Therefore, the way in which an individual views their gender, the beliefs that they hold regarding gender and academic performance, and whether these beliefs are triggered may affect performance. Similarly, the opinions of the evaluator can affect the results. Although standardized testing procedures can avoid overt differences in how test takers of different genders are treated, subtle differences can have a substantial effect. If the individual administering the relevant tests possesses gender-based stereotypes regarding performance, the way in which the test is administered and the evaluator's expectations may unintentionally bias the results (e.g., if an evaluator expects men to perform better on math tasks, the evaluator may be more encouraging and may score and interpret the results more favorably when evaluating a man than when evaluating a woman).

Gender Differences in Cognitive Assessment

Many research studies have found minor but consistent differences in the cognitive abilities of men and women. The degree to which the discrepancy in performance originates from biological differences, social biases, or a combination of both is a subject of controversy. Studies have found that, on average, men perform better on tasks of visuospatial functioning, working memory, verbal reasoning, and simple motor tasks compared with women, who tend to show advantages in tasks of face detection, verbal productivity (i.e., the amount of words generated within a time limit), and encoding new information. However, these differences are not consistent across the literature, and the etiology, magnitude, and practical implications of such differences are unclear. The majority of formal cognitive assessment measures utilize normative data from both men and women. If the normative data reveal gender differences on any one task, the use of gender specific norms is recommended for interpretation of that task to reduce bias. In other words, while differences in performance appear to naturally occur between men and women, bias in the interpretation of results is greatly minimized by the use of normative data across the majority of cognitive assessment measures. On tests of overall intelligence quotient, research similarly indicates that there are sometimes minor differences found between men and women on the performance of certain tasks (e.g., women tend to perform better on a test of working memory involving repetition and manipulation of digits, whereas men tend to perform better on another working memory task involving simple arithmetic). However, few if any significant differences have been found in the literature between men and women on overall intelligence quotient scores, suggesting that intelligence tests in general are not significantly biased by gender differences. Additionally, the research suggests that neurological and cognitive gender differences are overshadowed by individual differences.

In educational assessment, research has shown that women tend to earn better grades in school across all subjects but men tend to score better on standardized tests. On academic achievement assessment measures, women consistently outperform men on written tasks. While some studies have found that men tend to perform better on tasks involving math and sciences, others have found that women demonstrate better performance on these subjects. Gender bias in educational assessment has important implications. If there is a gender bias in the assessment of academic skills, it may result in inappropriate referrals or the denial of special-education services. In addition, gender identity may be particularly important in the case of educational assessment because of stereotype threat.

Gender Differences in Personality Assessment

Personality measures contain tests that evaluate disposition and psychopathology. The tests can be divided into categories known as projective and objective. Projective tests utilize ambiguous stimuli and interpret test takers' responses. Scoring is highly reliant on evaluator opinions. Objective tests are often in the form of multiple-choice self-reports and produce numerical ratings and utilize normative data. However, the distinction between these categories has become increasingly blurred since the 1950s (e.g., some projective measures utilize normative data). Gender is rarely directly addressed in the scoring procedures for projective testing, although the emphasis on evaluator opinion within the scoring method introduces susceptibility regarding any gender biases the evaluator might possess. In objective testing, gender has traditionally been considered as a dichotomous variable with gender-based normative data.

While some researchers have suggested that personality tests contain gender bias, this must be differentiated from bias in diagnostic thresholds, criteria, and applications. Leslie Morey, a prominent researcher in psychological assessment, defined two types of gender bias found in personality assessment. The first is assessment bias, in which the same symptoms or traits are described differently based on the gender of the test taker. For instance, the same characteristic might be described as assertion in men and as aggression in women. A second type of bias was described as criterion bias, which indicates that the diagnostic system or pathological construct is inaccurately gender specific. Criterion bias is particularly problematic for psychological measurements. Feminist psychology has suggested that personality constructs are based on an androcentric perspective, which could result in women appearing abnormal when compared with unisex normative data. Additionally, the criteria for psychological diagnoses might pathologize behaviors that are environmentally encouraged for women but not for men, such as dependency. Furthermore, some research has suggested that the way in which diagnostic criteria are categorized is gender biased. This can occur when items more associated with one gender are used for diagnostic purposes. For instance, research has suggested that men and women experience and report symptoms of depression differently. A test that contains items regarding tearfulness as a symptom of depression will likely result in increased levels of endorsement by women.

Research Directions

Research regarding gender differences in psychological measurement increased throughout the 20th and 21st centuries. This had a direct effect on testing procedure. For example, personality tests have increasingly utilized unisex normative data. Although most of the research has focused on cognitive and personality assessment, the early 21st century saw an increase in gender considerations in forensic assessment as well, including the first published adaptations of measures of risk developed specifically for women. While the empirical emphasis on gender in psychological measurement reflects a trend within the general field of psychology, the published literature in psychological assessment represents a limited (i.e., dichotomous) view of gender. Therefore, particularly given the important applications of psychological testing (e.g., academic performance, treatment placement), despite the increased empirical focus, the need for additional research in this area remains.

Rebecca A. Weiss and Christina Massey

See also Gender Bias in Research; Gender Bias in the *DSM*; Mental Health and Gender: Overview

Further Readings

Americans With Disabilities Act of 1990, Pub. L. No. 101-336, 42 U.S.C. 12111-12112 (1991).

Chrisler, J. C., & McCreary, D. R. (Eds.). (2010). *Handbook of gender research in psychology* (Vol. 2). New York, NY: Springer-Verlag.

Civil Rights Act of 1991, Pub. L. No. 102-166, 42 U.S.C. (1991).

Halpern, D. F. (2012). *Sex differences in cognitive abilities* (4th ed.). New York, NY: Psychology Press.

Holdnack, J. A., & Weiss, L. G. (2013). Demographic adjustments to WAIS-IV/WMS-IV norms. In J. A. Holdnack, L. W. Drozdick, L. G. Weiss, & G. L. Iverson (Eds.), *WAIS-IV, WMS-IV, and ACS* (pp. 171–216). Waltham, MA: Academic Press.

Johns, M., Schmader, T., & Martens, A. (2005). Knowing is half the battle: Teaching stereotype threat as a means of improving women's math performance. *Psychological Science, 16,* 175–179.

Morey, L. C., Warner, M. B., & Boggs C. D. (2002). Gender bias in the personality disorder criteria: An investigation of five bias indicators. *Journal of Psychopathology and Behavioral Assessment, 24,* 55–65. doi:10.1023/A:1014005308914

Psychological Measurements, Sexual Orientation Bias in

Psychological measurement is an important and powerful component of the mental health field. Extremely important educational, occupational, and clinical decisions are made on the basis of psychological evaluations, which are in turn often based heavily on specific psychological measurements. There are two potential points of bias in psychological measurement: (1) bias within the instruments themselves and (2) bias on the part of the clinician who is interpreting the test scores those instruments yield. This entry thoroughly examines those two points of potential bias in psychological measurement as related specifically to sexual orientation.

Bias in Psychological Instruments

Psychological instruments are widely used and carry a great deal of weight behind them. As many were developed in the mid- to late 20th century, both the language used within them and the particular way they have been used within the context of a larger evaluation were heavily influenced by the culture (mainly Western) of that time period. With the pervasiveness of heterosexism in Western culture, even those instruments developed or revised in the early 21st century are influenced in a potentially biased way against sexual minorities. The two primary ways the instruments themselves are biased are (1) the language and content of the actual measure items and (2) the limited knowledge about their applicability to sexual minority populations.

Item Content

Three primary problems can occur with the individual items and wording on psychological measures, as related to the potential bias against sexual minorities: (1) omission bias, (2) connotation bias, and (3) contiguity bias. Each of these has the potential to distort the way test scores come out for sexual minorities and, thus, can affect the way the tests are interpreted by professionals.

Omission bias refers to situations in which the wording of items does not take into consideration that the person taking the test may be a sexual minority, such as not offering the possibility of responding appropriately because the choices do not apply directly to the person. For example, if on a measure a question asks male respondents about their intimate relationships with female partners, this does not acknowledge that a sexual minority may have a different relationship constellation. The Minnesota Multiphasic Personality Inventory, second edition (MMPI-2), one of the most widely used measures of clinical and personality functioning, includes items that refer to "marriage" and "mother and father" in questions about children, both of which can exclude sexual minorities. Some widely used measures of psychological symptoms ask for relationship status with the options single, married, and divorced, and there are items about feeling shy or reserved in the presence of the opposite sex (obviously implying romantic shyness), all of which again do not directly apply to sexual minorities in the way the test developers intended. Because responses to items on these scales are meant to tap into specific psychological constructs, omitting the option that the respondent may be a sexual minority, and thus limiting their responses, can alter the test scores and interpretation of them in an unintended way.

Connotation bias refers to situations in which words relating to sexual minorities are presented within the same context as words describing psychopathology or deviance—for example, using the word *diagnose* as it relates to sexual minority status, such as an instrument that says it will "diagnose" sexual orientation, is necessarily equating sexual orientation to mental illness. Connotation bias can also occur when measures use lists that include sexual orientation among sexual disorders or deviant behavior. An example of this would be a test that purports to evaluate sexual orientation, child molestation, pedophilia, and other fetishes. The connotation of including sexual orientation within that list is that being a sexual minority is deviant and/or pathological.

Contiguity bias occurs when a scale used to measure sexual orientation is presented along with scales to measure pathology or deviance. Perhaps the most famous example of this is the MMPI, which is a measure of clinical and personality pathology. Originally, Scale 5 was meant to assess homosexuality; it is now a measure of level of adherence to traditionally masculine and feminine gender roles (though the test manual still includes the issue of assessing homosexuality, for historical reasons). Other scales on the MMPI include depression and schizophrenia, and literally the two scales that surround Scale 5 are psychopathic deviate (Scale 4) and paranoia (Scale 6). The fact that homosexuality was presented alongside these clearly pathological scales (and some argue that even the revised MMPI-2, which calls Scale 5 masculinity/femininity, certainly continues to stigmatize gender identity minorities and perhaps sexual minorities) presents a negative bias against sexual minorities.

Understanding how the content of measures can be biased against sexual minorities is important not only in the development of new measures but also in the revision of existing measures. It is important to note, however, that it is not so simple to just change the content of measures. When items are altered in any way, steps must be taken to ensure that the measure continues to be reliable and valid. If the alterations are significant enough, the entire process of norming (i.e., collecting data on a large set of people, so that when an individual is tested with the measure he or she can be compared with a large group of others) may need to be conducted again. This can be an arduous process, and much research that has been conducted on measures as they were could be rendered less relevant because of the changes. This is why some measures, even though they have been identified as biased, have not yet been altered.

Instrument Applicability

Perhaps more complicated than bias in specific item content is the fact that not much is known about the specific applicability of individual measures to sexual minority populations, simply because the research has not been done. Most normative samples do not even include information on sexual orientation, so it is unclear how representative these comparison groups truly are. Some have argued that measures should have separate normative data for sexual minority populations, though this is potentially problematic. For example, a measure of depression could be normed on a large sexual minority population, so that it is clearly applicable to sexual minorities; however, an individual who took the test would then be compared with this population, which is known to have higher rates of depression than the general population. That is, it may not be useful to know an individual's level of depression compared with other sexual minority individuals; it may be much more useful to know their level of depression compared with the larger general population. Other measures, however, may merit separate normative groups for sexual minorities, such as measures of sexual identity formation or other similar constructs.

Another component of how applicable a measure is to a sexual minority population is the fact that some working definitions of well-being, psychological adjustment, or positive mental health may be heterosexually biased, even if individual items within the measure are not. For example, if being married or having children is a benchmark of psychological health on a particular measure, then it is necessarily not applicable (at least not in an unbiased way) to sexual minorities. Although many may be able to and choose to get married and/or have children, these may not be signs within the sexual minority community of positive well-being. More important, the absence of them is not a sign of psychological maladjustment. The constructs that theoretically drive the individual measures need to be scrutinized for sexual orientation bias, in addition to the individual items.

Bias in the Use of Psychological Measurements

In addition to psychological measures being potentially biased themselves, the person using them has the potential to be biased against sexual minorities as well. With deeply ingrained heterosexist beliefs embedded in Western culture, even those clinicians who are sensitive to and aware of heterosexist bias have the potential to use psychological measures in a biased way.

One of the first and most basic ways in which a clinician can use psychological measures in a biased way against sexual minorities is in the initial selection of the tests themselves. Different tests measure different psychological constructs, and a clinician chooses tests based on often implicit assumptions and hypotheses about what is likely happening with the individual being tested. For example, some broad-based, multidimensional personality measures are meant for a nonclinical, low-psychopathology population. Others are meant to examine specific psychopathology. If a sexual minority individual being assessed is in current distress, biased assumptions may lead a clinician to choose, for example, the Millon Clinical Multiaxial Inventory, a measure that is particularly sensitive to personality disorders and has been found to have a tendency to overpathologize. In reality, the individual may have stress related directly to being a sexual minority, such as suffering many microaggressions or being discriminated against, for which the presenting distress would be logical and reasonable. Selecting tests is rarely straightforward, but there is great potential for bias against sexual minorities when measuring only internal pathology.

When interpreting test scores, clinicians often do not appreciate just how influenced they can be by culture. It is especially important to note that many different scores on psychological measures are culturally influenced for populations that have traditionally been oppressed and continue to suffer discrimination. Individuals who identify as sexual minorities in Western culture have a distinct history and ongoing pattern of being discriminated against, however subtly, and this influences how they may respond on certain measures. For example, a measure of paranoia may be generally elevated in this population, not because all sexual minorities are paranoid but because the measure itself includes items related to being wary of sharing too much information about oneself with strangers or keeping others at arm's length until one knows them better. These are reasonable traits to expect from someone who has had negative experiences disclosing their sexual orientation in the past or who has at least learned of the history of discrimination and abuse of sexual minorities. To conclude that an individual is paranoid because of slight elevation on this measure would be erroneous and biased.

Furthermore, there may be additional factors that should be considered when measuring general well-being, life satisfaction, psychological health, or other such general psychological constructs with sexual minorities. For example, while an individual's psychological structures may be fully intact, constructs specific to sexual minorities may be affecting their well-being. Sexual minority identity development, for example, is a process that in general does not need to be navigated by heterosexual individuals. How one's sexual minority identity is defined has developed over time, and how it is understood by the individual and others may certainly affect general well-being. Measures of life satisfaction may be lower than ideal because of identity struggles, and clinicians need to understand that this may play a role in overall well-being, so that they do not reach an erroneous conclusion, for example, that the individual is depressed. Another example is the level of "outness." How out or publicly open one is about one's sexual orientation is not a concern that most heterosexual individuals struggle with, but like sexual minority identity development, it may certainly play a role in the general well-being of sexual minorities. An inadvertent way clinicians can be biased against sexual minorities is by not considering constructs like these in the context of a psychological evaluation and thus not seeing the full picture of the person they are assessing.

A. Jordan Wright

See also Research: Overview; Sexual Orientation: Overview; Sexual Orientation as Research Variable; Sexual Orientation Dynamics in Clinical Training

Further Readings

American Psychological Association, Committee on Lesbian and Gay Concerns. (1991). Avoiding heterosexist bias in language. *American Psychologist, 46,* 973–974.

Chernin, J., Holden, J. M., & Chandler, C. (1997). Bias in psychological assessment: Heterosexism. *Measurement and Evaluation in Counseling and Development, 30,* 68–76.

Pope, M. (1992). Bias in the interpretation of psychological tests. In S. Dworkin & F. Gutierrez (Eds.), *Counseling gay men and lesbians: Journey to the end of the rainbow* (pp. 277–292). Alexandria, VA: American Counseling Association.

Prince, J. P. (1997). Assessment bias affecting lesbians, gay men, and bisexuals. *Measurement and Evaluation in Counseling and Development, 30,* 82–87.

Williams, C. L. (1987). Issues surrounding psychological testing of minority patients. *Hospital and Community Psychiatry, 38,* 184–189.

Psychopathy and Gender

Psychopathy refers to a personality disorder characterized by interpersonal manipulation, lack of empathy, callousness, and impulsivity and a risk-taking, parasitic, irresponsible, and socially deviant lifestyle. In the criminal justice system, a diagnosis of psychopathy is an important aspect of risk assessment, because research has shown that psychopathic offenders recidivate at about 2.5 times the rate of nonpsychopathic offenders. Much of the research on psychopathy has been conducted with male offender samples, given the substantially higher base rate of psychopathy in men, particularly incarcerated men. However, there is growing research on the extent to which the psychopathy construct extends to women as well as to subclinical (e.g., student, community, workplace) samples. This research suggests that although women tend to be much less psychopathic than men, the construct is a valid predictor of important outcomes in both male and female samples. However, female manifestations of psychopathy may be somewhat different from male manifestations, and such differences have implications for measurement and intervention. This entry begins with a classical description of psychopathy as well as the method of its measurement. Next, the expression of psychopathy is reviewed, as are the development models. The next section considers correlates and measurement of nonclinical psychopathy. The entry concludes by reviewing treatment options.

Classical Descriptions and Measurement of Psychopathy

In his seminal 1941 book *The Mask of Sanity*, psychiatrist Hervey Cleckley described a category of both male and female patients who appeared intelligent and rational and who did not suffer from psychosis or mood/anxiety disorders. However, despite their often charming and sincere outward presentation, these patients got into trouble repeatedly, seemingly incapable of learning from experience or of truly understanding the pain of their victims.

Since Cleckley's depiction of psychopathy, there have been numerous attempts to refine descriptions of this puzzling disorder and to better understand its causes, correlates, and response to treatment. Psychologist Robert Hare, in particular, has spent his career researching psychopaths, particularly in the context of violence and other criminal behavior. Hare also developed the Psychopathy Checklist—Revised (PCL-R), the instrument widely considered the gold standard in measuring psychopathy, particularly in forensic settings. Scores on the 20 PCL-R items are based on both interview and file information. For each item (e.g., lack of realistic, long-term goals; a grandiose sense of self-worth; criminal versatility), an individual is scored from 0 (*does not apply*) to 2 (*reasonably good match*). A cutoff score of 30 out of a possible 40 points is typically used for a diagnosis of psychopathy.

Based on this instrument, Hare has estimated that about 1% of the adult population would meet the criteria for a diagnosis of psychopathy, but that proportion is much higher in prison settings. About 15% to 30% of male offenders meet the PCL-R diagnostic criteria for psychopathy, whereas about 11% to 23% of female offenders meet the criteria. Although there is some overlap in these estimates, on average, PCL-R scores tend to be lower in female prison samples than in male prison samples.

In male offender samples, a PCL-R diagnosis of psychopathy is a robust predictor of recidivism, both violent and nonviolent, as well as the number and severity of institutional infractions. Although there is evidence that the PCL-R is reliable and valid for female offender samples, it might not have the same implications for risk assessment. For example, PCL-R scores are somewhat less predictive of female than of male recidivism and institutional noncompliance.

Expression of Psychopathy

Classical male psychopathy is well illustrated by the Canadian serial killer Clifford Olson, identified by Hare as a psychopath. A con artist and thief, Olson confessed to killing 11 boys and girls aged 9 to 18 years, then extracted $100,000 from the government for providing the locations of the bodies. Throughout his incarceration, Olson manipulated the legal system, taunted the families of his victims, sought media attention, and expressed no remorse for his crimes. However, the expression of psychopathy might be somewhat different in women. While psychopathy is related to alcohol and drug use in both genders, some evidence indicates that psychopathy is related to anxiety, negative emotionality, and self-harm to a greater extent in women than in men. In fact, some researchers have suggested that psychopathy and borderline personality disorder symptoms overlap in women to such an extent that borderline personality disorder may represent a female expression of psychopathy.

Furthermore, although psychopathy is associated with aggression and manipulation in both genders, women's aggression may take a different form from men's aggression. Women are more apt to employ tears, sexuality, and relational aggression rather than physical assault. Psychopathy is also associated with prostitution to a greater extent in women than in men. Cleckley's case study of "Anna" captures these distinctions well. This bright, articulate woman engaged in highly promiscuous behavior, sometimes stealing from her sexual partners. She played cruel practical jokes on her instructors and fellow students and was subsequently expelled from numerous institutions. Although never physically aggressive, Anna aggressed in other ways, for example, by urinating on her "friends'" evening gowns.

Studies have shown that women are more likely to aggress against people they know, particularly children and sexual partners, rather than against strangers. In his book *Without Conscience*, Hare described the psychopath who allowed her boyfriend to sexually assault her 5-year-old daughter because she was too tired to have sex herself. The female psychopath also may be more likely than the male psychopath to manipulate others into committing crimes or other socially deviant behaviors on her behalf. Thus, women's psychopathic, irresponsible and harmful behavior may be of a type that is less likely to result in a criminal record than men's behavior. Since previous criminal activity is a component of PCL-R psychopathy, women's scores may be lower than men's for reasons that are unrelated to the real levels of socially malevolent behavior.

Developmental Models of Psychopathy

Psychopathy is characterized by impulsive, reward-driven behavior. Hare's early research suggested that psychopaths show less of a physiological response to impending punishment (e.g., an electric shock) than do other people. Such findings are consistent with theories that children who are genetically predisposed to be unmotivated by punishment will be extremely hard to socialize and are more likely to develop psychopathic characteristics. In keeping with genetic theories, both criminality, in general, and psychopathy, in particular, show a genetic basis. Some theories posit that women require greater genetic and/or environmental influences to express psychopathic behavior, but evidence for such theories has been mixed.

Both male and female psychopaths are more likely to have a history of childhood neglect and/or abuse (physical or sexual) than nonpsychopathic controls, suggesting the role of interaction of the early environment with genetic factors. Among adolescent boys with conduct problems, those who have a history of childhood antisocial behaviors characterized by callous/unemotional traits, poor impulse control, and greater diversity in their misbehaviors are more likely to be diagnosed as psychopaths in adulthood compared with adolescent boys whose antisocial behavior had a later onset. For girls, childhood conduct problems are quite uncommon, but a similar category of girls can be identified but with an adolescent onset. That is, these girls have poor impulse control, callous/unemotional traits, and diverse antisocial behaviors and are more likely to be identified as psychopathic in adulthood, but their conduct problems have a delayed onset compared with boys. A recent study of detained youth identified as having callous/unemotional traits (considered a precursor to psychopathy) showed that girls were more likely than boys to report extreme levels of distress, such as anxiety and depression. The authors noted that these distressed adolescents may have different treatment needs than adolescents who more closely resemble the prototypical cold, unfeeling psychopath.

Evolutionary theories suggest that psychopathy is part of a "fast" and exploitive life strategy. Indeed, at higher levels of psychopathic traits, community men reported a greater willingness to use coercive and deceptive strategies to attain sex. In an undergraduate sample, psychopathy was associated with both fantasizing about short-term, anonymous, nonromantic, sexual activity and being more apt to engage in fantasized activities about deviant and anonymous sexual behavior. However, in a separate study of nonclinical, sexually deviant behaviors collected from an online sample, subclinical psychopathy was unrelated to a variety of sexually deviant behaviors after controlling for narcissism, Machiavellianism, and Big Five personality traits.

Measurement and Correlates of Nonclinical Psychopathy

There is evidence that psychopaths are not qualitatively different from nonpsychopaths. Rather, psychopathy appears to be dimensional in nature, with diagnosed psychopaths having extremely high levels of those characteristics associated with psychopathy. Thus, research on psychopathic offenders should translate downward to nonclinical samples, and findings about psychopathic traits in nonclinical samples should inform the forensic literature.

In community and student samples, self-report questionnaires are typically used to measure psychopathy. These instruments do not yield a psychopathy diagnosis but rather assess variance in the levels of psychopathic traits. In these samples, where there would be very few, if any, individuals who would meet the PCL-R criteria for a diagnosis of psychopathy, levels of psychopathic traits as assessed by self-report questionnaires have been found to be good predictors of plagiarism, cheating on multiple-choice exams, having many impersonal sexual relationships, and verbal, physical, and relational aggression. Men typically report substantially higher levels of psychopathy (about 1 standard deviation higher) than do women on these instruments, but associations with antisocial and aggressive behaviors are similar. One common method of assessing nonclinical psychopathy is through measuring the "dark triad" personality traits of narcissism, subclinical psychopathy, and Machiavellianism.

There has also been a recent interest in corporate psychopathy. A recent study investigated a mixed-gender sample of 203 managers and executives from several companies, and while psychopathy scores in this sample did not statistically differ, on average, from scores in community samples, there were proportionately more high scorers in the corporate sample. Interestingly, in this study, psychopathy was unrelated to gender but was related to high ratings of charisma and presentation style and low ratings of being a team player and overall performance, suggesting a level of adaptiveness in psychopathy in some contexts echoing evolutionary arguments for the utility of psychopathy. However, while these findings are intriguing and have garnered much media attention in recent years, the corporate psychopathy literature is relatively new and has been limited by difficulty in obtaining permission to conduct psychopathy research in business environments.

Treatment

At a clinical level, psychopathy has been long thought to be resistant to intervention. Indeed, a 1960s intensive therapeutic community for male offenders had the unexpected result that, although successful for the nonpsychopaths, the treated psychopaths re-offended at higher rates than the untreated psychopaths. Furthermore, in one review, the authors found that in both male and female samples (but predominantly male), psychopaths were less responsive to and more likely to drop out of treatment than nonpsychopaths. However, as the authors of this review emphasized, the fact that the psychopaths were less successful does not mean that they had no success. The fact that the therapeutic community, with its emphasis on empathy and shared responsibility, has not been widely effective in treating psychopathy should not be taken as evidence that no therapy will ever be successful with psychopaths. Hare suggests that to be successful with psychopaths, a treatment must focus on the benefits of socially and legally appropriate behavior to the psychopath.

Treatment with adolescents shows a similar but slightly more encouraging pattern. Again, youths with higher levels of psychopathy were less compliant with treatment and benefited less than their less psychopathic peers. However, the majority of studies reviewed showed some treatment success for psychopathic youth.

At this point, it is unclear whether female psychopaths would benefit from different treatment strategies from those offered to men or whether female psychopaths are generally more or less responsive to treatment than men. Given the gender differences in expressions of psychopathy, it seems a fruitful avenue of exploration.

Beth A. Visser and Jennifer Lodi-Smith

See also Antisocial Personality Disorder and Gender; Violence and Gender: Overview

Further Readings

Babiak, P., & Hare, R. D. (2006). *Snakes in suits.* New York, NY: Regan Books.

Cleckley, H. (1988). *The mask of sanity* (5th ed.). St. Louis, MO: Mosby.

Hare, R. D. (1993). *Without conscience.* New York, NY: Guilford Press.

Verona, E., & Vitale, J. (2006). Psychopathy in women. In C. J. Patrick (Ed.), *Handbook of psychopathy* (pp. 415–436). New York, NY: Guilford Press.

Visser, B. A., DeBow, V., Pozzebon, J. A., Bogaert, A. F., & Book, A. (2015). Psychopathic sexuality: The thin line between fantasy and reality. *Journal of Personality, 83,* 376–388.

Psychosexual Development

Psychosexual development refers to the biological, psychological, and sociocultural processes by which an individual develops sexually across the life span. It includes core sexual or gender identity—one's sense of self as female or male; sexual orientation—erotic interests in the same, other, or both sexes; and gender role—behaviors typically associated with women or men in a particular society. This entry focuses on the development of sexual and gender identity.

What it means to be female or male and how one develops an identity as a woman or a man are topics of long-standing debate. This is particularly true when one's gender role behaviors, sexual or gender identity, or sexual orientation are considered atypical for a specific culture. Simplistically, theories have emphasized biological (nature) or sociocultural (nurture) factors. This entry briefly examines the role of genes and hormones and reviews several psychosocial theories of psychosexual development. It concludes with a brief overview of psychosexual development across the life span. Much of the information in this entry can be referenced in much greater depth in the book *Gender Development* by Judith Owen Blakemore, Sheri Berenbaum, and Lynn Liben.

Biological Processes

Both genes and hormones have been hypothesized to account for psychosexual development. With a few exceptions, genes do not appear to be the causal mechanism for sexual differentiation in brain development. Adherents to a genetic position argue that specific genetic mechanisms exist but are as yet undetermined. We will use androgen insensitivity syndrome (AIS) as an example. First, recall that if the father contributes a Y chromosome at conception, the fetus develops as a male (46,XY), whereas an X chromosome from the father results in a female (46,XX). Until about 7 weeks' gestation, the fetus is sexually undifferentiated. At this time, the sex-determining region of the Y chromosome activates the production of testosterone, a male hormone from the steroid androgen category. This results in the development of male genitalia. Depending on the level of testosterone present in utero at this time, the 46,XY fetus ordinarily develops as a male. High levels of testosterone are needed for the penis and testes to develop.

Notably, sexual differentiation of the brain occurs after sexual differentiation of the gonads. However, in individuals with a disorder (or difference) of sexual development (DSD) known as AIS, the sex-determining region of the Y chromosome is fully functional, but the androgen receptors in the body are inactive. Thus, the fetus develops as phenotypically female despite having 46,XY chromosomes and high levels of testosterone in utero. When compared with genetic females (46,XX), those with AIS appear to be similar with regard to sexual orientation, marital status, and retrospective recall of childhood play activities.

There is much stronger evidence for the causal effect of hormones in psychosexual development. In studies with rodents and nonhuman primates, the prenatal administration of androgens has shown the most consistent sex differences. Female fetuses given androgen in utero develop masculinized behaviors postnatally. The effects of prenatal administration of estrogens, responsible for the development of female physiology, are less clear.

Experimental manipulations of these kinds are unethical in humans, so researchers have relied on studying DSD conditions. For example, females with congenital adrenal hyperplasia (CAH) have high levels of androgen beginning early in gestation and throughout the prenatal period. This is an important phase in brain development. Compared with other girls, even sisters, they tend to prefer masculine activities and interests as children. As adults, women with CAH are more interested in male-typical activities and careers and less interested in marriage and childbearing than women without CAH. Nonetheless, it must be noted that about 95% of these individuals maintain a female gender identity despite having masculine behaviors and interests.

In summary, based on studies of DSD, there is more evidence supporting a hormonal than a genetic basis for psychosexual differentiation. However, studies examining the biological bases of sexual development have used small, highly select samples. Therefore, definitive conclusions cannot be made. Furthermore, it is unclear how well the findings in studies of DSD or nonhuman organisms generalize to the entire population.

Psychosocial Processes

Psychosocial processes include, but are not limited to, psychoanalytic theory, learning and social learning theory, and cognitive developmental theory.

Psychoanalytic Theory

Sigmund Freud (1856–1939) was an Austrian neurologist who is considered the founder of psychoanalysis. Freud expounded five stages of psychosexual development, depending on the primary focus of a developing child's physiological preoccupation with sexual gratification, which he referred to as erogenous zones. The first of these five stages is oral, during which time infants younger than about 18 months old are preoccupied with libidinous gratification centered on the mouth, including breast suckling. The second stage is anal, from about 1½ to 3 years of age, with a focus on the anus, including control of the bowel and bladder. The third stage is phallic, when the genitalia (penis for boys and clitoris for girls) are the primary focus of pleasure. During this time, children aged 3 to 6 years develop an awareness of the physiological basis of the sexes as well as the gender characteristics associated with girls and boys and develop sexual attractions. Freud's fourth stage of psychosexual development is the latency stage, which lasts until puberty. The final stage is genital, from puberty through adulthood. The primary focus is on fulfillment of mature responsibilities and adult relationships, including marriage and parenthood.

During the phallic stage, Freud argued, parent-child relationships are altered in important ways. In the oral and anal stages, both sexes have a strong bond with the mother because of the nurturing she provides infants. However, in the latent stage, children come to see the parent of the same-sex as an adversary for the parent of the other sex. Freud referred to this competitive process as the Oedipus complex. Oedipus is a character from Greek mythology who killed his father and unwittingly married his mother.

As awareness of anatomical sex differences develops, boys come to believe that girls have been castrated. Boys suspect that they may be castrated if their fathers become aware of their nascent sexual attraction to their mothers. According to Freud, coping with castration anxiety causes a boy to identify with his father, enabling him to maintain a nonsexual relationship with his mother.

Freud argued that the psychoanalytic process differs in girls. During the phallic stage, girls come to believe that they have been castrated, resulting in penis envy. This causes a girl to transfer erotic interests to her father, creating an adversarial relationship with her mother. However, she represses this conflict for fear of losing her mother's love. She resolves the conflict by identifying with her mother. As adults, Freud asserted, women resolve penis envy by giving birth to a child, who psychically replaces the absent penis.

Some early female psychoanalysts sharply criticized Freud for ignoring the cultural effects of patriarchy and rejected the concept of penis envy. This criticism permeates contemporary psychoanalytic thinking, particularly among feminists. Another reproach underscores Freud's apparent obsession with sex, even in infants. An important observation is that Freud argued that humans are essentially bisexual and that homosexuality may be a normal biological variation despite being considered a social aberration.

The chief component of Freudian psychosexual development was identification with the same-sex parent. However, early experimental psychologists who tested these theories were unable to find support for them. Simply put, children generally were not found to be like their parents in personality or sex role behaviors. However, Freud's theory of psychosexual development was an important impetus to research and theory on the processes by which individuals come to identify as female or male, girl or boy.

Learning Theory

Learning theory emphasizes nurture and is based on operant conditioning. Children whose behaviors conform to sociocultural norms receive positive reinforcement, such as praise or rewards, which increases the frequency of these behaviors. Conversely, they may be punished for engaging in gender-atypical behaviors, which decreases the frequency of engaging in them. Relatedly, social learning theorists argue that gender-related behavior also is shaped by observing others as well as images, such as movies. Thus, children need not directly experience the positive reinforcement or punishment of other children. They learn typical gender-related behaviors by observing the treatment others receive. For example, a girl may learn to avoid playing with trucks because she sees another girl shunned or disciplined for doing so. A boy may acquire an aversion to playing with dolls because he sees a movie in which a boy is being taunted or rejected for engaging in these behaviors. Children tend to imitate the gender-related behavior of those with power and prestige as well as same-sex models. However, learning and social learning theories have been criticized for seeing children as too passive in the developmental process.

Social-Cognitive Theory

The American psychologist Lawrence Kohlberg (1927–1987) developed a cognitive developmental stage theory of psychosexual development known as gender constancy. He argued that children first come to awareness that they are a girl or a boy and subsequently attach meaning to the concepts. They then gravitate toward sociocultural activities associated with being a girl or a boy, which is socially reinforced. Reinforcement increases their preference for activities and sociocultural characteristics associated with their gender, which further solidifies their identity as a girl or a boy, respectively.

Researchers have found that gender constancy occurs first for self, then for others. Self-awareness of one's gender develops by about age 2 years, whereas identification of others as girls or boys occurs by about age 3 or 4 years. Furthermore, awareness that the categories are immutable must occur before gender constancy develops, even when physical appearances change. Arguably, full gender constancy generally does not develop until age 7 or 8 years. Importantly, some researchers have argued that age is irrelevant and that before gender constancy is achieved, children must first come to realize that each sex has distinct genitalia.

Developing Gender Identity

Until about age 2 years, children make mistakes in gender labeling. By the age of 2 to 3 years, children can accurately identify girls and boys, women and men. From ages 3 to 6 years, children develop knowledge about gender stereotypes, solidify gender preferences, and begin to attain gender constancy. Boys tend to receive more rigid, harsher training for gender role behaviors. Young adolescents tend to adhere to stricter gender stereotypes than their older peers. These stereotypes become more flexible in late adolescence, with greater tolerance and flexibility for oneself and others. However, they tend to perceive others, including adults, in stereotypical ways. Notably, peers and the media as well as parents influence gender flexibility or inflexibility. Adolescents also become acutely aware of sex roles and begin to recognize their sexual orientation. During adulthood, gender flexibility tends to increase with age. Individuals become more willing to make exceptions to gender stereotypes, particularly for themselves.

Furthermore, while research is still in its nascent stages, some scholars are exploring how psychosexual identity may influence gender identity for transgender and gender nonconforming (TGNC) people. Given that TGNC people do not identify with their sex assigned at birth, they may gravitate toward gender nonconformity from earlier ages, which then affects their psychosexual development. Future research can explore how Freudian or psychoanalytic theories can further explain TGNC identities in ways that are gender affirming and inclusive.

Robin M. Mathy

See also Gender Identity; Gender Role Behavior

Further Readings

Blakemore, J. E. O., Berenbaum, S. A., & Liben, L. S. (2009). *Gender development*. New York, NY: Psychology Press.

Freud, S. (1927). Some psychological consequences of the anatomical distinction between the sexes. *International Journal of Psychoanalysis, 8*, 133–142.

Freud, S. (1962). *Three essays on the theory of sexuality* (J. Strachey, Ed. & Trans.). New York, NY: Basic Books.

Freud, S. (1966). *The complete introductory lectures on psychoanalysis* (J. Strachey, Ed. & Trans.). New York, NY: W. W. Norton.

Hines, M., Ahmed, S. F., & Hughes, L. A. (2003). Psychological outcomes and gender-related development in complete androgen insensitivity syndrome. *Archives of Sexual Behavior, 32*(2), 93–101.

Hines, M., Brook, C., & Conway, G. S. (2004). Androgen and psychosexual development: Core gender identity, sexual orientation, and recalled childhood gender role behavior in women and men with congenital adrenal hyperplasia (CAH). *Journal of Sex Research, 41*(1), 75–81.

Kohlberg, L. (1966). A cognitive-developmental analysis of children's sex-role concepts and attitudes. In E. E. Maccoby (Ed.), *The development of sex differences* (pp. 82–172). Stanford, CA: Stanford University Press.

Öçal, G. (2011). Current concepts in disorders of sexual development. *Journal of Clinical Research in Pediatric Endocrinology, 3*(3), 105–114.

Psychosis and Gender

See Schizophrenia and Gender

Puberty

Puberty is a period of sexual maturation. It is a time when a child undergoes internal and external changes that begin the process of the physical capacity for sexual reproduction. It is a complex process that involves dramatic internal changes that begins when hormones (specialized substances released by glands) are produced by the body and signal the body to develop and change in certain ways. During puberty, sex hormones start to be produced at adult levels by glands in the body as signaled by the pituitary gland in the brain. The male hormone is known as androgen, and the female hormone is known as estrogen. Males and females produce both types of hormones, but androgens are produced in higher concentration in males and estrogens are produced in higher concentration in females. During puberty, adolescents also experience growth spurts as a result of an increased production of growth hormones that interact with the sex hormones. This entry discusses the specifics of puberty in girls and boys. The effects of puberty on a person's emotional well-being are then reviewed, and the entry concludes with a look at the physical and emotional effects caused by the time at which one goes through puberty.

Puberty in Girls

Puberty typically begins earlier in girls than in boys. Girls begin puberty at around age 11 years. However, the internal changes underlying this process in girls begin by about age 8 years. During this time, the body begins to produce estrogen. Estrogen is linked to numerous reproductive functions in women, including regulating the menstrual cycle, the thickening of the uterine wall to prepare the body for pregnancy, the shedding of that lining if the egg produced during the cycle is not fertilized, and others. It is especially implicated in puberty because it brings on the onset of menstruation. Also known as menarche, this event is a particularly important part of puberty as it is often considered as the signal that the female body is now capable of reproduction.

In addition to hormonal and internal changes, female puberty also includes the development of various secondary sex characteristics or visible external changes that signal maturity but are not directly involved in reproduction. This includes the development of breasts, the growth of pubic and underarm hair, changes in body shape such as the widening of the hips, growth spurt, and also facial and/or body acne.

Puberty in Boys

Boys typically begin puberty around age 13 or 14 years, but some internal changes begin earlier. At around age 11 years, boys experience changes in primary sex characteristics, triggered by the increased production of androgens. These changes include the accelerated growth of the penis and scrotum, along with the enlargement of the prostate gland and seminal vesicles, which produce semen. Semen is the fluid that carries sperm, and sexual maturity in boys is marked by spermarche, or a boy's first ejaculation.

Spermarche marks the production of viable sperm and usually occurs around the age of 13 years, when the body has begun producing sperm for more than a year. Initially, a boy's semen contains relatively few sperm, but the amount of sperm increases with age. Spermarche is also often signaled by nocturnal emissions or "wet dreams."

In addition to the hormonal changes and sexual maturity of the organs and gonads, boys experience various changes in secondary sex characteristics during puberty. These changes include the growth of pubic, underarm, and facial hair. The vocal cords and larynx in boys become longer and larger, which results in the deepening of their voices. Some of these external changes in boys can begin as early as age 11 or 12 years.

Puberty and Emotional Well-Being

Puberty is often associated with mood swings and other emotional challenges. This is partly due to surges in hormone production (e.g., higher levels of these hormones have been associated with anger and depression), as well as stresses in dealing with the rapid changes in body appearance and functioning. Adolescents entering puberty may not be aware of how to deal with the emerging need for hygiene or may experience embarrassment about the physical changes in their bodies. Especially for girls, normal changes in body shape such as the widening of the hips can bring about feelings of dissatisfaction and self-consciousness.

Pubertal Timing

The timing of puberty can also affect adolescents' experiences. Early-maturing boys tend to feel better about themselves because they are more likely to excel at sports, to be popular, and to have a more positive self-concept. However, they are also more likely to have difficulties in school, lower academic performance, and higher instances of risky behaviors. In the long term, early-maturing boys tend to be not only more responsible and cooperative as adults but also more conforming and less flexible.

Late-maturing boys tend to be at a disadvantage due to their smaller size. They are less successful at sports and are viewed as less attractive by their peers. However, they are less likely to engage in risky behaviors and have fewer problems at school. As adults, late-maturing boys tend to be more flexible and creative and have a better sense of humor.

Early-maturing girls tend to be more self-conscious and feel different from their peers.

However, they are usually more popular, especially among boys, and tend to start dating earlier. Early puberty in girls is linked to increased risk for earlier sexual activities and other risky behaviors. In the long term, early-maturing girls are at elevated risk for emotional problems and have lower academic achievement.

Late-maturing girls tend to be viewed as less popular and less attractive and may be overlooked in dating and have a relatively low social status. However, as they begin to mature, they tend to have greater satisfaction with their bodies and themselves than early-maturing peers. In the long term, late-maturing girls tend to have a more positive body image and might have fewer emotional problems than early-maturing girls.

Transgender adolescents face a range of unique issues during puberty, particularly in relation to the physiological changes for their assigned birth sex. For instance, a transgender girl may begin to develop a larger penis and scrotum, grow hair on her armpits or legs, or experience vocal chord changes. In recent years, there have been medical developments in puberty blockers or puberty suppressants for transgender children. These hormonal procedures suppress the body's production of estrogen or testosterone, which pauses any physiological changes that would occur during puberty. Some advocates suggest that blocking puberty in this way can be helpful to prevent psychological distress in transgender children, while others are fearful of the health risks of puberty suppression, due to the nascent amount of research.

Car Mun Kok and Maria Rosario T. de Guzman

See also Adolescence and Gender: Overview; Estrogen; Puberty Suppression; Testosterone; Transgender and Gender Nonconforming Adolescents

Further Readings

Allen, H., Blenning, C., Rindel, S., Selva, K., & Burleton, J. (2014). *Puberty blocking and hormone therapy needs of transgender adolescents.* Portland, OR: TransActive Gender Center. Retrieved from http://gendercreativekids.ca/wp-content/uploads/2014/01/TransActive-OHSC-Testimony.pdf

Archibald, A. B., Graber, J. A., & Brooks-Gunn, J. (2003). Pubertal processes and physiological growth in adolescence. In G. R. Adams & M. D. Berzonsky (Eds.), *Blackwell handbook of adolescence* (pp. 24–47). Malden, MA: Blackwell.

Feldman, R. (2008). *Development across the life span* (5th ed.). Upper Saddle River, NJ: Pearson.

Steinberg, L. (2006). *Adolescence* (7th ed.). New York, NY: McGraw-Hill.

Puberty Suppression

For transgender adults, medical interventions that help develop the physical characteristics of their experienced gender are the acknowledged and increasingly widely accepted effective choice of treatment. With regard to young transgender adolescents, there has been more reluctance to provide treatment with irreversible effects at a young age. Puberty suppression, however, with only reversible effects, has now become part of the clinical management protocols for transgender adolescents. It provides them with time and rest to make more definite decisions regarding gender reassignment, without the distress resulting from the development of puberty characteristics that are incongruent to their experienced gender identities. Dilemmas and concerns still exist concerning gonadotropin-releasing hormone analogs (GnRHa) for transgender adolescents. Despite this, there is now limited evidence that an approach that includes puberty suppression leads to favorable outcomes in young adulthood. This entry examines the early formation of the protocol of puberty suppression, including the criteria used to determine a patient's eligibility for such procedures. The entry then reviews some preliminary research evidence regarding the success of puberty suppression as well as some criticisms. The entry concludes by exploring the need for a multidisciplinary approach to puberty suppression as well as needs with regard to social transitioning.

Development of the Protocol

Since its introduction in the mid-1990s, puberty suppression has rapidly become an element of adolescent transgender care. Many clinics around the world have adopted its use, and it is now part of different clinical guidelines for treating transgender adolescents, like the "Standards of Care for the Health of Transsexual, Transgender and Gender Nonconforming People" of the World Professional Association for Transgender Health and the Endocrine Society's "Clinical Guidelines for Endocrine Treatment of Transsexual Person."

According to this approach, after careful psychological evaluation, suppression of puberty by means of GnRHa can be introduced. GnRHa were developed for treatment of central precocious puberty. Their use leads to complete suppression of the hypothalamic-pituitary gonadal axis, and the production of testosterone in natal boys and estrogen in natal girls is prevented. Suppression of puberty is meant to relieve the immediate stress accompanying puberty development in a direction transgender adolescents abhor. By avoiding the psychological stress, age-appropriate social and intellectual development should be enabled. Transgender adolescents can explore their desire for gender reassignment in a more reflective and less pressured manner without a preoccupation with biological puberty. In case an adolescent decides on medical gender reassignment, the arrest of further growth of secondary sex characteristics has lifelong advantages for the transgender adolescent's physical appearance. In case an adolescent does not want further gender reassignment, GnRHa treatment can be discontinued, and puberty of the natal sex restarts.

Eligibility Criteria

Eligibility criteria for puberty suppression are that the adolescent has demonstrated a long-lasting pattern of intense gender nonconformity or gender dysphoria that worsens with the onset of puberty. There should be no psychological, medical, or social problems that interfere with assessment or treatment, and the adolescent should have enough understanding of the effects of GnRHa to give informed consent. In some countries, there are age limits with regard to medical informed consent. It is also advised that there is parental or other social support. Physically, an adolescent should have some experience of their natal puberty (Tanner Stages 2–3). This has a diagnostic value because while in most prepubertal children gender dysphoria will desist, the likelihood that gender dysphoria will persist in pubertal adolescents is much higher.

Research Evidence

There is some research evidence of the success of puberty suppression in transgender care. One study showed that, compared with before-treatment functioning, transgender adolescents improved in their psychological and general functioning after a mean of 2 years' use of puberty suppression. Puberty suppression had no effect on gender dysphoria. Only after cross-sex hormones and gender affirming surgery was gender dysphoria resolved, a second study proved. This same sample of now young adults also showed that quality-of-life parameters were comparable with their same-age peers. Although these are promising results, it should be considered that they stem from only one clinic and constitute a highly selected sample of adolescents who were at baseline already functioning relatively well and growing up in a supportive environment.

Criticism

Despite its success, there is also criticism of puberty suppression. Some state that no medical intervention should be provided for minors with gender dysphoria, as young transgender adolescents may desist from their wish for gender reassignment during psychotherapy. Other potential risks of blocking pubertal development relate to the development of bone mass and growth, both typical events of hormonal puberty, and to brain development. Here again, there is now some evidence from follow-up studies that the benefits outweigh the risks, although more information and longer-term information is needed.

Multidisciplinary Approach

According to the guidelines, transgender adolescent care is preferably provided within a multidisciplinary specialized gender identity service. That way, mental health professionals and pediatric endocrinologists can collaboratively assess, educate, and decide about medical interventions. A supportive and open-minded attitude is most helpful when the mental health provider is assessing the gender dysphoria and eligibility for puberty suppression. Coexisting mental health concerns need to be assessed and treated. Autistic characteristics, which seem to occur more often in transgender adolescents than in the general population, can make this a challenging task. Transgender adolescents may also be vulnerable to experiencing social exclusion, leading to anxiety and depression, or may have families with difficulty accepting their gender dysphoria. They may profit from meeting with other transgender adolescents and their families; a supportive school environment is also of importance.

Social Transitioning

While on puberty suppression, most transgender adolescents decide to start living in the experienced gender role and change their name and pronoun. Some of them might have made this social gender transition at a younger age, although it should be considered that persistence rates of childhood gender dysphoria are relatively low and changing back to the natal gender role can be distressing. Social transitioning while on puberty suppression gives the adolescent the time to experiment in the experienced gender role before the more irreversible effects of prescribed estrogens or testosterone develop. In some cases, anxieties hold back an adolescent from making a social transition, and the time of puberty suppression is used to treat the psychological problems. Only when cross-hormones are started are there visible changes in physical appearance, and postponing social transitioning becomes more difficult. There are now countries where legal gender can be changed from age 16 years on and medical gender reassignment is not a necessary requirement.

Annelou L. C. de Vries

See also Adolescence and Gender: Overview; Gender Identity and Adolescence; Gender Identity and Childhood; Gender Nonconformity and Transgender Issues: Overview; Puberty; Transgender and Gender Nonconforming Adolescents

Further Readings

Cohen-Kettenis, P. T., Steensma, T. D., & de Vries, A. L. (2011). Treatment of adolescents with gender dysphoria in the Netherlands. *Child and Adolescent Psychiatric Clinics of North America, 20*(4), 689–700. doi:10.1016/j.chc.2011.08.001

Coleman, E., Bockting, W., Botzer, M., Cohen-Kettenis, P., DeCuypere, G., Feldman, J., . . . Zucker, K. (2012). Standards of care for the health of transsexual, transgender, and gender-nonconforming people, version 7. *International Journal of Transgenderism, 13*(4), 165–232. doi:10.1080/15532739.2011.700873

de Vries, A. L., McGuire, J. K., Steensma, T. D., Wagenaar, E. C., Doreleijers, T. A., & Cohen-Kettenis, P. T. (2014). Young adult psychological outcome after puberty suppression and gender reassignment. *Pediatrics, 134*(4), 696–704. doi:10.1542/peds.2013-2958

Hembree, W. C., Cohen-Kettenis, P., Delemarre-van de Waal, H. A., Gooren, L. J., Meyer, W. J., III, Spack, N. P., . . . Montori, V. M. (2009). Endocrine treatment of transsexual persons: An Endocrine Society clinical practice guideline. *Journal of Clinical Endocrinology and Metabolism, 94*(9), 3132–3154. doi:10.1210/jc.2009-0345

Steensma, T. D., McGuire, J. K., Kreukels, B. P., Beekman, A. J., & Cohen-Kettenis, P. T. (2013). Factors associated with desistence and persistence of childhood gender dysphoria: A quantitative follow-up study. *Journal of the American Academy of Child and Adolescent Psychiatry, 52*(6), 582–590. doi:10.1016/j.jaac.2013.03.016

Queer

The term *queer* is commonly used as an umbrella term for members of the lesbian, gay, bisexual, and transgender (LGBT) communities. Some individuals who do not identify closely with any of these terms but who also do not identify as heterosexual and cisgender choose the term *queer* as their identity descriptor. "Queer" is a nonspecific descriptor, which may refer to sexual orientation, gender identity, sexual practices, or some combination of these factors. In the common abbreviation *LGBTQ*, the *Q* typically stands for "queer" (although it previously referred to "questioning"). This entry discusses the history of the use of the term as well as related queer theory.

History of the Term

Queer originated as an adjective used to describe something odd or quaint. In the early 18th century, it began to take on a negative connotation. The term connoted otherness but not strictly in a sexual sense. Around the 1920s, the term *queer* began to be used in the United States and the United Kingdom as a derogatory term for homosexual. It was so widely used in this way that the U.S. Children's Bureau, among other organizations, used it in official publications. In its current usage, *queer* takes on a variety of meanings, some positive and some negative.

Queer as a Pejorative

Heterosexual identified individuals have used the term *queer* as a derogatory adjective to insult or threaten LGBT individuals or to insult other individuals who possess traits associated with LGBT identities (e.g., effeminate males). The term has also been used as a noun to describe individuals who are queer or perceived to be queer (e.g., a queer, queers). *Queer* has been used in popular culture as a pejorative, including in the childhood variant of the game tag known as "Smear the Queer" and a famous quote from the 1987 Stanley Kubrick film, *Full Metal Jacket* ("Only steers and queers come from Texas").

Reclaiming the Term *Queer*

Despite its use as a pejorative outside the LGBT community, within the LGBT community, *queer* has been seen as a more comprehensive alternative to the limiting *gay* and *lesbian* labels. The mainstream reclamation of the term *queer* came as a part of the Gay Pride movement, a cultural shift beginning in the 1980s and proceeding throughout the 1990s. The Gay Pride movement emphasized embracing one's identity and place in the LGBT community, rather than feeling shame and guilt. This movement challenged the status quo, and queer identified individuals resisted assimilation into the mainstream culture. In this context, the queer identity embraces concepts such as gender and sexual orientation fluidity, nontraditional forms of gender expression, and unconventional sexual and romantic relationships.

Queer Nation, an activist group formed in 1990 by members of the AIDS Coalition to Unleash Power, was one of the first groups to bring the newly reclaimed term to the attention of mainstream culture, both with their name and with the creation of the well-known chant "We're here; we're queer. Get used to it!" Queer Nation distributed a flier titled "Queers Read This" at the New York City Gay Pride Parade in the summer of 1990. The flier, featuring the group's manifesto, suggested that the use of the term *gay* was inappropriate and stated,

> When a lot of lesbians and gay men wake up in the morning we feel angry and disgusted, not gay. So we've chosen to call ourselves queer. Using "queer" is a way of reminding us how we are perceived by the rest of the world.

There has been a growing comfort with the term *queer* since the 1990s. In the 2000s, this is the preferred identity of many young LGBT individuals. Modern uses of the term *queer* as a positive identity marker include the popular 2000s television shows *Queer Eye for the Straight Guy* and *Queer as Folk*. The Queer Nation chant was also parodied in an episode of the sitcom *Arrested Development*.

However, there continues to be a subset of individuals who believe that the term *queer* cannot be separated from its roots in hate speech and should not be used to describe LGBT individuals. There is a fear that members of the out-group will not be familiar with the new connotation and therefore all uses of *queer* will be rendered derogatory. Furthermore, they argue that the term belongs to the heterosexuals and cannot be taken back; therefore, any use of the term by LGBT individuals serves to further reinforce the original pejorative, or as Audre Lorde (1983) said, "The master's tools will never dismantle the master's house" (p. 110). This ideological split tends to occur along generational lines, with older individuals—many of whom were victimized by this word in the past—tending to reject this reclamation.

Genderqueer

In recent years, many individuals have begun to identify as "genderqueer" or "gender queer," which is usually defined as an identity in which a person does not conform to societal gender role norms or does not identify as any gender. Synonyms of *genderqueer* include *gender nonconforming*, *agender*, *nonbinary*, *gender fluid*, or *third gender*. Similar to those who use *queer* to define their sexual orientation, many individuals may identify as genderqueer to symbolize that they are fluid with their gender, do not subscribe to rigid gender roles, or both.

Queer Theory

Queer has also taken on a different, but related, meaning in the fields of sociology, gender studies, and critical literary theory. In this context, the term denotes a subversion of heterosexual and cisgender norms. Feminist theorist Teresa de Lauretis is most often credited with coining the term *queer theory*. In 1991, she wrote that queer theory provided a possibility to "recast or reinvent the terms of our sexualities . . . construct another discursive horizon, another way of thinking the sexual" (p. iv). The field of queer theory developed out of women's and gender studies, predominantly in the most elite U.S. institutions of higher education. Queer theory has been heavily influenced by Judith Butler's work on gender performativity and fluidity, Eve Sedgwick's work on secrecy and disclosure, Andrew Parker's rereading of Karl Marx, Adrian Rich's broadening of the definition of lesbian sexuality, and Michel Foucault's history of homosexuality and sexuality in general, among other contributions. De Lauretis stated that the "queer" label denoted most consistently the refusal to acknowledge heterosexuality as the gold standard of sexuality against which all individuals should be measured; the questioning of the common conflation of lesbian, gay, and bisexual issues; and the acknowledgment of the intersection of racial, sexual, and gender performance.

In this usage, definitions of the term *queer* vary widely, and there is some debate as to who or what can be queer. In the narrowest sense, in queer theory, *queer* refers to the LGBT community as a whole and acts as a term indicating resistance to heteronormative and cisnormative societal structures and expectations. Individuals who may not identify as LGBT but who identify with queer practices, such as cross-dressing and nontraditional forms of sexual play or romantic relationships, may be considered queer in some contexts as well. In the broadest sense of the term, *queer* refers to a sort of limitless meta-identity that may incorporate a variety of marginalized identities. Queer theory aims not to replicate the same exclusionary identity politics that has characterized the mainstream; to this end, the boundaries of the term *queer* are fluid or nonexistent, such that no binary can be formed. As such, queer theorist Annamarie Jagose (1996) stated that "queer is less an identity than a *critique* of identity" (p. 131).

Queer theorists have deconstructed the prevailing belief in heterosexuality as a stable, naturally occurring norm from which LGBT individuals are deviant. Heterosexuality's frailty is revealed through interrogations of heterosexuality, rather than a focus exclusively on marginalized or pathologized identities. Through a queer lens, heterosexuality is seen as constantly defending itself against perceived attacks on its institutions (e.g., same-sex marriage, gay and transgender military service, gay Boy Scout leaders). This can be observed in the language used by those opposing same-sex marriage, who view themselves as acting in "defense of marriage." Furthermore, the binary division of heterosexuality and homosexuality is refuted, thus blurring the boundaries that heterosexuality, as an institution, works to maintain.

Advancements in queer theory in the 1990s coincided with and contributed to the increased use of the term *queer* in popular culture. Queer theorists differentiate the popular use of the term *queer* from their theoretical use of the term, although both loosely represent resistance to mainstream value systems that condemn certain identities and behaviors. However, queer theory has been criticized by some as being overly interested in the theoretical and intellectual, to the neglect of the real, lived experience of queer individuals. Although the rise of queer theory may have helped bring more public attention and awareness to queer issues, it has been argued that queer theorists, in their obsession with texts and signifiers, have done little to directly improve the quality of life of their subjects.

Lindsey S. Davis

See also Androgyny; Feminism: Overview; Gender Identity; Gender Nonconformity and Transgender Issues: Overview; Heteronormativity; Queerness; Sexual Identity; Sexual Orientation: Overview

Further Readings

Butler, J. (1993). *Bodies that matter: On the discursive limits of "sex."* New York, NY: Routledge.

de Lauretis, T. (1991). Queer theory: Lesbian and gay sexualities. *Differences: A Journal of Feminist Cultural Studies, 3*(2), ii–xviii.

Foucault, M. (1978). *The history of sexuality.* New York, NY: Vintage Books.

Halperin, D. (1995). *Saint Foucault: Towards a gay hagiography.* New York, NY: Oxford University Press.

Hirsch, M. (2000). *Queer theory and social change.* London, England: Routledge.

Jagose, A. (1996). *Queer theory: An introduction.* New York, NY: New York University Press.

Lorde, A. (1984). *Sister Outsider: Essays and speeches.* Berkeley, CA: Crossing Press.

Parker, A. (1991). Unthinking sex: Marx, Engels and the scene of writing. *Social Text, 9*(11), 28–45.

Rich, A. (1983). Compulsory heterosexuality and lesbian existence. In A. Snitow, C. Stansell, & S. Thompson (Eds.), *Powers of desire: The politics of sexuality* (pp. 177–205). New York, NY: Monthly Review Press.

Sedgwick, E. K. (1990). *The epistemology of the closet.* Berkeley: University of California Press.

QUEERNESS

Queerness is difficult to define because of the myriad ways in which the term has been used historically and contemporarily. Originally a word meaning "bizarre" or "strange," the term gained widespread use as a derogatory slur on LGBTQ people in the early 20th century. Today, it may refer to the ways in which certain people's gender expression, gender identity, or sexual orientation falls outside of what is considered the cisgender, heterosexual norm. Queerness, in this way, makes an attempt to decentralize mainstream discussions of what is considered normal, for example, traditional expressions of gender and sexual orientation. *Queer* is often used as an umbrella term for referring to LGBTQ people, and queerness refers to traits shared among people in the LGBTQ community. It is very important to note, however, that while the term *queer* has been reclaimed and is currently used in this way by some, many LGBTQ people in the early 21st century still regard *queer* as a derogatory term and do not use it to describe themselves.

This entry explores the social background behind the term *queer* and its effect within the LGBTQ community.

Romanticizing the Margins

In many ways, queerness is defined by what it is not. In much of the Western world, society adheres to a medically imposed gender binary based on visual genitalia at birth, as well as clearly defined expectations for romantic and sexual practices based on this designation. Being cisgender and heterosexual in this context is seen as the default or normal rather than as one among several options. As such, things falling outside this expectation are, inherently, queer. Cissexism and homonegativity have instilled a sense of shame and inherent queerness on identities that fall outside the cisgender and heterosexual norm. However, members of the LGBTQ community have made efforts to reclaim the word *queer* as a way of subverting the societal norm and, in effect, "romanticizing the margins" to which LGBTQ people have been relegated. Members of the LGBTQ community celebrate queerness as natural and beautiful and reject the idea that cisgender, heterosexual identities should be praised for being the norm. Queerness is made further complex when examining intersections of identity, for example, how race, ability, or size interact with cultural expectations of gender identity, gender expression, and sexual orientation.

Who Should Use the Terms *Queer* and *Queerness*?

It is important to recognize the impact that queer theory and queerness have had on the field of psychology; however, *queer* is not a universally reclaimed term. *Queer* still carries a negative meaning for many LGBTQ people, often for the same reasons that some LGBTQ people have chosen to reclaim it. Some may find that it romanticizes the margins to which they are relegated in a society that is cissexist and homonegative; however, the rhetoric highlighting the deviance of these individuals, particularly in the field of psychology, has been strong. As such, *queerness* as a term that highlights the ways in which LGBTQ identities are "separate" and "different" and fall outside the norm may not be empowering to LGBTQ individuals for whom being accepted as "normal" is important. Individuals who reject *queer* as a defining word may seek language that instead identifies LGBTQ identities as alternate and equally valid identities alongside cisgender and straight identities. In established terms like *queer theory*, it is considered appropriate to use the word *queer*. However, when attempting to refer to a larger LGBTQ group with an umbrella term, it is important to understand the audience to whom one is speaking, the degree to which one is seeking a truly inclusive umbrella term, and how that is applicable and important to the intended audience (e.g., In what circumstances is it important to refer to LGB and transgender people simultaneously, given the nonmutual exclusivity of these identities and the vastly different experiences entailed by each?).

Studying Queerness in Academia

Queerness in academia has mostly been studied in the context of queer theory. Queer theorists especially look at the ways in which queerness fails to match, meet, or exonerate the ideals set up by a cishetero, patriarchal society. In many ways, this approach to research dismantles the cissexist and heteronormative ideals that shape Western worldviews and societal expectations. *Queerness* thereby becomes an important word through which oppressive norms and transgressions can be explored and discussed. However, because of the charged history of the word as a slur against LGBTQ people, many object to the application of the term *queerness* to things that are not inherently about LGBTQ identities and experiences. For example, while an academic examination into the subversion of gender roles, such as expectations of chore division in cisgender, heterosexual couples, may "transgress" gender norms that dictate the typical or normalized responsibilities of men and women in a household, the degree to which this can be defined academically as queer is debatable. Some might argue that customs that subvert the expectations set up by a sexist, heteropatriarchical society are inherently queer. However, others might say that because of the historical usage of the term *queerness*, as well as the ways in which it has only just begun to be reclaimed by LGBTQ people, the term may not be applied to situations that do not involve LGBTQ people.

James C. Welch and Richard Q. Shin

See also Cissexism; Gender Expression; Gender Identity; Gender Nonconforming People; Heterosexism; Sexual Orientation: Overview

Further Readings

Bornstein, K. (1994). *Gender outlaws: On men, women, and the rest of us.* New York, NY: Routledge.

Butler, J. (1990). *Gender trouble: Feminism and the subversion of identity.* New York, NY: Routledge.

QUID PRO QUO

See Women's Issues: Overview; Workplace Sexual Harassment

Race and Gender

Race, or the phenotypic characteristics (e.g., skin color, hair texture, facial features, etc.) of human beings, and gender, the expression of their feminine and masculine characteristics, are two of the primary ways society organizes and structures the lives of people. Reciprocally, people largely organize their sense of themselves through the lenses of their race and gender and, as a result, form identities that are integrally linked to how they present to the wider world. Given the power of race and gender to affect the lived experiences, thinking, and behaviors of men, women, and transgender persons of multiple racial, ethnic, and class backgrounds, it is critical to understand the ways race and gender intersect to shape human psychology. In this entry, the concepts of race and gender are explored to inform the ways race and gender intersect to shape an individual's psychology. Examples of the external (i.e., the shared social and political meanings of race and gender) and internal (i.e., the processes by which individuals make meaning of their racial and gender identities) ways in which race and gender are understood to shape psychology are also presented.

Race as a Social Construct

Race is a central organizing idea that shapes much of human life across the world. Developed as a means to organize human beings in ways similar to the ways animals and plant life are categorized, phenotypic characteristics have been utilized to categorize the diversity expressed among human mammals. Currently, race is understood to be socially constructed because the value placed on racial groupings reflects a social and political rationale rather than distinct genetic differences. Historically, race has been conceptualized using three types of theories: (1) ethnicity, (2) class, and (3) nation.

Briefly, ethnicity-based theories of race suggest that racial differences are due to cultural variations. Following this logic, because cultural groups vary with regard to practices of living, such as religious or spiritual practices, food and cuisine, health and well-being practices, forms of relational and familial organization, and processes for managing death and dying, this cultural variation has been used to organize and categorize racial groups. Alternatively, class-based theories of race were developed to explain race or racial differences by focusing on the economic structures and processes that stratify the population into class statuses or levels. These theories use economic concepts such as the production, exchange, and consumption of commodities to explain the ways in which inequality manifests across racial groups. Finally, race has been conceptualized as based in the existence of a nation. Nation-based theories of race are born out of the idea of nation building, whereby the imperialist thrust by European government powers extended their reach beyond their borders, typically in countries or on land initially inhabited by indigenous persons of color.

An example is used to illustrate the three types of race theories and points to explanatory gaps. Persons of Indian cultural descent whose ancestors migrated to the Caribbean as indentured servants to the colonizing British, Dutch, and French share some cultural practices with the African-descent Caribbean persons whose ancestors were brought to the Caribbean during the 16th and 19th centuries as part of the trans-Atlantic slave movement. Culture sharing can be found in the cuisine, music, and spiritual practices of these groups, and thus the ethnicity-based theories have the potential to be explanatory. However, when the Siddis—an ethnic group of Bantu (African) descendants with African features who live in India and Pakistan—are considered, the ethnicity-based theories fall short. Brought to India to serve as indentured servants by Portuguese and Arab merchants, some Siddis identify as Sufi Muslims, Hindus, and Roman Catholic Christians. Though Siddis and Afro-Caribbeans are phenotypically similar and share culture with racially similar groups (Indian and Pakistani), their cultural experiences are not shared, and thus an ethnicity-based theory does not adequately explain their phenotypic similarities and cultural differences to define them as a racial group.

The Siddis and Afro-Caribbeans did share economic status (servant class), and for this reason, class-based theories could be explanative. How can their similar phenotypic characteristics and class status be explained? Ideas of a free market suggest that wealth is dependent on the exchange of goods and services based on the ability of producers to create a product that is desirable enough for people to choose to spend their capital (currency exchanged for labor) to purchase these goods and services. Accordingly, anyone can or should be able to be in the high or low economic classes (i.e., be a producer or a consumer) and accumulate wealth irrespective of their race or any other demographic characteristics. While this is logical, in the example of the African-descent Siddis and Afro-Caribbean persons, the fact is they were specifically chosen to function as servants and/or slaves (i.e., work on forced labor camps/plantations). In fact, scholars have unearthed race-based justifications (i.e., using phenotype characteristics as a rationale) that have been used to legitimize the exploitation and enslavement of particular groups, specifically those of African and Indian descent. For example, it was concluded that African-descent persons were especially suitable for physical labor because of their musculature and build, and Indian-descent persons had a natural inclination toward docility, which was deemed important for servants working in close proximity with Whites. It is important to note that, though considered legitimate during this time, the use of these characteristics along racial groupings as a classification and rationale for enslavement or servitude was racist. However, perhaps most obviously exemplifying the race-based rationale for placing African- and Indian-descent people in lower classes or castes (slave and servant) was the fact that their darker skin color identified them and made them visibly distinct from Whites, which could therefore reduce confusion and help maintain the social order.

Finally, nation-based theories of race are considered. As previously described regarding ethnicity and class-based theories, the nation-based explanation of race considers race, not geographic location, as indicative of a nation, such that the Dutch Antilles, the American or British Virgin Islands, or the French Antilles are extensions of their European governments and their power on foreign lands. In this vein, these satellite territories extended power from their racially White countries of origin and cultivated ideas of White supremacy. Moreover, because of the association of Whiteness with power, African- and Indian-descent persons were subordinate in these contexts.

Although they are historic, these theories of race continue to guide ideas about race in our society and inspire the development of contemporary perspectives by which to explore race. Notably, in 2014, Michael Omi and Howard Winant published the third edition of their seminal text *Racial Formation in the United States*, in which they continued to explore the concept of race as being created or formed. They articulated racial formation to occur in a variety of ways to facilitate critical understandings of "racial projects" that organize and characterize societal notions and practices relative to race. Racial projects take on varied forms, and some examples include laws and policies, ideas like a "postracial" society, colorblind ideologies, and even ideas such as the "New Jim Crow" proposed by Michelle Alexander.

Gender as a Social Construct

As with race, the meaning made of gender is based on social constructions that value male over female persons. Whether it relates to competition in sports, professionalism, or interpersonal relationships, people who exhibit conventional characteristics of the male gender, such as being independent/individualistic, strong, and bold, and utilizing direct verbal and/or brute force to resolve conflict, are deemed favorably. Whereas, whether sexually male or female, individuals exhibiting traditional feminine characteristics, like being relational, collaborative, and receptive, and acknowledging emotion and intuition as relevant forms of information to guide decision making, are considered less valuable.

The complexity of gender and the valuation of maleness and masculinity over femaleness and femininity can be exemplified in the societal and political responses to instances in which heterosexual and heteronormative notions of sexuality and gender are challenged. Gay men, lesbian women, bisexual men and women, and transgender women and men represent a challenge to traditional notions of maleness and femaleness because their gender and sexual identity and expression push against the boundary of individual actualization and the sociocultural prescriptions for gender and its expression. For example, a transgender woman, transitioning from male to female, is subjected to nonverbal and verbal discrimination, physical violence, and attack, as has been exemplified by the high rates of violence toward members of the transgender community. The violence is so prevalent that November 20 has been marked as the "Transgender Day of Remembrance," highlighting the fact that every 2 days, across the world, someone is killed as a result of not conforming to traditional gender role and expression expectations.

Since the lines of masculinity and femininity or maleness and femaleness are not finite, the permeability of the male/female dichotomy permits inquiry into essentialist notions of maleness and femaleness and has the potential to pose a threat for those privileged by systems of male supremacy. For instance, lesbian women who do not conform to stereotypical notions of what it means to be a non-feminine lesbian appear to challenge stereotypes of what it means to be a nonheterosexual woman. For instance, people may be more comfortable when a lesbian appears to fit a more stereotypical "butch" (i.e., traditionally male dress and behavioral patterns) ideal than when a lesbian identifies in a more "femme" way, with all the stereotypical activities and expression of conventional femaleness, while still preferring to have sexual relations with women. These expressions of gender and sexuality challenge ideas of maleness—particularly in identity (i.e., who gets to identify as a man) and behavior (i.e., whether performance, dress, and actions influence masculinity).

Race and gender intersect to shape the ways individuals are affected by their experiences in the world and the ways they think about themselves. Two areas in which these dynamics become apparent are in (1) the interaction individuals have with others (external), such as ethnoviolent acts, and (2) those they experience within themselves (internal), such as processes of identity development.

Ethnoviolence is defined as acts of verbal or physical attack on individuals due to their race and/or gender. Such attacks are an example of one's external interactions with others that are shaped by their racial and gender identities. This type of violence occurs when an individual has been targeted because of their racial and/or gender group membership. Unfortunately, there are numerous recent developments that can serve as examples. For instance, in the first few weeks of 2015, eight trans women of color were killed. The acts of violence demonstrated against them exemplify how the intersection of gender and race negatively affects people's lives. As epitomized in ethnoviolent acts toward them, transgender women of color are targeted because their gender does not conform to conventional notions of the cisgender male/female binary, while the color of their skin (i.e., being non-White) leads to systemic and interpersonal racism, placing them at higher risk for assault and/or murder.

While ethnoviolence may be a more blatant example, it expressly articulates the extremity to which White and male supremacy can be taken to affect the mental and physical well-being of people marginalized due to their race and/or gender, and as such it is a good example of external interactions or those between people. Alternatively, internal interactions are those that address the way individuals feel about themselves as a consequence of their racial and/or gender identities. Racial and gender identity scholars have developed models to conceptualize the ways a person comes to acknowledge and value their racial and gendered selves. Stage and status models of racial and gender identity development articulate the process by which an individual develops through several identity statuses, moving from being unaware of the role of race and/or gender in their lives to becoming a healthy and informed racial and/or gendered person. Janet Helms's work on the people of color model, White racial identity model, and womanist identity models; Nancy Downing and Kristin Roush's feminist identity model; and Aaron Devor's transgender identity model are examples of these stage and status models. What is notable about these models is that while they are descriptive of a progressive developmental process, they also propose that healthy development ends in one's sense of ownership and empowerment to reclaim the self from marginalizing and oppressive ideologies.

Models for racial and gender identity have also taken non–stage or status forms. Sandra Bem's widely publicized work on gender has gone uncontested as the focus continues to center on whether a person is high or low masculine or feminine, leading to four potential classifications: (1) undifferentiated, (2) androgynous, (3) masculine, or (4) feminine. Additionally, the Multidimensionality Model of Racial Identity articulated four dimensions of race: (1) salience, (2) centrality, (3) ideology, and (4) regard for one's race and racial group membership. Each dimension was identified and conceived as contributing to one's sense of racial identity.

Finally, researchers have begun to examine how intersectional identities affect psychological processes and outcomes, particularly those of historically marginalized groups (e.g., women of color, LGBTQ people of color) who experience identity in multiple ways. Some individuals possess identities with group values that often conflict with those of others (e.g., women of color might be taught that a feminist identity suggests that women should be independent and strong, while their immigrant ethnic communities teach them to be submissive to men). On the contrary, individuals with both privileged and historically oppressed identities may navigate other unique experiences and identities; for instance, White women may experience sexism, while not recognizing their racial privilege.

Wendi S. Williams

See also Femininity; Gay Men and Gender Roles; Gender Conformity; Gender Nonconforming Behaviors; Gender Role Socialization; Gender Socialization in Men; Gender Socialization in Women; Gender-Based Violence; Transgender and Gender Nonconforming Identity Development

Further Readings

Bailey, T. K., Williams, W. S., & Favors, B. (2014). African Americans. In E. J. R. David (Ed.), *Internalized oppression: The psychology of marginalized groups* (pp. 138–162). New York, NY: Springer.

Bem, S. L. (1993). *The lenses of gender: Transforming the debate on sexual inequality.* New Haven, CT: Yale University Press.

Ehrlich, H. J. (2009). *Hate crimes and ethnoviolence: The history, current affairs, and future of discrimination in America.* New York, NY: Westview Press.

Helms, J. (2007). *A race is a good think to have* (2nd ed.). Alexandria, VA: Microtraining Associates.

Lev, A. I. (2004). *Transgender emergence: Therapeutic guidelines for working with gender variant people and their families.* New York, NY: Routledge.

Miller, J. B. (1987). *Toward a new psychology of women.* Boston, MA: Beacon Press.

Moradi, B. (2005). Advancing womanist identity development. *The Counseling Psychologist, 33,* 225–253.

Omi, M., & Winant, H. (2015). *Racial formation in the United States.* New York, NY: Routledge.

Racial Discrimination, Gender-Based

Theoretical and empirical research on racism in the field of psychology has explored both the manifestations of racism in U.S. society and the psychological influence of racism on people of color (i.e., African American, Asian American, Latina/o, and Native American individuals). This entry provides a brief overview of some of the key terms in the field of psychology regarding racial discrimination, including *racism, racism-related stress*, and *racial microaggressions*. Then, it highlights the research on the psychological influence of racism on people of color, particularly the negative effects of stress associated with racism, with a specific focus on gendered racism.

Overview of Racial Discrimination

Psychologist James Jones has defined racism as prejudice and ethnocentrism based on race, which is reinforced by power against the socially designated inferior racial group and supported by individuals, institutions, and cultural mores. Jones conceptualized a multidimensional model of racism that includes three different types of racism: (1) individual, (2) institutional, and (3) cultural. Individual racism is the experience of racism on a personal level, such as being the target of a racial slur or a hate crime. This is also usually described as overt and conscious acts of racism. Institutional racism refers to the political, social, and institutional policies that discriminate against people of color and perpetuate inequality. Cultural racism refers to the practice of ethnocentrism, whereby the cultural values and practices of the dominant racial group are considered to be superior and those of racial minorities are assumed to be inferior. This form of racism is often invisible to people in the dominant group. In addition, researchers have defined internalized racism as holding negative racist stereotypes and beliefs that are accepted by people of color.

Racism can be perpetuated on an overt and conscious level in addition to a subtle and unconscious level. Previous research on racism focused on overt forms of discrimination. However, research on contemporary forms of racism has increased in the psychology literature in the past 15 years. Although some overt acts of discrimination have decreased, subtle and covert discrimination continues to persist. Some researchers have conceptualized racism as a daily life stressor known as racism-related stress. Research indicates that subtle and everyday forms of oppression serve as daily stressors in the lives of people of color. More recently, Derald Wing Sue has developed a framework to understand microaggressions, which are subtle forms of racial discrimination that take place in everyday interactions and convey negative racial insults toward people of color.

Effects of Racial Discrimination

A growing body of empirical research in psychology has found that both overt and subtle forms of racial discrimination have a negative effect on the psychological and physical health of people of color. Specifically, several systematic literature reviews and meta-analyses have found that racism and discrimination have a negative impact on a range of mental health outcomes including psychological distress, depression, anxiety, and well-being. In addition, the experience of perceived racism has been associated with a number of physical health issues, such as self-reported poor health, hypertension, increased risk for high blood pressure, substance use, and several other health issues.

There is a large body of research that has documented the negative effects of racial discrimination for people of color and gender discrimination for women across race and ethnicity. In addition, psychology researchers have found that individuals experience unique stressors based on the intersections of their race and gender. Social science researchers have offered a number of potential theories on the gendered nature of racial discrimination.

Approaches to Studying Intersections of Racial Discrimination and Gender

Interdisciplinary literature on the intersections of race and gender has been in existence for decades. A majority of the early research on the intersections of racial discrimination based on gender has focused on Black women's experiences with racism and sexism, or *gendered racism*, a term coined by sociologist Philomena Essed, which refers to the intersection of racism and sexism. However, research on gendered racism has extended to exploring the experiences of women of color from various racial/ethnic backgrounds. In addition, recent work has begun to explore gendered forms of racism that men of color experience. Researchers argue that women of color experience gendered and classed forms of racism that are based on the stereotypes and assumptions about womanhood that exist in contrast to White womanhood. For example, Black women have been stereotyped as strong, hardworking, domineering, and sexually promiscuous. Asian women have been stereotyped as weak, subservient, and sexually available. These stereotypes exist to marginalize and objectify women of color based on gender role expectations.

In the field of psychology, there are five ways in which researchers have traditionally explored intersections of gender and race as they relate to experiences of discrimination: (1) single axis, (2) comparative, (3) additive, (4) interactional, and (5) intersectional. Although these five approaches have been grounded in the research literature on race and gender, the approaches can intersect with other social identities, such as social class, sexual orientation, religion, and disability.

Single-Axis Approach

Much of the research on racial discrimination has utilized a single-axis approach, which assumes that racial discrimination is the primary form of oppression that affects the lives of people of color. Researchers typically explore the overall experiences of racial discrimination by people of color, without regard for the differential experiences based on gender or other social identity groups. Researchers also might control for gender or explore gender as a covariate. This approach tends to highlight the experiences of dominant members within a subordinate group, such as the experiences of men of color over women of color, because the single-axis approach minimizes within-group variability, which could lead to the reinforcement of a hierarchy of oppressions.

Comparative Approach

The second approach is the comparative approach. This approach explores racial discrimination based on gender. However, in this approach, gender is used as a categorical variable, and the objective is to compare the differences between men and women in their experiences of racial discrimination. Researchers have found differential experiences of racial discrimination based on gender. Specifically, some studies have found that men of color report a greater frequency of racial discrimination. However, other studies have found mixed results. Thus, it is difficult to explore meaningful differences when gender is treated as a categorical variable, because it oversimplifies the complex intersections between gender and race.

In addition, exploring racial discrimination by gender using a comparative approach is troublesome because the context in which racial discrimination is experienced is not considered. This assumes universality of racial experiences across genders, but because racial perceptions are often gendered, men and women of different races have different racial experiences in the context in which they live day to day. This shapes the kind of discrimination individuals may experience. For example, some men of color are stereotyped and assumed to be criminals, which affects the types of encounters they have in their everyday lives. In general, comparative research does not explain why the experiences of men and women of racial discrimination may differ, such as experiences of racism, sexism and patriarchy, male privilege, and gender role socialization.

Additive Approach

The third approach is the additive approach, which has been influenced by the concept of "double jeopardy." Originally articulated by Frances M. Beal to refer to the ways both racism and sexism affect the lived experiences of Black women, it was later expanded to refer to the experiences of women of color more broadly. This approach seeks to explore the impact of race and gender on individuals' experiences of discrimination separately and then seeks to explore the additive effects of these experiences. Thus, the purpose of this approach is to see which aspect of discrimination (race or gender) uniquely accounts for aspects of the outcome variable of interest. For example, some studies have explored the impact of both racial and gender discrimination on psychological distress for women of color. These studies have found that both racial and gender discrimination separately significantly predict psychological distress. This approach is helpful in better understanding the additive effects of racial and gender discrimination on the experiences of women of color, but it does not explore the interactive effects of both racial and gender discrimination.

Interactional Approach

The fourth approach to studying racial discrimination based on gender is an interactional approach that focuses on examining how gender and race interact to effect racial discrimination. The interactional approach proposes that sexism and racism interact with each other and cause unique experiences for women and men of color. The interactional approach is often used in conjunction with the additive approach. Many interactional research studies are also critiqued for their tendency to examine gender and race separately, because they lead to misleading findings. For example, when women are asked to choose whether race or gender affects their psychological distress more, researchers find that only sexism is reported to contribute to psychological distress and not racism. Though the interactional approach is more complex than the additive approach, it still tends to separate race from gender.

Intersectional Approach

The fifth approach to explore the intersection of racism and sexism is the intersectional approach, which argues that the optimal way to explore racism and sexism is to assess the intersectional and joint experiences of race and gender oppression. Initially conceptualized from Black feminist theory, intersectionality theory was developed with a focus on exploring the experiences of individuals with multiple marginalized identities and, hence, intersecting forms of oppression.

In the field of psychology, there has been an increase in using the intersectional approach to study race and gender discrimination. For example, some researchers have explored the psychological impact of gendered racism on the experiences of women of color. In quantitative research, researchers have found that there is a significant association between the frequency of gendered racism and psychological distress. In addition, coping strategies have been found to buffer against the negative effects of these experiences. However, findings have been mixed in uncovering the specific types of coping strategies that are most beneficial in mitigating the effects of gendered racism. More research is needed to further explore this aspect. Specifically, the increase in quantitative measures to assess gendered racism experienced by individuals based on the intersections of their race and gender is needed to continue to advance research in this area.

More recently, scholars have applied the construct of gendered racism to study the intersection of racial discrimination and gender experiences of men of color. Thus, this body of research focuses on the gendered forms of racism experienced by men of color, which can vary based on the stereotypes that exist about one's racial group. For example, many Blacks and Latinos experience stereotypes and assumptions of criminality and second-class citizenship, among others. In addition, psychology researchers have also begun studying the impact of gender roles and issues of masculinity in the exploration of gendered racial discrimination among men of color.

Research on the psychological impact of racial discrimination has been in existence for decades. More recently, there has been an increase in research on the differential racial discrimination experiences of individuals based on gender. This body of work has found that the impact of racial discrimination on individuals varies based on intersections with gender, ethnicity, and racial group. More research is needed that explores the intersections of perceived racism and gender to uncover the psychological impact of interlocking forms of oppression on marginalized groups.

Jioni A. Lewis, Marlene Williams, and Cecile A. Gadson

See also Intersectional Theories; Women of Color and Discrimination

Further Readings

Beal, F. (1970). Double jeopardy: To be Black and female. In T. Cade (Ed.), *The Black woman: An anthology* (pp. 90–100). New York, NY: Signet.

Bowleg, L. (2008). When Black + lesbian + woman ≠ Black lesbian woman: The methodological challenges of qualitative and quantitative intersectionality research. *Sex Roles, 59*(5/6), 312–325. doi:10.1007/s11199-008-9400-z

Essed, P. (1991). *Understanding everyday racism: An interdisciplinary theory.* Thousand Oaks, CA: Sage.

Jones, J. M. (1997). *Prejudice and racism* (2nd ed.). New York, NY: McGraw-Hill.

Lewis, J. A., & Neville, H. A. (2015). Construction and initial validation of the gendered racial microaggressions scale for Black women. *Journal of Counseling Psychology, 62*(2), 289–302. doi:10.1037/cou0000062

Pascoe, E. A., & Smart Richman, L. (2009). Perceived discrimination and health: A meta-analytic review. *Psychological Bulletin, 135*(4), 531–554. doi:10.1037/a0016059

Sue, D. W. (2010). *Microaggressions in everyday life: Race, gender, and sexual orientation.* Hoboken, NJ: Wiley.

Racial Discrimination, Sexual Orientation–Based

Racial and ethnic minority (REM) lesbian, gay, bisexual, transgender, and queer (LGBTQ) individuals represent a population with multiple marginalized statuses. Living at the intersection of two oppressed identities creates both unique and nuanced social locations for REM LGBTQ people. REM LGBTQ individuals often report disenfranchisement from their racial/ethnic communities due to their sexual orientation and gender identities, and similar exclusion from the LGBTQ community related to their REM identities. This entry presents theoretical frameworks for understanding the racism experiences of REM LGBTQ people in the LGBTQ community. In addition, a brief review of research pertaining to the unique racist discrimination experiences of REM LGBTQ individuals and associated mental and physical health consequences is provided. The entry concludes with a discussion of forms of resilience observed within this group and needed research.

Minority Stress and Intersectionality Theory

Ilan Meyer proposed minority stress theory (MST) to provide a framework for understanding the experiences of LGB individuals. MST postulates that people with oppressed identities, like REM LGBTQ individuals, experience distinctive stress and adverse life events related to their marginalized status or statuses, which can negatively affect mental and physical health outcomes. These stressors exist above and beyond general stressors, are persistent and stable, and are most often outside the control of the individual. Thus, racial/ethnic LGBTQ people are argued to exist in a racist, heterosexist, and transphobic societal context in which external (e.g., heterosexism) and internalized (e.g., internalized racism) stress processes are constantly experienced.

Intersectionality theory also presents a useful framework for understanding multiple marginalized identities. Intersectionality theory originally emerged from the work of Black feminist scholars. Intersectionality theory has been utilized to inform our understanding of how oppression operates in people with multiple marginalized identities. The additive approach argues that the effect of discrimination associated with each marginalized or minority identity has a cumulative impact. Terms such as *double jeopardy* or *triple jeopardy* capture this concept. For instance, a Native American bisexual woman would be posited to be the target of racism, heterosexism, and sexism based on her oppressed ethnic, sexual orientation, and gender identities. It is important to note that this list is not exhaustive and that other identities, such as social class and ability status, can also be salient. Alternatively, other scholars contend that a person's individual social identities, as well as their associated discrimination experiences, are not divisible into distinct identity units. This approach, termed the *intersectionality approach*, maintains that a person's experience is more than the sum of its parts. Importantly, both approaches to examining the experiences of REM LGBTQ people have been supported.

Racism Experiences of REM LGBTQ People

In the context of both MST and intersectionality theory, it becomes clear that REM LGBTQ people can be the target of multiple forms of discrimination due to their multiple minority identities. For instance, research has found that REM LGBTQ people report experiencing more heterosexist discrimination than White LGBTQ individuals. One explanation offered for this finding is that REM LGBTQ people experience heterosexism both outside and within their racial/ethnic communities. It is also possible that studies that assess for only one type of discrimination (e.g., heterosexism) also access forms of discrimination that are inclusive of not only the target identity of investigation (e.g., sexual orientation identity, gender identity) but the intersecting identities as well. Put simply, an REM LGBTQ person responding to a survey about discrimination in housing based on sexual orientation may report experiences related to their sexual orientation identity as well as their identity as an REM LGBTQ person. Indeed, prior studies have found that individuals with multiple marginalized identities are not always able to discern which of their identities or combination of identities was the focus of discrimination.

However, with regard to racism, emerging research has investigated the unique discrimination experiences of REM LGBTQ people. Racism serves to denigrate and subordinate REM people through ideologies, prejudicial attitudes, and discriminatory actions that perpetuate and justify unequal access to resources, privileges, and fair treatment. Racial discrimination can be overt or covert. More recently, covert or subtler forms of everyday racism have been increasingly referred to as *racial microaggressions* (e.g., being followed in a department store). Racism may also occur at both structural (e.g., racially segregated neighborhoods) and individual (e.g., being called a racist name, physical assault) levels.

REM LGBTQ individuals can be the targets of racism both within and outside the LGBTQ community. However, some scholars argue that the racism that LGBTQ people experience from others in the LGBTQ community can be particularly wounding because a core aspect of the self (i.e., racial or ethnic identity) is being maligned by individuals from whom an REM LGBTQ person might anticipate (or hope for) support and affirmation. In some instances, this is referred to as *horizontal oppression*. Disturbingly, a majority of REM LGBTQ people report having experienced some form of racism from the LGBTQ community, and certain commonalities in racist experiences within the LGBTQ community have been reported by REM LGBTQ people across research studies. For instance, REM LGBTQ people often report being called racist names, feeling like the "token" REM person in social groups and organizations, and having to educate White LGBTQ people about race and ethnicity issues. REM LGBTQ individuals also discuss that White LGBTQ individuals may take a color-blind approach to their race/ethnicity. Although this could be perceived to be an indicator of acceptance on the surface, this approach frequently serves to similarly negate the cultural experience of REM LGBTQ people. REM LGBTQ individuals also discuss being fetishized or objectified by others in the LGBTQ community based on their race and/or ethnicity. For instance, Asian/Asian American LGBTQ men report being exoticized and perceived as hypersexual or sexually submissive. Conversely, REM LGBTQ individuals also report being rejected as potential dating or sexual partners due to their race and/or ethnicity. All of these experiences can result in feelings of otherness and lack of acceptance. Importantly, experiences of racism also have negative implications for the mental and physical health of REM LGBTQ people.

Mental and Physical Health Consequences

Racial discrimination has been associated with greater overall psychological distress, anxiety, depression, and suicidality, and lower self-esteem for REM LGBTQ people. With regard to physical health, racism has been found to be positively related to high-risk sexual behavior among REM LGBTQ people, and some REM LGBTQ individuals report a higher likelihood of substance use compared with their heterosexual REM and White LGBTQ counterparts. Furthermore, REM LGBTQ people report that they believe that racism in the LGBTQ community has significantly interfered with their ability to live full and satisfying lives. Beyond these external forms of discrimination, and consistent with MST, the internalization of racism has also been found to be related to negative mental health outcomes (e.g., distress). Consequently, REM LGBTQ people's mental health is negatively affected not only by the racist incidents themselves but also by the internalization of the devaluing messages about REM LGBTQ people that are central to racism.

Resiliency Factors

Given the evidence that the majority of REM LGBTQ people experience racism in the LGBTQ community, and that these experiences have negative implications for the mental and physical health of this group, scholars have attempted to identify resiliency factors and coping strategies that may ameliorate the effects of racism in this population. In addition, it is important not to overly pathologize REM LGBTQ people and to appropriately highlight observed strengths. For instance, researchers have discussed how REM LGBTQ people may utilize the skills that they have acquired to address one form of discrimination (e.g., heterosexism) to cope with another form (e.g., racism). REM LGBTQ people may also utilize role-flexing strategies, whereby individuals orient themselves to a more valued identity in a particular milieu. With role flexing, REM LGBTQ people may avoid direct stigmatization by reorienting themselves to an identity (race/ethnicity or sexual orientation) that will be more valued and supported in a given environment. Indeed, REM people are believed to cultivate bicultural competencies that allow them to operate in both minority and majority contexts. Other strategies that have been explored with REM LGBTQ individuals include participation in collective action/activism (e.g., reading literature relevant to one's identities, mentoring), seeking social support, developing spirituality, and directly challenging the discrimination.

Future Considerations

Although the psychological research summarized in this entry focused on the experiences of REM LGBTQ people, it is critical to highlight that available research with this group continues to be sparse. Most research with LGBTQ populations is focused on the experiences of White LG people. Furthermore, what little research with REM LGBTQ people that does exist tends to examine the experiences of African American or Latino men. Thus, research with other REM GBQ men (e.g., Asian/Asian American) and REM LBQ women and transgender people of any racial/ethnic minority identity is sorely needed. Likewise, studies with REM LGBTQ samples tend to be more narrowly focused on disease, symptomatology, and risky sexual behaviors (e.g., HIV/AIDS, substance use). Although these studies may address important health concerns, they may also reflect a bias about the subject matter that is most germane to this population. Clearly, more studies are needed that investigate other health-related outcomes and the well-being of REM LGBTQ individuals. In sum, REM LGBTQ people represent a diverse and vibrant community. More research is needed that captures the full breadth and scope of this population and their lived experiences.

Cirleen DeBlaere and Franco Dispenza

See also Dual Minority Status; Exoticization of LGBTQ People of Color; Hate Crimes Toward LGBTQ People; Heterosexism; Homophobia; Intersectional Identities; Intersectional Theories; LGBTQ People of Color and Discrimination

Further Readings

Balsam, K. F., Molina, Y., Beadnell, B., Simoni, J., & Walters, K. (2011). Measuring multiple minority stress: The LGBT People of Color Microaggressions Scale. *Cultural Diversity and Ethnic Minority Psychology, 17,* 163–174. doi:10.1037/a0023244

Cole, E. R. (2009). Intersectionality and research in psychology. *American Psychologist, 64,* 170–180. doi:10.1037/a0014564

DeBlaere, C., Brewster, M. E., Bertsch, K. N., DeCarlo, A. L., Kegel, K. A., & Presseau, C. (2014). The protective power of collective action for sexual minority women of color: An investigation of multiple discrimination experiences and psychological distress. *Psychology of Women Quarterly, 38,* 20–32. doi:10.1177/0361684313493252

Fukuyama, M. A., & Ferguson, A. D. (2000). Lesbian, gay, and bisexual people of color: Understanding cultural complexity and managing multiple oppressions. In R. M. Perez, K. A. DeBord, & K. J. Bieschke (Eds.), *Handbook of counseling and psychotherapy with lesbian, gay, and bisexual clients* (pp. 81–105). Washington, DC: American Psychological Association.

Harper, G. W., Jernewell, N., & Zea, M. C. (2004). Giving voice to emerging science and theory for lesbian, gay, and bisexual people of color. *Cultural Diversity and Ethnic Minority Psychology, 10,* 187–199. doi:10.1037/1099-9809.10.3.187

Huang, Y. P., Brewster, M. E., Moradi, B., Goodman, M., Wiseman, M., & Martin, A. (2009). Content analysis of literature about LGB people of color: 1998–2007. *The Counseling Psychologist, 38,* 363–396. doi:10.1177/0011000009335255

Meyer, I. H. (2003). Prejudice, social stress, and mental health in lesbian, gay, and bisexual populations: Conceptual issues and research evidence. *Psychological Bulletin, 129,* 674–697. doi:10.1037/0033-2909.129.5.674

Singh, A. A., & McKleroy, V. S. (2011). "Just getting out of bed is a revolutionary act": The resilience of transgender people of color who have survived traumatic life events. *Traumatology, 17,* 34–44. doi:10.1177/1534765610369261

RAPE

A rape occurs when the statute of the state where a sexual act takes place defines that act as rape. How academicians define rape may be very different from a particular state's legal definition. A general definition of rape would be nonconsensual contact or penetration of a person's mouth, vagina, or anus by another's body part (e.g., finger, hand, penis) or an object (e.g., bottle, weapon). Rape also occurs when a person is made to contact or penetrate another person. Similarly, what constitutes consent can also vary based on statute. In general, consent exists when a person both knowingly and willingly participates in sexual activity. It requires a person be aware that the decision is being made, understand the potential consequences of the decision, and have the ability to refuse. There can be no coercion (e.g., threats, verbal intimidation), trickery (e.g., by the use of drugs or alcohol), or force (e.g., physical force). Importantly, giving consent to one sexual act does not mean giving consent to all sexual acts. Consent needs to be continuously given as a sex act evolves. For example, a person may consent to one type of penetration (e.g., oral) and withdraw consent for further sexual acts.

Estimates of how prevalent rape is depends on how it is defined. For most of American history, state statutes on rape have been derived from the English common law definition, which was based on certain assumptions of what a "real" rape looked like. This entry begins by reviewing the statistics on rape, the common law definition of rape, and "real" rape myths. It then explores how legal definitions have changed over time as a result of social movements. Finally, there is a short discussion of the current social climate.

Incidence and Prevalence

There are two main issues with estimating the incidence and prevalence of rape: (1) underreporting to the police and (2) unknown victims. First, official statistics, such as those from the Federal Bureau of Investigation's Uniform Crime Reporting (UCR) program, rely on reports to the police. Historically, the UCR's definition of rape is similar to the common law definition (the definition was updated in 2013). The UCR estimated 83,425 incidents in the United States during 2011, which is a prevalence rate of 52.7 rapes per 100,000 female inhabitants. This estimate underrepresents the number of rapes because it restricts rape to women victims only and because the majority of rapes are never reported. For example, it is estimated that less than 5% of women in college report their victimization to the police.

The solution to this issue is to use self-report data (i.e., people are asked about their victimization experience directly). As part of the Bureau of Justice Statistics, the National Crime Victimization Survey (NCVS) surveys approximately 90,000 households about the frequency, characteristics, and consequences of various victimizations (e.g., robbery, burglary, rape). Unlike the UCR, the NCVS defines rape in a way that includes men and also estimates the number of attempted rapes (called sexual assaults). In 2013, the NCVS found 300,170 incidents of rape and sexual assault, which is a rate of 1.1 per 1,000 people aged 12 years and older.

Importantly, both the UCR and NCVS indicate a decrease in the incidence and prevalence of rape in recent years. The UCR reports a 12.4% decrease between 2002 and 2011. The NCVS estimated that female rape declined by 58%, from 5.0 victims per 1,000 females aged 12 years or older in 1995 to 2.1 per 1,000 in 2010.

The NCVS also underestimates the number of rapes because of the second issue with collecting data about rape—what Mary P. Koss referred to as the "hidden rape victim." Hidden victims include both the people who do not report to the police and the many individuals who do not understand that they have been victimized. To capture data on these individuals, Koss and colleagues created the Sexual Experiences Survey. This instrument asks a series of behaviorally specific questions to determine if individuals have experienced unwanted sexual contact (e.g., kissing), sexual coercion (e.g., pressured to have sexual intercourse), attempted rape (e.g., attempt to forcibly have unwanted sexual intercourse), or completed rape (e.g., forced to have unwanted sexual intercourse). Her 1987 national study of college women found that almost half of them (46.3%) had had some form of sexual victimization, 23.2% had had unwanted sexual contact, 11.5% had experienced sexual coercion, 10.1% had experienced an attempted rape, and 6.5% had been raped within the past year alone.

The Centers for Disease Control and Prevention adapted this behaviorally specific model in the National Intimate Partner and Sexual Violence Survey (NISVS). This is a national random-digit telephone survey of adults aged 18 years and older. It asks about any unwanted sexual experiences (e.g., being flashed, being groped). It also includes all three components of consent (i.e., coercion, trickery, and being physically forced), includes different forms of penetration (e.g., oral, with a body part, with an object), and allows for an understanding of rape where the victim can be penetrated or be forced to penetrate another individual. In 2011, 19.3% of women and 1.7% of men reported being raped during their lifetime. A larger number, 43.9% of women and 23.4% of men, experienced other forms of unwanted sexual contact. With the most inclusive definition of rape and the behavior self-report measure, it is this estimate that is frequently used by public policy initiatives such as the call to action put out by the White House Council on Women and Girls in 2014.

Statistics show that some individuals are more vulnerable than others. The risk of first rape is highest for both men and women prior to the age of 18 years. Men who are raped are more likely to be raped when they are 12 years old or younger. Women are more likely to be victimized than men and are at highest risk when they are unmarried, live in urban areas, have a low income, and are unemployed. People of color are more likely to be raped than Whites, with American Indian/Alaskan Natives having the highest risk of victimization. More than a third of women who were raped as a child are revictimized in adulthood.

Alcohol is also frequently involved in the occurrence of rape. The Centers for Disease Control and Prevention's National Violence Against Women Survey found that approximately 20% of women and 38% of men were using alcohol when they were victimized. Alcohol has been found to be a risk factor for sexual assault among college students, with approximately half of all rapes involving the victim and/or the perpetrator knowingly or unknowingly consuming alcohol prior to the assault.

Common Law Definition

From 1642 to the mid-20th century, most American statutes followed the English common law definition of rape, which was "illicit carnal knowledge of a female by force and against her will." This limited rape in the legal statutes to penile penetration of the vagina committed by a man on a woman. Notably, rape could not occur within a marriage. In application, the key to conviction was clear indication that the victim did not give consent. Proof of nonconsensual sex included indication that the woman resisted (usually documented by physical injury to the victim), that she cried out during the attack, that she immediately filed a report with the police, and that she had corroborating testimony from a witness. With a few exceptions, most statutes would reflect this definition until the social movements in the 1970s.

"Real" Rape Myth

The common law understanding of rape created an idea of what a "real" rape victim and a "real" rape would look like. Feminists argue that the "real" rape myth derives from two interrelated assumptions about women: (1) that they are sexually promiscuous and (2) that women would lie about their desire to have sex in order to appear virtuous or to punish a man. Because of the need to show that sex was nonconsensual for rape to have occurred, women were under a heavy burden to prove that they had not wanted sex and were not just lying about it later.

As such, a woman's character was central to her claim of rape. The belief was that a "real" rape victim (someone who was actually raped, not just lying about it later) needs to be sexually conservative (i.e., either a virgin or a virgin until marriage). Her dress and behavior were also considered indications of her underlying desire to have sex (e.g., dressing provocatively, being out late at night, and flirting all were indicators that she consented).

Characteristics of the rapist were also important. The perpetrator needed to be someone whom the victim would not be seen as desiring, making the social status of the man relevant. Because of a woman's promiscuous nature, rape by someone she knew was also suspect. This results in two powerful myths of a "real" rapist—a non-White male who is a stranger.

Finally, the victim's behavior during and after the rape itself was called into question. To prove that she did not actually want sex and that she was not now lying about it, she was required to resist and show evidence of resistance. In the absence of this, there needed to be an overt explanation for why she could not resist, such as the presence of a weapon. She was also expected to immediately report the attack to the police.

These "real" rape myths are problematic because the majority of rapes do not reflect them. According to the NCVS, from 2005 to 2010, 78% of rapes were perpetrated by a family member, friend, or acquaintance. Only 58% of female survivors had any kind of physical injury. Only 11% of attackers had a weapon. A common response to rape is the experience of tonic immobility, which is the inability to move. The UCR indicates that the group arrested most for rape are White males between 18 and 30 years. Because most rapes actually do not reflect these stereotypes, rape victims are often not believed by courts, the police, and people in general, resulting in few rapists being adjudicated.

Rape Law Reform

Early reform movements centered on attempts to challenge rape statutes derived from the common law definition of rape that reinforced "real" rape myth assumptions. This movement was composed primarily of two groups with divergent motivations: (1) Feminist groups were motivated to eliminate "real" rape myths, while (2) victims' rights groups wanted to adjudicate more perpetrators. This movement created several important changes.

First, early state statutes required evidence of nonconsent and that the victim was not lying about a consensual act, either through proving that she had resisted "in the utmost"—usually by showing physical injuries—or by providing corroborating evidence or testimony. This corroboration requirement existed for no other crime besides rape. Because the majority of rapes do not result in extreme injury and occur in private, few rapes could be adjudicated.

Today, all states have statutes that define situations under which consent is not possible. For example, each state has its own legal age of consent. While this varies from state to state, the age of consent falls between 14 and 18 years. Other factors that may preclude the possibility of consent include illness, disability, being unconscious, or being under the influence of alcohol or other drugs. These changes expanded the number of cases that could go to trial.

Second, two other reforms also centered on issues of consent but focused on court procedures. One of these was the removal of the "Hale warning," adopted from Mathew Hale, a 17th-century English justice, who doubted women's veracity in rape cases. Prior to the 1980s, in many states, the judge needed to provide the Hale warning to the jury: "an accusation easily to be made, hard to be proved, and harder yet to be defended by the party accused, tho' never so innocent."

The other was the creation of rape shield laws that were designed to prohibit the use of a woman's sexual history as evidence in trial. This was an attempt to counteract the belief that women who have consented previously (either to their attacker or simply in consensual relations in the past) were likely to have consented this time as well. Most states currently have some type of rape shield law; however, many have allowable exceptions. For example, in the state of Colorado, the woman's previous sexual history with the perpetrator is allowable into evidence.

Third, the definition of rape was challenged. Again, a primary assumption about rape is that it is an act against a woman's will. Statutes were frequently gender specific, excluding male victims and female perpetrators. While the NISVS reports that almost all (98%) rapists are male and the majority of victims are women, some women do perpetrate and some men are victims. Statutes also frequently did not allow for same-sex rape. Recognition of these factors led many states to change their statutes to be gender neutral. Furthermore, no state uses marriage as an exemption from prosecution for rape—though some states make it harder to prosecute marital rape than do others.

Current Social Climate

Despite these changes to rape statutes, "real" rape myths continue to exist, affecting society's treatment of victims and the number of cases going into trial. Many court officials and juries still expect victims to show injuries, and a victim's sexual history still often enters into decisions. Politicians make comments about rape being more or less "legitimated" based on its circumstances. Current social movements are still attempting to dismantle assumptions about a woman signaling consent based on her personal characteristics or actions before, during, or after the assault.

Bridget K. Diamond-Welch

See also Acquaintance Rape; Campus Rape; Date Rape; Rape Culture; Revictimization; Sexual Assault; Sexual Assault, Survivors of; Sexual Coercion; Slut Shaming; Spousal Rape; Stranger Rape

Further Readings

Anderson, I., & Doherty, K. (2008). *Accounting for rape.* London, England: Routledge.

Black, M. C., Basile, K. C., Breiding, M. J., Smith, S. G., Walters, M. L., Merrick, M. T., . . . Stevens, M. R. (2011). *The National Intimate Partner and Sexual Violence Survey (NISVS): 2010 summary report.* Atlanta, GA: Centers for Disease Control and Prevention, National Center for Injury Prevention and Control.

Brownmiller, S. (1975). *Against our will: Men, women, and rape.* New York, NY: Simon & Schuster.

Caringella, S. (2009). *Addressing rape reform in law and practice.* New York, NY: Columbia University Press.

Fisher, B. S., Diagle, L. E., & Cullen F. T. (2010). *Unsafe in the ivory tower: The sexual victimization of college women.* Thousand Oaks, CA: Sage.

Koss, M. P., Gidycz, C. A., & Wisniewski, N. (1987). The scope of rape: Incidence and prevalence of sexual aggression and victimization in a national sample of higher education students. *Journal of Counseling and Clinical Psychology, 55,* 162–170.

Lees, S. (1996). *Carnal knowledge: Rape on trial.* London, England: Hamish Hamilton.

Stevenson, K., (2000). Unequivocal victims: The historical roots of the mystification of the female complainant in rape cases. *Feminist Legal Studies, 8,* 343–366.

Rape Culture

Although its use and definition vary across fields, *rape culture* is a term broadly used to describe the normalization and pervasiveness of rape-supportive attitudes and sexual violence in a society. Rape culture is shaped by cultural practices that overtly and/or implicitly condone, excuse, or tolerate rape and sexual violence. Initially, the notion of rape culture was developed within feminist theory and was tied to misogyny and the sexual objectification of women. However, the term is also used more broadly to describe the normalization and lack of public effort in addressing the high rates of sexual violence (e.g., police reluctance to handle rape cases), and the high prevalence of rapes occurring in prisons. Cultural influences often tied to maintaining rape culture include the media (e.g., how sexual violence cases are covered in the news), advertising (e.g., how advertisements display women and sexual coercion), and popular culture, such as music, television, and movies. Behaviors and attitudes tied to rape culture include victim blaming, sexual objectification of women, and trivializing the impact of rape on the rape survivor (i.e., an individual who has experienced rape or sexual violence). It has been found that individuals exhibiting attitudes consistent with rape culture are at increased likelihood of exhibiting other discriminatory attitudes and behaviors, such as homophobia, sexism, and racism, indicating that attitudes consistent with rape culture correlate with other types of discrimination. In this entry, the origin and meaning of rape culture are first discussed. Victim blaming and the stigma associated with reporting rapes are then examined. Finally, the entry explores how rape culture is prevalent both on college campuses and in popular culture.

Origin and Meaning

The concept of rape culture was first introduced in the 1970s in the United States by feminists who began to address women's sexuality and reproductive rights. During the 1970s, feminists started raising public awareness of rape prevalence, which had previously been largely ignored on a societal level. In 1975, the movie *Rape Culture*, directed by the American film producer Margaret Lazarus, was released. This movie discussed the prevalence of rape and the role of popular media in shaping attitudes toward sexual violence. Having formulated the term *rape culture*, this film brought the concept of rape culture to broader awareness. In feminist theory, rape culture is understood to be a result of pervasive misogyny (i.e., contempt or dislike for, or prejudice against women) and the normalization of rape-supportive attitudes. Following the escalation in the number of employed women in the 1960s, feminist theory argued that women's increased role in public life was perceived as an attack on traditional gender roles. Rape was understood then as a way to demonstrate power and reinforce patriarchy through fear.

In the 1970s, feminists conceptualized rape from the perspective of the woman, and emphasized the loss of control and helplessness that victims often feel. Rape was considered a means of enforcing traditional gender roles and maintaining a social hierarchy ruled by men. Previously, much due to psychoanalytic theory, rape had been conceptualized as a result of overwhelming sexual impulses; thus, it was thought that men who raped were simply unable to control their sexual urges. Second-wave feminists challenged the attribution of uncontrollable sexual impulses to the male prerogative, and rape was reconceptualized from a sexual to a violent act and from uncontrollable behavior to a deliberate act intended to demonstrate dominance and control over women. It was emphasized that the implications of rape culture extend well beyond the individuals experiencing rape and apply to all women. Rape or fear of rape was described as something women have to deal with on a daily basis and to which they have to adjust their behavior. For instance, fear might lead women to engage in precautionary behaviors such as not going out alone at night, limiting their opportunities to be actively engaged in the public sphere. Although strongly associated with feminist theory, rape culture is used to describe any environment in which rape is accepted and normalized—regardless of the gender of the survivor. For instance, the high prevalence and apparent acceptance of rape in prisons has been described as rape culture.

Victim Blaming and Stigma

Historically, women have often been blamed for sexual victimization. Victim blaming refers to the role of the rape survivor and describes how the individual experiencing sexual violence is held responsible for the incident. Blame is commonly attributed to a survivor of rape by questioning whether a rape actually took place and by indicating that there was something the victim did to tempt or seduce the rapist. Following the conceptualization of rape culture, victim blaming is seen as systemic and deeply integrated in our society; it is embedded and manifested in the normalized ways we talk about sexual violence and rape survivors. A frequent example of victim blaming is to attribute the rape to the victim's clothing, such as wearing a short skirt. The reasoning is that if a woman is dressed "provocatively," as determined by males, she must want sex.

In court cases involving sexual violence, the survivor's clothing and sexual history are often discussed and sometimes actively used by prosecutors to form the opinions of jury members. It is commonly reported that women's testimonies in rape cases are doubted and scrutiny is given to questions regarding their clothing, alcohol intake, and sexual history. For instance, if a woman is found to have had numerous previous sexual partners or to have engaged in a variety of sexual experimentation, a prosecutor might use this as an argument against the truthfulness of the woman's statement. In what is known as the "skinny jeans defense," an Australian jury acquitted an alleged rapist on the defense that the survivor's jeans were too tight for the accused to forcibly take them off her. It was argued that the survivor must have helped the accused take her jeans off or taken them off herself. Therefore, it could not have been rape.

Furthermore, any sign of acquiescence or consent is frequently used to undermine the belief that a rape occurred. There are examples of court cases in which the prosecutor has questioned whether it is at all possible to rape a woman without her consenting and in which it has been argued that women are able to fight a rapist off or at least scream to get help or scare him away. Notably, this is very different from how other assault crimes are handled. For instance, it is commonly advised that individuals experiencing a violent mugging should give up whatever the perpetrator of the crime wants and refrain from resisting or fighting back. It is assumed that resisting puts a person at heightened risk for harm. In comparison, this assumption does not appear to apply to rape cases, in which compliance is often seen as an indication of consent.

Furthermore, women are often held responsible for preventing rape, through being encouraged to make themselves less vulnerable to sexual victimization. For instance, women are often encouraged not to walk alone at night, not to get drunk, and to wear clothing that covers them up—to avoid being raped. A culturally established belief holding that the burden of avoiding rape is on women is a sign of rape culture, as it indicates that the high prevalence of rape is normalized. Victim blaming contributes to stigmatization of individuals experiencing sexual violence, and it is believed to have a bearing on whether or not survivors disclose or report rapes and other incidents of sexual violence. Blame or fear of being blamed for rape might lead to shame and fear of reporting. It is difficult to accurately establish report rates of sexual abuse and rape; however, it is known that these incidents are vastly underreported.

Rape Culture on College Campuses

The high prevalence of rapes and sexual assaults on college campuses started to receive public attention during the beginning of the 2000s. Rape culture on campuses was especially discussed in relation to colleges in the United States, Canada, and Great Britain. In the United States, it has been found that more than half the women in college report having experienced at least one unwanted sexual experience and that in college dating relationships, experiences of male sexual aggression are common for women. The high prevalence of sexual violence in college campuses has been referred to as an epidemic in the United States, where nearly one in five women report having experienced attempted or completed rape during their freshman year in college. College rapes often occur between acquaintances and often involve date rapes and rape of women who are in some way incapacitated.

Many survivors of college rape have come forth publicly and described how they were not taken seriously when trying to report their abuser. Often, there has been reluctance among college administrations to address the high prevalence of rape on campuses and to protect the alleged rapists while disregarding the rape survivors. This reluctance has been tied to colleges attempting to protect their image, portraying their campuses as safe and their students as successful and courteous. The documentary *The Hunting Ground* (2015) addresses the lack of administrative engagement in addressing rape culture in colleges and portrays survivors of college rapes. *Carry That Weight* (2014–2015), also called the Mattress Performance, is an art performance carried out by Emma Sulkowitcz. She reported being raped by a fellow student while at Columbia University; however, her report did not have any consequences for the alleged rapist. Sulkowitcz's case and performance sparked a substantive debate about campus sexual assaults and the disinclination of colleges to acknowledge this challenge.

Sexual Violence in Popular Culture

Rape culture is also prevalent in and maintained by popular culture, such as film, media reporting, and advertisements. It has been argued that media coverage of sexual violence cases pursues sensationalism rather than meaningful news reporting and as a result stereotypes sexual victimization. For instance, it is frequently the case that incidents involving false rape accusations receive vaster media coverage than actual rape cases. This undue presentation contributes to preserving the myth that false accusations of rape are common, in turn making it more difficult for rape survivors to disclose. In fact, the rates for false accusations related to sex crimes are lower than 10% and are no higher than for other types of crimes.

Furthermore, forcible sex is often romanticized in movies or television. Women are often portrayed as initially resisting a man initiating sex, before giving in and seemingly enjoying the sexual encounter. These depictions undermine the significance of consent and validate nonconsensual sex. Additionally, they indicate that not only will the woman eventually consent but she will also enjoy it. These instances are examples of rape culture, as they are normalized and socially accepted portrayals of women and sexuality.

Anniken Lucia Willumsen Laake and Cynthia Calkins

See also Campus Rape; Date Rape; Hostile Sexism; Misogyny; Patriarchy; Rape; Sexism; Slut Shaming

Further Readings

Brownmiller, S. (2013). *Against our will: Men, women and rape*. New York, NY: Open Road Integrated Media.

Connell, N., & Wilson, C. (1974). *Rape: The first sourcebook for women by New York radical feminists* (pp. 27–28). New York, NY: New American Library.

Donat, P. L., & D'Emilio, J. (1992). A feminist redefinition of rape and sexual assault: Historical foundations and change. *Journal of Social Issues, 48*(1), 9–22.

Higgins, L. A., & Silver, B. R. (1991). *Rape and representation*. New York NY: Columbia University Press.

Lazarus, M. (Director & Producer), & Wunderlich, R. (Producer). (1975). *Rape culture* [Documentary]. New York, NY: Cambridge Documentary Films.

Rutherford, A. (2011). Sexual violence against women: Putting rape research in context. *Psychology of Women Quarterly, 35*(2), 342–347.

Reliability and Gender

When developing a tool to measure any physical or psychological trait, the degree to which the tool actually measures what it is supposed to with sufficient consistency is of the utmost concern. From a measurement perspective, the "actually measures what it is supposed to" part of the previous statement refers to a property of instruments called *validity*, whereas the "with sufficient consistency" part refers to a property called *reliability*. Both of these properties are equally important from a test development standpoint, and establishing reliability is a prerequisite for assessing validity. This entry discusses reliability within the context of classical test theory (CTT). First, reliability is defined conceptually, followed by a discussion of the importance of ensuring that psychological instruments contain items that are equally reliable for both males and females.

Defining Reliability

Tests or procedures that are reliable yield scores that are highly consistent and stable. That is, for a perfectly reliable test, an individual taking the test 10 times would get the exact same score all 10 times. However, psychological, social, and behavioral phenomena are seldom measured perfectly, and it becomes incumbent on the test designer to understand and explain why, for whom, and under what circumstances lack of reliability occurs.

CTT holds that for any test, a person's observed score consists of two unrelated parts: (1) true score (the "signal" of interest) and (2) error (the "noise" that interferes with the signal). Error can be either systematic (every person's score has the same amount of noise) or random (the amount of noise differs for every test taker). The goal of any test developer is to develop items that maximize the contribution of the true score (the signal) to an individual's responses and minimize both types of error (the noise). Systematic error can often be identified and corrected for (i.e., taken out of respondents' scores); however, random error by its very nature is unpredictable and nonreproducible and, consequently, cannot be disentangled from a person's true score. Psychometricians aim to develop measurement instruments that purely measure the construct of interest; that is, they want tests that are less susceptible to both systemic and random error.

Reliability in Classical Test Theory

Within the framework of CTT, there are several ways of assessing reliability, all of which are aimed at providing a single estimate on which to judge the precision and/or stability of the scores associated with a test. This single number sometimes represents a ratio indicating how much signal there is relative to how much noise there is in a set of responses (i.e., signal/[signal + noise]), with the signal representing the degree to which respondents answer similar questions in similar ways.

Other times it can represent a correlation between (a) repeated assessments of the same individual and (b) alternate (yet equivalent) versions of the same test. In all cases, the goal is to provide the researcher with some estimate of the test's precision. It is important for researchers to know this information and, furthermore, to establish whether measurement instruments are equally reliable across genders (and usually across ethnic groups as well), a task that can be accomplished by testing for what is called measurement invariance.

Reliability Across Genders

Measurement invariance testing involves sequentially testing whether several properties about a set of responses can be equated across different groups. The most restrictive level of invariance involves testing whether two groups have the same amount of error in their scores. For example, imagine a group of people who completed a measure of happiness. Some people might have been in a worse mood than normal when they took the test, and their scores might have been much higher if measured on a "normal" day. Likewise, some individuals might have been in a much better mood than normal when taking the test, and their scores might have been significantly lower if measured on a normal day. In general, these fluctuations from participants' "true" response are expected to negate one another, as shown in Figure 1.

Several things should be noted in this figure: (a) all six individuals' "true" standing on happiness is the same, (b) the average of the observed scores and error scores for the males is the same as for the females, and (c) there is literally twice as much error contributing to the females' scores relative to the males' scores. Such a pattern would usually fail the statistical test of equal reliability between groups. Failing this test is problematic because it signals bias in the instrument, meaning that one group is being measured better or more precisely than the other. In this case, the instrument can be said to measure happiness more precisely for the males relative to the females. This is problematic because the reliability of an instrument influences the degree to which inferences drawn using the instrument can be considered valid. That is, the correlation between a test (e.g., happiness) and an outside criterion to which it is theoretically related (e.g., suicide ideation) cannot exceed the reliability of the test. Returning to the example, if the males' reliability estimate was equal to .90, then the maximum it could correlate with suicide ideation would be .81 (assuming suicide ideation was measured perfectly). Similarly, if the females' reliability estimate was equal to .70 (generally the lowest acceptable value), the highest it could correlate with suicide ideation would be .49.

This example would draw one to rightly conclude that males and females are equally happy; however, it would also wrongly lead one to the

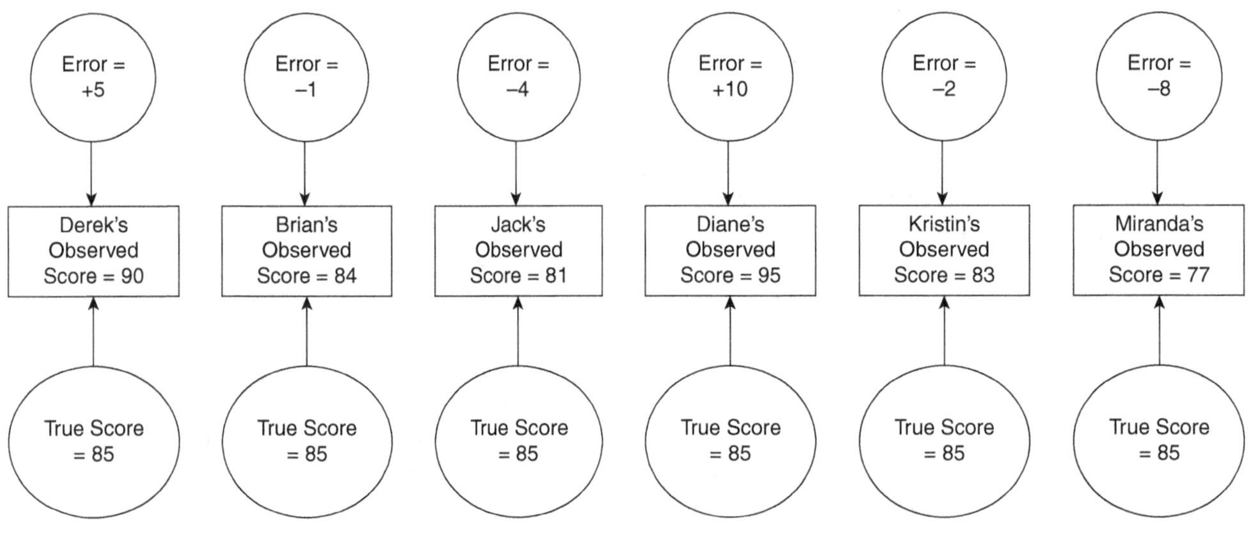

Figure 1 Contribution of True Score and Error to Observed Scores for Males Versus Females

conclusion that the relationship between happiness and suicide ideation is stronger for males than for females. Such an inference would not be valid as the observed correlations differ not because of the relationships between the constructs themselves but, rather, due to differences in how reliably they were measured between the two groups.

Willie J. Hale and Augustine Osman

See also Ethics in Gender Research; Gender Bias in Research; Research Methodology and Gender; Validity and Gender

Further Readings

Kline, T. (2005). *Psychological testing: A practical approach to design and evaluation.* Thousand Oaks, CA: Sage.

Raykov, T., & Marcoulides, G. (2011). *Introduction to psychometric theory.* New York, NY: Routledge.

Reparative Therapy

See Sexual Orientation Change Efforts

Reproductive Cancer and Mental Health in Men

Cancer diagnosis and treatment, especially when affecting the reproductive organs, can have deleterious effects on men's mental health. Reproductive cancers are those in which the disease originates in the reproductive organs. The most common male reproductive cancers are prostate, testicular, and penile cancers. Prostate cancer accounts for more than a quarter of all cancers diagnosed in men, compared with testicular (1%) and penile (0.2%) cancers, which occur at much lower rates, though prevalence varies based on age and geographic region. Disparities in prevalence rates across racial groups are evident in reproductive cancer. African American men have the highest rate of being diagnosed with prostate cancer compared with other racial/ethnic groups, while testicular cancer occurs more often in White males. Although relatively rare, penile cancer has a slightly higher incidence rate in African American men. Additionally, cultural differences in men might also affect reproductive health. Among minority groups, language barriers, increased medical mistrust, and religiosity—specifically the belief that cancer has a spiritual meaning—might influence and delay decisions to seek medical care.

The physical and psychological demands of such cancers present new physical and psychological circumstances to which men must adjust. The presence of a psychological disorder has been identified as an indicator of adjustment to cancer, and elevated prevalence of psychological disorders, including symptoms of depression and anxiety, are documented in samples of men with reproductive cancers in comparison with the general population. Such mental health disturbances can occur discretely around the time of diagnosis and treatment or persistently across longer durations.

This entry focuses on the prevalence of psychological distress in men with reproductive cancer, as well as common factors related to diagnosis and treatment that influence adjustment and mental health. Specifically, the roles of sexuality and one's sense of self, the social environment, and psychological coping in mental health after a male reproductive cancer diagnosis are reviewed. This entry concludes with a brief discussion of psychological interventions in the cancer context.

Psychological Distress and Mental Health Problems

The prevalence of diagnosable psychological disorders is elevated among cancer patients, including adjustment disorders, depression and related mood disorders, and anxiety disorders (including acute and posttraumatic stress disorders). Although research demonstrates that men diagnosed with reproductive cancer are at heightened risk for distress and dysfunction, the majority appear to adjust well. In fact, the preponderance of patients do not develop symptoms meeting the diagnostic threshold for psychopathology. Therefore, depressive or anxiety-related symptoms are commonly used indicators of mental health problems or psychological distress.

Current estimates of distress symptoms vary widely across cancers. Estimates of psychological distress in men with prostate cancer are between 24% and 31%, while the upper estimates of distress rates in men with testicular cancer (13% to 39%) and penile cancer (5% to 50%) tend to be higher. Such wide-range estimates reflect the limited number of studies that have assessed psychological distress, as well as variation in how distress is operationalized and measured and when symptoms are assessed (e.g., at diagnosis vs. 5 years postdiagnosis).

Psychological distress is multifaceted and exerts negative effects across psychological, physical, and social domains. Such effects are interrelated. For instance, depressive symptoms predict nonadherence to medication and noncompletion of medical treatment. Significant attention has been given to identifying the factors that predict mental health problems in men with reproductive cancer. In addition to disease-related factors (e.g., incontinence, erectile dysfunction, fatigue, infertility), often exacerbated by cancer treatment, the influence of gender norms, stress and coping processes, and relationship dynamics has been identified.

Predictors of Psychological Distress

Sexual Functioning and Treatment-Related Side Effects

Impairment in sexual functioning resulting from medical treatments for reproductive cancer, such as surgery or radiation therapies, is a strong predictor of psychological distress. Surgical removal or radiation of the affected body tissue can result in damage to the surrounding healthy nerves. The profile of sexual side effects varies as a function of cancer type, stage of disease, and treatment method. For instance, patients who undergo a radical prostatectomy (surgical removal of the prostate) commonly experience reduction or loss of orgasm, diminished sexual desire, and/or erectile dysfunction; men who have one or both testicles removed (orchiectomy) may experience infertility, body image concerns, reduced libido, or difficulties with ejaculation. With penile cancer, an effort is made to preserve the physical integrity of the penis, but men with even minimal surgery may experience significantly impaired sexual functioning.

Treatment for reproductive cancer can result in other physical side effects that can contribute to distress. For instance, following radiation therapy for prostate cancer, men often report urinary and/or bowel incontinence. Like changes in sexual function, these problems can often worsen after treatment, before some improvement in function is restored. Hormone therapies may also be used. Deprivation of testosterone can help reduce prostate tumor growth. However, low testosterone can contribute to decreased muscle/bone mass, erectile dysfunction, enhancement of breast tissue, and decrease in libido. Finally, chemotherapy has a negative impact on mood. Physical symptoms experienced during chemotherapy, such as hair loss, persistent fatigue, nausea, and pain, can increase distress even long after treatment is completed.

Gender Role Norms and Sexual Orientation

The experience of male reproductive cancer often clashes with and can even undermine men's masculine schemas or gender role ideals. A traditional view of masculinity places an emphasis on restricted emotional expression, assertion of control, and strength. The experience of reproductive cancer, including the diagnosis and treatment-related side effects, challenges this view of masculinity. For instance, cancer itself is an illness that men might interpret as invoking weakness. Embarrassment and fear may prevent disclosure of the illness, and survivors may develop a sense of being less of a man. Physical side effects such as incontinence or impotence might be met with feelings of powerlessness and shame.

Masculine gender role norms, such as stoicism, may result in masking emotional distress and delay help seeking for physical symptoms or psychological distress. Delays in diagnosis or treatment allow the cancer more time to spread to other areas of the body, which will require more aggressive treatment and result in reduced chances of survival. Fears of being perceived as weak may prevent men from seeking help for depression or anxiety. Men with traditional views of masculinity may be more likely to seek help if treatment is framed as a way to promote or preserve other aspects of their masculinity. For example, a husband whose symptoms prevent him from working may be more amenable to help if he views assistance as an important step in resuming his role as a provider.

Changes in sexual function, sexual organs, or sexual motivation can alter men's sexual self-schema, or how they view their sexuality and sexual behaviors. Men with more traditional schemas are more vulnerable to depression when experiencing sexual dysfunction after treatment. Male reproductive cancers exert unique stress on the masculine identity, and special attention to the discrepancy between gender role identity and physical deficit is needed. Masculine identity can be successfully renegotiated when men reframe the altered functioning (e.g., viewing bodily changes as a normal part of cancer treatment while expanding their masculine values and balancing hope of recovery with acceptance of current functioning).

Although little research has sought to identify the needs and experience of sexual minority men with reproductive cancer, gay and bisexual men likely have unique needs and experiences. In the case of prostate cancer, for instance, there is indication that gay men are less likely to be screened for prostate cancer and more likely to have lower health-related quality of life after diagnosis when compared with general groups of patients, particularly with regard to mental and sexual function. It is important to consider that gay and bisexual men disproportionately experience risk factors for declining quality of life and psychological adjustment, including experiencing health-damaging social conditions such as prejudice, stigma, violence, and discrimination. They tend to have poorer health care access, lower likelihood of health insurance coverage, and limited access to culturally competent health care providers. More consideration is needed to understand the unique intersections of sexual orientation and the experiences of reproductive cancer in men.

Social Support

The impact of having support from others, or social support, on mental health and adjustment to cancer has been studied extensively and is one of the strongest predictors of mental health outcomes. In general, emotionally supportive relationships set the stage for better adjustment to reproductive cancer, whereas criticism, social constraints, and social isolation impart risk. Satisfying interpersonal relationships can provide a forum for emotional expression and processing, practical assistance in managing illness, and reinforcement of one's sense of meaning, joy, and connectedness. Support can encourage positive health behaviors or minimize risky behaviors and diminish physiological reactivity to stress. When compared with those reporting less support, men receiving more social support exhibit more effective coping, higher self-esteem and life satisfaction, and fewer depressive symptoms. At the same time, an unsupportive or socially constrained environment (e.g., others withdrawing, showing discomfort or criticism while discussing concerns, changing the topic of discussion) may lead individuals to feel isolated and misunderstood, which in turn can intensify psychological distress.

Social support can take various forms. Researchers and clinicians have pointed to three forms of support that have particular importance to psychological distress: (1) *emotional* (e.g., expressing difficult emotions to a supportive other), (2) *instrumental* (e.g., assistance with household chores), and (3) *informational* (e.g., learning about options for sperm banking) support. While instrumental and informational support are most commonly utilized in response to physical changes and information needs from medical professionals, respectively, greater levels of emotional support are consistently associated with lower levels of distress in men with reproductive cancer.

Coping With Cancer-Related Demands

The way in which an individual copes with a stressor, such as a cancer diagnosis, can affect psychological distress. Coping includes cognitive and behavioral efforts to manage, tolerate, or reduce the impact of situations perceived (or appraised) as stressful. Appraisal of the situation involves evaluating the significance of the stressor (primary appraisal) as well as evaluating the controllability of the stressor and available coping resources (secondary appraisal). For instance, loss of fertility due to cancer treatment might only be distressing if a man perceives this as a threat to his goals or if he believes he will not be able to handle the associated challenges.

Action-oriented or problem-focused coping is more likely to be used if men view a cancer diagnosis as a challenge. This type of coping involves any action aimed at lessening a problem (e.g., addressing erectile dysfunction by seeing a sexual rehabilitation specialist). Such efforts are often associated with better psychological adjustment. Alternatively, emotion-focused coping includes efforts to manage internal reactions to cancer. For instance, in response to fears about cancer recurrence, men might attempt to change the way they think about the worry, distance themselves from worried thinking patterns (e.g., rumination), or seek emotional support from others. Although avoidance coping, including strategies to escape from difficult feelings, denial of the circumstance, disengagement from others, or creation of a temporary distraction, can often be helpful in the short term, it may lead to increased psychological distress over time.

Behavioral Interventions

Although treatment of mental health problems with pharmacologic approaches is productive, substantial progress has been made in demonstrating the efficacy of psychosocial interventions in reducing mental health problems after a cancer diagnosis. Various behavioral approaches have been tested in clinical trials, with particular emphasis on the use of cognitive behavioral therapy and the enhancement of coping skills. More recently, attention has been given to testing therapeutic approaches that include partners and target communication skills, redefinitions of intimacy, and regulation of emotions. Such approaches have demonstrated small to moderate effects on quality of life and psychological outcomes for prostate cancer patients and their partners.

Despite the promise of psychosocial interventions for mental health, limited work has been done with men with reproductive cancers. Most clinical applications in this area have focused on men with prostate cancer, with very few studies centered on testicular or penile cancers. Approaches that incorporate masculine gender norms and foster effective emotion regulation are warranted. Future research for targeted subgroups, such as young adults with testicular cancer, should consider the importance of the patient's developmental stage.

Future Directions

Psychological distress in men with reproductive cancer is influenced by a range of factors. While psychosocial interventions hold promise, systematic screening for distress in clinical settings and provision of adequate referral for treatment services remain a challenge. Design and implementation of screening procedures to identify men experiencing psychological distress and those at increased risk for distress will require increased knowledge of the biological, social, psychological, and cultural factors that contribute to mental health problems after reproductive cancers.

Significant work is needed to better understand the role of sociodemographic characteristics (socioeconomic status, race/ethnicity) in the disparities in psychological distress among men with reproductive cancer. Finally, while this entry briefly explored the factors underlying psychological distress, distress itself might have a unique impact on cancer progression over time. Understanding the reciprocity of psychological and biological disease processes can contribute to a new research frontier.

Katie Darabos, Sean J. Ryan, and Michael A. Hoyt

See also Health Issues and Gender: Overview; Masculinity Gender Norms; Masculinity Ideology and Norms; Men's Health; Mental Health and Gender: Overview; Sexual Dysfunction; Sexuality and Men

Further Readings

American Cancer Society. (2013). *Sexuality for the man with cancer*. Washington, DC: Author. Retrieved from http://www.cancer.org/acs/groups/cid/documents/webcontent/002910-pdf.pdf

Hoyt, M. A., & Stanton, A. L. (2012). Adjustment to chronic illness. In A. S. Baum, T. A. Revenson, & J. E. Singer (Eds.), *Handbook of health psychology* (2nd ed., pp. 219–246). New York, NY: Taylor & Francis.

Katz, A. (2010). *Man, cancer, sex*. Pittsburgh, PA: Hygeia Media.

Maddineni, S. B., Lau, M. M., & Sangar, V. K. (2009). Identifying the needs of penile cancer sufferers: A systematic review of the quality of life, psychosexual and psychosocial literature in penile cancer. *BMC Urology, 9*(8), 1–6. doi:10.1186/1471-2490-9-8

Mulhall, J. P. (2008). *Saving your sex life: A guide for men with prostate cancer*. Chicago, IL: Hilton.

Sadonsky, R., Basson, R., Krychman, M., Moralas, A. M., Schover, L., Wang, R., & Incrocci, L. (2000). Cancer and sexual problems. *Journal of Sexual Medicine, 7*, 349–373. doi:10.1111/j.1743-6109.2009.01620.x

Reproductive Cancer and Mental Health in Women

Reproductive cancers are diseases in which abnormal cells divide uncontrollably and destroy body tissue in organs related to reproduction or sex. For women, these cancers affect organs such as the vagina, the uterus, the cervix, the ovaries, the fallopian tubes, and other surrounding areas. Accordingly, the most common forms of reproductive cancer are vaginal cancer, uterine cancer, cervical cancer, ovarian cancer, vulvar cancer, and fallopian tube cancer. Breast cancer is sometimes considered a reproductive cancer.

In general, reproductive cancers are hard to detect until they have been developed in the body, as symptoms tend not to develop in the earlier stages of cancer. There are screening tests that can be used to detect breast cancers (e.g., mammogram X-rays) and some reproductive cancers (e.g., Pap smear lab tests during pelvic exams). However, because symptoms do not develop, people are diagnosed with cancer usually based on confirmation by a biopsy—a procedure in which small pieces of tissues are removed to test for cancer.

In recent years, there has been an increase in awareness of women's breast cancer across the United States, which has been coupled with an increase in research on women's breast cancer in general. Studies have also examined breast cancer survivors' mental health processes and psychological well-being, including their coping mechanisms as well as the potential for symptoms like depression, anxiety, or body image issues. In contrast, there is far less societal awareness about women's reproductive cancers, and there are few studies that examine how such cancers affect women's mental health. This entry examines the research that exists on different reproductive cancers in women, the mental health of women who have reproductive cancer, and some cultural considerations regarding the proliferation of reproductive cancer in women.

Types of Reproductive Cancer in Women

Vaginal Cancer

Vaginal cancer is a rare type of cancer that affects about 1 of every 1,100 women. The National Cancer Institute (NCI) estimated that in 2016 there were an estimated 4,620 new cases of vaginal cancer in the United States and approximately 950 deaths were attributed to this disease. The most common type of vaginal cancer is squamous cell carcinoma, which occurs in the squamous cells that make up the epithelial lining of the vaginal wall. Approximately 15% of vaginal cancers are adenocarcinomas, which occur in the glandular, or secretory, cells in the epithelial wall. Most vaginal adenocarcinomas develop in women after menopause. A rare type called clear cell adenocarcinoma has been linked to fetal exposure to diethylstilbestrol. Other types of vaginal cancer include melanomas, which occur in the lower and/or outer parts of the vagina, and sarcomas, which begin in the soft tissue deep in the vaginal wall.

Vaginal cancers often do not exhibit signs or symptoms in the early stages. In addition to a palpable mass, individuals may experience unusual vaginal discharge or bleeding, painful intercourse and urination, constipation, and pelvic pain. Treatment options for precancers of the vagina include laser therapy and various topical treatments. Invasive vaginal cancer is primarily treated with radiation therapy and surgery, as well as chemotherapy for the treatment of advanced disease.

Uterine Cancer

Cancers of the uterine body include endometrial carcinomas and uterine sarcomas. Endometrial carcinoma, which affects the inner lining of the uterine corpus, is the most common female reproductive organ cancer in the United States. Uterine sarcomas begin in the myometrium, or muscle layer, of the uterus. The NCI estimated that in 2016 there were approximately 60,000 new diagnosed cases of uterine cancer and approximately 10,500 deaths due to this cancer.

Symptoms of uterine cancer may include unusual vaginal bleeding and discharge. Advanced stages of uterine cancer may include pelvic pain, unanticipated weight loss, and evidence of a palpable mass. The primary treatment option for women with uterine cancer is surgery. Depending on the type and severity of the disease, a combination of hormonal therapy, radiation therapy, and chemotherapy may also be used.

Cervical Cancer

Cervical cancers occur in the epithelial lining of the cervix. The most common types include squamous cell carcinomas, which begin in the exocervix (the area closest to the vagina), and adenocarcinomas, which occur in the glandular cells lining the endocervix (the area closest to the uterus). Adenosquamous carcinomas, or mixed carcinomas, are a rare type of cervical cancer that include features of both squamous cell carcinoma and adenocarcinoma. Invasive cervical cancers often develop from precancerous changes that are highly preventable when found early. Because of available screening tests and vaccines aimed specifically at the human papillomavirus, early diagnosis is associated with high survival rates and high quality of life after treatment. The NCI estimated that in 2016 there were approximately 12,990 new cases and 4,120 deaths were attributed to cervical cancer.

Symptoms associated with cervical cancer do not occur until the cancer has become invasive. These symptoms may include unusual bleeding and discharge, and pain during intercourse. Primary treatment options for women with early to late stages of cervical cancer may include surgery or a combination of radiation therapy and chemotherapy. Advanced stages of cervical cancer may be treated with chemotherapy alone.

Ovarian Cancer

Ovarian cancer can develop in three types of cells within the ovaries. Tumors may form in (1) the epithelial cells, which cover the outer layer of the ovary; (2) germ cells, which produce eggs; and (3) stromal cells, which produce hormones. It is estimated that women have a lifetime risk of 1 in 70 of developing ovarian cancer. The NCI estimated approximately 22,280 new cases of ovarian cancer in the United States in 2016.

Early stages of ovarian cancer typically have no overt symptoms. Some individuals may experience abdominal swelling, difficulty eating, bloating, early satiety, or urinating frequently or urgently. Treatment options often include two or more combinations of treatment such as surgery, hormone therapy, targeted therapy, radiation therapy, and chemotherapy. Surgery is the primary treatment for ovarian cancer. Targeted drugs have been used to shrink tumors or to slow the growth of cancer cells. Administering chemotherapy directly into the abdomen appears to improve survival for some patients with advanced stages of the cancer.

Vulvar Cancer

Vulvar cancer most often affects the labia majora (outer skin folds) and labia minora (inner skin folds), which protect the vaginal opening. Vulvar cancer can less often affect the clitoris or Bartholin glands, which produce the mucus that lubricates the vagina. The NCI estimated approximately 5,950 new diagnosed cases in the United States and approximately 1,110 deaths due to vulvar cancer in 2016.

Specific to the type of vulvar cancer, symptoms may range from no symptoms to itching, soreness, changes in color around the vulva (pink, red, white, or other colors other than the normal skin color), a bump or distinct mass, pain, discharge, bleeding, or open sores. Treatment options include surgery, radiation therapy, and chemotherapy. In more advanced stages of cancer, chemotherapy may be combined with radiation to shrink the tumor prior to surgery.

Fallopian Tube Cancer

Fallopian tube cancer results from an abnormal proliferation of cells in the fallopian tubes, which allow a woman's eggs (ova) to pass from the ovaries to the uterus. It is one of the rarest malignancies of the female gynecological tract and accounts for approximately 1% of all gynecological cancers.

Symptoms may include abdominal pain, vaginal bleeding, and vaginal discharge. Treatment typically involves surgery in combination with chemotherapy and radiation therapy. In the early stages of the cancer, one or both of the fallopian tubes may be removed, along with one or both of the ovaries. Surgery may also involve removing the uterus, cervix, or nearby tissue.

Women's Reproductive Cancers and Mental Health

Previous studies have found that anywhere from one fourth to one half of all people who are diagnosed with cancer experience significant physical issues, with common concerns including pain, fatigue, and difficulties in functioning. Women may especially experience these symptoms, with many researchers considering that these experiences manifest when women experience significant psychosocial stress. Studies also reveal how cancer survivors experience common mental health problems such as anxiety and depression, with research supporting the suggestion that mental health outcomes vary according to the various stages of coping with cancer. For example, psychological symptoms may differ for women when they are first diagnosed with reproductive cancers, when they are undergoing treatment, and when they enter remission and become survivors of reproductive cancers. Some studies find that age of onset influences how women with reproductive cancers cope psychologically. For instance, for young women without children who are diagnosed with cancer, mental health concerns may be related to their perceptions or fears of future reproductive issues. Furthermore, research finds that reproductive cancers, particularly for women who receive chemotherapy treatment, result in an array of physical symptoms such as weight gain, hair loss, sexual dysfunction, and difficulties in daily functioning. These symptoms can create even more psychological difficulties for survivors, which oftentimes exacerbate the physical symptoms even more.

Cultural Considerations

Though the literature on women's reproductive cancer is scarce, there is a growing scholarship on the cultural factors affecting women of different cultural groups. First, studies have supported the fact that for both Black and White women, the experiences of being pregnant, breastfeeding, and oral contraceptive use predicted lower instances of reproductive cancer. For Asian women, both parity and gravidity are associated with ovarian cancer risk, in that the more times a woman has been pregnant and the more times a woman has given birth, the more the chance of being diagnosed with ovarian cancer decreases. Research with Alaska Native women has found that age at first menstruation may increase the risk for reproductive cancer across women of all age groups. Some studies with lesbian and bisexual women of various racial groups (who have been diagnosed with reproductive cancer) find that gender norms may influence patients' perceptions of health care facilities; some women reported how heterosexism and gender role norms preclude them from feeling supported or included in group therapy or treatment facilities. Finally, emerging studies reveal that transgender men (e.g., men who were born with female reproductive organs) are significantly less likely to be up-to-date on Pap smear tests and other preventive cervical screening care that may increase their chances of detecting reproductive cancer in the earlier stages. Future studies can examine some of the cultural and gender identity–related reasons why transgender men are not being screened or seeking treatment—including transphobic experiences with health care systems and medical practitioners, fear of being viewed less as a man, or lack of knowledge about reproductive health or cancers.

Kirklyn Escondo, Andrew Zarate, and Kevin L. Nadal

See also Health Issues and Gender: Overview; Lesbians and Health; Women's Health

Further Readings

Anderson, K. N., Schwab, R. B., & Martinez, M. E. (2014). Reproductive risk factors and breast cancer subtypes: A review of the literature. *Breast Cancer Research and Treatment, 144,* 1–10.

Quinn, G. P., & Vadaparampil, S. T. (2012). *Reproductive health and cancer in adolescents and young adults.* Dordrecht, Netherlands: Springer.

Turkington, C., & Edelson, M. (2005). *The encyclopedia of women's reproductive cancer.* New York, NY: Infobase.

Wiggins, D. L., Monzon, C., & Hott, B. R. (2014). The impact of reproductive cancers on women's mental health. In D. L. Barnes (Ed.), *Women's reproductive mental health across the lifespan* (pp. 283–300). New York, NY: Springer.

Reproductive Rights Movement

Reproductive and sexual rights have had a long history of struggle across the United States. In most countries, they are still a contentious issue; yet they continue to be at the forefront of cultural transformation and women's development. Only since the early 2000s has the concept of gender joined the discourse around reproduction, sexuality, and rights. Thus, this entry analyzes how gender has permeated and shaped the reproductive rights movement. Concepts of reproductive health, reproductive rights, and reproductive justice are explored in light of the notion of gender in an increasingly interconnected and diverse world.

Reproductive Health and Rights

Reproductive health requires accurate knowledge, safety, responsibility, freedom, and appropriate services, as well as the means to access them in order to address all reproductive matters throughout one's life span. To guarantee the above, people need the ability to exercise reproductive rights, a notion that has been promoted during conferences of the United Nations and international nongovernmental organizations since the 1990s. As a result of these conferences' resolutions and recommendations, many initiatives were taken to improve women's health and to reduce societal barriers due to reproduction. Developing nations saw an influx of nongovernmental organizations that aimed at empowering women by reducing the number of unplanned pregnancies. Years later, and mainly due to the AIDS epidemic, men were introduced as target recipients of reproductive and sexual health services.

In the United States, the narrative of reproductive health and rights centered for many years on a woman's right to make decisions about her pregnancy—a subject that continues to be a highly divisive topic among Americans. These divisions are more evident by political affiliation and by sex. For example, more women and Democrats favor women's right to choose how to manage their reproductive rights than do men and Republicans. At the same time, differences in opinion vary regarding abortion, depending on specific circumstances such as gestational period and reasons to terminate a pregnancy, among others. Over the years, there has been an increasing awareness that middle-class, heterosexual, and White women of reproductive age are not the only ones in need of rights, services, and empowerment in matters of reproduction and sexual health. Furthermore, it has been evident that rights alone do not guarantee access to needed services, and as a result of a deepening economic inequality in the country, many vulnerable populations have not had their needs met in terms of their reproductive health. For example, rates of cervical cancer, maternal mortality, infant mortality, teenage pregnancy, and syphilis are all higher among some ethnic minority and low-income populations. Likewise, ethnic minority women's organizations have demonstrated how oppression, discrimination, and exploitation have created barriers to reproductive health and rights. Consequently, reproductive rights advocates have broadened the scope of their focus to include ethnic minorities, low-income groups, teenagers, undocumented immigrants, LGBTQ (lesbian, gay, bisexual, transgender, and queer) people of all ages, older populations, as well as men in general. Within this range, there is also a variety of reproductive health concerns. This shift in focus gave birth to the reproductive justice movement, which emphasizes sociopolitical and economic inequalities as the root of reproductive injustice. Hence, reproductive justice encompasses both reproductive rights and reproductive health.

Despite the fact that reproductive justice is an inclusive movement that seeks equality for diverse populations, the majority of those actively involved in this movement continue to be female. Women tend to organize and attend conferences around the United States more than men do, bringing reproductive rights and justice to the forefront of academia, community organizing, alternative media, and societal engagement. Women are the ones appearing in court hearings and protests every time a new law that threatens reproductive health and justice appears. They are organized in think tanks that attempt to change public policy and unjust laws, and they are overrepresented as direct service employees in nonprofit organizations promoting reproductive health, education, and rights. Despite this, women are underrepresented in the decision-making levels of government and the media. Even though reproductive health and justice affect and involve all of society, the struggle still lies mainly on women. Fortunately, support has been found among LGBTQ activists—both men and women—who see the movement beyond their individual struggles.

In addition to the inequities that sparked the reproductive justice movement as highlighted above, a gender inclusive reproductive justice involves scenarios such as

- transgender men who become pregnant;
- gay men and infertile couples who hire a surrogate mother to start a family;
- lesbian/bisexual women who are artificially inseminated;
- men who donate their sperm, and their potential legal obligations with their offspring;
- paid maternal and paternal leave for new parents;
- men's increased involvement in child rearing and men who want to be stay-at-home dads, even if temporarily;
- workplace accommodations for breastfeeding for low-wage earners and fast-food workers; and
- reproductive health services for imprisoned populations.

All the situations listed, among others, would require a paradigm shift in which reproductive matters are not the realm and responsibility of women alone but of society as a whole. Therefore, this goal necessitates a revision of the notion of masculinity and the role of men in reproduction and child rearing, as it is already happening in a few countries (e.g., Sweden). The U.S. government may consider examining and potentially adopting some of the policies of these other nations to improve reproductive health, rights, and justice in the United States.

Mónica M. Alzate

See also Breastfeeding; Surrogacy; Women's Health; Workplace and Gender: Overview

Further Readings

Alzate, M. M. (2009). The role of sexual and reproductive rights in social work practice. *Affilia: Journal of Women and Social Work, 24*(2), 108–119. doi:10.1177/0886109909331695

Bennhold, K. (2010, June 9). In Sweden, men can have it all. *New York Times*. Retrieved from http://www.nytimes.com/2010/06/10/world/europe/10iht-sweden.html

Mohapatra, S. (2012). Achieving reproductive justice in the international surrogacy market. *Annals of Health Law, 21*(1), 191–200.

Research: Overview

Empirical research on gender and gender-related topics (e.g., gender identity, sexual orientation, gender expression) has a long and contentious history, particularly within psychology. Deeply shaped by social, political, and historic contexts, scientific inquiry on gender has been situated within—and has often reproduced and legitimated—racial and (dis)ability hierarchies, religious and moral paradigms, hetero- and cisnormativity, and deceptively simple gender categories and binaries. Psychologists have produced both powerful examples of research for gender justice and liberation and scientific "cover stories" that have been used to legitimate social oppression and exclusion throughout the history of research on gender. Depending on by whom, why, how, and toward what end the projects are undertaken, empirical research on sex, gender, and sexuality has been liberatory, historic, surprising, essentialist, and/or pathologizing.

The entries under the Research category review a set of the epistemological, theoretical, and methodological concerns that have plagued gender research both in the past and today. Some comment on significant historic texts (e.g., "The Kinsey Scale"); some document the significance of key policy decisions that have reversed the long-standing exclusion of women from clinical trials (e.g., "Sampling Bias and Gender"); and others recognize the importance of research that "normalizes" a wide range of sexual preferences and attractions (e.g., "Sexual Orientation as Research Variable"). A number of essays are straightforward entries—for instance, on the problem of gender-biased language or the importance of validity and reliability when assessing gender constructs. Others explore ongoing debates within the field for which there are no clear guidelines at the moment (e.g., "Transgender Research, Bias in" and "Heteronormative Bias in Research").

An aim of this overview is to appreciate the entries that have clear answers and also relish the entries that pose willful challenges to the field. That is, it encourages a critical eye toward the scientific process, looking back and forward. This overview opens by first sketching a brief history of the ways in which bias (gender, heteronormative, racial/ethnic, transgender), conferred through White and able-bodied standards, has shaped the types of research questions asked and methodologies implemented. It then outlines current theoretical and methodological debates within research on gender and gender-related topics. The intent is not to be exhaustive but instead to highlight some of today's most pressing and core issues in gender research.

Historical Overview of Psychological Research on Sex, Gender, and Sexuality

The definition, meaning, and measurement of gender have varied dramatically, and with controversy, throughout the history of psychological research. Across much of the 20th century, research on "gender" denoted the psychological study of the experiences of cisgender women and to a lesser extent cisgender men, with the aim of "correcting" the historic imbalance that had privileged the study of cisgender undergraduate White men as the "standard" psychological subject. In 1968, Naomi Weisstein, an early pioneer in activist feminist psychology, published "Psychology Constructs the Female," in which she argued, "Psychology has nothing to say about what women are really like, what they need and what they want, especially because psychology does not know" (p. 135). At that point, Weisstein challenged psychology's lack of appreciation for social context, its bias toward male theorists and frameworks, and the prevalence of biologically based theories (an argument that still resonates today). "Psychology Constructs the Female" was considered the opening shot across the bow for second-wave feminism in psychology. A festschrift of commentaries on the piece, collected 25 years later, in 1993, was published in *Feminism and Psychology*, where Weisstein got the last word: "Let us return to an activist, challenging, badass, feminist psychology" (p. 244).

Following on her heels, through the last quarter of the 20th century, second-wave feminist psychologists effectively exposed the androcentric nature of the discipline, demonstrating that psychological theory and science were based largely on the experiences of men (principally White, middle-class, heterosexual, able-bodied, cisgender men), resulting in a dearth of psychological inquiry into areas of social experience unique to or significant for women (e.g., domestic violence, reproductive health, gender stereotyping). Critical feminist psychologists including Rhoda Unger allied with feminist philosophers of science to interrogate the "science" of psychology. Many argued against positivist contentions that psychological practice is value neutral or fully "objective," articulating that gender bias permeates the research process in the formulation of research questions (e.g., using biased theory), study design (e.g., operational definitions, selection of participants), interpretation of data (e.g., ignoring alternative explanations), and communication of findings (e.g., focusing on gender differences as opposed to gender similarities).

Critiques of Biological Determinism and Differentiation Between Sex and Gender

With greater emphasis on women's experience within psychological inquiry, feminist psychologists drew attention to structural inequities and violence, gender disparities, and forms of discrimination. Two big questions were being floated: Are there differences? And if so, from where do they derive? Turning to the social and developmental conversations about gender, fueled by the groundbreaking work of Carol Gilligan's *In a Different Voice* (1982), many young feminist psychologists sought to validate and honor what came to be considered "essential" sex differences, suggesting that inequality existed between men and women as a result of the devaluation of female attributes (e.g., cooperation and relationality) within a male-dominated society. Rising alongside the "difference" paradigm, other feminist psychologists, including Rachel Hare-Mustin and Jeanne Marecek, challenged the "alpha bias" of the focus on gender "difference," casting empirical doubt on whether these aggregated differences actually existed.

In the midst of these debates, gender psychologists were extremely instrumental in peeling away the conflation of biology, social relations, socialization, and power hierarchies. While it may be difficult to appreciate it now, it was conceptually mind-blowing to be able to distinguish sex and gender, to speak of date rape and marital rape, and to articulate sexual harassment as a violation of, not intrinsic to, women's work. Many contributed to the important and still significant distinction between sex and gender: Sex was identified as a set of biological and psychological characteristics that constitute "male" and "female" bodies, while gender referred to the social and cultural meanings attached to male and female bodies, attributing greater power and status to men, as well as an individual's sense of self as a gendered being.

The conceptual separation of sex and gender raised tautological questions about masculinity and femininity as exclusively belonging to individuals who are assigned male and female sex at birth, respectively. Positioning gender as a social construct further led to an expansion of gender-related research to include gender roles (i.e., expected social positions based on one's sex assigned at birth), gender traits (i.e., attributes associated with social beliefs of masculinity and femininity), and gender ideologies (i.e., beliefs about the essential nature of male and female bodies). The field was generating conceptual and methodological tools to theorize, in the language of Unger, "gender as a verb," not as a noun.

Yet despite these significant conceptual advancements, by distinguishing sex and gender, new conceptual problems arose. At its base, social science research reified gender categories and thereby stabilized sex/gender binaries. By focusing on sex differences, second-wave feminist psychology—particularly the more mainstream work based in liberal feminist ideology—was often used to legitimate essentialist notions that men and women were fundamentally distinct and should be treated as "equal." While many resisted this framework, the "difference" paradigm took hold in the popular culture, flattening questions of power differentials, homogenizing groups, and obscuring important differences within sex/gender categories. The mainstream strain of this work perpetuated the belief that only two sexes and genders existed—one from Venus and one from Mars. Gender was still caught in the vice of complementarity, with the male and female categories viewed as neatly compatible pieces of a puzzle.

As gender binaries were not challenged within the field, heterosexuality was tightly secured as the "appropriate" expression of sexuality and was guaranteed the designation as the "normal," unchallenged standard for gender/sexuality research. That is to say, while serious excavation of sex/gender was undertaken within the psychology of the 1970s and 1980s, research on sexual orientation was still primarily pathologizing, reflecting both cisnormative and heteronormative assumptions. As the entries on transgender and heteronormative bias demonstrate, early psychological conceptualizations of gender identity and sexual orientation both stabilized what was normative and pathologized transgender identities and same-sex sexuality. Important exceptions include pioneers Rich Savin-Williams, Beverly Greene, Greg Herek, and others. The entry "Heteronormative Bias in Research" reports that "a content analysis of the 139 research studies from the late 1960s to early 1970s showed that 88% of the research assumed the psychopathology of homosexuality." Thus, it is not surprising that until the 1970s, for example, many psychologists focused on diagnosing homosexuality with the motivation that the diagnostic criteria would lend themselves to a "cure." While the American Psychological Association declassified homosexuality as a psychological disorder in 1972, as of 2017, gender dysphoria—identifying with a gender other than the one assigned at birth—remains a psychological disorder in the *Diagnostic and Statistical Manual of Mental Disorders, Fifth Edition* (*DSM-5*). As a result, psychology has perpetuated essentialist notions regarding the congruous and assumed "natural" relationship between sex assigned at birth, gender identity, and sexual desire.

Conceptualizing Intersections of Oppression and Privilege

The emphasis placed on differentiating *between* women and men—on "uncovering" sex differences—tended to reinforce complementarity and also mute the rich, contradictory, and wild diversity of experiences that exist *within* and *among* individuals in these categories. One major critique of mainstream feminist psychology in the 20th century was that the category "women" commonly stood as a monolith category, referencing—without explicating—heterosexual, White, financially stable, nondisabled, cisgendered females. Research studies, for instance, on work, marriage, and child rearing privileged images of strong and autonomous women who were workers and mothers, casting a shadow over girls and women with disabilities, older women, women of color, women of low socioeconomic status, lesbians, and bisexual women.

At the same time when some researchers in the 1970s and 1980s were insisting that women, and gender, be taken seriously, others were beginning to interrogate the important intersections of multiple identities and positionalities, in particular gender, race, class, and disability. In 1975, Stephanie Shields challenged beliefs of biological determinism in a leading essay in the *American Psychologist* titled "Functionalism, Darwinism, and the Psychology of Women: A Study in Social Myth, and From the Arena of Comparative Psychology." In 1978, Ethel Tobach, with her critical biologist colleague Betty Rosoff, initiated the *Genes and Gender* series to challenge the infiltration of sexist and racist assumptions in the field of evolutionary psychology and genetic determinism. In 1983, Althea Smith and Abigail Stewart published "Approaches to Studying Racism and Sexism in Black Women's Lives" in the *Journal of Social Issues*. The same year, Kay Deaux published *Women of Steel*, an ethnography of female blue-collar workers in the steel mining industry. Later in the decade, in 1988, Michelle Fine and Adrienne Asch published the first volume of *Women and Disabilities*.

As these "marginalized" population studies were beginning to be published, exploring communities that psychology had left in the shadows, new, brilliant, and somewhat biting forms of social critique also began to emerge from within the field. Bonnie Strickland, later president of the American Psychological Association, published a chapter on coming out as a lesbian in the South, "Under the Confederate Flag." Nancy Russo initiated a long and important portfolio of work challenging the presumed benefits of key heterosexual institutions, namely marriage and childbearing. Russo documented the differential health consequences of marriage for women and men: the positive mental health effects of marriage for men and the negative effects for women, the negative consequences of (unwanted) pregnancy and the positive consequences of (wanted) abortion. In the early 1990s, Pam Reid authored "Poor Women in Psychological Research: Shut Up and Shut Out," and Lillian Comas-Dias forged new theoretical and empirical paths by integrating critical work on colonialism, oppression, gender, and race/ethnicity into the quite traditional field of psychotherapy research. This was a thrilling intellectual and political moment for sex/gender/sexuality researchers.

The last decade of the 20th century witnessed a virtual explosion of work on gender and disability, class, sexuality, and race/ethnicity. The intersections were rich, but the categories were relatively secure. Influenced by queer theory, critical race theory, disability studies, and postcolonial theory, however, new scholarship emerged in which "damage-centered research" was challenged and "desire-focused research" was advocated, and gender/sex/sexuality categories began to explode and become more fluid. Multiple methods offered new, if provisional, strategies for moving forward through the categorical uncertainty and ambivalence. In the following section, each of these key research "moves" in the field is considered.

Entering the Damage/Desire Dialectic

Similar to the history of research on race, disability, and class, the legacy of damage-centered research in sex/gender scholarship in psychology focuses on "deficits" and on outcomes such as internalized self-hatred, low self-esteem, depression, helplessness, and suicide ideation. More recently, however, there has been an explosion of pleasure-oriented research—largely outside psychology—in which questions of desire, yearning, and joy sit at the core of the inquiry. This debate is old—and hot. For a moment, let us revisit the history of this dialectic in the field, to avoid, perhaps, polar swings between damage- and desire-oriented research and generate instead some interesting theoretical and empirical assemblages that recognize the consequences of oppression and also the rich, vibrant desires and forms of resistance enacted in what indigenous scholar Gerald Vizenor calls "survivance."

Some readers may remember the feminist debates on danger and desire, a dialectic that has haunted feminism throughout history. Many have argued that the alcohol prohibition movement from 1920 to 1933 was based on a danger/victim narrative about alcohol, exacerbating violence against women. In 1982, at the Barnard Conference on Sexuality, the Feminist Sex Wars flared along the same dialectic—arguments about danger (of pornography) versus pleasure. At the conference, scholar-activists including Carol Vance, author of *Pleasure and Danger*, confronted the rising tide of the Women Against Pornography movement. Gayle Rubin raised and contested the "vanilla" sacred ring of what was considered "appropriate" sex, even raising questions of cross-generational sexuality. The debates were inflamed.

In 1988, on the heels of the Feminist Sex Wars, Fine published "The Missing Discourse of Desire" in the *Harvard Educational Review*, drawn from a critical ethnography of sexuality education classes, in which once again she found a repetition of the dominant discourses focusing on female victimization, (im)morality, illness, disease, unwanted pregnancy, and prevention—but not on desire, wanting, yearning, masturbation, oral sex, orgasm, or young women's capacity to say "yes." Then, as now, critical interrogations of desire were few and far between within the vast landscape of sexuality research. Sara McClelland and Fine have more recently written on "thick desire," inviting researchers to consider social science investigations of structural and intimate enactments of oppression and desire. The point is that these two dynamics—danger and pleasure—should not be positioned as opposites but as conjoined. Researchers cannot privilege one over the other, rehearsing the errors enacted by researchers who focus on "deficits" versus "resilience."

However, there has been a small, rising wave of desire-focused research that nevertheless recognizes oppression and structural violence. Not surprisingly, funding is difficult. Federal and private philanthropy dollars typically target "problems," not joy—and certainly not sexual joy. Nevertheless, Planned Parenthood researchers have documented the positive health benefits of masturbation and orgasm; social psychologist Christin Bowman has authored a prize-winning essay on female masturbation, and critical race theorist Jennifer Nash has written a series of provocative books and essays, for example, *The Black Body in Ecstasy: Reading Race, Reading Pornography*, "Desiring Desiree," and "Black Anality."

Yet the tensions between damage- and pleasure-based research persist: On one side, one hears about "violence against women," the "objectification of women," the "vulnerability of women with disabilities," and depression and suicide ideation among LGBTQ youth; on the other, one reads research that privileges "desire," resilience, and "women's agency." Echoes of this struggle can be heard in critiques of Title IX mandates for university responses to sexual violence grievances on campus (assuming that he is guilty and she is a victim), the need for trigger warnings in classrooms (assuming that students are vulnerable), the patronizing sexual harassment codes that limit sex relations between faculty and students (denying that power is sexy and denying women students' agency), debates about the legalization of prostitution (sex workers vs. trafficked women), and the arguments between the pro- and antisexualization movements.

Given that psychology as a discipline has long focused on damage, struggle, oppression, and pathology—coming from both conservative and progressive researchers—the question is "Can gender/sexuality research focus *less* on damage and *more* on desire?" Can research enter the theoretical and methodological space where researchers engage the dialectics of oppression and desire? Psychologist William Cross has written extensively about the ideological bias and scientific (in)validity of damage-focused research. His early interest was in Black psychology and the fetishism of "self-hatred." In later writings, Cross and colleagues (Fine and McClelland), argued that a focus on "damage" alone undermines the strength and resilience of individuals and marginalized communities and obscures the structural causes of negative outcomes. These writers have called for a research that documents oppression and also desire. This call, however, has been resisted by more than a few. The fear is that, in the popular imagination, evidence of joy invalidates evidence of oppression. Researchers have been hostage to the belief that conditions are considered unequivocally oppressive only if damage can be documented. Thus, there is a rightful fear that if psychologists explore pleasure in deeply unjust circumstances, they risk losing an analysis of the scarring consequences of oppression. For now, psychologists look forward to psychological frameworks that enable them to document both oppression and resistance, pain and joy, while they enter the rich landscape of desire/pleasure, and its knotty relationship to cumulative structural violence.

Considering Gender and Gender-Related Categories and Binaries

A second challenge raised by these entries involves the question of categories and binaries, which are increasingly fluid and multiple. In the early 21st century, there is a growing recognition among scholars, educators, policymakers, activists, and especially youth that binaries rooted in normative categories and/or in exclusions no longer map easily onto the complex lives of people. Queer theory, the transgender movement, and genderqueer youth, as well as UndocuQueer, #BlackLivesMatter, sex-positive girls' movements, Pussy Riot, and other social movements forged at complex intersections are challenging the binaries of male/female, straight/gay, masculine/feminine, and even gender conforming/nonconforming. Questions have emerged around the fluidity and classification of identities, casting doubt on the usefulness of binary gender distinctions and raising fundamental questions regarding the validity, reliability, and ethics of identity measurements and categorizations. This can be considered a politically exciting, if empirically "awkward," moment, when categories that social scientists have taken for granted are being challenged and scrutinized by the very people who know best—young and old who are living bodies at the sex/gender/sexuality "margins."

Many of the entries in this section on research and gender highlight the conceptual and methodological challenge of studying categories that are rapidly shifting, changing, and being contested. Both confusion and disagreement exist on how best to define, operationalize, and measure various gender-related topics. For instance, it is commonly assumed that sexual orientation comprises desire, behavior, and identity. However, there are flaws to this argument (e.g., if an individual identifies as gay and engages in same-sex sexual activity but has some opposite-sex sexual attraction, they would still be gay, despite their attraction). Given this, how is sexual orientation to be conceptualized and operationalized? Are men who have sex with other men considered "gay" even while they identify as heterosexual? How is Lisa Diamond's findings that some women shift their sexual identities over time and across situations accounted for? At this point in history, such complexity challenges the construct validity and reliability of quantitative measures of sexual orientation.

The risk of losing the richness of a psychological phenomenon pertains to all quantitative measures. However, within research on gender, forced gender categorization and gender-related categorizations—quantitative and qualitative—raise practical, ethical, and political concerns as research circulates through popular culture. Practically, gender, for example, is simultaneously an embodied performance of one's sense of self as well as the means through which one is read by the outside world. The "doing" of gender is context dependent and results from intra-individual variation as well as larger societal gender norms. A woman may "femme up" her mannerisms while at work but express herself with a more masculine demeanor when in the company of friends. A person may also have intra-individual differential feelings as masculine or feminine. A genderqueer person, for example, may choose to accentuate masculine aspects of themselves one day and feminine aspects the next. If the fluidity, multiplicity, and variability (between and within persons) are taken seriously, a commitment to construct reliability may itself be viewed as problematic.

The intersection of gender identity and gender expression highlights the ethical and political concerns of categorizing bodies and identities. Transgender individuals are commonly described as gender *nonconforming*. Yet through his masculine presentation, affect, and mannerisms, a trans man likely feels that—and may be perceived as if—he is *conforming* to his gender identity as a man. Automatically categorizing trans individuals as gender nonconforming both invalidates their self-determined identity and potentially inaccurately characterizes how they are perceived in the world. Thomas Teo argues that social scientists have a responsibility to produce work that does not simply reproduce and "pass on" the stereotypes that float in the larger culture—in order not to further oppress and inflict what he describes as *epistemological violence*. Nonbinary transgender identities (e.g., agender individuals, genderqueer individuals) often do not identify with and/or use the terms *masculinity* and *femininity* to characterize their gender. Requiring them to "check off" their sex assigned at birth and/or gender identity may feel like imposing binary assignations on them and enacts epistemological violence. Yet psychologists who study gender and gender-related topics confront a complex situation: How can they use binary assignations (e.g., in surveys, experiments) while these categories are in the midst of radical destabilization? Political movements often rely on identity politics, and yet lives embody and enact far more complexity.

Using Multiple Methods to Help Carve a Path Forward

As a provisional and admittedly inadequate response, researchers turn to method and ask, "To what extent might multiple methods and measures support, for now, the transitional conceptual space in which they find themselves, to honor the fluidity and 'stretchiness' of constructs within sex/gender/sexuality studies?" Given the instability/unreliability (for researchers) or the exciting fluidity of categories (for real people), and the rich intersections of lives, many researchers are moving toward multiple measures and multiple methods to interrogate sexualities. The groundbreaking work of oral histories gathered by Burt Kohler and more recently Phil Hammack on the lives of gay men, the quantitative and qualitative assessments of intimacy among gay couples by David Frost, the use of mapping of lesbian economies and geographies by Jack/Jen Geiseking, and the social media analyses of Monique Ward reflect the exciting new innovative methodologies that researchers are engaging to open up the field of sex/gender/sexuality studies. All of these researchers are innovating methods and relying on multiple methods to map onto the rich, varied, and diverse gender/sexuality identities that populate contemporary culture.

Two recent studies raise important questions and radically exciting possibilities for this historic intermoment, between categories and disruptions. *Gender conforming* and *nonconforming* are terms used to describe individuals who present and express their gender in ways that counter the expectations based on their sex assigned at birth. Although gender expression is not commonly assessed within psychological research, the measures that do exist often implement Likert scales that ask participants to place themselves on a continuum between "masculine" and "feminine." Recognizing that *masculinity* and *femininity* are loaded terms that carry different meanings across time, across place, and within individuals, Stephanie Anderson coupled traditional quantitative scales with qualitative narrative prompts in her work on the intersections of gender expression and race in experiences of antigay discrimination. Specifically, she asked participants to tell stories about how they embody their gender. In taking a multimethod approach, she was better able to account for the fluidity of gender presentation, while evaluating the epistemological utility of gender conformity scales and the criteria that constitute categorizing an individual as gender conforming or gender nonconforming. In a participatory action research project titled "What's Your Issue?" María Elena Torre, David Frost, Allison Cabana, and a team of LGBTQ youth researchers engaged the complicated terrain and the potentially high stakes of labeling and defining oneself. In a national survey on LGBTQ youth experience, they asked young people to place themselves on masculine and feminine continuums; however, they also provided space for youth to comment on the use of masculine and feminine language to describe their gender expression. In acknowledging the messiness of gender measurement on their survey, they conceptually expanded the definition of gender and attended to the potential of survey items to inflict epistemological violence.

These are serious debates within the field, and social movements are far ahead of social science. There is no consensus except that there are many genders and sexualities—that context matters, people change over time, and there are wild variations among identities, behaviors, and attractions. How psychologists respond to these questions determines who gets included within research, and yet these decisions carry enormous social and political consequences for the individuals and groups with whom the research is conducted. A key challenge for researchers lies in their desire to generate meaningful and valid questions even as people, social movements, and history are challenging, dismantling, and unpacking the very categories on which they rely. These nuanced analyses and variations are significant for exploding homogeneous categories and recognizing the differential lived consequences of oppression, and they also yield significant implications for policy and for intervention. At this moment, researchers are interested in a social science that can appreciate the significance of these identity categories even as they complicate how these identity categories are embodied, enacted, internalized, and resisted—but never fully abandoned.

Stephanie M. Anderson and Michelle Fine

See also Ethics in Gender Research; Gender Bias in Research; Heteronormative Bias in Research; Measuring Gender Identity; Reliability and Gender; Research Methodology and Gender; Transgender Research, Bias in

Further Readings

Bowleg, L. (2008). When Black + lesbian + woman ≠ Black lesbian woman: The methodological challenges of qualitative and quantitative intersectionality research. *Sex Roles, 59*(5–6), 312–325.

Cahill, C. (2007). Repositioning ethical commitments: Participatory action research as a relational praxis of social change. *ACME: An International E-Journal for Critical Geographies, 6*, 360–373.

Chmielewski, J. F., Belmonte, K., Fine, M., & Stoudt, B. (2016). Intersectional inquiries with LGBT and nonconforming youth of color: Participatory research on discipline disparities at the race/sexuality/gender nexus. In R. Skiba, K. Mediratta, & K. Rausch (Eds.), *Inequality in school discipline: Research and practice to reduce disparities* (pp. 171–188). London, England: Palgrave Press.

Comas-Díaz, L. E., & Greene, B. E. (1994). *Women of color: Integrating ethnic and gender identities in psychotherapy*. New York, NY: Guilford Press.

Fine, M. (2012). Troubling calls for evidence: A critical race, class and gender analysis of whose evidence counts. *Feminism & Psychology, 22*(1), 3–19.

Frost, D. M., & Meyer, I. H. (2012). Measuring community connectedness among diverse sexual minority populations. *Journal of Sex Research, 49*(1), 36–49.

Gieseking, J. J. (2013). Where we go from here: The mental sketch mapping method and its analytic components. *Qualitative Inquiry, 19*(9), 712–724.

McClelland, S. I., & Fine, M. (2008). Writing on cellophane: Studying teen women's sexual desires, inventing methodological release points. In K. Gallagher (Ed.), *The methodological dilemma: Creative, critical and collaborative approaches to qualitative research* (pp. 232–260). London, England: Routledge.

Nadal, K. L., Issa, M., Leon, J., Meterko, V., Wideman, M., & Wong, Y. (2011). Sexual orientation microaggressions: "Death by a thousand cuts" for lesbian, gay, and bisexual youth. *Journal of LGBT Youth, 8*(3), 1–26.

Shields, S. A. (2008). Gender: An intersectionality perspective. *Sex Roles, 59*(5), 301–311.

Tate, C. C., Youssef, C. P., & Bettergarcia, J. N. (2014). Integrating the study of transgender spectrum and cisgender experiences of self-categorization from a personality perspective. *Review of General Psychology, 18*(4), 302–312.

Tolman, D. L. (2012). Female adolescents, sexual empowerment and desire: A missing discourse of gender inequity. *Sex Roles, 66*(11–12), 746–757.

Torre, M. E., & Fine, M. (2010). A wrinkle in time: Tracing a legacy of public science through community self-surveys and participatory action research. *Journal of Social Issues, 67*(1), 106–121.

Weis, L., & Fine, M. (2012). Critical bifocality and circuits of privilege: Expanding critical ethnographic theory and design. *Harvard Educational Review, 82*(2), 173–201.

Weisstein, N. (1968). *Kinder, kuche, kirche as scientific law: Psychology constructs the female* [Rev. and expanded ed.]. Boston, MA: New England Free Press.

Weisstein, N. (1993). Power, resistance and science: A call for a revitalized feminist psychology. *Feminism & Psychology, 3*, 239–245. doi:10.1177/0959353593032011

Research Methodology and Gender

Research methods are tools psychologists use to investigate a domain of interest (e.g., gender roles). They allow researchers to describe phenomena, measure specific constructs (often called variables), or test hypotheses. Different methods have strengths and weaknesses, depending on the researcher's goal. Methods can be divided into two categories: quantitative and qualitative. Some researchers use one type of method exclusively, whereas others use one or the other, depending on the research question; still others combine both types within the same project. This entry provides an overview of commonly used quantitative and qualitative methods, the assumptions behind each type, and the advantages and disadvantages of each.

Quantitative Methods

The main goal of quantitative methods is often to test hypotheses, although they can also be used to describe a phenomenon of interest or to develop new ways of measuring a particular construct. They capture data at the aggregate level and assume that the results are generalizable to all members of a population (e.g., working mothers). Therefore, questions of sampling (who is represented in a study), validity (how well the measures used assess the constructs under investigation), and reliability (how well the measures used assess the constructs over time or across different people) are important.

Major Data Collection Methods

There are two main data collection methods in quantitative approaches to studying gender: surveys and experiments. Surveys can include open- or closed-ended questions asking a large number of people to self-report on their experiences. Surveys are designed to test questions of relationships (Is X associated with Y?) and not questions of causality (Does X cause Y?). However, longitudinal surveys (in which participants respond to a survey at multiple times) can test questions of order. Surveys are useful for examining the relationships between different constructs, as well as in measurement development and descriptive research projects. Depending on the sample, they also allow a researcher to maximize external validity (the degree to which they are measuring phenomena in "the real world").

Experimentation involves the manipulation of at least one variable to examine its effect on another. Experiments test questions of causality and maximize internal validity (control of outside factors that might affect an outcome of interest). As such, most experiments take place in researchers' laboratories. Experiments usually rely on random assignment, meaning that participants have no greater chance of being assigned to one experimental condition than to another. However, field experiments, which take place in a real-world setting, are often quasi-experimental because they often cannot rely on complete random assignment to conditions. Although gender would be difficult (if not impossible) to manipulate, experimentalists may include it in their analyses as a variable that affects other variables, or they may manipulate psychological processes believed to be related to gender. For example, traditional beliefs about women's roles might have different effects on women's behavior than on men's behavior. By manipulating these beliefs, experiments can test if they result in different behaviors for all people, as well as whether the effects are different for women versus men.

Advantages and Disadvantages of Quantitative Approaches

Advantages of quantitative methods include (relative) ease of data collection from larger samples, control of outside factors that affect an outcome of interest (in experiments), and the ability to generalize one's findings to a larger population of interest. Disadvantages may include decreased ability to capture rich descriptions of complex phenomena, overinterpretation of the generalizability of findings (e.g., not carefully considering the limitations of one's sample in terms of class, race, sexuality, or other important differences), and decreased external validity. This latter critique is most often made of laboratory studies, although simply because a study lacks external validity it does not mean that the findings are not of theoretical or practical importance.

Qualitative Methods

Qualitative methods are preferred when the researcher wants rich and complex descriptions of a given phenomenon. They aim to capture the individual's unique experience and thoughts or to provide rich and in-depth description of a phenomenon of interest. Qualitative methods tend to be about generating concepts and theory rather than testing hypotheses. The researcher's role in the process is often an integral part of the analysis. The thoroughness of analysis of a given phenomenon and representation of its complexity are more important than generalization or replicability.

Major Data Collection Methods

Interviewing and focus groups are the most common qualitative methods (note that while content analysis is popular, it often involves quantifying qualitative data, and so it is not included here). Interviews include questions that aid participants in speaking in depth about particular issues or experiences and can vary in their level of structure. Focus groups are group-level interviews. Usually, there are one or two moderators and several participants. Ideally, the dynamics of the group should be carefully managed by the moderator, with group members facilitating rather than suppressing one another's contributions. Sampling is a critical issue in qualitative studies because the decision about who speaks about a phenomenon will have direct consequences on the findings.

Advantages and Disadvantages of Qualitative Approaches

A major advantage of qualitative approaches is their ability to capture and describe participants' experiences in more depth and detail than is possible (or even sometimes desirable) in surveys or experiments. This makes them very useful for discovering and capturing important (even if idiosyncratic) details and generating theory. Disadvantages include a lack of generalizability, that analyses are subject to researchers' interpretations (though some claim that they are no more "subjective" than quantitative methods, so this may be more perception than fact), and the fact that qualitative methods are often relatively labor intensive.

When considering research methods (both quantitative and qualitative) in gender psychology, it is important to attend to the degree to which researchers assume that gender is a binary category and the degree to which the method and analyses reflect this assumption. Increasingly, researchers are attending to the ways in which they can capture the constructed, contested, and nonbinary aspects of gender. Finally, it is important to note that all methods offer distinct advantages and disadvantages and that researchers should offer justification for their methodological approach and explain how it is well suited to answer their research question.

Nicola Curtin and Mukadder Okuyan

See also Measuring Gender; Measuring Gender Identity; Measuring Gender Roles; Measuring Sexual Orientation; Research: Overview

Further Readings

Dillman, D. A., Smyth, J. D., & Christian, L. M. (2014). *Internet, phone, mail, and mixed-mode surveys: The tailored design method.* Hoboken, NJ: Wiley.

Ellsworth, P. C., Carlsmith, J. M., & Gonzales, M. H. (1990). *Methods of research in social psychology* (2nd ed.). New York, NY: McGraw-Hill.

Howitt, D. (2010). *Introduction to qualitative methods in psychology.* Harlow, England: Prentice Hall.

Willig, C. (2013). *Introducing qualitative research in psychology.* Berkshire, England: McGraw-Hill Education.

Revictimization

Revictimization is most commonly thought of as experiencing physical or sexual assaults in adulthood after experiencing childhood sexual or physical abuse. However, some people also view revictimization simply as experiencing multiple interpersonal victimizations (physical or sexual assaults) perpetrated by different people, no matter the age. Revictimization is to be distinguished from polyvictimization, which is defined as having experienced two or more types of traumatic and/or stressful experiences. This entry briefly reviews the consequences of revictimization, the risk for revictimization, and recommendations for future directions to increase knowledge of revictimization.

Consequences of Revictimization

Revictimization is associated with a range of negative outcomes including increased substance use and substance-related problems as well as potentially risky sexual behaviors, such as higher numbers of partners and earlier age of first intercourse. People who experience revictimization are more likely to report physical health conditions; psychological symptoms such as depression, posttraumatic stress disorder, and anxiety; and interpersonal problems than people who experience single or no victimization. These problems are also often more severe for people who experience revictimization than for people with single or no victimization history.

Risk for Revictimization

Revictimization is most commonly studied in adult women based on childhood histories of sexual or physical abuse. Studies have shown that women with a history of childhood sexual abuse are up to three times more likely than women without a history of childhood sexual abuse to be assaulted again in adulthood. However, women who report only physical abuse in childhood also report high rates of victimization in adulthood. Therefore, it appears that any experience of childhood abuse increases the risk for subsequent revictimization. Researchers are also starting to pay more attention to the period of adolescence for such women, as some studies are finding that experiencing interpersonal victimization during adolescence further increases the risk for revictimization in adulthood.

Less attention has been given to men who experience childhood sexual or physical abuse as well as adult men who report being victims of interpersonal violence. Therefore, little is known about revictimization risk in men. However, some studies have found that men are not at elevated risk for revictimization as compared with women.

Potential Mechanisms of Revictimization

Though the phenomenon of revictimization is well documented, the mechanism by which the risk for revictimization increases remains less well understood. A number of factors have been theorized to contribute to the risk for revictimization, including environmental variables, cognitive functioning, problematic interpersonal skills, risk detection, coping skills, self-attributions such as self-blame and self-esteem, and symptomatology and psychological adjustment.

For example, some people suggest that childhood abuse may interfere with typical development of affect regulation, which leads to adopting emotional numbing or avoidance coping strategies. These avoidance coping strategies may in turn lead to deficits in risk detection abilities—the capacity to notice external (e.g., a dating partner's threatening behaviors) and internal (e.g., one's own feelings of fear or discomfort) danger cues. Deficits in risk detection abilities then place childhood abuse survivors at increased risk of not responding to dangerous situations. Individuals with abuse histories may also engage in maladaptive coping mechanisms such as increased substance use and engagement in risky sexual behaviors that might place them in dangerous situations more often.

Others point to the fact that childhood abuse may lead to negative expectations that relationships involve harm and violence. Children exposed to violence may learn that violent tactics are acceptable and effective, be less sexually assertive, and be more influenced by power and gender dynamics that lead to violence. They may also fail to learn social and coping skills, leading to interpersonal problems and conflict in later relationships. All these factors may lead to repeated experiences of intimate partner violence.

Future Directions

Very little is known about the heterogeneity of revictimization survivors. To date, revictimization research has largely involved adult women who experience violence perpetrated by men. Studies have typically not included men who experience revictimization or individuals who experience revictimization by same-sex perpetrators. It is also unclear whether revictimization risk varies by racial/ethnic groups or by age. Understanding these nuances about revictimization will help identify contributing factors that increase the risk of experiencing revictimization.

In addition, as the mechanisms of revictimization risk are better understood, we can begin to design programs to prevent revictimization. The criminal justice and public health costs resulting from interpersonal violence are staggering. Therefore, preventing revictimization is one of the best ways to decrease long-term criminal justice and public health costs.

Ann T. Chu

See also Date Rape; Intimate Partner Violence; Physical Abuse; Rape; Sexual Abuse; Sexual Assault

Further Readings

Breitenbecher, K. H. (2001). Sexual revictimization among women: A review of the literature focusing on empirical investigations. *Aggression and Violent Behavior,* 6(4), 415–432.

Classen, C. C., Palesh, O. G., & Aggarwal, R. (2005). Sexual revictimization: A review of the empirical literature. *Trauma, Violence, & Abuse,* 6(2), 103–129.

Cloitre, M. (1998). Sexual revictimization: Risk factors and prevention. In V. M. Follette, J. I. Ruzek, & F. R. Abueg (Eds.), *Cognitive-behavioral therapies for trauma* (pp. 278–304). New York, NY: Guilford Press.

Messman-Moore, T. L., & Long, P. J. (2000). Child sexual abuse and revictimization in the form of adult sexual abuse, adult physical abuse, and adult psychological maltreatment. *Journal of Interpersonal Violence, 15*(5), 489–502.

Role Models and Gender

Role models are individuals who are looked up to or admired, often in a domain in which one hopes to achieve success. They may be individuals whom one has a personal relationship with, such as an advanced peer, teacher, or coach, or famous figures one does not know personally. Role models serve as examples of what one can aspire to as well as sources of inspiration. Role models who share one's gender identity have traditionally been thought to be more efficacious, especially in contexts in which one's gender is in the minority, although evidence suggests that this is not always the case. A great deal of empirical work has focused on the benefits of female role models for women and girls, particularly in fields in which they are underrepresented (e.g., politics or science, technology, engineering, and mathematics [STEM] fields). This entry briefly introduces these benefits as well as how role model gender relates to what is known about who makes successful role models. The entry concludes with a brief overview of the circumstances in which gender-matched role models have not been found to be better than role models of another gender.

Importance of Role Model Similarity

Role models who are seen as similar to the self are more likely to be perceived as relevant to the self. Perceived similarity can also increase the likelihood that a role model's success seems attainable. Both self-relevance and attainability are key attributes of effective role models. Role models who are seen as similar to the self are also more motivating and inspiring than role models who are seen as dissimilar. Gender is one dimension that can influence perceptions of similarity, but sharing other characteristics including race and ethnicity or even smaller details such as hobbies or an alma mater may also increase feelings of similarity with a potential role model.

Benefits of Same-Gender Role Models

Many men and women report preferring role models who share their gender identity, and there is evidence that gender-matched role models have benefits, particularly for women in domains in which their abilities are negatively stereotyped (e.g., STEM, leadership). Relatively little work has focused on who makes effective role models for men and boys, but there is some evidence that gender matching may have less impact on them than it does on women and girls.

Compared with male role models, female role models improve women's performance on experimental tasks in which negative stereotypes about their abilities are salient, such as difficult math tests or public speaking. Successful professional women can increase women's self-rated performance and the extent to which they aspire to future involvement in a field. Female professors weaken women's implicit stereotypes associating certain fields with males, and both female professors and female peers can increase the extent to which women identify with these fields. Female peer role models have also been shown to improve women's implicit or automatic attitudes toward a field and to increase women's confidence in their abilities.

Although experimental and field studies have demonstrated several benefits of female role models for women, evidence from large-scale field studies looking at the effects of teacher and professor gender has been mixed. While some studies have found that same-gender teachers and professors enhance students' academic performance and make it more likely that they will persist in a field or domain, others find no effects or even negative effects.

Caveats

Although current knowledge indicates that same-gender role models have a positive impact, evidence also suggests that same-gender role models are not always better than role models who are not matched by gender. In some situations, same-gender role models can even be detrimental. Extremely successful female role models can be intimidating and make women feel worse about themselves than male role models who are equally successful. Additionally, female role models who are highly stereotypical of male-dominated fields such as computer science can decrease women's interest and expectations that they can succeed in the field just as much as stereotypical male role models do. Male role models who defy stereotypes of these fields, on the other hand, increase women's interest and perceptions of future success. These findings suggest that role models who are not matched by gender can still be effective as long as the perceiver feels similar to the role model on other dimensions. Conversely, same-gender role models may be ineffective if perceivers feel dissimilar to them in other ways. Same-gender role models can also backfire when they are highly counterstereotypical if their combination of success and counterstereotypical traits makes emulating their achievements seem unattainable. For example, extremely feminine role models in STEM fields decrease girls' interest and self-rated ability in these fields compared with female role models who display more gender neutral traits. Less is known about circumstances that may make same-gender role models more or less effective for men and boys.

Sianna Alia Ziegler and Sapna Cheryan

See also Career Choice and Gender; Gender Stereotypes; STEM Fields and Gender; Stereotype Threat and Gender; Stereotype Threat in Education; Women and Leadership

Further Readings

Cheryan, S., Siy, J. O., Vichayapai, M., Drury, B. J., & Kim, S. (2011). Do female and male role models who embody STEM stereotypes hinder women's anticipated success in STEM? *Social Psychological and Personality Science, 2*(6), 656–664. doi:10.1177/1948550611405218

Dasgupta, N., & Asgari, S. (2004). Seeing is believing: Exposure to counterstereotypic women leaders and its effect on the malleability of automatic gender stereotyping. *Journal of Experimental Social Psychology, 40*(5), 642–658. doi:10.1016/j.jesp.2004.02.003

Lockwood, P. (2006). "Someone like me can be successful": Do college students need same-gender role models? *Psychology of Women Quarterly, 30*(1), 36–46. doi:10.1111/j.1471-6402.2006.00260.x

Lockwood, P., & Kunda, Z. (1997). Superstars and me: Predicting the impact of role models on the self. *Journal of Personality and Social Psychology, 73*(1), 91–103. doi:10.1037/0022-3514.73.1.91

Romantic Relationships in Adolescence

Adolescence is the period of development between childhood and adulthood, a period of transition and new opportunities. Many of these opportunities are tied to a growing need for balancing autonomy and connection with significant others. The formation and subsequent navigation of romantic relationship experiences in adolescence provide the ideal vehicle for tackling this challenge. Although past research has focused on identifying important features of these early romantic relationships, researchers are only now beginning to understand these relationships in their developmental context and how they differ from relationships with parents and friends during this developmental period. This entry summarizes current thoughts on how romantic relationship partners influence each other in adolescence and how different expectations over roles in romantic relationships cause some unique gender differences across a variety of sexual orientation identities.

Influence of Partner Characteristics

Most adolescents have been involved in some type of romantic experience by the time they are 18 years old. These experiences range from desired encounters to short-term and often shallow trysts, to deep, meaningful relationships. In total, romantic relationships provide a unique setting in which adolescents begin applying skills learned from interactions with parents and peers in a more intimate, emotional, and private manner. Often, peer groups influence partner selection, but group dynamics can also change as a result of dating patterns within circles of friends. For example, dating decreases the time spent with friends, which can disrupt peer groups' feelings of connectedness and belonging. This is especially true if not all friends begin dating at the same time or for sexual minority adolescents who may not reveal their sexual orientation identities to their same-sex friends, which may cause them to feel more distant. While both genders may hide their feelings of insecurity and loss from their friends, it is likely that males will act out while females turn their negativity inward. In addition, because females emotionally mature faster, they may be more prone to the negative ramifications of being "left out" of dating than same-age male peers. Furthermore, sexual minority youths may pursue and engage in unfulfilling heterosexual romantic relationships or avoid dating altogether, which may augment the negative consequences of being left out. Therefore, individuals are influenced by their own and others' romantic experiences, which can lead to further changes in friendship dynamics.

At the individual level, there is a debate over the extent to which dating partners' characteristics influence adolescents in romantic relationships. More specifically, it is important to identify characteristics that can negatively affect the partner's adjustment through adolescence compared with qualities that promote healthy development. Prior research has indicated that heterosexual females' working models of relationships are related to their own behavior as well as their partner's, but the association does not seem to be as strong for males. This likely indicates that females are more attuned to the relationship and can adapt their expectations according to their current experience. Alternatively, females may simply be selecting partners who match their preconceived working model. Males are probably not as tuned into dyadic behavior or may enter relationships with less clearly defined working models, reflecting males' slower emotional maturity.

Prior research has also indicated that in heterosexual relationships males tend to have greater influence and power in the relationship than females. It is known that males typically feel more pressure toward initiation of romantic relationships and fear of rejection, but these worries rarely translate into more than fleeting levels of anxiety. Females, on the other hand, are much more likely to forgo their own identity once in a relationship, often at the cost of their own mental health. There is even suggestion that long-term difficulties with adult relationships can be tied back to the willingness to develop a submissive style in romantic relationships in adolescence. In terms of same-sex relationships, less is known regarding how power dynamics influence later mental health. Future work can aid our understanding greatly by identifying how individual and dyadic characteristics affect males and females uniquely in same-sex, other-sex, and both-sex orientations.

Different Expectations for Relationships by Gender in Adolescence

Another aspect of adolescent romantic relationships in which females and males differ is the expectations from the relationship in general and the partner specifically. Common perceptions have been confirmed by research; females place more emphasis on intimacy compared with males. Additionally, females are more concerned with close attachment and caring behaviors in heterosexual romantic relationships than males. Correspondingly, females are more willing to tolerate relational victimization from partners in striving to maintain and increase closeness. Taken to an extreme, females may endure emotional and physical abuse at higher rates to maintain perceived intimacy and attachment rather than exit problematic relationships. However, little research on such intimacy has been done to further explore this discrepancy. Do females have higher expectations in terms of intimacy and connectedness than males, or are males lacking the maturity necessary to develop such influential qualities essential for intimacy? Perhaps as adolescents develop, these gender differences decrease as males and females mature through navigating romantic experiences and learn healthier ways to increase intimacy and attachment.

Furthermore, female teens have been found to be more negatively affected when in a relationship that does not meet their expectations or needs than males. However, it is not known whether this is because females enter heterosexual relationships with higher or more rigid expectations, which may not be met within their romantic experience, than males, or whether females are more emotionally invested in the relationship, which contributes to more psychological and emotional damage when the relationship fails to live up to their expectations.

Often, sexual minority adolescents engage in intense same-sex friendships rather than in same-sex romantic relationships. In addition, it is common for sexual minority teens to skip dating and enter a relationship, or accelerate the transition from close friendship to a romantic relationship. Little is known regarding the differential expectations for sexual minority youth and the subsequent influence on individual development.

There is less known about how adolescents form preconceived ideas of relationship expectations. It seems worthwhile to identify what adolescents consider to be the most important aspects of their relationship both prior to its beginning and throughout its duration. In addition to females seeking emotional support and intimacy, it is hypothesized that males more commonly seek the physical aspects of a relationship. The extent of the expectations for the physical development of the relationship is likely to differ by gender. In addition, sexual minority adolescents may idealize a relationship, especially if they have been withholding their sexual identity for some time. As previously mentioned, this may translate to rapid progression when a relationship begins or may lead to feelings of disappointment when expectations are not met. The discrepancy between what partners consider as most essential can reveal how adolescents form and change their expectations as they develop.

Jessica Kansky and Chris Hafen

See also Children's Social-Emotional Development; Friendships in Adolescence; Gender Norms and Adolescence; Sexuality and Adolescence

Further Readings

Collins, W. A., Welsh, D. P., & Furman, W. (2009). Adolescent romantic relationships. *Annual Review of Psychology, 60,* 631–652.

Diamond, L. M., & Lucas, S. (2004). Sexual-minority and heterosexual youths' peer relationships: Experiences, expectations, and implications for well-being. *Journal of Research on Adolescence, 14,* 313–340.

Diamond, L. M., Savin-Williams, R. C., & Dube, E. M. (1999). Sex, dating, passionate friendships, and romance: Intimate peer relations among lesbian, gay, and bisexual adolescents. In W. Furman, B. B. Brown, & C. Feiring (Eds.), *The development of romantic relationships in adolescence* (pp. 175–210). New York, NY: Cambridge University Press.

Furman, W., Ho, M. J., & Low, S. M. (2007). The rocky road of adolescent romantic experience: Dating and adjustment. In R. C. M. E. Engels, M. Kerr, & H. Stattin (Eds.), *Friends, lovers and groups: Key relationships in adolescence* (pp. 61–80). London, England: Wiley.

Savin-Williams, R. C. (1996). Dating and romantic relationships among gay, lesbian, and bisexual youths. In R. C. Savin-Williams & K. M. Cohen (Eds.), *The lives of lesbians, gays, and bisexuals: Children to adults* (pp. 166–180). Fort Worth, TX: Harcourt Brace.

Seiffge-Krenke, I. (2011). Coping with relationship stressors: A decade review. *Journal of Research on Adolescence, 21,* 196–210.

Simpson, J. A. (1990). Influence of attachment styles on romantic relationships. *Journal of Personality and Social Psychology, 59,* 971–980.

Romantic Relationships in Adulthood

Gender roles are pervasive in how adult heterosexual romantic relationships unfold and are enacted. Given that adult romantic relationships are more interdependent in that adults often share responsibilities such as income, a home, and children, issues of power and the implications of each person's role are going to have a greater impact.

The different scripts for each gender are evident from the initiation of the relationship through the continued sexual encounters that a couple share. This entry provides a brief overview of the traditional scripts assigned to heterosexual men and women, and the liberties and restrictions that they each entail. It then discusses the pros and cons of the negotiation and sharing of these roles in gay, lesbian, and other nonheteronormative relationships.

Traditional Establishment of Gendered Romantic Scripts

The establishment of romantic scripts became more mainstream during 12th-century France and was framed as a knight's public admiration of an often married noble lady of the court who was above his social station (i.e., "put on a pedestal"). The knight would publicly praise the lady's key virtues—youth, beauty, and sexual modesty—and was devoted to her from afar. This courtly love changed in the Middle Ages to become more scandalous and physical, but it served to establish the basis of modern gendered romantic roles; the man is framed as the active pursuer who must woo the woman, and the woman is relegated to be the passive responder and gatekeeper to the man's advances. Although these prescriptive ideologies have changed in modern society, there remain strong gender roles in heterosexual romantic relationships.

Traditional Gendered Script for Men

Men are socialized from a young age to be agentic, independent, and aggressive in accomplishing their goals. The male role is defined in part as antithetical to the perceived fragility, emotionality, and dependence of both women and homosexual men. This role is rigid and isolating for men, who are raised to be emotionally reserved but yet are expected to be comfortable with the expressivity and interdependence that characterize romantic relationships with women.

The onus is on men to both initiate and win over (or woo) the woman so that she will become sexually available to him. This "wooing" of a woman is rooted firmly in a benevolent sexism within the notion that women are morally better, fragile creatures who deserve to be treasured and protected by men. Although superficially positive, this content ultimately serves to frame women as less competent ("weak but wonderful") and unequal to men.

The wooing process has also become complicated in an age in which the abolishment of gender roles has begun, but it is still unclear what our expectations of each woman are toward traditional chivalry. For example, if John asks Mary out to dinner, he is then in the precarious position of deciding whether he should offer to pay. Historically, the romantic script suggested that the man should always be the provider; however, that was in the context of women being economically disadvantaged. John is left with the options of offering to pay (and risk offending Mary if she views this as a sexist move) or suggesting to split the check (and risk suggesting to Mary that he is either cheap or that this is not a "date" and he does not have romantic feelings for her).

Sexual interaction in romantic relationships is also strongly tied to the male role, as evidenced by the double standard that men's status increases with the number of sexual partners whereas women's decreases (i.e., men with sexual experience are "studs," whereas women are "sluts"). Specifically, men are expected not only to be the initiators of all sexual contact but also to take the lead in the sexual activities that unfold throughout the relationship. Although the male role allows men the freedom to act in accordance with their desires, they are also burdened by the anxiety of social rejection and sexual performance while not feeling entitled to the emotional closeness of romantic relationships.

Traditional Gendered Script for Women

Women are socialized from a young age to believe that they are genetically predisposed for relationships and that romantic relationships, in particular, should be central to their lives and validating to their identity as a woman. This bias is also visible in the communal way in which women are socialized (e.g., to put others' needs/feelings first, to be accommodating and pleasant, and ultimately to maintain harmonious interactions). In romantic relationships, this translates to women initiating a relationship in indirect ways, by enhancing their appearance to look "beautiful" or through subtly giving a look signaling for a man to approach. Although the woman's role is predominantly passive and framed as responding to men's advances, it does allow for the limited power of being sexual gatekeepers of when and under what circumstance sexual activity occurs. In this script, the definition of a woman's value is a function of her beauty (in that a more beautiful woman will have more male competition for her attention), a lack of sexual activity (a woman's virginity is considered valuable, whereas a man's virginity is not), and the selectivity with which she does engage in sexual activity. Sexual economics specifies that women are more likely to exchange this commodity (sex) for valuable currency from male partners, such as love, affection, commitment, money, desirable experiences, and/or gifts. Although not burdened with the pressure of initiation and rejection that men face, this general passivity limits women in both approaching potential partners and asserting their needs generally within the relationship.

Relationship Scripts in Gender Nonconforming Relationships

Initial research into gay and lesbian relationships sought to impose roles parallel to those found in traditional heterosexual relationships. Specifically, these typologies are "femme" and "butch" for lesbians, with the femme paralleling the traditional feminine role and the butch playing the traditional masculine role. For gay men, these roles are "bottoms" and "tops," suggesting that power distinction lies in who is submissive versus dominant during sex. This dichotomy is forced and inaccurate because there are many different subtypes of gay and lesbian people, suggesting that an imposition of heterosexual gendered roles and their allocation of power is irrelevant. Although these types of relationships will be discussed later in terms of homosexual ones, the negotiation of roles would apply to any relationship in which they were not perceived as having already been allocated (e.g., egalitarian heterosexual, homosexual, trans*).

For example, because in nonheterosexual relationships one partner's virginity is not perceived as more valuable, these relationships also lack the heterosexual gendered roles of "sexual gatekeepers" and "sexual initiator." Accordingly, the similar gender role socialization for both partners suggests greater egalitarianism in the agentic and communal traits that each partner can adopt in both the initiation and the progression of a romantic sexual relationship. For example, many lesbians have indicated that they reject the notion of an active versus passive partner and tend to share these roles equally. Similarly, gay men report that either they or their partners are equally likely to initiate sexual intimacy in a new relationship.

This difference is also reflected in the different scripts that homosexual relationships follow for their initiation. For example, gay men have been found to include sexual activity in their first-date scripts and to often pursue new partners while in an open relationship with their current partner. Conversely, lesbian relationship initiation is more likely to stem from friendship and to lack the casual dating phase that precedes the escalation to commitment.

This is not to suggest, however, that gay or lesbian relationships have less conflict, rather that they may simply face different sources of it. For example, along with the greater freedom in role adoption comes the additional burden of having to negotiate the specific roles within a given relationship, and the implications for self-identity. In this sense, Terri, as an example, may have been the more communal person in a previous relationship with Pat but is currently less so in their current relationship, which may require some adjustments and identity renegotiation. Despite the potential discomfort of the negotiation process, relationship satisfaction increases when partners are high in both stereotypically masculine and stereotypically feminine traits. The benefits may stem from many sources, including the notion that masculinity is associated with more strategic relationship maintenance behaviors whereas femininity is associated with more routine relationship maintenance behaviors.

Finally, any noncisgendered person operating in a heteronormative society may also face the additional confusion of being unsure whether the person they are romantically attracted to may share in this attraction. This uncertainty may lead to individuals being more passive in the relationship initiation phase, not out of gender role dictates but rather due to the possibly negative consequences associated with the potential partner's rejection.

These negative consequences could range from having their sexual identity or orientation made public (being publicly "outed") to violence on the potential partner's behalf at the suggestion that they may be anything other than heterosexual. Men in particular, due to the rigidity and fragility of the masculine role, may be more likely to react negatively and with violence than women.

Marie-Joelle Estrada

See also Gay Men and Romantic Relationships; Heterosexual Romantic Relationships; Lesbians and Romantic Relationships

Further Readings

Baumeister, R. F., & Vohs, K. D. (2004). Sexual economics: Sex as female resource for social exchange in heterosexual interactions. *Personality and Social Psychology Review, 8,* 339–363.

Marshall, T. C. (2010). Gender, peer relations, and intimate romantic relationships. In J. C. Chrisler & D. R. McCreary (Eds.), *Handbook of gender research in psychology* (pp. 281–310). New York, NY: Springer.

Rudman, L. A., & Glick, P. (2008). Love and romance. In *The social psychology of gender: How power and intimacy shape gender relations* (pp. 204–230). New York, NY: Guilford Press.